Implementing and Administering a Microsoft® Windows® 2000 Directory Services Infrastructure

Exam 70-217

Implementing and Administering a Microsoft® Windows® 2000 Directory Services Infrastructure

Exam 70-217

First Edition

Kenneth C. Laudon, Series Designer
Brian Hill, MCSE, MCSA

The Azimuth Interactive MCSE/MCSA Team
Carol G. Traver, Series Editor
Kenneth Rosenblatt
Robin Pickering
Russell Polo
David Langley
Kevin Jensen, MCSE
Mark Maxwell
Stacey McBrine, MCSE, MCSA
Barbara Ryan
Richard Watson, MCSE, MCSA

Upper Saddle River, New Jersey, 07458

Senior Vice President/Publisher: Natalie Anderson
Acquisitions Editor: Steven Elliot
Marketing Manager: Steven Rutberg
Assistant Editor: Allison Marcus
Editorial Assistant: Jasmine Slowick
Editorial Assistant: Jodi Bolognese
Marketing Assistant: Barrie Reinhold
Media Project Manager: Joan Waxman
Production Manager: Gail Steier de Acevedo
Editorial Production Project Manager: Tim Tate
Associate Director, Manufacturing: Vincent Scelta
Manufacturing Buyer: Tim Tate
Art Director: Pat Smythe
Design Manager: Maria Lange
Interior Design: Kim Buckley
Cover Designer: Jill Little
Cover Photo: Richard Laird/Getty Images
Associate Director, Multimedia: Karen Goldsmith
Manager, Multimedia: Christy Mahon
Full Service Composition: Azimuth Interactive, Inc.
Quality Assurance: Digital Content Factory Ltd.
Printer/Binder: Banta Book Group, Menasha
Cover Printer: Phoenix Color Corporation

Credits and acknowledgments borrowed from other sources and reproduced, with permission, in this textbook appear on appropriate page within text.

10 9 8 7 6 5 4 3 2 1
0-13-142208-1

To our families,
for their love, patience,
and inspiration.

Brief Contents

Contents

About This Series

Welcome to the Laudon MCSE/MCSA Certification Series!

You are about to begin an exciting journey of learning and career skills building that will provide you with access to careers such as Network Administrator, Systems Engineer, Technical Support Engineer, Network Analyst, and Technical Consultant. What you learn in the Laudon MCSE/MCSA Certification Series will provide you with a strong set of networking skills and knowledge that you can use throughout your career as the Microsoft Windows operating system continues to evolve, as new information technology devices appear, and as business applications of computers continue to expand. The Laudon Certification Series aims to provide you with the skills and knowledge that will endure, prepare you for your future career, and make the process of learning fun and enjoyable.

Microsoft Windows and the Networked World

We live in a computer networked world—more so than many of us realize. The Internet, the world's largest network, now has more than 500 million people who connect to it through an estimated 171 million Internet hosts. The number of local area networks associated with these 171 million Internet hosts is not known. Arguably, the population of local area networks is in the millions. About 60% of local area networks in the United States are using a Windows network operating system. The other networks use Novell or some version of UNIX Netware (Internet Software Consortium, 2003). About 95% of the one billion personal computers in the world use some form of Microsoft operating system, typically some version of Windows. A growing number of handheld personal digital assistants (PDAs) also use versions of the Microsoft operating system called Microsoft CE. Most businesses—large and small—use some kind of client/server local area network to connect their employees to one another, and to the Internet. In the United States, the vast majority of these business networks use a Microsoft network operating system—either an earlier version called Windows NT, or the current version called Windows 2000. Many will soon upgrade to Windows Server 2003.

The Laudon MCSE/MCSA Certification Series prepares you to participate in this computer-networked world and, specifically, the world of Microsoft Windows 2000 and XP Professional client operating systems, as well as Windows 2000 Server and Server 2003 operating systems.

Laudon MCSE/MCSA Certification Series Objectives

The first objective of the Laudon MCSE/MCSA Certification Series is to help you build a set of skills and a knowledge base that will prepare you for a career in the networking field. There is no doubt that in the next five years, Microsoft will issue several new versions of its network operating system, and new versions of Windows client operating system. In the next five years—and thereafter—there will be a steady stream of new digital devices that will require connecting to networks. Most of what you learn in the Laudon Series will provide a strong foundation for understanding future versions of the operating system.

The second objective of the Laudon MCSE/MCSA Certification Series is to prepare you to pass the MCSE/MCSA certification exams and to receive certification. Why get certified? As businesses increasingly rely on Microsoft networks to operate, employers want to make sure their networking staff has the skills needed to plan for, install, and operate these networks. While job experience is an important source of networking knowledge, employers increasingly rely on certification examinations to ensure their staff has the necessary skills. The MCSE/MCSA curriculum provides networking professionals with a well-balanced and comprehensive body of knowledge necessary to operate and administer Microsoft networks in a business setting.

There is clear evidence that having the MCSE/MCSA certification results in higher salaries and faster promotions for individual employees. Therefore, it is definitely in your interest to obtain certification, even if you have considerable job experience. If you are just starting out in the world of networking, certification can be very important for landing that first job.

The Laudon Series teaches you real-world, job-related skills. About 90% of the work performed by MCSE/MCSAs falls into the following categories, according to a survey researcher (McKillip, 1999):

- Analyzing the business requirements for a proposed system architecture.
- Designing system architecture solutions that meet business requirements.

- Deploying, installing, and configuring the components of the system architecture.
- Managing the components of the system architecture on an ongoing basis.
- Monitoring and optimizing the components of the system architecture.
- Diagnosing and troubleshooting problems regarding the components of the system architecture.

These are precisely the skills we had in mind when we wrote this Series. As you work through the hands-on instructions in the text, perform the instructions in the simulated Windows environment on the CD-ROM, and complete the problem solving cases in the book, you will notice our emphasis on analyzing, designing, diagnosing, and implementing the Windows software. By completing the Laudon MCSE/MCSA Certification Series, you will be laying the foundation for a long-term career based on your specialized knowledge of networks and general problem solving skills.

Preparing you for a career involves more than satisfying the official MCSE/MCSA objectives. As you can see from the list of activities performed by MCSE/MCSAs, you will also need a strong set of management skills. The Laudon MCSE/MCSA Certification Series emphasizes management skills along with networking skills. As you advance in your career, you will be expected to participate in and lead teams of networking professionals in their efforts to support the needs of your organization. You will be expected to describe, plan, administer, and maintain computer networks, and to write about networks and give presentations to other business professionals. We make a particular point in this Series of developing managerial skills such as analyzing business requirements, writing reports, and making presentations to other members of your business team.

Who Is the Audience for This Book?

The student body for the Laudon MCSE/MCSA Certification Series is very diverse, and the Series is written with that in mind. For all students, regardless of background, the Series is designed to function as a *learning tool* first, and, second, as a compact reference book that can be readily accessed to refresh skills. Generally, there are two types of software books: books aimed at learning and understanding how a specific software tool works, and comprehensive reference books. This series emphasizes learning and explanation and is student-centered.

The Laudon MCSE/MCSA Certification Series is well suited to beginning students. Many students will just be starting out in the networking field, most in colleges and training institutes. The Series introduces these beginning students to the basic concepts of networking, operating systems, and network operating systems. We take special care in the introductory chapters of each book to provide the background skills and understanding necessary to proceed to more specific MCSE/MCSA skills. We cover many more learning objectives and skills in these introductory lessons than are specifically listed as MCSE/MCSA objectives. Throughout all Lessons, we take care to *explain why things are done*, rather than just list the steps necessary to do them. There is a vast difference between understanding how Windows works and why, versus rote memorization of procedures.

A second group of students will already have some experience working with networking systems and Windows operating systems. This group already has an understanding of the basics, but needs a more systematic and in-depth coverage of MCSE/MCSA skills they lack. The Laudon MCSE/MCSA Certification Series is organized so that these more experienced students can quickly discover what they do not know, and can skip over introductory Lessons quickly. Nevertheless, this group will appreciate the emphasis on explanation and clear illustration throughout.

A third group of students will have considerable experience with previous Microsoft operating systems such as Windows NT. These students may be seeking to upgrade their skills and prepare for the Windows 2000/XP/2003 MCSE/MCSA examinations. They may be learning outside of formal training programs as self-paced learners, or in distance learning programs sponsored by their employers. The Laudon MCSE/MCSA Certification Series is designed to help these students quickly identify the new features of new versions of Windows, and to rapidly update their existing skills.

Laudon Series Skills and MCSE/MCSA Objectives

In designing and writing the Laudon Certification Series, we had a choice between organizing the book into lessons composed of MCSE/MCSA domains and objectives, or organizing the book into lessons composed of skills needed to pass the MCSE/MCSA certification examinations (a complete listing of the domains and objectives for the relevant exam will be found inside the front and back covers of the book). We chose to organize the book around skills, beginning with introductory basic skills, and building to more advanced skills. We believe this is a more orderly and effective way to teach students the MCSE/MCSA subject matter and the basic understanding of Windows network operating systems.

Yet we also wanted to make clear exactly how the skills related to the published MCSE/MCSA objectives. In the Laudon Series, skills are organized into Lessons. At the beginning of each Lesson, there is an introduction to the set of skills covered in the Lesson, followed by a table that shows how the skills taught in the Lesson support specific MCSE/MCSA objectives. All MCSE/MCSA objectives for each of the examinations are covered; at the beginning of each skill discussion, the exact MCSE/MCSA objective relating to that skill is identified.

We also recognize that as students approach the certification examinations, they will want learning and preparation materials that are specifically focused on the examinations. Therefore, we have designed the MCSE/MCSA Interactive Series (on CD ROM) to follow the MCSE/MCSA domains and objectives more directly. Students can use these tools to practice answering MCSE/MCSA examination questions, and practice implementing these objectives in a realistic simulated Windows environment.

What's Different About the Laudon Series—Main Features and Components

The Laudon MCSE/MCSA Certification Series has three distinguishing features that make it the most effective MCSE/MCSA learning tool available today. These three features are a graphical illustrated 2-page spread approach, a skills-based systematic approach to learning MCSE/MCSA, and an interactive *multi-channel pedagogy.*

Graphical illustrated approach. First, the Laudon Series uses a graphical, illustrated approach in a convenient *two-page spread format* (see illustration below). This makes learning easy, effective and enjoyable.

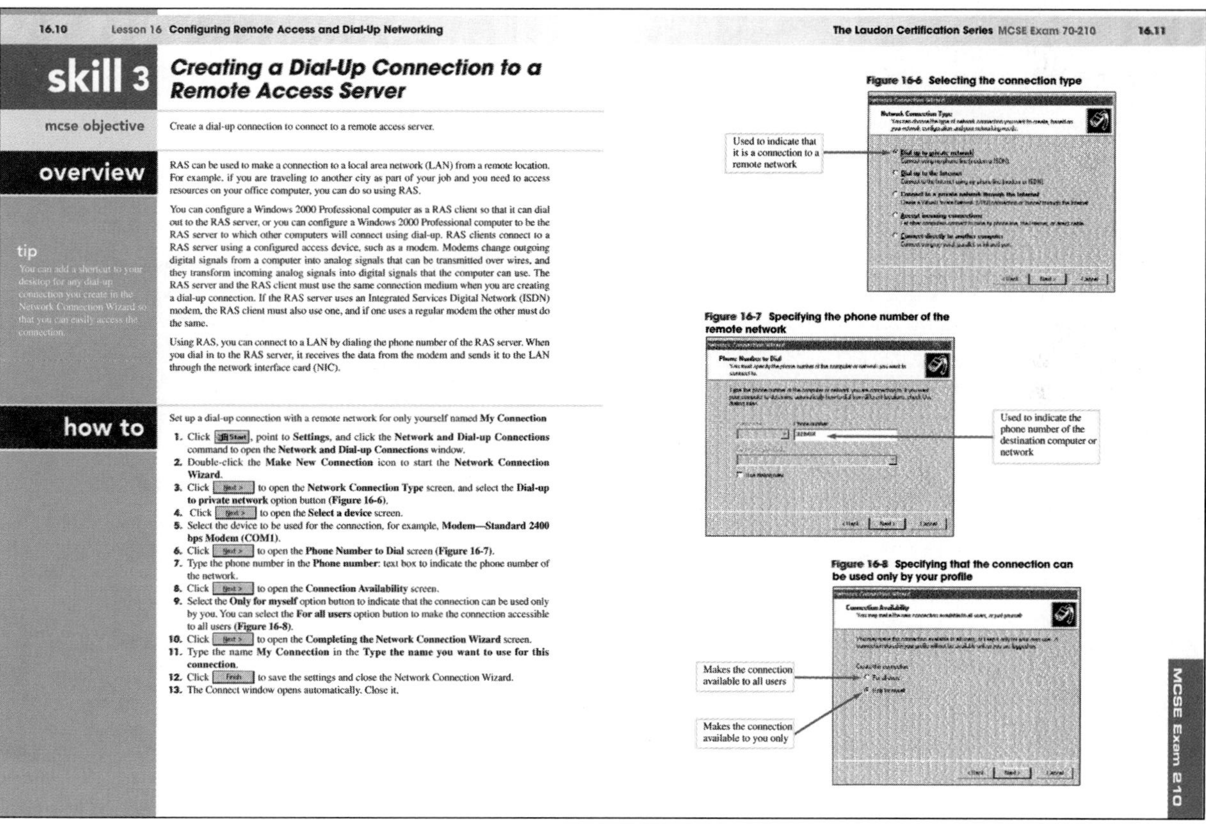
16.10 Lesson 16 **Configuring Remote Access and Dial-Up Networking**

skill 3 ***Creating a Dial-Up Connection to a Remote Access Server***

mcse objective

Create a dial-up connection to connect to a remote access server.

overview

RAS can be used to make a connection to a local area network (LAN) from a remote location. For example, if you are traveling to another city as part of your job and you need to access resources on your office computer, you can do so using RAS.

You can configure a Windows 2000 Professional computer as a RAS client so that it can dial out to the RAS server, or you can configure a Windows 2000 Professional computer to be the RAS server to which other computers will connect using dial-up. RAS clients connect to a RAS server using a configured access device, such as a modem. Modems change outgoing digital signals from a computer into analog signals that can be transmitted over wires, and they transform incoming analog signals into digital signals that the computer can use. The RAS server and the RAS client must use the same connection medium when you are creating a dial-up connection. If the RAS server uses an Integrated Services Digital Network (ISDN) modem, the RAS client must also use one, and if one uses a regular modem the other must do the same.

Using RAS, you can connect to a LAN by dialing the phone number of the RAS server. When you dial in to the RAS server, it receives the data from the modem and sends it to the LAN through the network interface card (NIC).

tip

You can add a shortcut to your desktop for any dial-up connection you create in the Network Connection Wizard so that you can easily access the connection.

how to

Set up a dial-up connection with a remote network for only yourself named **My Connection**

1. Click [Start], point to **Settings**, and click the **Network and Dial-up Connections** command to open the **Network and Dial-up Connections** window.
2. Double-click the **Make New Connection** icon to start the **Network Connection Wizard.**
3. Click [Next >] to open the **Network Connection Type** screen, and select the **Dial-up to private network** option button **(Figure 16-6).**
4. Click [Next >] to open the **Select a device** screen.
5. Select the device to be used for the connection, for example, **Modem—Standard 2400 bps Modem (COM1).**
6. Click [Next >] to open the **Phone Number to Dial** screen **(Figure 16-7).**
7. Type the phone number in the **Phone number**: text box to indicate the phone number of the network.
8. Click [Next >] to open the **Connection Availability** screen.
9. Select the **Only for myself** option button to indicate that the connection can be used only by you. You can select the **For all users** option button to make the connection accessible to all users **(Figure 16-8).**
10. Click [Next >] to open the **Completing the Network Connection Wizard** screen.
11. Type the name **My Connection** in the **Type the name you want to use for this connection.**
12. Click [Finish] to save the settings and close the Network Connection Wizard.
13. The Connect window opens automatically. Close it.

The Laudon Certification Series MCSE Exam 70-210 16.11

Figure 16-6 Selecting the connection type

Figure 16-7 Specifying the phone number of the remote network

Figure 16-8 Specifying that the connection can be used only by your profile

Each two-page spread is devoted to a single skill. On the left-hand side of the two-page spread, you will find a conceptual overview explaining what the skill is, why it is important, and how it is used. Immediately following the conceptual overview is a series of *How To Steps* showing how to execute the skill. On the right hand side of the two-page spread are screen shots that show you exactly how the screen should look as you execute the skills. The pedagogy is easy to follow and understand.

In addition to these main features, each two-page spread contains several *learning aids*:

- *More:* a brief section that explains more about how to use the skill, alternative ways to perform the skill, and common business applications of the skill.
- *Tips:* hints and suggestions to follow when performing the skill placed in the left margin.
- *Caution:* brief sections that tell you about the pitfalls and problems you may encounter when performing the skill placed in the left margin.

At the end of each Lesson, students can test and practice their skills using three end-of-Lesson features:

- *Test Yourself:* a multiple-choice examination that tests your comprehension and retention of the material in the Lesson.
- *Projects: On Your Own:* short projects that test your ability to perform tasks and skills in Windows without detailed step-by-step instructions.
- *Problem Solving Scenarios:* real-world business scenarios to help you analyze or diagnose a networking situation. The case generally requires you to write a report or prepare a presentation.

Skills-based systematic approach. A second distinguishing feature of the Laudon MCSE/MCSA Series is a *skills-based* systematic approach to MCSE/MCSA certification by using five integrated components:

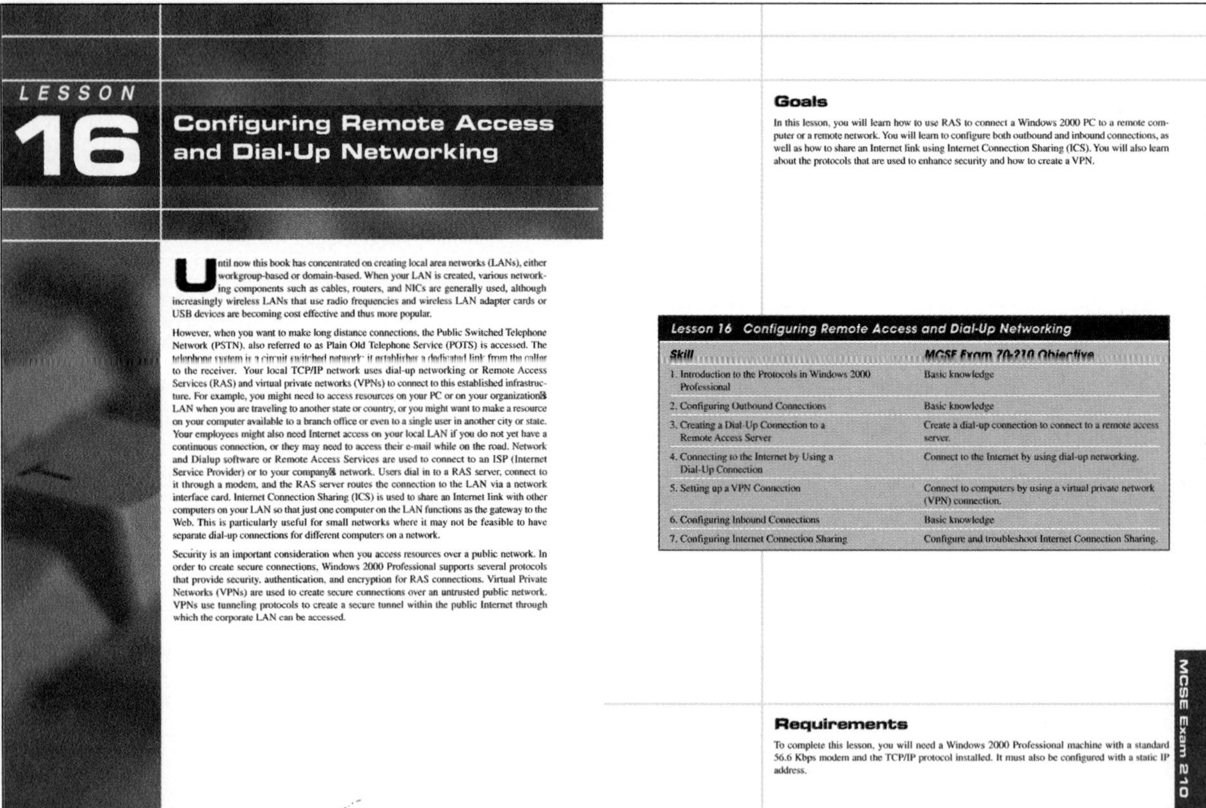

LESSON 16

Configuring Remote Access and Dial-Up Networking

Until now this book has concentrated on creating local area networks (LANs), either workgroup-based or domain-based. When your LAN is created, various networking components such as cables, routers, and NICs are generally used, although increasingly wireless LANs that use radio frequencies and wireless LAN adapter cards or USB devices are becoming cost effective and thus more popular.

However, when you want to make long distance connections, the Public Switched Telephone Network (PSTN), also referred to as Plain Old Telephone Service (POTS) is accessed. The telephone system is a circuit switched network: it establishes a dedicated link from the caller to the receiver. Your local TCP/IP network uses dial-up networking or Remote Access Services (RAS) and virtual private networks (VPNs) to connect to this established infrastructure. For example, you might need to access resources on your PC or on your organization's LAN when you are traveling to another state or country, or you might want to make a resource on your computer available to a branch office or even to a single user in another city or state. Your employees might also need Internet access on your local LAN if you do not yet have a continuous connection, or they may need to access their e-mail while on the road. Network and Dialup software or Remote Access Services are used to connect to an ISP (Internet Service Provider) or to your company's network. Users dial in to a RAS server, connect to it through a modem, and the RAS server routes the connection to the LAN via a network interface card. Internet Connection Sharing (ICS) is used to share an Internet link with other computers on your LAN so that just one computer on the LAN functions as the gateway to the Web. This is particularly useful for small networks where it may not be feasible to have separate dial-up connections for different computers on a network.

Security is an important consideration when you access resources over a public network. In order to create secure connections, Windows 2000 Professional supports several protocols that provide security, authentication, and encryption for RAS connections. Virtual Private Networks (VPNs) are used to create secure connections over an untrusted public network. VPNs use tunneling protocols to create a secure tunnel within the public Internet through which the corporate LAN can be accessed.

Goals

In this lesson, you will learn how to use RAS to connect a Windows 2000 PC to a remote computer or a remote network. You will learn to configure both outbound and inbound connections, as well as how to share an Internet link using Internet Connection Sharing (ICS). You will also learn about the protocols that are used to enhance security and how to create a VPN.

Lesson 16 Configuring Remote Access and Dial-Up Networking

Skill	*MCSE Exam 70-210 Objective*
1. Introduction to the Protocols in Windows 2000 Professional	Basic knowledge
2. Configuring Outbound Connections	Basic knowledge
3. Creating a Dial-Up Connection to a Remote Access Server	Create a dial-up connection to connect to a remote access server.
4. Connecting to the Internet by Using a Dial-Up Connection	Connect to the Internet by using dial-up networking.
5. Setting up a VPN Connection	Connect to computers by using a virtual private network (VPN) connection.
6. Configuring Inbound Connections	Basic knowledge
7. Configuring Internet Connection Sharing	Configure and troubleshoot Internet Connection Sharing.

Requirements

To complete this lesson, you will need a Windows 2000 Professional machine with a standard 56.6 Kbps modem and the TCP/IP protocol installed. It must also be configured with a static IP address.

MCSE Exam 210

- Main Book—organized by skills.
- Student Project Book—for practicing skills in realistic settings.
- Examination Guide—organized by MCSE/MCSA domains and objectives to practice answering questions representative of questions you are likely to encounter in the actual MCSE/MCSA examination.
- Interactive multimedia CD ROM—organized by MCSE/MCSA domains and objectives—that allows students to practice performing MCSE/MCSA objectives in a simulated Windows environment.
- Powerful Website—provides additional questions, projects, and interactive training.

Within each component, the learning is organized by skills, beginning with the relatively simple skills and progressing rapidly through the more complex skills. Each skill is carefully explained in a series of steps and conceptual overviews describing why the skill is important.

The CD ROM is especially useful to students who do not have access to a Windows network on which they can practice skills. It also is useful to all students who want to practice MCSE/MCSA skills efficiently without disturbing an existing network. Together, these five components make the Laudon Certification Series an effective learning tool for students, increasing the speed of comprehension and the retention of knowledge.

Interactive media multi-channel learning. A third distinguishing feature of the Laudon MCSE/MCSA Certification Series is interactive media *multi-channel* learning. Multi-channel learning recognizes that students learn in different ways, and the more different channels used to teach students, the greater the comprehension and retention. Using the MCSE/MCSA Interactive Solutions CD ROM, students can see, hear, read, and actually perform the skills needed in a simulated Windows environment on the CD ROM. The CD ROM is based directly on materials in the books, and therefore shares the same high quality and reliability. The CD ROM and Website for the book provide high levels of real interactive learning—not just rote exam questions—and offer realistic opportunities to interact with the Windows operating system to practice skills in the software environment without having to install a new version of Windows or build a network.

Supplements Available for This Series:

1. Test Bank

The Test Bank is a Word document distributed with the Instructor's Manual (usually on a CD). It is distributed on the Internet to Instructors only. The purpose of the Test Bank is to provide instructors and students with a convenient way for testing comprehension of material presented in the book. The Test Bank contains forty multiple-choice questions and ten true/false questions per Lesson. The questions are based on material presented in the book and are not generic MCSE questions.

2. Instructor's Manual

The Instructor's Manual (IM) is a Word document (distributed to Instructors only) that provides instructional tips, answers to the Test Yourself questions and the Problem Solving Scenarios. The IM also includes an introduction to each Lesson, teaching objectives, and teaching suggestions.

3. PowerPoint Slides

The PowerPoint slides contain images of all the conceptual figures and screenshots in each book. The purpose of the slides is to provide the instructor with a convenient means of reviewing the content of the book in the classroom setting.

4. Companion Website

The Companion Website is a Pearson learning tool that provides students and instructors with online support. On the Laudon MCSE/MCSA Certification Series Companion Website, you will find the Interactive Study Guide, a Web-based interactive quiz composed of fifteen or more questions per Lesson. Written by the authors, there are more than 255 free interactive questions on the Companion Website. The purpose of the Interactive Study Guide is to provide students with a convenient online mechanism for self-testing their comprehension of the book material.

About This Book

Exam 70-217 Implementing and Administering a Microsoft Windows 2000 Directory Services Infrastructure

This book covers the subject matter of Microsoft's Exam 70-217. The focus in this book is on Windows 2000 directory services infrastructure. You will learn about a variety of tools that are used to implement, configure, and administer Windows 2000 directory services, which are implemented through a database known as Active Directory. You will be introduced to the architecture of Active Directory, as well as its components and physical and logical structure. You will also learn how to manage and troubleshoot Active Directory, ensuring that you can implement a network that runs smoothly.

The following knowledge domains are discussed in this book:

- Installing and Configuring Active Directory.
- Installing, Configuring, Managing, Monitoring, and Troubleshooting DNS for Active Directory.
- Configuring, Managing, Monitoring, Optimizing, and Troubleshooting Change and Configuration Management.
- Managing, Monitoring, and Optimizing the Components of Active Directory.
- Configuring, Managing, Monitoring, and Troubleshooting Security in a Directory Services Infrastructure.

How This Book Is Organized

This book is organized into a series of Lessons. Each Lesson focuses on a set of skills you will need to learn in order to master the knowledge domains required by the MCSE/MCSA examinations. The skills are organized in a logical progression from basic knowledge skills to more specific skills. Some skills—usually at the beginning of Lessons—give you the background knowledge you will need in order to understand basic operating system and networking concepts. Most skills, however, give you hands-on experience working with Windows XP Professional and, in some cases, Windows 2000 Server. You will follow step-by-step instructions to perform tasks using the software.

At the beginning of each Lesson, you will find a table that links the skills covered to specific exam objectives. For each skill presented on a 2-page spread, the MCSE/MCSA objective is listed.

The MCSE/MCSA Certification

The MCSE/MCSA certification is one of the most recognized certifications in the Information Technology world. By following a clear-cut strategy of preparation, you will be able to pass the certification exams. The first thing to remember is that there are no quick and easy routes to certification. No one can guarantee you will receive a certification—no matter what they promise. Real-world MCSE/MCSAs get certified by following a strategy involving self-study, on-the-job experience, and classroom learning, either in colleges or training institutes. Below are answers to frequently asked questions that should help you prepare for the certification exams.

What Is the MCP Program?

The MCP program refers to the Microsoft Certified Professional program that certifies individuals who have passed Microsoft certification examinations. Certification is desirable for both individuals and organizations. For individuals, an MCP certification signifies to employers your expertise and skills in implementing Microsoft software in organizations. For employers, MCP certification makes it easy to identify potential employees with the requisite skills to develop and administer Microsoft tools. In a recent survey reported by Microsoft, 89% of hiring managers said they recommend a Microsoft MCP certification for candidates seeking IT positions.

What Are the MCP Certifications?

Today there are seven different MCP certifications. Some certifications emphasize administrative as well as technical skills, while other certifications focus more on technical skills in developing software applications. Below is a listing of the MCP certifications. The Laudon MCSE/MCSA Certification Series focuses on the first two certifications.

- *MCSA:* Microsoft Certified Systems Administrators (MCSAs) administer network and systems environments based on the Microsoft Windows® platforms.
- *MCSE:* Microsoft Certified Systems Engineers (MCSEs) analyze business requirements to design and implement an infrastructure solution based on the Windows platform and Microsoft Server software.
- *MCDBA:* Microsoft Certified Database Administrators (MCDBAs) design, implement, and administer Microsoft SQL Server™ databases.
- *MCT:* Microsoft Certified Trainers (MCTs) are qualified instructors, certified by Microsoft, who deliver Microsoft training courses to IT professionals and developers.
- *MCAD:* Microsoft Certified Application Developers (MCADs) use Microsoft technologies to develop and maintain department-level applications, components, Web or desktop clients, or back-end data services.
- *MCSD:* Microsoft Certified Solution Developers (MCSDs) design and develop leading-edge enterprise-class applications with Microsoft development tools, technologies, platforms, and the Windows architecture.
- *Microsoft Office Specialist:* Microsoft Office Specialists (Office Specialists) are globally recognized for demonstrating advanced skills with Microsoft desktop software.
- *MCP:* Microsoft certified Professionals

What Is the Difference Between MCSA and MCSE Certification?

There are two certifications that focus on the implementation and administration of the Microsoft operating systems and networking tools: MCSA and MCSE. The MCSA credential is designed to train IT professionals who are concerned with the management, support, and troubleshooting of existing systems and networks (see diagram below).

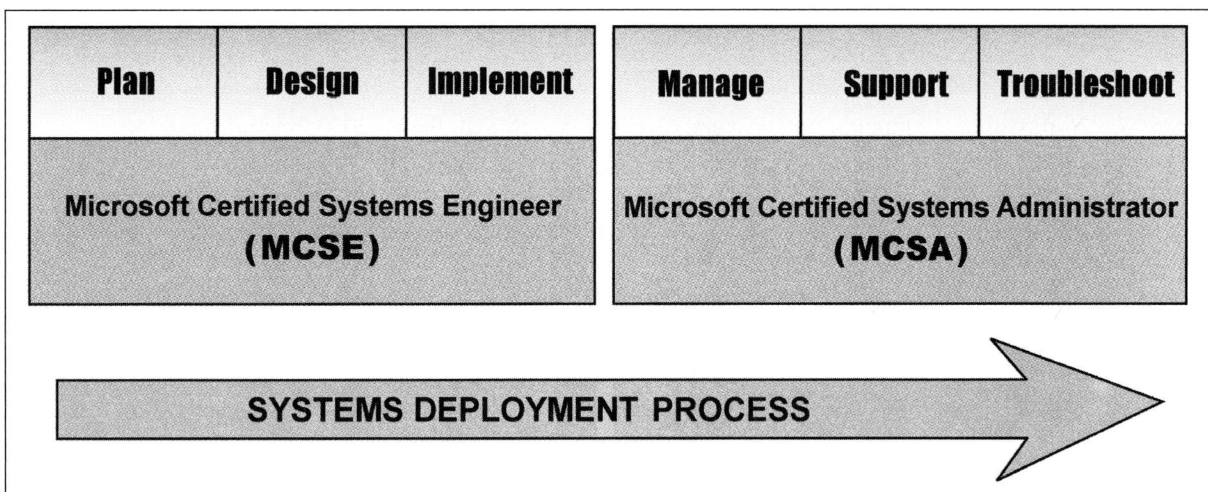

MCSA prepares you for jobs with titles such as Systems Administrator, Network Administrator, Information Systems Administrator, Network Operations Analyst, Network Technician, or Technical Support Specialist. Microsoft recommends that you have six to twelve months experience managing and supporting desktops, servers, and networks in an existing network infrastructure.

The MCSE certification is designed to train IT professionals who are concerned with the planning, designing, and implementation of new systems or major upgrades of existing systems. MCSE prepares you for jobs with titles such as Systems Engineer, Network Engineer, Systems Analyst, Network Analyst, or Technical Consultant. Microsoft recommends that you have at least one year of experience planning, designing, and implementing Microsoft products.

What Does the MCSA on Windows 2000 Require?

MCSA candidates are required to pass a total of four exams: three core exams and one elective exam. The list below shows examinations that are included in the MCSA track.

Core Exams (3 Exams Required)

(A) Client Operating System (1 Exam Required)

- *Exam 70-210:* Installing, Configuring, and Administering Microsoft Windows 2000 Professional

  or
- *Exam 70-270:* Installing, Configuring, and Administering Microsoft Windows XP Professional

(B) Networking System (2 Exams Required)

- *Exam 70-215:* Installing, Configuring, and Administering Microsoft Windows 2000 Server

  and
- *Exam 70-218:* Managing a Microsoft Windows 2000 Network Environment

Elective Exams (1 Exam Required)

- *Exam 70-028:* Administering Microsoft SQL Server 7.0
- *Exam 70-081:* Implementing and Supporting Microsoft Exchange Server 5.5
- *Exam 70-086:* Implementing and Supporting Microsoft Systems Management Server 2.0
- *Exam 70-088:* Implementing and Supporting Microsoft Proxy Server 2.0
- *Exam 70-214:* Implementing and Administering Security in a Microsoft Windows 2000 Network
- *Exam 70-216:* Implementing and Administering a Microsoft Windows 2000 Network Infrastructure
- *Exam 70-224:* Installing, Configuring, and Administering Microsoft Exchange 2000 Server
- *Exam 70-227:* Installing, Configuring, and Administering Microsoft Internet Security and Acceleration (ISA) Server 2000, Enterprise Edition
- *Exam 70-228:* Installing, Configuring, and Administering Microsoft SQL Server 2000 Enterprise Edition
- *Exam 70-244:* Supporting and Maintaining a Microsoft Windows NT Server 4.0 Network

As an alternative to the electives listed above, you may substitute the following third-party certification combinations for an MCSA elective:

CompTIA Exams: *CompTIA A+* and *CompTIA Network+*
CompTIA A+ and *CompServer+*

What Is the MCSE Curriculum for Windows 2000?

MCSE candidates are required to pass a total of seven exams: five core exams and two elective exams. The list below shows the examinations that are included in the MCSA track.

Core Exams (5 Exams Required)

(A) Client Operating System (1 exam required)

- *Exam 70-210:* Installing, Configuring, and Administering Microsoft Windows 2000 Professional

  or
- *Exam 70-270:* Installing, Configuring, and Administering Microsoft Windows XP Professional

(B) Networking System (3 Exams Required)

- *Exam 70-215:* Installing, Configuring, and Administering Microsoft Windows 2000 Server
- *Exam 70-216:* Implementing and Administering a Microsoft Windows 2000 Network Infrastructure

  and
- *Exam 70-217:* Implementing and Administering a Microsoft Windows 2000 Directory Services Infrastructure

(C) Design (1 Exam Required)

- *Exam 70-219:* Designing a Microsoft Windows 2000 Directory Services Infrastructure
- *Exam 70-220:* Designing Security for a Microsoft Windows 2000 Network
- *Exam 70-221:* Designing a Microsoft Windows 2000 Network Infrastructure
- *Exam 70-226:* Designing Highly Available Web Solutions with Microsoft Windows 2000 Server Technologies

Elective Exams (2 Exams Required)

- *Exam 70-019:* Designing and Implementing Data Warehouses with Microsoft SQL Server™ 7.0
- *Exam 70-028:* Administering Microsoft SQL Server™ 7.0
- *Exam 70-029:* Designing and Implementing Databases with Microsoft SQL Server™ 7.0
- *Exam 70-056:* Implementing and Supporting Web Sites Using Microsoft Site Server 3.0
- *Exam 70-080:* Implementing and Supporting Microsoft Internet Explorer 5.0 by Using the Microsoft Internet Explorer Administration Kit
- *Exam 70-081:* Implementing and Supporting Microsoft Exchange Server 5.5
- *Exam 70-085:* Implementing and Supporting Microsoft SNA Server 4.0
- *Exam 70-086:* Implementing and Supporting Microsoft Systems Management Server 2.0
- *Exam 70-088:* Implementing and Supporting Microsoft Proxy Server 2.0
- *Exam 70-214:* Implementing and Administering Security in a Microsoft Windows 2000 Network
- *Exam 70-218:* Managing a Microsoft Windows 2000 Network Environment
- *Exam 70-219:* Designing a Microsoft Windows 2000 Directory Services Infrastructure
- *Exam 70-220:* Designing Security for a Microsoft Windows 2000 Network
- *Exam 70-221:* Designing a Microsoft Windows 2000 Network Infrastructure
- *Exam 70-222:* Migrating from Microsoft Windows NT 4.0 to Microsoft Windows 2000
- *Exam 70-223:* Installing, Configuring, and Administering Microsoft Clustering Services by Using Microsoft Windows 2000 Advanced Server
- *Exam 70-224:* Installing, Configuring, and Administering Microsoft Exchange 2000 Server
- *Exam 70-225:* Designing and Deploying a Messaging Infrastructure with Microsoft Exchange 2000 Server
- *Exam 70-226:* Designing Highly Available Web Solutions with Microsoft Windows 2000 Server Technologies
- *Exam 70-227:* Installing, Configuring, and Administering Microsoft Internet Security and Acceleration (ISA) Server 2000 Enterprise Edition
- *Exam 70-228:* Installing, Configuring, and Administering Microsoft SQL Server™ 2000 Enterprise Edition
- *Exam 70-229:* Designing and Implementing Databases with Microsoft SQL Server™ 2000 Enterprise Edition
- *Exam 70-230:* Designing and Implementing Solutions with Microsoft BizTalk® Server 2000 Enterprise Edition
- *Exam 70-232:* Implementing and Maintaining Highly Available Web Solutions with Microsoft Windows 2000 Server Technologies and Microsoft Application Center 2000
- *Exam 70-234:* Designing and Implementing Solutions with Microsoft Commerce Server 2000
- *Exam 70-244:* Supporting and Maintaining a Microsoft Windows NT Server 4.0 Network

What About Windows Server 2003?

Windows Server 2003 is the latest release of Microsoft's family of network operating systems. In early 2003, Microsoft began releasing the full requirements for the MCSE and MCSA examinations on Microsoft Windows Server 2003. The MCP program will offer an upgrade path consisting of one or two exams that will enable current MCSEs and MCSAs on Windows 2000 to update their respective certification to the Windows Server 2003 track. You should check with the Microsoft Certification Program official Website at: **http://www.microsoft.com/traincert/mcp/default.asp** for the latest information. Microsoft recommends that until the software and examination requirements are released, individuals should continue to pursue training and certification in Windows 2000, because the skills acquired for Windows 2000 are highly relevant to, and provide a solid foundation for, Windows 2003 Server. To retain certification, MCSEs and MCSAs on Windows 2000 will *not* be required to pass Windows 2003 Server exams. If you are training on a Windows 2000 network for Windows 2000 certifications, you should continue to do so.

Do You Need to Pursue Certification to Benefit from This Book?

No. The Laudon MCSE/MCSA Certification Series is designed to prepare you for the workplace by providing you with networking knowledge and skills regardless of certification programs. While it is desirable to obtain a certification, you can certainly benefit greatly by just reading these books, practicing your skills in the simulated Windows environment found on the MCSE/MCSA Interactive Series CD ROM, and using the online interactive study guide.

What Kinds of Questions Are on the Exam?

The MCSE/MCSA exams typically involve a variety of question formats.

(a) Select-and-Place Exam Items (Drag and Drop)

A select-and-place exam item asks candidates to understand a scenario and assemble a solution (graphically on screen) by picking up screen objects and moving them to their appropriate location to assemble the solution. For instance, you might be asked to place routers, clients, and servers on a network and illustrate how they would be connected to the Internet. This type of exam item can measure architectural, design, troubleshooting, and component recognition skills more accurately than traditional exam items can, because the solution—a graphical diagram—is presented in a form that is familiar to the computer professional.

(b) Case Study-Based Multiple-Choice Exam Items

The candidate is presented with a scenario based on typical Windows installations, and then is asked to answer several multiple-choice questions. To make the questions more challenging, several correct answers may be presented, and you will be asked to choose all that are correct. The Laudon Certification Series Test Yourself questions at the end of each Lesson give you experience with these kinds of questions.

(c) Simulations

Simulations test your ability to perform tasks in a simulated Windows environment. A simulation imitates the functionality and interface of Windows operating systems. The simulation usually involves a scenario in which you will be asked to perform several tasks in the simulated environment, including working with dialog boxes and entering information. The Laudon Certification Series Interactive Media CD-ROM gives you experience working in a simulated Windows environment.

(d) Computer Adaptive Testing

A computer adaptive test (CAT) attempts to adapt the level of question difficulty to the knowledge of each individual examinee. An adaptive exam starts with several easy questions. If you get these right, more difficult questions are pitched. If you fail a question, the next questions will be easier. Eventually the test will discover how much you know and what you can accomplish in a Windows environment.

You can find out more about the exam questions and take sample exams at the Microsoft Website:
http://www.microsoft.com/ traincert/mcp/default.asp.

How Long is the Exam?

Exams have fifty to seventy questions and last anywhere from 60 minutes to 240 minutes. The variation in exam length is due to variation in the requirements for specific exams (some exams have many more requirements than others), and because the adaptive exams take much less time than traditional exams. When you register for an exam, you will be told how much time you should expect to spend at the testing center. In some cases, the exams include timed sections that can help for apportioning your time.

What Is the Testing Experience Like?

You are required to bring two forms of identification that include your signature and one photo ID (such as a driver's license or company security ID). You will be required to sign a non-disclosure agreement that obligates you not to share the contents of the exam questions with others, and you will be asked to complete a survey. The rules and procedures of the exam will be explained to you by Testing Center administrators. You will be introduced to the testing equipment and you will be offered an exam tutorial intended to familiarize you with the testing equipment. This is a good idea. You will not be allowed to communicate with other examinees or with outsiders during the exam. You should definitely turn off your cell phone when taking the exam.

How Can You Best Prepare for the Exams?

Prepare for each exam by reading this book, and then practicing your skills in a simulated environment on the CD ROM that accompanies this series. If you do not have a real network to practice on (and if you do not build a small network), the next best thing is to work with the CD ROM. Alternatively, it is very helpful to build a small Windows 2000 network with a couple of unused computers. You will also require experience with a real-world Windows 2000 network. An MCSE/MCSA candidate should, at a minimum, have at least one year of experience implementing and administering a network operating system in environments with the following characteristics: a minimum of 200 users, five supported physical locations, typical network services and applications including file and print, database, messaging, proxy server or firewall, dial-in server, desktop management, and Web hosting, and connectivity needs, including connecting individual offices and users at remote locations to the corporate network and connecting corporate networks to the Internet.

In addition, an MCSE candidate should have at least one year of experience in the following areas: implementing and administering a desktop operating system, and designing a network infrastructure.

Where Can You Take the Exams?

All MCP exams are administered by Pearson VUE and Prometric. There are 3 convenient ways to schedule your exams with Pearson VUE:

- Online: **www.pearsonvue.com/ms/**
- Toll Free in the US and Canada: call (800) TEST-REG (800-837-8734). Or, find a call center in your part of the world at: **http://www.pearsonvue.com/contact/ms/**
- In person: at your local test center. Pearson VUE has over 3,000 test centers in 130 countries. To find a test center near you, visit: **www.pearsonvue.com**

To take exams at a Prometric testing center, call Prometric at (800) 755-EXAM (755-3926). Outside the United States and Canada, contact your local Prometric Registration Center. To register online with Prometric, visit the Prometric web site, **www.prometric.com**.

How Much Does It Cost to Take the Exams?

In the United States, exams cost $125 USD per exam as of January, 2002. Certification exam prices are subject to change. In some countries/regions, additional taxes may apply. Contact your test registration center for exact pricing.

Are There Any Discounts Available to Students?

Yes. In the US and Canada, as well as other select regions around the globe, full-time students can take a subset of the MCP exams for a significantly reduced fee at Authorized Academic Testing Centers (AATCs). For details on which countries and exams are included in the program, or to schedule your discounted exam, visit **www.pearsonvue.com/aatc**.

Can You Take the Exam More Than Once?

Yes. You may retake an exam at any time if you do not pass on the first attempt. But if you do not pass the second time, you must wait fourteen days. A 14-day waiting period will be imposed for all subsequent exam retakes. If you have passed an exam, you cannot take it again.

Where Can I Get More Information about the Exams?

Microsoft Websites are a good place to start:

MCP Program (general): **http://www.microsoft.com/traincert/mcp/default.asp**

MCSE Certification: **http://www.microsoft.com/traincert/mcp/mcse/default.asp**

MCSA Certification: **http://www.microsoft.com/traincert/mcp/mcsa/default.asp**

There are literally thousands of other Websites with helpful information that you can identify using any Web search engine. Many commercial sites will promise instant success, and some even guarantee you will pass the exams. Be a discriminating consumer. If it were that easy to become an MCP professional, the certification would be meaningless.

Acknowledgments

A great many people have contributed to the Laudon MCSE/MCSA Certification Series. We want to thank Steven Elliot, our editor at Prentice Hall, for his enthusiastic appreciation of the project, his personal support for the Azimuth team, and his deep commitment to the goal of creating a powerful, accurate, and enjoyable learning tool for students. We also want to thank David Alexander of Prentice Hall for his interim leadership and advice as the project developed at Prentice Hall, and Jerome Grant for supporting the development of high-quality certification training books and CDs for colleges and universities worldwide. Finally, we want to thank Susan Hartman Sullivan of Addison Wesley for believing in this project at an early stage and for encouraging us to fulfill our dreams.

The Azimuth Interactive MCSE/MCSA team is a dedicated group of technical experts, computer scientists, networking specialists, and writers with literally decades of experience in computer networking, information technology and systems, and computer technology. We want to thank the members of the team:

Kenneth C. Laudon is the Series Designer. He is Professor of Information Systems at New York University's Stern School of Business. He has written twelve books on information systems and technologies, e-commerce, and management information systems. He has designed, installed, and fixed computer networks since 1982.

Carol G. Traver is the Senior Series Editor. She is General Counsel and Vice President of Business Development at Azimuth Interactive, Inc. A graduate of Yale Law School, she has co-authored several best-selling books on information technology and e-commerce.

Kenneth Rosenblatt is a Senior Author for the Series. He is an experienced technical writer and editor who has co-authored or contributed to over two dozen books on computer and software instruction. In addition, Ken has over five years experience in designing, implementing, and managing Microsoft operating systems and networks.

Robin L. Pickering is a Senior Author for the Series. She is an experienced technical writer and editor who has co-authored or contributed to over a dozen books on computers and software instruction. Robin has extensive experience as a Network Administrator and consultant for a number of small to medium-sized firms.

Russell Polo is the Technical Advisor for the Series. He holds degrees in computer science and electrical engineering. He has designed, implemented, and managed Microsoft, UNIX, and Novell networks in a number of business firms since 1995. He currently is the Network Administrator at Azimuth Interactive.

David Langley is an Editor for the Series. David is an experienced technical writer and editor who has co-authored or contributed to over ten books on computers and software instruction. In addition, he has over fifteen years experience as a college professor, five of those in computer software training.

Kevin Jensen is a Technical Consultant and Editor for the Series. He is a Systems Consultant, Trainer, Administrator, and Independent Technical Editor. Kevin's industry certifications are MCSE on Windows 2000, Microsoft Certified Trainer (MCT), Certified Novell Engineer (CNE), Certified Netware Instructor (CNI), and Certified Technical Trainer (CTT). Kevin has specialized in enterprise network management, design, and interoperability between different network operating systems.

Mark Maxwell is a Technical Consultant and Editor for the Series. He has over fifteen years of industry experience in distributed network environments including TCP/IP, fault-tolerant NFS file service, Kerberos, Wide Area Networks, and Virtual Private Networks. In addition, Mark has published articles on network design, upgrades, and security.

Brian Hill is a Technical Consultant and Editor for the Series. His industry certifications include MCSE 2000, MCSA, CCNP, and CCDP. Brian is Lead Technology Architect and a Bootcamp instructor for Techtrain, Inc. His Windows 2000 experience spans back as far as the first Beta releases. He is also the author of *Cisco: The Complete Reference*.

Acknowledgments (cont'd)

Stacey McBrine has spent more than 18 years configuring and supporting DOS and Windows based personal computers and local area networks, along with several other operating systems. He is certified as an MCSE for Windows NT 4.0, and was one of the first 2000 persons in the world to achieve MCSE certification for Windows 2000. He has brought his real world experience to the classroom for the last 5 years as a Microsoft Certified Trainer. He holds several other certifications for Cisco, Linux, Solaris, and Security.

Barbara Wilson Ryan has over 20 years of experience in technical education, teaching application software and network operating systems to students in the United States and Southeast Asia. Her recent focus has been on the Windows NT and Windows 2000 operating systems, both at the education and technical support levels. She has authored technical site-based courses, technical online courses, and computer operating system documentation.

Richard Watson has worked in the industry for 10 years, first as a Checkpoint Certified Security Engineer (CCSE), and then as a Lead Engineer for a local Microsoft Certified Solution Provider. Among his many other industry certifications are MCSE on Windows 2000 and NT4, Microsoft Certified Trainer (MCT), Cisco Certified Network Associate (CCNA), and IBM Professional Server Expert (PSE). Richard is currently the President of Client Server Technologies Inc., which provides network installation and support, website design, and training in Beaverton, Oregon.

Quality Assurance

The Laudon MCSE/MCSA Certification Series contains literally thousands of software instructions for working with Windows products. We have taken special steps to ensure the accuracy of the statements in this series. The books and CDs are initially written by teams composed of Azimuth Interactive Inc. MCSE/MCSA professionals and writers working directly with the software as they write. Each team then collectively walks through the software instructions and screen shots to ensure accuracy. The resulting manuscripts are then thoroughly tested by an independent quality assurance team of MCSE/MCSA professionals who also perform the software instructions and check to ensure the screen shots and conceptual graphics are correct. The result is a very accurate and comprehensive learning environment for understanding Windows products.

We would like to thank the primary member of the Quality Assurance Team for his critical feedback and unstinting efforts to make sure we got it right. The primary technical editor for this book is Michael Aubert. Michael Aubert is a technical editor and technical author with over seven years of experience. He has also worked as an independent consultant and engineer on a variety of enterprise-level projects for clients in the United States. Michael's professional certifications include Microsoft Certified Systems Engineer (MCSE), Microsoft Certified Database Administrator (MCDBA), and Microsoft Certified Solution Developer (MCSD). His main areas of expertise include network engineering and security, directory services design, database administration, and solution architectures, including Microsoft .NET.

Other Books in the Laudon MCSE/MCSA Certification Series

Installing, Configuring, and Administering Microsoft® Windows® 2000 Professional Exam 70-210
ISBN 0-13-142209-X

Installing, Configuring, and Administering Microsoft® Windows® 2000 Server Exam 70-215
ISBN 0-13-142211-1

Implementing and Administering Microsoft® Windows® 2000 Network Infrastructure Exam 70-216
ISBN 0-13-142210-3

Managing a Microsoft® Windows® 2000 Network Environment Exam 70-218
ISBN 0-13-144744-0

Designing Security for a Microsoft® Windows® 2000 Network Exam 70-220 ISBN 0-13-144906-0

Installing, Configuring, and Administering Microsoft® Windows® XP Professional Exam 70-270
ISBN 0-13-144132-9

Managing and Maintaining a Microsoft® Windows® Server 2003 Environment Exam 70-290
ISBN 0-13-144743-2

Implementing, Managing, and Maintaining a Microsoft® Windows® Server 2003 Network Infrastructure Exam 70-291

Planning and Maintaining a Microsoft® Windows® Server 2003 Network Infrastructure Exam 70-293

Planning, Implementing, and Maintaining a Microsoft® Windows® Server 2003 Active Directory Infrastructure Exam 70-294

LESSON 1

Introducing Active Directory Services in Windows 2000 Server

Active Directory (AD) is Microsoft Windows 2000 Server's directory service. A directory service is a database that stores information about users and resources in a network and provides ways to access and distribute that information. Active Directory is one of the core features that makes Windows 2000 Server suitable for network administration in large organizations. Active Directory helps you more efficiently perform network administration tasks such as designing a network structure; adding, removing, and locating users and resources on a network; and managing users and resources.

The network administration features of Active Directory are based on the concepts of domains, groups, and user management first introduced with the Microsoft Windows NT operating system. However, Active Directory enhances these concepts to enable management of large domains and networks. In this lesson, we'll give you an overview of these network administration features.

You'll also need to understand some basics about Active Directory's architecture and where it fits within the architecture of Windows 2000. Active Directory is composed of layers of processes that work in mutual coordination with many interfaces and protocols to facilitate data exchange between servers and clients. Each layer consists of components that help in the proper functioning of the operating system by maintaining a smooth flow of information and data between all the layers and subsystems that are a part of the Active Directory architecture.

In this lesson, we'll also explain Active Directory's use of objects. In Active Directory, users, groups, sites, domains, and other directory components are all considered objects. Active Directory maintains a list of these objects, and stores the list in a directory database. When you search for a user account in a network, Active Directory uses the directory database to locate the object.

We'll also examine both the logical and physical structure of Active Directory. The logical structure reflects the administrative structure of an organization. The physical structure reflects the actual locations of objects in a network. The logical and physical structures are not related to one another.

Active Directory is based on concepts such as the global catalog, trust relationships, and Domain Name System (DNS). The global catalog stores information about objects in a forest, which is a collection of domains that share a common schema, global catalog, and configuration (described more fully in Skill 5). Active Directory uses information from the global catalog to locate objects in the forest. A trust relationship is a logical link between two domains that allows resources to be shared between the two domains. DNS is Windows 2000's primary method of resolving names for computers in a network into IP addresses, which is required in order to log on to a domain.

To ensure smooth functioning of a network, you need to plan the implementation of Active Directory. This requires organizing objects in a domain in a manner that simplifies access to objects and makes the task of administering these objects easier. We'll finish the lesson by going over the three main stages of Active Directory implementation: planning the domain structure, determining the domain name, and designing the site structure.

Goals

In this lesson, you will be introduced to Active Directory and its functions, features, and architecture. You will learn about Active Directory objects, components, and concepts. This lesson also covers planning a domain structure, domain namespace, and site structure.

Lesson 1 Introducing Active Directory Services in Windows 2000 Server

Skill	*Exam 70-217 Objective*
1. Introducing Active Directory	Basic knowledge
2. Identifying the Functions and Features of Active Directory	Basic knowledge
3. Introducing Active Directory Architecture	Basic knowledge
4. Introducing Active Directory Objects	Basic knowledge
5. Examining the Logical and Physical Structure of Active Directory	Basic knowledge
6. Examining More Active Directory Concepts	Basic knowledge
7. Planning a Domain Structure	Basic knowledge
8. Planning a Domain Namespace	Basic knowledge
9. Guidelines for Planning a Site Structure	Basic knowledge

Requirements

There are no special requirements for this lesson.

skill 1 Introducing Active Directory

exam objective

Basic knowledge

overview

A **directory service** is a database that stores information about users, groups, domains, and other resources (all referred to as *objects*) on a network, and provides ways to centrally access and administer that information. In Windows 2000 Server, the directory service is referred to as **Active Directory** or **AD (Figure 1-1)**. Active Directory provides a unique identity for all of its objects. Using this unique ID (known as a SID, or Security ID), an object can then be allowed or denied access to resources individually. Due to the centralized nature of Active Directory, you can access and administer the directory service globally, unlike decentralized models (also known as Peer-to-Peer), which require changes to several databases in order to effect a global change.

Active Directory's structure reduces the administrative effort required to complete day-to-day administrative tasks such as managing users and resources. For instance, Active Directory allows you to group objects and then assign network permissions to these groups rather than to individual objects. Administrators can also delegate the ability to perform common tasks to other users or groups. As a result, tasks, such as adding users on the network and assigning access permissions to network resources, are less cumbersome.

Windows NT introduced the concept of a directory service based on **domains**—collections of network resources grouped together under a single domain name and security boundary—that provide a single point of authentication for all the users on a network. However, the domain concept, as executed in Windows NT has several limitations that prevent it from being used effectively in large networks. For example, in Windows NT, the writable copy of the directory resides on a single server known as the Primary Domain Controller (PDC). All the other domain controllers (known as BDC's, or Backup Domain Controllers) store read-only copies of the database. Having only one writable copy of the database leads to a single point of failure for write operations (such as changing a password). In Windows 2000, all domain controllers are considered to be equal—except for those that handle certain specific roles discussed later in this lesson—providing more scalability and redundancy. Another limitation of Windows NT is that trust relationships between domains must be built manually, using one-way, non-transitive trusts. Trusts are required in order for a user from one domain to access resources in another domain. Managing all the different trust relationships in a large organization can be very time-consuming. Unlike Windows NT, in Active Directory, most trust relationships within a single forest are created automatically. This makes it possible for Active Directory to provide scalability in large business organizations.

Figure 1-1 Active Directory

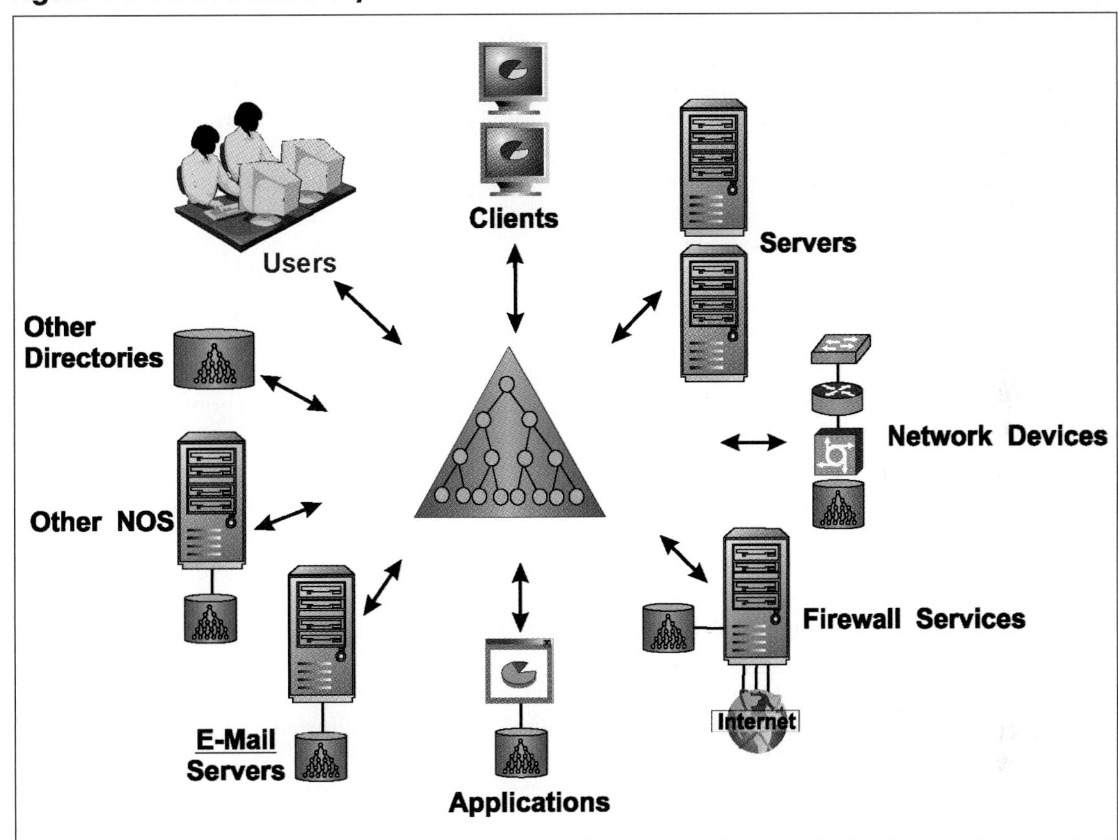

skill 2 Identifying the Functions and Features of Active Directory

exam objective

Basic knowledge

overview

Active Directory has a number of features that make it a reliable and secure directory service for a business setting. It provides policy-based administration, data security, extensibility, scalability, and information replication, and is compatible with other directory services. The following is a brief overview of each of these features (**Table 1-1**):

- Policy-based administration: Active Directory makes network administration easier by allowing administrators to manage users and computers using group policies. A **group policy** is a set of rules that apply to a part of the directory structure such as an OU, Domain, or Site. Using this feature, an administrator can make complex modifications to the user's environment, assign rights, configure network security, and even install software to collections of users or computers.
- Increased security of information: The Windows 2000 operating system supports protection of both stored data and network data. In Windows 2000, stored data can be protected using Encrypting File System (EFS) and permissions. User account information, domain-related password restrictions, and permissions for a user to access network resources—all three can be controlled by security policies that you can implement via group policy settings.
- Integration with Domain Name Service (DNS): DNS is a naming service that can translate host names into numeric IP addresses. AD uses standard DNS naming conventions for domains.
- Extensibility: Active Directory allows nearly any type of information to be added to the database as a function of having an extensible schema. The schema in Active Directory can be viewed as the "rulebook" that AD plays by. The **schema** contains a list of all possible object types (called Object Classes), the data fields those objects contain (known as attributes), and the relationships that are allowed between the objects. Because the schema is extensible, you can add new attributes (such as an Employee ID field) to existing objects, or even create entirely new classes of objects, to suit your company's needs. Since the schema is such an important piece of AD, it should be protected from unauthorized modifications. For this reason, AD (by default) only allows members of the Schema Administrators group write access to the schema.
- Scalability: Active Directory can store anywhere from a small number to millions of objects. An object automatically inherits the rights of the section into which it is placed.
- Information replication: Active Directory automatically replicates the contents of its database across every domain controller in the domain.
- Compatibility with other directory services: Active Directory is based on protocols, such as Lightweight Directory Access Protocol (LDAP), HTTP, and Name Service Provider Interface (NSPI), so it is compatible with other directory services that use these protocols. LDAP is used to exchange information between the directories and applications.

more

The domain controller stores schema information, configuration information, and the information about directory objects and their features in a directory called the **directory database**. Each domain controller for each domain replicates this information.

Table 1-1 Features of Active Directory

Feature	Description
Policy-based administration	Makes network administration easier by allowing administrators to manage users and computers using group policies.
Security	Supports protection of both stored data and network data.
Integration with Domain Name Service (DNS)	Uses standard DNS naming conventions for domains.
Extensibility	Allows nearly any type of information to be added to the database as a function of having an extensible schema.
Scalability	Can store anywhere from a small number to millions of objects.
Information replication	Automatically replicates the contents of its database across every domain controller in the domain.
Compatibility with other directory services	Based on protocols, such as Lightweight Directory Access Protocol (LDAP), HTTP, and Name Service Provider Interface (NSPI), so it is compatible with other directory services that use these protocols.

skill 3 Introducing Active Directory Architecture

exam objective

Basic knowledge

overview

It will be helpful to you to understand some basics about the architecture of Active Directory and where it fits within the architecture of Windows 2000. Windows 2000 architecture has two primary layers: user mode and kernel mode. The kernel mode layer consists of several components, including the Executive, the Hardware Abstraction Layer (HAL), the microkernel, and a set of kernel mode drivers. These components make it possible for the kernel mode layer to function properly. The **user mode** is the interface between the application and the kernel mode. It accepts requests from the application and forwards them to the kernel for processing. The components of the user mode are as follows:

- **Environment subsystems** provide interfaces for applications to interact with the kernel and Integral subsystems. The environment subsystem components can make such applications run by providing Application Programming Interfaces (APIs) that are used in the other operating systems, compiling them for Windows 2000, and then passing the applications to executive services in the kernel mode for processing. The most commonly used APIs in the environment subsystems are Win32, Win16, and POSIX (Portable Operating System Interface) (used primarily for Unix-based applications)
- **Integral subsystems** perform important operating system functions such as security and session management. The integral subsystem contains a security subsystem, which receives logon requests and initiates the logon authentication process; a workstation service, which enables a client computer to access the network; and a server service, which allows a Windows 2000 computer to share network resources. Active Directory is located within the security subsystem **(Figure 1-2)**.

The **kernel mode** layer communicates with the system data and hardware in order to process any input/output requests made by a user. This layer operates in a protected area of memory and is responsible for executing I/O requests. It also prioritizes hardware and software interrupts based on the precedence of the application or service making the request. An **interrupt** is a request for attention from the processor coming from hardware devices. When an interrupt is generated, the processor suspends its current operations and saves the status of its work. Then it gives control to a special routine called the interrupt handler, which contains the instructions for dealing with the particular situation that caused the interrupt. Interrupts can be generated by various hardware devices to request service or report problems. The kernel mode has four major components:

- the **Executive**, which performs I/O functions, object management, and security functions. The Executive has a number of subcomponents. For instance, the Security Reference Monitor subcomponent of the Windows 2000 Executive provides security guidelines for the user mode by providing the authentication and authorization processes, thus making Active Directory secure;
- the **microkernel**, which manages the computer's processors;
- **kernel mode drivers**, which take requests from the operating system and translate them into hardware functions; and
- the **Hardware Abstraction Layer (HAL)**, which provides the interface between the other software layers and the core hardware, allowing the Windows 2000 operating system to run on multiple hardware platforms.

These components make it possible for the kernel mode layer to function properly.

Figure 1-2 Location of Active Directory within the Windows 2000 architecture

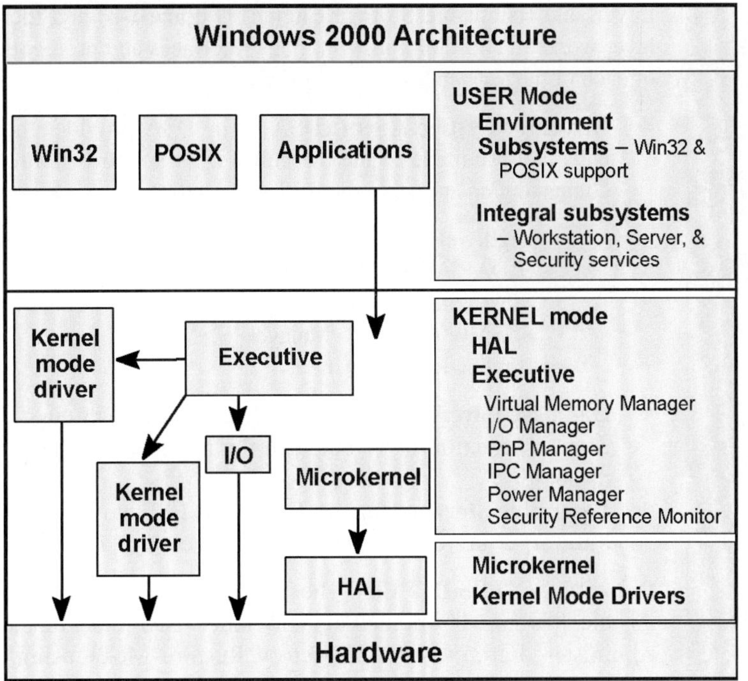

skill 3 Introducing Active Directory Architecture (cont'd)

exam objective

Basic knowledge

overview

Active Directory itself is made up of three service layers (Directory System Agent, Database Layer, and Extensible Storage Engine) **(Figure 1-3)** and the underlying Data Store. Each layer works in coordination with many interfaces and protocols. Below is a fuller description of each of the service layers, and the Data Store.

- **Directory System Agent (DSA):** The DSA provides the interface for the application calls that are made to the directory. DSA supports the following protocols that enable clients to gain access to the Active Directory:
    - Lightweight Directory Access Protocol / Active Directory Service Interface (LDAP/ADSI)
    - Messaging API (MAPI)
    - Security Accounts Manager (SAM)
    - Replication (REPL)
- **Database Layer:** Access calls to the database go through the Database Layer, which acts as an abstraction layer between the applications that make the access calls and the database.
- **Extensible Storage Engine (ESE):** The ESE has a direct contact with the records in the directory data store. It is based on an object's relative distinguished name attribute.

Data Store (NTDS.DIT file): The records making up the Active Directory database reside in this file. It is stored by default in the \Winnt\NTDS folder on the domain controller and can be administered from Active Directory Restore Mode using NTDSUTIL, located in the System32 folder in the Winnt folder.

Figure 1-3 Active Directory architecture

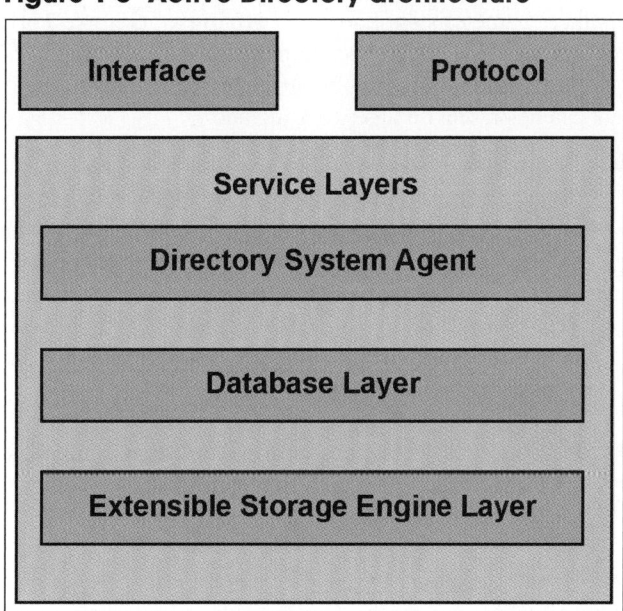

skill 4

Introducing Active Directory Objects

exam objective

Basic knowledge

overview

Active Directory treats each domain resource as an **object**. Each object is represented by distinct characteristics known as **attributes (Figure 1-4)**. The attributes help you locate objects in a domain. For example, to locate a computer in a network, you will use the computer name or description attribute of the object. The types of Active Directory objects that can be present on a network include:

- **User accounts** store the logon information of users in a domain. A domain acts as a security boundary: assuming no trusts are in place, users may only access objects within their own domains. Some of the details a user account may include are user logon name, password, and the user's first name, last name, telephone number, and e-mail address.

- You use **contacts** to store information about any person or organization that has business relations with your organization. This information includes name, address, telephone number, and e-mail address.

- **Computer objects** store information about computers that are members of a domain. This information includes computer name, description, and other attributes discussed in more detail in later lessons.

- **Groups** are objects used to apply permissions across large numbers of users, computers, and even other groups. While groups are not strictly containers (at least, not in the same manner as an OU, for instance), groups have membership lists that define which objects are members of the group. You use groups to organize users and resources into units in order to manage them more efficiently. For instance, instead of assigning rights and permissions to each user separately, you can assign rights and permissions to a group of users at once.

- **Published folders** are shared folders that have been listed in Active Directory. When you publish a folder in AD, you create an object that stores a pointer to the folder. Other network users may then use this pointer to access the shared folder.

- A **printer** is also represented by an object that contains a pointer to the printer on a computer. On a Windows 2000 print server, Windows 2000 automatically detects and publishes printers to Active Directory. However, you must manually publish a printer connected to a computer that is either not part of an Active Directory domain, or is attached to a down-level (pre-Windows 2000) print server.

- **Domain controllers** are Windows 2000 Server computers that authenticate user logon attempts and exchange the directory information with other domain controllers. This process of exchanging directory information is known as **replication**. In Active Directory, domain controllers use **multimaster replication** to exchange directory information with other domain controllers in a domain. In this type of arrangement, no single domain controller is responsible for replication, and all the domain controllers in a domain act as peers while replicating directory information. Although a domain controller replicates all the directory information, it immediately replicates important information, such as disabling of user accounts, to other domain controllers.

  Each Domain Controller is represented by a Domain Controller object in Active Directory. You can store the Domain Name System (DNS) name, pre-Windows 2000 name, operating system version, location, and name of the administrator in this object.

Figure 1-4 Objects and their attributes

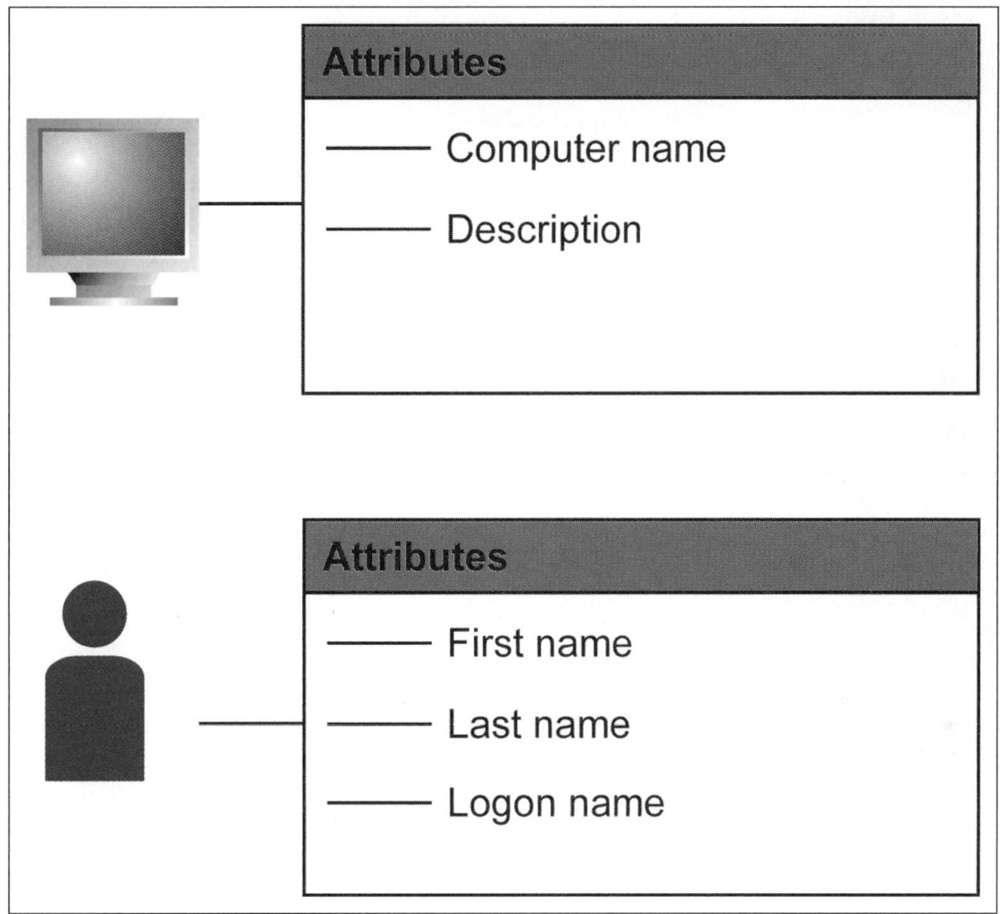

skill 4 Introducing Active Directory Objects (cont'd)

exam objective

Basic knowledge

overview

Domain controllers also handle a user's interactions with a domain such as locating objects and logon requests. While only a single domain controller is required per domain, you should usually ensure that at least two domain controllers are present for each domain. Having additional domain controllers in a domain ensures that directory information is available even if one of the domain controllers is unavailable. Additional domain controllers also share the load of the existing domain controller.

- **Organizational units (OUs)** are container objects that can store groups, users, computers, and other OUs. An OU is used to allow for organization of objects in the domain, delegation of control over a small portion of the domain, and application of group policy. An OU is the smallest unit in the domain with which you can delegate administration of users and resources in an OU to an authorized user or group of users. Only one OU exists by default in each domain—namely, the Domain Controllers OU. It is recommended that you create additional OUs to represent your organization based on your administrative needs. For instance, if you have an administrator responsible for each department, you would create an OU structure based on department. Keep in mind that OUs are domain specific, meaning each domain has its own OU structure.

Figure 1-5 shows a typical network hierarchy, while **Figure 1-6** displays how those objects would be represented onscreen by Windows 2000.

more

In Active Directory, you use names to locate objects in a network. The naming conventions that Active Directory supports for naming objects are as follows:

Distinguished name (DN): A unique name for every object in a network. It includes the name of the domain that holds the object and the complete path to the object through the container hierarchy, for instance: CN=JDoe, OU=Sales, DC=Corp, DC=Com.

Relative distinguished name (RDN): RDN is derived from the DN. The RDN of an object is simply the object's name, for instance: CN=Jdoe.

Globally unique identifier (GUID): A unique 128-bit number assigned to an object at the time of its creation. A GUID of an object does not change even when you move or rename the object.

User principal name (UPN): An easy-to-remember name of a user account. It is made up of the first name and last name attributes of a user and the UPN suffix, which is usually the DNS name of the domain where the user is situated. **Figure 1-7** displays examples of the naming conventions.

caution

In an OU, two objects cannot have the same RDN.

Figure 1-5 A typical network hierarchy

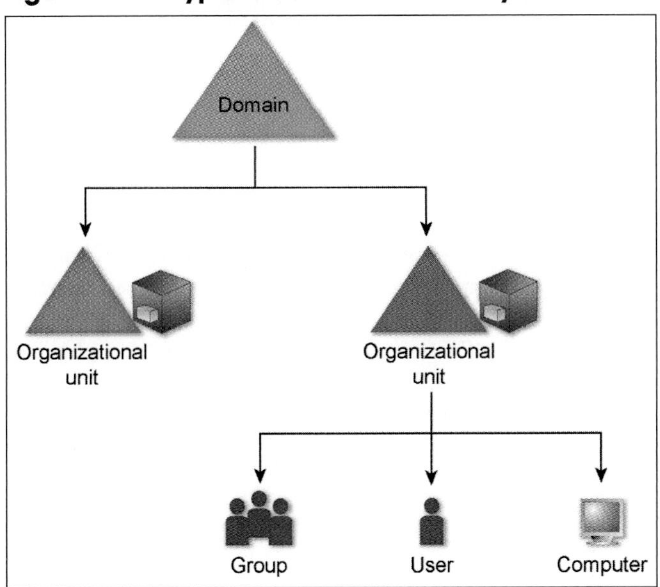

Figure 1-6 Network objects

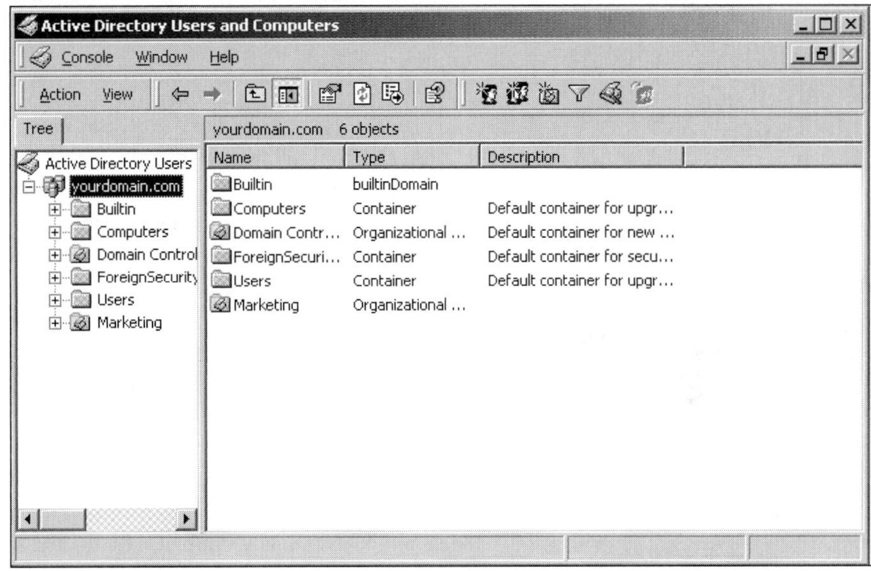

Figure 1-7 Examples of naming conventions

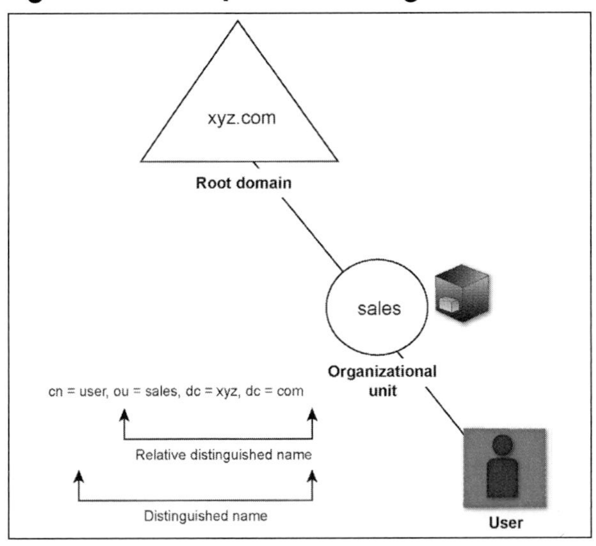

skill 5 Examining the Logical and Physical Structure of Active Directory

exam objective

Basic knowledge

overview

The objects of Active Directory can be organized logically or physically in a network. The **logical structure** consists of domains, trees, and forests. Besides being Active Directory objects, OUs are also part of the logical structure. When resources are grouped logically, you can locate a resource using its name regardless of its physical location. The **physical structure** of Active Directory is made up of sites. Domain controllers are also part of the physical structure, as well as being Active Directory objects.

Following is a list of each component of the logical structure and its characteristics:

Domains

In Active Directory, domains represent the core unit of the logical structure. You use domains to represent the administrative boundaries of your organization **(Figure 1-8)**. As you have already learned, a domain is a security boundary: only users with permission can access the objects of the domain. A domain stores information only about the objects that it contains. A domain can span multiple physical locations.

Trees

A **tree** is a hierarchical collection of one or more domains. A tree is formed when you add one or more child domains to the top-level domain, which is also known as the root of the tree **(Figure 1-9)**. The characteristics of trees are as follows:

- A tree follows a **contiguous naming scheme** where every **child domain**, or subdomain, in the tree derives its name from the **root domain** (the first domain of a domain tree).
- An implicit two-way transitive trust exists between the parent domains and child domains of a domain tree. An implicit two-way transitive trust is a type of logical link that is automatically established between domains for sharing resources.

Forests

A **forest** is a collection of domains that share a common schema, global catalog, and configuration **(Figure 1-10)**. Forests have the following characteristics:

- All domains in a forest share a common schema and a common global catalog. This enables all the domains within a forest to contain uniform information. As a result, all the users of a forest have access to the latest information about objects in the forest. As you learned in Skill 2, the schema defines the type of objects and the type of information pertaining to the objects that can be stored in Active Directory. The **global catalog** contains all objects in all domains of the forest, but only contains a small number of attributes of each object.
- Although domains in a forest operate independently, they are able to communicate with each other because all domains in a forest share a common schema.
- All domains in a forest share a common global catalog.
- Forests follow a **disjointed naming scheme** where the names of domain trees may not be related to one another.
- In a forest, an implicit two-way transitive trust exists between the root domains of domain trees and the root of the forest.

Figure 1-8 A domain structure in an organization

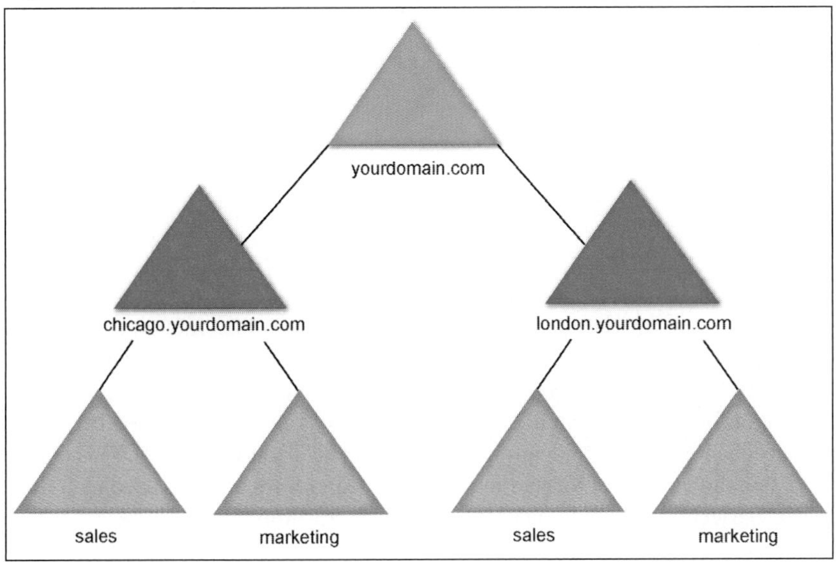

Figure 1-9 A tree structure in Active Directory

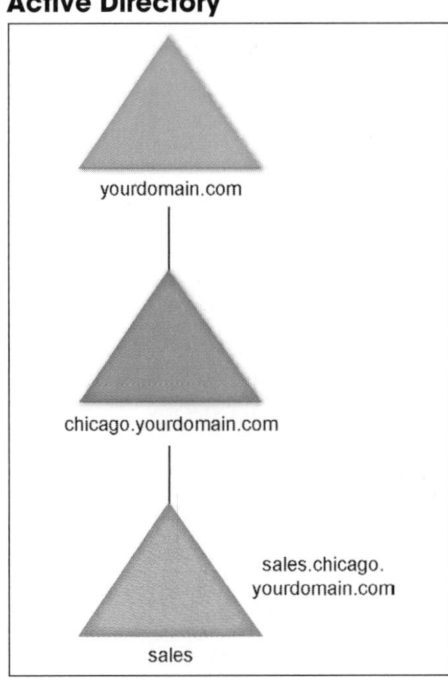

Figure 1-10 A forest structure in Active Directory

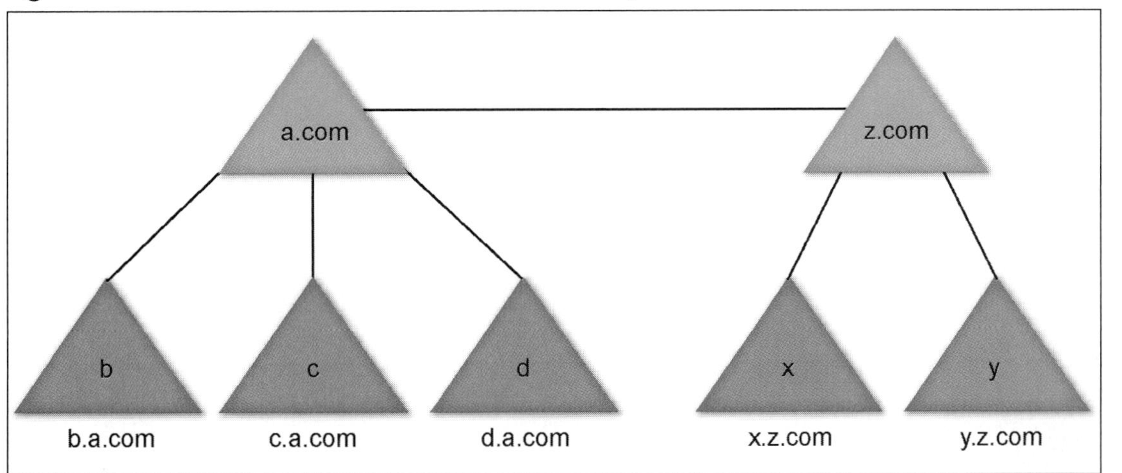

skill 5 Examining the Logical and Physical Structure of Active Directory *(cont'd)*

exam objective

Basic knowledge

overview

Sites

A site is a logical representation of a physical location within Active Directory. Subnets are always associated with sites in order to allow clients to determine which site they belong to. Subnets are AD objects containing a collection of IP addresses that are associated with a single physical location **(Figure 1-11)**. When a user logs on to a domain, in order to authenticate the logon request, the client's IP address is cross referenced with the subnet object assigned to each site in order to determine which site the client belongs to. This allows the client to use a domain controller located in its physical site. Sites are also used to control replication traffic between physical locations. Because the logical structure of Active Directory is different from the physical structure, a site can span multiple domains and a domain can span multiple sites. For example, suppose you have an organization located in a three-story building. Each floor is configured as a site. The first floor houses two domains: ACCT and DEV. The DEV domain also exists on the second floor. The site on the first floor spans multiple domains and the DEV domain spans multiple sites.

Figure 1-11 Structure of a site

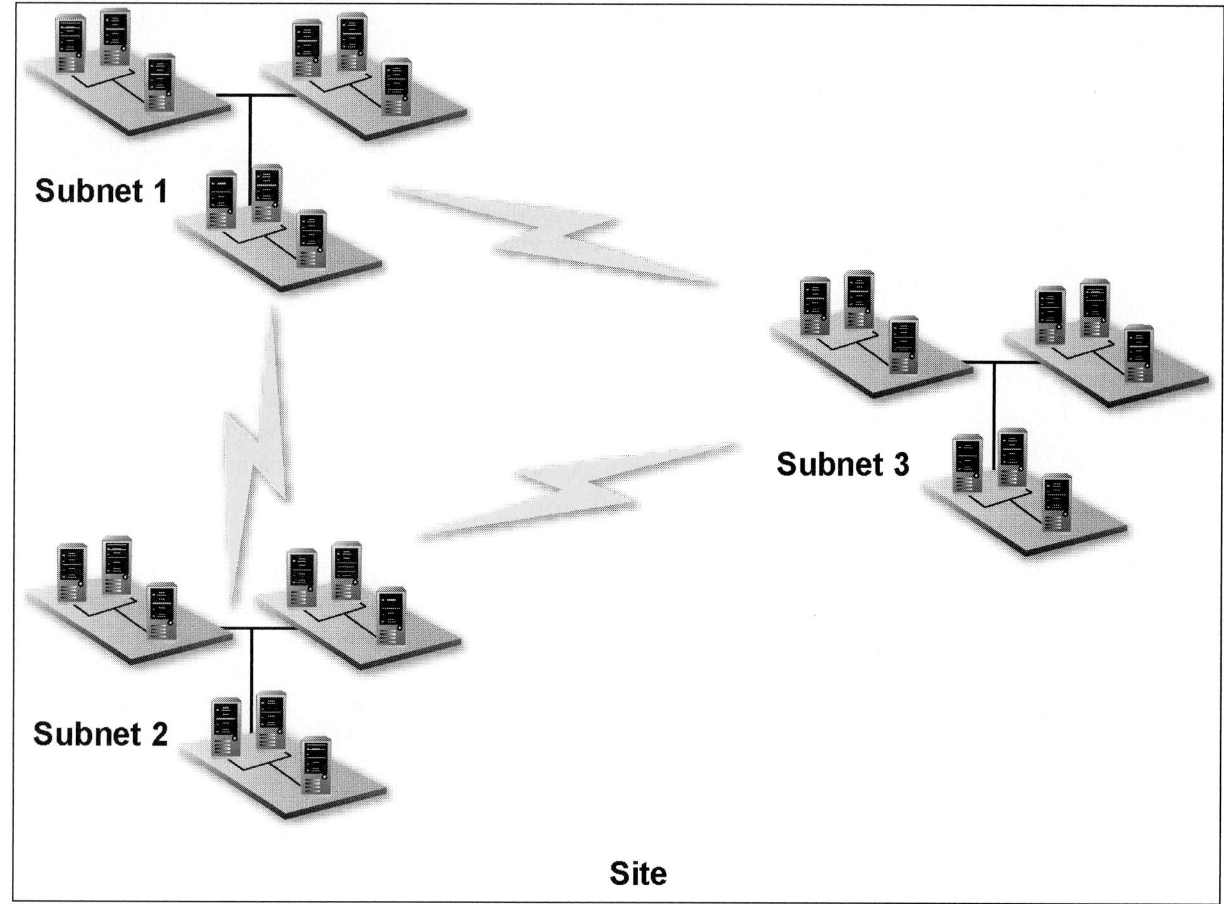

skill 6 Examining More Active Directory Concepts

exam objective Basic knowledge

overview

In previous Skills, we have mentioned global catalogs, trust relationships, and DNS. Each of these allows Active Directory to organize, manage, and locate objects, as well as maintain a stable and easy-to-administer network. In this Skill, we will look at each of these concepts further.

Global catalog

The global catalog stores information about all objects in a forest. By default, the global catalog is created on the first domain controller in a forest. This domain controller is known as a **global catalog server**. Whenever information about objects is updated, to ensure that users have access to the latest information about objects, a global catalog server exchanges this information with other global catalog servers in a forest. In a single domain, the global catalog server stores information about all objects of that domain. In multiple domains, the global catalog server stores a full replica of information about objects belonging to its domain and a partial replica of information of objects belonging to other domains **(Figure 1-12)**. The partial replica stores object information most frequently used in search operations by the users of the domain to which the global catalog server belongs. For example, the partial replica can contain object information such as a user's first name and logon name, as well as machine names.

You can add additional global catalog servers in a forest to provide backup to the default global catalog server. Additional global catalog servers also share the load of the existing global catalog server. Global catalog servers also participate in logons in native mode by performing UPN lookups, as well as providing universal group (defined below) storage. A UPN (User Principal Name) lookup is required when a user chooses to logon with their UPN **(Jdoe@corp.com)** instead of simply using his or her logon name and selecting the domain from the drop-down list. A **universal group** can contain global groups, other universal groups, and user accounts from any domain in a domain tree or forest. Universal groups are only available in native mode. A global catalog also handles user and program-related queries about objects. Because a global catalog stores information about all the objects in a forest, a query about an object can be resolved by the global catalog in the domain in which the query originated. As a result, queries are resolved quickly without generating unnecessary network traffic.

tip

If a global catalog server is not available, a user can log on to the local computer using a local account.

Trust relationship

A **trust relationship** is a logical link between two domains. Active Directory supports two general types of trusts: one-way non-transitive and two-way transitive. One way transitive trusts operate exactly like Windows NT trusts, which operate exactly like people. For example, if I trust you, then you get to drive my car. With a one way trust, if Domain A (known as the "trusting" domain) trusts Domain B (known as the "trusted" domain), then Domain B can be allowed access to Domain A's resources. However, just because Domain A trusts Domain B does not mean that Domain B trusts Domain A. In order for Domain B to trust Domain A, an additional trust must be created. This is the one-way nature of the one-way non-transitive trust. The term **transitive** means that the trust follows through; conversely, **non-transitive** means that it does not follow through. For example, if we are using one-way non-transitive trusts, and Domain A trusts Domain B, which trusts Domain C, then Domain A **does not** trust Domain C. This is, again, like people. If I trust you, then you get to drive my car. However, just because you trust Bob that does not mean that I trust Bob. In order for Bob to drive my car, I would have to specifically trust Bob. The one-way non-transitive trust relationships of Windows NT allow for a lot of flexibility and control; however, they can be confusing and difficult to manage. For this reason, Windows 2000 builds its default trusts as

Figure 1-12 Function of the global catalog server in multiple domains

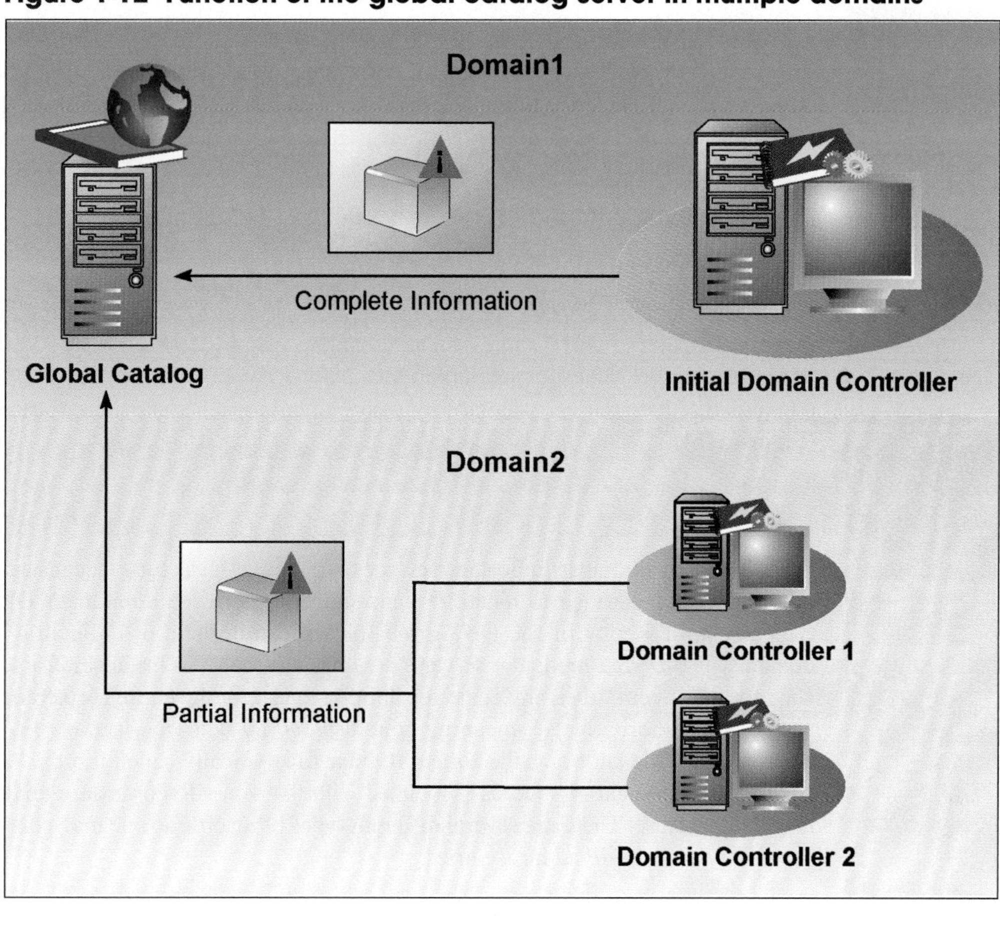

skill 6

Examining More Active Directory Concepts *(cont'd)*

exam objective

Basic knowledge

overview

two-way, transitive trusts. With these trusts, the end result is that every domain in a forest automatically trusts every other domain in a forest, by default. Keep in mind, however, that domains are still security boundaries. In other words, just because a trust exists does not automatically mean that a user from a given domain has access to resources from the other domain, only that the user can be given access to those resources **(Figure 1-13)**.

Table 1-2 lists the differences between the two types of trust relationships.

Domain Name System (DNS)

Active Directory uses DNS as its name resolution service. **Name resolution** is the process of mapping a name to an IP address. The computer running this service is known as a **DNS name server**. DNS helps computers to locate other computers in a network. DNS organizes domains in a hierarchical structure by using a naming scheme called **domain namespace (Figure 1-14)**.

more

DNS is one of the most important services for Active Directory, because computers in a domain use this service to locate domain controllers in the domain. A DNS server will typically hold a copy of the DNS zone for a given domain or collection of contiguous domains. The **DNS zone** is the server's area of authority. For instance, if a server holds the zone for "corp.com," then any name resolution request for the entire corp.com domain can be answered "authoritatively," meaning conclusively, by that DNS server. The DNS zone is contained in a file known as the **zone database file**, typically called just the "Zone file." The zone file will contain all records associated with that zone. Records are individual entries in the DNS database. There are several different types of records a zone may contain, and not all are strictly name-to-IP address entries.

Figure 1-13 Trust relationships in a network

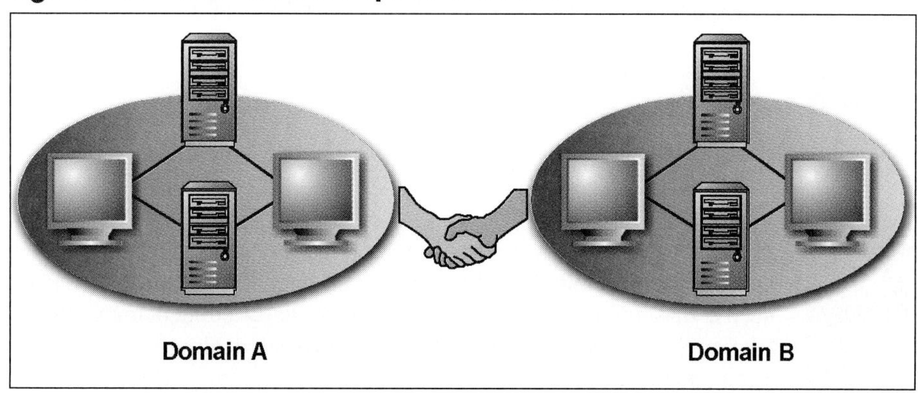

Table 1-2 Differences between the two types of trust relationships

Two-way transitive trust	One-way non-transitive trust
This is the type of trust that is automatically established between a parent and child domain, and between the root domains of each tree and the root domain of the forest. This functionality means that all domains in a forest automatically trust all other domains in the same forest.	This type of trust has the same functionality as Windows NT trusts. You can establish explicit one-way non-transitive trusts between Windows 2000 domains and Windows NT domains, between a Windows 2000 domain and a Kerberos realm, and between Windows 2000 domains in different forests.
When two domains are joined by this type of trust, each domain acts as a trusting domain, as well as a trusted domain.	When two domains are joined by this type of trust, one domain acts as a trusting domain and the other as a trusted domain. The trusted domain has the ability to gain access to the trusting domain's resources.
A transitive trust flows to other domains in a domain tree, even if they are not directly related to each other. For example, domains A and B are part of the same domain tree but are not directly related. Domains A and B have subdomains, C and D, respectively. Because the four domains are part of the same forest, all four domains will automatically be bound by an implicit two-way transitive trust.	This type of trust is restricted to the trusting and trusted domains only, and does not flow to any other domain in a forest. For instance, domains A and B are joined by an explicit one-way nontransitive trust. This trust relationship will not flow to any other domains.

Figure 1-14 Domain namespace hierarchy

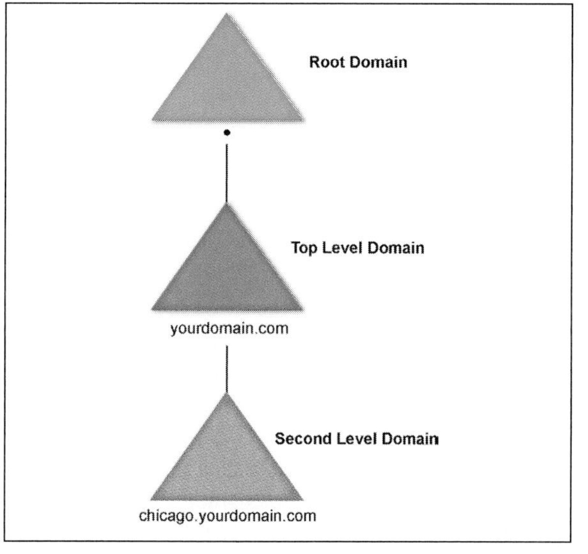

skill 7 Planning a Domain Structure

exam objective

Basic knowledge

overview

Planning a domain structure is an integral part of Active Directory implementation. In Active Directory, unlike Windows NT, domain structure is primarily dependant on administrative needs. In Windows NT, domains were typically created for each physical location. In Windows 2000, sites are used to control issues dealing with physical location (such as replication and logon traffic), and domains are simply administrative boundaries. For this reason, it is typically suggested that you keep a single domain model if at all possible.

Domain models can be broadly classified into two categories: single domain model and multiple domain model (**Figure 1-15**). While planning a domain structure, you can use either of the two domain models. To decide between the two domain models, you need to compare the advantages of both of the domain models.

A **single domain model** is easy to manage and administer because the administrative boundary is clearly defined. It is suitable for any organization that follows a truly centralized administrative model. In general, if your company does not require at least one of the three specific benefits (listed below) of a multi-domain model, you should probably use a single domain model. A single domain is easier to set up because only a single domain must be configured. A single domain model is also significantly easier to administer in most cases.

A **multiple domain model** is typically appropriate in only three specific situations: separation of domain level administrative privileges, separation of account policies (Password, account lockout, and Kerberos), and (rarely) control of localized traffic.

For separation of domain level administrative control, multiple domains are required. For instance, if your company consists of four divisions, and each division includes a group of administrators that are solely responsible for domain level changes (such as domain level group policies, delegation of control, and creation of the domain's OU structure) with no guidance from any central administrative entity, then a multiple domain model (with four domains, in this case), makes sense. However, if your company operates on a centralized or partially decentralized (also known as a hybrid) administrative model, a single domain, with OUs for delegation, is typically more appropriate and reduces administrative overhead. For instance, if your company has five locations, each with an administrative group responsible for administration related to that location, as well as a central administrative group responsible for policies and procedures that apply to the entire company, a single domain model, utilizing OUs and Sites for each specific location, is more appropriate.

caution

Always attempt to restrict the number of domains in your structure to the minimum absolutely necessary. Use OUs instead of additional domains for application of group policy and delegation of control.

For separation of account policies, you first must understand the impact of these policies. Your account policies are simply a subsection of group policy that contains the Password, Account Lockout, and Kerberos policies. The account policies section of group policy is a particularly important consideration in your domain model because these three policies, and only these three policies, can only be applied at the domain level. In other words, if you want one division of your company to only require 4 character passwords while the other division requires much more secure 8 character passwords, you will require two separate account policies to enable those features, which means you will also require a separate domain for each division. Separation of account policies is typically the most common valid reason for a multiple domain model, whether in real life or on an exam.

Finally, for control of localized traffic, you will typically use sites. However, sites will only reduce the amount of domain replication traffic between locations. If you require a complete reduction of domain-level replication traffic (i.e. no replication traffic should cross the WAN links), you may be forced to use a multiple domain model. The only method to absolutely ensure that a change to the domain database in one location will not replicate to another location is to make each location a separate domain. Please be aware that this is an exceedingly rare requirement, and is almost never a correct solution to bandwidth problems on an exam.

Figure 1-15 Domain models

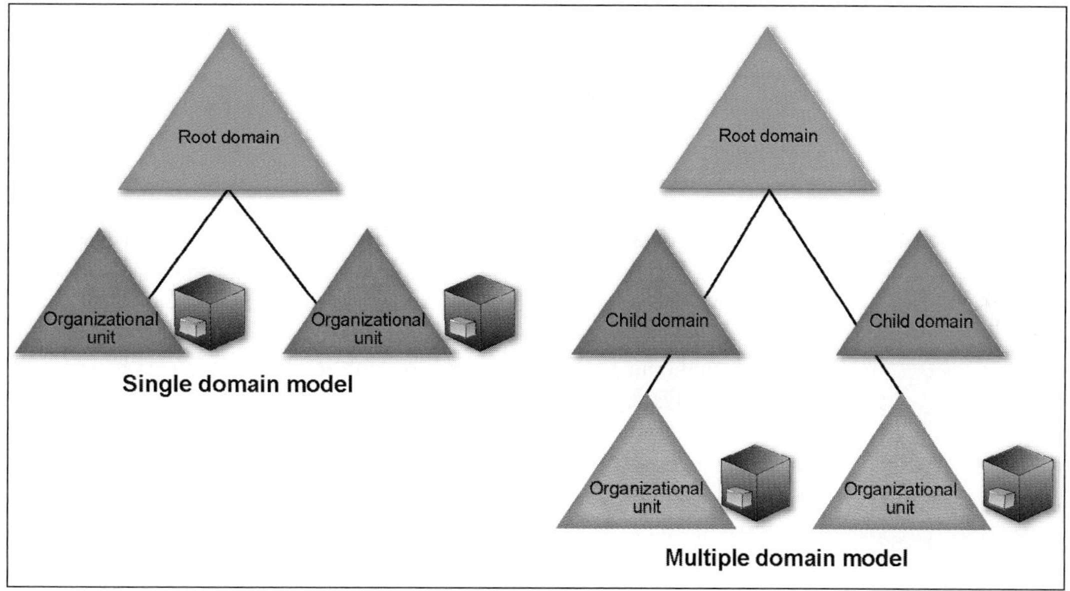

skill 8 Planning a Domain Namespace

exam objective

Basic knowledge

overview

In Active Directory, domains are named using DNS names. You need to choose a unique domain name for your organization and register it with an organization that manages Internet DNS namespaces. This organization adds an entry pointing to the authoritative name servers for your domain on the top-level name servers on the Internet (the .com servers, for instance). You can also use this domain name to host the Web site of the organization on the Internet.

There are three types of DNS namespaces: internal, external, and hybrid. Internal namespaces are not resolvable by hosts who are using public (Internet) DNS servers. These namespaces are only used for internal clients, and are well suited to hosting AD due to an increase in security. External namespaces are resolvable from any client on the Internet. This is required for Internet accessible resources, such as web sites, but is typically a poor choice for hosting AD due to the potential lack of security they can impose. A hybrid namespace design provides the best of both worlds by dividing your namespace into two zones: one for public access and one for private access. One method of using a hybrid namespace involves delegating a DNS subdomain as the root of your internal structure. For instance, you might use yourdomain.com for public access, putting it on a public server accessible from the Internet, and private.yourdomain.com for internal access, putting this zone on a private server located behind a **firewall**, which is a combination of hardware and software security systems that secures a network from unauthorized access from outside the network. This method is shown in **Figure 1-16**. Another method for providing a hybrid namespace involves creating two disconnected zones for the same name. Using this method, two separate zones for a domain (yourdomain.com, for instance) exist on two separate servers. You place the publicly accessible records on the external server, which is outside of the firewall, and both the public and private records on the internal server, which is behind the firewall. This solution reduces naming confusion among users, but can be somewhat difficult to manage due to duplication of effort whenever a public resource is modified. This solution is shown in **Figure 1-17**.

While naming domains, you need to follow certain guidelines:

- All AD domain names should be static. In Windows 2000, the only way to rename an AD domain is to remove AD and recreate the domain from scratch.
- A domain name should be short, simple, and easy to remember. You should use standard DNS characters for naming the domains. The Windows 2000 operating system supports the following standard DNS characters: A-Z, a-z, 0-9, and the hyphen. Each domain name in a DNS namespace should be unique. It is recommended that you ensure uniqueness, even when using an internal namespace, by registering the domain name.
- Including the periods, domain names should not exceed 63 characters. The **Fully Qualified Domain Name (FQDN)** can be up to 255 characters. Domain names are not case-sensitive; therefore, the domain name xyz.com is the same as XYZ.COM.

tip

Internet Assigned Numbers Authority (IANA) is the organization responsible for the worldwide DNS namespace.

caution

You should use Unicode characters only if all the servers running the DNS service support Unicode. While Windows 2000's DNS service supports Unicode, most DNS servers do not.

more

To decide between having the same or different internal and external DNS names, you need to understand their advantages and disadvantages. The advantages and disadvantages of using the same internal and external DNS names as opposed to using separate internal and external DNS names appear in **Tables 1-3** and **1-4**.

Figure 1-16 Hybrid namespace with DNS subdomain

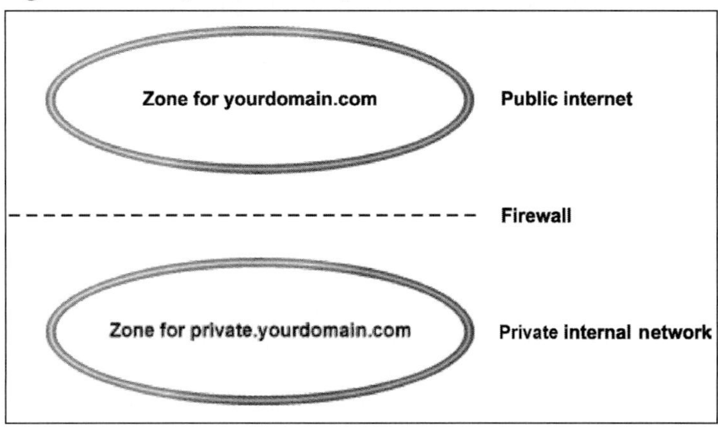

Figure 1-17 Hybrid namespace with two disconnected zones

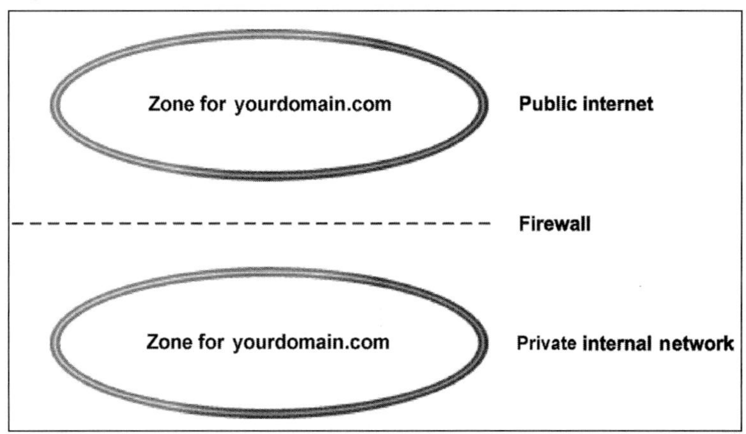

Table 1-3 Advantages and disadvantages of using the same internal and external DNS names

Advantages	Disadvantages
Only one DNS name needs to be registered.	Results in a complex DNS configuration, due to duplication of effort.

Table 1-4 Advantages and disadvantages of using separate internal and external DNS names

Advantages	Disadvantages
The difference between internal and external resources is clear.	Two different naming conventions can be confusing for users.
Easy to manage since separate zones exist for internal and external resources.	Requires registration of multiple DNS names with an Internet DNS (if the internal and external names are not contiguous). When you use separate internal and external namespaces, by default, logon names and e-mail IDs of users are different. You may change this functionality by adding alternative UPN suffixes in the Active Directory Domains and Trusts console.

skill 9 Guidelines for Planning a Site Structure

exam objective

Basic knowledge

overview

Once you have planned the domain namespaces, you need to plan a site structure for your organization. A site maps to the physical structure of an organization. Sites participate actively in the user logon and authentication process, and play an important role in the directory replication process. Directory replication can take place within a site or between sites, but generally occurs more frequently within a site than between sites. Within a site, Active Directory automatically generates a path for replication among domain controllers in the same domain using a hybrid mesh topology, as shown in **Figure 1-18**. This path is known as **replication topology**. Replication between sites (Inter-Site replication) can be manually configured, while replication within a site (Intra-Site replication) is always automatic.

NOTE: If you disable AD's automatic creation of connection objects (discussed in later lessons) by manually creating connection objects, you can control intra-site replication. However, this is not only not recommended, you should ignore this fact on the 70-217 exam, as most of the questions expect you to believe that intra-site replication is always automatic.

While planning a site structure for an organization that is spread across geographical locations, you should conform to the following guidelines:

tip

It is quite simple to design a site structure for any organization that is using a single local area network (LAN). Because the local area connections are fast, the entire LAN can be a single site.

- While planning sites, you need to decide which domain controller the computers on a given subnet should use. To optimize logon traffic, you should typically ensure the availability of at least one domain controller per site.
- To optimize inter-site replication, you should configure replication so that it occurs when the network traffic is light.
- Configure a powerful server as the preferred **bridgehead server** for inter-site replication. The bridgehead server is the only server in a site allowed to replicate to other sites. This functionality reduces the amount of replication traffic between sites, as all servers are not attempting to replicate with all other servers; however, it also increases the load on the bridgehead server. Note that if you do not choose a preferred bridgehead, the KCC will choose one for you, but it is best to choose the most powerful DC in a site for this role manually **(Figure 1-19)**.
- Ensure that you place your domain controllers in their proper sites. By default, clients will choose the correct site each time they get a new IP; however, DC's only choose a site when they are first created, and must be manually moved thereafter. This can lead to a problem if you build all of your DC's in a central location.

Figure 1-18 Replication within a site using a ring topology

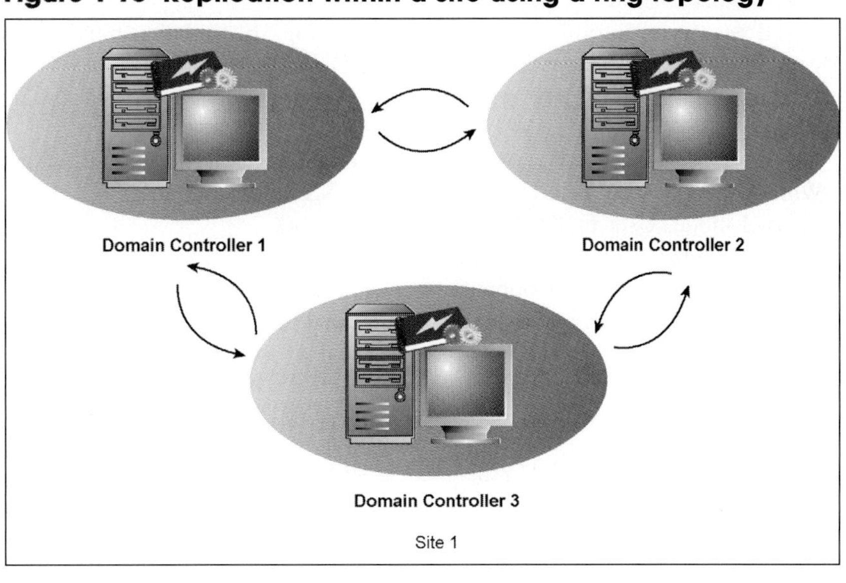

Figure 1-19 Using a bridgehead server for inter-site replication

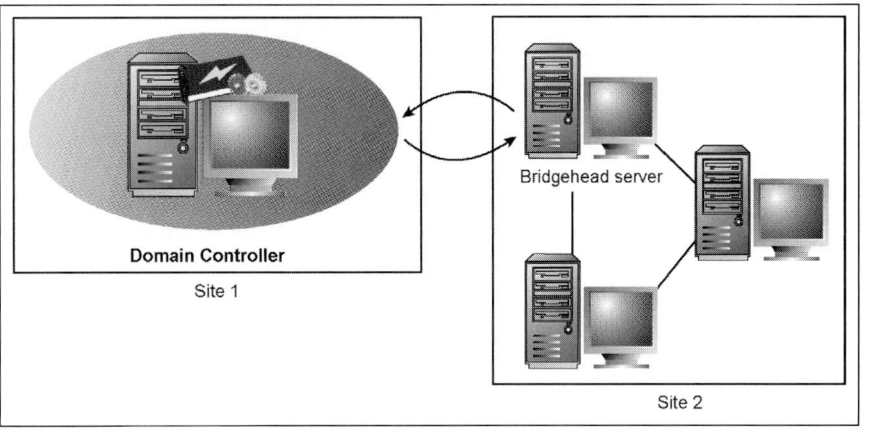

Summary

- Active Directory is a directory service (a database that stores information about users and resources in a network) and is one of the core features that makes Windows 2000 Server suitable for network administration in large organizations.
- Features of Active Directory include policy-based administration, increased security of information using Encrypting File System, integration with Domain Name Service (DNS), extensibility, scalability, information replication, and compatibility with other directory services.
- The two layers in Windows 2000 Architecture are the user mode and the kernel mode. User mode has two components: environment subsystem and integral subsystem. The kernel mode has four components: Windows 2000 Executive, device drivers, microkernel, and Hardware Abstraction Layer.
- Active Directory is a combination of service layers and many interfaces and protocols that work in mutual coordination. Active Directory has four major components: Directory System Agent, Database Layer, Extensible Storage Engine, and Data Store.
- Active Directory objects include user accounts, contacts, groups, published folders, published printers, computers, domain controllers, and organizational units (OUs).
- There are two ways of classifying Active Directory components: logical and physical.
- The logical structure consists of domains, OUs, forests, and trees, and the physical structure consists of sites and domain controllers.
- Active Directory is based on concepts of a global catalog, trust relationships, and Domain Name System (DNS).
- The global catalog stores a partial copy of all objects in a forest.
- A trust relationship is a logical link between two domains.
- DNS helps computers to locate other computers in a network.
- As a part of implementing Active Directory, you need to plan a domain structure. Active Directory supports two domain models: single domain model and multiple domain model.
- Active Directory uses DNS as its name resolution service. There are three types of DNS namespaces: internal, external, and hybrid. You can implement either the same internal and external DNS names for your domain or keep different DNS names for your domain.
- To implement Active Directory, you need to plan a site structure. A site is a group of subnets that are connected by a high-speed network connection.

Key Terms

Active Directory
Attributes
Bridgehead server
Child domain (subdomain)
Computer objects
Contacts
Contiguous naming scheme
Data Store (NTDS.DIT file)
Database Layer
Directory database
Directory service
Directory System Agent (DSA)
Disjointed naming scheme
Distinguished name (DN)
DNS name server
DNS zone
Domain
Domain controller
Domain Name System (DNS) name
Domain namespace
Environment subsystem
Executive
Extensible Storage Engine
Firewall
Forest
Fully Qualified Domain Name (FQDN)
Global catalog
Global catalog server
Globally unique identifier (GUID)
Group
Group policy
Hardware Abstraction Layer (HAL)
Interrupt
Integral subsystem
Kernel mode
Kernel mode drivers
Logical structure
Microkernel
Multimaster replication
Multiple domain model
Name resolution
Object
Organizational unit (OU)
Physical structure
Published folders
Relative distinguished name (RDN)
Replication
Replication topology
Root domain
Schema
Shared folders
Single domain model
Site
Subnets
Tree
Trust relationship
Unicode characters
Universal group
User accounts
User mode
User principal name (UPN)
Zone database file

Test Yourself

1. What is the function of schema information?
   a. Collecting information of all the data objects in a domain. The information is domain-specific and is not replicated to the other domains.
   b. Describing the logical structure of the directory along with the information of replication topology. The schema then replicates the information to all domains in the tree or forest.
   c. Exchanging information between the directories and applications in the Microsoft Management Console (MMC).
   d. Defining the objects that can be created in the directory, and their attributes.
2. Which of the following are the container objects in Active Directory? (Choose all that apply).
   a. OU
   b. Group
   c. User account
   d. Contact
   e. Shared folder
3. Which of the following components provides security guidelines for the user mode?
   a. NTDSUTIL tool
   b. Security Accounts Manager
   c. Directory System Agent
   d. Security Reference Monitor
4. Identify the correct statement.
   a. DSA builds a relationship between the parent-child in the directory and provides the interface for the directory access calls.
   b. Database Layer has direct contact with the records in the directory data. It is based on the object's relative distinguished name attribute.
   c. Extensible Storage Engine is controlled by a database engine called the Extensible Storage Engine database engine, stored by default in the \Winnt\NTDS folder on the domain controller.
   d. Data Store Layer permits access calls made to the database to go through it. This is located between the applications and the database.
5. Which of the following are functions of additional domain controllers? (Choose all that apply)
   a. Acts as a logical link between two domains.
   b. Provides backup to the first domain controller.
   c. Handles interaction between the users and the domain.
   d. All of the above.
6. Which of the following components are part of the Active Directory physical structure? (Choose all that apply)
   a. Domains
   b. Sites
   c. Domain controllers
   d. Trees
7. Which of the following statements are correct about an OU? (Choose all that apply)
   a. Container objects that can store domains.
   b. Smallest units to which administrative authority can be delegated.
   c. Part of the Active Directory physical structure.
   d. Represent the functional structure of an organization.
8. In a multiple domain scenario, a global catalog server stores a:
   a. Full replica of objects belonging to other domains.
   b. Full replica of all objects in a forest.
   c. Full replica of objects belonging to its domain.
   d. None of the above.
9. The implicit two-way transitive trust is automatically established between: (Choose all that apply)
   a. Domains of a tree.
   b. Domains across forests.
   c. A Windows 2000 domain and a Windows NT domain.
   d. OUs in a domain.
10. An explicit one-way nontransitive trust will be established when a:
    a. Child domain is created under an existing domain.
    b. Domain tree is added to an existing forest.
    c. Windows 2000 and a Windows NT domain are manually linked.
    d. New domain is added to an existing tree.
11. Which of the following are advantages of a single domain model? (Choose all that apply)
    a. Easy to set up.
    b. Easy to manage.
    c. Suitable for networks storing large numbers of objects and resources.
    d. Supports distant physical locations.
    e. Suitable for independently functioning divisions.
12. Which of the following situations require a multiple domain model? (Choose all that apply)
    a. A small-sized organization with autonomous divisions.
    b. A mid-sized organization using separate security policies for various groups of users.
    c. A mid-sized organization that has branches connected by a slow link.
    d. A small-sized organization that has branches connected by a fast link.
13. You will keep the internal and external DNS names the same when you want: (Choose all that apply)
    a. A single DNS zone.
    b. To implement single logon.
    c. A simple configuration for the DNS server.
    d. To register one DNS name.

14. Which of the following guidelines should be followed while planning a domain namespace? (Choose all that apply)

a. Domain names should remain static.
b. Domain names should be descriptive.
c. Each domain name in a DNS namespace should be unique.
d. Domain names should not exceed 255 characters.

15. Which of the following guidelines should be followed while planning a site structure? (Choose all that apply)

a. Configure replication within a site so that it occurs when the network traffic is light.
b. Use a bridgehead server for inter-site replication.
c. Place domain controllers in the proper sites.
d. Install a global catalog server for replication between sites.

Problem Solving Scenarios

1. You work as an administrator with the London branch of Spearhead Consultants. Active Directory forms the backbone of the network infrastructure at the London branch. This branch has three divisions: Sales, Marketing, and Administration. The Administration division is divided into the Accounts division and the Human Resource division. The Administration division uses a different security policy because it deals with confidential information. The London branch recently purchased a new building that will house the Software Development division and the E-learning division. The two buildings of the London office are connected by a WAN link. Both the Software Development division and the E-learning division are autonomous units and require separate security policies. Based on this information, plan a domain structure and a site structure for the London branch.

2. Surfthenet is an Internet Solution Provider (ISP) with 150 employees. The company has two main divisions: Human Resources and Accounts. The Human Resources division handles recruitment and payroll. The Accounts division handles distribution of salaries to employees and financial matters for the company. Surfthenet follows a uniform security policy and centralized method of administration. Surfthenet's network has been hacked several times recently. Since Active Directory provides excellent security against Internet hacking, Surfthenet's management has decided to implement Active Directory in the organization. You work in the systems administration department, and your boss instructs you to create an Active Directory implementation plan that he can present to the CEO of the company. Prepare a presentation with your suggestions about the domain model to use, a domain structure, a suitable domain namespace, and a site structure for Surfthenet.

LESSON

2 Implementing Active Directory

Implementing Active Directory allows you to manage the network structure in an organization. The implementation process involves installing Active Directory, transferring operations master roles between domain controllers, and creating organizational unit (OU) structures. You install Active Directory to create additional domain controllers, domains, subdomains, or forests. Verification of Active Directory installation enables you to make sure that all the Active Directory components, such as the database and DNS components, are successfully installed.

During installation of Active Directory, you designate a Windows 2000 Server as a domain controller. Once the installation is complete, some domain controllers are designated as operations masters. These operations masters are assigned specific tasks for managing Active Directory forests and domains. Operations masters (also known as **FSMO**s, or Flexible Single Masters of Operation) are required because certain operations to the AD structure have permanent effects. If a conflict (such as two domain controllers attempting to make the same modifications to AD at the same time) were involved in one of these changes, disastrous effects could result. An example of such a task is modifications performed on the schema. Since AD has no functionality for deleting changes to the schema (only disabling), conflicting changes could partition the schema, which is extremely difficult to repair.

By default, Active Directory assigns the domain-wide operations master roles (RID Master, Infrastructure Master, and PDC Emulator) to the first domain controller in the domain, and the forest-wide operations master roles (Schema Master and Domain Naming Master) to the first domain controller in the forest. The domain-wide roles are performed by one domain controller in each domain, while the forest-wide roles are performed by one domain controller in the forest. Sometimes, due to technical problems, the operations master may be unavailable, or you might want to change the default operations master role assignments. In such situations, Active Directory allows you to transfer (when the original master is still functional) or seize (when the original master is unrepairable) the operations master roles to other domain controllers in the domain.

The implementation of Active Directory also involves creating OU structures. OUs are container objects that can store groups, users, computers, and other OUs. You create OUs under domains to represent the business and functional structure of your organization in a manner that is easy to administer. A good practice for OU design is to design for group policy application first and delegation of control secondarily. In most cases, you will find that once you design for group policy, no further structural modifications are necessary.

Goals

In this lesson, you will learn to install Active Directory, as well as to verify the installation. This lesson also introduces you to operations master roles. Additionally, you will learn to view and transfer these roles and implement an organizational structure within a domain.

Lesson 2 Implementing Active Directory	
Skill	***Exam 70-217 Objective***
1. Installing Active Directory	Install forests, trees, and domains. Install and configure DNS for Active Directory.
2. Verifying Active Directory Installation	Verify and troubleshoot Active Directory installation.
3. Introducing Operations Master Roles	Basic knowledge
4. Viewing the Operations Master Role Assignments for a Domain	Basic knowledge
5. Transferring Operations Master Roles	Transfer operations master roles. Seize operations master roles.
6. Implementing an Organizational Unit Structure within a Domain	Implement an organizational unit (OU) structure. Create and manage objects manually or by using scripting.

Requirements

To complete the skills in this lesson, you will need to have administrative rights on a Windows 2000 Server computer on a network. At least one of this machine's hard disks must be configured to use the NTFS file system. You will also need the Windows 2000 Server installation CD. For Skill 5, you will need an additional Windows 2000 Server domain controller joined to the domain you created in Skill 1.

skill 1 Installing Active Directory

exam objective

Install forests, trees, and domains. Install and configure DNS for Active Directory.

overview

To organize objects in a domain and to implement the planned domain structure, domain namespace, and site structure, you need to install Active Directory on a Windows 2000 Server using the Active Directory Installation Wizard. When you install Active Directory for the first time, you create the root domain, a new domain tree, as well as a new forest, and you designate a Windows 2000 Server computer as a domain controller. When you create a domain, by default, the domain is configured to run in **mixed mode**, which allows the coexistence of Windows NT 4.0 backup domain controllers (BDCs) and Windows 2000 Server domain controllers (DCs). If your network consists of only Windows 2000 domain controllers, you can switch to **native mode**. This mode supports only Windows 2000 domain controllers.

During the Active Directory installation, three components are installed: Domain Name System (DNS) service, database and database log files, and shared system volume. **Table 2-1** describes each component in detail. You need to log on as an administrator on the Windows 2000 server before you run the Active Directory Installation wizard.

caution

You can switch from mixed mode to native mode, but this process is irreversible. For this reason, ensure that there are no plans to add NT 4 domain controllers before switching.

how to

Create a domain on a Windows 2000 Server computer and install Active Directory using the Active Directory Installation Wizard.

1. Click Start, point to **Programs**, point to **Administrative Tools**, and then click the **Configure Your Server** command.
2. Select "Active Directory" from the left menu and then select "Start the active directory wizard".
3. The **Welcome to the Active Directory Installation Wizard** screen appears. Click Next >.
4. The **Domain Controller Type** screen appears. On this screen, you specify the role for the server. The **Domain controller for a new domain** option button is selected by default **(Figure 2-1)**. Click Next > to designate the server as a domain controller in a new domain.
5. The **Create Tree or Child Domain** screen appears. On this screen, you specify if you want to create a new domain tree or a new child in an existing domain tree. The **Create a new domain tree** option button is selected by default. To accept the default selection, click Next >.
6. The **Create or Join Forest** screen appears. On this screen, you specify whether you want to create a new forest of domain trees or place the domain tree in an existing forest. The **Create a new forest of domain trees** option button is selected by default. To accept the default selection, click Next >.
7. The **New Domain Name** screen appears. Type a domain name, such as **mydomain.com** in the **Full DNS name for new domain** text box **(Figure 2-2)**, and click Next >.
8. The **NetBIOS Domain Name** screen appears. In the **Domain NetBIOS name** text box, the domain name appears by default. To accept the default domain NetBIOS name, click Next >.
9. The **Database and Log Locations** screen appears. The default location, **C:\WINNT\NTDS**, appears in the **Database location** and **Log location** text boxes. To accept the default location, click Next >.
10. The **Shared System Volume** screen appears. The default location, **C:\WINNT\SYSVOL**, is already specified in the **Folder location** text box. To accept the default location, click Next >.

tip

You can also start the Active Directory Installation wizard by running the DCPROMO command from the command prompt.

tip

To optimize Active Directory performance and allow for restoration to the point of failure, you should place the database and log files on separate hard disks.

tip

The shared system volume (the sysvol folder) must be located on an NTFS disk.

Table 2-1 Components installed during Active Directory installation

Component	Description
Domain Name System (DNS) service	DNS can be installed before or while you are installing Active Directory. Windows 2000 clients query a DNS server to locate domain controllers in a domain (down-level clients still use NetBIOS naming to find domain controllers). DNS is a required component of AD, as the SRV records added during the install not only help Windows 2000 clients locate domain controllers, they also allow new domain controllers to verify the domain and locate other domain controllers when adding new domain controllers to an existing domain. If the SRV records are not added, you will have great difficulty locating the domain controllers from any Windows 2000 machine. In this case, the easiest solution is often to enable dynamic DNS on your zone (in the properties dialog of the zone), and from a command prompt on the DNS server, run "ipconfig /registerdns". You can also simply restart the Netlogon service on your domain controller.
Database and database log files	During installation, a database and database log files are created by default. The directory database stores the information of all the objects in a domain. Database log files store messages that are used to track the operations performed on the directory database. In a transaction log based database (like AD and Exchange), the transaction logs keep track of every change made to the database (in AD, for up to 10MB of changes, by default). You should place logs on a separate disk to increase performance whenever possible.
Shared system volume	The shared system volume is a folder structure that is present on all Windows 2000 domain controllers and is created during Active Directory installation. This folder structure stores a copy of public files of domains such as scripts and group policy objects. The contents of this folder are automatically replicated by the File Replication Service (FRS) to all the domain controllers in a domain.

Figure 2-1 Creating a new domain

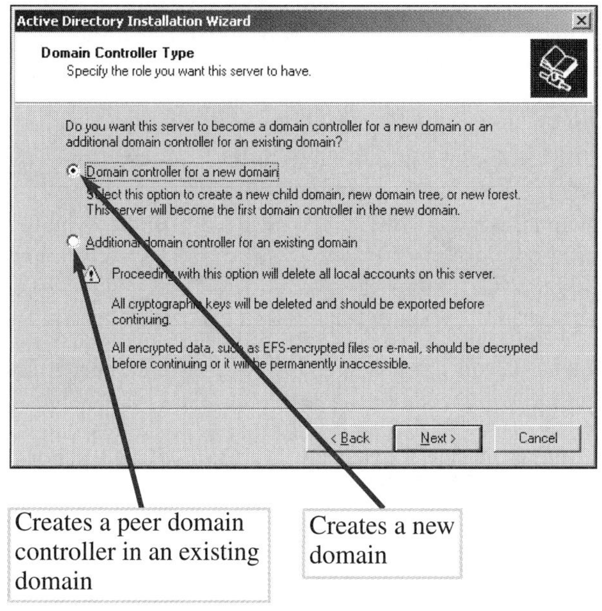

Figure 2-2 Specifying a DNS name for the new domain

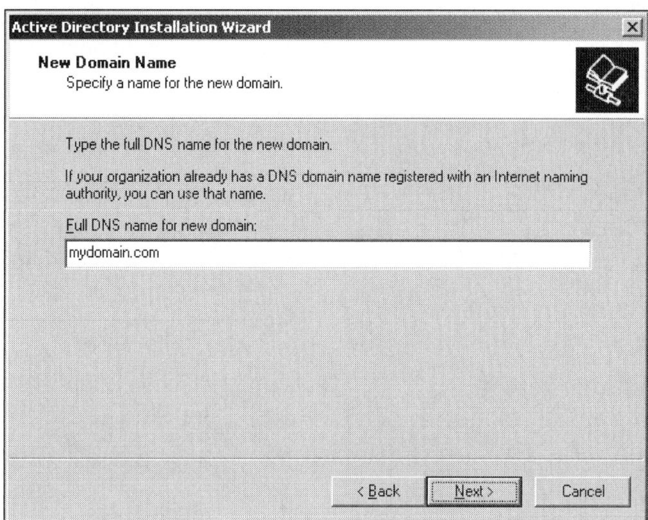

skill 1 Installing Active Directory (cont'd)

exam objective

Install forests, trees, and domains. Install and configure DNS for Active Directory.

how to

11. If you have not yet installed a DNS server, or your DNS server is configured with dynamic DNS disabled, the **Active Directory Installation Wizard** message box will appear **(Figure 2-3)**, reminding you to install and configure a DNS server. To proceed with the installation of the DNS server, click OK.
12. The **Configure DNS** screen appears. The **Yes, install and configure DNS on this computer (recommended)** option button is selected by default. Click Next >.
13. The **Permissions compatible with pre-Windows 2000 servers** option button is selected by default. Click Next >.
14. Type a password in the **Password** text box, and click Next >.
15. The **Summary** screen containing the list of options you have selected appears. Review the contents of this screen, and click Next >.
16. The **Configuring Active Directory Installation** progress indicator appears as the Active Directory service is being installed. This process takes several minutes, during which you will be prompted to place the Windows 2000 Server CD-ROM in your CD-ROM drive. When the **Completing the Active Directory Installation Wizard** screen appears, click Finish.
17. You have promoted a Windows 2000 Server to a domain controller and installed Active Directory on this domain controller for the domain. A message box requesting your confirmation about restarting the computer appears.
18. Click Restart to restart the computer. Any changes you made to the computer during the installation will be saved permanently. When you reboot the computer, the changes will be automatically applied to your computer.

tip

Note that the password entered in step 14 (the Active Directory Restoration Mode password) is not the same as your standard administrator password. It is used whenever you boot into Active Directory Restore mode or the Recovery Console.

more

In addition to creating a new domain, tree, and forest, the Active Directory Installation Wizard helps you deal with the expansion of your organization. For instance, if a new division has been added to your organization or your organization has opened a new overseas branch, you might want to create new domains or domain trees. To add a subdomain to another domain, you select the **Domain controller for a new domain** option button, and then select the **Create a new child domain in an existing domain tree** option button **(Figure 2-4)**. To add a domain tree to a forest, you select the **Domain controller for a new domain** option button, select the **Create a new domain tree** option button, and then select the **Place this new domain tree in an existing forest** option button **(Figure 2-5)**.

Even though domain controllers in Windows 2000 are created after setup is complete, you can still automate the creation of a domain controller by using Dcpromo.exe in an unattended installation answer file. Microsoft outlines two methods for automating Windows 2000 setup and domain controller setup. In the first method, you add the required setup instructions to your answer file in the Setup file [DCInstall] and [GUIRunOnce] sections. In the second method, you use the Setup file [GUIRunOnce] section to initiate the promotion of a domain controller through a separate answer file. For more details on these processes, see Microsoft Knowledge Base article 224390.

tip

Do not be alarmed if the boot process takes longer and general performance of your server declines after installing AD. This is normal, and is caused by the additional demands of loading and running a complex database like AD.

Figure 2-3 Active Directory Installation Wizard message box

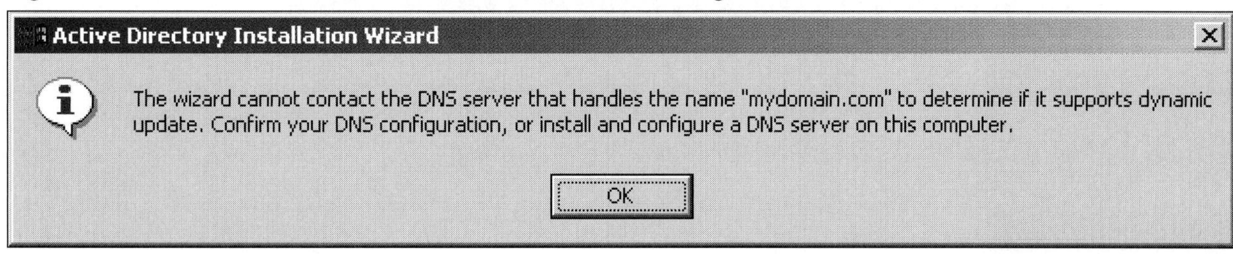

Figure 2-4 Adding a domain to another domain

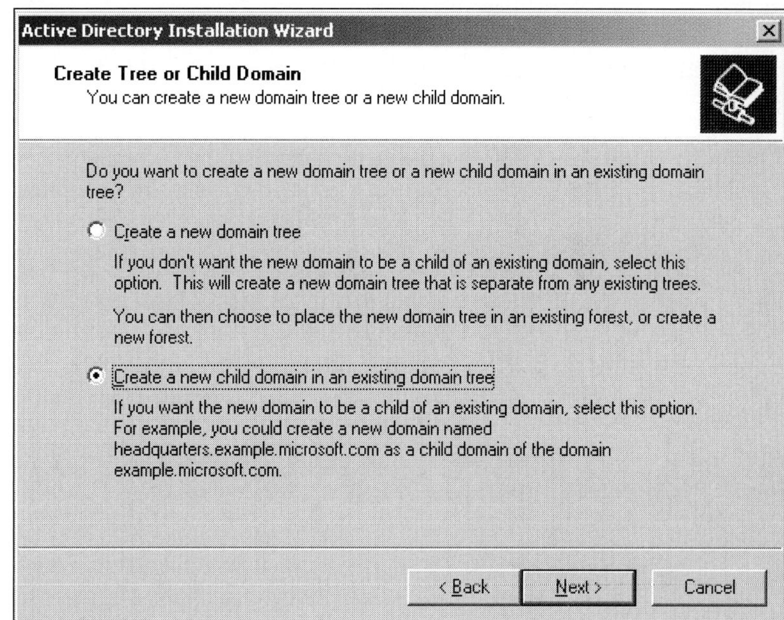

Figure 2-5 Adding a new domain tree to an existing forest

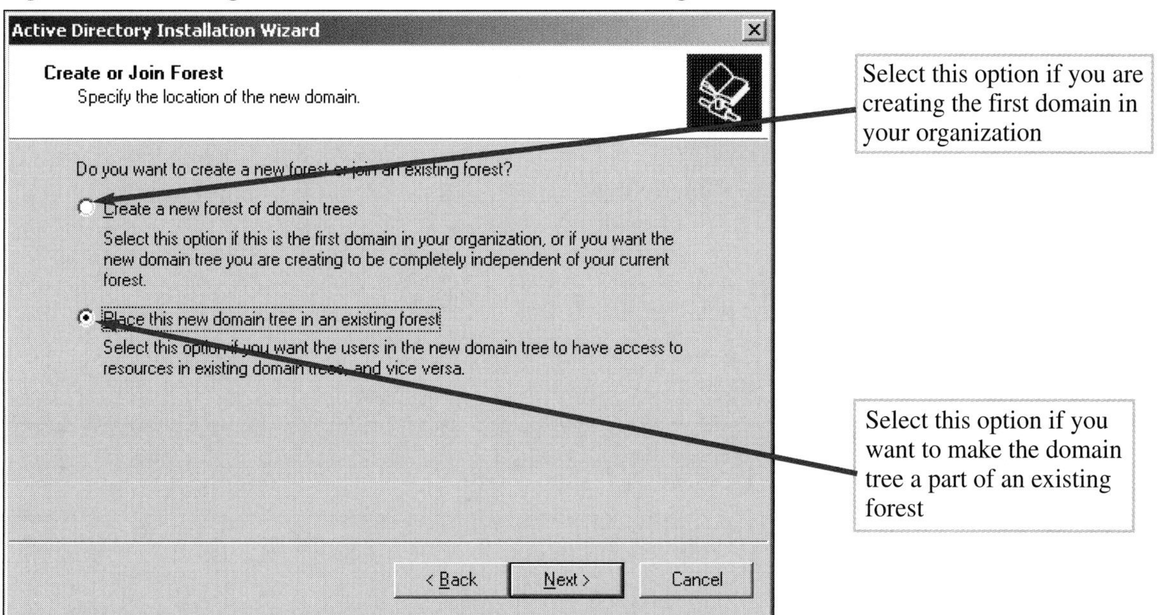

skill 2 Verifying Active Directory Installation

exam objective

Verify and troubleshoot Active Directory installation.

overview

Once you have installed Active Directory, you may need to add additional Active Directory domain controllers. When you install Active Directory a new domain controller, the installation process requests installation-critical information from Active Directory. Therefore, you need to verify Active Directory installation to ensure that these components are successfully installed.

You can verify the installation of Active Directory using the **Active Directory Users and Computers console**. In addition to verifying the Active Directory installation, the Active Directory Users and Computers console, which is an administrative tool, helps in creating and deleting objects, setting their permissions, and modifying their properties. The primary objects controlled by this console are organizational units (OUs), Windows 2000 user accounts, group accounts, computer accounts, and published printers. To verify Active Directory installation, you verify the presence of:

- The domain that you specified during Active Directory installation **(Figure 2-6)**.
- The presence of your new domain controller in the Domain Controllers OU.

In addition to the Active Directory Users and Computers console, presence of the Active Directory Domains and Trusts and Active Directory Sites and Services consoles in the Administrative Tools menu also verifies the successful installation of Active Directory. Descriptions of these administrative tools are given below:

- **Active Directory Domains and Trusts console:** This console helps in managing the trust relationships between two or more domains in the same forest or different forests. **Figure 2-7** shows the Active Directory Domains and Trusts console. You can use this console to:
  - Provide interoperability with other domains.
  - Switch from mixed mode to native mode.
  - Transfer the domain naming master role from a domain controller to another domain controller.
  - Add or remove alternate User Principal Name (UPN) suffixes to user logon names.
- **Active Directory Sites and Services console:** You use this console to create sites, create subnets, move domain controllers to the correct sites, configure servers as Global Catalog servers, and create site links. This information is used by Active Directory to decide the method of replication of directory information and to process service requests.

tip

It is possible for AD to install but the DNS modifications required to support AD to be missing. To check this, look in your DNS console, in the zone for your domain, and look under the "underscore" subdomains (such as "_msdcs") for Service Resource Location (SRV) records. If you are not familiar with the DNS console, you can also validate DNS from a command prompt by typing "nslookup". Then at the special prompt, type "lst srv domain.com", where "domain.com" is the name of your domain.

Figure 2-6 Verifying the presence of a domain

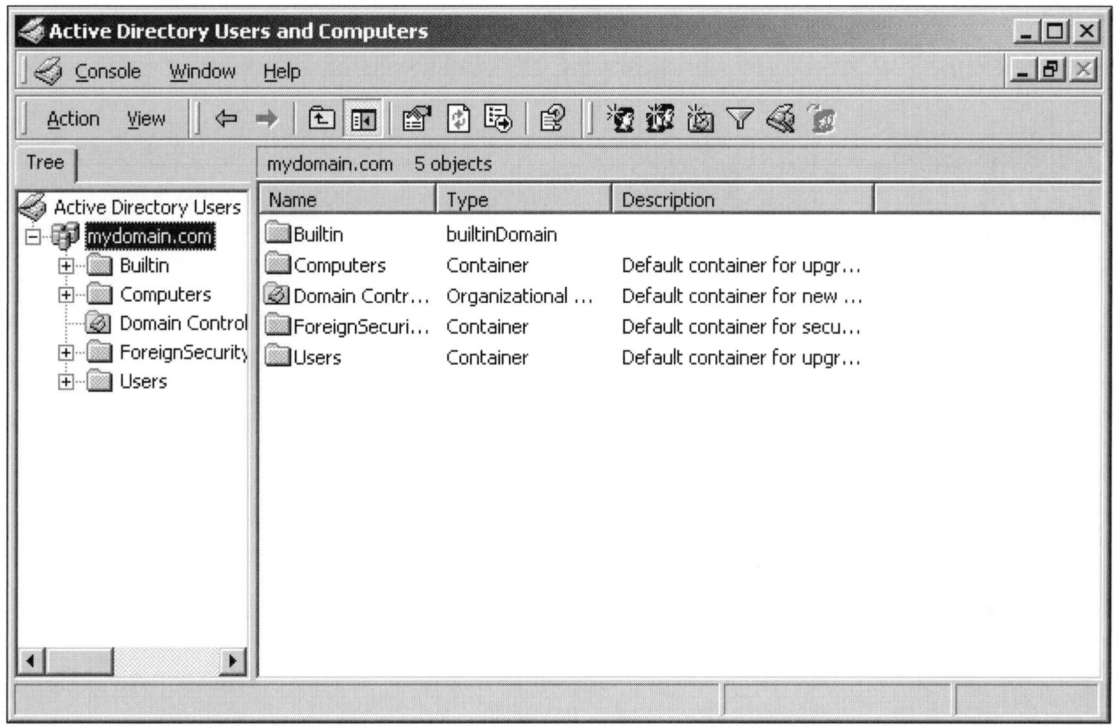

Figure 2-7 Active Directory Domains and Trusts

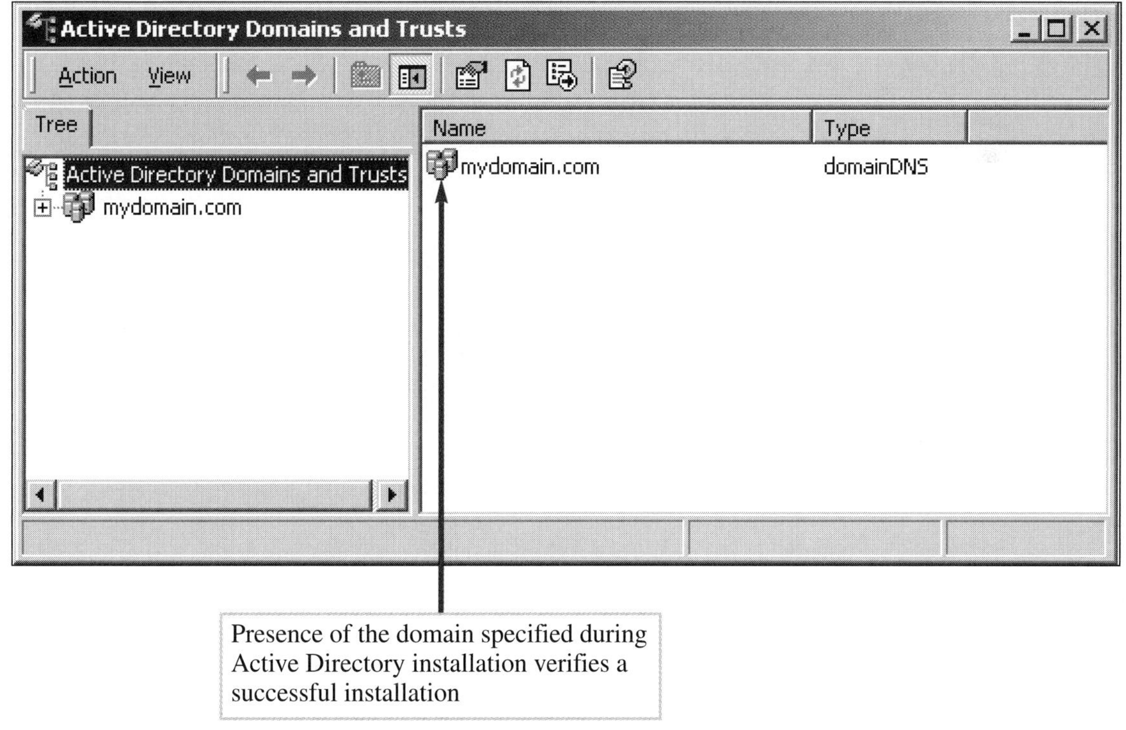

skill 2 Verifying Active Directory Installation (cont'd)

exam objective

Verify and troubleshoot Active Directory installation.

how to

Verify the installation of Active Directory.

1. Click Start, point to **Programs**, point to **Administrative Tools**, and then click the **Active Directory Users and Computers** command. The **Active Directory Users and Computers** console appears.
2. Double-click the <domain_name.com> node in the left pane of the console to expand it. The contents of the node are displayed.
3. To view the domain controller, click the **Domain Controllers** OU. The domain controller appears in the right pane (**Figure 2-8**).
4. Click the **Close** button to close the **Active Directory Users and Computers** console.
5. Verify that the system volume was created and shared. Click **Start**, click **Run**, type **%systemroot%\sysvol**, and then click **OK**. The **Sysvol** folder should appear, and you should see four folders: Domain, Staging, Staging Areas, and Sysvol. Close the Sysvol folder.
6. Verify that the Active Directory database and log files were created. Click **Start**, click **Run**, type **%systemroot%\ntds**, and then click **OK**. The NTDS folder should appear, and you should see the following files and folder: Drop, edb.chk, edb.log, ntds.dit, res1.log, res2.log, and Temp.edb.
7. Close the NTDS folder.

tip

If you used mydomain.com as your domain name, the node will be called mydomain.com.

more

In addition to the three default consoles, you can also install an additional tool called the **Active Directory Schema snap-in**, which permits you to view and modify the schema. A schema defines the type of objects and the type of information pertaining to the objects that can be stored in Active Directory. To install the Active Directory Schema snap-in, run the **AdminPak** program from the **I386** folder of the **Windows 2000 Server installation CD**. The **Windows 2000 Administration Tools Setup** wizard appears. Follow the instructions that appear in the **Windows 2000 Administration Tools Setup** wizard. Click the **Start** button, and then click the **Run** command. The **Run** dialog box appears. In the **Open** text box, type **mmc**, and then click the **OK** button. An empty **Microsoft Management Console (MMC)** appears. Click the **Add/Remove Snap-in** command on the **Console** menu. The **Add Remove Snap-in** dialog box appears. To display a list of available snap-ins, click the **Add** button. The **Add Standalone Snap-in** dialog box appears. Double-click **Active Directory Schema** from the list of available snap-ins, and then click the **Close** button. To close the **Add/Remove Snap-in** dialog box, click the **OK** button. To save this console, click the **Save** command on the **Console** menu. The **Save As** dialog box appears. By default, this console will be saved in the Administrative Tools menu. To specify a name for the snap-in, type **Active Directory Schema** in the **File name** text box, and then click the **Save** button. **(Figure 2-9)**.

Figure 2-8 Verifying the presence of a domain controller

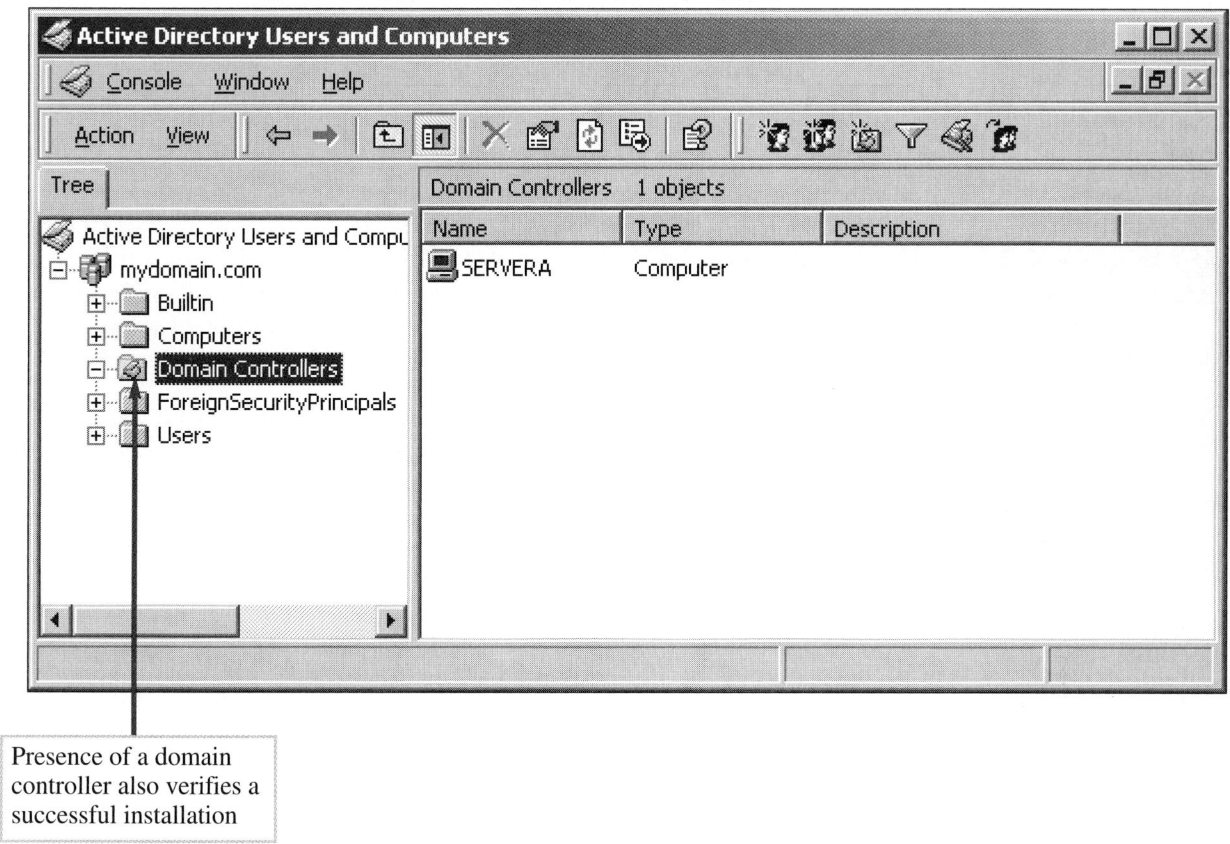

Presence of a domain controller also verifies a successful installation

Figure 2-9 Active Directory Schema snap-in installed

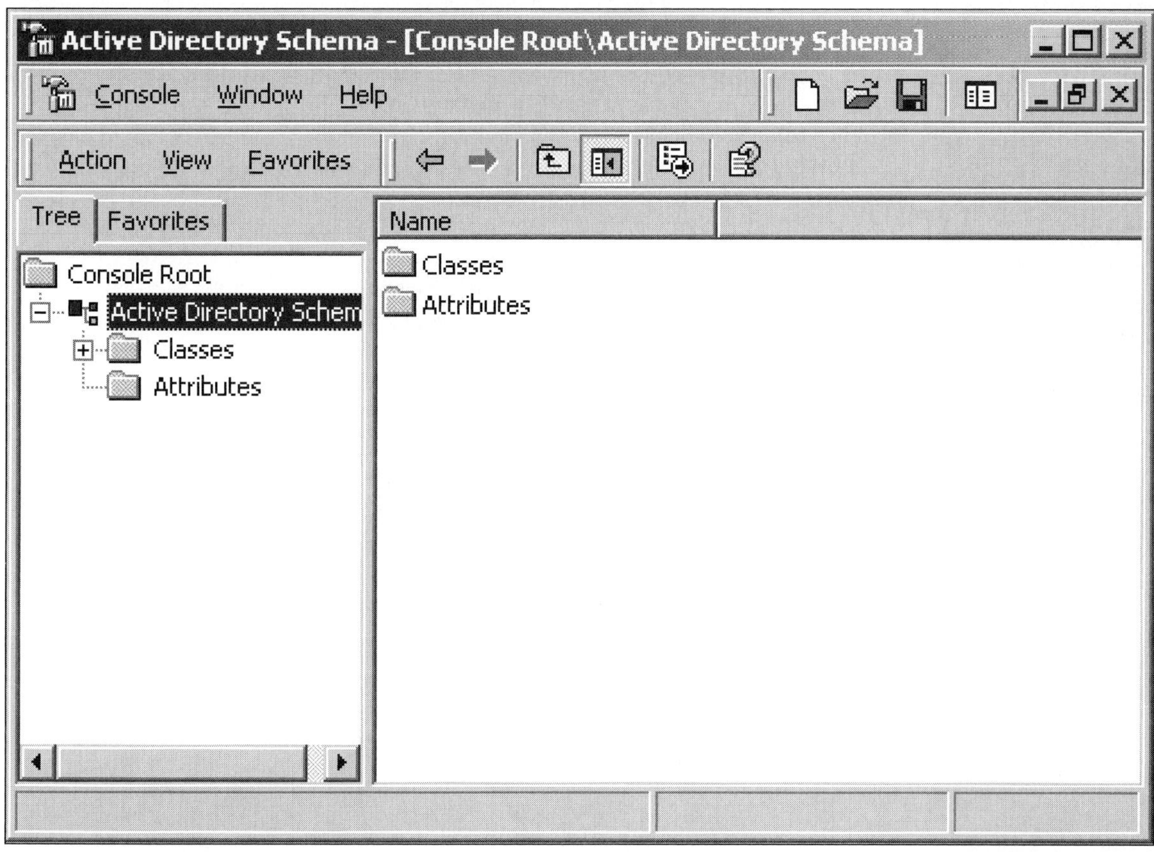

Exam 70-217

skill 3 Introducing Operations Master Roles

exam objective

Basic knowledge

overview

caution

By default, the first domain controller in the forest root domain holds the Infrastructure Master role and will be a Global Catalog server. In a single domain environment, this is not a problem, as the Infrastructure Master has no functionality. But in a multi-domain environment, always ensure that these roles are kept on separate servers, as the Infrastructure Master will not function properly if it is also a Global Catalog server.

While most functions in Active Directory use a true multi-master replication model, with all domain controllers having the ability to modify AD, a few specific types of events in AD must be controlled using a single-master model, with only a single domain controller able to modify the data. Each of these special functions is controlled by servers known as FSMOs (Flexible Single Masters of Operations), commonly called **operations masters**. These functions are split into two general types, as listed below:

- **Forest-wide operations master roles:** The two forest-wide FSMO roles are the **Schema Master** and the **Domain Naming Master**. Each of these roles may reside on only a single server for the entire forest. By default, both roles will be held by the first domain controller created in the root domain of the forest. **Table 2-2** lists the forest-wide operations master roles and their descriptions.
- **Domain-wide operations master roles:** The three domain-wide roles are **PDC Emulator**, **RID Master**, and **Infrastructure Master**. Each of these roles may reside on only a single domain controller in each domain. By default, all three roles will be placed on the first domain controller created in each domain. **Table 2-3** lists the domain-wide operations master roles and their descriptions.

When you create the first domain in a new forest, by default, all five operations master roles are assigned to the first domain controller in that domain. Active Directory assigns only the domain-wide operations master roles to the first domain controller of any subsequent child domains that you create in the forest.

more

tip

More information about FSMO roles can be obtained from Microsoft Knowledge Base article 197132.

tip

More information about FSMO placement can be obtained from Microsoft Knowledge Base article 223346.

tip

It is important that both of the domain controllers should be direct replication partners of the standby operations master domain controller.

Listed below are guidelines for planning operations master roles for per-forest roles.

- It is typically a good idea to assign the two forest-wide roles a high-uptime server. Backups of this machine are of special importance.
- As a rule, the schema master and the domain naming master roles should be assigned to a single domain controller of one of the domains in the forest.

Listed below are the guidelines that you should follow while planning operations master roles for per-domain roles.

- You should have at least one additional domain controller to act as a standby operations master for other operations masters. In case a domain controller fails, the standby domain controller can be manually configured to seize the failed domain controller's roles.
- In general, assign both the relative ID master and the PDC emulator roles to the same domain controller. If necessary, these roles can be assigned to separate domain controllers to reduce the load on the PDC emulator if the domain is large; however, you should ensure that these servers are always capable of communicating with each other.
- Do not assign the infrastructure master role to a domain controller that is hosting the global catalog service if there is more than one domain. A global catalog stores information about objects in a tree or a forest. Whenever this information changes, the global catalog updates the information through replication. Therefore, the global catalog always contains the latest information about objects. If you assign the infrastructure master role to a domain controller hosting the global catalog, the infrastructure master will not function properly, as there are no "phantom" references for it to update.

Table 2-2 Forest-wide operations master roles and their descriptions

Forest-wide operations master roles	Description	Problems if the FSMO fails	Transferred at
Schema master role	The domain controller holding the schema master role has write permissions for the directory schema. You can have only one schema master in the entire forest at any point in time.	Unless the failure occurs during a schema modification, there will be little to no problems. However, you cannot modify the schema until you bring the schema master back online or seize the role using ntdsutil.exe.	Active Directory Schema console
Domain naming master role	The domain controller holding the domain naming master role can add or remove domains in a forest. Only one domain naming master role can exist in the entire forest.	No domains may be added or removed from the forest until this server is back online or the role is seized using ntdsutil.exe.	Active Directory Domains and Trusts console

Table 2-3 Domain-wide operations master roles and their descriptions

Forest-wide operations master roles	Description	Problems if the FSMO fails	Transferred at
Relative ID master role	This domain controller allocates sequences of relative IDs to each of the various domain controllers in its domain. This role is needed to ensure unique blocks of RIDs that are assigned to each domain controller, assuring that each object within the domain will have a unique SID.	If no RID master or standby RID master is available, your domain controllers may run out of RID. Therefore, you will be unable to create new objects until you bring the server back online or the role is seized using ntdsutil.exe.	Active Directory Users and Computers console
PDC emulator role	The domain controller holding this role receives preferential replication of security changes and acts as the time synchronization master for the domain. It also processes password change requests from down-level clients in the domain and replicates updates to Windows NT backup domain controllers.	If PDC emulator fails, you may experience various problems especially: Replication to NT4 domain controls may stop, down-level clients may be unable to change passwords, and clocks may fall out of sync, which, once they are more than five minutes off, will cause the domain to deny database changes. Resolve these problems by restoring the domain controller holding this role or by using ntdsutil.exe to seize the role.	Active Directory Users and Computers console
Infrastructure master role	The domain controller holding the infrastructure master role updates cross-domain references. When you reference an object from another domain, the reference must be updated on the referencing domain any time a change occurs. The Infrastructure Master makes a list of references to objects that do not exist in its database, and updates those references when changes occur.	Initially, failure of the Infrastructure Master role may not cause noticeable problems. In a multi-domain environment, however, cross-domain references will not update, which will lead to errors when modifying groups with members from other domains. Resolve this problem by restoring the domain controller holding this role or by seizing the role using ntdsutil.exe.	Active Directory Users and Computers console

skill 4

Viewing the Operations Master Role Assignments for a Domain

exam objective

Basic knowledge

overview

You need to identify and view the domain controllers that hold the operations master roles in order to monitor the operations master roles. Regular monitoring of the operations masters roles in a domain or forest enables you to determine the performance and load on each of the operations masters. This in turn enables you to decide the roles that need to be transferred to other domain controllers. You can view all the domain-wide operations master role assignments using the Active Directory Users and Computers console. You use the Active Directory Schema snap-in and the Active Directory Domains and Trusts console to view the schema master and the domain naming master roles.

how to

View the domain-wide operations master role assignments.

1. Click Start, point to **Programs**, point to **Administrative Tools**, and then click the **Active Directory Users and Computers** command. The **Active Directory Users and Computers** console appears.
2. Right-click the **Active Directory Users and Computers** node, and then click the **Operations Master** command on the shortcut menu. The **Operations Master** dialog box opens with the **RID** tab activated by default **(Figure 2-10)**.
3. The name of the domain controller holding the relative ID master role appears in the **Operations master** text box. This text box is present on all the tabs and displays the name of the domain controller holding that particular role.
4. To identify the domain controller holding the PDC emulator role, click the **PDC** tab.
5. To identify the domain controller holding the infrastructure master role, click the **Infrastructure** tab.
6. Click OK to close the **Operations Master** dialog box.
7. Click the **Close** button X to close the **Active Directory Users and Computers** console. You have identified the domain controllers holding the domain-wide operations master roles.

more

To view the **schema master** role assignment, right-click the **Active Directory Schema** node in the **Active Directory Schema** console, and then click the **Operations Master** command on the shortcut menu. This displays the **Change Schema Master** dialog box, and the name of the domain controller holding the schema master role appears in the **Current Operations Master** section **(Figure 2-11)**.

To view the domain naming master role assignment, right-click the **Active Directory Domains and Trusts** node in the **Active Directory Domains and Trusts** console, and click the **Operations Master** command on the shortcut menu. This displays the **Change Operations Master** dialog box, where the name of the domain controller holding the domain naming master role appears in the **Domain naming operations master** box **(Figure 2-12)**.

Figure 2-10 Viewing the default domain-wide operations master role assignments

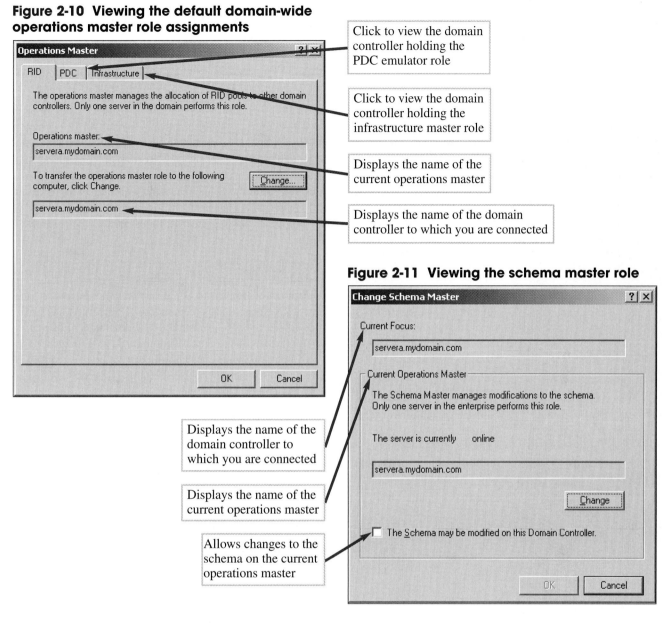

Operations Master

RID | PDC | Infrastructure

The operations master manages the allocation of RID pools to other domain controllers. Only one server in the domain performs this role.

Operations master:

servera.mydomain.com

To transfer the operations master role to the following computer, click Change.

Change...

servera.mydomain.com

OK Cancel

Click to view the domain controller holding the PDC emulator role

Click to view the domain controller holding the infrastructure master role

Displays the name of the current operations master

Displays the name of the domain controller to which you are connected

Figure 2-11 Viewing the schema master role

Change Schema Master

Current Focus:

servera.mydomain.com

Current Operations Master

The Schema Master manages modifications to the schema. Only one server in the enterprise performs this role.

The server is currently online

servera.mydomain.com

Change

The Schema may be modified on this Domain Controller.

OK Cancel

Displays the name of the domain controller to which you are connected

Displays the name of the current operations master

Allows changes to the schema on the current operations master

Figure 2-12 Viewing the domain naming master role

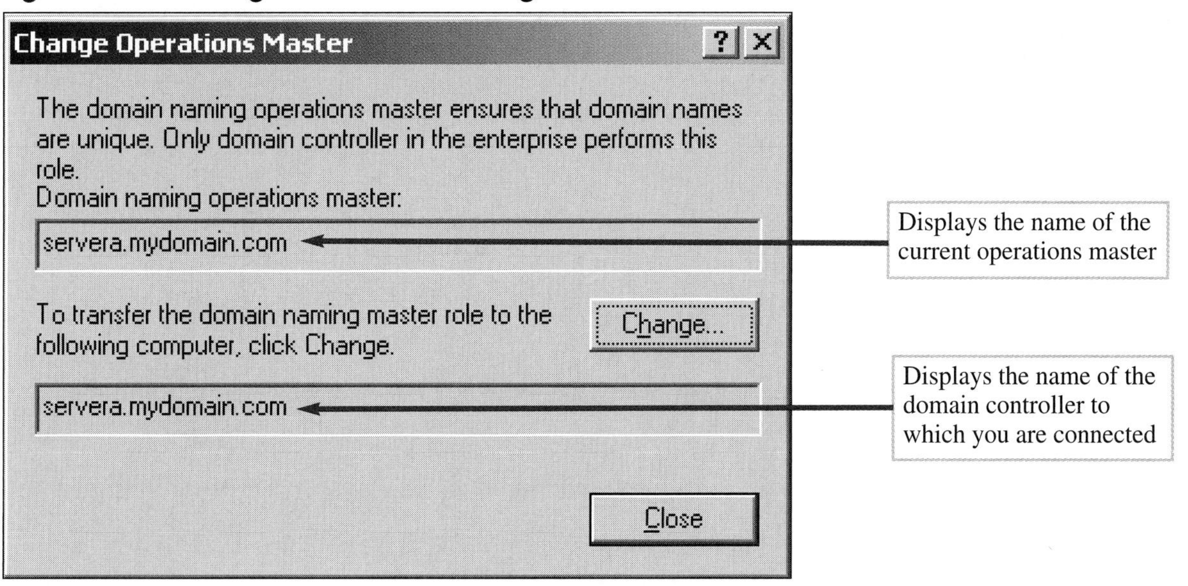

skill 5 Transferring Operations Master Roles

exam objective

Transfer operations master roles. Seize operations master roles.

overview

After identifying the domain controllers holding the operations master roles, you can now easily transfer the roles between domain controllers. You need to transfer the operations master roles under the following two conditions:

- You want to change the default operations master because the domain controller is unavailable for replication.
- The performance of the domain controller holding the operations master role is deteriorating due to excess load.

You can transfer operations master roles between the domain controllers within a forest, as well as within domains with the assistance of the original operations master. To transfer an operations master role from one domain controller to another, ensure that both domain controllers are available and connected to each other through the network. Transferring an operations master role is a two-stage process. First, you connect to the new domain controller that will hold the role, and then you transfer the role to the domain controller that is identified for the role. You use the Active Directory Users and Computers console to transfer the relative ID master, PDC emulator, and infrastructure master roles. You use the Active Directory Domains and Trusts console to transfer the domain naming master role.

caution

To restore a domain controller whose roles have been seized, you must first format the hard disk and reload the Windows 2000 Server operating system.

Sometimes, due to system failure, an operations master may be unavailable. If there is any chance of recovering the operations master, you should; otherwise, you can force the transfer of the operations master role to a Windows 2000 Server without the cooperation of the existing owner of the roles. This process is also called seizing the role. **Table 2-4** lists the effects

Table 2-4 Failure of operations master roles—the effects and corrective actions

Operations master role failures	*Effect*	*Corrective action*
Schema master failure	Temporary unavailability of a domain controller holding this role will affect the administrators only if they are trying to modify the schema or install an application that modifies the schema during installation.	If the operations master is unavailable for an indefinite period, you can seize the role to a Windows 2000 standby operations master. Before seizing the schema master role, you first must remove the current operations master from the network, and then verify that the copy of the schema on the new operations master is updated with the rest of the domain controllers in the forest.
Domain naming master failure	Temporary unavailability of a domain controller holding this role will affect the administrators only if they are trying to add a domain to the forest or remove a domain from the forest.	If the operations master is unavailable for an indefinite period, you can seize the role to a Window 2000 standby operations master. Before seizing the domain naming master role, you first should remove the current operations master from the network, and then verify that the new operations master is updated with the latest information.
Relative ID master failure	Temporary unavailability of a domain controller holding this role will affect the administrators only if they are creating an object, and the domain in which they are creating the object runs out of relative identifiers.	If the operations master is unavailable for an indefinite period, you can seize the role to a Window 2000 standby operations master. Before seizing the relative ID master, a utility known as Repadmin is used to verify whether the new operations master has received any updates performed by the previous role holder, and then to remove the current operations master from the network.
PDC emulator failure	Even temporary unavailability of this role affects network users and administrators.	In case of PDC emulator failure, you may need to immediately seize the role to a Window 2000 standby operations master if the domain has clients without Windows 2000 client software, or if the domain contains Windows NT backup domain controllers. Before seizing the PDC emulator master, remove the current operations master from the network and verify that the new operations master is up-to-date. When the original PDC emulator master becomes available, you can return the role to the original domain controller.
Infrastructure master failure	Temporary unavailability of a domain controller holding this role will affect the administrators only if they have recently moved or renamed a large number of accounts.	If the operations master is unavailable for an indefinite period, you can seize the role to a domain controller that is not a global catalog, but is well connected (usually in the same site) to a global catalog. Before seizing the infrastructure master, remove the current operations master from the network and verify that the new operations master is up-to-date. When the original infrastructure master becomes available, you can return the role to the original domain controller.

skill 5 Transferring Operations Master Roles *(cont'd)*

exam objective

Transfer operations master roles. Seize operations master roles.

overview

of unavailability of operations master roles and the actions to be taken in case the roles become unavailable. You can use the **NTDSUTIL** command from the command prompt to seize any operations master role. **Table 2-5** lists the sequence of commands to seize a schema master role and descriptions of these commands.

how to

Transfer the PDC emulator role from one domain controller to another domain controller.

1. Log on as an **Administrator** to the second domain controller joined to the domain you created in Skill 1.
2. Click Start, point to **Programs**, point to **Administrative Tools**, and then click the **Active Directory Users and Computers** command. The **Active Directory Users and Computers** console appears.
3. In the console tree, right-click the **Active Directory Users and Computers** node, and then click the **Connect to Domain Controller** command on the shortcut menu. The **Connect to Domain Controller** dialog box appears.
4. To specify the new domain controller that will hold the PDC emulator role, click the name of the second domain controller (ServerB), on the list of domain controllers displayed at the bottom of the **Connect to Domain Controller** dialog box, and then click OK **(Figure 2-13)**.
5. Right-click the **Active Directory Users and Computers** node, and then click the **Operations Masters** command on the shortcut menu. The **Operations Master** dialog box appears.
6. To start the process of transferring the PDC emulator role, click the **PDC** tab.
7. To transfer the PDC emulator role, click Change... on the PDC tab. A message box asks you to confirm the transfer of the PDC operations master role **(Figure 2-14)**.
8. Click Yes. A message box indicating the successful transfer of the operations master role appears.
9. Click OK to close the message box.
10. Click OK to close the **Operations Master** dialog box.
11. Click the **Close** button to close the **Active Directory Users and Computers** console. You have transferred the PDC role from the domain controller you created in Skill 1 to another domain controller.

tip

This skill requires a second domain controller joined to the domain you created in Skill 1.

more

Apart from transferring the per-domain operations master and the domain naming master roles, you might need to transfer the schema master role. You use the Active Directory Schema snap-in to transfer the schema master role. To begin, open the **Active Directory Schema** snap-in, right-click the **Active Directory Schema** node, and then click the **Change Domain Controller** command on the shortcut menu. The Change Domain Controller dialog box appears. To specify the new domain controller that will hold the schema master role, select the **Specify Name** option button, type the name of the domain controller, and then click the **OK** button. Right-click the **Active Directory Schema** node, and then click the **Operation Master** command on the shortcut menu. The **Change Schema Master** dialog box appears. To transfer the schema master role to the new domain controller, click the **Change** button. A message box asking you to confirm the transfer of the schema master role appears. Click the **Yes** button. Another message box indicating the successful transfer of the operations master role appears. Click the **OK** button to close the message box.

Table 2-5 Sequence of commands to seize operations master roles

Sequence of commands	Description
1. Type **roles** at the NTDSUTIL prompt	Displays the FSMO maintenance prompt
2. Type **connections** at the FSMO maintenance prompt	Connects to a specific domain controller
3. Type **connect to server** followed by the Fully Qualified Domain Name (FQDN) at the server connections prompt	Connects to the specified server, DNS name, or IP address
4. Type **quit** at the server connections prompt	Quits the server maintenance prompt
5. Type **seize <name of the role>** at the FSMO maintenance prompt	On the connected server, overwrites the role that you specify in place of <name of the role>
6. Type **quit** at the FSMO maintenance prompt	Quits the FSMO maintenance prompt
7. Type **quit** at the NTDSUTIL prompt	Quits the utility and displays the command prompt

Figure 2-13 Specifying the new operations master

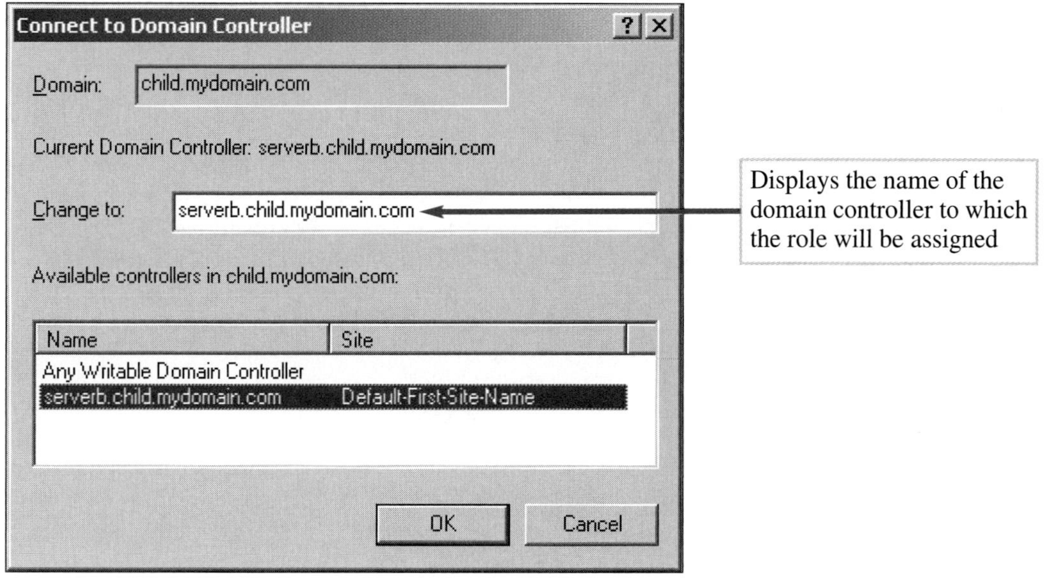

Figure 2-14 Transferring the PDC emulator role

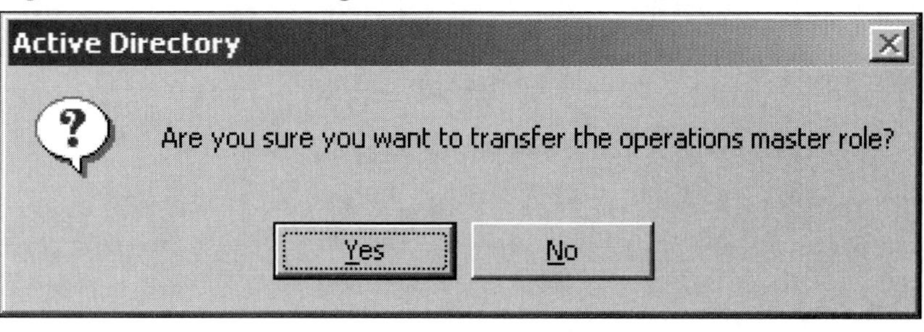

skill 6 Implementing an Organizational Unit Structure within a Domain

exam objective

Implement an organizational unit (OU) structure. Create and manage objects manually or by using scripting.

overview

Planning and creating an organizational unit (OU) structure is the last activity you perform to complete the implementation of Active Directory. OUs are structures used to organize objects within the domain into logical groups, simplifying administration of large numbers of objects. You can manage users easily and efficiently in an OU. In a multiple-domain model, each domain implements its own OU hierarchy, independent of the OU structures in other domains. Creating OUs enables you to:

- Apply group policy to a particular group of users or computers independently of other groups of users and computers in other OUs.
- Structure a domain according to the departments and locations in your organization. Without OUs, all users are maintained in a single list under a domain. This is particularly problematic in extremely large organizations, where a list of 60,000 + users can be a nightmare to manage otherwise.
- Delegate administrative control of network resources to users.
- Accommodate any changes that are likely to take place in the structure of your organization. Reorganizing users between OUs requires significantly less time and effort than reorganizing users between domains.
- Organizational units simplify the viewing and administration of directory objects within a domain. Therefore, you should plan an OU structure carefully so that the organizational units represent your organization in a meaningful and manageable way. They also allow the administrator to have easy access to all the objects at any level of hierarchy. (***Note:*** OUs and Containers are different in very major ways. Visually, an OU has a book icon inside of its folder icon [see the MKTG OU in **Figure 2-18** for an example], while a container does not. Functionally, an OU may be created and deleted, and group policies can be applied to OUs. Containers exist by default, cannot be deleted, and may not have group policy applied to them.)

tip

Try to keep your OU structure to three levels deep, or less, for simplification purposes.

There are three standard models available for designing OUs: business function-based, geographical-based, and business function and geographical-based. The important thing to keep in mind is that OUs are for administrative organization and should be designed with ease of administration in mind.

You use the business function-based model to create an OU structure that reflects the various business functions within an organization. In **Figure 2-15** the top level OUs, Sales and Manufacturing, and the second level OUs, Cars and Trucks, represent the business divisions and the functional divisions, respectively. You use the geographical-based model to create an OU structure that represents the location of branches of an organization. In **Figure 2-16** the top level OUs, North Chicago and South Chicago, and the second level OUs, Field Blvd. and Washington Blvd., represent the geographical regions and the physical locations within the regions, respectively. You can also combine the business function and the geographical-based models to create an OU structure that reflects the various business functions within the different branches of an organization. In **Figure 2-17** the top level OUs, North London and South London, and the second level OUs, Sales and Manufacturing, represent the regions and the functional divisions, respectively.

You use the Active Directory Users and Computers console to create OUs. When you create an OU in a domain, by default, it is created in the first available domain controller. Information about the OU is then replicated to all domain controllers in that domain.

Figure 2-15 A business function-based OU structure

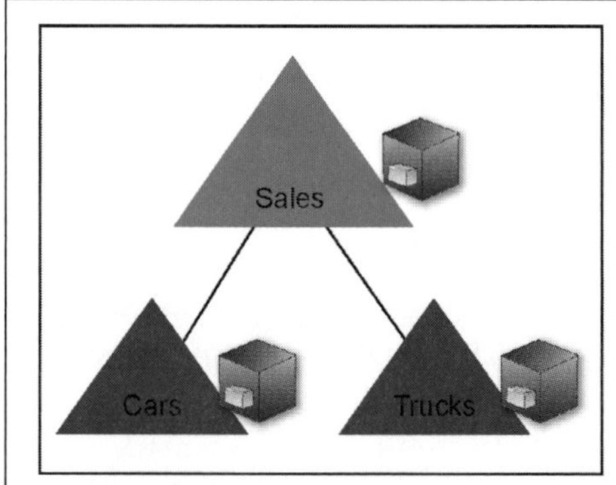

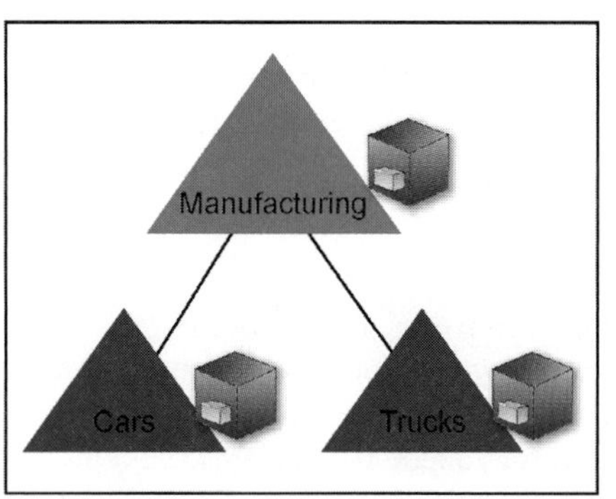

Figure 2-16 A geographical-based OU structure

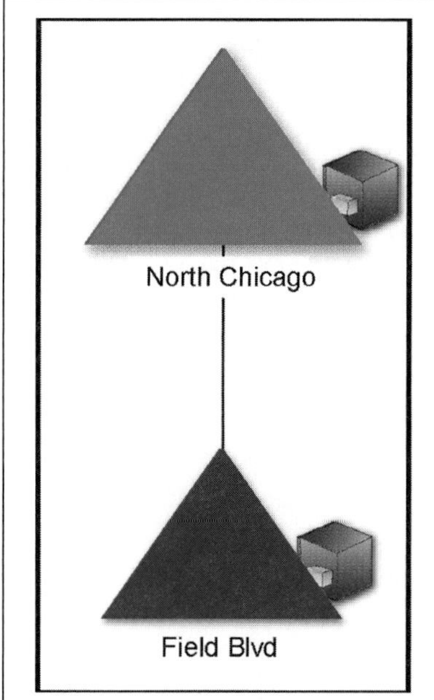

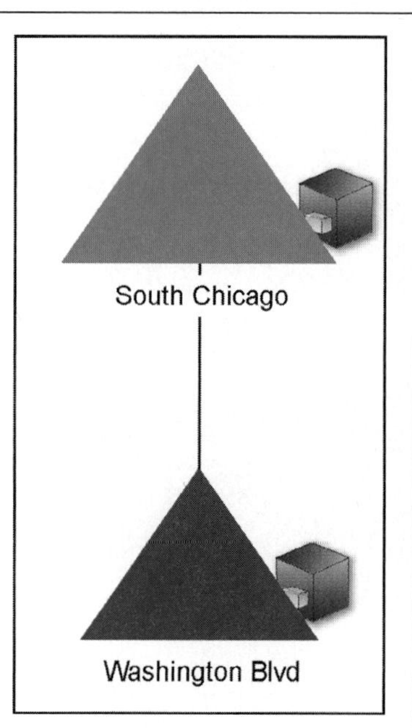

Figure 2-17 A business function and geographical-based OU structure

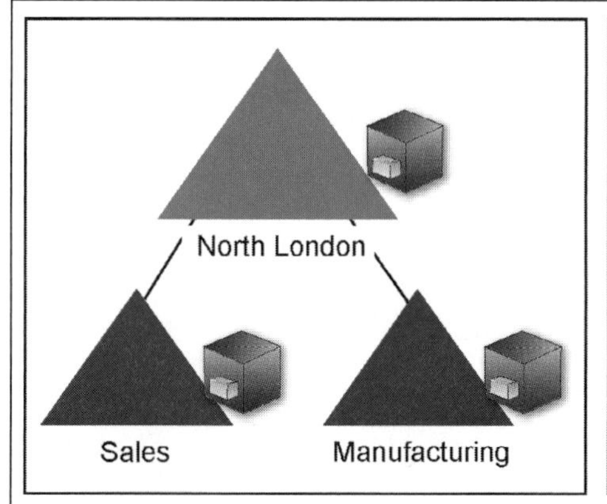

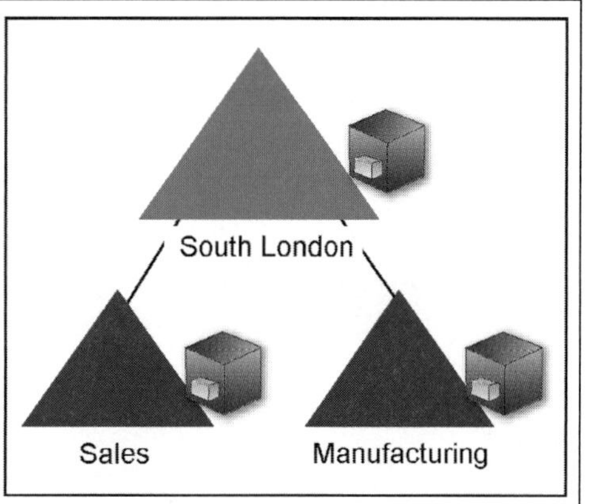

skill 6 Implementing an Organizational Unit Structure within a Domain (cont'd)

exam objective

Implement an organizational unit (OU) structure. Create and manage objects manually or by using scripting.

how to

Create an OU in a domain.

1. Click **Start**, point to **Programs**, point to **Administrative Tools**, and then click the **Active Directory Users and Computers** command. The **Active Directory Users and Computers** dialog box appears.
2. In the console root, click the location where you want to create the OU. Here, click the mydomain.com node to select a domain.
3. Click **Action** on the menu bar, point to **New**, and then click the **Organizational Unit** command. The **New Object – Organizational Unit** dialog box appears.
4. Type **MKTG** in the **Name** text box to specify the name of the OU, and then click OK **(Figure 2-18)**. The new OU appears in the right pane of the console root.
5. Click the Close button ☒ to close the **Active Directory Users and Computers** console. You have created an OU, called MKTG, in the domain mydomain.com.

tip

You can also click an OU if you want to create a nested OU, which is an OU created within an OU.

more

Each OU that you create contains a set of default properties. Apart from the default properties, each OU has additional properties, such as a description. The properties of an OU are **attributes** that you use to locate the OU. You can set the properties of an OU using the Active Directory Users and Computers console. To set the properties of an OU, open the console, select the OU, and then click the **Properties** command on the **Action** menu. The **Properties** dialog box for the selected OU appears **(Figure 2-19)**. You can specify the description and other details for the OU here. To set the properties, click the **Apply** button, and then click the **OK** button.

Figure 2-18 Creating an organizational unit

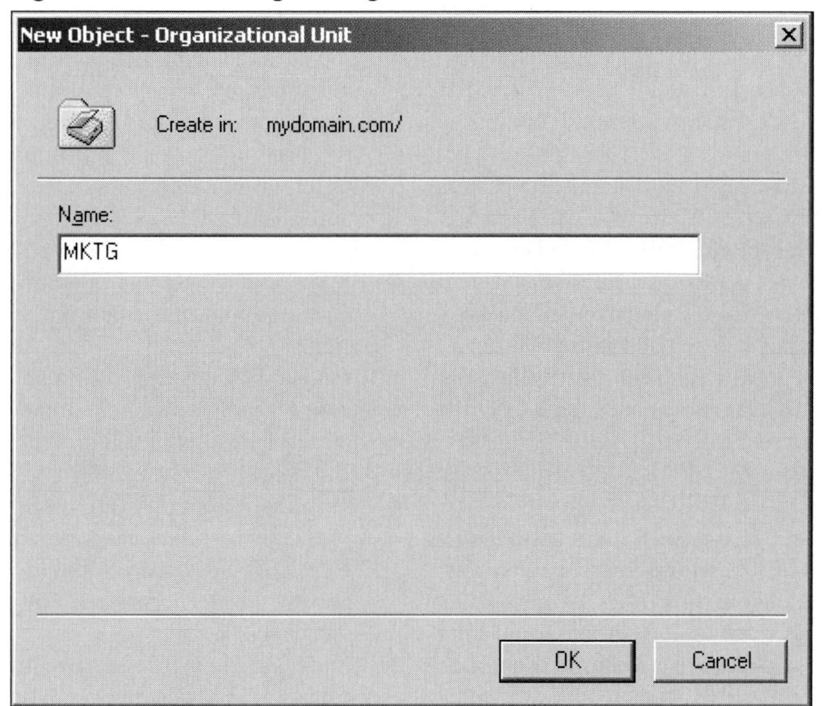

Figure 2-19 Properties dialog box

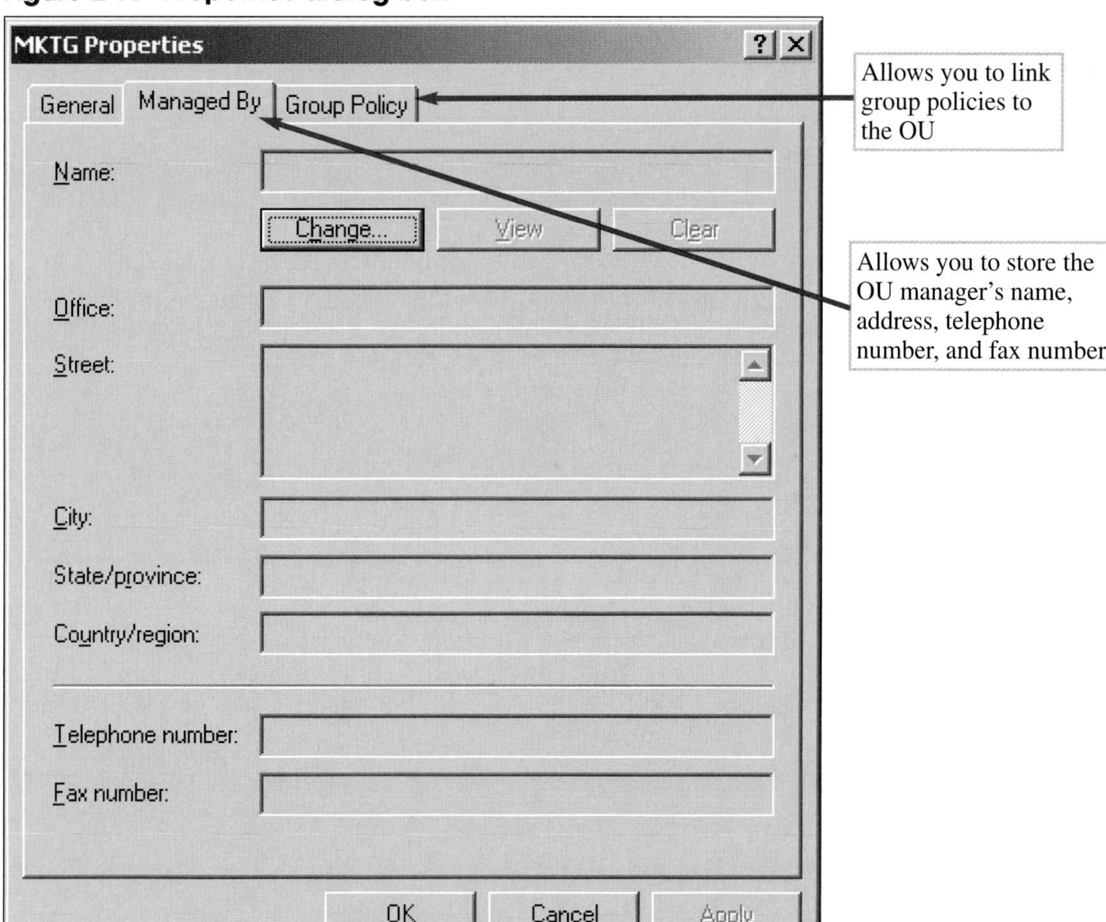

Summary

- You install Active Directory using the Active Directory Installation wizard. When you install Active Directory for the first time, you create the root domain, a new domain tree, and a new forest; furthermore, you designate a Windows 2000 Server as a domain controller.
- You install DNS services, database and database log files, and shared system volume during Active Directory installation.
- You verify Active Directory installation to ensure that any Active Directory components you add in the future are correctly installed. The tools available for the verification of Active Directory installation are the Active Directory Users and Computers console, the Active Directory Domains and Trusts console, the Active Directory Sites and Services console and the DNS console.
- Operations master roles can be classified into two categories: forest-wide operations master roles and domain-wide operations master roles. Forest-wide operations master roles can be further classified into schema master role and domain naming master role. Domain-wide operations master roles are also subdivided into three categories: relative ID master role, primary domain controller (PDC) emulator role, and infrastructure master role.
- You need to identify the domain controllers that hold the operations master roles to decide which roles need to be transferred to different domain controllers.
- You need to transfer the operations master roles if the operations master is unavailable for replication, or if the performance of the domain controller holding the operations master role is deteriorating due to excess load.
- When you transfer an operations master role assignment, you move the role from one domain controller to another.
- You should consider seizing an operations master role only if you are positive that the operations master will never be available again. You use the NTDSUTIL command to seize any operations master role.
- Organizational units (OUs) are objects that can store other objects such as users, groups, computers, and other OUs. OUs are used to divide a domain into logical groups in order to organize large numbers of objects effectively.
- There are three standard models for designing OU structures: business function-based, geographical-based, and business function and geographical-based. You use the Active Directory Users and Computers console to create OUs.

Key Terms

Active Directory Domains and Trusts console
Active Directory Schema snap-in
Active Directory Sites and Services console
Active Directory Users and Computers console
Database log files
Domain naming master role
Domain-wide operations master roles
Forest-wide operations master roles
Infrastructure master role
Mixed mode
Native mode
NTDSUTIL
Operations master roles
Primary domain controller (PDC) emulator role
Relative ID master role
Schema master role
Shared system volume
Single master roles

Test Yourself

1. Which of the following components are created during Active Directory installation? (Choose all that apply)
   a. DHCP Servers
   b. Database and database log files
   c. Contacts
   d. Shared system volume

2. To verify Active Directory installation, you check the presence of: (Choose all that apply)
   a. Computers in the first domain.
   b. The domain specified during Active Directory installation.
   c. Groups in the root domain.
   d. A domain controller in the Domain Controller OU.

3. Identify the forest-wide operations master roles from the following: (Choose all that apply)
   a. Relative ID master
   b. Schema master
   c. Domain naming master
   d. Infrastructure master

4. Which of the following statements about operations master roles is correct? (Choose all that apply)
   a. When the first domain is created in a new forest, by default, all the operations master roles are assigned to the first domain controller in that domain.
   b. Each domain in a forest can have only one relative ID master, PDC emulator, and infrastructure master.
   c. The schema master and the domain naming master roles cannot be assigned to a single computer.
   d. Each domain in a forest will have both domain-wide and forest-wide operations master roles.
   e. In a forest, no two domain controllers can perform the same forest-wide operations master role.

5. You can view all the domain-wide operations master role assignments using the Active Directory Users and Computers console.
   a. True
   b. False

6. Which following situation requires seizing an operations master role?
   a. The performance of the operations master role is deteriorating.
   b. An operations master will become permanently unavailable.
   c. The domain controller is no longer hosting the global catalog.
   d. The connectivity between the parts of a network is not available.

7. You need to create OUs in order to: (Choose all that apply)
   a. Structure a domain according to the departments and locations in your organization.
   b. Implement different account policies for different groups of users.
   c. Apply top level administrative privileges to different divisions of your company.
   d. Delegate administrative control over network resources to users.
   e. Accommodate any changes that are likely to take place in the structure of your organization.

Projects: On Your Own

1. Install Active Directory and create a child domain.
   a. Start the **Active Directory Installation** wizard.
   b. Select the option to create a new domain.
   c. Select the option to make the new domain part of another domain.
   d. Specify the name of the parent domain.
   e. Accept the default options displayed on subsequent screens of the wizard.
   f. Check the **Summary** check box to confirm change.

2. Verify Active Directory installation for a domain.
   a. Open the **Active Directory Users and Computers** console.
   b. Check the existence of the child domain created in the above exercise.
   c. Check the **Domain Controllers** folder for the existence of a domain controller object.
   d. Use the **DNS console** and **nslookup.exe** to ensure that SRV records for your domain have been added.

3. View the domain-wide operations master role assignments.
   a. Open the **Active Directory Users and Computers** console.
   b. Open the **Operations Master** dialog box.
   c. View the relative ID master, PDC emulator, and infrastructure master roles.

Problem Solving Scenarios

1. Your company has recently upgraded to Windows 2000. As your company's Network Administrator, you have the task of managing the domain structure of the network, as well as the related upgrade process. At the moment, you have five Windows NT 4.0 domains: Corporate, Admin, IT, Sales, and Manufacturing. The Admin and Sales departments do not require separate domain identities, since the number of users for these domains is comparatively low and the administrative overhead for maintaining separate domains for these departments is high. Secondly, you want to have complete control over all administrative tasks from a single point that is ideally the corporate domain. Prepare a PowerPoint presentation outlining your plan of action for tackling the situation described.

2. Your company network is based on Windows 2000, and you are running the ADS domain structure. The domain structure is as follows: The root domain is company.msft and it has three child domains: branch1.company.msft, branch2.company.msft, and mktg.company.msft.

The domain controller in the root domain, named RDC1, holds the forest-wide Operations Masters. This domain also has one additional domain controller. Similarly, the domain-wide roles are held by respective Domain Controllers in each domain. Also, there is one additional domain controller in each domain.

The domain controller for the mktg.company.msft domain recently failed, and you have received complaints from users that they can neither change their passwords nor access other domains.

You must put the domain structure back in operation as soon as possible. List the steps you will follow to achieve this.

LESSON 3

Integrating the Domain Name System with Active Directory

On a TCP/IP network, computers and other devices (collectively known as hosts) use IP addresses to connect and communicate with each other. It is difficult to remember these IP addresses due to their numerical format. You can overcome this problem by using names instead of IP addresses. These names act as aliases for the IP addresses and are valid when you use them to refer to a TCP/IP host on a network; however, names must eventually be resolved to an IP address.

In Windows 2000, Domain Name System (DNS) is the native method for resolving host names to IP addresses. DNS forms an integral part of the Windows 2000 operating system. In addition to using DNS to resolve names on the network, Windows 2000 also uses it for locating different services on the network.

Some of the new features in Windows 2000's implementation of DNS are quite advanced, and significantly reduce administrative effort required for managing your DNS infrastructure. These new features are briefly mentioned below, and expanded upon later in the lesson:

- Dynamic DNS (DDNS) Support. Windows 2000 fully supports dynamic DNS as described in RFC 2136, providing for automatic registration of various records by compliant hosts or DHCP servers.
- Windows 2000 also supports secure dynamic updates of DNS, only allowing (by default) an update to a record by the host who originally registered that record. This reduces the chance of name spoofing in the network. However, this mechanism is only compatible with Windows 2000 DNS servers, as it is not compliant with secure updates as defined by RFC 3007 (though it is similar to the method defined in RFC 2743).
- Active Directory Integrated Zones: Windows 2000 supports a new type of zone, Active Directory Integrated (ADI), which eliminates both the standard text-based zone files and the entire zone-transfer process by inserting all records for a zone as objects in the AD database. This functionality brings about several benefits, most notably, a reduction in zone transfer traffic, automatic replication, increased replication security, and multi-master replication of DNS modifications.
- Incremental Zone Transfers: Windows 2000 also includes support for Incremental Zone Transfers (IXFR) as defined in RFC 1995. IXFR allows DNS servers to simply transfer changes to the zone, rather than transferring the entire zone for each change. This significantly reduces network traffic related to zone transfers.
- Service Location Record Support: Windows 2000 supports Service Location (SRV) records, as defined in RFC 2782, to allow DNS to be used to resolve specific types of services (such as LDAP), as well as names. This is at the core of Windows 2000's native support of DNS, as the ability to search for a type of service is critical to the logon process.

Note that even though DNS is now the native name resolution method, that does not mean that NetBIOS names (and the WINS servers that resolve them) are obsolete. While it is possible to rely solely on DNS for name resolution in Windows 2000, many applications (including DFS) and down-level operating systems (like Windows NT) still require NetBIOS name resolution.

Goals

In this lesson, you will learn to install and configure DNS on your system. You will also learn to use the DNS console to create zones, configure zones for dynamic updates, and enable zone transfers. Additionally, you will learn to set debug properties for the DNS server to create an efficient and reliable DNS for the network of your organization. Finally, you will learn to troubleshoot DNS problems.

Lesson 3 Integrating the Domain Name System with Active Directory

Skill	*Exam 70-217 Objective*
1. Introducing DNS	Basic knowledge.
2. Describing DNS Zones and DNS Server Roles	Basic knowledge.
3. Installing the DNS Service	Install and configure DNS for Active Directory.
4. Planning the Zones in DNS	Basic knowledge.
5. Creating Lookup Zones	Integrate Active Directory DNS zones with existing DNS infrastructure.
6. Delegating Zones	Create and configure DNS records.
7. Configuring Dynamic DNS	Install and configure DNS for Active Directory. Configure zones for dynamic updates and security-enhanced dynamic updates.
8. Implementing Zone Replication and Zone Transfer in Servers	Manage, monitor, and troubleshoot DNS.
9. Setting Debugging Options for DNS Servers	Manage, monitor, and troubleshoot DNS.
10. Troubleshooting DNS Problems	Manage, monitor, and troubleshoot DNS.

Requirements

To complete the skills in this lesson, you need administrative rights on two Windows 2000 Server computers (Server1 and Server2) that do not have DNS service or Active Directory installed. You will also need the fully functioning domain controller for the mydomain.com domain created in Lesson 2.

skill 1 Introducing DNS

exam objective

Basic knowledge

overview

DNS is a hierarchical, distributed, and scalable database that contains various entries known as records. In order to understand the workings of DNS and how DNS performs all its functions, you first need to understand the structure of DNS.

The structure of DNS is defined by the **DNS namespace**. The DNS namespace is a hierarchical arrangement of contiguous domains. This hierarchical structure consists of a root domain, top-level domains, second-level domains, any number of potential subdomains, and various records (such as Host name records, also known as "A" records). **Table 3-1** describes this hierarchical structure.

To fully identify a host in the DNS hierarchy, you use a **Fully Qualified Domain Name (FQDN)**, which is a segmented name that uses a host name together with its domain names, separated by dots. A FQDN completely identifies a host on a TCP/IP network such as the Internet. For example, **computer1.domain1.mydomain.com.** is an FQDN that indicates that "." is the root domain, **com** is a top-level domain, **mydomain** is a second-level domain, **domain1** is a child domain, and **computer1** is the name of the host computer.

Understanding the DNS hierarchy makes it easy to understand the way DNS works to resolve host names to IP addresses, and IP addresses to host names. To perform all this in a Windows 2000 network, DNS requires two main components: resolver and name server.

Resolver

Resolver runs on the DNS client computers and is the service used to request resolution of a name from a DNS server. During the process of DNS name resolution, if the client cannot resolve the destination host name on its own (either from the DNS name cache or the hosts file), the resolver sends a query to the server configured as the primary DNS name server, requesting the required data. The receiving DNS server may then issue queries of its own to higher level DNS servers in order to resolve the name.

This process is best described with an example. Imagine you are attempting to resolve www.prenhall.com from your home PC. Your computer (the resolver) will issue a recursive query to your primary DNS server for the address www.prenhall.com. A recursive query is simply asking the DNS server to "find" the answer. Since you issued a recursive query to your primary DNS server, that server will then do the majority of the work for you. First, the DNS server will look in its cache to see if it had already resolved this record (for another client, perhaps). If the record is not listed in the cache, the DNS server will then typically issue an iterative query to the root (".") DNS servers (listed in a file known as "root hints").

Issuing an iterative query is like asking the server to give you directions to someone who can answer your query. The root servers, named A.root-servers.net through M.root-servers.net, contain records pointing to each top-level domain on the Internet. These servers will respond back to your DNS server, informing it that while they do not know what the correct IP address for www.prenhall.com is, your DNS server should ask the .com servers, as they might know. Your DNS server then sends the same query to the .com servers, who would then tell it to ask the prenhall.com DNS server. Your DNS server then queries the prenhall.com DNS server, which responds with the IP address listed in the host record for www.prenhall.com. Your DNS server then adds this information to its cache, and finally responds to your original query.

Table 3-1 Hierarchical structure used in DNS

Levels of hierarchy	Description
Root domain	The root domain is located at the top of the hierarchy and is represented by a period ".".
Top-level domain	The top-level domains are the first branches that emerge from the root. They indicate the type of organization that owns the domain. For example, the ".com" domain is meant for commercial organizations and the ".org" domain is meant for not-for-profit organizations.
Second-level domain	The second-level domains are located below the top-level domains and are used to identify specific organizations within the top-level domains. A common example of a second-level domain is yahoo.com.
Subdomain	The subdomains (also known as child domains) are branches that emerge from a given second-level domain. For example, in www.support.microsoft.com, support is a child domain of the microsoft second-level domain.
Host name	The host names identify a specific computer on the network.

skill 1

Introducing DNS (cont'd)

exam objective

Basic knowledge

overview

While the above example describes the differences in the two main query types pretty well, both of these query types, along with an additional type known as an inverse query, are also described below:

- **Recursive:** When a client sends a recursive query to the DNS server, the DNS server looks for the record in its database. If the DNS server does not contain the matching record, it forwards the query to other DNS servers until a matching entry is found. The reply containing the resolved IP address is returned to the DNS server. The client waits until the query is resolved, and the DNS server sends the resolved query back to the client. However, if the name server is not able to find the requested data or the specified domain name, the name server replies with an error message **(Figure 3-1)**.
- **Iterative:** The client queries a DNS server and instructs the server that it expects the best answer the server can provide without seeking help from other DNS servers. If a local DNS server cannot resolve an iterative query, the query is referred to the root-level DNS server. The root-level DNS server then sends a pointer containing the IP address of the suitable DNS server in the namespace to resolve the answer. These pointers sent by the root-level DNS server to the local DNS server are called referrals, and the referrals are the expected answers for iterative queries. Recursive and iterative queries are also called forward lookup queries.
- **Inverse**: In this query, the client sends a request to a name server to resolve an IP address to a name. IP address to name lookups are commonly used by server applications (web traffic logs and security applications, for instance) to find the originating domain for a given client.

Name server

A DNS name server is simply a server with the DNS server service installed and running. While a name server usually also includes one or more zone files (DNS databases) used for authoritatively resolving queries to one or more zones, this is not required. Servers that have no zone files are typically used to cache requests for large numbers of clients, and are known as "caching only" servers.

Figure 3-1 Resolving a forward lookup query

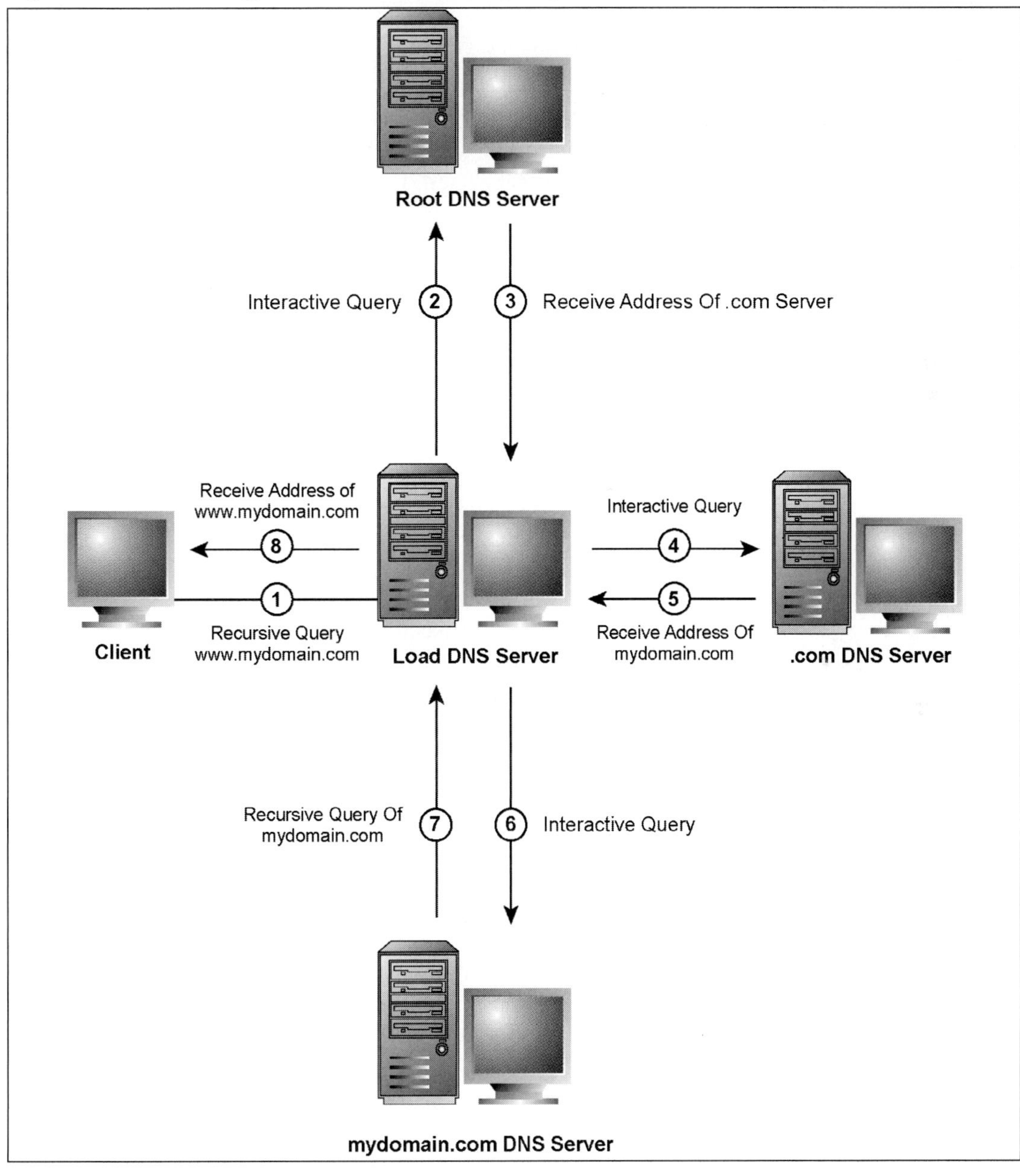

skill 2 Describing DNS Zones and DNS Server Roles

exam objective Basic knowledge

overview

DNS is based around the concept of **zones**. Zones are an area of authority consisting of one or more contiguous domains. When a server contains a particular zone, it is said to be authoritative for that zone, meaning that any query it receives for that zone can be answered with direct knowledge; no other servers must be asked.

Each zone on a DNS server is defined by a **zone file**. Zone files are typically text-based databases that contain all of the **resource records** associated with the zone. Depending on the type of zone, these resource records may vary, but usually the zone file is primarily composed of "A" (Address, sometimes called host) records **(Figure 3-2)**.

Zones are broken into two primary types: Forward Lookup and Reverse Lookup. Forward lookup zones are your standard DNS zones. They are used primarily for resolving name-to-IP lookups using A records. Reverse lookup zones are used for inverse queries, and typically resolve IP-to-name lookups using PTR (pointer) records.

In addition, zones can be defined by their sub-type, primary, secondary, or Active Directory integrated (ADI). The primary zone will always be contained on a single server, and is typically referred to as the only "writable" copy of the zone (see Tip). Your primary zone should typically be contained on a secure server (meaning behind your firewall) to reduce the risk of modification to the zone by unauthorized parties. The server hosting the primary copy of your zone is known as the **primary server**. The primary server's job is simply to make updates to the zone, as well as transfer the zone to the secondary servers. **Secondary servers** are servers containing a "read-only" copy of the zone known as a **secondary zone**. These servers are typically used to handle the bulk of the queries against the zone. Secondary servers will retrieve a copy of the zone from the primary server and will check for updates to the zone (once every 15 minutes, by default). If an update is detected, the secondary will request a copy of the changes and copy them down using a process known as a zone transfer. In a zone transfer, the server sending the zone transfer is known as the **master**, and the server receiving the transfer is known as the **slave**.

Next, ADI servers contain an ADI zone. ADI zones are special in that they do not have a zone file, per se. The resource records in the zone file in an ADI zone are converted into AD objects and copied into Active Directory. All domain controllers, therefore, have a complete copy of an ADI zone. You may then make these domain controllers DNS servers, and they will automatically replicate changes to the DNS zone. Each ADI DNS server (which must be a domain controller) will have a full writable copy of the zone, essentially making them all "primary" servers for the zone. You may still have secondary servers (which contain a secondary copy of the zone and are not required to be domain controllers) in an ADI zone, though they are usually not required. The secondary servers simply treat *one* of your ADI servers as the primary and perform zone transfers as if it were a standard primary server.

Finally, there is one type of server, briefly mentioned earlier, that does not contain a zone. This type of server is known as a **caching-only** server. While all servers (and clients) cache lookups, a caching-only server is used only for caching lookups. This is usually useful in situations where DNS traffic is clogging a WAN link. In this case, if you installed a secondary server in the location, you would still be generating excess traffic due to zone transfers. However, if you install a caching-only server, the server will simply cache lookups (which reduces traffic) and will not perform zone transfers, so no additional traffic is generated.

tip

The zone database files are stored with the file extension .dns in the %\system32\dns folder on the hard disk of a DNS server.

tip

Secondary zones are actually writable copies of the zone as well; however, by default, secondary zones are overwritten by the primary zone every 15 minutes, so changes made to a secondary zone are inconsequential.

caution

The terms "primary" and "secondary" servers have different connotations depending on the context the terms are used in. In DNS, the primary server is the server with the primary zone, and the secondary servers are servers with secondary zones. On a client PC, each PC has entries in its IP configuration for a primary name server and a secondary name server. In this case, the primary is the server that the client will contact first to resolve names (and usually contains a secondary copy of the zone); the secondary server is the server the client will use if its primary server is unavailable.

Table 3-2 Types of resource records

Type of resource record	Represented in a DNS database file as	Description
Start of Authority	(SOA)	Identifies the primary DNS server for the zone that has authority over the data in the domain; first recorded in the DNS database file and added by DNS automatically when a zone is created.
Name Server	(NS)	Identifies the additional name servers that have been assigned to the zones in the domain; added automatically by DNS when a zone is created.
Address (Host)	(A)	Lists the host's name-to-IP address mapping for a forward lookup zone.
Canonical Name (Alias)	(CNAME)	Used to assign more than one name to a single host.
Mail Exchanger	(MX)	Identifies which mail exchanger can be contacted for other specified domains.
Service Location (Service)	(SRV)	Identifies which servers are hosting a particular service.
Pointer	(PTR)	Points to another part of the domain namespace; lists the host's IP-to-name address mapping for a reverse lookup zone.

Figure 3-2 Resource records in a zone database file

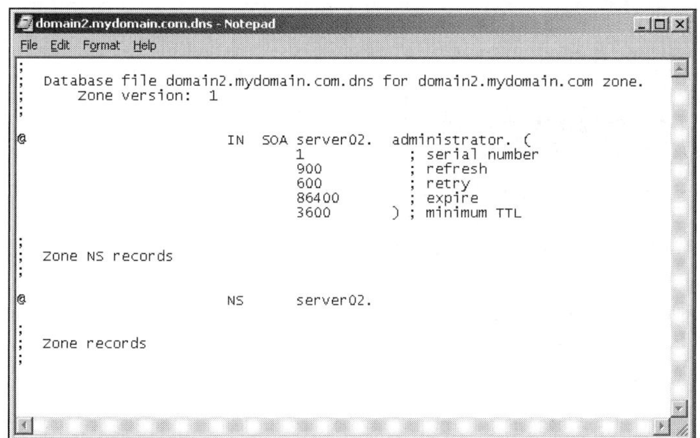

```
domain2.mydomain.com.dns - Notepad
File Edit Format Help
;
;  Database file domain2.mydomain.com.dns for domain2.mydomain.com zone.
;      Zone version:  1
;

@                     IN  SOA server02.  administrator. (
                              1            ; serial number
                              900          ; refresh
                              600          ; retry
                              86400        ; expire
                              3600       ) ; minimum TTL

;
;  Zone NS records
;

@                         NS      server02.

;
;  Zone records
;
```

Figure 3-3 Master name server concept

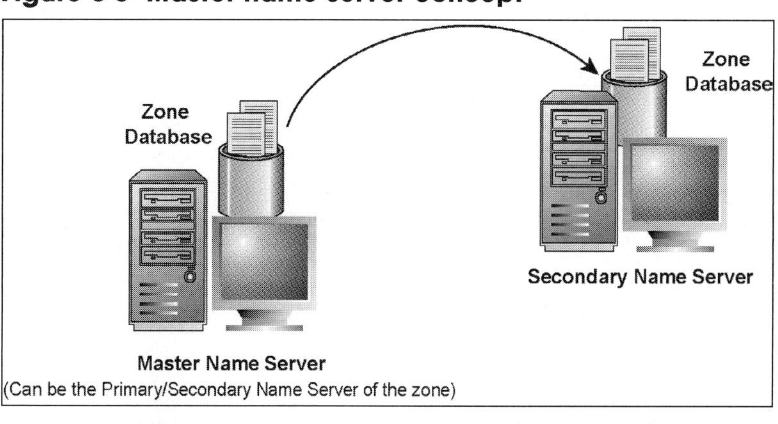

skill 3 Installing the DNS Service

exam objective

Install and configure DNS for Active Directory.

overview

To implement a DNS server on a computer running Windows 2000 Server, you need to install the Microsoft DNS Server service. DNS will perform automatic mappings between FQDNs and IP addresses, enabling users in your network to efficiently use the network resources. You can implement multiple DNS servers in your Windows 2000 network.

caution

Make sure that the TCP/IP protocol is configured with a static IP address and the address listed for the primary name server is the **same** as your static IP address.

how to

Install the DNS service on Server1.

1. Log on to the computer as an Administrator.
2. Insert the **Windows 2000 Server** CD into the CD-ROM drive.
3. Click Start, point to **Settings**, and then click the **Control Panel** command to open the **Control Panel** window.
4. Double-click the **Add/Remove Programs** icon to open the **Add/Remove Programs** window.
5. Click the **Add/Remove Windows Components** button to add DNS as a Windows component **(Figure 3-4)**. This displays the **Windows Components Wizard** window.
6. Select the **Networking Services** check box to add DNS as one of the services on the network **(Figure 3-5)**.
7. Click Details... to display the list of networking services that can be installed on the computer. The **Networking Services** window is displayed.
8. Select the **Domain Name System (DNS)** check box in the **Subcomponents of Networking Services** list to select DNS as the service to be installed **(Figure 3-6)**.
9. Click OK to close the Networking Services dialog box.
10. Click Next > in the **Windows Components Wizard** to install DNS. The wizard displays the files being configured to install the required components.
11. The last screen of the wizard informs you that the steps in the wizard have been completed successfully. To close the Windows Components Wizard, click Finish.
12. Click Close to close the **Add/Remove Programs** window.
13. Close the Control Panel window.

more

Once the DNS server service is installed on a Windows 2000 Server, the command for opening the DNS management console is added to the **Administrative Tools** menu. To open the DNS management console, click **Start**, point to **Programs**, point to **Administrative Tools**, and then click the **DNS** command. The DNS console tree displays the zones for the domain created automatically during DNS installation.

Figure 3-4 Accessing the Add/Remove Programs window

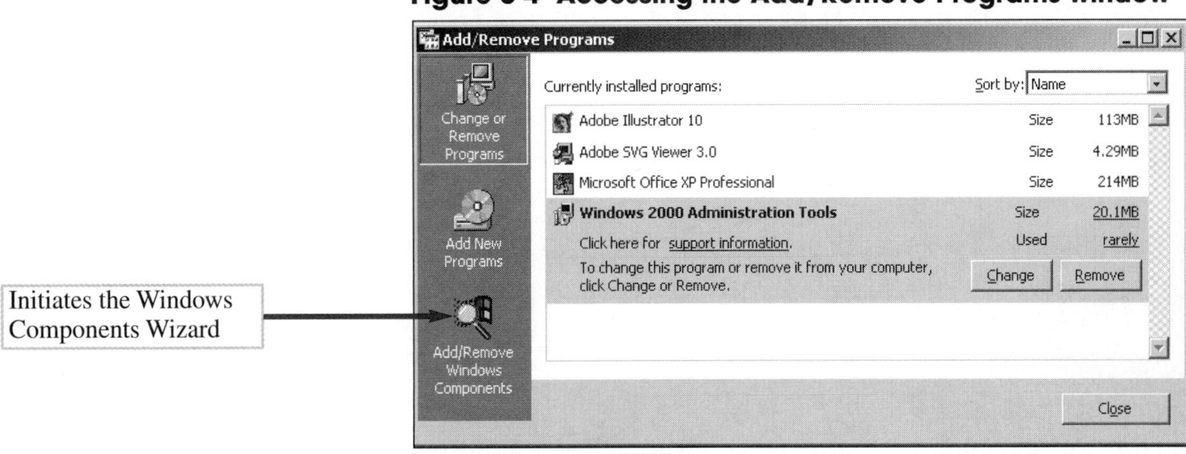

Figure 3-5 Adding or removing Windows 2000 components

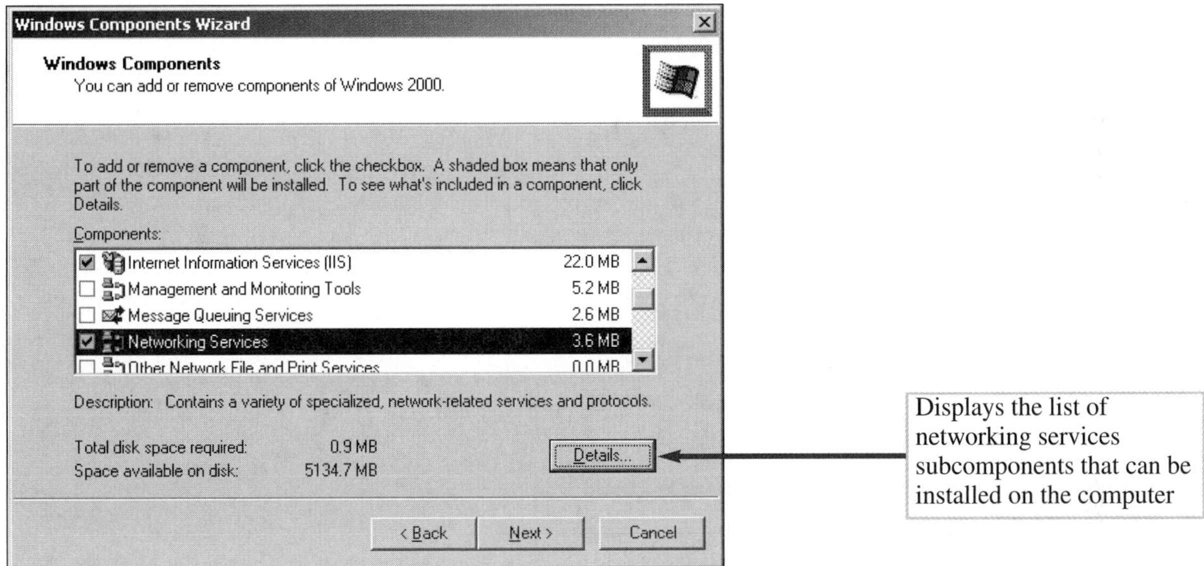

Figure 3-6 Adding or removing subcomponents of Networking Services

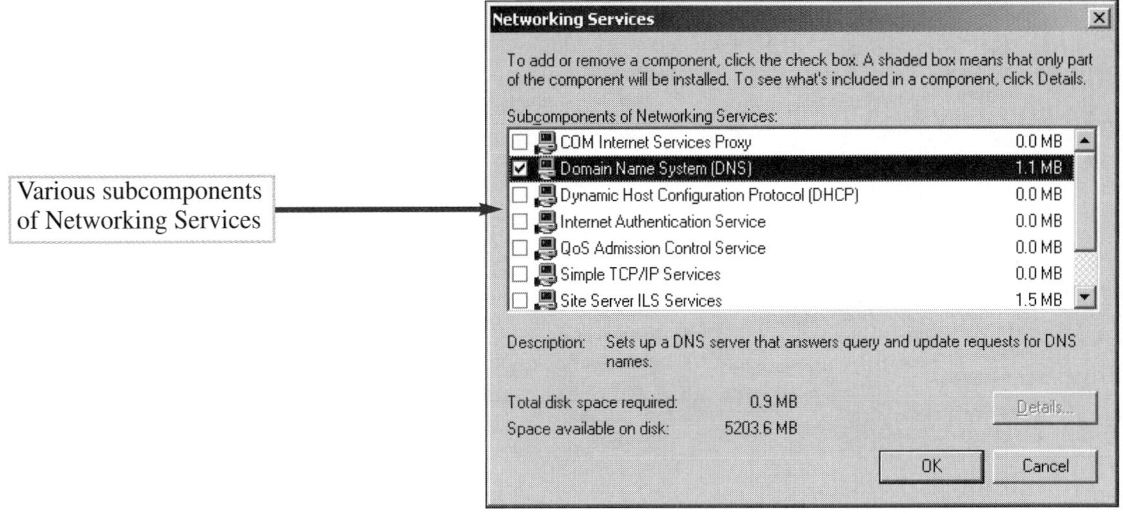

skill 4 Planning the Zones in DNS

exam objective

Basic knowledge

overview

Once DNS is installed, you need to configure it. To effectively implement DNS, you need to design a zone strategy. This strategy involves determining the number and types of zones you need and how you will divide the DNS namespace into one or more zones. **Figure 3-7** illustrates the strategy you should follow while planning zones in the DNS structure.

The steps to follow while planning the zones are described below.

1. Determine the types of zones on a network

The first step in planning the zones is to determine the type of zone that suits your requirements. You can create three types of zones in Windows 2000: **standard primary zones**, **standard secondary zones**, and **Active Directory-integrated zones**. **Table 3-3** describes the different types of zones used in DNS.

2. Determine the types of zone transfers

The next step in planning the zones on a DNS network is to select a zone transfer technique. Since the standard primary zone contains the latest resource records, any change in the standard primary zone should be reflected in all standard secondary zones. To reflect the changes, you need to synchronize the standard secondary zones with the primary zone. This process of synchronization is called a zone transfer. Windows 2000 supports two types of **zone transfers**. A brief description of these zone transfers is covered in **Table 3-4**.

The zone transfer process can occur in one of the following two ways:

- The primary server notifies the secondary servers about a change in the primary zone.
- The secondary server queries the primary server for changes when the refresh interval of the secondary server expires.

3. Set the number of zones on the network

After you select a zone transfer method, plan the number of zones the network will contain. The number of zones is not restricted to the number of DNS servers in a domain because one DNS server can manage many domains. For smaller organizations, a single zone is ideal. For larger organizations, the number of zones depends upon resource records and client requests. Consider a scenario where an organization, ABCD, Inc., has its headquarters in San Francisco and branch offices in Phoenix, New York, Atlanta, and Chicago. The network administrator has divided the network into one domain with these four subdomains: phoenix.abcd.com, newyork.abcd.com, atlanta.abcd.com, and chicago.abcd.com. This namespace could be contained in a single zone, as it is contiguous, but in this example, each server is receiving large quantities of queries. In order to reduce overhead, the namespace has been divided into four zones. Each branch has a DNS server and the DNS server's respective zones. **(Figure 3-8)**.

4. Determine the zone replication strategy

This strategy depends upon the size of the organization and the geographical location of the organization's DNS servers. Replicating zone data offers the following advantages:

- Distribution of the name resolution workload among multiple DNS servers.
- Fault tolerance for the zone data. If the primary server is unable to process queries, a copy of its replicated zones remains available.

tip

To choose the number of delegated zones, you should first identify how the traffic is distributed in your network. Use the System Monitor and Network Monitor to analyze traffic patterns, especially on a low-speed network.

Table 3-3 Types of zones used in DNS

Type of zone	Description
Standard primary zone	When a DNS server is the primary server for a zone, the zone type is configured as standard primary. All updates are made on the primary zone, which stores the master copy of the zone in the form of a text file. The primary server either answers all client queries or delegates them to other servers.
Standard secondary zone	When a DNS server is the secondary server for a zone, the zone type is standard secondary. The changes in the standard primary zone are replicated through a one-way zone transfer on the secondary zone. In other words, a standard secondary zone is a copy of an existing standard primary zone.
Active Directory-integrated zone	When the zone data is stored and replicated as a part of the Active Directory database, the zone type is Active Directory-integrated. The zone can be specified as an Active Directory-integrated zone only if it is configured on a domain controller.

Table 3-4 Types of zone transfers

Type of zone transfer	Description
Full zone transfer (AXFR)	The entire DNS server database is copied from the primary to the secondary DNS server to update the zone data. This is used for older DNS servers that do not support IXFR (such as NT 4). If the DNS server does not have a history of the zone changes, it uses the AXFR method for zone transfer.
Incremental zone transfer (IXFR)	Only the intermediate changes in the DNS database are replicated to the secondary DNS servers. The IXFR method is much less bandwidth intensive for large zones.

Figure 3-7 Strategy for planning the zones

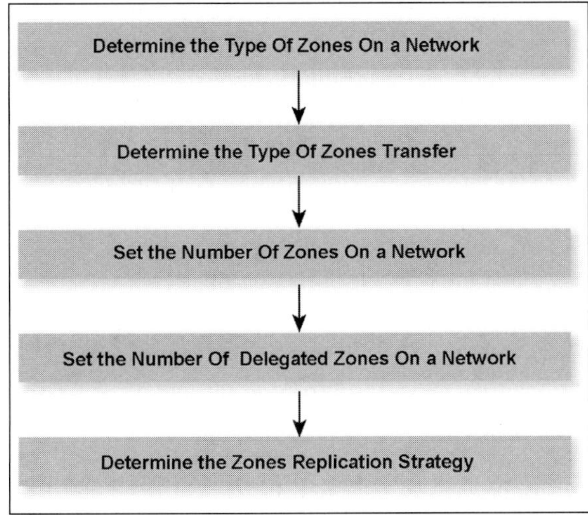

Figure 3-8 Number of zones in a network

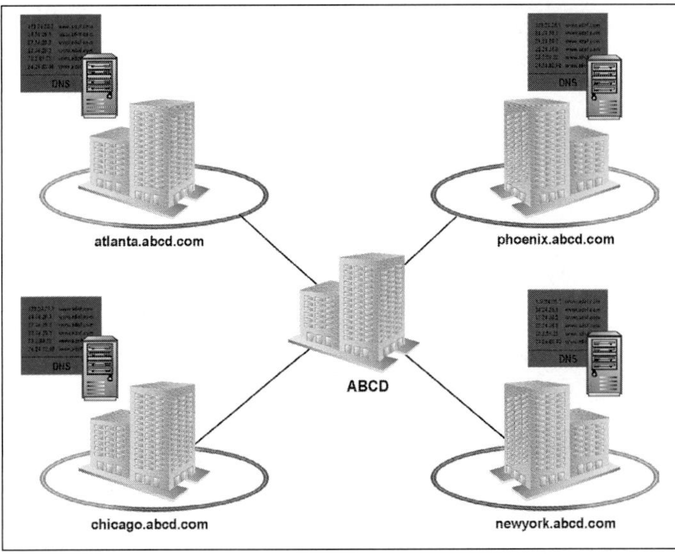

skill 4 Planning the Zones in DNS (cont'd)

exam objective

Basic knowledge

more

It is preferable to use Active Directory-integrated zones for internal DNS zones in most cases. The features of Active Directory-integrated zones are described below.

- **Multimaster update model and enhanced security features:** In this model, any ADI DNS server can be designated as a primary source of data for the zone. The Active Directory database stores the master copy of the zone information. Since this database is fully replicated to all domain controllers on the network, all ADI DNS servers have a copy of the data and are capable of updating the zone data. An extra security feature of Active Directory-integrated zones is that you can use Access Control List (ACL) to restrict access to specific zones or resource records in the zone.
- **Automatic replication and synchronization of zones based on changes in the Active Directory domain:** Each time a zone is modified, the zone is replicated to other domain controllers automatically. If a DNS server is down, any domain controller with DNS can perform updates and process the client requests
- **Simplification of DNS and Active Directory maintenance:** In Active Directory-integrated zones, Active Directory and DNS data are replicated together based on Active Directory replication schedules. This reduces a lot of additional effort that you might have to put in while managing standard zones, where zone data is independent of Active Directory data and needs to be replicated separately.
- **More efficient and secure Active Directory replication:** Processing of Active Directory replication is based only on updates; hence only relevant changes are circulated. In addition, all Active Directory replication is encrypted, and replication between sites is automatically compressed. This results in improved replication efficiency and security.

Figure 3-9 Zone delegation

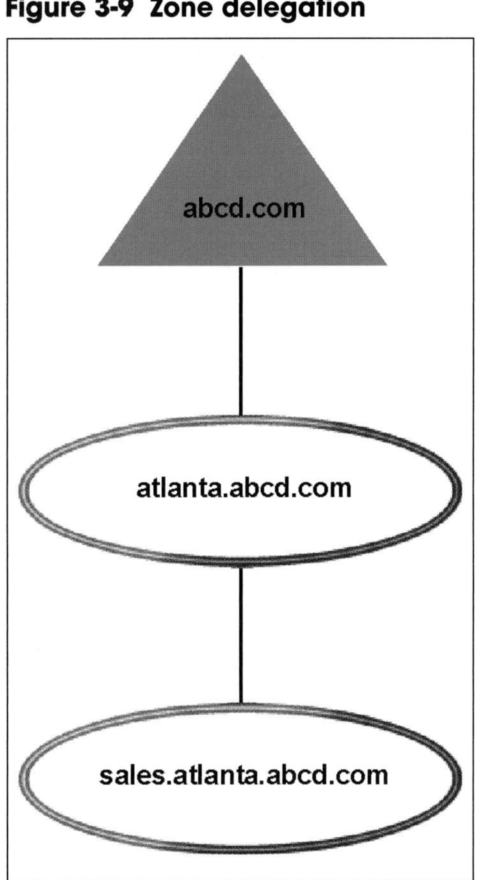

skill 5 Creating Lookup Zones

exam objective

Integrate Active Directory DNS zones with existing DNS infrastructure.

overview

Zones are the organizational units of the DNS namespace representation. You can use zones to store records of network resources logically within the namespace. You can search for these network resources by creating lookup zones. The two types of zones that can be created in DNS are **forward lookup zones** and **reverse lookup zones**. When the DNS server receives a query, the DNS server uses either of the two lookup zones to resolve the query.

Forward lookup zones help to resolve forward lookup queries. In this process, a client requests resolution of a query by proceeding from the highest- to the lowest-level domains. The name server attempts to resolve the name to an IP address. If the name server succeeds, it responds to the client computer by sending the IP address. However, if the name server is unable to resolve the query, it forwards the query to other name servers in the hierarchy. This process continues until the name server finds the server that is authoritative for the domain you are seeking. The authoritative server responds to the query and returns the IP address to the local name server.

how to

Create a forward lookup zone on an additional server named Server1.

1. Log on to Server1 as the Administrator.
2. Click Start, point to **Programs**, point to **Administrative Tools**, and then click the **DNS** command. This will display the **DNS** console.
3. Right-click the Forward Lookup Zone folder and then click the **New Zone** command on the shortcut menu. The New Zone Wizard initiates to guide you through the steps of creating a forward lookup zone.
4. The first screen of the wizard defines a zone and identifies the purpose of the wizard, as shown in **Figure 3-10**. Click Next > to proceed to the next screen.
5. The next screen displays the three types of zones that can be created. The **Standard primary** option button is selected by default **(Figure 3-11)**. Click Next > to proceed to the next screen where you will specify the details for the standard primary zone.
6. Type **domain1.mydomain.com** in the **Name** text box to specify the name of the standard primary zone and click Next >.
7. The **Create a new file with this file name** option button is selected by default and the text box displays the name of the zone file that will be used to store zone-related information as **domain1.mydomain.com.dns**. Click Next > to view the summary screen of the New Zone Wizard.
8. The summary screen displays the details of the new zone **(Figure 3-12)** Click Finish to complete the procedure for creating the forward lookup zone.
9. The details pane of the DNS console displays the new forward lookup zone **(Figure 3-13)**.
10. Right-click on the name of your server at the top of the left pane and select properties. The **Properties** dialog box will appear.
11. Click on the **Forwarders** tab.
12. On the **Forwarders** tab, select the check box to enable forwarders.
13. Type in the IP address of the server that is hosting the mydomain.com zone, click the **Add** button, and click **OK**. This configures your server to use the mydomain.com server to resolve addresses that are not in the server's zone files.

Repeat these steps on Server2 for the domain2.mydomain.com domain.

tip

You can also copy an existing zone file from another computer. To use an existing zone file, you must stop the DNS service, copy the file to the **%SystemRoot%-\system32\dns** folder on the destination server, and then restart the service.

Figure 3-10 Welcome screen of the New Zone Wizard

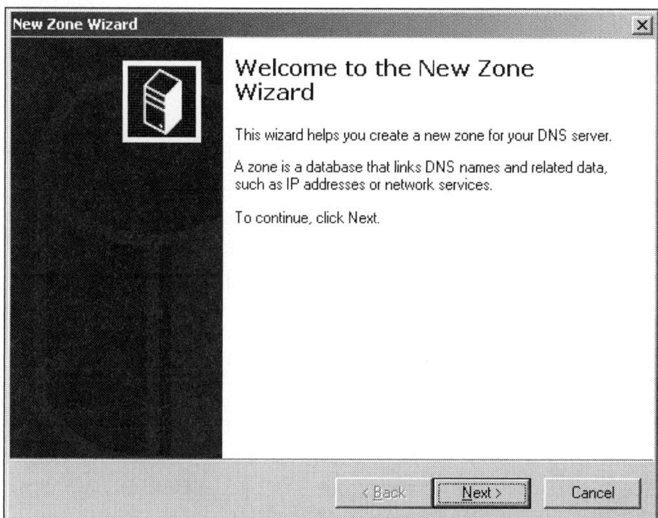

Figure 3-11 Selecting the type of zone to be created

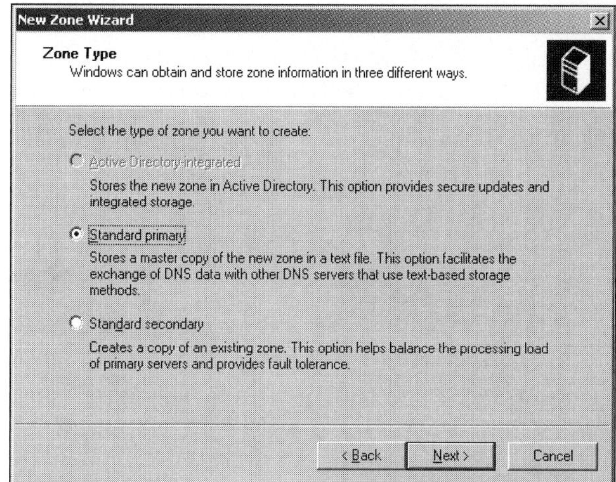

Figure 3-12 Settings of the new forward lookup zone

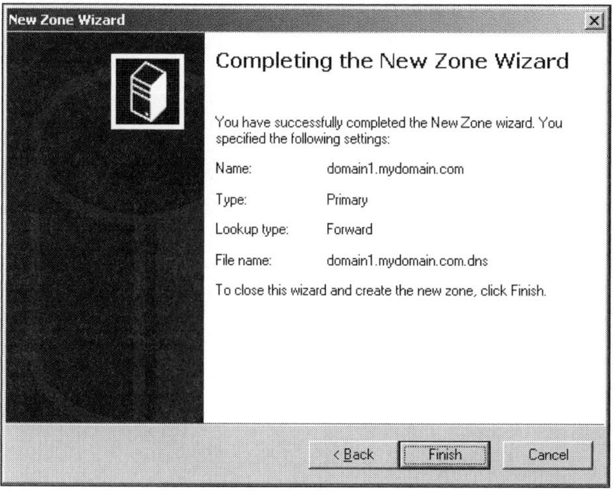

Figure 3-13 The new forward lookup zone in the DNS console

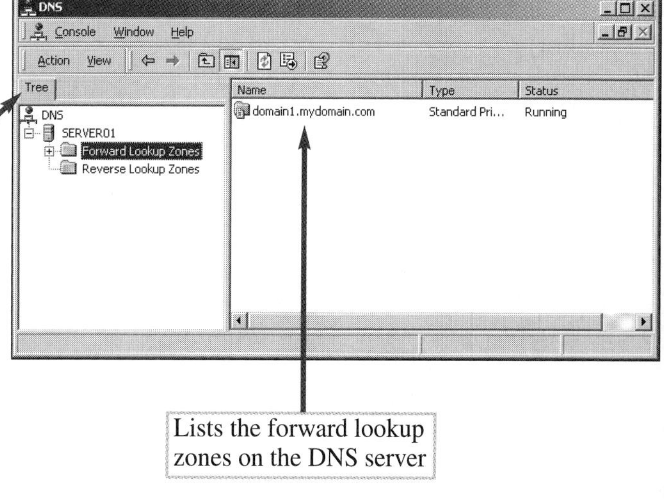

skill 5 Creating Lookup Zones (cont'd)

exam objective

Integrate Active Directory DNS zones with existing DNS infrastructure.

more

Reverse lookup zones are used to address reverse lookup queries. They provide the DNS name for the IP address sent by the client. Since the DNS database is indexed by name and not by IP address, the way reverse lookup queries are performed is different from the way forward lookup queries function. To ease the problem of resolving IP addresses to names, a special domain called **in-addr.arpa** was created for DNS. This domain also follows a hierarchical naming scheme, but is based on IP addresses instead of names.

The subdomains of the in-addr.arpa domain are named after the numerals specified in an IP address. The main difference between the in-addr.arpa domain and other domains in DNS is that the order of octets in the IP address of the in-addr.arpa domain is reversed. For example, a network ID 135.45.1 on a network would be saved as 1.45.135.in-addr.arpa in the in-addr.arpa domain **(Figure 3-14)**. The reversal occurs because IP addresses become more specific from left to right, while domain names get more specific from right to left.

The process of creating a reverse lookup zone is similar to the one for creating a forward lookup zone. You need to right-click the **Reverse Lookup Zones** folder in the DNS console tree and then click the **New Zone** command to initiate the New Zone Wizard.

Reverse lookup zones are required to run troubleshooting tools such as **NSLookup**. NSLookup is a command-line utility that can be used to test the DNS domain namespace. NSLookup is installed with TCP/IP. In addition, you use reverse lookup zones to resolve the names of clients accessing your resources. For instance, when viewing web statistics, the statistics application typically performs a reverse lookup to give you the domains of the clients that accessed the server.

Figure 3-14 Specifying the network ID of the reverse lookup zone

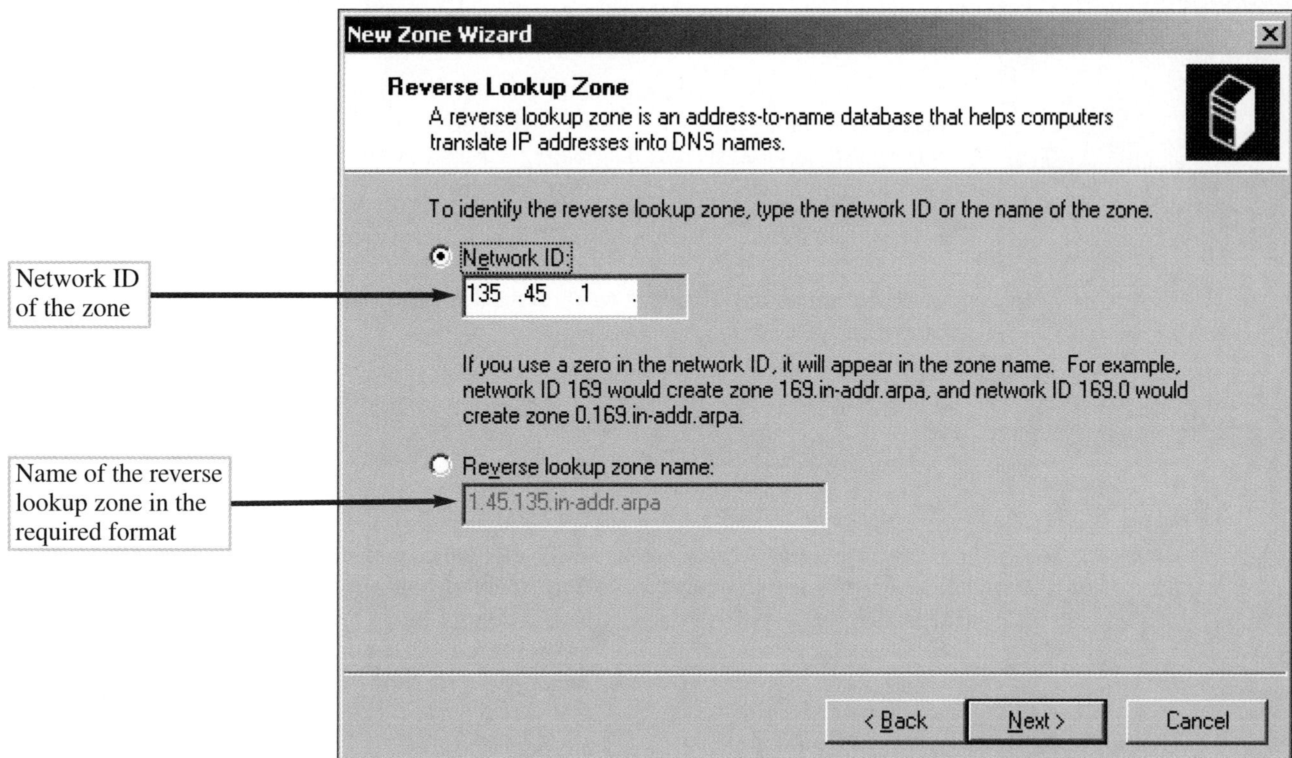

skill 6 Delegating Zones

exam objective

Create and configure DNS records.

overview

You can add more domains, in the form of subdomains, within an existing domain. When you do this, the subdomains can remain a part of the same zone and can be managed as a part of the original zone records. Alternatively, the subdomains can be delegated to other zones created to support the subdomains.

Delegation is the process of assigning responsibility of a section of the DNS namespace to a separate zone. In an expanding network, you can delegate zones to ensure proper management of DNS services such as distributing the load of one large DNS database to multiple servers to improve DNS name resolution performance.

You can create a **zone delegation** using the New Delegation Wizard in the DNS console. To do this, first identify the domain that you want to delegate. Then, create an NS (name server) resource record for the server that will host the delegated zone. Finally, add the name server to create a zone delegation.

caution

While creating a zone delegation, ensure that the host record for the server that will host the delegated zone exists in the DNS table.

how to

Create a zone delegation for our two new subdomains, domain1 and domain2, on Server A.

1. Log on as Administrator to the server hosting the mydomain.com domain.
2. In the DNS console tree, right-click **mydomain.com**, the domain for which you want to create a zone delegation, in the details pane, and then click the **New Delegation** command on the shortcut menu. The **New Delegation Wizard** opens.
3. Click [Next >] to proceed to the next screen.
4. To specify a name for the delegated zone, type **domain1** in the **Delegated domain** text box on the **Delegated Domain Name** page. The **Fully qualified domain** name text box is filled automatically **(Figure 3-15)**.
5. Click [Next >] to open the **Name Servers** screen.
6. Click [Add] on the **Name Servers** screen to specify the name server that will host the delegated zone. The **New Resource Record** dialog box appears **(Figure 3-16)**.
7. Enter the IP address and name (Server1.domain1.mydomain.com) for Server1.
8. Click [OK] to close the **New Resource Record** dialog box.
9. The **Name Servers** screen of the wizard displays the name of the server that will host the delegated zone **(Figure 3-17)**.
10. Click [Next >] to display the summary screen that lists the details of the new zone delegation.
11. Click [Finish] to complete the procedure for creating a zone delegation. You have now delegated the DNS management of the domain domain1.mydomain.com to Server1.

Repeat these steps for domain2.mydomain.com.

more

The DNS console of Windows 2000 provides you with options to create different types of resource records. You can add a resource record for a zone by right-clicking the zone to which you want to add the record and selecting the type of record you want to add. You can also view the resource records for a zone in the details pane by clicking the zone in the DNS console tree.

Figure 3-15 Specifying the delegated domain

New Delegation Wizard
Delegated Domain Name
Specify the name of the domain you want to create.
Authority for the domain you create will be delegated to a different zone.
Delegated domain:
domain1
Fully qualified domain name:
domain1.mydomain.com
< Back
Next >
Cancel
Displays the FQDN as soon as you specify the name of the delegated domain

Figure 3-16 Specifying the Name Server

New Resource Record
Name Server (NS)
Server name:
Server01.domain1.mydomain.com
Browse...
Resolve
IP address:
Add
192.168.1.1
Remove
Up
Down
OK
Cancel
Used to specify the IP address of the computer that will become an authoritative name server for this zone
Used to query and resolve the FQDN of the server specified in the Server name text box

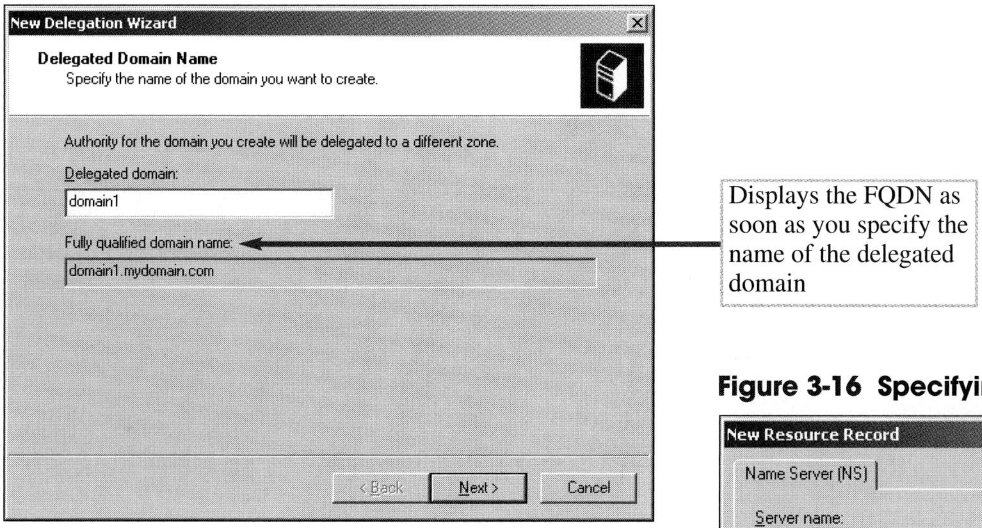

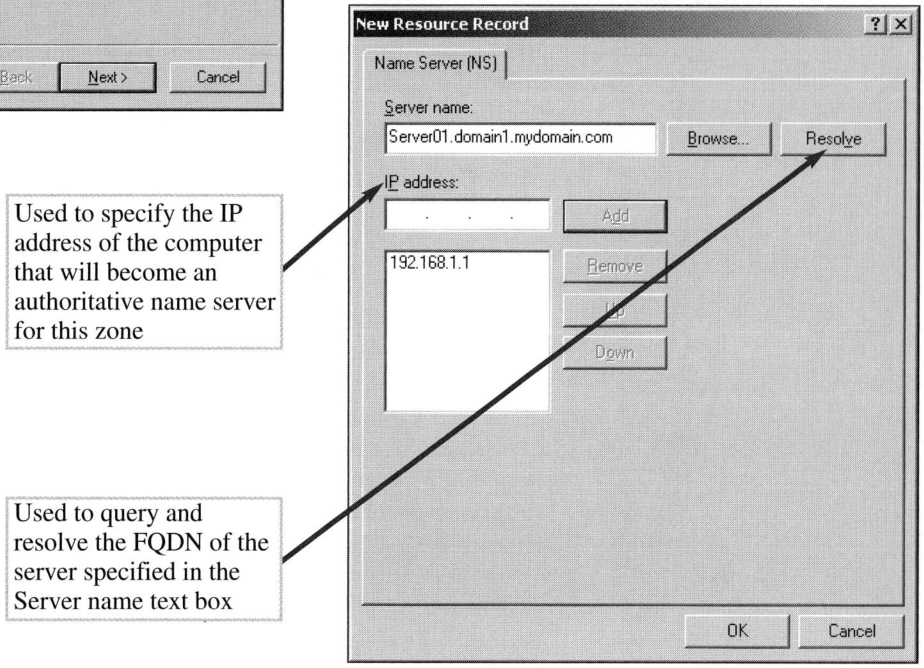

Figure 3-17 Specifying the Name Server to host the delegated zone

New Delegation Wizard
Name Servers
You can select one or more name servers to host the delegated zone.
Specify the names and IP addresses of any DNS servers you want to have host the delegated zone.
Server Name
IP Address
Server01.domain1.mydomain.com.
[192.168.1.1]
Add...
Edit...
Remove
< Back
Next >
Cancel
Displays the list of servers that would host the delegated zone
Add servers to this list
Modify the properties of a listed server
Remove servers from this list

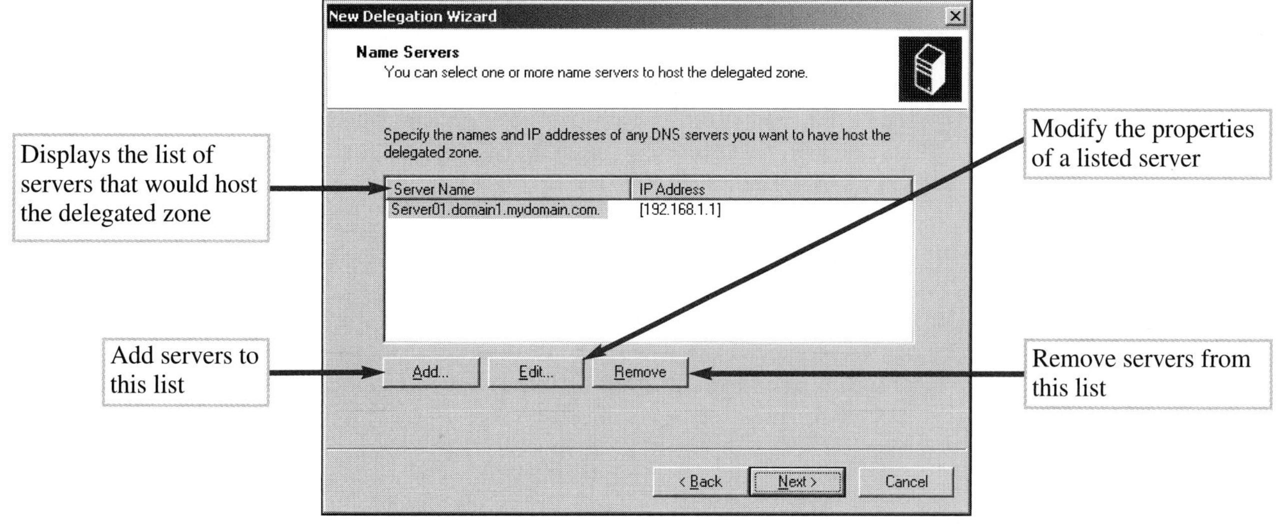

skill 7 Configuring Dynamic DNS

exam objective

Install and configure DNS for Active Directory. Configure zones for dynamic updates and security-enhanced dynamic updates.

overview

In DNS, any change in the domain needs to be updated manually in the zone database file on the primary name server. **Dynamic Domain Name System (DDNS)** is the dynamic update capability included in Windows 2000 DNS. Using DDNS, clients and/or **Dynamic Host Configuration Protocol (DHCP)** servers on a network may automatically update the zone file. In order for DDNS to function, the DNS server must support DDNS (Windows 2000 DNS and BIND 8.1.1 both support DDNS), and either the clients or the DHCP servers must support DDNS (only Windows 2000 clients and DHCP servers support DDNS).

You can also set aging and scavenging features for zones. Aging and scavenging features remove old and unused resource records so that they don't accumulate and later cause problems for the DNS zone. This is not an issue with a manually configured DNS zone but when using DDNS, it is possible for a PC to register a record and then be permanently removed from the domain. If scavenging is not enabled, records created in this type of scenario will remain on the DNS server indefinitely.

tip

While BIND 8.1.1 technically supports DDNS, there are some bugs in the implementation of this version of BIND. For this reason, version 8.2.2 or higher is suggested.

how to

Configure a zone for DDNS and set its aging and scavenging features. Also, set the properties for the SOA resource records of the zone.

1. Log on to Server1 as Administrator.
2. In the DNS console tree, double-click the Forward Lookup Zones folder to view the list of forward lookup zones in the details pane.
3. Right-click the zone **domain1.mydomain.com** in the details pane and then click the **Properties** command on the shortcut menu. The **Properties** dialog box for the forward lookup zone is displayed.
4. Select **Yes** in the **Allow dynamic updates** list box, as shown in **Figure 3-18**. Another option, **Only Secure Updates**, appears only if the zone type is Active Directory-integrated. This option allows only dynamic updates that use secure DNS for the zone. Secure updates specify that only the users, groups, or computers that have the right to write to the record (typically, only the PC that initially registered the record) have the permission to update the record.
5. Click [Aging...]. The **Zone Aging/Scavenging Properties** dialog box is displayed. This dialog box is used to specify aging and scavenging properties for the resource records of the zone.
6. Select the **Scavenge stale resource records** check box and type **15** in the **Refresh interval** text box to specify the refresh interval as 15 days, as shown in **Figure 3-19**. The refresh interval specifies the period of time in which the server will accept a refresh (an update to the timestamp) or an update (an update to the actual record data and the timestamp). The record will not be scavenged until both the no-refresh and refresh intervals expire, in this case, 22 days from now. Click [OK] to close this dialog.
7. Click [Yes] in the **DNS** message box to apply the settings to the standard primary zone.
8. Click the **Start of Authority (SOA)** tab in the **Properties** dialog box to specify the options for the SOA resource records for the zone.
9. To specify one hour as the refresh interval, type **1** in the **Refresh interval** text box and select **hours** in the corresponding list box.

tip

The SOA resource record is always the first resource record for any zone. It indicates the primary DNS server for the zone.

Figure 3-18 Configuring a zone for DDNS

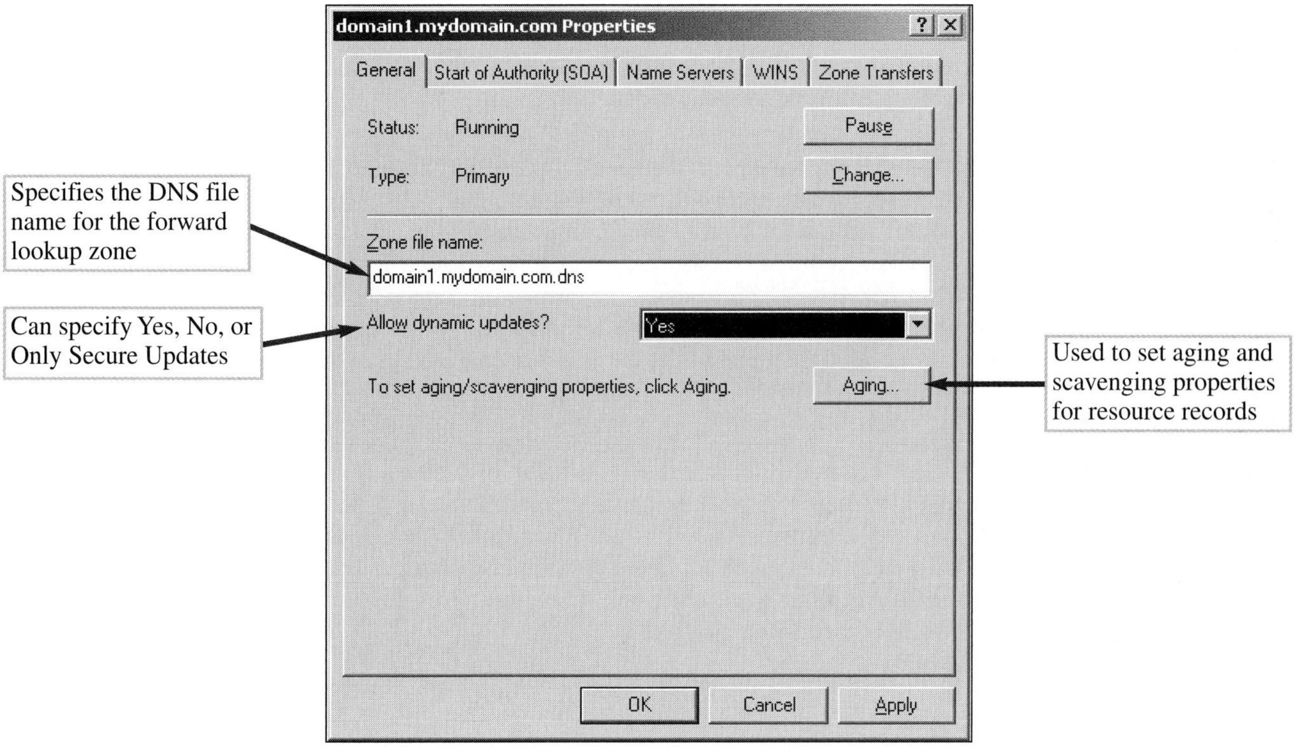

domain1.mydomain.com Properties

General | Start of Authority (SOA) | Name Servers | WINS | Zone Transfers

Status: Running — Pause

Type: Primary — Change...

Zone file name: domain1.mydomain.com.dns

Allow dynamic updates? Yes

To set aging/scavenging properties, click Aging. — Aging...

OK | Cancel | Apply

Specifies the DNS file name for the forward lookup zone

Can specify Yes, No, or Only Secure Updates

Used to set aging and scavenging properties for resource records

Figure 3-19 Setting aging/scavenging properties for a zone

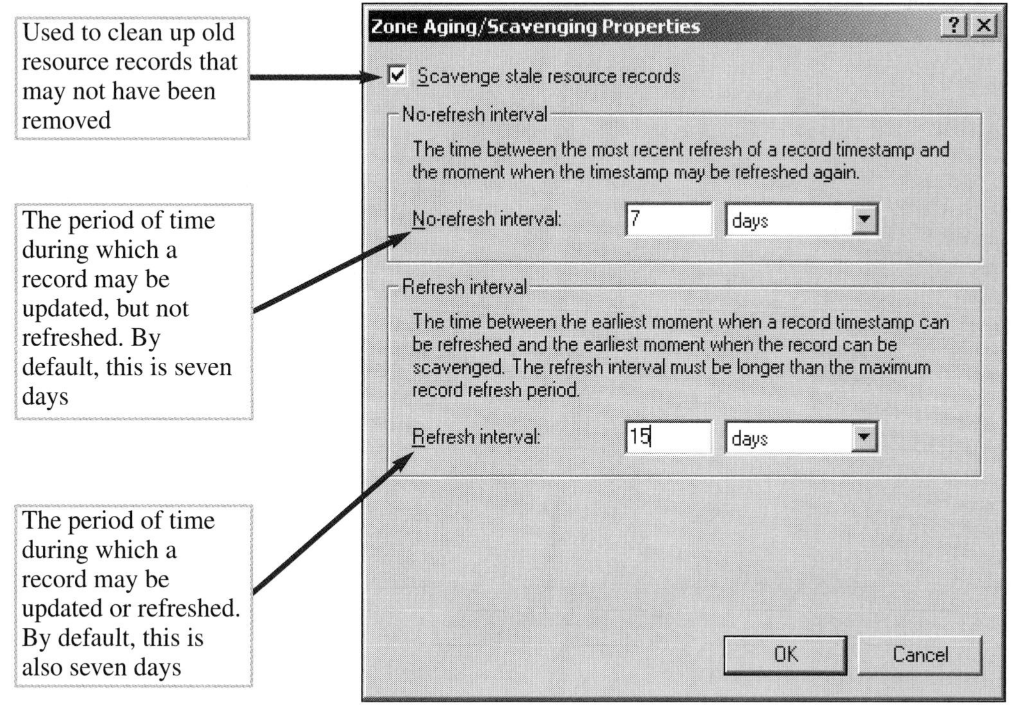

skill 7 Configuring Dynamic DNS (cont'd)

exam objective

Install and configure DNS for Active Directory. Configure zones for dynamic updates and security-enhanced dynamic updates.

how to

10. To specify ten days as the Time-To-Live (TTL) interval, type **10** in the first section of the **TTL for this record** text box **(Figure 3-20)**. This interval indicates how long the DNS servers are allowed to cache information about this record after the information is returned from DNS. The default TTL value is one hour.

11. Click OK to close the **Properties** dialog box for the forward lookup zone. You have configured DDNS for this zone, set its aging and scavenging features, and specified the properties of the SOA resource records of the zone.

more

In a DNS-based network supporting Active Directory, it is preferred that you use Active Directory-integrated zones. You can change the standard primary zones to Active Directory-integrated. To do so, click Change... in the **Properties** dialog box for the zone. This displays the **Change Zone Type** dialog box, where you select the **Active Directory-integrated** option button **(Figure 3-21)**.

You can set aging and scavenging features for all Active Directory-integrated zones by right-clicking the DNS server, and then clicking the **Set Aging/Scavenging for all zones** command on the shortcut menu. However, for standard primary zones, you need to manually configure each zone by selecting the zone and setting its properties.

Figure 3-20 Setting SOA properties for a zone

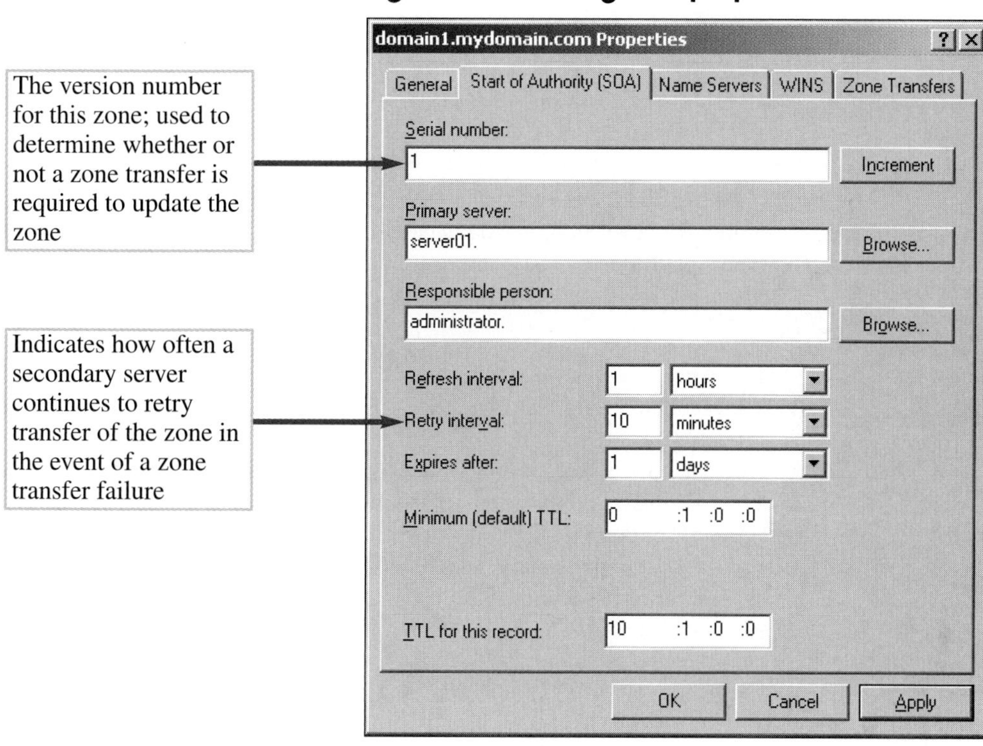

Figure 3-21 Changing the zone type

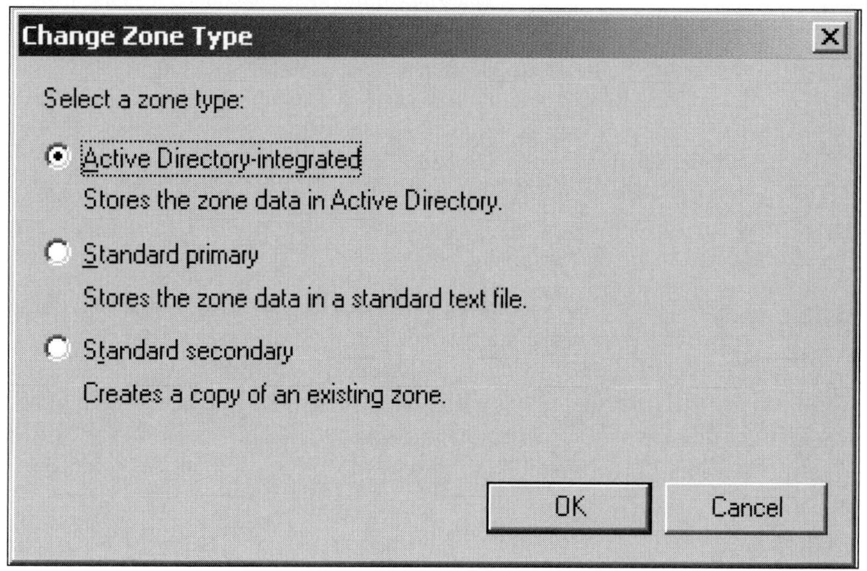

skill 8 Implementing Zone Replication and Zone Transfer in Servers

exam objective

Manage, monitor, and troubleshoot DNS.

overview

Zone replication is the process of replicating zone data to a secondary zone, and the process is commonly known as a zone transfer. Zone transfers are important in order to ensure that the latest changes to the database are reflected correctly on the secondary DNS servers. The two possible methods of performing a zone transfer are listed below and summarized in **Table 3-5**:

Standard zone replication is simply the act of copying the entire text-based DNS database (in AXFR) or changes to the database (IXFR) to all secondary servers. This process is known as a zone transfer. Standard zone transfers are performed in plain text (unencrypted), are typically uncompressed, and are typically performed at static intervals (once every15 minutes by default). Standard replication is used in standard primary/secondary DNS architectures, as well as between Active Directory-integrated DNS servers and secondary servers for the ADI zone. With a standard primary zone, if the server hosting the primary zone is unavailable, new name registrations and updates to existing records will fail, as only the primary server can modify the database.

Active Directory zone replication technique is used for ADI zones. With an ADI zone, each domain controller may act as a primary DNS server. The records in the primary zone files are stored in Active Directory as AD objects, and zones are replicated following Active Directory's multi-master update model. All the domain controllers in the network are positioned as peers in the multi-master update model. Therefore, even if one DNS server is down, name registration is not obstructed because manual and dynamic updates are allowed on each DNS server.

tip

Active Directory-integrated zones do not require the process of zone transfer to enable zone replication because zones are replicated automatically along with Active Directory replication. The only case in which zone transfers are used in an ADI zone is when a server is configured to hold a secondary copy of the ADI zone.

You can enable zone replication by using the process of zone transfers. You can specify servers to participate in the zone transfer process in the DNS console. A zone transfer is required when the:

- Refresh interval for the zone expires, and the secondary server's serial number in its copy of the SOA, is not equal to the serial number in the primary server's copy of the SOA. This event indicates a change to the database has occurred and needs to be replicated.
- Secondary server is notified of zone changes by its master server.
- DNS server service is started on a secondary server for the zone.
- DNS console is used on a secondary server for the zone to manually initiate a transfer from its master server.

In Windows 2000 Server, when a new DNS server is added and configured as a secondary server in the network, it always performs a full zone transfer (AXFR) to obtain and replicate a complete copy of the zone. Subsequently, DNS service supports incremental zone transfer (IXFR) that requires less traffic on the network and enables faster zone transfers. However, it is still possible for a secondary server that supports IXFR to use AXFR on occasion. An example of this would be when the secondary server notices a database error.

Table 3-5 Methods of performing zone transfers

Type of zone transfer	Description
Standard zone replication	◆ Copies the entire text-based DNS database or changes to it to all secondary servers ◆ Performed in plain (unencrypted) text ◆ Performed at regular intervals ◆ Used in standard primary/secondary DNS architectures and between Active Directory-integrated DNS and servers and secondary servers for the ADI zone
Active Directory zone replication	◆ Used for ADI zones ◆ Records in the primary zone files are stored as AD objects ◆ Zones are replicated following following Active Directory's multi-master update model ◆ Name registration is not compromised by the failure of one DNS server

skill 8 Implementing Zone Replication and Zone Transfer in Servers *(cont'd)*

exam objective

Manage, monitor, and troubleshoot DNS.

how to

Specify the servers to take part in zone replication.

1. Display the **Properties** dialog box for the forward lookup zone **mydomain.com**.
2. Click the **Name Servers** tab.
3. Click [Add] to add name servers to the list. The **New Resource Record** dialog box is displayed.
4. Type in the name and IP addresses for Server1 and Server2 and click **Add**.
5. Click [OK] to close the **New Resource Record** dialog box and return to the **Name Servers** tab. The **Name Servers** tab displays the new server added to the Name Servers list **(Figure 3-22)**.
6. Click the **Zone Transfers** tab to specify the zone transfer properties.
7. Click the **Only to servers listed on the Name Servers tab** option button to specify that the zone transfer should occur only for the servers listed on the **Name Servers** tab **(Figure 3-23)**.
8. Click [OK] to complete the procedure and close the **Properties** dialog box.

caution

In our DNS configuration, no secondary copies of any zones exist, so this exercise just shows you how to specify which servers should be allowed to request a zone transfer (although, in this case, no transfer will occur). By default, any server that requests a zone transfer from the primary will receive the zone transfer, making this step an optional one used to increase the security of the DNS infrastructure.

more

DNS notification is a feature of the DNS service. It uses a notify-pull mechanism for notifying a selected set of secondary servers for a zone whenever the zone is updated. After the notification reaches the notified servers, they can start the zone transfer process and pull changes from the notifying server to update the zone.

DNS notification is not required for Active Directory-integrated zones since DNS data gets refreshed automatically when Active Directory replicates.

To enable DNS notification, open the **Zone Transfers** tab of the **Properties** dialog box for a zone and click [Notify...]. You can then set the options for informing the secondary servers of a zone change so that these servers can start the zone transfer process. In the **Notify** dialog box, select the **Automatically notify** check box, and then select the **Servers listed on the Name Servers tab** option button to specify that only the servers listed on the **Name Servers** tab should be notified **(Figure 3-24)**.

Figure 3-22 The list of name servers to participate in zone transfer

Figure 3-23 Specifying servers for zone transfer

Figure 3-24 Enabling DNS notification

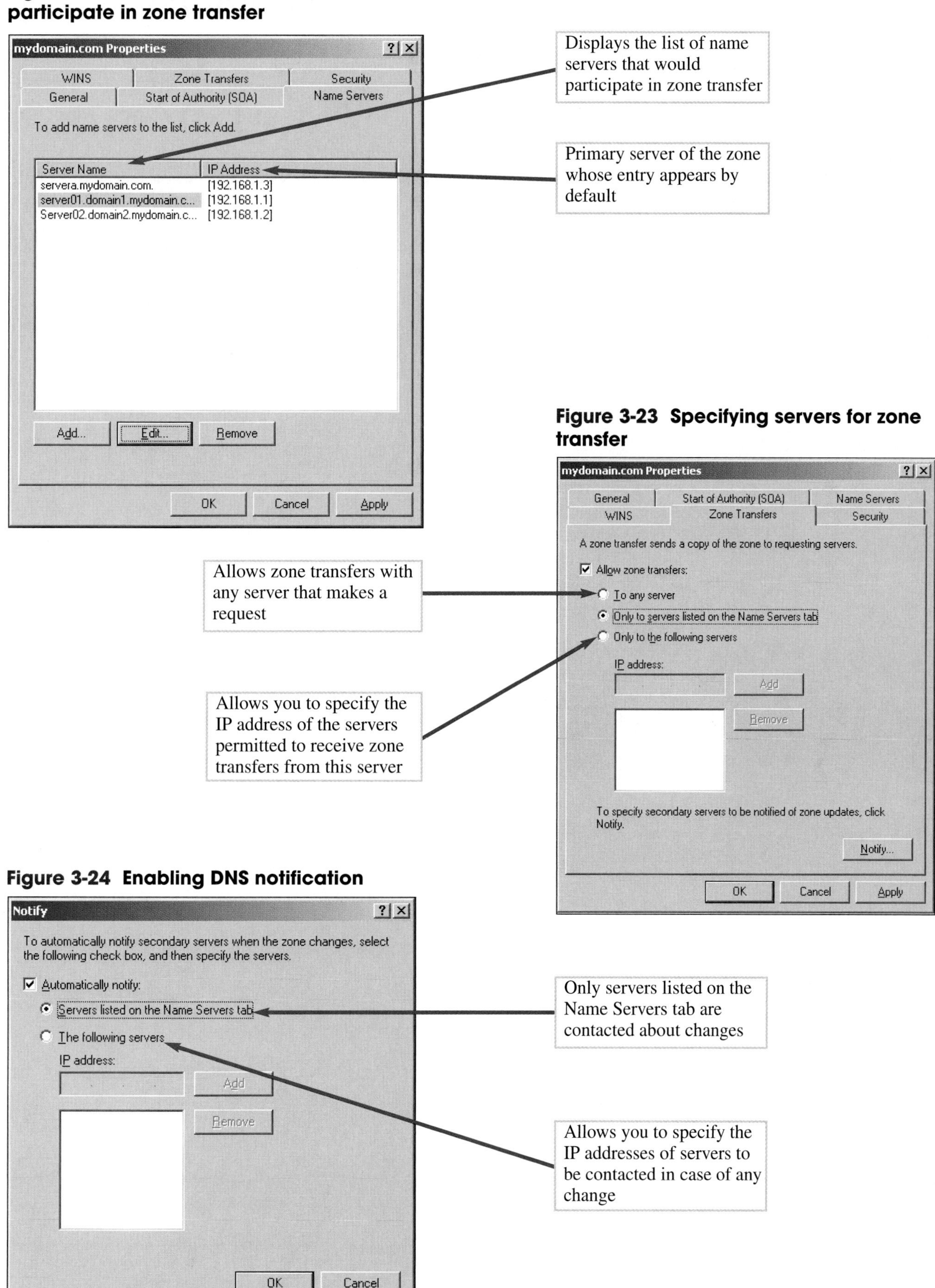

skill 9 Setting Debugging Options for DNS Servers

exam objective

Manage, monitor, and troubleshoot DNS.

overview

Windows 2000 Server provides two ways to monitor DNS servers. First, a default log of DNS server event messages is stored in the **DNS server log.** The DNS server log contains basic events logged by the DNS server service, including the status of the starting and stopping of the DNS server. You can view the DNS server log using Event Viewer. You can also use Event Viewer to view and monitor client-related DNS events **(Figure 3-25)**.

Second, you can set debug options in the DNS console to create a temporary trace log as a text-based file of DNS server activity. This file, known as **DNS.LOG**, is created and stored in the **%systemroot%\System32\Dns** folder. All debug options are disabled by default. You can selectively enable these options so that the DNS server service performs additional trace-level logging of selected types of events or messages for the purpose of general troubleshooting. **Table 3-6** describes the debug logging options that you can employ for the DNS server.

caution

Debug logs consume a lot of disk space and some processor and memory resources, and should be used only temporarily when detailed information about server performance is required.

how to

Set debug options for the DNS Server.

1. In the DNS console tree, right-click Server1, and then click the **Properties** command on the shortcut menu. The **Properties** dialog box for the domain opens.
2. Click the **Logging** tab.
3. Select the **Query** check box to log the queries received by the DNS server service from the clients.
4. Select the **Receive** check box to log the number of DNS query messages received by the DNS server service **(Figure 3-26)**.
5. Click OK to close the **Properties** dialog box. You can now view the log file **DNS.LOG** to view the queries that will be logged after you have set the debug options.

Figure 3-25 DNS Server log in Event Viewer

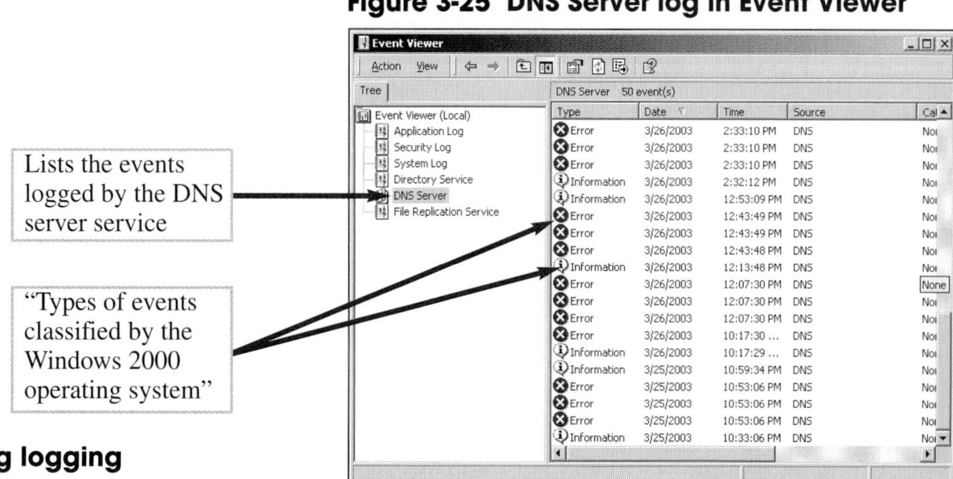
Lists the events logged by the DNS server service
"Types of events classified by the Windows 2000 operating system"

Figure 3-26 Setting debug logging options for the DNS Server

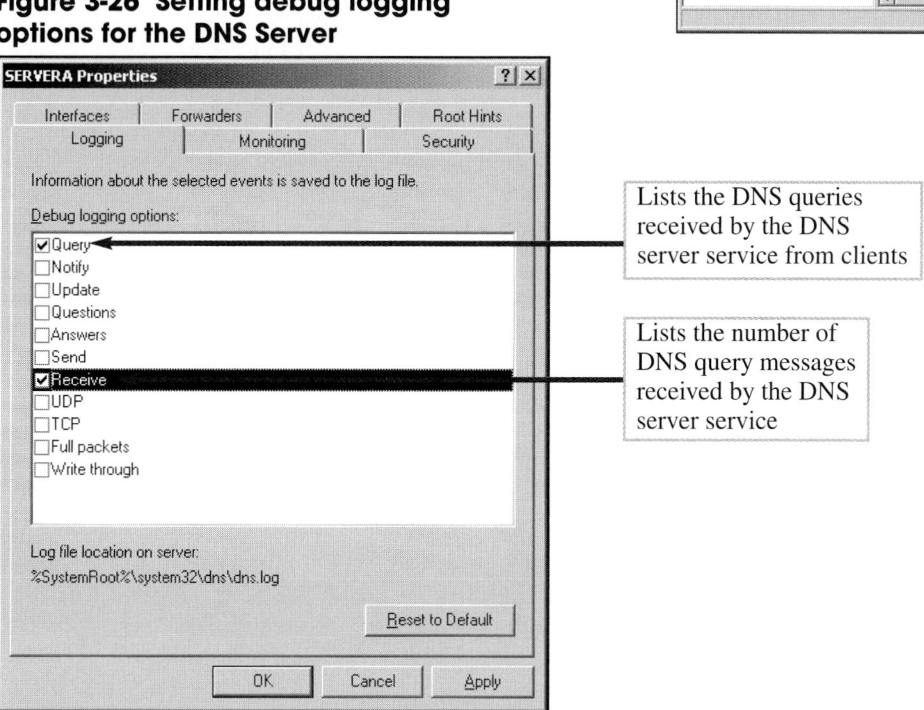
Lists the DNS queries received by the DNS server service from clients
Lists the number of DNS query messages received by the DNS server service

Table 3-6 Debug logging options for the DNS server

Logging options	Description
Send	Lists the number of DNS query messages that the DNS server has sent.
Update	Lists the dynamic updates sent to the DNS server service by other computers.
Notify	Lists the notification messages that other servers have sent to the DNS server service.
Questions	Lists the contents of the question section for each DNS query message that the DNS server service processes.
Answers	Lists the contents of the answer section for each DNS query message that the DNS server service processes.
Full Packets	Lists the number of full packets that the DNS server service has written and sent.
Write Through	Lists the number of packets written through by the DNS server service and back to the zone.
UDP	Lists the number of DNS requests that the DNS server service has received over a UDP port.
TCP	Lists the number of DNS requests that the DNS server service has received over a TCP port.

skill 10 Troubleshooting DNS Problems

exam objective

Manage, monitor, and troubleshoot DNS.

overview

The primary concern of a DNS administrator is to determine whether the DNS server is performing its query resolution tasks successfully. Occasionally, there might be problems in Active Directory, which would require troubleshooting of the DNS service. The three important areas that you need to focus on as a DNS administrator are DNS Clients, DNS Server, and DNS Zones. To troubleshoot DNS problems, you need to understand these areas in detail.

DNS Client Troubleshooting: The purpose of a DNS environment is defeated if the clients face problems in using the DNS server to resolve their queries. **Table 3-7** describes the causes and solutions of a typical problem that clients generally face.

DNS Server Troubleshooting: You need to troubleshoot a DNS server in case it is not able to resolve queries for DNS clients correctly. **Table 3-8** lists an example of a DNS server problem and the probable causes and solutions of the problem.

DNS Zone Troubleshooting: All the DNS queries in a zone are resolved using the zone file. Any problem in a zone invariably results in a problem in resolving DNS queries. Zone problems must be rectified to ensure smooth administration and functioning in a DNS environment. For example, when loading the zone file, a DNS server may receive an error message indicating that it could not load the zone. This message could imply that there is a database error with the zone file. The descriptions of some possible DNS zone-related problems are listed below:

- **Zone is paused at the DNS server:** You can verify whether a zone is started at a DNS server by using the **Properties** dialog box for the zone.
- **Problems in zone-transfer:** For the zone transfer process to occur successfully, both the source and destination servers involved in the zone transfer process must be connected to each other.
- **Version of the zone file is the same at both the source and destination servers:** The zone transfer process occurs only if the versions of the zone file at the two servers are different. You can determine the version of a zone file by using the serial number of the zone. Each time the zone file changes, the value of the serial number is incremented to indicate a new version of the zone file. You can manually increment the serial number to initiate the zone transfer process at the secondary server.
- **The authoritative zone data in the zone file is incorrect:** If you manually edit zone files, remember that resource records must be used according to standard record usage and formatting guidelines as specified in the Request for Comments (RFCs) for DNS. Use the DNS server event log to find out the source of the failed zone transfer.

tip

By default, zones are started when they are created at a DNS server. Only the zones that have been paused earlier need to be restarted.

more

Requests for Comments (RFCs) are a regularly growing series of technical reports, proposals for protocols, and protocol standards used by the Internet community. RFCs contain definitions of routing standards and are published by the Internet Engineering Task Force (IETF), as well as other open research groups. You may read, suggest modifications to, or even propose a new RFC at no charge. To read any RFC, visit www.rfc-editor.org.

Table 3-7 A typical DNS client problem with its probable causes and solutions

Problem	Causes	Solutions
When you try to access a Web site using Microsoft Internet Explorer, you receive the error message "Unknown host <hostname> error message".	1. The DNS client does not have a valid IP address configuration for the network.	1. Use the IPCONFIG command at the command prompt to verify that the client has a valid IP address, subnet mask, and default gateway for the network where it is used. If a problem is detected in the IPCONFIG command output, modify the TCP/IP properties of the client to use valid IP address configuration settings.
	2. The DNS client is unable to contact its configured DNS servers.	2. Identify the IP addresses of the configured DNS servers. Next, verify whether or not the server is responding. To rectify the network connectivity problem, verify that all your network connections are properly configured.
	3. The DNS server used by the client has no listing for the host name. This indicates that the DNS server loaded a zone file that does not contain the address resource record for the host name.	3. Verify that the DNS server used by the client loads the zone file containing a resource record for the host name. This can be verified by opening the DNS console and selecting the appropriate zone.
	4. The DNS client and/or DNS server has cached a negative response for the host name.	4. On the client, run the command ipconfig /flushdns (on Windows 2000), restart the DNS client service (Windows NT), or reboot. On the DNS server, stop and restart the DNS server service.

Table 3-8 A typical DNS server problem, with its probable causes and solutions

Problem	Causes	Solutions
When a client tries to access a DNS server, an error message indicating no response from the server is displayed.	1. The DNS server is on the network but not responding to DNS queries from clients.	1. To verify whether the DNS server is functioning properly, first attempt to ping the DNS server by using the IP address listed for the DNS server using the ipconfig /all command. If the ping is successful, then verify that the DNS server service is functioning by examining the services console on the DNS server.
	2. The DNS server has been limited to use a specific list of IP addresses to service its clients. The server IP address used by clients to contact it is not in the list of restricted IP addresses.	2. Use the Interfaces tab in the Properties dialog box of the server to configure the list of IP addresses.
	3. The DNS server has been configured to disable the use of its automatically created, default reverse lookup zones. ***Note:*** This error only shows up in the nslookup utility, and should have no bearing on forward lookups by the clients.	3. You can manually disable the creation of these zones by performing advanced changes to the server registry. It must be verified that such changes have not been made to the registry and the default reverse lookup zones exist on the server.

Summary

- Domain Name System (DNS) is the primary naming system of Windows 2000. The main tasks of DNS in an Active Directory environment include resolving host names to IP addresses and locating different services on the network.
  - The DNS structure is defined by the DNS namespace, which is a hierarchical grouping of names, representing the arrangement of domains in the DNS.
  - The topmost domain in the DNS namespace hierarchy is called the root domain, which is followed by the top-level domains and second-level domains. Second-level domains can also contain subdomains.
  - A Fully Qualified Domain Name (FQDN) fully identifies a TCP/IP host on the Internet. It is a combination of domain names together with the host name.
  - The process of DNS name resolution involves a resolver that makes a request and the name server that answers that request. The resolver can use recursive, iterative, and inverse queries to make a request to the name server.
- A DNS database is divided into zones that contain information about domains and their resources.
  - The information about each zone is stored in a separate file called a zone database file. A zone database file consists of resource records that contain information about the resources in a DNS domain.
  - DNS servers can be used as primary name servers, secondary name servers, and caching-only name servers.
- Planning a zone strategy involves determining the types of zones and zone transfers on a network, setting the number of zones and delegated zones, and finally, determining the zone replication strategy.
- The two primary types of zones that can be used in DNS are forward lookup zones and reverse lookup zones. Forward lookup zones help to resolve forward lookup queries. Reverse lookup zones enable reverse lookup queries.
- Dynamic Domain Name System (DDNS) is the dynamic update capability included in DNS.
- Zone replication is the process of replicating zone data to all secondary zones at each server.
- DNS notification is a feature of the DNS service that uses a push mechanism for notifying a selected set of secondary servers for a zone whenever the zone is updated.
- Windows 2000 Server enables you to set up debugging options to monitor DNS servers. Normal DNS server event messages are stored in the DNS server log and can be viewed using Event Viewer. Debug messages are stored in a special log file in the %systemroot%\System32\Dns folder.
- The three important areas that you might need to troubleshoot as a DNS administrator are DNS Client, DNS Server, and DNS Zones.

Key Terms

DNS namespace
Fully Qualified Domain Name (FQDN)
Resolver
Recursive query
Iterative query
Inverse query
Name server
Zone
Zone of authority
Root domain
Zone database file
Resource record
Primary name server
Primary DNS server
Secondary name server
Secondary DNS server
Master name server
Caching-only name server
Standard primary zone
Standard secondary zone
Active Directory-integrated zone
Zone transfer
Access Control List (ACL)
Forward lookup zones
Reverse lookup zones
in-addr.arpa
NSLookup
Zone delegation
Dynamic Domain Name System (DDNS)
DHCP Server
Zone replication
Standard zone replication
Active Directory zone replication
DNS notification
DNS server log
Event viewer
Requests for Comments (RFCs)

Test Yourself

1. Which of the following best describes a subdomain?
   a. It is the domain located at the top of the namespace and represented as ".".
   b. It is the first branch domain that emerges from the root.
   c. It identifies a specific organization within the top-level domain.
   d. It is the branch that emerges from a second-level domain.

2. Your organization is migrating from a Microsoft Windows NT 4.0 network to a Windows 2000 environment. One Windows NT 4.0 Server computer is already hosting a primary DNS zone and you want to retain the zone settings in the new setup. Which of the following would you perform to enable DNS to retain its current settings and prepare you to install Active Directory after migration?
   a. Upgrade DNS on Windows NT to Windows 2000 DNS Service.
   b. Install the Active Directory client for Windows NT 4.0 on the Windows NT 4.0 DNS server.
   c. Install a Windows 2000 Server. Configure the DNS server as a secondary server to the Windows NT 4.0 DNS server. Complete the zone transfer process, and make the Windows 2000 DNS server the primary zone.

3. Which of the following resource records are added by DNS automatically when a zone is created? Choose all that apply.
   a. Start of Authority (SOA) records
   b. Domain records
   c. Host records
   d. Name server records
   e. Alias records

4. Which of the following is required before you install Active Directory?
   a. DNS must support incremental zone transfers.
   b. DNS must support the dynamic update protocol.
   c. DNS must reside on a Windows 2000 domain controller.
   d. DNS must contain at least one secondary zone.
   e. DNS must support SRV records.

5. Which of the following zone types would you create if you wanted to add an additional server to an existing Active Directory-integrated zone?
   a. Active Directory-integrated
   b. Standard primary
   c. Standard secondary
   d. Reverse lookup

6. Which of the following queries are used to query a name server to obtain the name of a computer by providing its IP address?
   a. Forward lookup query
   b. Reverse lookup query
   c. Recursive query
   d. Iterative query

7. Which of the following is a valid reason for delegating a subdomain?
   a. To circumvent the DNS database limit of 40,000 records.
   b. To synchronize all the standard secondary zones with the primary zone.
   c. To add additional servers for resolving queries to an existing zone.
   d. To divide the DNS database into smaller, more manageable parts.

8. You are the administrator of a Windows 2000 Active Directory-integrated network. Your network is a single domain-multiple site network, where sites are connected by using high-speed T1 lines. In this network, a single DNS server is used for host name resolution. Changes in the objects and their details occur on this network frequently. What should you do to ensure that the data about the domain namespace remains up-to-date across the network?
   a. Specify a serial number for the DNS name server in the domain.
   b. Specify a retry interval for the DNS name server in the domain.
   c. Specify a shorter default TTL value for the records on the DNS name server in the domain.
   d. Specify the aging/scavenging properties for stale resource records in the DNS name server.

9. Which of the following is a characteristic of DDNS?
   a. Assigns IP addresses to clients.
   b. Automatically configured when DNS is installed on a machine acting as a DHCP server.
   c. Configured through the DNS console by creating a resource record.
   d. Allows computers to register and dynamically update resource records in the zone.

10. You need to set aging/scavenging features for all the zones on a DNS server that uses standard primary zones. You select Set Aging/Scavenging for all zones from the shortcut menu of the DNS server. You also ensure that the Scavenge stale resource records check box is selected for the zones. However, you notice that scavenging is not taking place as required. Why?
    a. You can set aging/scavenging only for Active Directory-integrated zones.
    b. You need to set aging/scavenging for each standard primary zone manually.
    c. You can set aging/scavenging for only standard secondary zones.
    d. You also need to specify the server in the Name Servers tab.

11. Under which of the following conditions do standard zone transfers take place? Choose all that apply.
   a. When DNS service is started on the primary server.
   b. When the refresh interval of a zone expires.
   c. When notification of changes made to the primary zone is sent to the secondary server.
   d. When the DNS service is started on a secondary server.
   e. When each domain controller acts as a primary DNS server.

12. DNS notification should be used only when:
   a. Secondary DNS servers exist in a zone.
   b. Primary DNS servers exist in a zone.
   c. Active Directory-integrated zones exist.
   d. Forward lookup queries are used.

13. Which of the following command-line utilities can be used in troubleshooting DNS problems? Choose all that apply.
   a. IPCONFIG
   b. DCPROMO
   c. NTDSUTIL
   d. NSLOOKUP
   e. REPADMIN

Projects: On Your Own

1. Install DNS service on your network to provide domain name resolution and easy access to other resources and computers in the network. In order to do this, you need to create a standard primary forward lookup zone named Market.XYZ.com on the XYZ DNS server for your network. Also, create a standard reverse lookup zone with the IP address 208.142.155.
   a. Log on as an Administrator on a domain controller.
   b. Insert the Windows 2000 Server disc into the CD-ROM drive.
   c. Install DNS using the Windows Components Wizard.
   d. Open the **DNS** console.
   e. Access the **Forward Lookup Zones** container and initiate the New Zone Wizard.
   f. Create a standard primary zone named Market.XYZ.com.
   g. Access the **Reverse Lookup Zones** container and initiate the New Zone Wizard.
   h. Create a standard primary zone with the IP address 208.142.155.

2. Configure the Market.XYZ.com zone for DDNS, set its aging and scavenging features, and set the properties for the SOA resource records of the zone.
   a. Open the **Properties** dialog box of the Market.XYZ.com zone.
   b. Set the option to allow dynamic updates.
   c. Open the **Zone Aging/Scavenging Properties** dialog box.
   d. Specify the refresh interval for the resource records as 12 days.
   e. Open the **Start of Authority (SOA)** tab.
   f. Specify the refresh interval for the secondary servers as **30** minutes and the **Time-To-Live (TTL)** value for the SOA resource record as 10 days.

3. Specify the servers that will take part in zone replication and transfer.
   a. Open the **Properties** dialog box of the Market.XYZ.com zone.
   b. Open the **Name Servers** tab.
   c. Add a secondary server named SECXYZ with the IP address 208.142.155.130.
   d. Open the **Zone Transfers** tab.
   e. Specify the option that zone transfer should occur only for the servers listed in the **Name Servers** tab.
   f. Open the **Notify** dialog box to set notification for this server.

Problem Solving Scenarios

1. You are planning to implement the Windows 2000 Active Directory Infrastructure. As per the current setup, which relies on Windows NT 4.0 and NetBIOS Name Resolution, there is one remote location, which is part of the network but is connected by a slow WAN link. During the planning phase, you realize the importance of the Domain Naming System with respect to the Active Directory implementation. Draft a memo outlining the steps you need to take to ensure a proper name resolution infrastructure for Active Directory services to be installed and configured.

2. Your network currently uses Standard Zones on the DNS servers. After implementing ADS, you realize that the Replication traffic is becoming a major reason for concern with regards to the Directory Replication traffic as well as the Name Resolution and Zone Transfer traffic. Also, currently you update the zone database files manually whenever a new client is added/removed on the network. You would now like to update this process as well. Prepare a plan of action specifying the steps you need to take to resolve these issues.

LESSON

4

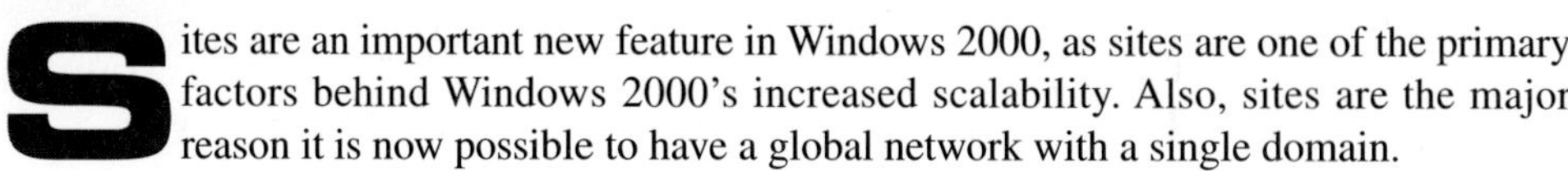

Configuring Site Settings and Inter-Site Replication

Sites are an important new feature in Windows 2000, as sites are one of the primary factors behind Windows 2000's increased scalability. Also, sites are the major reason it is now possible to have a global network with a single domain.

Sites are logical representations of your physical network within Active Directory. As such, site layout tells Active Directory how your network is physically built. Site links connect each site, telling Active Directory which sites are connected to each other, and to a degree, what type of connectivity is used between those locations. Active Directory then uses this information to determine how replication should occur, which domain controllers should respond to user requests, which global catalog server to contact, and which servers are closest to the end user for site aware applications (such as DFS).

Sites are a critical component within Active Director; therefore, all AD administrators should have a solid understanding of how to design and implement site topologies.

Goals

In this lesson, you will learn to create sites and subnets, link the sites, and designate a site license server and global catalog server. You will also learn to configure site link attributes and verify replication topology using the AD Sites and Services console, as well as configure the server settings for a site in order to meet the business requirements of an organization.

Lesson 4 Configuring Site Settings and Inter-Site Replication

Skill	Exam 70-217 Objective
1. Creating Sites to Develop a Directory Structure	Create sites, subnets, site links, and connection objects.
2. Configuring a Subnet	Create sites, subnets, site links, and connection objects.
3. Creating Site Links	Create sites, subnets, site links, and connection objects.
4. Configuring Site Link Attributes	Create sites, subnets, site links, and connection objects.
5. Creating Site Link Bridges	Create sites, subnets, site links, and connection objects.
6. Configuring Connections in Active Directory	Create sites, subnets, site links, and connection objects.
7. Selecting a Bridgehead Server for Inter-Site Replication	Monitor, optimize, and troubleshoot Active Directory performance and replication.
8. Checking Replication Topology	Monitor, optimize, and troubleshoot Active Directory performance and replication.
9. Creating a Server Object in a Site	Configure server objects. Considerations include site membership and global catalog designation.
10. Managing Server Objects	Configure server objects. Considerations include site membership and global catalog designation.
11. Designating a Global Catalog Server	Configure server objects. Considerations include site membership and global catalog designation.
12. Designating a Site License Server	Basic knowledge

Requirements

To complete this lesson, you will need administrative rights on ServerA, the Windows 2000 Server computer that is the domain controller for the mydomain.com domain you created in Lesson 2.

skill 1 Creating Sites to Develop a Directory Structure

exam objective

Create sites, subnets, site links, and connection objects.

overview

A site is a logical representation of your physical structure. In general, sites are physical locations (buildings), but there are cases in which a single site might span multiple buildings, such as in a CAN (Campus Area Network). In general, a site can be thought of as a location where all computers are "well-connected". This essentially means that all computers in a single site should be connected by high-speed, reliable, cost-effective links. Typically, the only links that meet all of the criteria of a "well-connected" link are Local Area Network (LAN) links.

Site membership, at least in most cases, is defined by your IP structure. Since in a routed IP network, each physical location will typically have its own addressing range, it is therefore a fairly simple proposition to have AD examine the IP address of a client in order to determine which site the client is a member of. AD defines the address ranges associated with each site by examining the subnet object associated with each site. A subnet object is simply an object created in AD that is assigned a range of IP addresses and is associated with a site.

Sites are very easy to create in Active Directory. When you install Active Directory on a Windows 2000 Server, Windows 2000 Server creates the first site by default. This site is named Default-First-Site and is created in the Sites container. To manage a small LAN, one site is sufficient. For large environments, however, you may be required to create additional sites manually. An example of a large environment can be a big firm with various physical locations. You can create different sites for each of these locations.

You create a site using the Active Directory Sites and Services console.

tip

While you can rename the default first site, it typically is a better idea to create new sites and leave the default site as an empty site in your design. This is because the default-first-site name is where a domain controller is placed if it cannot locate its correct site. By leaving the default-first-site empty, it will always be very easy to find "orphaned" domain controllers.

how to

Create a site.

1. Log on to **ServerA** as an **Administrator**.
2. Click **Start**, point to **Programs**, point to **Administrative Tools**, and then click the **Active Directory Sites and Services** command. The **AD Sites and Services** console opens.
3. Right-click the **Sites** folder, and then click the **New Site** command in the console tree. The **New Object-Site** dialog box opens.
4. Type **TestSite1** in the **Name** text box to specify a name for the site.
5. Select the site link object **DEFAULTIPSITELINK (Figure 4-1)**, and click **OK**. This opens an **Active Directory** message box that lists the tasks you need to perform in order to complete the configuration of the newly created site **(Figure 4-2)**. Windows 2000 provides **DEFAULTIPSITELINK** as the default site link. The **AD Sites and Services** console ensures that every site is placed in at least one site link.
6. Click **OK** in the **Active Directory** message box.
7. The new site, **TestSite1**, now appears in the tree of the **AD Sites and Services** console **(Figure 4-3)**.

more

Renaming a site is as simple as renaming a file or a folder. Right-click the site, click the **Rename** command, and type the new name.

Figure 4-1 Creating a site

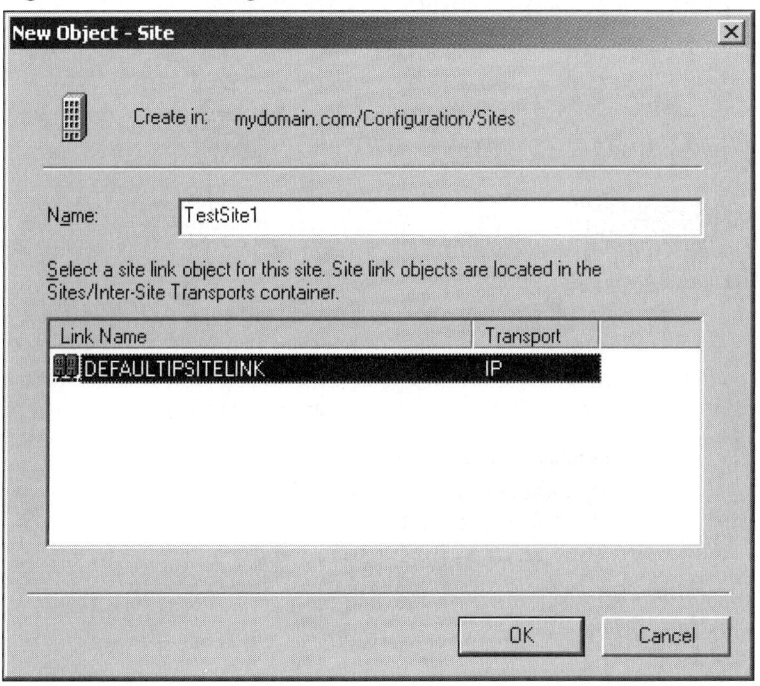

Figure 4-2 New site object notification window

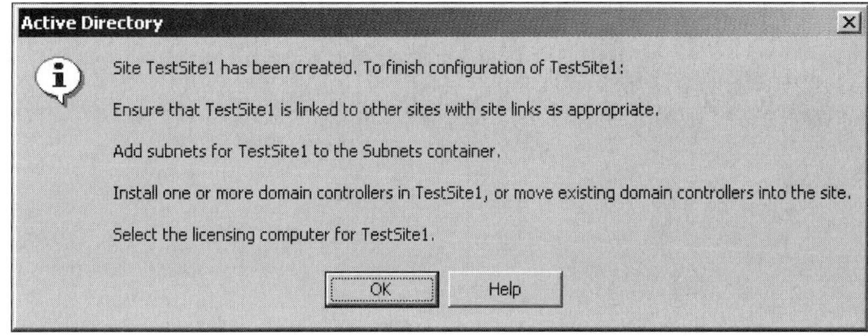

Figure 4-3 New site in the AD Sites and Services console

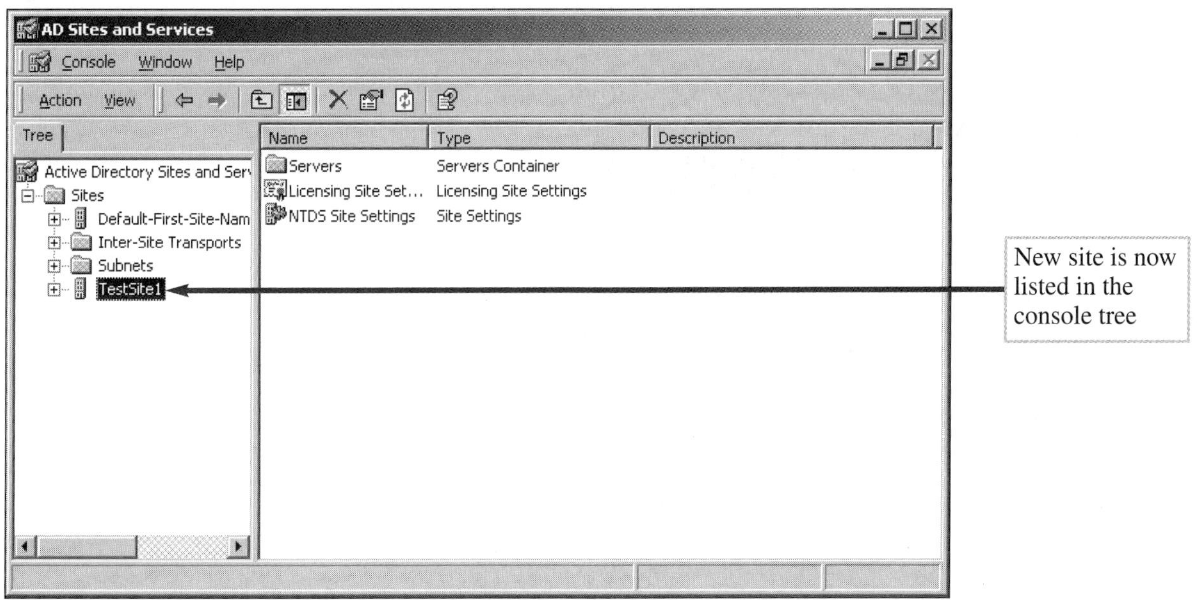

skill 2 Configuring a Subnet

exam objective

Create sites, subnets, site links, and connection objects.

overview

There are two common definitions of a **subnet**. In networking, a subnet is defined as a collection of host computers on a TCP/IP network in which the computers are not separated by routers. This definition is also typically called a segment. However, in AD, a subnet is simply a range of IP addresses **(Figure 4-4)**, and may or may not match your physical subnets. For instance, imagine you have a single building composed of four large floors. On each floor, you have approximately 250 hosts. You may have a router or layer-3 switch on each floor dividing the floors into four physical subnets, 192.168.4.0/24, 192.168.5.0/24, 192.168.6.0/24, and 192.168.7.0/24. However, since these are all in one building, and each subnet is separated by routed LAN links instead of WAN links, the entire building should really be a single AD site with a single AD subnet. This can be accomplished by assigning an AD subnet of 192.168.4.0/22, which will include every address between 192.168.4.0 and 192.168.7.255. You then associate this subnet with the site for your building, and from that point on, AD will automatically know that any PC with an IP address in that range is a member of that particular site.

tip

If IP addressing confuses you, you may want to spend some time reading up on IP network design before continuing. A good, free resource for IP addressing is available at **learntosubnet.com**.

An IP address is unique for each computer communicating by using TCP/IP. An IP address identifies the location of a host computer on a network in the same way that a street address identifies a house on a city street. Each IP address has two sections: a network address and a host address. The network address indicates the network on which the computer is running, and the host address uniquely identifies a given host on a TCP/IP network.

A subnet mask helps to distinguish the network address from the host address and determines where the network ID ends and the host address begins in an IP address. In the previous example, with the 192.168.5.0/24 address block, for instance, the subnet mask is notated by the /24. This is known as Classless Inter-Domain Routing, or CIDR, notation. The /24 simply denotes that there are 24 binary ones in the subnet mask and is the same as saying 255.255.255.0 in the standard dotted decimal subnet mask representation. When creating a subnet object, you have the opportunity to see the mask displayed in both formats. If you do not know the subnet mask and the subnet address of your subnet, run the **ipconfig/all** command to view the details of the subnet. The ipconfig command displays the TCP/IP configuration on the computer. You can use the ipconfig command to get host computer TCP/IP configuration information, including the IP address, subnet mask, default gateway, DNS server(s), WINS server(s), NBT node type, domain suffix, and most other configured TCP/IP parameters.

As already mentioned, AD uses the IP address of client PCs and member servers to associate them with the correct sites. However, the primary component of a site is a list of domain controllers that exist in the specified site. For placement of domain controllers, AD attempts to find a match between the machine's IP address and a subnet object *only during the initial promotion process*. The server must be manually moved between sites from then on. If the server's IP address does not correspond to any of the subnet objects defined in AD, then AD will simply place that domain controller in the Default-First-Site (domain controllers that fall victim to this functionality are referred to as "orphaned"). For this reason, your first domain controller will always be placed in this site. You must make sure you manually move any "orphaned" domain controllers to their appropriate sites once you create them in order to generate a correct replication topology.

Figure 4-4 Assigning a subnet to a site

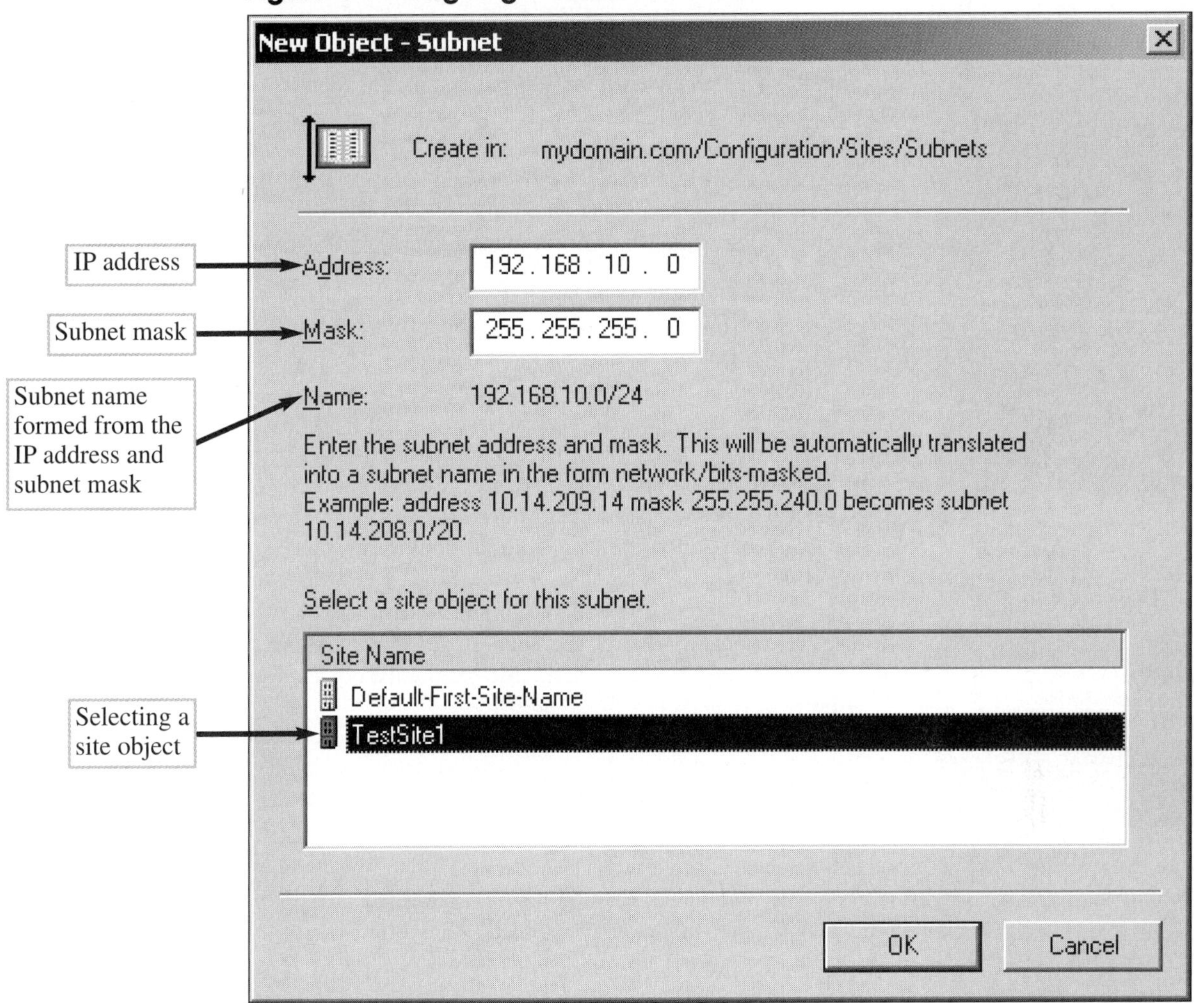

skill 2 Configuring a Subnet *(cont'd)*

exam objective

Create sites, subnets, site links, and connection objects.

overview

An easy way to roll out large numbers of domain controllers without having to manually move them to the appropriate sites is to follow the steps below:

1. Create your first domain controller for each site at a central location.
2. Ship these servers to their appropriate remote locations.
3. Create site objects for each location, create and associate subnet objects to the sites, and create site links as needed.
4. Manually move the first server for each site out of the Default-First-Site and into its correct site.
5. Drop ship the rest of the servers to their appropriate remote site and install them there.

Following these steps allows AD to perform the initial database replication locally (over LAN links rather than WAN links), while automatically placing all servers (after the first for each site) in the appropriate site.

how to

Create a subnet and associate it with a site.

1. Right-click the Subnets folder under the **Sites** container in the **AD Sites and Services** console. Then, click the **New Subnet** command. The **New Object-Subnet** dialog box opens.
2. Type the IP address **192.168.10.0** in the **Address** text box.
3. Type the subnet mask **255.255.255.0** in the **Mask** text box.
4. Click the **TestSite1** option in the **Site Name** list box to associate the subnet with this site (**Figure 4-4**), and click OK.
5. The new subnet appears in the AD Sites and Services console tree (**Figure 4-5**).

more

You can associate a subnet with a different site by right-clicking the subnet, and then clicking the **Properties** command. The **Properties** dialog box will open. You can use the **Site** list box in this dialog box to associate the subnet with a different site.

Figure 4-5 New subnet in the AD Sites and Services console

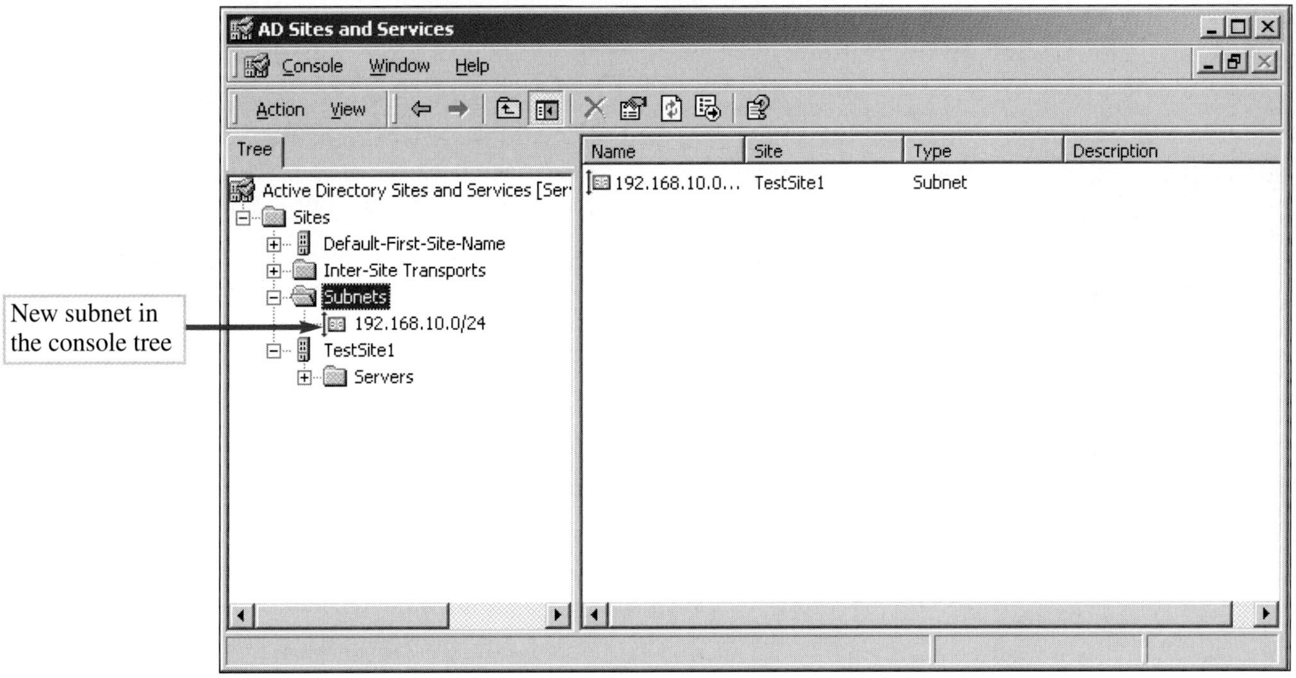

New subnet in the console tree

skill 3 Creating Site Links

exam objective

Create sites, subnets, site links, and connection objects.

overview

Site links are connections between sites that form the core of Active Directory **inter-site replication**. You need to create links between two sites before replication can occur. In the absence of a site link, you cannot make connections between the computers in the two sites. Site links are not generated automatically and need to be created using the **AD Sites and Services** console. A site link can contain more than two sites, but this is typically not advised unless you have a mesh topology between the sites in question. In general, it is best to create site links as necessary in order to match the physical topology of your network.

When you install Active Directory on a Windows 2000 Server, the Active Directory Installation Wizard automatically creates a site link named DEFAULTIPSITELINK in the IP container. You can rename the DEFAULTIPSITELINK object according to your preference.

When creating site links, you have the option of using either the Simple Mail Transfer Protocol (SMTP) or Internet Protocol (IP) as the transport protocol (**Figure 4-6**).

SMTP replication essentially sends AD replication as attachments in encrypted e-mail messages. SMTP replication has the advantage of being asynchronous, which means that it is not time sensitive. This makes it useful in situations where the link separating sites is slow or unreliable. SMTP also has no difficulty passing through Network Address Translation (NAT) devices to get to a particular destination. However, SMTP is rarely used because it may only be used for replication between different domains. SMTP is never a valid choice for a site link when you need to replicate information between different sites in the same domain. Finally, SMTP is a bit complicated to configure, as it requires e-mail servers (Exchange is preferred) that are encryption capable (Key Management Server is used with Exchange to provide this functionality), and also requires a Certificate Authority (CA) to issue the certificates used by the SMTP server to generate the encryption.

tip

RPC over IP (or simply RPC) and IP are synonymous terms in the Sites and Services console.

IP replication actually means Remote Procedure Call (RPC) over IP. RPC is a common protocol in Microsoft products, and has a few distinct advantages and disadvantages. RPC is fairly efficient (at least compared to SMTP) and provides for rapid data transfer over reasonably fast, reliable links. On the other hand, RPC is synchronous, which means it is very time sensitive, and is typically a poor choice for slow, unreliable links. In addition, since RPC chooses random port numbers after the initial session establishment phase and references these port numbers in the packet's RPC header, RPC can not be translated by NAT devices. However, these points are mostly moot in real life, as RPC is the only protocol choice available for replicating changes within a single domain.

Figure 4-6 Contents of the Inter-Site Transports folder

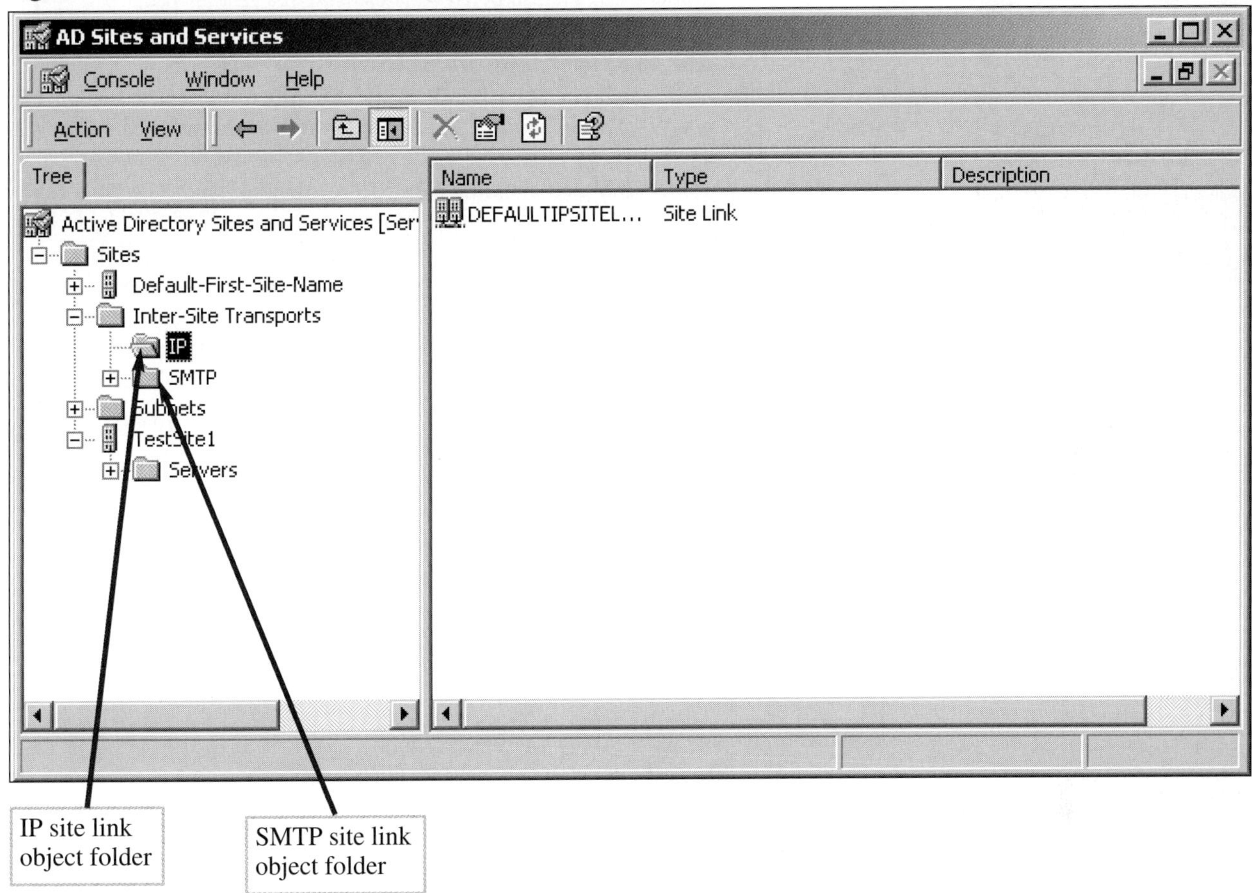

skill 3

Creating Site Links (cont'd)

exam objective

Create sites, subnets, site links, and connection objects.

how to

Create a site link to facilitate a connection between sites using the IP transport.

1. You need two sites to create a site link. **TestSite1** will be one of these two sites. Create a second site, **TestSite2**, using the **AD Sites and Services** console.
2. Double-click the Inter-Site Transports folder in the **AD Sites and Services** console to expand it. This displays both the IP and SMTP folders under the Inter-Site Transports folder.
3. Right-click the IP folder, and then click the **New Site Link** command. The **New Object-Site Link** dialog box opens.
4. Type **TestSiteLink1** in the **Name** text box to specify the name for the site link.
5. Click the **TestSite1** option in the Sites not in this Site link list box, and click [Add>>] to add a site to the site link.
6. Click the **TestSite2** option, and click [Add>>] to add another site **(Figure 4-7)**.
7. Click [OK] to close the **New Object-Site Link** dialog box.
8. The new site link appears in the **AD Sites and Services** console **(Figure 4-8)**.

more

You can also add or remove a site from an existing site link. To add a site to a site link, right-click the site link to which you want to add the site. Click the **Properties** command to access the **Properties** dialog box. Select the site from the **Sites not in this Site link** list box in the **General** tab, click [Add>>] to add the site to the site link, and click [OK] to apply the changes **(Figure 4-9)**. You can configure the following options in the **Properties** dialog box.

- **Description**, which describes the site link.
- **Sites not in this Site link**, which displays the available sites. You can add the sites for the site link from this list box.
- **Sites in this Site link**, which displays the sites in the site link. You can remove the sites in the site link from this list box.
- **Cost**, which Active Directory uses to decide which route to use when replicating information. The cheapest available route is used based on the overall cost.
- **Replicate every**, which is the interval at which replication takes place over this link.
- **Change Schedule**, which is used to change replication schedules while the site link is available for replication.

Figure 4-7 Creating a site link

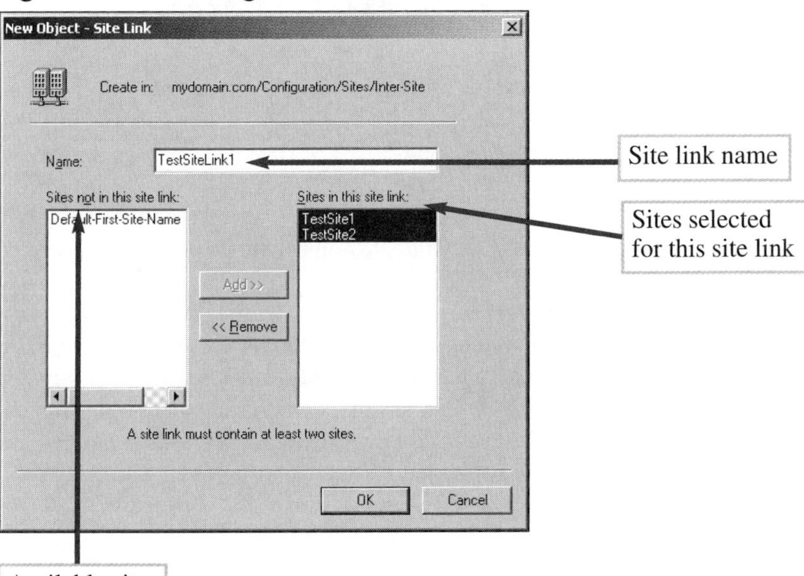

Figure 4-8 New site link in the IP site link object folder

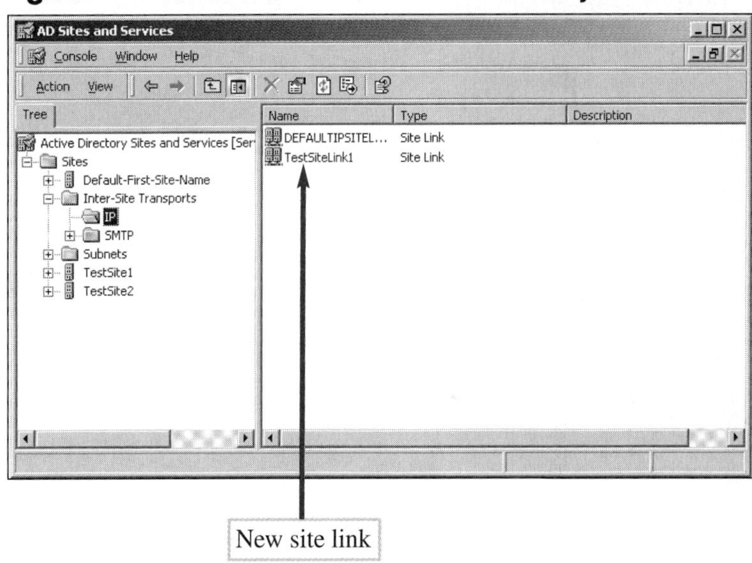

Figure 4-9 Specifying properties for a site link

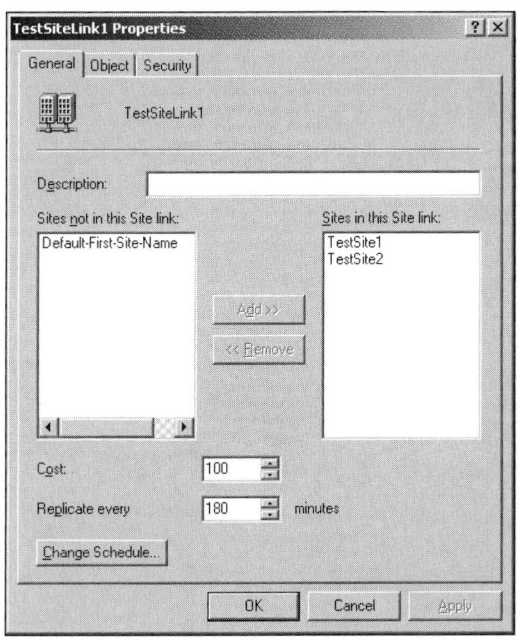

skill 4

Configuring Site Link Attributes

exam objective

Create sites, subnets, site links, and connection objects.

overview

After you create site links, you need to configure inter-site replication. To do this, you need to configure the following **site link attributes**:

- **Site link cost:** The cost field in a site link is used when Active Directory needs to determine which is the best of two possible replication paths. If there are two or more replication paths to a given site, Active Directory will add the costs associated with all site links along each path and use the path that has the lowest final value. For instance, imagine that you have three sites, A, B, and C. Site links exist between site A and B (Site link A-B), between B and C (Site link B-C), and between site A and C (Site link A-C), creating a small, fully meshed topology. In this case, if a change occurs at site A, Active Directory needs to be able to determine the most efficient method of replicating that change to C. Should it replicate with B and let B replicate with C, or should it replicate directly to C? Assuming the links have the same approximate bandwidth available, the default costs (100 per link) on your site links will suffice, causing AD to replicate directly to C, as the A-C path costs 100 and the A-B-C path costs 200. However, what if the direct link to C is a fractional T-1 running at a mere 256 Kbps, while the links from A to B and B to C are 1.544 Mbps T-1 links? In this case, you need to modify the costs of your site links so that AD can choose the best path, in this case, A-B-C. For this example, you would simply need to increase the cost of site link A-C to something larger than 200. However, in a much larger environment, it is much easier to use a cost "scale" based on available bandwidth to create relational costs than to try to think through every possible path (which is error prone at best). Typically, it is recommended to use a mathematically derived scale, starting with the maximum cost value (32,767) for your slowest link and dividing the cost by 2 each time your bandwidth doubles. For example, imagine that in your network, your slowest link is 64Kbps. You would apply the maximum cost of 32,767 to all 64Kbps links. For 128Kbps links, you would divide that cost by 2, giving those links a cost of 16,384 (you actually divide 32,768 by 2, since 32,767 will not divide evenly). Moreover, 256Kbps links get a cost of 8,192, while 512Kbps links get a cost of 4,096, and so on, until you get to 2Gbps links with a cost of 1. Using a scale like this, you never have to worry about a link's cost not being relational to the bandwidth it provides. Note that the default site link cost is 100, and the maximum site link cost is 32,767 **(Figure 4-10)**.
- **Replication frequency:** You can control the frequency at which inter-site replication occurs by specifying a value (an integer) for the replication frequency. Active Directory will check for replication updates after the specified duration. The replication interval ranges from a minimum of 15 minutes to a maximum of 10,080 minutes (equal to one week's time). For any replication to occur, a site link has to be available. In other words, the interval only applies within the "window" of time provided by the link's schedule. If a site link is unavailable when the replication update is scheduled, replication will not occur. The default site link replication frequency is 180 minutes.
- **Replication availability information:** You also need to specify the availability of a site link for replication. Simple Mail Transfer Protocol (SMTP) is asynchronous: it ignores all schedules by default. Therefore, for most practical scenarios, the schedule on SMTP site links serve no purpose. You need to configure site link replication availability on SMTP site links only if the site link is using scheduled connections, the SMTP queue is not on a schedule, and there is no intermediary, such as a proxy server, involved in the exchange of information between servers.

tip

In most smaller networks, redundant paths are rare. If your network does not have any redundant paths, then there is no need to concern yourself with site link costs. Simply use the defaults.

Figure 4-10 Setting the Cost field

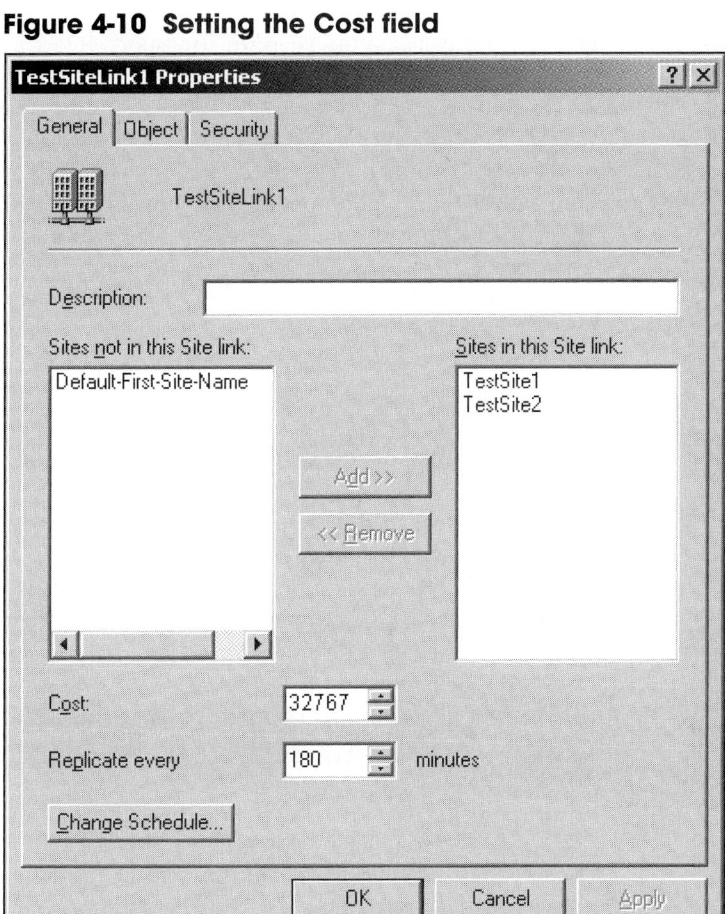

skill 4 Configuring Site Link Attributes (cont'd)

exam objective

Create sites, subnets, site links, and connection objects.

how to

Configure the site link attributes: site link cost, replication frequency, and replication availability.

1. Click the IP folder under the Inter-Site Transports folder in the **AD Sites and Services** console.
2. In the Details pane, right-click the site link **TestSiteLink1**, and then click the **Properties** command. The **TestSiteLink1 Properties** dialog box opens to the **General** tab.
3. Type **40** as the value for the cost of replication in the **Cost** spin box.
4. To configure site link replication frequency, type **120** in the **Replicate every** spin box to represent the number of minutes between two replications **(Figure 4-11)**. Replication will now occur every two hours. Note that the value is processed as the nearest multiple of 15.
5. To configure site link replication availability, click Change Schedule... . The **Schedule for TestSiteLink1** dialog box opens. A blue rectangle indicates that replication will be available during this time, whereas a white rectangle indicates that replication will not be available.
6. Click the **Replication not available** radio button to remove the default replication schedule.
7. Click the rectangle that corresponds to Sunday 12 A.M., drag it to the end of the row, and click the **Replication Available** option button. Similarly, click the rectangle that corresponds to Saturday 12 A.M., drag it to the end of the row **(Figure 4-12)**, and click the Replication Available button again. This will make the connection available at all times on Saturday and Sunday.
8. Click OK to close the dialog box.
9. You have changed the cost, replication frequency, and replication availability for the site link **TestSiteLink1**. Click OK to apply these properties.

tip

Remember that the lower the value, the higher the priority. For example, the cost of a T1 link might be 80, while the cost of a dial-up link might be 1920.

more

You can choose to ignore inter-site replication schedules for both the IP and SMTP transport folders. To do this, right-click the IP folder under the Inter-Site Transports folder in the **AD Sites and Services** console. Then click the **Properties** command to access the **IP Properties** dialog box. Select the **Ignore Schedules** check box on the **General** tab of the **IP Properties** dialog box **(Figure 4-13)**. If the **Ignore Schedules** check box is selected, replication is always available over all links for this inter-site transport. You can follow the same steps to ignore inter-site replication schedules for the SMTP transport folder (though SMTP will typically ignore schedules regardless of your settings).

Figure 4-11 Modifying the cost of replication and replication frequency

Specifying site link cost

Specifying replication frequency

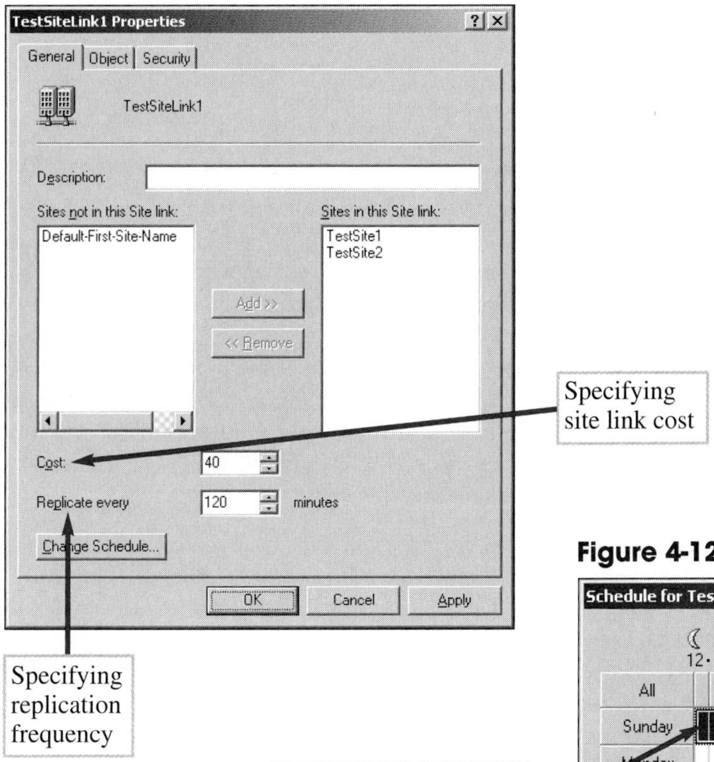

Figure 4-12 The Schedule for TestSiteLink1 dialog box

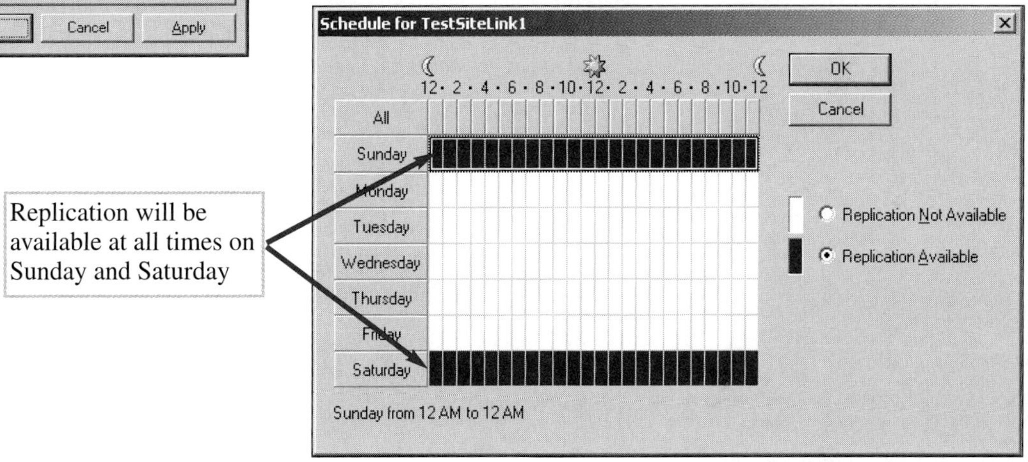

Replication will be available at all times on Sunday and Saturday

Figure 4-13 The IP Properties dialog box

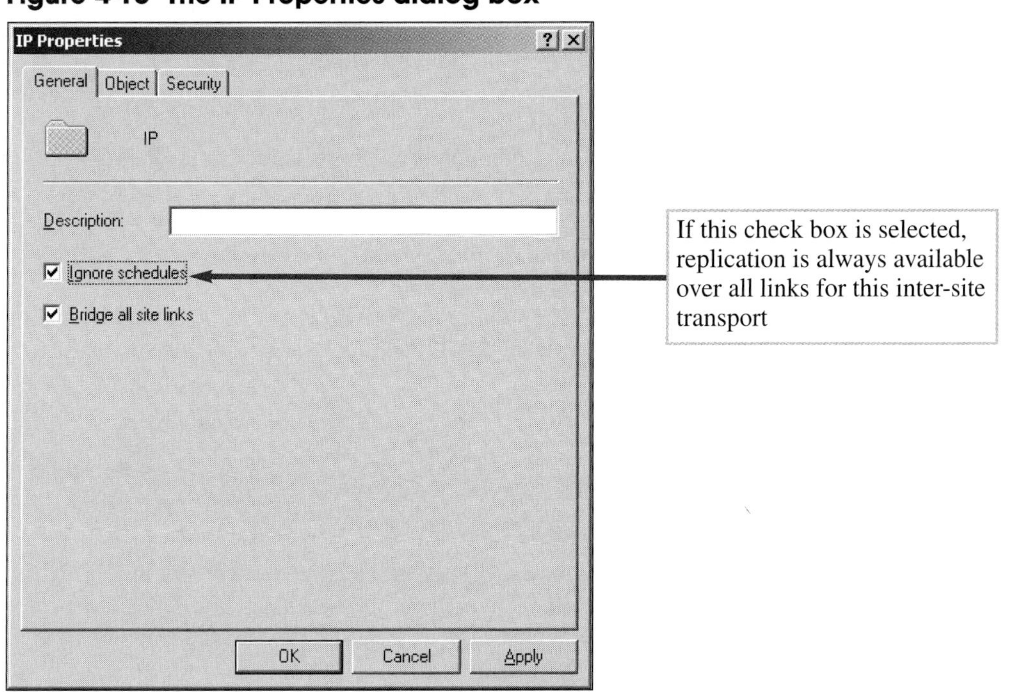

skill 5 Creating Site Link Bridges

exam objective

Create sites, subnets, site links, and connection objects.

overview

Site link bridges are a means of linking two or more indirectly connected sites for replication. Site link bridges help replicate your network configuration for efficient routing of network traffic. By default, all site links use the same transport and are automatically bridged. Such site links are also called transitive. Microsoft gives a scenario in which the routing tables on your routers do not allow each DC to communicate with every other DC, and in this case, they suggest disabling automatic bridging and configuring manual site links. In 99% of those cases, I would instead suggest you fix your routing tables, as that is the most effective and least painful solution. However, if you are in a crunch for bandwidth, disabling site-link bridging can reduce replication traffic in some cases. Although in most cases, you would be better advised to simply leave the default site link bridging settings in place.

tip

Once automatic site link bridging is disabled, all of your site link bridges must be manually created if they are required.

For an example of when disabling site link bridging can save some bandwidth, in **Figure 4-14**, we have a situation in which all replication traffic between site D and any other site must travel through site A. If site link bridging remains enabled, then any change occurring in site D will be replicated to site A, site B, and site C in three separate replication sessions, sending the exact same replication data across D's WAN link three times. It would be more efficient to simply let site D replicate with site A and let site A replicate those changes to sites B and C. To enable this functionality in this example, you would simply disable site link bridging, and *would not* create any manual bridges. This tells AD that it has no direct replication path from D to B or C, so it replicates with A (which does have a path), and lets A replicate to the other two sites. There is a catch, of course: Replication of changes initiated at site D will now require more time (up to 3 hours more, using the default interval) in order to reach sites B or C, and vice versa.

Since all site links are bridged by default, manual creation of site link bridges is effectively disabled if the **Bridge All Site Links** check box remains enabled. Therefore, you need to switch off automatic bridging before creating site link bridges manually.

how to

Disable automatic bridging and create a site link bridge.

1. Right-click the IP folder under the Inter-Site Transports folder in the **AD Sites and Services** console.
2. Click the **Properties** command to open the **IP Properties** dialog box.
3. Click the **Bridge All Site Links** check box to clear it and disable automatic bridging.
4. Click [OK] to close the dialog box.
5. Right-click the IP folder under the Inter-Site Transports folder in the **AD Sites and Services** console.
6. Click the **New Site Link Bridge** command.
7. The **New Object-Site Link Bridge** dialog box opens.
8. Type **TestBridge1** in the **Name** text box.
9. Click the **DEFAULTIPSITELINK** option in the **Site links not in this site link bridge** list box, and then click [Add>>]. **DEFAULTIPSITELINK** is added to the list of site links in the site link bridge.
10. Click the **TestSiteLink1** option, and click [Add>>] to add another site link (**Figure 4-15**).
11. Click [OK]. A new site link bridge (**Figure 4-16**) has been created.

tip

If you only have two site links they will automatically be added to the "Site links in this site link bridge" list box.

caution

A site link bridge must contain at least two site links.

more

You can revert to automatic bridging for all site links for inter-site transport within a bridge by right-clicking the IP or SMTP folder and opening the Properties dialog box. Select the Bridge All Site Links check box on the General tab of the IP or SMTP Properties dialog box.

Figure 4-14 Using a site link bridge effectively

Router
256 K link
Router
Site A
Site D
Router
Site B
Site C

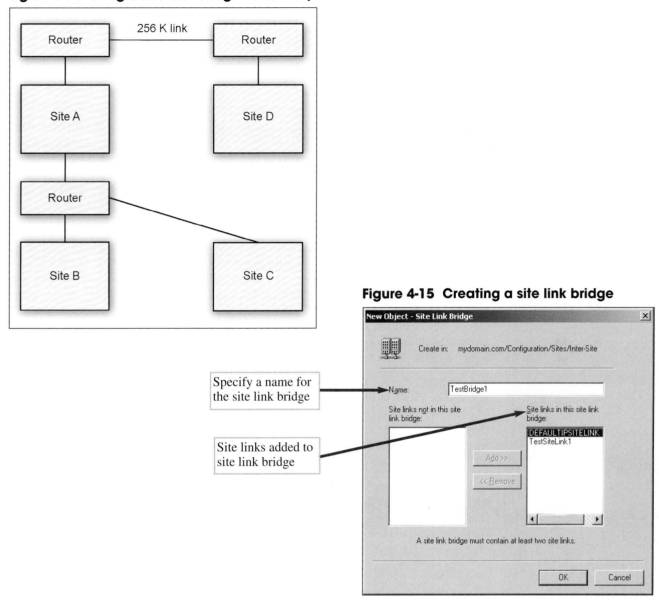

Figure 4-15 Creating a site link bridge

New Object - Site Link Bridge
Create in: mydomain.com/Configuration/Sites/Inter-Site
Specify a name for the site link bridge
Name: TestBridge1
Site links not in this site link bridge:
Site links added to site link bridge
Site links in this site link bridge:
DEFAULTIPSITELINK
TestSiteLink1
Add >>
<< Remove
A site link bridge must contain at least two site links.
OK
Cancel

Figure 4-16 New site link bridge in the IP site link object folder

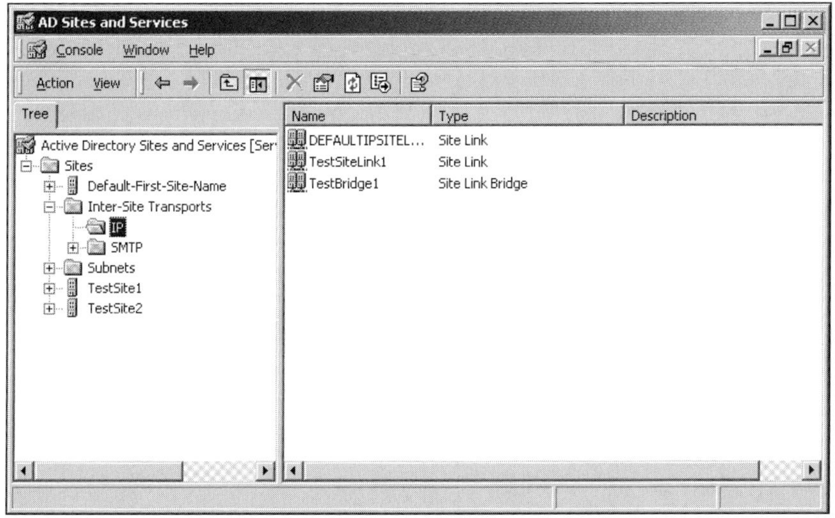

Exam 70-217

skill 6 Configuring Connections in Active Directory

exam objective

Create sites, subnets, site links, and connection objects.

overview

Connections are created automatically in Active Directory with the help of the **Knowledge Consistency Checker (KCC)**. KCC is an Active Directory process responsible for creating connection objects. **Connection objects** are the one-way, individual communications channels that the KCC typically creates between individual servers for replication. Whereas site links correspond to connections between sites, connection objects correspond to connections between servers.

The KCC automatically builds connection objects as necessary within a site based on what is known as the "three hop" or "15 minute" rule. Essentially, the KCC builds a replication topology out of connection objects within each site so that no matter which server a change occurs on, replication to all other servers in a site will occur within a three-server span. For instance, the KCC might build a replication topology so that when a change occurs to Server A, it will be replicated to Server C, which will replicate the change to Server E, which will replicate the change to Server F (**Figure 4-17**). In this case, Server C would be Server A's only **direct replication partner**. Similarly, Server E would be Server C's direct replication partner. Server A is *not* Server C's partner as the connection objects are one-way.

tip

You can manually force replication for *any* connection object by right-clicking on the object and selecting "Replicate Now." However, remember that connection objects are one-way.

Note that the "15 minute" rule and "three hop" rule are one and the same. The 15 minute part is based on AD's intra-site replication schedule. When a change occurs, AD will set a 5-minute timer. Once the timer expires, it will notify its direct replication partners of all changes that occurred during this time. These servers, after pulling the needed changes, will set their own five minute timers and repeat the process. Therefore, each hop takes around five minutes, and within 15 minutes, all servers in the site should have a given change.

Due to the KCC's enforcement of the "three hop" rule, domain controllers are not necessarily connected to all other domain controllers within their site. Rather, each domain controller is connected to just enough domain controllers in order to satisfy the rule and provide some slight overlap for redundancy. This functionality reduces overhead by reducing the number of connections each server must keep up with.

Additionally, the KCC uses site links to determine which sites are connected, and then only builds connection objects between the bridgehead for a given site and the bridgeheads for all other connected sites. Connections between sites do *not* follow the three-hop limitation.

Finally, while you can create connection objects manually, this practice is highly discouraged. When the KCC creates a connection object, it keeps track of the connection. If there is a problem with the connection object, the KCC will then automatically create new connections as necessary to restore the replication topology. However, when you create a manual connection object, you essentially tell the KCC that you are going to keep track of communications between those servers. This means that the KCC's error handling functionality is disabled for that connection, and you must manually deal with any problems that may occur. You should create connections manually only if you are sure the connection is required and you want the connection to remain until you manually delete it. You must also make sure you use the correct transport if you create connections manually. By default, manual connections use the RPC transport.

Figure 4-17 One possible replication topology built by the KCC

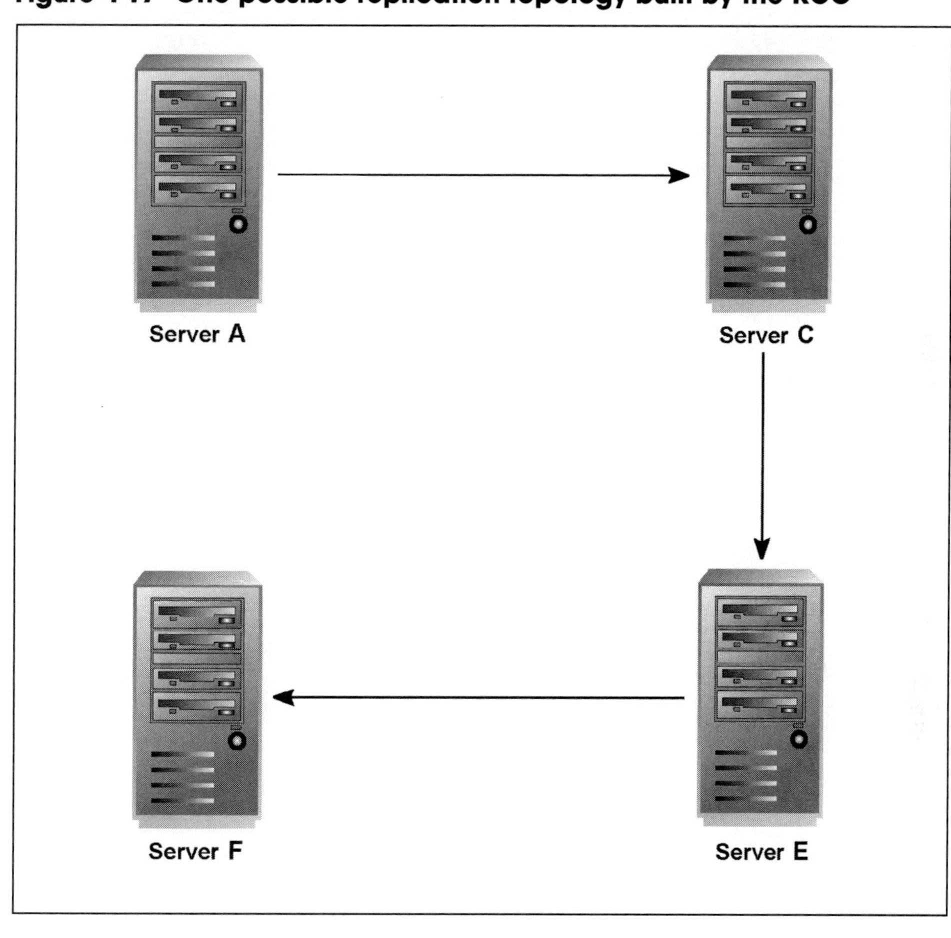

skill 6 Configuring Connections in Active Directory *(cont'd)*

exam objective

Create sites, subnets, site links, and connection objects.

how to

Add a new connection and force replication over the connection.

1. Click the Servers folder under the **Default-First-Site-Name** site in the **AD Sites and Services** console.
2. Click **ServerA** under the Servers folder. The **NTDS Settings** object is displayed.
3. To add a new connection, right-click the **NTDS Settings** object, and then click the **New Active Directory Connection** command. The **Find Domain Controllers** dialog box opens with the list of available domain controllers.
4. Click **ServerA** in the list of servers in the **Find Domain Controllers** dialog box **(Figure 4-18)** to create a connection in this server, and then click OK. The **New Object-Connection** dialog box opens.
5. Type **TestCon1** as the name for the new connection object in the **Name** field **(Figure 4-19)**, and click OK. The new connection will be displayed in the Details pane.
6. To force replication over **TestCon1**, right-click **TestCon1** in the Details pane, and click the **Replicate Now** command **(Figure 4-20)**. This command forces replication with the domain controller in which the connection is created to all other sites for which site links are available.

tip

This particular lab is simply designed to show you how to create a connection object. In real life, you would not create replication connections from ServerA to ServerA.

more

When you create site links and configure their replication availability, cost, and replication frequency, you automatically provide KCC with information about what connection objects to create in order to replicate directory data between sites (inter-site). In addition to creating your own connection objects, you can also modify the replication settings for automatically generated connection objects. However, once you modify such a connection, it becomes a manual connection and carries all of the difficulties associated with any other manual connection.

Figure 4-18 Choosing a domain controller to create a connection object

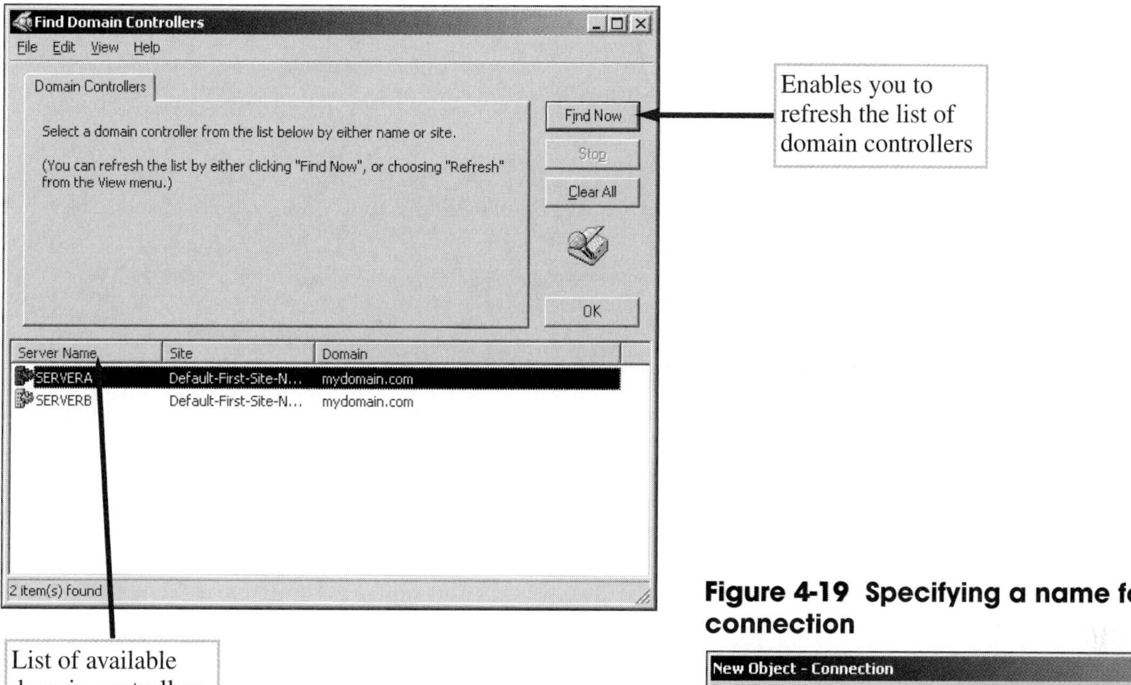

Figure 4-19 Specifying a name for the new connection

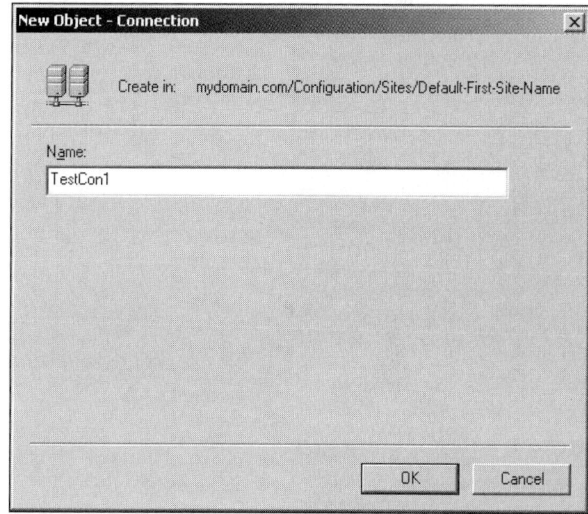

Figure 4-20 Forcing replication on a connection object

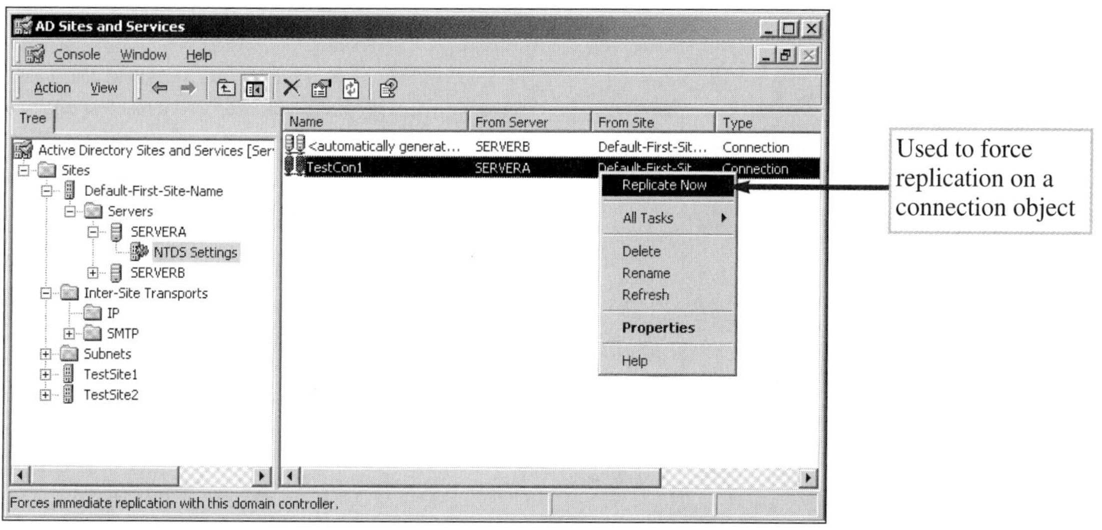

Exam 70-217

skill 7

Selecting a Bridgehead Server for Inter-Site Replication

exam objective

Monitor, optimize, and troubleshoot Active Directory performance and replication.

overview

When performing inter-site replication, the most important consideration is usually usage of bandwidth. As mentioned in the previous skill, the KCC will typically only create connection objects between **bridgehead servers** for inter-site replication. This functionality reduces traffic by limiting the number of connections established between sites.

As with most of its calculations, the KCC does not require any input from you in order to create these connection objects. However, you can also give the KCC a list of one or more preferred bridgehead servers to choose from. If one or more servers are designated as preferred bridgeheads, the KCC will choose one of those servers to perform the bridgehead role if possible. This allows you to designate servers on a high-speed backbone as the bridgehead servers for a particular site.

A topic that shows up in Microsoft materials (including the 70-217 test) quite often is the selection of the proper bridgehead server when using a Microsoft Proxy Server. Microsoft suggests designating the proxy server as the preferred bridgehead server. While this is the correct answer on the test, as AD cannot replicate *through* a NAT device, it is not a good choice in real life. In order to designate the proxy server as the site's preferred bridgehead, you have to promote your proxy server (which, in this case, is your firewall) to a domain controller, which is not a good idea from a security perspective. Instead, if you need to replicate AD across the Internet, you can reduce your security risk substantially by using a tunneling protocol, such as Layer 2 Tunneling Protocol (L2TP), to create a Virtual Private Network (VPN) link between sites. By using a tunnel for replication traffic, NAT is not performed on the replication session, and replication works as advertised.

how to

Select a bridgehead server for inter-site replication.

1. In the **AD Sites and Services** console, right-click ServerA under **Default-First-Site-Name**, and then click the **Properties** command. The **Properties** dialog box for the server opens.
2. To specify a transport for inter-site data transfer, click the **IP** option in the **Transports available for inter-site data transfer** list box, and then click Add>> (**Figure 4-21**).
3. Click OK to close the **Properties** dialog box for the server.

more

You can assign multiple preferred bridgeheads to each site, and the KCC will always attempt to choose a bridgehead from this list. However, if there is a problem and the KCC cannot choose a bridgehead from your list of preferred bridgeheads, it *will not* choose another bridgehead, and replication will fail. See Knowledge Base article 271997 for more information.

Figure 4-21 Specifying a preferred bridgehead server

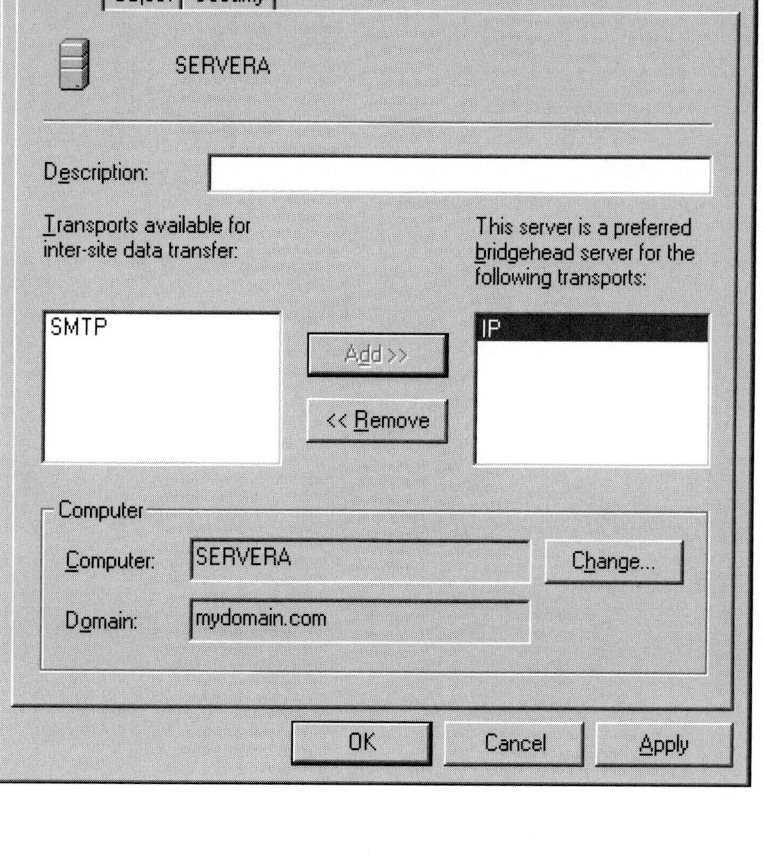

skill 8 Checking Replication Topology

exam objective

Monitor, optimize, and troubleshoot Active Directory performance and replication.

overview

Occasionally, you may make a major change that significantly affects your replication topology such as shutting down multiple domain controllers. While the KCC does periodically check the topology to ensure replication can be performed, in cases in which you caused a major change to occur, you can speed the process by forcing topology regeneration. This process is known as triggering the KCC, and can be performed fairly easily from within Active Directory Sites and Services.

When you trigger the KCC, the KCC examines the current connection objects and recalculates the topology based on server availability. For inter-site connections, the Inter-site Topology Generator (ISTG) is also triggered. The ISTG is a special service in AD that is used to check for the availability of domain controllers in remote sites and calculate the best replication paths between sites using the cost fields of the site links. Once the ISTG determines the best paths and available servers, the KCC then builds necessary inter-site connection objects using this information.

You can use the Active Directory Replication Monitor to monitor the replication process on single or multiple domain controllers in a domain. Using the replication monitor, you can also see a graphical view of your connection objects to each server, giving you a visual way to analyze your replication topology. You can install the Replication Monitor from the Support\Tools folder on the Windows 2000 Server CD.

how to

Force a recalculation of the replication topology by triggering the KCC using the **AD Sites and Services** console.

1. Double-click ServerA in the **AD Sites and Services** console.
2. Under ServerA, right-click the **NTDS Settings** object, point to **All Tasks**, and then click the **Check Replication Topology** command (**Figure 4-22**).
3. The **Check Replication Topology** message box appears, informing the user that Active Directory has checked the replication topology (**Figure 4-23**).
4. Click OK to close the message box.

Figure 4-22 Checking replication topology

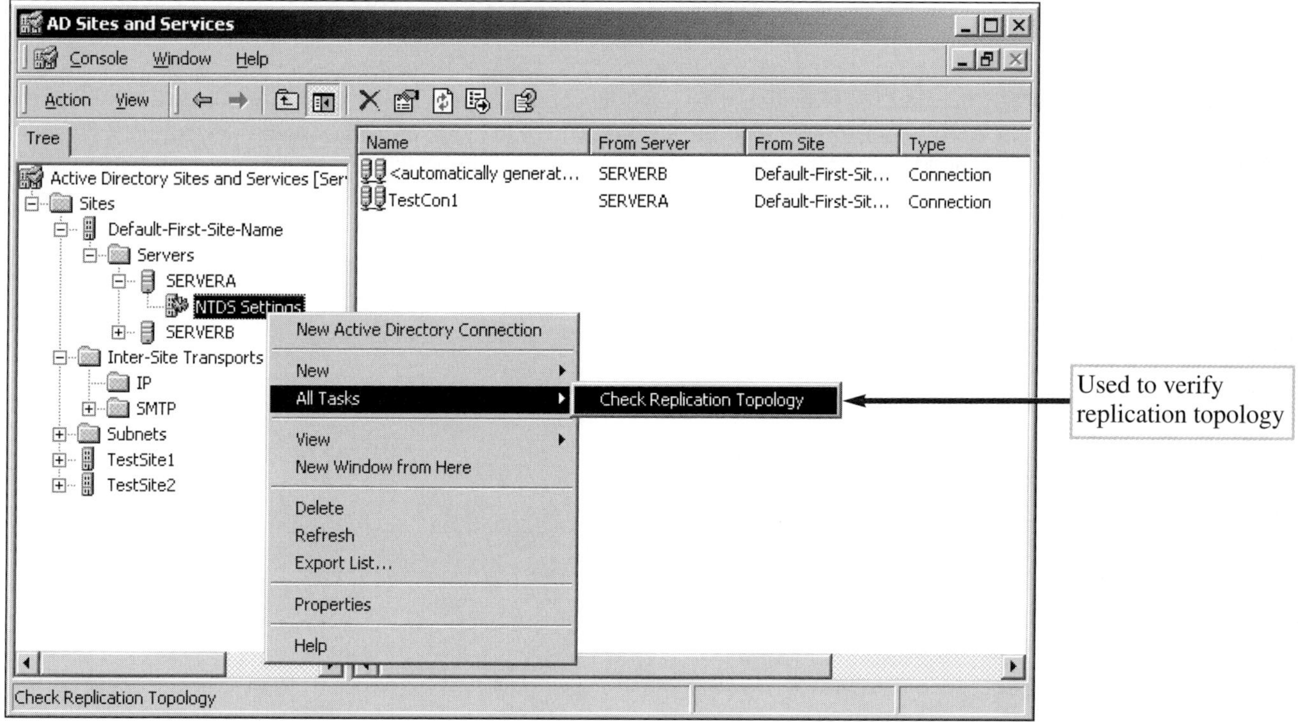

Figure 4-23 Check Replication Topology message box

skill 8 Checking Replication Topology (cont'd)

exam objective

Monitor, optimize, and troubleshoot Active Directory performance and replication.

more

Ineffective replication may result in a decrease in Active Directory performance. It may also result in poor directory information or unavailability of domain controllers. Some replication problems and their solutions are discussed in **Table 4-1**.

Table 4-1 Troubleshooting Replication Issues

Problem	Solution
A remote site uses a slow, unreliable connection, causing failures in replication.	An SMTP site link is preferred if a link is slow and unreliable. SMTP uses asynchronous replication, which means that the data is not time sensitive. While SMTP site links will use a larger amount of bandwidth overall, they are not affected nearly as much by link reliability as RPC, meaning that fewer retransmissions will be required on an unreliable link. This can actually improve performance, regardless of the additional bandwidth used. However, keep in mind that SMTP can only be used for inter-site replication between *different domains*. If this link exists between two sites in the same domain, then your only true solution to the problem is to purchase a faster, more stable link.
Directory information altered at domain controllers in one site is not being updated in domain controllers in other sites regularly.	The cause of this problem is usually a combination of a large replication interval and a short replication window in the site link schedule. Increase the time range for replication to occur or the frequency of replication within that time range. In case the replication is occurring through a site link bridge, check all site links in the bridge to isolate the site link that is restricting replication.
Replication traffic between sites is using a disproportionate amount of bandwidth on WAN links, causing problems with time-sensitive, business critical applications that also use the link.	This problem can have several possible causes, and therefore several possible solutions. Check each of the following: • Ensure that your site links mirror your replication topology. A common mistake is to use a single site link (such as the default site link) to connect all sites. A single site link should only be used when you have a fully meshed network. In any other case, AD will generate an incorrect topology and bandwidth waste can occur. • Ensure that domain controllers are placed in the correct sites. If domain controllers are all placed in a single site (another common mistake), then all replication will be intra-site replication, which is neither schedulable nor compressed. • If you are using a hub-and-spoke (also known as a star) topology, disabling site link bridging can usually reduce bandwidth consumption. Realize, however, that the tradeoff is that it takes longer for changes to be completely replicated. • If none of the previous solutions resolves the problem, modify your site link schedules so that replication is only allowed during off-peak hours. Be aware that this is a drastic measure and may cause issues on its own (such as a user account created at one site not replicating to another site until the next business day).
Replication of directory information has stopped.	Ensure that site links connect your sites to each other. If they do not, create site links as necessary to mirror your physical topology.

skill 9 Creating a Server Object in a Site

exam objective

Configure server objects. Considerations include site membership and global catalog designation.

overview

Server objects are representations of your domain controllers (and in some cases, member servers) in the Sites and Services console. AD will automatically create a server object for each domain controller you install. Server object placement is *extremely* important to proper topology generation, as the location of each server object is what AD uses to determine which site each server exists in. This is the sole information the KCC uses to determine the replication topology. As mentioned at the beginning of the lesson, AD will automatically place each server in the site that is associated with the subnet object that matches the server's IP address structure. However, this is performed *only* once, at domain controller creation, and is *never* changed by AD thereafter. Therefore, if you promote all of your domain controllers before you create the appropriate site and subnet objects for your network, you will need to manually move the objects into the correct sites in order to allow the KCC to generate the proper replication topology.

Note that while you can manually create server objects for your domain controllers, you should almost never need to. AD will create server objects for you automatically, and unless there is a fairly major database problem or a significant case of mistaken deletion, you shouldn't need to manually create them. The only other valid case of the need for manual server object creation is when running a site-aware application on a member server.

tip

In addition to AD, other products also can use AD sites to choose local servers. These applications are known as site-aware. At present, however, most of these applications (such as domain-based DFS) already run on domain controllers, so they will already have server objects to represent them.

how to

Create a server object in a site.

1. In the **AD Sites and Services** console, double-click the **TestSite1** site.
2. Right-click the Servers folder, point to **New**, and then click the **Server** command. The **New Object-Server** dialog box opens.
3. Type **TestServer1** in the **Name** text box **(Figure 4-24)**, and click OK.
4. The new server object appears in the **AD Sites and Services** console **(Figure 4-25)**.

Figure 4-24 Creating a server object

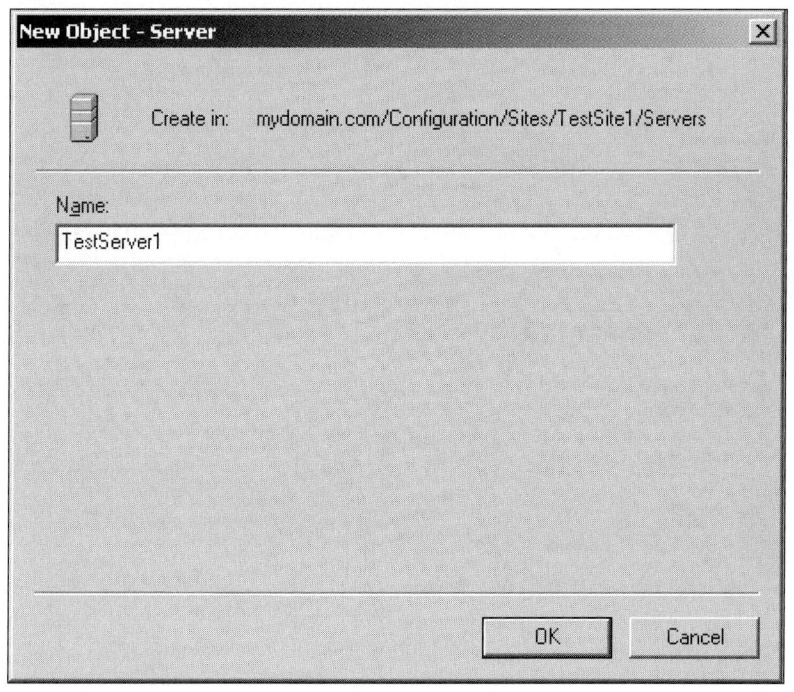

Figure 4-25 New server object in the site

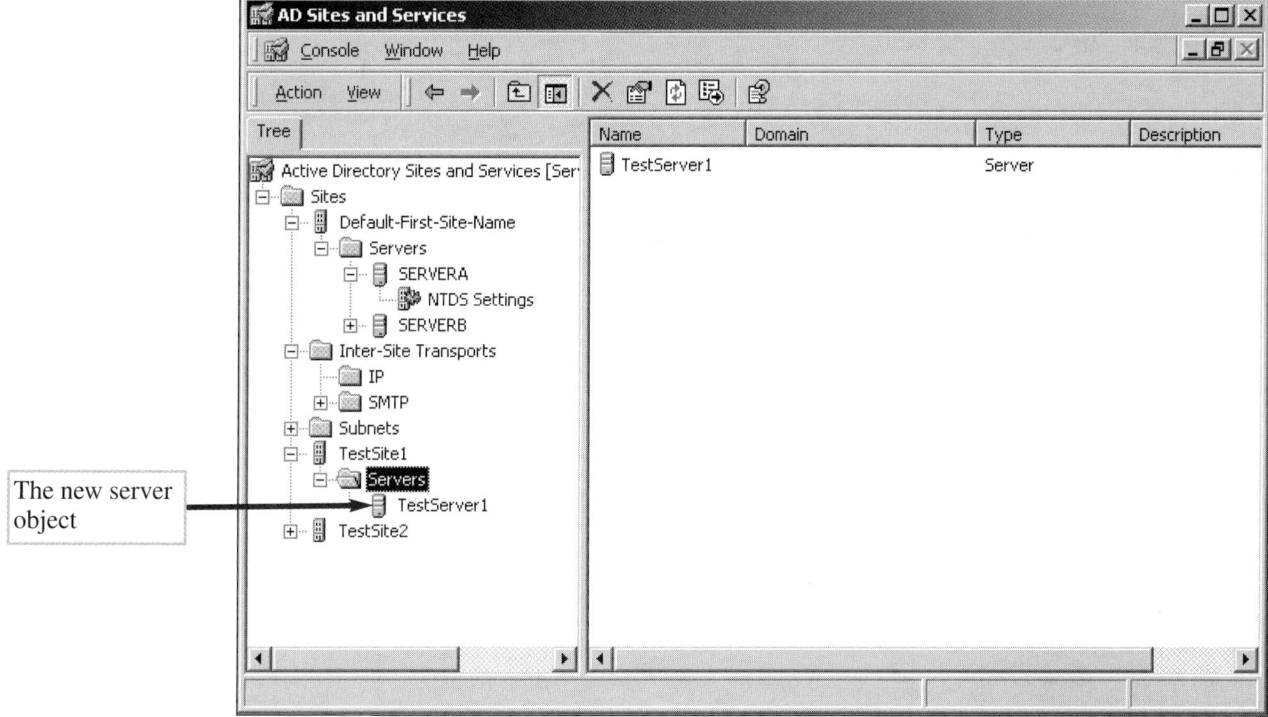

skill 10 Managing Server Objects

exam objective

Configure server objects. Considerations include site membership and global catalog designation.

overview

As an administrator, you need to manage server settings for a site as part of your maintenance tasks. You need to control replication and ensure that users are able to log on within a reasonable amount of time. In order to accomplish these tasks and create an efficient replication topology, you will occasionally need to move server objects between sites. Similarly, you may also need to identify non-functional servers and remove them from the sites.

You can move or remove server objects from Active Directory only if you have domain administrator rights.

tip

If a domain controller is demoted to a member server before being decommissioned, AD will remove its server object automatically. However, if the server simply fails, you will need to manually remove it.

how to

Move a server object between sites.

1. In the **AD Sites and Services** console, right-click **TestServer1** under the **TestSite1** folder, and then click the **Move** command. The **Move Server** dialog box opens.
2. Click the **TestSite2** option in the **Site Name** list box to select the site to which you want to move the server object (**Figure 4-26**)
3. Click OK. The server object appears in its new location in the **AD Sites and Services** console (**Figure 4-27**).

more

You can also remove a non-functional server object from a site. However, be very sure before you remove a server object from a site permanently.

Figure 4-26 Moving the server object to a different site

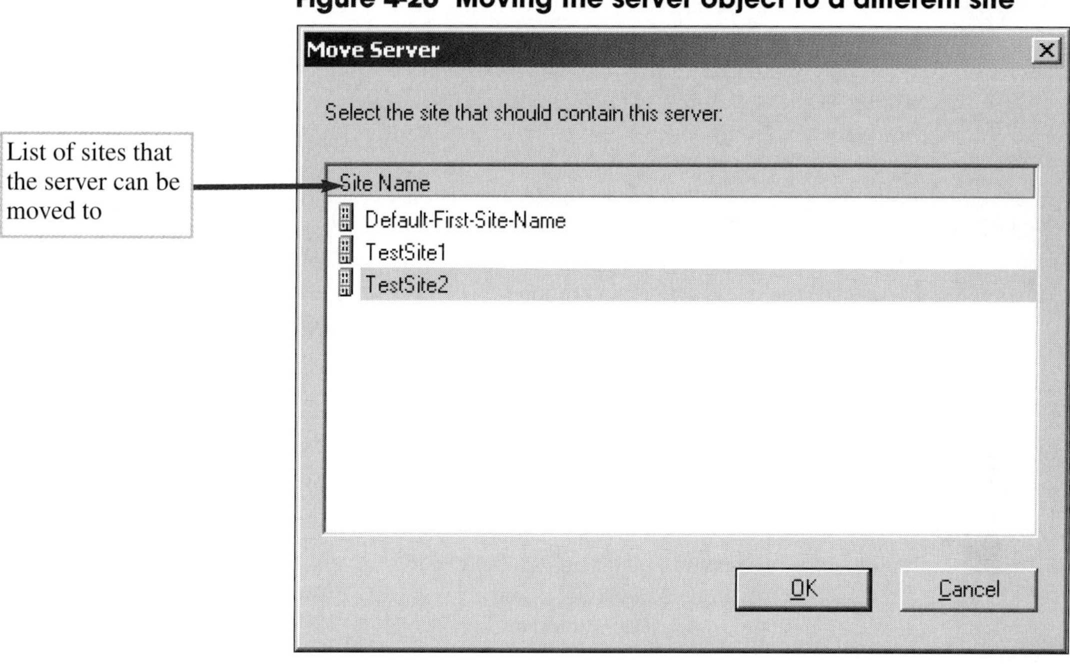

Figure 4-27 The server at its new location

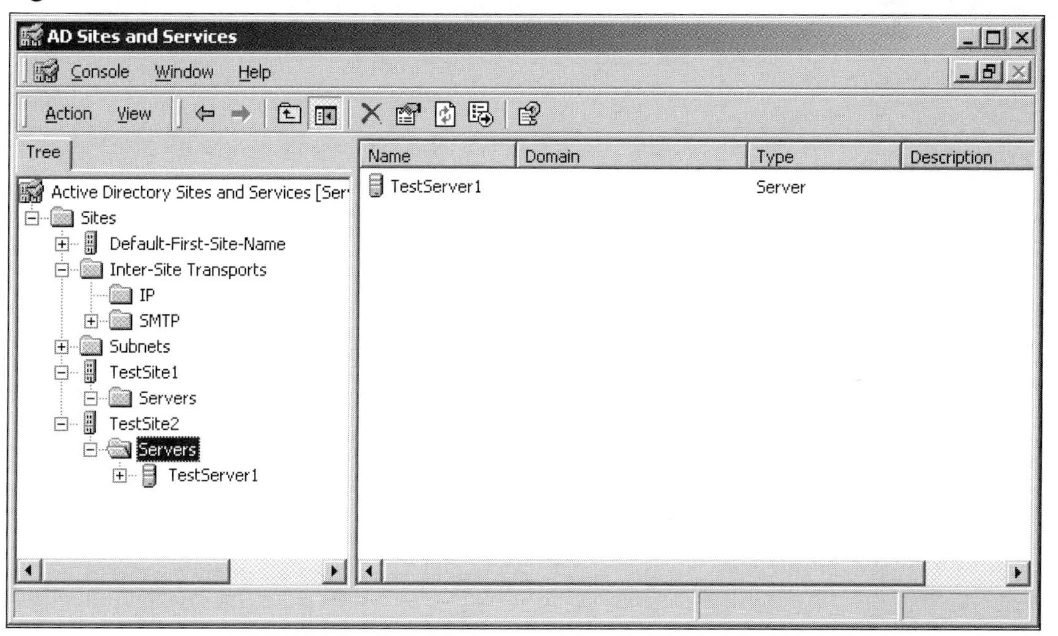

skill 11 Designating a Global Catalog Server

exam objective

Configure server objects. Considerations include site membership and global catalog designation.

overview

A **global catalog** is a database that stores a full, writable copy of the directory data for its own domain and a partial, read only copy of the directory databases for every other domain in the forest. The global catalog is stored on domain controllers that are designated as **global catalog servers**. Global catalog servers are required in Active Directory to facilitate enterprise searching, User Principal Name (UPN) lookups, and Universal group storage. Windows 2000 automatically creates the first global catalog server on the first domain controller installed to the forest. While there is only one global catalog server in a forest by default, there is no limit to the number of global catalog servers. However, you should keep in mind that every global catalog server requires more storage space to hold its database, and that global catalog servers replicate forest-wide, consuming additional bandwidth above and beyond that of a standard domain controller. In a native mode domain, Windows 2000 clients must have access to a global catalog server in order to log on.

tip

The only exception to this I rule is the Domain Administrators group. Members of the Domain Administrators group are allowed to log on to the network in all conditions by default.

Due to the important roles the global catalog servers play in AD, it is suggested that at least one global catalog server be placed in every physical site.

You can assign any domain controller as a global catalog server by setting the **Global Catalog** property in the **AD Sites and Services** console.

In addition to designating additional global catalog servers, you can also remove the global catalog server role from an existing global catalog server. This removes all of the information the server was storing that relates to other domains. However, whenever you remove the global catalog role, the size of the AD database on that server does not decrease. Instead, the database is now filled with a lot of additional "empty" space. In order to reduce the size of the database, you should reboot into directory services restore mode on the server in question, and compact the database (also known as an Offline Defrag) with the NTDSUtil tool. The steps for this process are available on Microsoft's web site at: http://www.microsoft.com/technet/prodtechnol/ad/windows2000/maintain/opsguide/Part2/ADOGdApB.asp?frame=true#p. Always ensure that you have a current backup before using the NTDSUtil tool.

how to

Designate a domain controller as a global catalog server.

1. Right-click the **NTDS Settings** object under the domain controller **Server01** in the **AD Sites and Services** console, and then click the **Properties** command. The **NTDS Settings Properties** dialog box opens.
2. Select the **Global Catalog** check box to make this domain controller a global catalog server (**Figure 4-28**), and then click OK.

more

Although all domain controllers can be configured as global catalog servers, you need to strike a balance when designating these servers. The global catalog maintains a subset of the directory information available within each domain. This information helps by allowing queries to be handled by the nearest global catalog server, and thus saves time and bandwidth. However, each additional global catalog server increases the amount of replication overhead within a network.

Figure 4-28 Designating a global catalog server

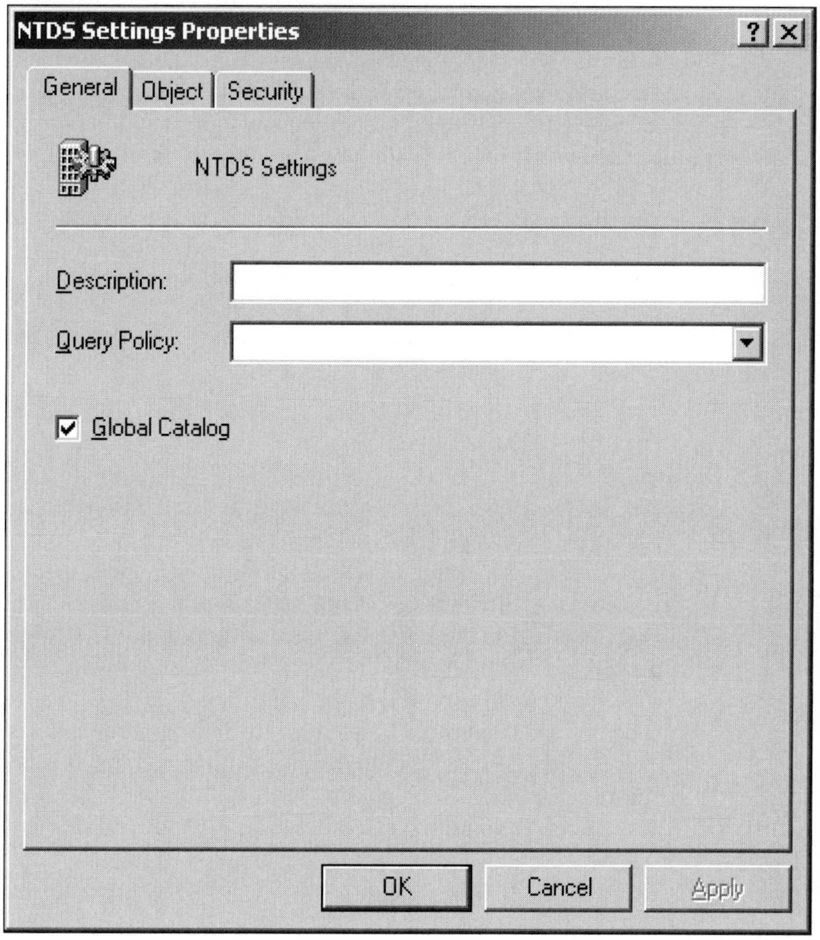

skill 12 Designating a Site License Server

exam objective

Basic knowledge

overview

A software license gives you the legal right to use a software application or program. For each software program that you use, you need a license, which is granted to you and documented in the software's license agreement. The Microsoft BackOffice licensing model governs licensing for Client Access Licenses (CALs) in relation to Microsoft Windows Server products. CALs are licenses allowing client machines to access a server product's features, and are typically sold on a one-per-connection (per server) or one-per-client (per seat) model.

The **site license server** in Windows 2000 gives an administrator the ability to monitor license purchases, deletions, and usage of the software to ensure an organization's legal compliance with the BackOffice software license agreement. In Windows 2000 Server, the License Logging service in a site replicates this licensing information to a centralized database on the site license server for the site. The site license server is usually the first domain controller created for the site.

tip

Although it is not compulsory for a site license server to be a domain controller, it is preferred that they be in the same site for optimal performance. In a large organization with multiple sites, the site license server in each site collects licensing information for that site separately.

how to

Designate a site license server.

1. Click the **TestSite1** folder in the **AD Sites and Services** console. The details pane displays the **Licensing Site Settings** object.
2. Right-click the **Licensing Site Settings** object, and then click the **Properties** command. The **Licensing Site Settings Properties** dialog box opens.
3. Click Change... in the **Licensing Computer** section. The **Select Computer** dialog box opens.
4. Click **ServerA (Figure 4-29)**, and then click OK to close the **Select Computer** dialog box and display the **Licensing Site Settings Properties** dialog box.
5. Click OK to assign the **ServerA** domain controller as the licensing computer **(Figure 4-30)**. The **Licensing Site Settings Properties** dialog box will close.
6. Close the **AD Sites and Services** console.

more

A site administrator or an administrator for the site license server can view the licensing details for an entire site by accessing the **Licensing** console from the **Administrative Tools** menu. The **Licensing** console enables you to manage client access licensing for an enterprise. It also helps in administering and tracking licensing data for a site in the centralized licensing database on the site license server.

Figure 4-29 Selecting a computer for site licensing

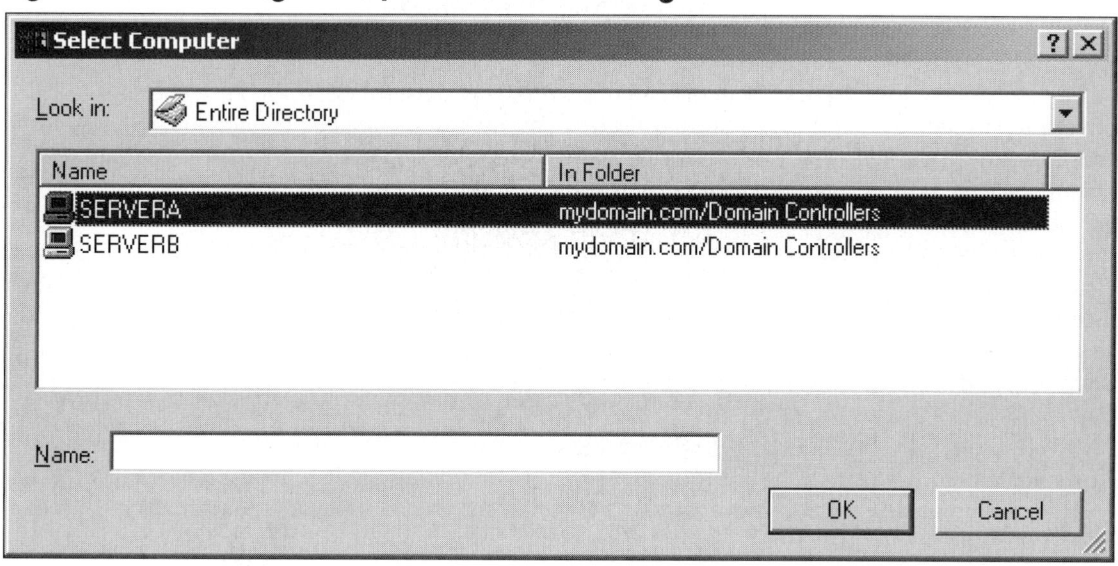

Figure 4-30 Specifying the licensing computer

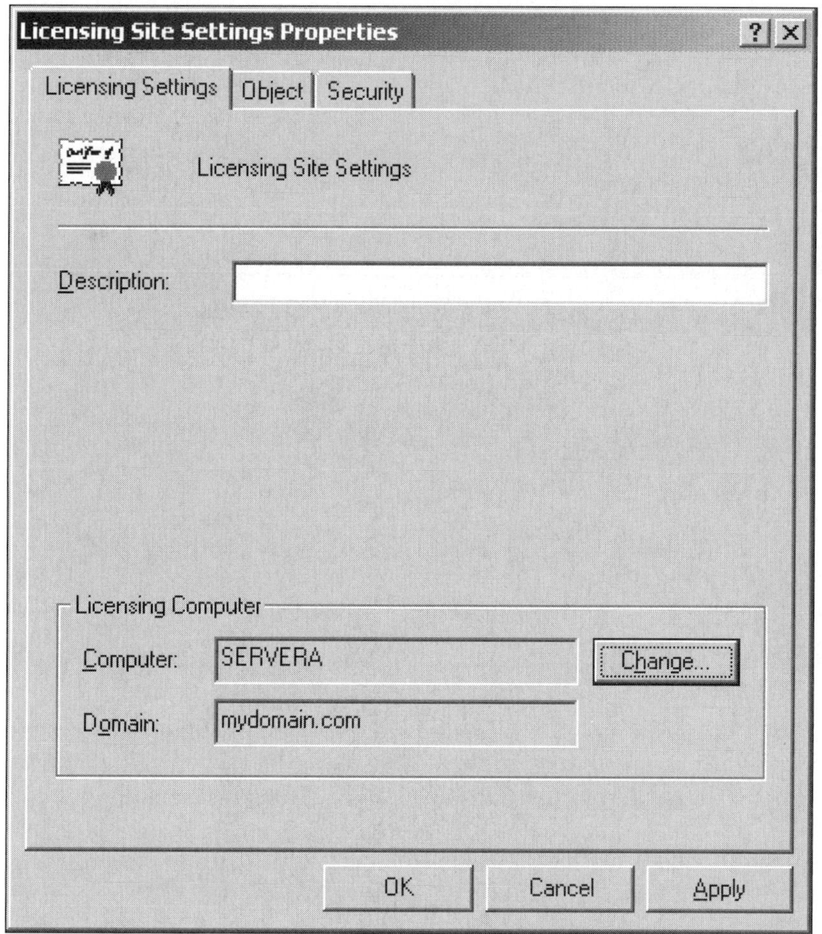

Summary

- Objects such as sites, subnets, site links, servers, and connection objects that form the physical structure of Active Directory control the replication of data among domain controllers within a domain, as well as between domains. These objects help AD operate within the boundaries of the physical structure of your organization.
- Sites define the physical layout of the network for Active Directory by organizing domain controllers and clients in relation to a physical location.
- A subnet is a range of addresses associated with a site. Subnets define boundaries for a site.
- Site links are a means of linking two or more sites for replication purposes.
- Inter-site replication is the process of copying information from one site to another. Inter-site replication is always compressed for changes in excess of 50KB, and is controllable through replication schedules and intervals.
- Intra-site replication is replication between domain controllers in a single site. Intra-site replication is always uncompressed, and is uncontrollable (replication will occur around 5 minutes after each change).
- A site link's cost, replication interval, and replication schedule can all be configured to modify inter-site replication behavior.
- By default, all site links are transitive. However, the automatic bridging features of AD can be disabled for special situations.
- The KCC creates connection objects automatically. However, you can manually add and delete connections or even force replication over a connection if required.
- Bridgehead servers are the main link for exchange of directory information between sites. Although you can specify more than one preferred bridgehead server, only one will act as the active preferred bridgehead server at any time.
- You can use the AD Sites and Services console to verify replication topology, which is a method of manually triggering a KCC computation. This process checks only for objects created automatically and does not affect manually created connection objects. Global catalog servers are required in Active Directory to facilitate enterprise searching, User Principal Name (UPN) lookups, and Universal group storage.
- You need to assign a domain controller, preferably the first, as the site license server for a site. In Windows 2000 Server, the License Logging service in a site replicates the licensing information on the centralized database of the site license server.

Key Terms

Site
Subnets
Site links
SMTP replication
IP replication
Inter-site replication
Intra-site replication
Site link attributes
Site link bridges
Transitive site links
Connections
Connection objects
Knowledge Consistency Checker
Bridgehead server
Replication topology
Global catalog servers
Site license server

Test Yourself

1. Which of the following is a basic function of a site within Active Directory?
   a. Sites are used to group subnets and domain controllers together so that Active Directory can be replicated efficiently.
   b. Sites are used to group all subnets together based on the efficiency of a network.
   c. Sites are used to hold all domain controllers together for the purpose of managing them.
   d. Sites are used to define boundaries for subnets.
2. Which of the following is a function of subnets in Active Directory?
   a. Subnets interact with site links and site link bridges to route replication traffic.
   b. Subnets are used to allow AD to determine which site a client is a member of.
   c. Subnets facilitate Active Directory replication with the help of domain controllers.
   d. Subnets help to locate domain controllers.
3. Which of the following tasks do you need to perform at the time of creation of a site link?
   a. The site link cost must be configured.
   b. The site replication frequency must be set.

c. The replication schedule must be configured.
d. At least two sites must be added to the site link.

4. Which of the following is the main function of a site link?
a. A site link combines a set of subnets connected using high-speed networking.
b. A site link is used to provide a logical path between sites so domain controllers in different sites can replicate.
c. Site links are used to specify the best network route to use for replication.
d. Site links serve as a focal point for replication between sites.

5. A site license server is required to be a domain controller.
a. True
b. False

6. Site A is connected to Site B by a LAN; Site B is connected to Site C by a T1 line; Site C is connected to Site D by an ISDN line; Site D is connected to Site A by a 56K dial-up connection. Site A is also connected to Site C by an ISDN connection. Link costs for each connection are shown below.

Site link	Link cost
AB	2
BC	4
CD	7
AC	7
AD	16

Which of the following is the best site link bridging configuration for replicating traffic between Site A and Site D using the lowest-cost route?
a. Create a site link bridge ABCD to route replication traffic from A to D.
b. No further links are required; Site A and Site D are connected via site link AD.
c. Create a site link ACD to route replication traffic from Site A to Site D.
d. Create a site link using two Site AD links; this will double the speed at which replication occurs.

7. You can modify the replication schedule for an automatically generated connection.
a. True
b. False

8. Which of the following is the basic function of a bridgehead server?
a. It serves as the main server used for inter-site replication.
b. It links domain controllers for replication.
c. It serves as the main server used for replication within a site.
d. It links sites together for replication.

9. Which of the following options would you choose if you need to reduce the load of a domain that is generating excessive replication traffic, which represents about 32% of all traffic for several subnets?
a. Modify the replication schedules for all automatically generated connections so that replication occurs during off-hours.
b. Manually create connection objects to route replication traffic over underutilized subnets.
c. Redistribute the replication load over underutilized subnets and create new site links and site link bridges.
d. Create a new set of connection objects and set their replication schedules for off-hours.

10. Which of the following will be the outcome when you remove all of the global catalog servers from a native mode domain with all Windows 2000 clients?
a. The Active Directory replication traffic stops.
b. No one but domain administrators will be able to log on to the domain.
c. You will be able to access any Active Directory information.
d. The replication load on Active Directory increases since it must create more connection objects to handle increased replication traffic.

11. It is recommended that there be at least one global catalog in every site.
a. True
b. False

Projects: On Your Own

1. Create a site and a subnet:
a. Log on as an Administrator.
b. Open the **AD Sites and Services** console.
c. Create a new site, **StudentSite1**, using the site link object **DEFAULTIPSITELINK**.
d. Create a new subnet using the IP address **10.10.6.1** and subnet mask **255.255.0.0**.
e. Select the site **StudentSite1** to associate with this subnet.

2. Configure a site link and set its attributes:
a. Open the **AD Sites and Services** console.
b. Create a new site, **StudentSite2**, using the link object **DEFAULTIPSITELINK**.
c. Create a new site link, **StudentSiteLink1**. Add the sites **StudentSite1** and **StudentSite2** to this link.
d. Set the site link cost to **80** and the site link replication frequency to **120**. Make the connection available at

all times on Saturday and Sunday and between 6 P.M. and 8 A.M. on weekdays.

3. Create a server object in a site, and then move it to another site:

a. Create a new server object **StudentServer1** in the site **StudentSite1**.

b. Move the server object **StudentServer1** to a different site, **StudentSite2**.

Problem Solving Scenarios

1. You have been assigned the task of administering a newly installed Windows 2000 ADS-based network. There are five domains, named OurCompany.com, BR1.OurCompany.com, BR2.OurCompany.com, and so on. The OurCompany.com domain is the root domain, while all others are child domains.

Currently, as per the default installation, all domains are on one site. The OurCompany.com domain uses the IP range 210.14.15.x/24, BR1 uses 210.14.15.x/24, BR2 uses 210.14.16.x/24, BR3 uses 210.14.17.x/24 and BR4 uses 210.14.18.x/24. All of these domains are connected via WAN links.

Write a memo describing the steps required to properly configure sites and subnet objects to optimize replication and ADS performance.

2. You administer a Windows 2000 ADS-based network, which contains four sites named A, B, C, and D. Site A and Site D are connected via a 128 kbps link, Site A and Sites B and C are connected via 64 kbps links. Due to increased operations on ADS, the amount of data being replicated from site D has substantially increased. As of now, since Site D has no direct connection with either Site B or Site C, all replication traffic gets routed twice through Site A. This results in an overloaded network at Site A.

You are required to resolve the overload issue. Prepare a document describing the steps you need to take to do so.

LESSON

5 Administering User Accounts

In Microsoft Windows 2000 Server, Microsoft Active Directory stores information about all users in a domain. User information is stored in the form of **user accounts**, which consist of information like the user logon name, first name, last name, and password. A user account is a form of identification of a user in a domain that lets the user gain access to resources on a network or on a local machine. There are three types of user accounts that Windows 2000 Server provides: local user accounts, domain user accounts, and built-in user accounts.

Local user accounts are created to enable a user to log on only to a specific computer and to gain access only to the resources on that computer. Conversely, domain user accounts are meant to allow users to log on to a domain and gain access to network resources. Finally, built-in user accounts are created by default during the installation of Windows 2000 Server and are used typically by administrators. Other users can also use them to gain access to network resources. Examples of built-in accounts are Administrator and Guest.

As part of your duties as administrator, you need to maintain the user accounts. This includes performing tasks, such as modifying user accounts, and resetting passwords. For each user account, Windows 2000 automatically creates a user profile the first time the account is used to log on to a computer. User profiles contain a user's personal data, desktop settings that define the user's work environment, network connections that are established when the user logs on to the network, and so on, all of which are applied each time the user logs on to the system. The three types of user profiles include local user profiles, roaming user profiles, and mandatory user profiles.

Windows 2000 provides the My Documents folder as the default location for users to store their data. However, Windows 2000 Server allows you to select another location, called the home folder, as the default location for storage.

Goals

In this lesson, you will learn about the various types of user accounts and user profiles in Windows 2000 Server. You will learn to create the local and domain user accounts, set user account properties, and maintain user accounts. You will also learn to create a roaming user profile and a home folder.

Lesson 5 Administering User Accounts

Skill	*Exam 70-217 Objective*
1. Planning Strategies for Creating User Accounts	Create and manage objects manually or by using scripting.
2. Creating a Local User Account	Create and manage objects manually or by using scripting.
3. Creating a Domain User Account	Create and manage objects manually or by using scripting.
4. Setting User Account Properties	Create and manage objects manually or by using scripting.
5. Introducing User Profiles	Basic knowledge
6. Creating a Roaming User Profile	Basic knowledge
7. Creating a Home Folder on a Server	Basic knowledge
8. Maintaining User Accounts	Create and manage objects manually or by using scripting.

Requirements

During this lesson, you will need to have administrative rights on a domain controller and a member server. As a prerequisite, you should know how to create and share folders, and change their desktop settings. You should also have administrator rights for using the machines.

skill 1 Planning Strategies for Creating User Accounts

exam objective

Create and manage objects manually or by using scripting.

overview

A **user account** is a form of identification for a user on a Windows 2000 network. A user account is used to build the user ticket (also known as a TGT, or Ticket Granting Ticket). The user ticket contains a list of the **Security IDs (SIDs)** associated with the user account and all groups that user account is a member of. The user ticket is used to prove that the user account is valid, and is used to construct session tickets. When the user wishes to access a resource, the operating system sends the user ticket to the domain controller with a special Kerberos request. The session ticket is presented to the specific machine controlling the resources (such as a file server, for instance) as a form of identification. The resource server will compare the SIDs in the token to a **Discretionary Access Control List (DACL)** on the resource. DACLs are composed of **Access Control Entries (ACEs)**. Each ACE contains the SID of a user account or group and the permissions applied to it.

tip

In addition to scripting, you can also create user accounts in batches from a CSV (Comma Separated Values) or LDIF (LDAP Importation File) file using the utilities csvde.exe or ldifde.exe.

You can create user accounts manually or by writing scripts. To create accounts manually, you use the Active Directory Users and Computers console. To script a user account, you need to be familiar with at least one scripting language such as VBScript or JScript.

It is very important to plan the process of creating user accounts before actually creating them. Planning will reduce the time you will take to create the required user accounts and will simplify the management of these accounts. The parameters that you need to plan for before creating user accounts are naming conventions, password requirements, and account options.

A naming convention is important for several reasons. A good naming convention makes it easy for users to remember their logon names, while also providing for cases in which two users are named the same (such as John P. Doe and John S. Doe). **Table 5-1** lists the factors that you need to take into consideration while deciding on a naming convention for your organization.

Each user account will typically have a password, as passwords can prevent unauthorized user access to a domain or a computer. **Table 5-2** describes standards for using passwords.

Table 5-1 Factors to be considered for naming conventions of user accounts

Factors	Details
Local user accounts	Create unique local user account names for every user on the user's local machine. As a general rule, you should only create local accounts for computers that are *not* members of a domain.
Domain user accounts	Create a unique logon name for every user in the directory. You also need to ensure that the user's full name is unique to the OU where you create the domain user account.
Character limit in user names	The user logon names you create should consist of no more than 20 uppercase or lowercase characters. This is because Windows 2000 recognizes only the first 20 characters even if more characters are entered.
Case-insensitivity	Since user logon names are not case-sensitive, you might use a combination of alphanumeric and special characters to help uniquely identify user accounts.
Invalid characters	There are certain invalid characters that you cannot use in user logon names. These include: " [ ] / \ = , + ! * ? < > :
Employees with same names	The naming convention should ensure that users with the same name can be differentiated. To accomplish this, you might use a combination of the user's first name and initials to form the user logon names. For example, the user logon names for two users named Mary Ann could be Marya and Maryann. You can also use other ways to distinguish users with the same name.
Employee type identification	In some organizations, you may have to distinguish employees by their category or division. For example, a user named Kelly Greg, who works in the Sales division, could have a user logon name KellyG-Sales. A more common approach is to identify temporary employees with an underscore, such as bobsmith for the temporary employee named Bob Smith. This allows you to sort the user list by name and have all temporary employees gravitate to the top of the list.
E-mail compatibility	Ensure the compatibility of the user principal name with e-mail accounts, as some e-mail applications do not accept certain characters such as spaces.

Table 5-2 Factors to be considered while specifying passwords

Factors	Details
Password for Administrator	An administrator account should always have a complex password to prevent unauthorized access to the account.
Controlling the passwords	As an administrator, you can decide whether you want to assign unique passwords for user accounts and prevent users from changing them, or allow users to choose their own passwords.
Picking the password	Always use passwords that are not very easy to guess. For example, it is not as easy to guess a password that has a combination of letters and numerals. Second, passwords should not be related to anything personal. For instance, even though Sandra721 might seem like a strong password, if Sandra is a person you know and July 21st is her birthday, it is a particularly poor choice. Next, when you use a new password, don't use passwords that are similar to the passwords you were using earlier. Finally, and perhaps most importantly, teach your users these tips to help secure passwords network-wide.
Maximum character limit	Windows 2000 supports passwords of up to 127 characters. However, you should typically refrain from creating passwords with over 14 characters, as Windows 98 only supports 14 character passwords. For increased security, passwords should always have at least eight characters.
Valid characters	To form a password, you can select characters from these groups: uppercase and lowercase letters, numerals, and non-alphanumeric characters. Passwords *are* case-sensitive.

skill 1

Planning Strategies for Creating User Accounts *(cont'd)*

exam objective

Create and manage objects manually or by using scripting.

overview

It is also important to consider the following options before creating user accounts.

- **Log On To:** This option enables you to specify which computers a user can log on to. By default, users are allowed to log on to any computer in the domain. However, you can enter specific computer names (NetBIOS names) into this field to limit which PCs this user account can log on to.
- **Logon Hours:** The logon hours section lets you specify which hours of the day and days of the week a user can log on. This is primarily used in high security environments where users must be allowed access only during business hours.
- **Account Expires:** This section allows you to predefine when this user account will expire. The user account will still exist; however, it will be disabled after this date, making it unusable for login. This is useful when you have large numbers of contract employees who only need access for a specific period of time.

These options can be specified on the **Account** tab in the **Properties** dialog box for a user account **(Figure 5-1)**. To display this dialog box, right-click any user object in the **Active Directory Users and Computers** console and then click the **Properties** command.

caution

The "Logon To" portion of AD is one of several that still require the use of legacy NetBIOS naming. In order for this option to function, NetBIOS names must be resolvable either through broadcast, LMHosts, or WINS.

more

If you know how to write scripts, you will find that scripting user accounts is a fast process since it requires no interaction with any Active Directory GUI. A key advantage of using scripts to create user accounts is that you can add a large number of user accounts at one go. Creating user accounts manually could become a time consuming process where you would need to specify various properties in different tabs for each account. In such a case, by using scripts, you can create a script that specifies various parameters of the account. Here, you are not required to provide values to the options manually as all parameters are included in the script file.

You can use **Active Directory Services Interfaces (ADSI)** to create scripts. ADSI is a fully programmable automation object available for administrators.

tip

Any time you create new accounts, regardless of the method used, you need to have permission to create new objects in the destination organizational unit (OU).

Figure 5-1 Specifying user account properties

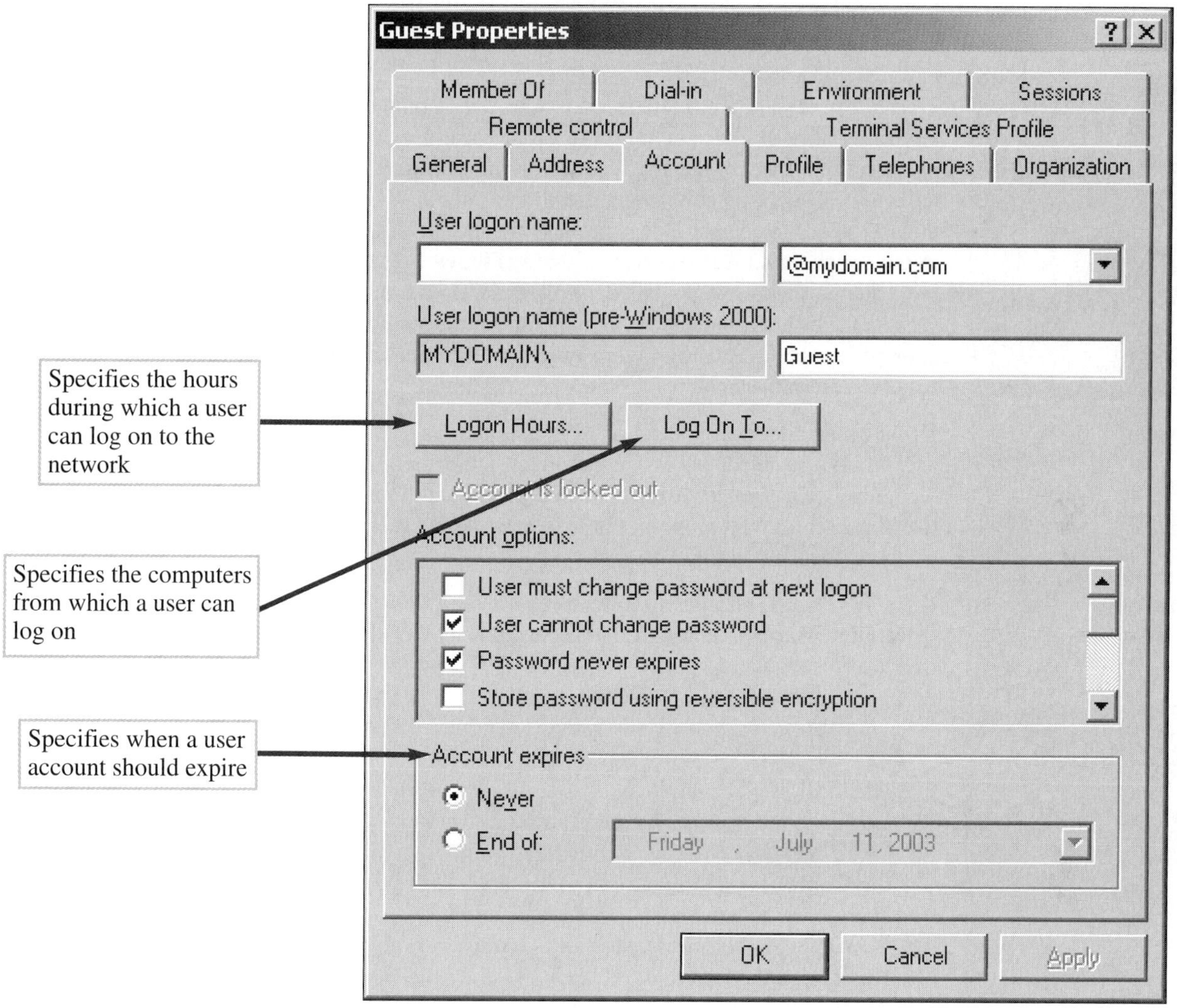

Guest Properties

Member Of | Dial-in | Environment | Sessions

Remote control | Terminal Services Profile

General | Address | Account | Profile | Telephones | Organization

User logon name:

@mydomain.com

User logon name (pre-Windows 2000):

MYDOMAIN\ Guest

Specifies the hours during which a user can log on to the network → Logon Hours...

Specifies the computers from which a user can log on → Log On To...

Account is locked out

Account options:

- User must change password at next logon
- User cannot change password
- Password never expires
- Store password using reversible encryption

Specifies when a user account should expire → Account expires

- Never
- End of: Friday , July 11, 2003

OK Cancel Apply

skill 2 Creating a Local User Account

exam objective

Create and manage objects manually or by using scripting.

overview

caution

You cannot create local user accounts on a domain controller.

tip

In general, you should avoid creating local accounts on computers that are members of a domain.

Local user accounts are created so that users log on only to a specific computer, and access the resources only on that computer. In order for a user using a local user account to access resources on other computers (without having to enter a separate username and password), a local user account must be created with the same name and password on all computers that the user needs to access. This is because the local user account that you create is stored only in the computer's local security database **(Figure 5-2)**, and Windows 2000 Server does not replicate the account to domain controllers. When a user logs on to a computer, the computer uses its local security database to authenticate the local user account. Similarly, when a user attempts to access a workgroup resource, the computer providing the resource authenticates the user account against its local accounts database.

If you create a local user account on a computer that requires access to domain resources, the user will not be able to access the resources in the domain. This is because the domain will not recognize local user accounts. Also, the domain administrator will not be able to administer the local user account properties or assign access permissions to the user for domain resources using the local computer.

If you have administrative rights, you can use the **Local Users and Groups** snap-in within the **Computer Management** console to create, delete, or disable local user accounts on a local computer.

how to

Create a local user account.

1. Log on to the member server as an Administrator.
2. Click **Start**, point to **Programs**, point to **Administrative Tools**, and then click the **Computer Management** command. This displays the **Computer Management** console.
3. Double-click the **Local Users and Groups** snap-in to view the Users folder.
4. Right-click the Users folder, and then click the **New User** command. This will display the **New User** dialog box.
5. Type **DonnaS** in the **User name** text box.
6. Type **Donna Smith** in the **Full name** text box.
7. Type **helloworld** in the **Password** text box.
8. Re-type **helloworld** in the **Confirm Password** text box.
9. Select the **User must change password at next logon** check box. This ensures that once the password is changed, only the user will know the password **(Figure 5-3)**.
10. Click **Create** to create the user account. The new local user account for Donna Smith is displayed in the Details pane of the **Computer Management** console.
11. Click the **Close** button to close the New User dialog box.
12. Close the **Computer Management** console.

Figure 5-2 Local security database

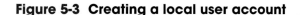

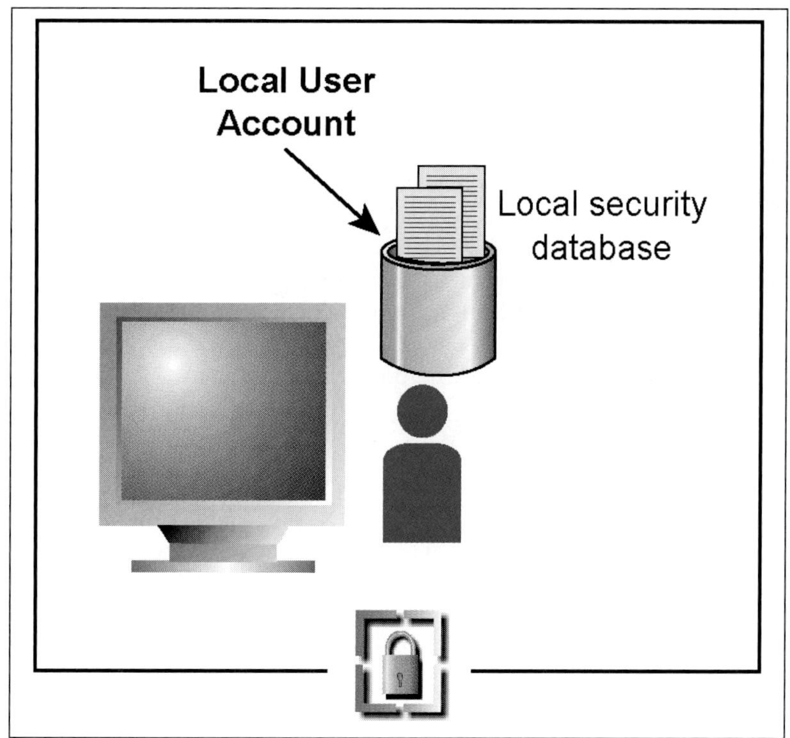
Local User Account
Local security database

Figure 5-3 Creating a local user account

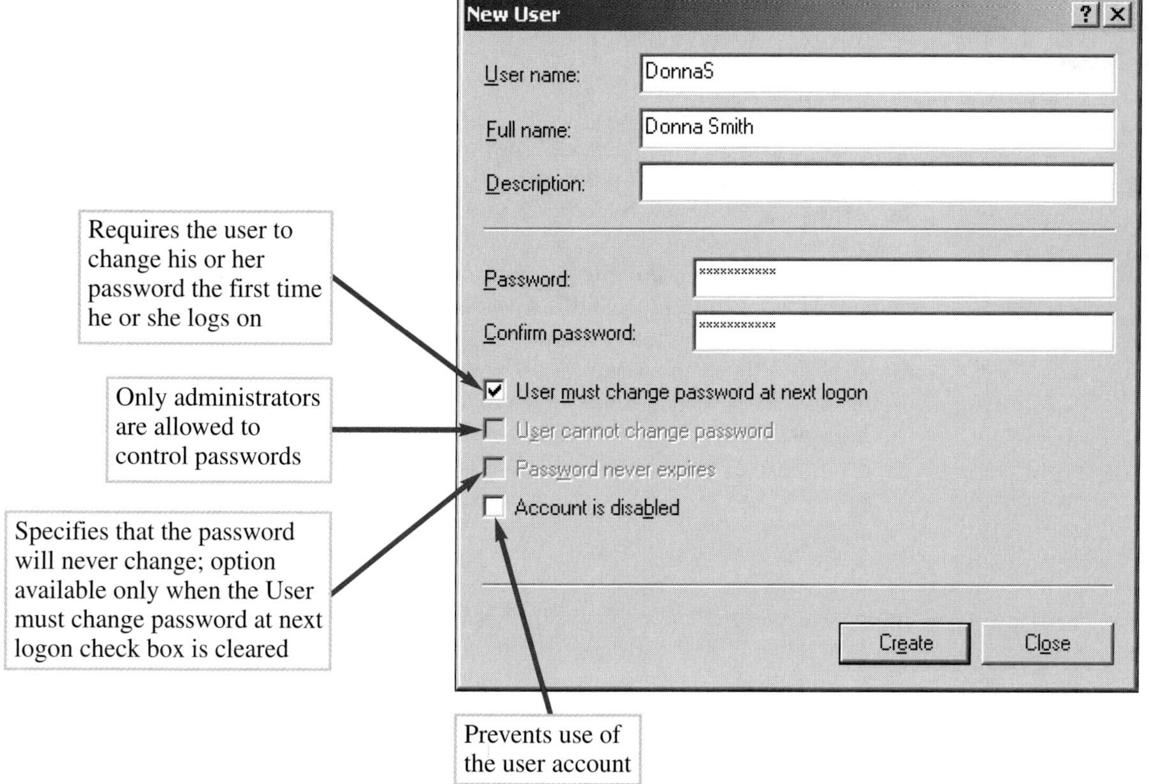
New User
User name: DonnaS
Full name: Donna Smith
Description:
Password:
Confirm password:
User must change password at next logon
User cannot change password
Password never expires
Account is disabled
Create
Close
Requires the user to change his or her password the first time he or she logs on
Only administrators are allowed to control passwords
Specifies that the password will never change; option available only when the User must change password at next logon check box is cleared
Prevents use of the user account

skill 3 Creating a Domain User Account

exam objective

Create and manage objects manually or by using scripting.

overview

You use a **domain user account** to log on to a domain and access network resources. You can create a domain user account in an OU on a domain controller, as shown in **Figure 5-4**. The domain controller then replicates the new user account information to all of the other domain controllers in the domain. After replication, all of the domain controllers in the domain will be able to authenticate the user during logon. In addition, all trusting domains may now allow the user account to gain access to their resources. You can use the **Active Directory Users and Computers** console to create domain user accounts.

During the logon process, a user provides a logon name and password (or, alternately, inserts his or her smartcard and provides a PIN). Windows 2000 Server uses this information to authenticate the user and build a user ticket that contains the user's identification and security settings. The purpose of the user ticket is to identify the user account in order to build session tickets, which are then used to identify the user to the domain member computers on which the user tries to access resources. An access token is then generated to identify the user and the groups to which the user belongs on the local computer. The access token remains available for the duration of the logon session.

Active Directory domain names are usually the full DNS name of the domain. However, for backward compatibility, each domain also has a pre-Windows 2000 name that is used by computers running pre-Windows 2000 operating systems. The pre-Windows 2000 domain name can be used to log on to a Windows 2000 domain from computers running pre-Windows 2000 operating systems. Thus, the same format can also be used to log on to a Windows 2000 domain from computers running Windows 2000.

how to

Create domain user accounts.

1. Log on to the domain controller as an Administrator.
2. Click Start, point to **Programs**, point to **Administrative Tools**, and then click the **Active Directory Users and Computers** command. This will display the **Active Directory Users and Computers** console.
3. Right-click the **Users** folder, point to **New**, and click the **User** command. This will display the **New Object-User** dialog box.
4. Type **Jack** in the **First name** text box.
5. Type **M** in the **Initials** text box and **Willis** in the **Last name** text box. Note that Jack's full name gets filled into the **Full name** text box automatically.
6. Type **JWillis** in the **User logon name** text box. Note that a pre-Windows 2000 logon name is automatically created. This name is the same as the user logon name (**Figure 5-5**).

Figure 5-4 Domain user account

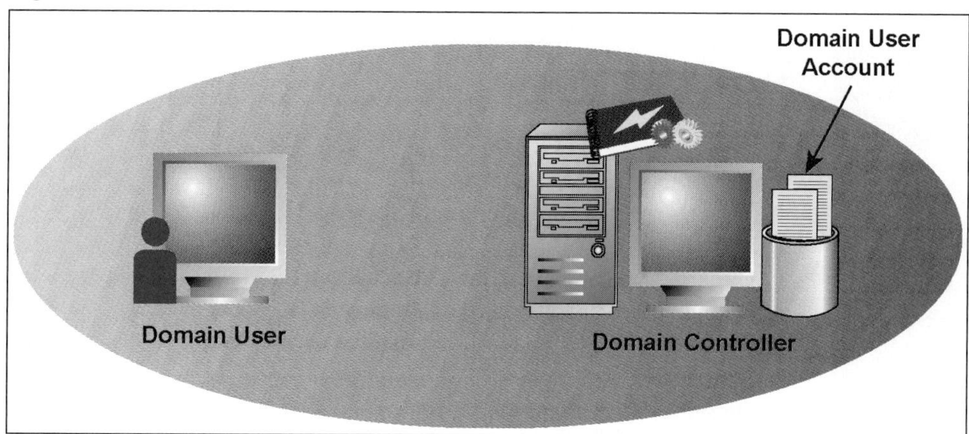

Figure 5-5 Creating a domain user account

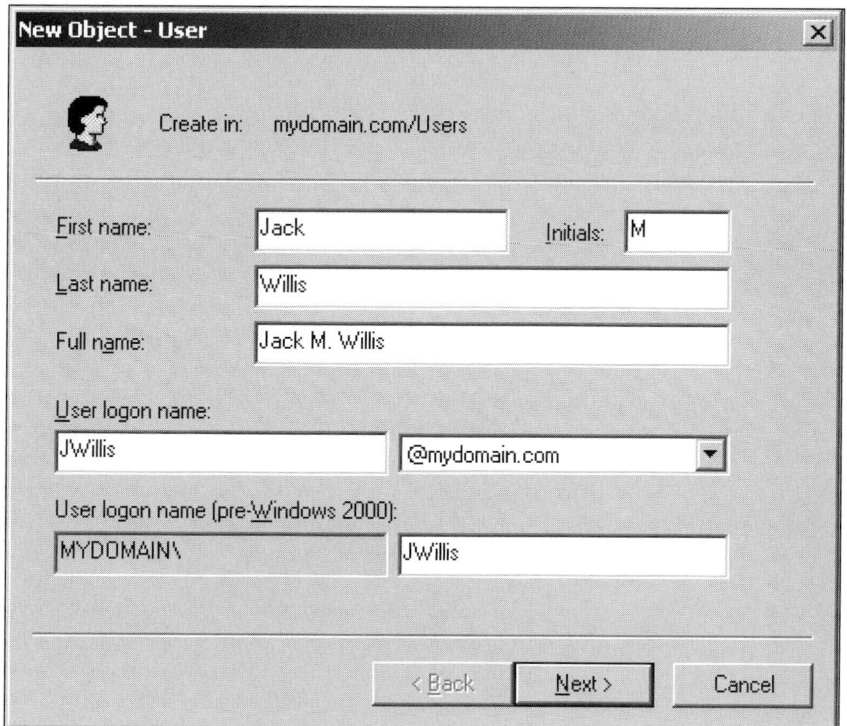

skill 3 Creating a Domain User Account (cont'd)

exam objective

Create and manage objects manually or by using scripting.

how to

7. Click [Next >] to display the options that enable you to specify the user's initial password.
8. Type an appropriate password in the **Password** text box.
9. Retype the password in the **Confirm password** text box.
10. Select the **User must change password at next logon** check box, as shown in **Figure 5-6**.
11. Click [Next >]. The **New Object-User** dialog box displays the options you have configured for this user account (**Figure 5-7**).
12. Click [Finish] after verifying that the user account options are correct. You can click [< Back] to modify the user details and settings. The Details pane of the **Active Directory Users and Computers** console displays the user account you have created (**Figure 5-8**).
13. Similarly, create another user account for **Barbara J. Clarke** with the user logon name **BClarke**.

more

You can use the Administrator **built-in user account** to perform administrative tasks. You can also use it to gain access to network resources. You can use the built-in Administrator account to perform administrative tasks like creating and managing user accounts, assigning permissions to user accounts to access resources, and so on. You can use the built-in Guest account to give users access to resources for a short time. The Guest account is disabled by default.

Figure 5-6 Specifying password for a new domain user account

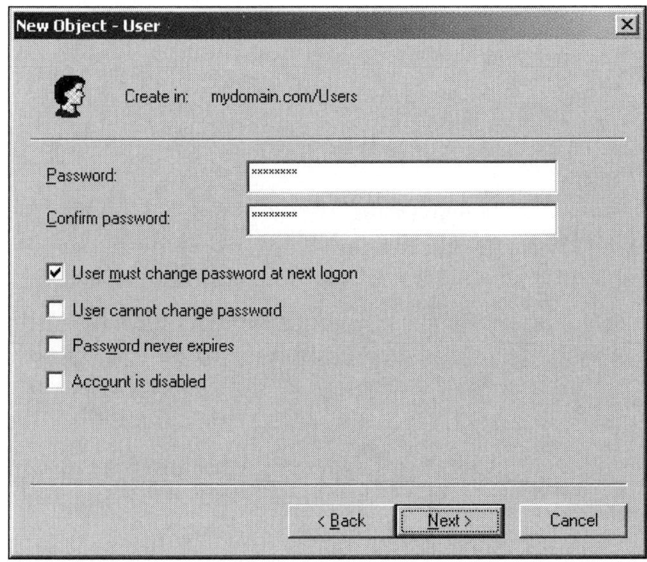

Figure 5-7 Summary screen for a new domain user account

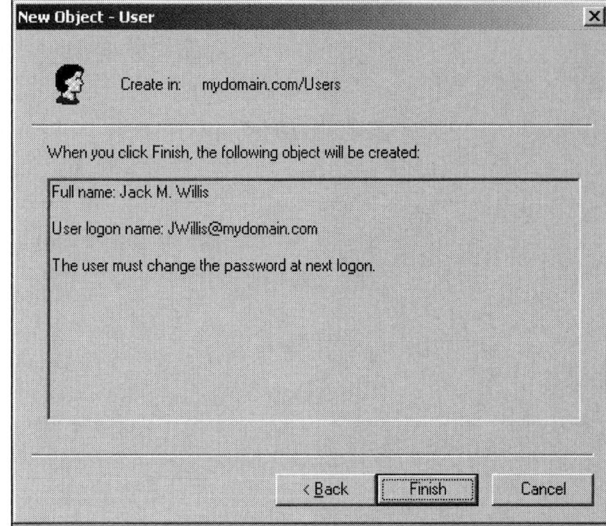

Figure 5-8 The new user in the Active Directory Users and Computers console

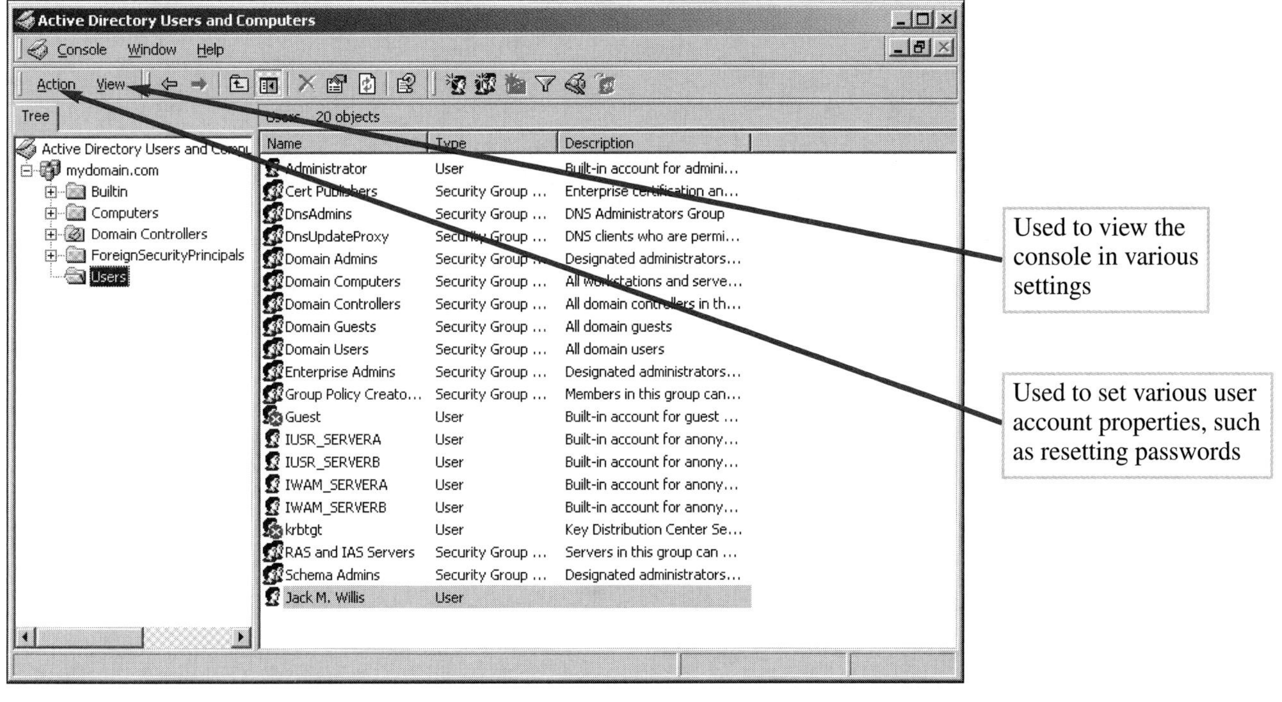

skill 4 Setting User Account Properties

exam objective

Create and manage objects manually or by using scripting.

overview

Every user account you create has a set of default properties associated with the account. You can configure personal information, logon settings, dial-in settings, and Terminal Services settings for a user.

The personal properties that you define for a domain user account are useful when searching for users. Therefore, if you want to be able to search for users based on very specific information, you should always provide as much detailed information for each domain user account as possible.

The Logon settings enable you to specify the logon hours for a user. As mentioned previously, this enables you to restrict the hours during which a user can remain logged on to the network.

You can also modify the dial-in settings for a user account. Dial-in settings for a user account specify if and how a user can make a dial-in connection to the network from a remote location.

Finally, you can specify Terminal Services settings for a user account. Terminal Services provides the ability to connect to a server from a remote location, as well as run a session as if you were physically sitting at the machine. The terminal services client sends the equivalent of keystrokes and mouse movements (input events) to the terminal server, the terminal server runs applications in response to these events, and then the terminal server sends screenshots of the session back to the PC. For an overly simplified example, terminal services is similar to a server-based "PC anywhere" application. Terminal Services provides a multi-session environment that allows remote computers (or Windows terminals) access to Windows-based programs running on the server. Windows 2000 Server includes Terminal Services Client software to support 16- and 32-bit Windows-based clients.

Note that you can save a lot of time in a large environment by filling out the common fields shared between user accounts in a "template" account. A template account is a disabled account used as a template for creating other accounts. After filling out the appropriate fields, you can now copy the account by right clicking on the account and choosing copy. This creates a new account with most of your pre-defined fields already filled in.

A description of the tabs of the **Properties** dialog box for a domain user account is provided in **Table 5-3**.

tip

For domain users, account properties are an example of object attributes.

Table 5-3 Tabs in the Properties dialog box of a domain user account

Tabs	Purpose
General	Stores the user's personal details, which include first name, last name, display name, description, office location, telephone numbers, e-mail address, home page, and additional Web pages.
Address	Stores the user's contact information, which includes street address, post office box, city, state or province, zip or postal code, and country or region details.
Account	Stores the user's account properties, such as user logon name, logon hours, account options, account expiration, and computers available for logging on.
Profile	Enables an administrator to set a profile path, logon script path, and home folder.
Telephones	Stores the user's home, pager, mobile, fax, and IP telephone numbers and any specific comments about these.
Organization	Stores the user's title, department, and company name, and the name of the user's manager.
Remote Control	Enables an administrator to configure the Terminal Services remote control settings.
Terminal Services Profile	Enables an administrator to configure the Terminal Services user profile.
Member Of	Stores the groups to which the user belongs.
Dial-in	Stores the dial-in properties for the user account such as access permissions and callback options.
Environment	Enables an administrator to configure the Terminal Services startup environment.
Sessions	Specifies the Terminal Services timeout and reconnection settings.

skill 4

Setting User Account Properties

(cont'd)

exam objective

Create and manage objects manually or by using scripting.

how to

Set domain user account properties such as personal information and logon hours.

1. Click the **Users** folder in the **Active Directory Users and Computers** console. The list of user accounts is displayed in the Details pane.
2. Right-click **Jack M. Willis** and click the **Properties** command. This will display the **Properties** dialog box for **Jack M. Willis**.
3. Type **ABC Consultants** in the **Office** text box.
4. Type **JWillis@abc.com** in the **E-mail** text box **(Figure 5-9)**.
5. Click the **Account** tab to specify the logon hours for Jack.
6. Click Logon Hours... . The **Logon Hours for Jack M. Willis** dialog box is displayed.
7. Select the entire area and click the "Logon denied" option to remove the default access times.
8. Drag from the rectangle that corresponds to Monday 2 P.M. to the rectangle that corresponds to Friday 10 P.M.
9. Click the **Logon Permitted** option button to specify Jack's logon hours as 2 P.M. through 10 P.M., Monday through Friday **(Figure 5-10)**.
10. Click OK to close the **Logon Hours for Jack M. Willis** dialog box.
11. Click OK to close the **Properties** dialog box and apply these settings.

tip

A blue rectangle corresponding to an hour indicates that the user can log on during that hour, and a white rectangle indicates that the user cannot log on during that hour.

more

You can also restrict users so that they can only log on to specific computers. To do this, open the **Properties** dialog box for a user account. Click Log On To... on the **Account** tab to open the **Logon Workstations** dialog box. Click the **The following computers** option button to specify the computer. Type the Computer's NetBIOS name in the **Computer name** text box and click Add to specify the computer from which the user can log on. Click OK to close the **Logon Workstations** dialog box. Click OK to close the **Properties** dialog box and apply these settings.

caution

To restrict the computers from which a user can log on to a domain, NetBIOS over TCP/IP (NBT) must be enabled.

Figure 5-9 Specifying user account properties

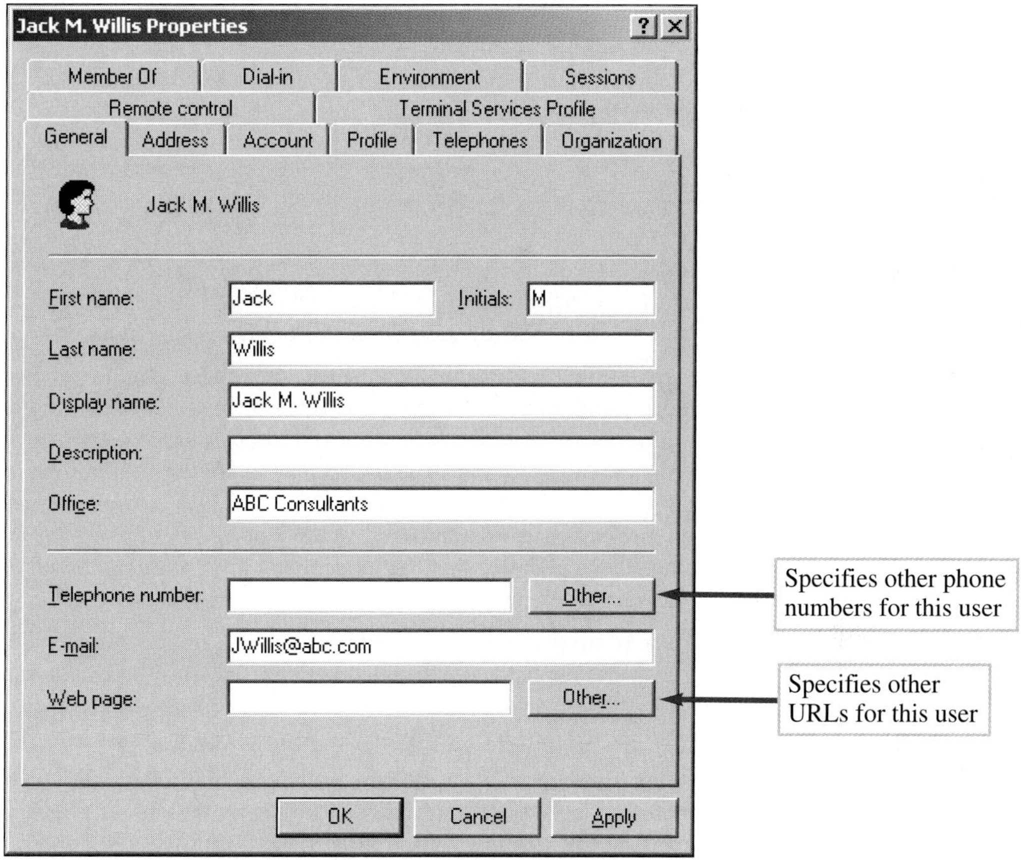

Figure 5-10 Specifying logon hours for a user account

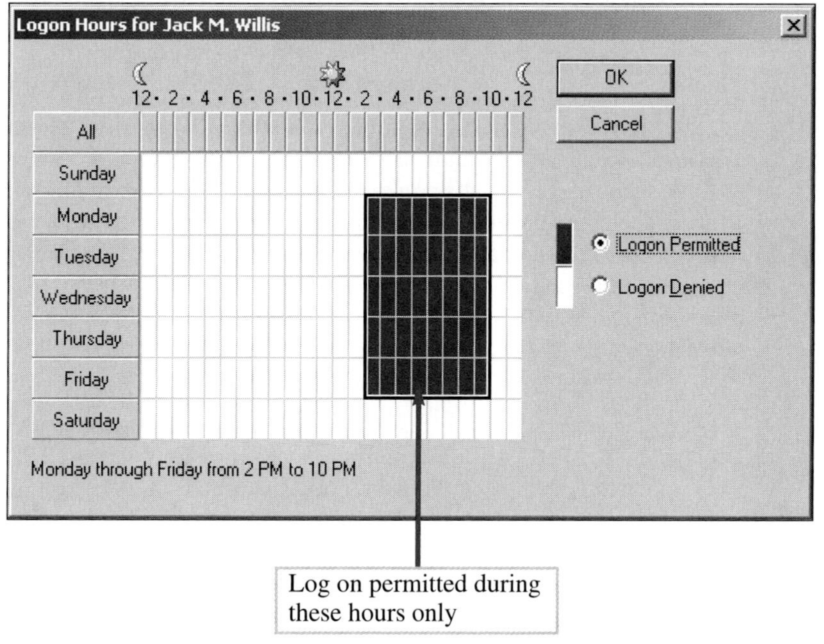

skill 5 Introducing User Profiles

exam objective

Basic knowledge

overview

A **user profile** is a collection of data that includes a user's personal data, desktop settings, printer connections, network connections that are established when the user logs on to the network, and other specified settings. In general, you can think of user profiles as collections of the user's settings. User profiles help in providing a consistent desktop environment each time you log on to the computer, which may be defined by you or your system administrator.

User profiles also enable multiple users to work from the same computer or a single user to work from multiple computers on a network without changing any of the settings. Even if multiple users use the same computer, the users can view their individual desktop settings whenever they log on. A user can customize the desktop environment without affecting another user's settings. Also, user profiles can be stored on a server so that users can use them on any computer running Microsoft Windows NT 4.0 or Windows 2000. User profiles also store the application settings of applications that comply with Microsoft's Windows 2000 software development guidelines.

User profiles are stored in the Documents and Settings folder. **Table 5-4** displays the configuration settings associated with a user profile, along with the source where you can specify these settings in Windows 2000. There are three types of user profiles: local user profiles, roaming user profiles, and mandatory user profiles.

A **local user profile**, as the name suggests, is limited to the computer you log on to and is stored on the system's local hard disk. It is created the first time you log on to a computer by copying the settings in the "default user" profile, and is the default type of profile. Any changes you make to your local user profile are also specific to the computer on which you made the changes. Local user profiles are stored in the folder C:\Documents and Settings*user_logon_name* where C:\ is the system drive name and *user_logon_name* is the name the user uses to log on to the system. For example, a user might add a picture in the My Pictures folder. Windows 2000 modifies the user profile accordingly to reflect the changes so that the next time the user logs on the picture will be present in the user's My Pictures folder. **Figure 5-11** displays the contents of a sample individual user profile folder.

A **roaming user profile** is helpful when a user has to work on multiple computers on a network. To enable a roaming profile, you must first configure a network path to the roaming profile in the user account's properties. Then, under the user profiles tab in system properties, change the user's profile type to roaming. The profile is then available to the user from all the computers in the domain. Any changes the user makes to the roaming user profile also get updated on the server. Users can view their individual settings from any computer on the network, unlike with a local user profile, which exists only on the computer on which it was created.

When the user logs on, Windows 2000 copies the roaming user profile from the network server to the client computer and temporarily applies the roaming user profile settings to that computer. The first time a user logs on to a computer, Windows 2000 copies all user profile files to the local computer. The subsequent times that a user logs on, Windows 2000 compares only the locally stored user profile files and the roaming user profile files on the server, and copies only the files that have changed since the last time the user logged on. When a user logs off, Windows 2000 copies the changes made to the local copy of the roaming user profile back to the network server. Be aware that roaming profiles can and typically do consume large amounts of network bandwidth. This is due to users' habits, which typically include creating folder structures either on the desktop or in the "My Documents" folder and placing large quantities of data in these locations. Since both folders are part of the user profile, it is very easy for your users to create very large user profiles, which then use large amounts of bandwidth whenever they need to be transferred.

tip

If you want to ensure that all users get specific settings by default the first time they log on to a machine, you can configure a profile with the appropriate settings and copy those settings to the "default user" profile using the User Profiles tab under system properties.

tip

If you are upgrading from a previous version of Windows, profiles may be located in an alternate location such as %SystemRoot%\Profiles.

Table 5-4 Configuration settings associated with a user profile

Configuration settings	Source in Windows 2000
All user-definable settings	Windows Explorer, Control Panel
All user-specific program settings affecting the user's Windows environment, such as Calculator, Notepad, Clock, and Paint	Accessories
Per-user Program settings for programs written specifically for Windows 2000 and designed to track program settings	Windows 2000-based programs
Items stored on the Desktop and Shortcut elements	Desktop contents
All user-definable computer screen colors and display text settings	Display Properties
Application data and user-defined configuration settings	Application data and registry hive
Any user-created mapped network drives	Mapped network drive
Links to other computers on the network	My Network Places
Network printer connection settings	Printer settings
Any bookmarks placed in the Windows 2000 Help system	Online user education bookmarks

Figure 5-11 A sample user profile folder

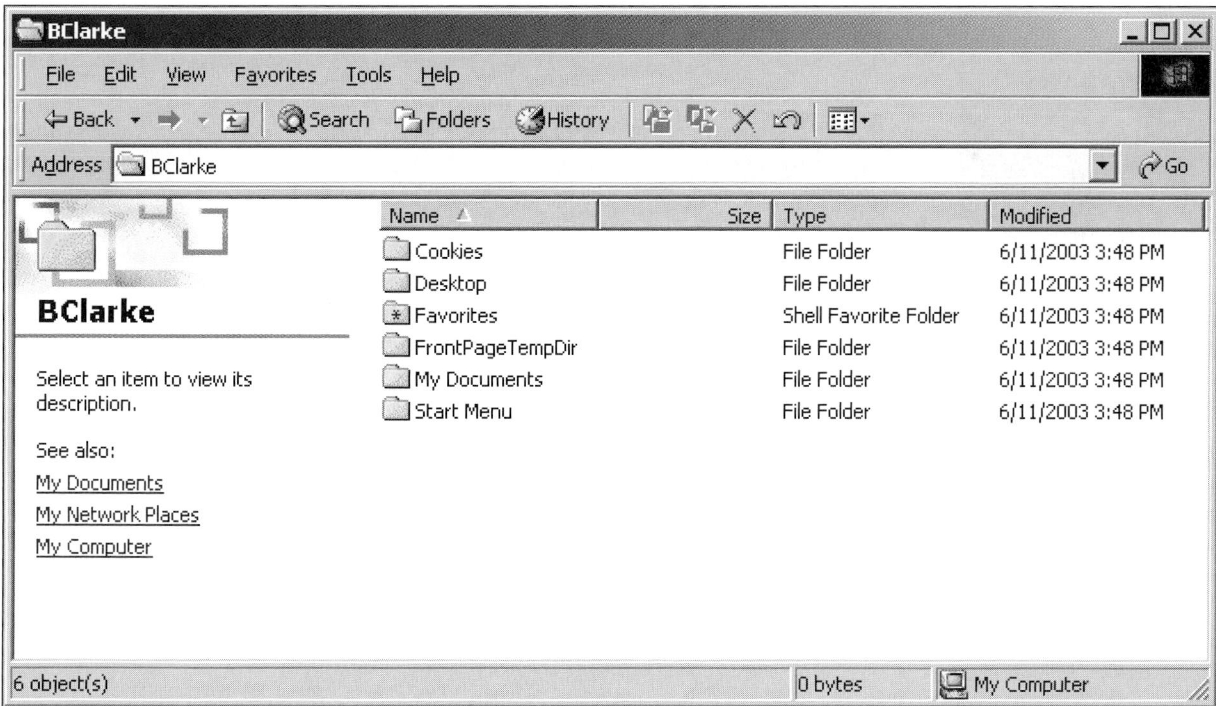

skill 5

Introducing User Profiles *(cont'd)*

exam objective

Basic knowledge

overview

A **mandatory user profile** is a type of roaming profile used to specify particular settings for individuals or a group. A mandatory user profile does not permanently save the desktop settings made by a user. Users can choose their own desktop settings for the computer they are logged on to, but none of these changes are saved when they log off. The mandatory profile settings are applied to the local computer each time the user logs on.

Mandatory user profiles can prove beneficial as an administrative tool because you can create a default user profile that is suited specifically for a user's tasks. For example, you can keep one user profile for all data entry operators. You can also specify the default user settings that will remain the same for all the user profiles. However, you should realize that users typically do not appreciate mandatory user profiles. It is best to warn the users before making their profiles mandatory.

caution

Only system administrators can make changes to mandatory user profiles.

You can set up a mandatory user profile for specific users. These users will be able to modify the desktop settings while they are logged on, but none of these changes will actually be retained when they log off.

Creating a mandatory user profile involves the same steps as creating a roaming profile, with one exception. After creation of the roaming profile, you must go into the appropriate network share point and rename the ntuser.dat file to ntuser.man.

more

The **All Users folder** in C:\Documents and Settings is used to modify all profiles applied to this individual machine. **(Figure 5-12)**. Any changes made to the All Users folder will apply to every profile of every user that logs in to this machine. For instance, if you want to make a certain icon available on everyone's start menu, you can simply add the icon to the start menu folder under the All Users folder.

Table 5-5 gives a brief explanation of each folder in an individual user profile. Notice that some folders appear shaded. This implies that these folders are hidden. Hidden folders are not visible by default. You have to access the Folder Options menu item under the Tools menu in Windows Explorer to view hidden files and folders.

Figure 5-12 Contents of the Documents and Settings folder

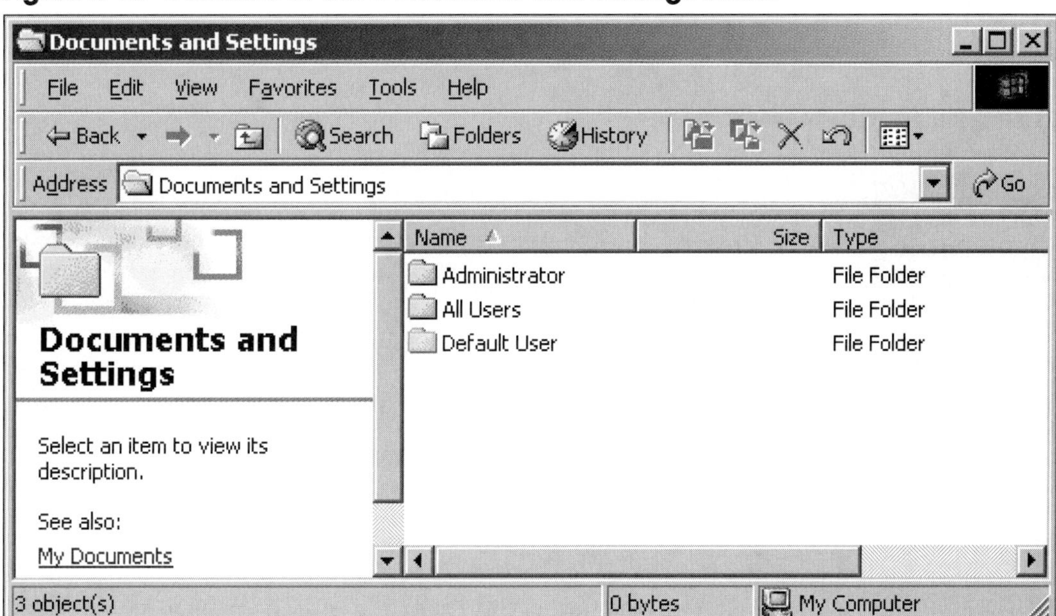

Table 5-5 Contents of a sample user profile folder

Folder name	Contents
Desktop	Contains desktop items like folders and program shortcuts.
Start Menu	Contains shortcuts to program items such as Microsoft Internet Explorer.
My Documents	Contains documents added or created by the user.
Favorites	Contains shortcuts to favorite sites on the Internet.
My Pictures	Contains the picture files stored by the user.
Local Settings	Contains Application data, History, and Temporary files.
Cookies	Contains user information and preferences such as logon data.
FrontPageTempDir	This is a temporary folder used by Microsoft FrontPage.
NetHood	Contains shortcuts to My Network Places items. This is a hidden folder.
PrintHood	Contains shortcuts to printer folder items. This is a hidden folder.
Recent	Contains shortcuts to the most recently used documents and accessed folders. This is a hidden folder.
SendTo	Contains shortcuts to document-handling utilities such as access to the floppy drive. This is a hidden folder.
Templates	Contains user template items such as ones created in Microsoft Word and Microsoft Excel.
Application Data	This is a hidden folder that contains program-specific data, such as a custom dictionary. Program vendors decide what data should be stored in this folder.
NTUSER.DAT file	This is a hidden file that stores user registry settings. It also has a corresponding log file named ntuser.dat.log.

skill 6 Creating a Roaming User Profile

exam objective

Basic knowledge

overview

You can create standard roaming user profiles for specific groups of users. To do this, you need to configure the desired desktop environment and copy the standard profile to the user's roaming user profile location. You need to consider certain factors before setting up a roaming user profile.

- Always create standard roaming user profiles on the file server you back up most frequently. This helps you to trace copies of the latest roaming user profiles.
- Place the roaming user profile folder on a member server instead of a domain controller in order to improve logon performance. Copying roaming user profiles between the server and client computers can tie up many system resources. Keeping profiles on the domain controller can therefore delay the authentication of users by the domain controller.

Standard roaming user profiles provide certain benefits. For example, you can provide a standard desktop environment to multiple users with similar job profiles. These users typically use the same network resources. For example, you can provide a standard desktop to all users in the Accounts section of an organization.

You can also provide users with the standard work environment that they require for performing their jobs. Similarly, you may also remove applications and connections that some users do not require.

Standard roaming user profiles also help you to streamline troubleshooting. The system support team, for example, being familiar with the user profile settings, would be able to identify solutions for problems more efficiently.

To create a standard roaming user profile, first create a shared folder on the server. Next, create a user profile template with the appropriate configuration. Then, copy the user profile template to the shared folder on the server and specify the users who will have access to the profile. Finally, specify the path to the profile template in the user account.

how to

Create a roaming user profile and set up a standard roaming user profile.

1. Log on to the domain controller as an **Administrator**.
2. Create a shared folder named TestProfiles in the C:\ folder and assign **Full Control** to the **Everyone** group on the domain controller. The standard roaming user profile will reside in this shared folder.
3. Now, create a user profile template using the account of Jack M. Willis. To do this, click the Users folder in the **Active Directory Users and Computers** console.
4. Right-click **Jack M. Willis** and click the **Properties** command. This will display the **Properties** dialog box for Jack M. Willis.
5. Click the **Member Of** tab, and click [Add]. The **Select Groups** dialog box displays.
6. Click the **Print Operators** option in the **Name** list box **(Figure 5-13)**, and click [OK] to make Jack a member of **Print Operators** group so that he can log on to the domain controller. Domain Controllers have enhanced security, and only allow administrative and operator groups the logon locally right. This step is not required when creating most user accounts.

caution

To create a roaming user profile for a user account, you either need administrative rights for the container in which the user account is stored, or write permissions to the user account.

Figure 5-13 Adding a user to a group

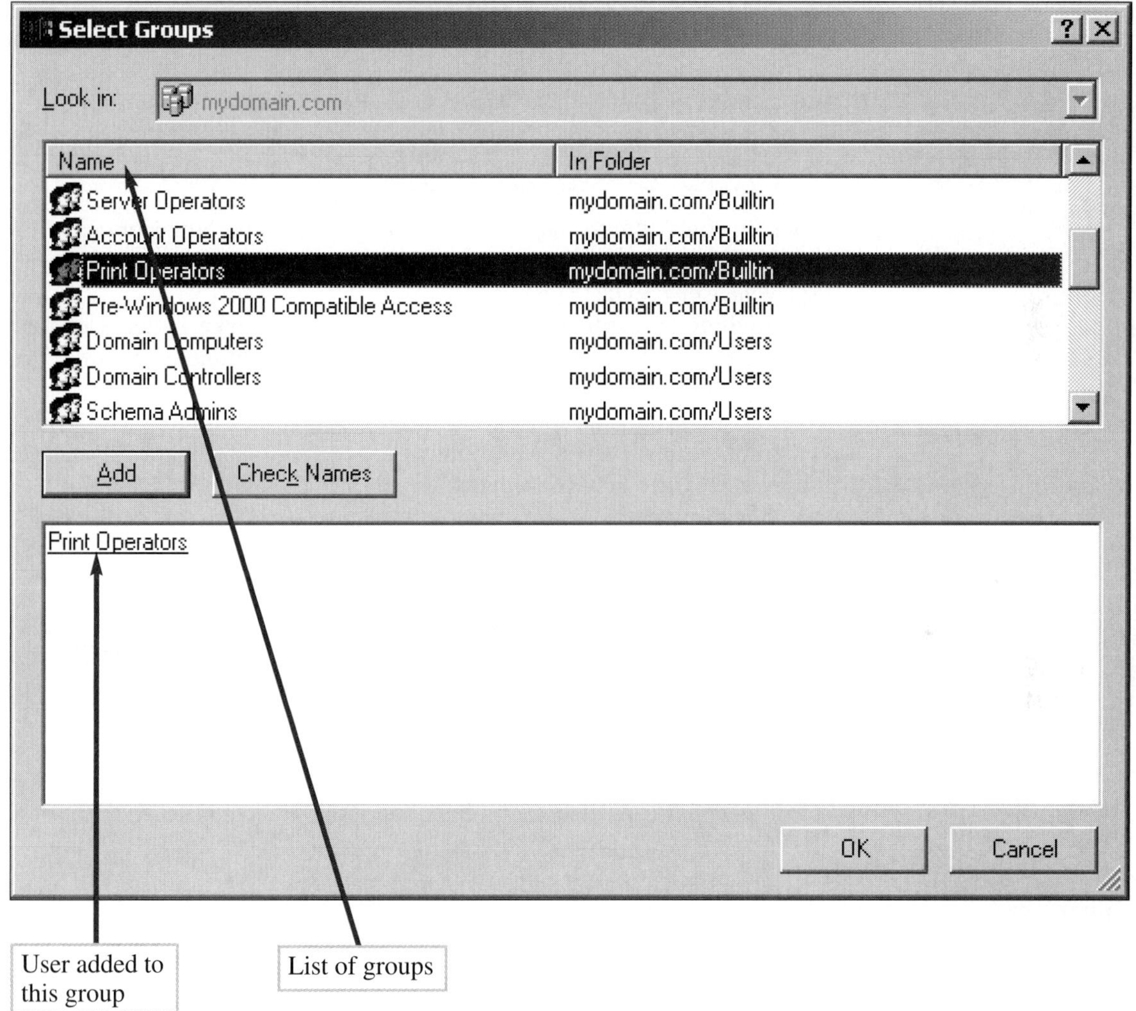

skill 6 Creating a Roaming User Profile (cont'd)

exam objective

Basic knowledge

how to

7. Log off of Windows 2000 and log on as **JWillis**. A local user profile is automatically created for Jack Willis. Change the current color scheme of the desktop from **Windows Standard** to **Spruce** by right clicking the desktop and accessing the **Properties** dialog box. Jack's user profile will be used as the user profile template for the standard roaming user profile. Log off of Windows 2000.
8. Log on as **Administrator** and open the **Active Directory Users and Computers** console.
9. Add another user, **Barbara J. Clarke**, to the **Print Operators** group.
10. Double-click **System** in the **Control Panel** to open the **System Properties** dialog box. Click the **User Profiles** tab to initiate the process of copying the user profile template to the shared folder TestProfiles **(Figure 5-14)**.
11. Under **Profiles stored on this computer,** click **computername\Jwillis**, where **computername** is the name of your computer, and then click [Copy To...]. This will display the **Copy To** dialog box.
12. Type **\\<domain_controller name>\testprofiles\BClarke** in the **Copy profile to** text box. BClarke is the folder that will contain the roaming user profile for Barbara **(Figure 5-15)**.
13. To specify Barbara as the user who will have access to the profile, click [Change...] under the **Permitted to use** section. The **Select User or Group** dialog box is displayed.
14. In the **Select User or Group** dialog box, select **Barbara J. Clarke** from the **Name** column, and click [OK] to close the dialog box **(Figure 5-16)**. Barbara J. Clarke has now been specified as user who is permitted to use the profile.
15. Click [OK] to close the **Copy to** dialog box.
16. Click [OK] to close the **System Properties** dialog box.
17. Open the **Properties** dialog box for **Barbara J. Clarke** from the **Active Directory Users and Computers** console. Click the **Profile** tab to specify the path to the roaming user profile for Barbara J. Clarke.
18. Type **\\ServerA\testprofiles\BClarke** in the **Profile path** text box **(Figure 5-17)**, and click [OK].
19. Log on as **BClarke** to test the roaming profile from another machine on the network.

tip

Using the variable %username% instead of the user's logon name automatically replaces the variable with the user account name and is useful when copying template accounts.

more

A mandatory user profile is a roaming user profile that is read-only (no changes can be saved). Although users might modify the desktop settings of the computer they are using, the changes are lost when they log off. Mandatory profile settings are applied to local client computers every time a user logs on. You can assign one mandatory profile to multiple users who require the same desktop settings — for example, data entry operators.

You can create a mandatory user profile using the hidden file **NTUSER.DAT**. This file stores the Windows 2000 Server system settings (registry entries in the HKEY_CURRENT_USER hive) that apply specifically to individual user accounts and user environment settings. To change this file to a read-only file so that it can be used as a mandatory user profile, rename the file **NTUSER.MAN**.

Figure 5-14 Accessing the list of user profiles

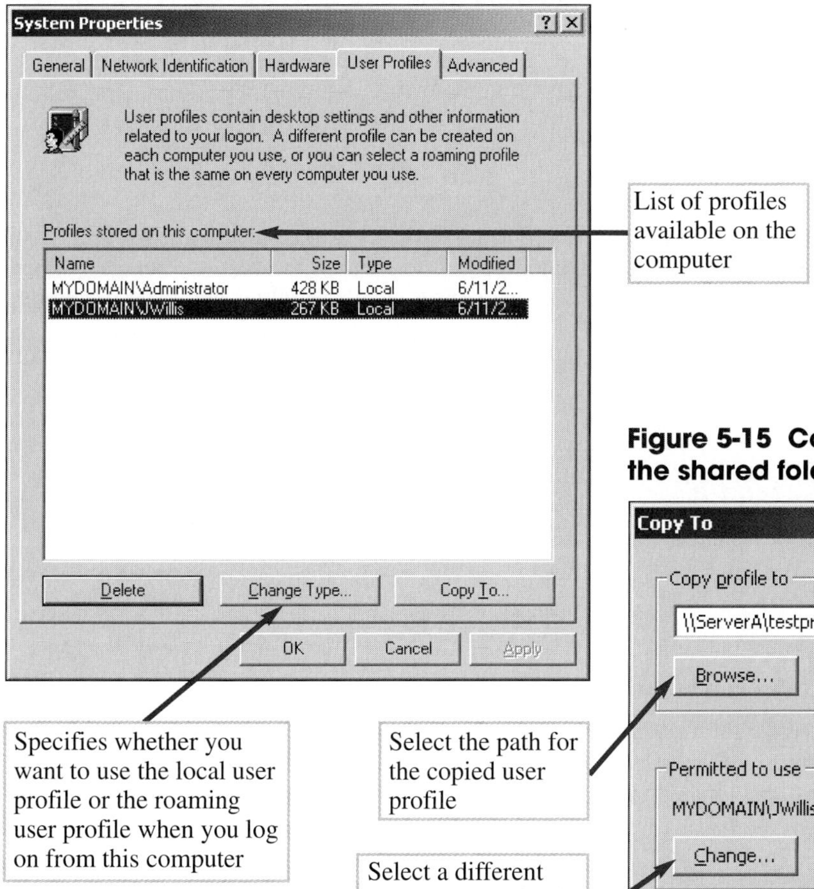

List of profiles available on the computer

Specifies whether you want to use the local user profile or the roaming user profile when you log on from this computer

Figure 5-15 Copying the user profile template to the shared folder

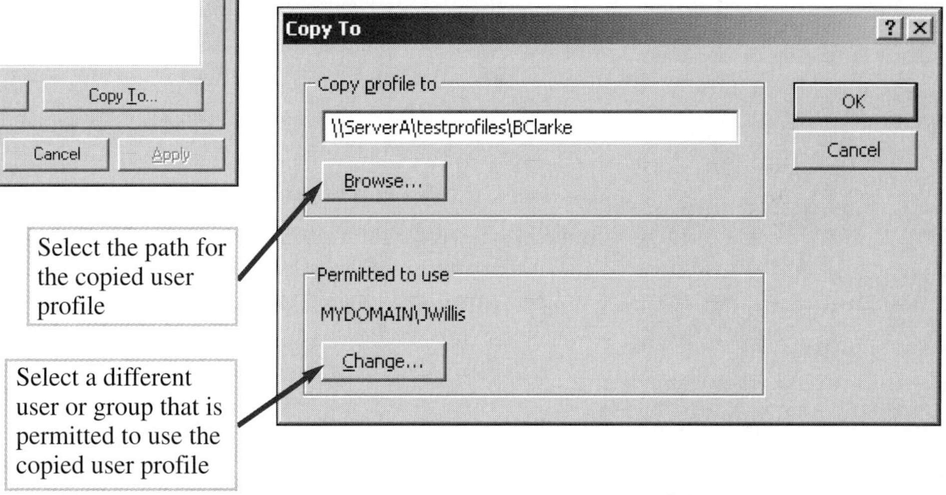

Select the path for the copied user profile

Select a different user or group that is permitted to use the copied user profile

Figure 5-16 Permitting a user to use the profile

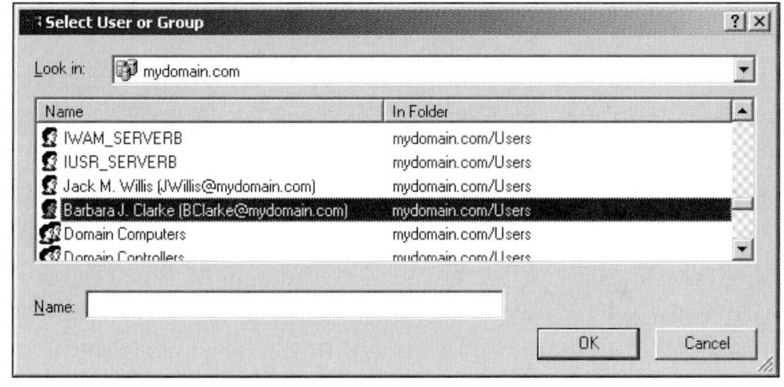

Figure 5-17 Specifying the path to the roaming user profile

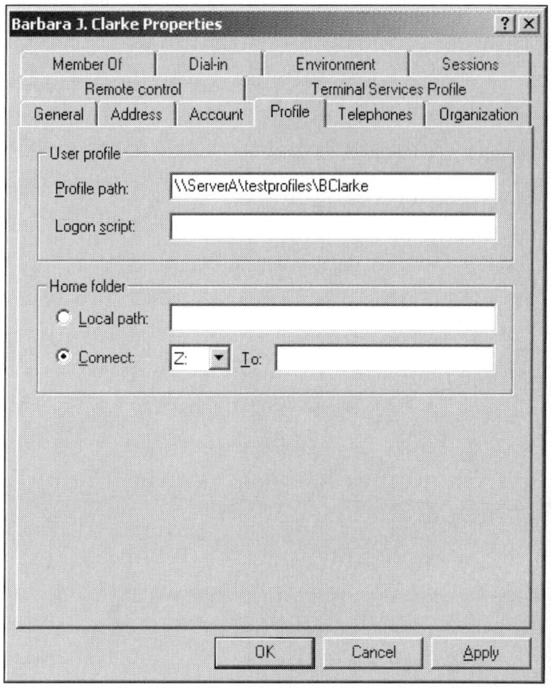

skill 7 Creating a Home Folder on a Server

exam objective

Basic knowledge

overview

The My Documents folder is the default location for users to store their data. Windows 2000 Server also allows you to specify a home folder as the default location for storage. A home folder is generally used when users want to store data in a folder that is not computer dependent and is easily accessible from any computer on the network. Most importantly, the home folder usually exists on a server, which mean it is typically backed up nightly as part of the server backup schedule.

Ideally, you can store the home folders of all users on a network server because it provides you with certain benefits. You can centralize the administration of user documents, and users can access their home folders from any computer on the network. Also, users can locate the home folders from a client computer using any Microsoft operating system.

caution

Always store home folders on an NTFS volume so that you can use NTFS permissions to provide security to user documents. Using FAT volumes will restrict you to apply only shared folder permissions.

how to

Create a home folder for a user in a shared folder on a member server.

1. Create a shared folder called "**test1 in C:**" on the server and assign **Full Control** to the **Users** group. This shared folder will contain the home folder JWillis for Jack.
2. Double-click the **Users** folder in the **Active Directory Users and Computers** console.
3. Right-click **Jack M. Willis** and click the **Properties** command. This will display the Properties dialog box for **Jack M. Willis**.
4. Click the **Profile** tab (**Figure 5-18**).
5. Click **Connect** in the **Home folder** section, and click the drive letter **Z:** in the list box to specify the drive for the existing network share.
6. In the **To** text box, type **\\<ServerA\test1\JWillis** as the path for the home folder.
7. Click OK. **Figure 5-19** displays the folder JWillis under **test1**. The home folder **JWillis** is automatically created in the **test1** folder.

caution

You need to create a shared folder before specifying the path for the home folder.

more

By storing a home folder in a shared folder on a file server, administration tasks, such as backing up user documents, are also centralized. The size of the home folder does not affect network traffic during logon since the home folder does not belong to any roaming user profile.

Figure 5-18 Specifying the path of the home folder

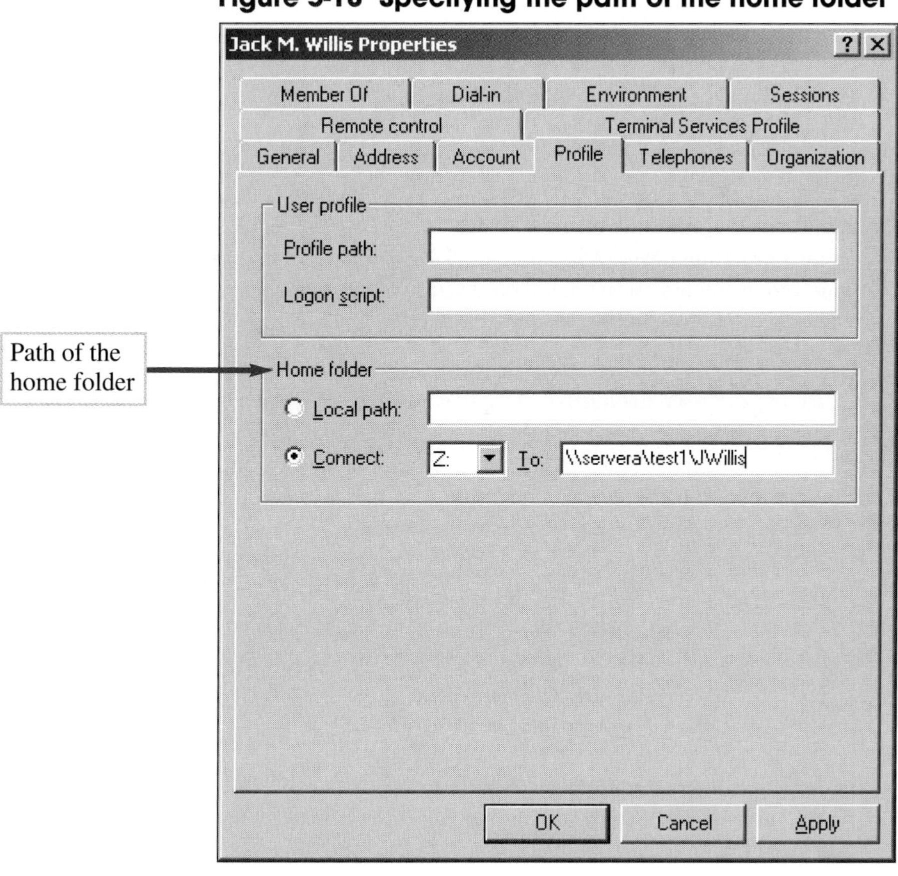

Figure 5-19 Home folder for a user

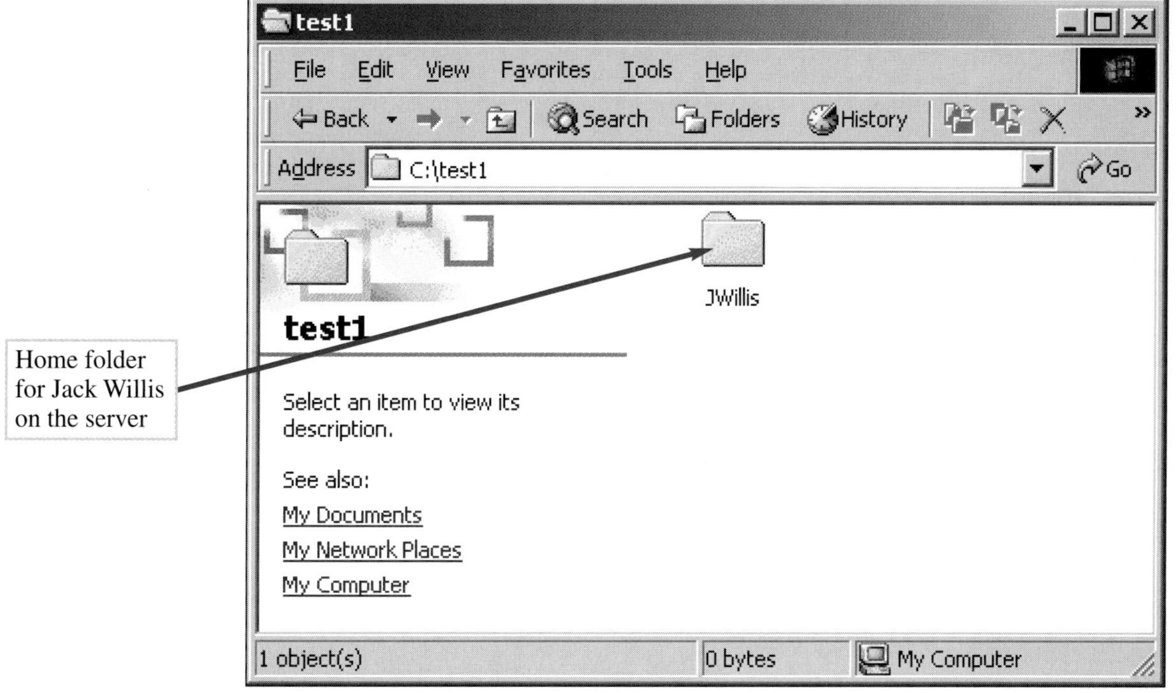

skill 8 Maintaining User Accounts

exam objective

Create and manage objects manually or by using scripting.

overview

As a network administrator, you are required to maintain user accounts based on the needs of your organization. Maintenance of these user accounts includes tasks such as modifying user accounts, resetting passwords, and unlocking user accounts. **Figure 5-20** displays the **Action** menu, which contains some of the properties you need to set as an administrator. To access the **Action** menu, right-click the user account in the Details pane.

You can modify user accounts in the following ways:

- **Rename a user account** — Rename an account when you want to maintain the rights, permissions, and group memberships of a particular user account and transfer the account to a different user. For example, if a new employee takes the place of another employee in a particular position, you can simply rename the account by changing the first, last, and user logon names to those of the new employee.
- **Disable or enable a user account** — Disable an account for security reasons when a user does not need the account for a certain period. For example, you can disable the account for a user when the user goes on vacation. When the user returns, you would enable the user account so that the user can log on to the network just as before. Note that when a user account is disabled, the Action menu displays the Enable Account command. Similarly, when a user account is enabled, the pop-up menu displays the Disable Account command.
- **Delete a user account** — Delete a user account when you no longer require it. For instance, you can delete an account when a user leaves the company and you are sure that you cannot make use of the account by renaming it.

Note that to modify user accounts, you need a minimum of write permissions on the user account. You can view permissions set on AD objects by clicking the Advanced Features option under the view menu in the Active Directory Users and Computers console.

You can reset passwords when a user's password expires before the user has a chance to change it. In some cases, users might even forget their passwords. You do not have to remember the old password to reset a password. After the administrator or the user sets a password for a user account, the password is not viewable to anybody, including the administrator. This protects passwords from being made available to other users and thereby prevents other users and the administrator from logging on as another user.

Windows 2000 Server can lock out user accounts for users who violate a security policy. For example, if a security policy states that the maximum number of failed logon attempts per user is three and a user exceeds the specified limit, Windows 2000 Server will lock the user account for that user and display an error message. In such a case, you could be required to unlock the user account.

tip

Disabling a user account is typically preferable to deleting a user account. If you delete the account, and the user is re-hired or another user is hired into the position, you must manually recreate all aspects of the account. However, if you had simply disabled the account, all you would need to do is enable (and possibly rename) the account.

Figure 5-20 Options in the Action menu

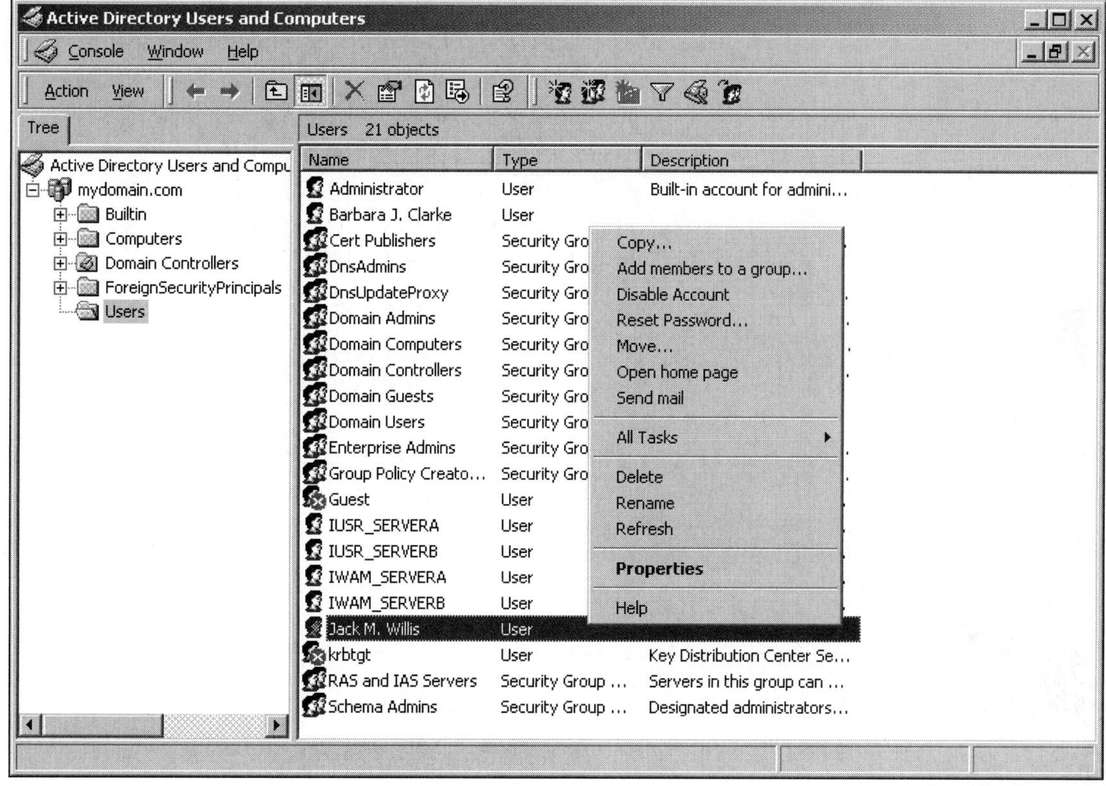

skill 8

Maintaining User Accounts *(cont'd)*

exam objective

Create and manage objects manually or by using scripting.

how to

Maintain a user account by first disabling and then enabling the account, and resetting the password.

1. Right-click the user account for Jack M. Willis in the **Active Directory Users and Computers** console. Note that since his account is currently enabled, the command **Disable Account** is visible.
2. Click the **Disable Account** command. The **Active Directory** message box is displayed, stating that the account has been disabled.
3. Click OK to close the message box **(Figure 5-21)**. You can see a red "X" marked on the account, as shown in **Figure 5-22**.
4. Right-click **Jack M. Willis** again. You can now see the **Enable Account** command.
5. Click the **Enable Account** command. The **Active Directory** message box appears, stating that the account has been enabled.
6. Click OK to close the message box. Note that the red "X" marked on the account earlier is not visible now.
7. Right-click the entry for **Jack M. Willis**.
8. Click the **Reset Password** command. This will display the **Reset Password** dialog box.
9. Type a password in the **New password** text box.
10. Re-type the password in the **Confirm password** text box.
11. Select the **User must change password at next logon** check box, as shown in **Figure 5-23**.
12. Click OK. An **Active Directory** message box is displayed, stating that the password has been changed.
13. Click OK to close the message box.
14. Close the **Active Directory Users and Computers** console.

more

To unlock a user account, identify the locked user account marked with a red "X" in the Details pane of the Users folder. Right-click the user account and open the **Account** tab of the **Properties** dialog box. You will see that the **Account is locked out** check box is selected. Clearing the check box will unlock the user account. Please note that the **Account is locked out** check box will be active only for a user whose user account has been locked. You cannot manually lock out a user account.

Figure 5-21 Active Directory message box

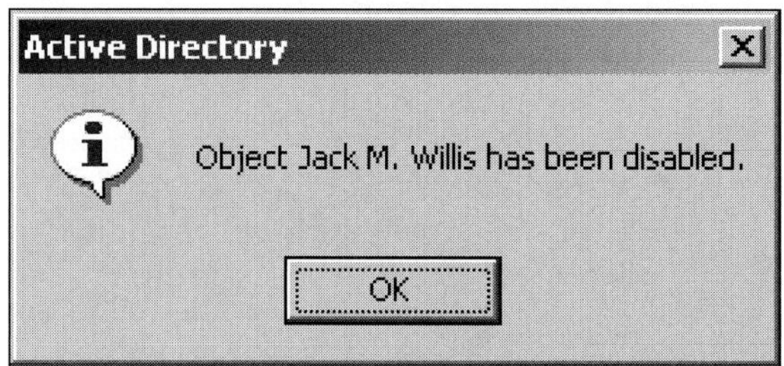

Figure 5-22 The disabled user account

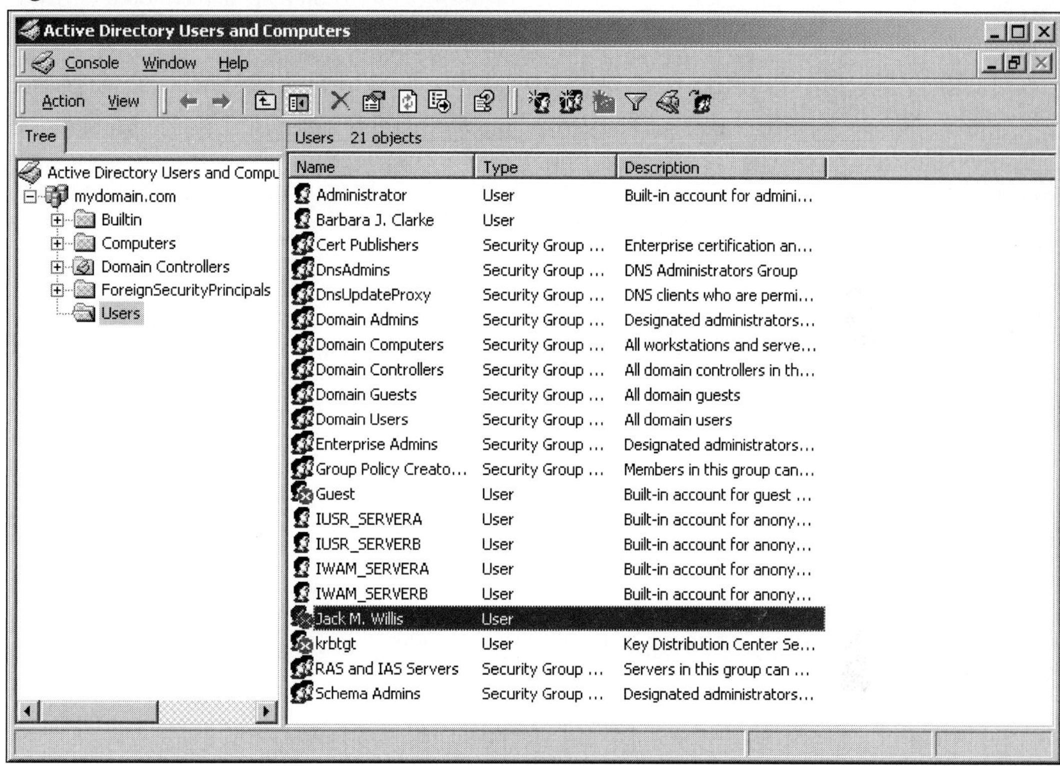

Figure 5-23 Resetting user password

Summary

- A user account is a form of identification of a user on a Windows 2000 network. A user account includes information, such as user logon name, password, contact details, profile details, and Terminal Services settings.
- You can create user accounts manually or by writing scripts. To create accounts manually, you use the Active Directory Users and Computers console. To write script for a user account, you need to be familiar with at least one scripting language such as VBScript or JScript.
- In Windows 2000 Server, there are three types of user accounts: local user accounts, domain user accounts, and built-in user accounts.
- Local user accounts allow users to only log on to the computer on which the local user account is created. This also implies that users gain access to only those resources that are present on the local machine. You can use the Computer Management console to create local user accounts.
- Domain user accounts allow users to log on to the network from any computer in the domain and gain access to network resources. You can use the Active Directory Users and Computers console to create domain user accounts.
- Built-in user accounts are created by default during the installation of Windows 2000 Server. Examples of built-in user accounts are the Administrator and Guest accounts. Built-in user accounts cannot be deleted.
- User profiles contain settings that define the user environment and are applied when a user logs on to a system. Types of user profiles include local user profile, roaming user profile, and mandatory user profile.
- A local user profile is created the first time you log on to a computer and is stored on a system's local hard disk.
- You can use roaming user profiles where users work on multiple computers. A roaming user profile is available to its user from all the computers in the domain.
- A mandatory user profile is a read-only roaming profile that can be used to specify particular settings for an individual or an entire group of users.
- Windows 2000 provides a home folder for the storage of files in a directory other than the My Documents folder.
- As a system administrator, you need to constantly maintain user accounts. This includes performing tasks such as modifying user accounts, resetting passwords, and unlocking user accounts.

Key Terms

Active Directory Services Interfaces (ADSI)
All Users folder
Built-in user accounts
Domain user accounts
Home folder
Local user accounts
Local user profile
Mandatory user profile
Roaming user profile
User account
User profile

Test Yourself

1. Which of the following consoles would you use to create domain user accounts manually?
   a. Active Directory Users and Computers console
   b. Active Directory Domains and Trusts console
   c. AD Sites and Services console
   d. Computer Management console

2. Which of the following pieces of information does a user account include? Choose all that apply.
   a. User logon name
   b. Callback options
   c. Terminal Services startup environment
   d. Licensing details

3. A user account:
   a. Provides standard desktop settings.
   b. Identifies the user in order to validate access to domain resources.
   c. Centralizes administration of user documents.
   d. Simplifies troubleshooting. Records the audit of the actions performed by the account.

4. Which of the following is the correct sequence for creating a standard roaming user profile?
   1. Copy the user profile template to the shared folder on the server and specify the users who will have access to the profile.

2. Create a shared folder on the server.
3. Create a user profile template with the appropriate configuration.
4. Specify the path to the profile template in the user account.

a. 1, 3, 2, 4
b. 2, 3, 1, 4
c. 4, 3, 1, 2
d. 1, 2, 3, 4

5. Which of the following consoles can you use to create local user accounts?
a. Active Directory Domains and Trusts console
b. Computer Management console
c. Distributed File System console
d. Active Directory Users and Computers console

6. Keith logs on to the network and changes his desktop settings to reflect a new screensaver that one of his friends sent to him. The next time Keith logs on to the same computer, his system does not activate the new screen saver. Which of the following user profiles seem to be applied to Keith's user account?
a. Roaming
b. Mandatory
c. Local
d. Home

7. You are the network administrator of ABC.com. You need to create user accounts for three freelancers who will work in the organization in shifts. Which of the following options would you set to restrict them so that they can access their machines only during a particular period?
a. Logon Hours option
b. Dial-in settings
c. Terminal Services
d. Access token

8. Which of the following would you use to create user accounts by writing scripts?
a. Active Directory Domains and Trusts console
b. Computer Management console
c. Active Directory Services Interfaces
d. Active Directory Users and Computers console

9. Which of the following statements is true?
a. You can create local user accounts on a domain controller.
b. The Guest account is disabled by default.
c. To restrict the computers from which a user can log on to a domain, NetBIOS must be disabled.
d. The All Users folder contains the folders that create the individual user profiles.

10. Which of the following statements is true about a home folder?
a. Provides a consistent desktop environment.
b. Identifies a system or a user on Windows 2000.
c. Should remain within specified size constraints as it affects the network traffic during logon.
d. Can be stored in a shared folder on a file server.

11. Which of the following is the valid reason for storing home folders on an NTFS volume?
a. Provide enhanced security to user documents.
b. Apply shared folder permissions.
c. Speed up the authentication of users by the domain controller.
d. Provide a standard desktop environment to multiple users with similar jobs.

12. Which of the following is required when creating a roaming user profile for a user account?
a. A fully shared folder
b. A read-only shared folder
c. A local NTFS partition
d. Administrator rights

13. Which one of the following options is always visible in the pop-up menu of a user account irrespective of the status of the account?
a. Disable Account.
b. Enable Account.
c. Account is locked out.
d. Reset Password.

14. Which of the following statements about passwords is correct?
a. You require the old password to reset a password.
b. Passwords are readable.
c. The user password is visible to the administrator.
d. Both the administrator and the user can set a password for a user account.

15. Which of the following is true about user profiles?
a. A mandatory user profile is a roaming user profile, which you can change.
b. A user can log on to only that user's computer.
c. User profiles are stored in the All Users folder.
d. Multiple users can log on to one computer.

Projects: On Your Own

1. Create a domain user account and specify the account options.
   a. Log on as **Administrator**.
   b. Open the **Active Directory Users and Computers** console.
   c. Create a domain user account for **TestStudent1**, using the user name **TStudent1** and password **password**. Also, make sure the user is asked to change the account password the first time the user logs on.
   d. Specify the logon hours for **TestStudent1** as **10 AM-6 PM**, **Monday-Friday**. Also restrict **TestStudent1** to use only the user's computer in order to log on to the domain.
2. Create a standard roaming user profile template for a user and specify a user TestStudent2 who will have access to the profile.
   a. Log on as **Administrator**.
   b. Create a shared folder, **TestShare1**, on the server.
   c. To create the user profile template for **TestStudent1**, first make him a member of **Print Operators** group.
   d. Log off as **Administrator** and log on as **TStudent1**.
   e. Change the current color scheme of the desktop to customize the template.
   f. Log off as **TStudent1** and log on as **Administrator**.
   g. Create a user account for **TestStudent2** and add the user to the **Print Operators** group.
   h. Copy the user profile of **TestStudent1** to the shared folder **TestShare1**.
   i. Specify **TestStudent2** as the user who is permitted to use the profile.
   j. Specify the path to the roaming user profile in the user account properties of **TestStudent2**.
3. Create a folder and configure it as the home folder for a user.
   a. Log on as **Administrator**.
   b. Create a folder **TestShare2** in **C:** folder and make it fully sharable.
   c. Open **Active Directory Users and Computers**.
   d. For user **TestStudent1**, configure **TestShare2** as the home folder.

Problem Solving Scenarios

1. You have been assigned the task of configuring two user accounts named Andrew Wilson and Simon Fraser. You need to restrict the users from logging on to the network between 7:00 PM and 9:00 AM from Mondays through Fridays. You also have to allow logons on Saturdays and Sundays only from 10:00 AM to 12:00 NOON.

Write a memo explaining the procedure you will follow to solve this problem. Specify which tool will be used to achieve the desired results.

2. You administer a network of 25 desktop users. The network is made up of a Windows 2000 ADS domain named DesignUsers. One user, Peter Williams, frequently moves around the network and uses multiple workstations during the course of his work. You want his desktop settings to follow him to whichever workstation he logs on to. Another user, Nicole, who is subordinate to Peter Williams, has a similar requirement but with a difference: she should not be able to change her settings once configured. Draft a plan of action explaining how you will achieve the described setup

LESSON

6 Implementing Groups in Active Directory

Active Directory simplifies network management by providing facilities that enable you to organize users in correlated groups. A group is a collection of users, computers, contacts, and other groups.

Creation of groups allows administrators to delegate specific administrative privileges and tasks to the groups. It also helps to assign collective access permission to the members of a group. For example, an administrator can define an Accounts group that contains all the users of the domain belonging to the Accounts department. This will make it easier for the administrator to assign access rights to the entire Accounts department, rather than assigning permission to each user individually.

There are two types of groups: distribution and security. To use groups effectively for administrative purposes, you need to devise group strategies that address the type of group scope you would use to group the users and network resources. You can specify the scope as global, domain local, or universal.

Windows 2000 Active Directory provides three classes of default groups: predefined global, built-in domain local, and special identity. These default groups have a predefined common set of user rights or group memberships that determine the type of tasks that a group member can perform.

Goals

In this lesson, you will learn to plan group strategies based on the various types and scopes of groups. You will learn to create groups and set group properties. Then, you will learn about the default groups provided by Active Directory. Finally, you will learn to access the administrative tools using the Run as command.

Lesson 6 Implementing Groups in Active Directory

Skill	***Exam 70-217 Objective***
1. Introducing Groups	Basic knowledge
2. Planning Group Strategies	Basic knowledge
3. Creating Groups	Create and manage objects manually or by using scripting.
4. Setting Group Properties	Create and manage objects manually or by using scripting.
5. Modifying Group Properties	Create and manage objects manually or by using scripting.
6. Creating Local Groups	Create and manage objects manually or by using scripting.
7. Introducing Default Groups	Basic knowledge
8. Starting a Program Using the Run as Command	Basic knowledge

Requirements

To complete the skills of this lesson, you will need administrative rights on ServerA, the domain controller for the mydomain.com domain, and a member server in the domain (here called Server01). Make sure that domain user accounts for Barbara J. Clarke with the user logon name BClarke and Charlie James with the user logon name CJames are set up on the domain controller (ServerA). Similarly, make sure that local user accounts for John Abraham with JohnA as the user logon name and Jim Howard with the user logon name JimH are set up on the member server (Server01).

skill 1 Introducing Groups

exam objective

Basic knowledge

overview

A **group** in Active Directory is a collection of users, computers, contacts, and other group objects within a forest. Users in a group are assigned rights and permissions, which help them to access network resources such as files, folders, and applications.

In Active Directory, multiple users can be part of a single group. Alternately, one user can be part of multiple groups. Creating groups ensures that the administrator does not need to assign similar permissions to each individual user separately **(Figure 6-1)**.

While creating a group, as an administrator, you need to specify two basic settings: the group type and the scope for the group.

There are two types of groups: distribution groups and security groups.

- **Distribution groups:** These groups are used primarily for sending e-mail messages to a group of users. Distribution groups cannot be used to set security permissions.
- **Security groups:** These groups are used to assign permissions to access or share the resources on a network. Security groups possess all the features of a distribution group and can also be used for nonsecurity-related purposes.

Once you have selected the group type, you need to select the group scope. There are three types of group scopes that can be assigned to groups in a network. These are domain local, global, and universal. **Figure 6-2** illustrates the various group types and group scopes available in Windows 2000.

- **Domain local:** This group scope is generally used to grant access rights to network resources such as printers and shared folders. The distinguishing feature of domain local groups is they may include members from any domain. In other words, domain local groups have an open membership. However, domain local groups are only visible in their own domain. This means that the domain local group can only be given access to resources located in the domain in which the domain local group has been created.
- **Global:** This group scope is used to group the users who share similar roles in the organization. In most typical environments, a global group is created for each job function or title. A Global group may only contain members from its own domain. However, a global group is visible in all domains in the forest.
- **Universal:** Universal groups are a new scope of group designed for use under very specific conditions. Universal groups can contain members from any domain and are visible in all domains. Universal groups are also unique in that they are stored entirely on global catalog servers, which means that a change to the membership of a universal group will cause global catalog replication throughout the entire forest. Universal groups are only available in native mode.

caution

You can switch from mixed mode to native mode, but this process is irreversible. You should switch to native mode only if all your Windows NT domain controllers have been upgraded to Windows 2000, and you do not plan to add any more NT 4 domain controllers. You can change the domain mode using the Active Directory Domains and Trusts console on the Administrative Tools menu.

Figure 6-1 Benefits of creating a group

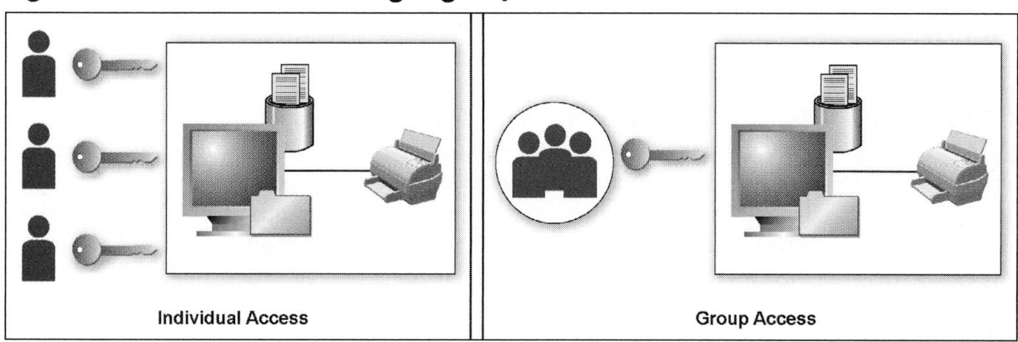

Figure 6-2 Group types and scopes

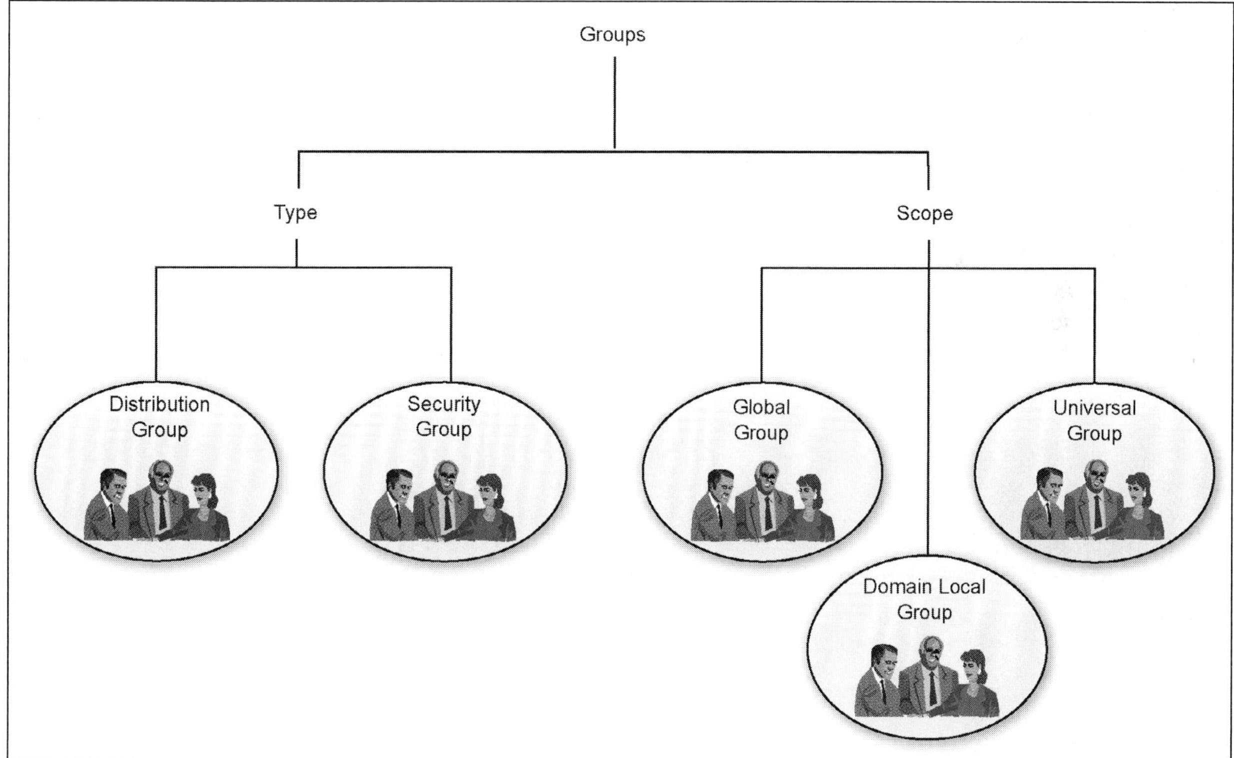

skill 1

Introducing Groups (cont'd)

exam objective

Basic knowledge

overview

The actual use and scope of groups depend on the mode in which you are running your domain. The two domain modes you can use to run a Windows 2000 domain are the mixed mode and the native mode. **Mixed mode** allows coexistence of Windows NT and Windows 2000 domain controllers in the same domain and is the default domain mode when you install Active Directory. **Native mode** supports only Windows 2000 domain controllers. **Table 6-1** describes the effect of the two domain modes on different group scopes.

more

A group can be a part of other groups in a network. The process of adding a group to other groups or consolidating the groups within a network is called **nesting**. You can add user groups as well as groups of other network resources, such as computers and contacts, to create a consolidated group. Nesting can simplify the management of a network. For example, you can create different global groups for the network administrators of the various branches of your organization and then nest all these global groups to form a worldwide network administrators group. You can thus use the worldwide network administrators group to assign required rights and permissions.

However, as an administrator, you need to exercise caution while nesting groups within a network. You should adequately document access permissions to users and their group membership to reduce accidental group allocations and to eliminate redundant inclusion of user accounts in groups. Moreover, more than a single level of nesting is not advisable in a network since troubleshooting a problem in a network that implements multiple levels of nesting is complicated.

Table 6-1 Effect of domain modes on group scopes

Group Scopes	Parameters	Mixed Mode	Native Mode
Universal	Members include	Not available	Accounts, global groups, and universal groups from any domain.
	Can be included as a member of	Not available	Other groups in any domain.
	Used for	Not available	Allowing access to resources in any domain.
	Conversion to other group types	Not available	Not available
Global	Members include	Accounts from the same domain	Accounts and other global groups from the same domain.
	Can be included as a member of	Local groups in any domain	Global, Local, Domain Local, and Universal groups in its own domain, and Local, Domain Local, and Universal groups in any other domain.
	Used for	Organizing user accounts by position.	Organizing user accounts by position.
	Conversion to other group types	Not available	Universal group, provided that the global group is not a member of any other group having global scope.
Domain local	Members include	Accounts and global groups from any domain.	Accounts, global groups, and universal groups from any domain and domain local groups from the same domain.
	Can be included as a member of	Not available	Other domain local groups in the same domain.
	Used for	Assigning permissions to gain access to resources in the same domain.	Assigning permissions in order to gain access to resources in the same domain.
	Conversion to other group types	Not available	Universal group, provided that none of the members of the domain local group have domain local scope.

skill 2 Planning Group Strategies

exam objective Basic knowledge

overview

Groups are generally formed to consolidate network objects that share common characteristics such as hierarchy or functional requirements. To use groups effectively for administrative purposes, you need to devise group strategies before creating groups in a network. Devising a group strategy involves deciding the type of group scope you would use to group the users and network resources. The selection of a strategy depends on the functional environment of your organization.

Even if you have a single domain, consider using the global and domain local groups strategy to assign permissions to network resources. **Figure 6-3** and **Table 6-2** illustrate this strategy, in which you create separate global groups for the sales, marketing, and production personnel, and use a domain local group for the sales data.

tip
The Microsoft rule is a very important concept for the test. You can summarize the rule using the acronym AGDLP, which stands for: Accounts go into Global groups, which go into Domain Local groups, which are assigned Permissions.

This strategy is known as "the Microsoft rule", and is the preferred strategy for building and using groups. Essentially, you build one global group for each position or job function. For instance, you might create a "Sales Associate Level 1-G" global group to organize all Level 1 Sales Associates. The "G" in the name helps you easily identify the global groups when looking at a list of groups. These groups are used to organize users, as all users with a particular job function should generally gain the same access permissions.

Then, each time you create a share, you create (typically) four separate domain local groups for different levels of access to the share. For instance, if you had a Sales Data share, you would create four domain local groups for the share, "Sales Data Read-DL", "Sales Data Write-DL", "Sales Data Modify-DL", and "Sales Data FullControl-DL". You would then assign the proper permissions for the Sales Data share to each individual domain local group.

Finally, you would make the global group or groups members of the appropriate domain local group. For instance, if your Level 1 Sales Associates need Write access to the Sales Data share, then you would add the "Sales Associate Level 1-G" global group to the "Sales Data Write-DL" domain local group. Because all Level 1 Sales Associates are members of the global group, and the global group is a member of the "Sales Data Write-DL" domain local group, all Level 1 Sales Associates gain Write access to the share.

The benefits of using the Microsoft rule include modularity, ease of modification, and a reduction in the size of the global group list. In terms of modularity, for instance, you can assign your file server admins the ability to create domain local groups and tell them to create your four domain local groups, as well as assign the appropriate permissions any time they create a new share. These admins can then do so without having to worry about who, specifically, gains access to those shares.

In terms of 'ease of modification', suppose that one of your global groups is a member of a domain local group that is giving them improper access to a resource. To resolve this problem, you do not need to modify any permissions, or assign users to different groups. You simply need to remove the global group from the membership list of the domain local group in question, and then add it to the appropriate domain local group.

Finally, reduction in the size of the global group list is a very important piece in a multi-domain environment. When you go to add a group from a different domain to one of your domain groups, you will see a list of all global groups from the other domain. If you were *not* using the Microsoft Rule, then one global group would have typically been built for each level of access to each resource, meaning that, in a large organization, you could literally have *thousands* of global groups to sort through. With the rule, however, you will only see one global group for each position level, which at most is going to add up to a few hundred global groups.

Figure 6-3 Strategy for creating global and domain local groups

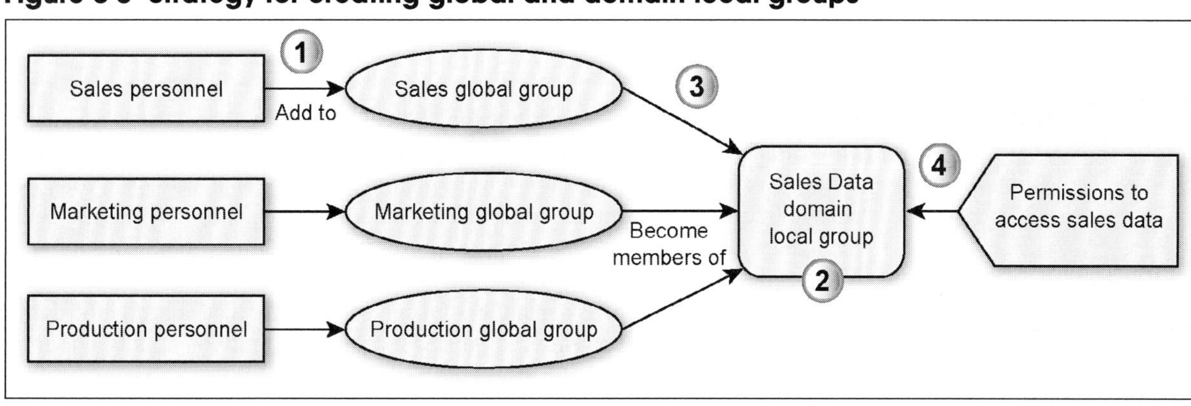

Table 6-2 Strategy for creating global and domain local groups

Step number	Procedure	Example
1	Assign users who share a common job profile to global groups.	An organization has three departments: sales, marketing, and production. The personnel working in these departments need access to the sales data that contains data on all sales transactions and money accrued to the company from its products. As a part of implementing the group strategy, you can create three global groups in the domain: Sales, Marketing, and Production.
2	Create a domain local group for shared resources or a group of resources, such as files and printers, to which users need access.	Create a domain local group called Sales Data that will contain the details of all sales transactions and money accrued to the company.
3	Add global groups to the domain local group.	Add the global groups Sales, Marketing, and Production as members of the domain local group, Sales Data.
4	Assign permissions to the domain local group to enable the members to access the required resource.	Grant appropriate rights and permissions to the domain local group to enable the members to access the sales data. The users from the sales, marketing, and production departments will now be able to access the sales data because their global groups are members of the Sales Data domain local group.

skill 2 Planning Group Strategies (cont'd)

exam objective

Basic knowledge

overview

If you want to use the universal group scope to create groups in the network, you can try the following strategies (**Table 6-3**):

- Before creating universal groups, ensure that the memberships of those groups will not change frequently. Universal groups are stored on global catalog servers, and changes to the memberships of universal groups are therefore replicated to all global catalog servers in the entire forest.
- Never add a user account as a member of a universal group. Instead, add global groups as members of universal groups. Again, this is for replication. If you remove a user account from a universal group, the universal group must then replicate, as its membership list has changed. However, if you remove a user account from a global group, which is a member of a universal group, the universal group's membership is not impacted. Therefore, the only replication that occurs is for the change in the global group, which is domain-wide instead of forest-wide.
- Universal groups are designed to be used for one specific situation: when you need multiple users in multiple domains to have the *same access* to multiple resources in multiple domains. For instance, if you have five groups in five domains that need the same access to 20 shares in those five domains, then you would use a universal group to reduce the effort required in building the group memberships. In this case, you would add the five global groups to the universal group, and then add the universal group to the 20 domain local groups with the proper permissions applied.

Table 6-3 Strategies for using the universal group scope to create groups in the network

Strategy	Reasoning
Ensure that the membership of the groups will not change frequently.	Changes to the membership of universal groups are replicated to all global catalog servers in the forest because universal groups are stored on global catalog servers.
Do not add a user account as a member of a universal group; add global groups as members of universal groups.	Prevents unnecessary forest-wide replication. Removing a user account from a universal group requires the group to replicate because the group's membership has changed. Removing a user account from a global group results in domain-wide replication only.
Use universal groups for the specific circumstance for which they are intended.	Universal groups are designed to allow multiple users in multiple domains to have the same access to multiple resources in multiple domains.

skill 3 Creating Groups

exam objective

Create and manage objects manually or by using scripting.

overview

Groups can be used effectively to manage large numbers of users and resources. In the following tasks, we will create a global distribution group and add members to this group using the Active Directory Users and Computers console in Windows 2000 Active Directory. It is important to realize that creating any type or scope of group follows these same steps. However, even in small environments, it is advised that you follow the Microsoft rule for creating groups and assigning permissions. While it takes a little more work to set up, in the long run it reduces effort to such a large degree that the extra setup effort is worth it.

tip

Use the Users container or an Organizational Unit (OU) in the Active Directory Users and Computers console to create groups.

how to

Create a group.

1. Log on to the domain controller as an Administrator.
2. Click **Start**, point to **Programs**, point to **Administrative Tools**, and then click the **Active Directory Users and Computers** command. This will display the **Active Directory Users and Computers** console.
3. Right-click the Users folder, point to **New**, and then click the **Group** command. The **New Object-Group** dialog box opens.
4. In the **Group name** text box, type **Group1**.
5. In the **Group scope** section, click the **Global** option button. This specifies the group as a global group.
6. In the **Group type** section, click the **Distribution** option button. This specifies the group as a distribution group (**Figure 6-4**).
7. Click **OK** to complete the procedure for creating a group. **Figure 6-5** displays the new group in the **Active Directory Users and Computers** console.

tip

The name must be unique in the domain where the group is being created. Note that the option for the pre-Windows 2000 group name is filled automatically.

more

Some groups may become redundant with changes in the organization. You should make sure to delete the groups that are no longer required. This helps you maintain security and prevents you from accidentally assigning permissions to groups and resources that are no longer required in your organization. Windows 2000 Active Directory uses the **SID** or **Security Identifier** to identify a particular group and assign permissions to it. SID is a unique number that identifies each security object in Active Directory. When a group is deleted, the SID of that group is also deleted and is never used by Windows 2000 again. Hence, you need to keep in mind that you cannot recreate and restore the settings of a deleted group.

To delete a group, right-click the group in the details pane of the **Active Directory Users and Computers** console and click the **Delete** command. Then, click **Yes** in the **Active Directory** message box that appears to delete the group. You can also move and rename user groups based on changes in the organization structure.

caution

You cannot delete a group if even one member has the group set as his or her primary group. The default primary group of all users is Domain Users. Primary groups apply only to users who log on to the network through Macintosh Services or to users who run POSIX-compliant applications. You must change the primary group only if you use these services.

Figure 6-4 Creating a group

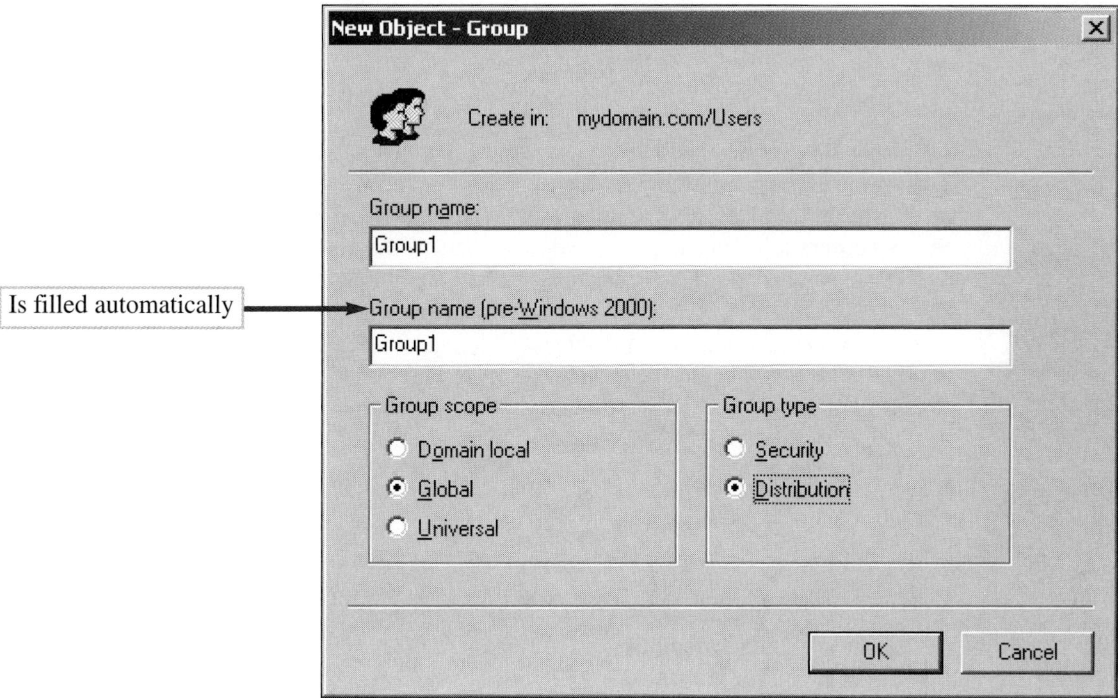

Figure 6-5 The new group in the Active Directory Users and Computers console

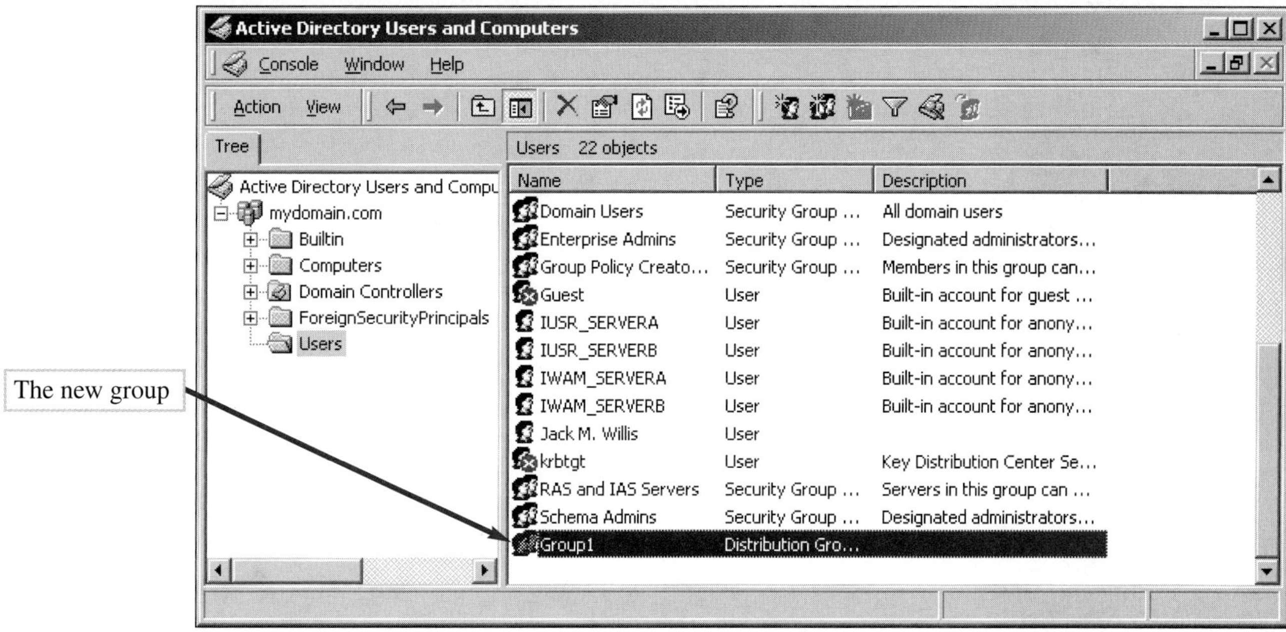

skill 4 Setting Group Properties

exam objective

Create and manage objects manually or by using scripting.

overview

Once you have created a group, you can set its properties by accessing the **Properties** dialog box for the group. The various tabs used to set the properties of a group include:

- **General tab:** Describes the scope and type assigned to the group.
- **Members tab:** Enables you to add members of the domain to the group. Members of a group can include user accounts, contacts, other groups, or computers.
- **Member Of tab:** Enables you to add the group to other groups in the domain or universal groups in other domains in the forest.
- **Managed By tab:** Enables you to specify the user or contact person managing the group.
- **Object tab:** Specifies the path of the group within the domain.
- **Security tab:** Enables you to specify permissions for the group, defining who can and cannot modify the group.

how to

Add members to a group and specify a manager for the group.

1. Right-click **Group1** in the **Active Directory Users and Computers** console and click the **Properties** command. This will display the **Properties** dialog box for **Group1**.
2. Click the **Members** tab in the **Properties** dialog box.
3. Click [Add...] to open the **Select Users**, **Contacts**, **Computers**, **or Groups** dialog box.
4. Click **Barbara J. Clarke** in the **Name** list.
5. Click [Add] to add this user to the group, Group1. The added member appears at the bottom of the dialog box (**Figure 6-6**).
6. Click [OK] to close the dialog box. The **Properties** dialog box now displays the member of the group, as shown in **Figure 6-7**.
7. To specify the manager of the group, click the **Managed By** tab.
8. Click [Change...] to open the **Select User or Contact** dialog box.
9. Click **Administrator** in the **Name** list in the **Select User or Contact** dialog box, and then click [OK] to close the dialog box. The **Name** text box displays the group manager (**Figure 6-8**).
10. Click [OK] to close the **Properties** dialog box.

tip

Rather than adding one user at a time, you can use the [Shift] or [Ctrl] key to select and add a specific range of user groups or accounts to the group.

Figure 6-6 Selecting users for the group

Select Users, Contacts, Computers, or Groups
Look in:
mydomain.com
Name
In Folder
Barbara J. Clarke (BClarke@mydomain.com)
mydomain.com/Users
Domain Computers
Domain Controllers
Schema Admins
Enterprise Admins
Cert Publishers
Domain Admins
Add
Check Names
Barbara J. Clarke (BClarke@mydomain.com)
OK
Cancel
Domain from which users and groups can be added
The new member in the bottom pane

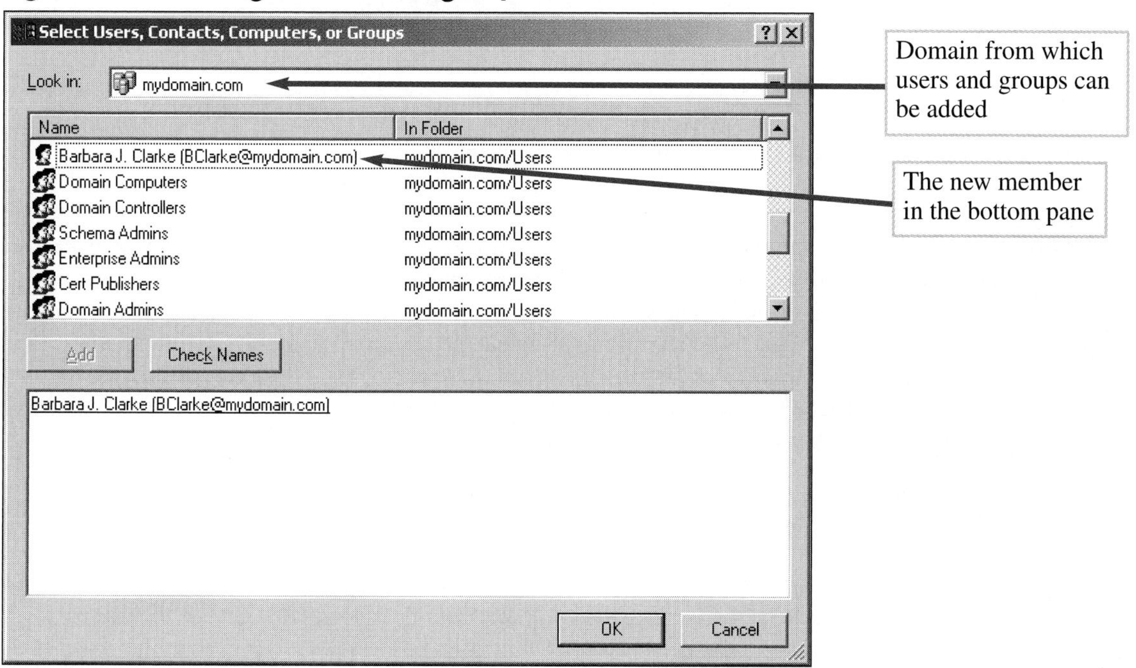

Figure 6-7 Member of the group

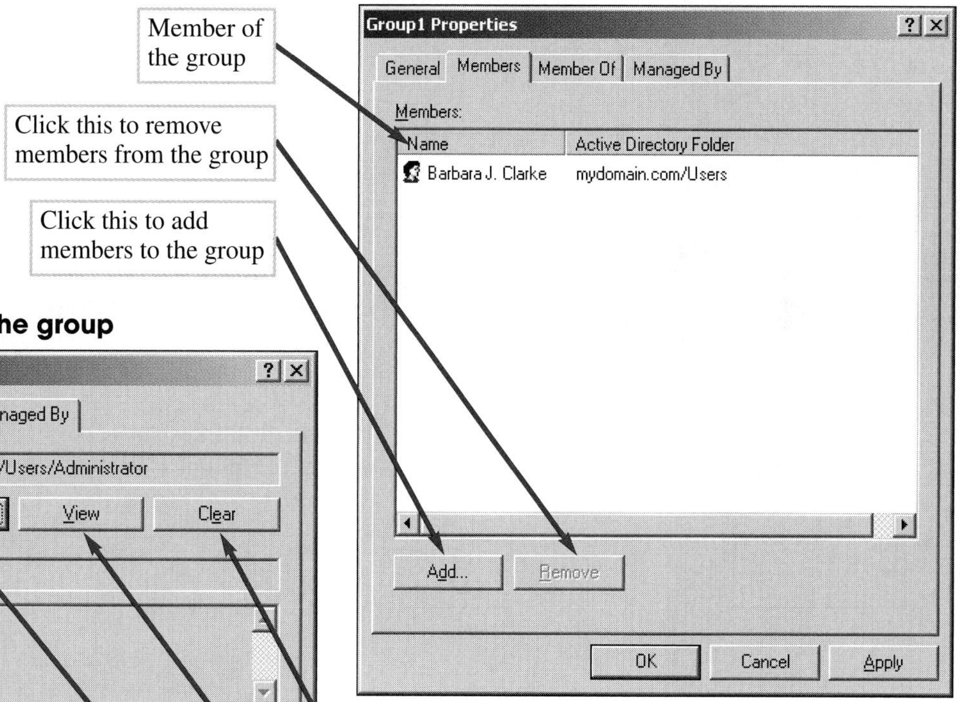

Group1 Properties
General
Members
Member Of
Managed By
Members:
Name
Active Directory Folder
Barbara J. Clarke
mydomain.com/Users
Add...
Remove
OK
Cancel
Apply
Member of the group
Click this to remove members from the group
Click this to add members to the group

Figure 6-8 Manager of the group

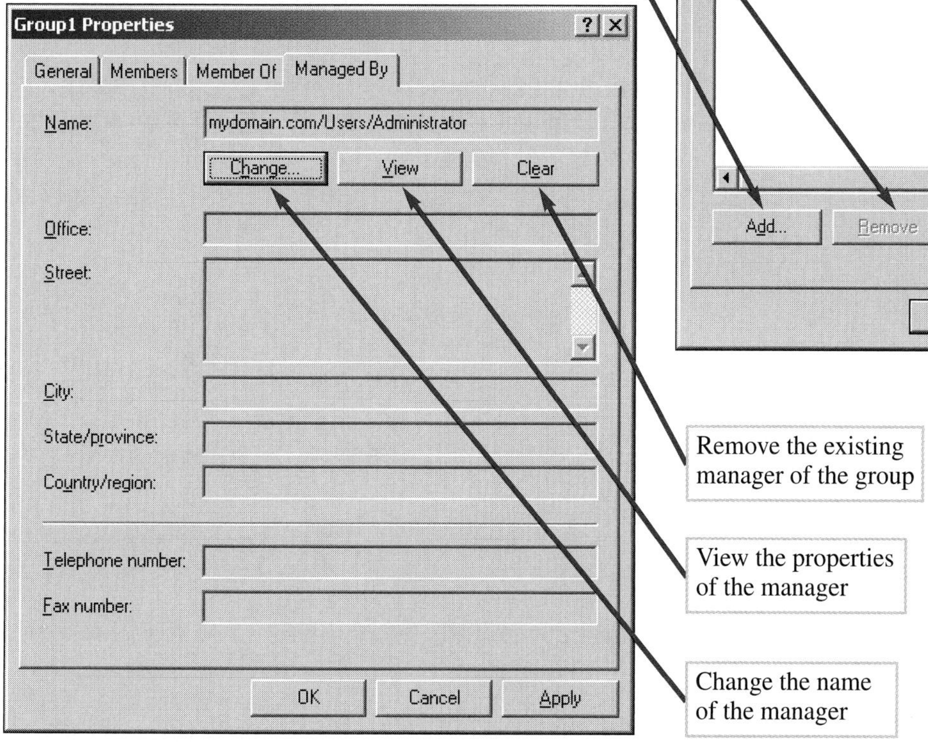

Group1 Properties
General
Members
Member Of
Managed By
Name:
mydomain.com/Users/Administrator
Change...
View
Clear
Office:
Street:
City:
State/province:
Country/region:
Telephone number:
Fax number:
OK
Cancel
Apply
Remove the existing manager of the group
View the properties of the manager
Change the name of the manager

skill 5 Modifying Group Properties

exam objective

Create and manage objects manually or by using scripting.

overview

Changes in the requirements of an organization may call for modifying the properties of groups. For example, when a network is restructured, the administrator may need to change the scope of a group. You need to keep two things in mind while planning the modification of group scopes. First, a domain local group can be converted to a universal group only if the domain local group does not contain another domain local group. Secondly, a global group can be changed to a universal group only if the global group is independent and not a member of another group.

Similarly, with occasional changes in the role of a group, you may also need to change a group type correspondingly. For example, a company hires trainees to work on a particular project and adds them to a distribution group so that they can communicate via e-mail. Later, when these trainees are transferred into various departments, they need to access various resources on the network depending on their roles. You should then change their distribution group to a security group and appropriate permissions should be assigned to the group. This would call for a change in the type and the scope of the existing group.

It is important to note here that group scopes and types can be changed only when Windows 2000 Active Directory is operating in the native mode. If your domain is in mixed mode, you first need to change the domain to native mode before changing the group scope and type. Remember that this process is irreversible.

tip

Windows 2000 Active Directory allows for the changing of group scopes only when it is operating in the native mode.

how to

Change the type and scope of a group. (You can perform this task only if your domain is in the native mode.)

1. Right-click **Group1** in the **Active Directory Users and Computers** console and click the **Properties** command. This will display the **Properties** dialog box for **Group1**.
2. In the **Group scope** section, click the **Universal** option button to change the group scope.
3. In the **Group type** section, click the **Security** option button to change the group type **(Figure 6-9)**.
4. Click OK to close the **Properties** dialog box.
5. Close the **Active Directory Users and Computers** console. **Figure 6-10** displays the modified properties of the group.

Figure 6-9 Changing the properties of a group

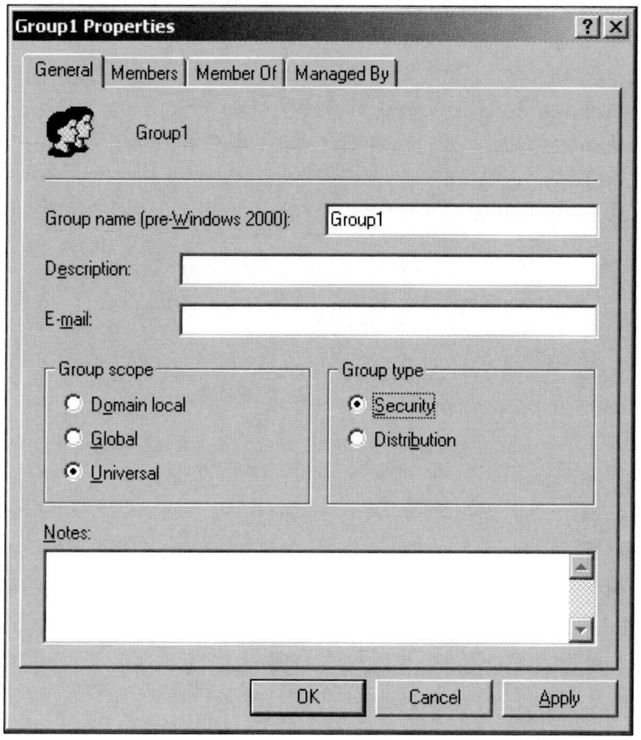

Group1 Properties

General | Members | Member Of | Managed By

Group1

Group name (pre-Windows 2000): Group1

Description:

E-mail:

Group scope: Domain local / Global / Universal (selected)

Group type: Security (selected) / Distribution

Notes:

OK | Cancel | Apply

Figure 6-10 Changed properties of the group

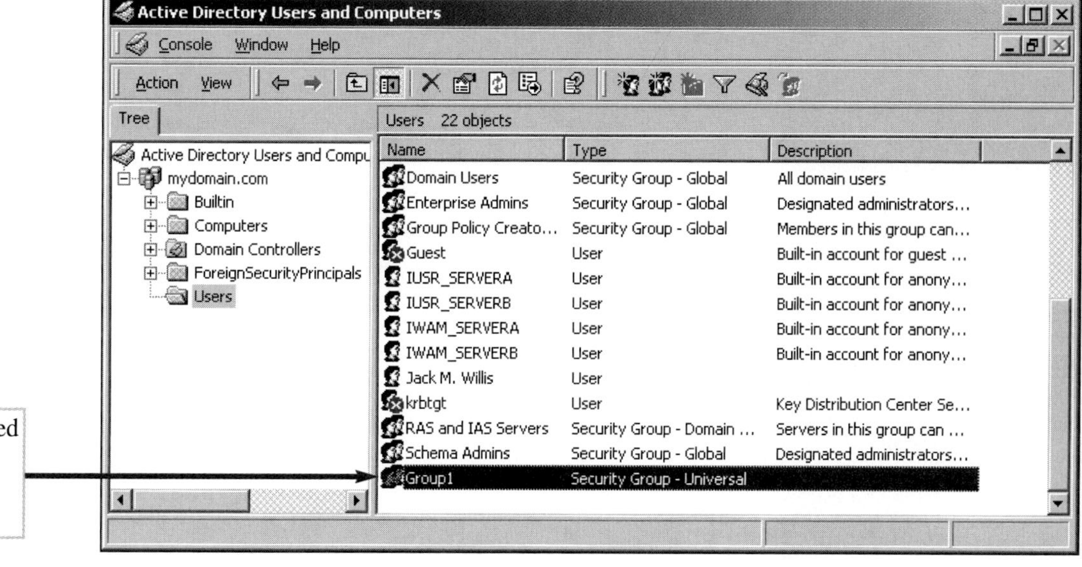

skill 6 Creating Local Groups

exam objective

Create and manage objects manually or by using scripting.

overview

You may find that groups with a domain local scope are sometimes referred to as local groups. However, there is a vast difference between a local group and a domain local group. Unlike a domain local group, which is a collection of user accounts from a domain, a local group is used to manage local user accounts on a single server or a stand-alone computer. In other words, groups with a local scope are called **local groups**. The access of these groups is limited to the resources located in the computer in which the group has been created. Local groups are useful for restricting user access to network resources in a workgroup environment.

To create local groups, you use the Local Users and Groups snap-in in the Computer Management console. Additionally, you can delete, rename, or even add members to the local group by accessing the shortcut menu of the local group in the Computer Management console.

how to

tip

Use a unique name for the local group. The name can contain 256 characters but cannot contain the following characters: \/[]:|<>+=;,?*

Create a local group.

1. Log on to the member server (Server01) as an **Administrator**.
2. Click Start, point to **Programs**, point to **Administrative Tools**, and then click the **Computer Management** command. This will display the **Computer Management** console.
3. Double-click the **Local Users and Groups** node to view the Groups folder.
4. Right-click the Groups folder and click the **New Group** command. The **New Group** dialog box is displayed.
5. In the **Group Name** box, type **LocalGroup1**.
6. Click Add... to open the **Select Users or Groups** dialog box.
7. Click **JohnA** in the **Name** list to add this user to the list of members in the group **(Figure 6-11)**. Note that you do not have the option to add a member while creating a domain local group on a domain controller.
8. Click OK to close the **Select Users or Groups** dialog box. The name of the member appears in the **Members** list in the **New Group** dialog box **(Figure 6-12)**.
9. Click Create to create the group.
10. Click Close to close the **New Group** dialog box.
11. Close the **Computer Management** console.

more

caution

Although global and universal groups can be made members of a local group, a local group cannot become a member of any other group.

You generally create local groups when the number of users is small and Active Directory is not installed on the network. It is important to remember that you can use local groups only on computers running Windows 2000 Professional and member servers running Windows 2000 Server. Local groups cannot be created on domain controllers because domain controllers use the Active Directory database instead of the local user database. Moreover, local groups can be used only on the computer where the local groups exist.

Built in local groups are stored in the Groups folder in the Local Users and Groups snap-in in the Computer Management of stand-alone servers, member servers, and computers running Windows 2000 Professional. **Table 6-4** describes some of the built-in local groups.

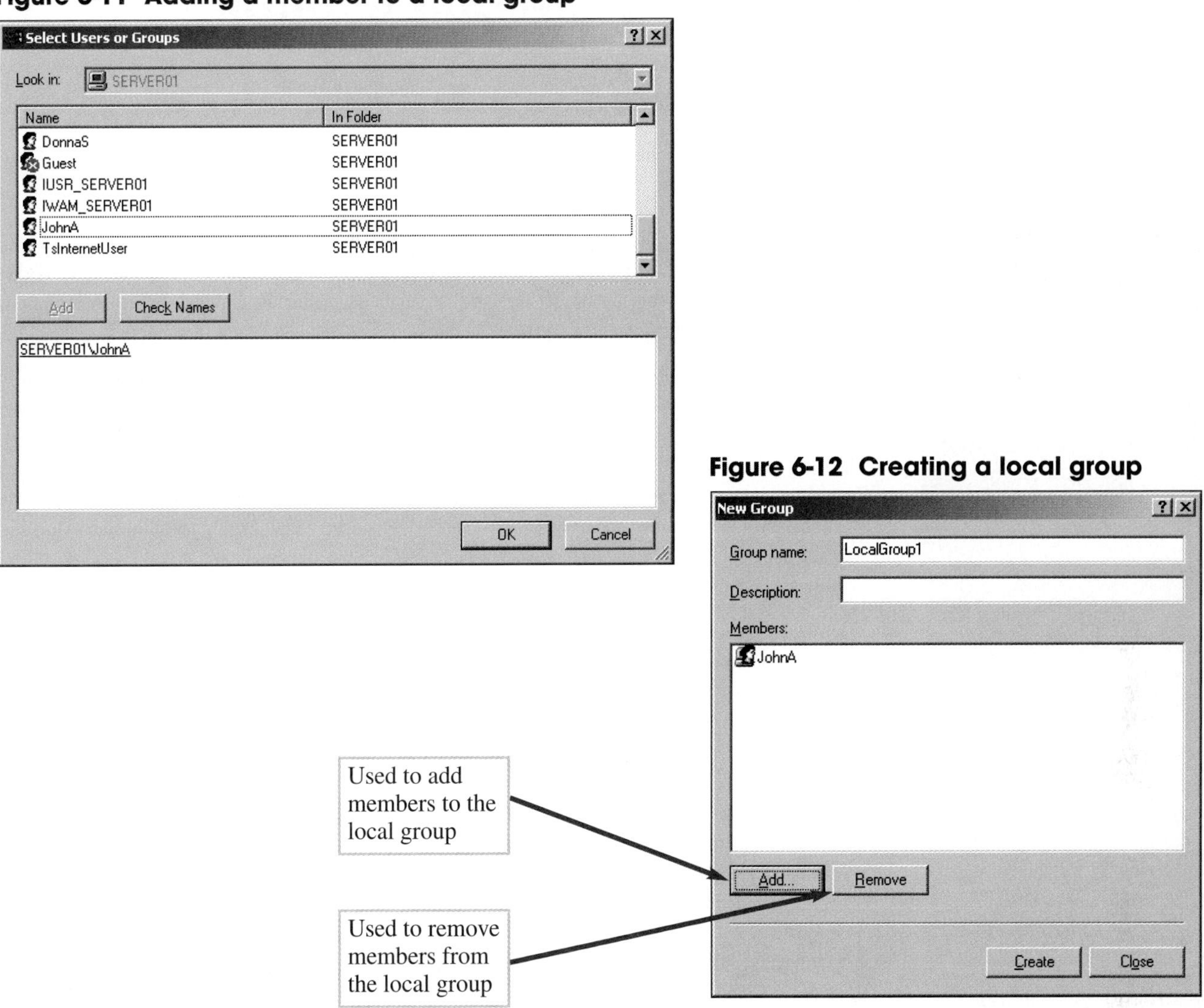

Figure 6-11 Adding a member to a local group

Figure 6-12 Creating a local group

Table 6-4 Built-in local groups

Built-in local groups	Description
Administrators	Used to provide full access to the local computer. The built-in Administrator account for a computer is a member of this group by default.
Guests	Used to manage guest accounts in a computer. Members cannot make permanent changes to the desktop settings. The built-in Guest account for a computer is a member of this group by default.
Users	Used to manage general user access in a computer. By default, all local user accounts created in a computer are added to this group.
Backup operators	Used to manage backup and restore procedures of the data in the computer.
Replicator	Used to include the service account for file replication. User accounts should not typically be added to this group.
Power Users	A group for power users, or user accounts that should have more privileges than standard users. Power users are allowed to share resources and perform other semi-administrative tasks.

skill 7 Introducing Default Groups

exam objective

Basic knowledge

overview

Windows 2000 Active Directory provides three classes of default groups: global, domain local, and special identity. These default groups have a predefined common set of user rights or group memberships, which determine the type of tasks that a user or a group member of each group can perform.

tip

These groups can vary from computer to computer, depending on the services installed in the network.

Global groups: These groups, also known as predefined global groups, consolidate common types of user accounts. Active Directory creates predefined global groups in the Users container in the Active Directory Users and Computers console. These groups have predefined group memberships. However, the domain-wide rights and privileges need to be assigned to the members of these groups. These rights can be assigned either by assigning user permissions to predefined global groups or by adding these global groups to domain local groups.

Some commonly used predefined global groups are described below.

- **Domain Admins:** This group is added to the Administrators built-in domain local group so that members of this group can manage resources and perform administrative tasks on any computer in the domain. The Administrator account is a member of this group by default.
- **Domain Users:** This group is added to the users built-in domain local group and manages all domain user accounts. The Administrator, Krbgt, TsInternetUser, Guest, IUSR_computer_name, and IWAM_computer_name accounts are default members. Each new domain user account automatically becomes a member of this group.
- **Domain Guests:** This group is added to the Guests built-in domain local group and contains all domain guest accounts. The Guest account is a member of this group by default.
- **Enterprise Admins:** This group is used to add users who need administrative control to manage resources in the network. The Administrator account is a member of this group by default.

Figure 6-13 displays some common predefined global groups.

Figure 6-13 Commonly used predefined global groups

Active Directory Users and Computers

Console Window Help

Action View

Tree

Active Directory Users and Compu
mydomain.com
Builtin
Computers
Domain Controllers
ForeignSecurityPrincipals
Users

Pre-defined global groups in the Users container

Users 22 objects

Name	Type	Description
Administrator	User	Built-in account for admini...
Barbara J. Clarke	User	
Cert Publishers	Security Group - Global	Enterprise certification an...
DnsAdmins	Security Group - Domain ...	DNS Administrators Group
DnsUpdateProxy	Security Group - Global	DNS clients who are permi...
Domain Admins	Security Group - Global	Designated administrators...
Domain Computers	Security Group - Global	All workstations and serve...
Domain Controllers	Security Group - Global	All domain controllers in th...
Domain Guests	Security Group - Global	All domain guests
Domain Users	Security Group - Global	All domain users
Enterprise Admins	Security Group - Global	Designated administrators...
Group Policy Creato...	Security Group - Global	Members in this group can...
Guest	User	Built-in account for guest ...
IUSR_SERVERA	User	Built-in account for anony...

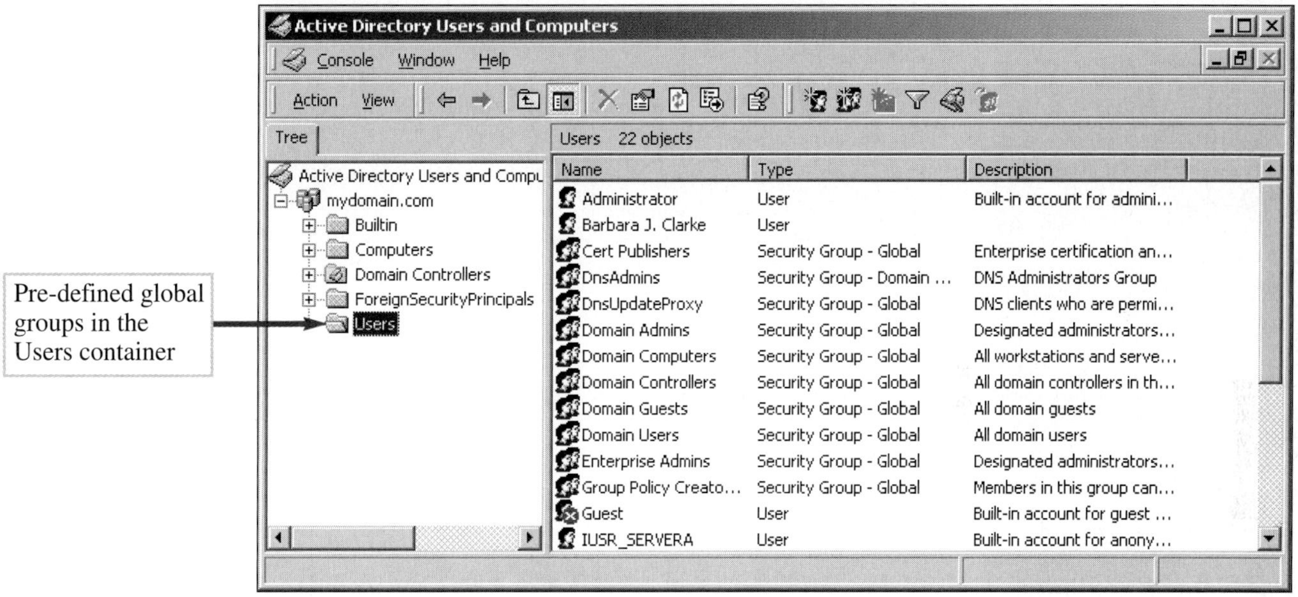

skill 7 Introducing Default Groups *(cont'd)*

exam objective

Basic knowledge

overview

In addition to predefined global groups, Windows 2000 also comes with predefined domain local groups, and special identity groups.

- **Domain local groups:** These groups in Windows 2000 Active Directory are also known as built-in groups and exist in the **Builtin** container in **the Active Directory Users and Computers** console. An administrator can add users to these groups to perform management tasks on domain controllers, as well as in Active Directory. **Table 6-5** describes some of the built-in domain local groups.
- **Special identity groups:** Special identity groups are present on all Windows 2000 computers and are logically grouped based on their actions instead of the groups to which they belong. These groups are defined and controlled by the operating system itself. Some of the special identity groups are described in **Table 6-6**.

Table 6-5 Built-in domain local groups

Built-in domain local groups	Description
Administrators	Used to provide full access to any domain member computer in the domain. The Administrator user account and the Domain Admins predefined global group are members of this group by default.
Guests	Includes guest accounts in the domain. The Guest account and the Domain Guests predefined global group are members of this group by default.
Users	Used to manage general user access. The Interactive pre-Windows 2000 groups, the Authenticated Users group and the Domain Users pre-defined global group are the members of this group.
Account operators	Used to create, modify, and delete user accounts and groups. However, members do not have rights to modify the Administrators group or any operator group.
Backup operators	Used to back up and restore any domain member computer using Windows backup.
Server operators	Used to perform general server management tasks such as sharing disk resources and backing up and restoring files on any domain member computer.
Print operators	Used to set up and manage network printers on any domain member computer.
Replicator	Used to include the service account for file replication. User accounts should not typically be added to this group.
Pre-Windows 2000 Compatible Access	Used to provide backward compatibility for Windows NT RAS servers or any other pre-Windows 2000 applications accessing the domain database. To allow Windows NT RAS server to use null sessions to access the domain database, add the Everyone group to this group. This group has pre-defined read access to the entire AD database.

Table 6-6 Special identity groups

Special identity groups	Description
Anonymous Logon	Includes users who are logged on to a computer without going through Windows 2000 security authentication.
Authenticated Users	Contains all users that have logged in. To prevent anonymous access to a resource, use this group instead of the Everyone group.
Creator Owner	Includes the user account of the user who created a resource or the user account that currently owns the specified resource. For example, if a member of the Administrators group creates a resource, the Administrators group is the owner of the resource.
Dialup	Includes any user who currently has a dial-up connection.
Everyone	Contains all users. Ensure that the Guest account is disabled when assigning permissions to the Everyone group. If enabled, the Guest account will acquire all rights assigned to the Everyone group. By default, the Everyone group is assigned full control to many resources. While it is common practice to *remove* the Everyone group's permissions, ensure that you *never deny* the Everyone group. Deny entries take precedence over allow entries, so if you deny the Everyone group, no one (including administrators) will have access.
Interactive	Contains a user account for any user who is currently locally logged on to the computer. Members of this group gain access to resources on the computer on which they are currently working. Use this group to specify that anyone who can access the computer locally can access resources on the computer. ***Note***: Certain services (Terminal Services and IIS, in particular) also provide remote users with a local logon. Any users using these services are considered to be logged on locally, and will be members of this group.
Network	Includes all users connecting to this computer across the network.

skill 8 Starting a Program Using the Run as Command

exam objective

Basic knowledge

overview

As a principle, you should avoid running a computer using the Administrator account. By doing this, you protect your network from some significant security risks. You should log on as a member of the Users or Power Users group for routine tasks. To perform an administrative task or to start a program while you are logged on as a user, you can use the Run as command. The **Run as command** allows you to access programs and other Windows 2000 administrative tools temporarily without logging off as the current user.

Note that there are certain applications, most notably Windows explorer, which cannot be accessed under a different user context. To access the application with administrator privileges, you must log on as an Administrator.

To start any program or any other Windows 2000 utility using the Run as command, you need:

- Appropriate user account and password information to log on to the computer.
- Existence of the program or the Windows 2000 utility on the system.

If you try to start a program or a Windows 2000 utility—such as an MMC console or Control Panel item—from a network location using the Run as command, the program may fail if the user account used to connect to the network share is different from the user account used to start the program. To resolve this problem, ensure that both user accounts have permissions to access the resource.

Before using the Run as command on your system, ensure that the RunAs service is actually running on your computer. You can set the RunAs service to start automatically at system startup by using the RunAs Service option in the Services console on the Administrative Tools menu.

Applications and desktop items that are initiated by Windows 2000 through a backend process cannot be started with the Run as command. Examples of the desktop items with this issue include Windows Explorer, My Computer, and the Printers folder (all of which use Explorer.exe).

tip

Although the Run as command is generally used to run programs as an administrator, other users having multiple accounts with alternate logging permissions can also use this command to access administrative programs.

how to

Use the **Run as** command to access the **Computer Management** console.

1. Log on to the domain controller as **BClarke**.
2. Click **Start**, point to **Programs**, and then point to **Administrative Tools**.
3. Pressing the **[Shift]** key, right-click the **Computer Management** command to view the shortcut menu.
4. Click the **Run as** command **(Figure 6-14)**. This displays the **Run As Other User** dialog box.
5. Click the **Run the program as the following user** option button.
6. In the **User name** text box, type an appropriate user name.
7. In the **Password** text box, type the appropriate password **(Figure 6-15)**.
8. Click **OK**. The **Computer Management** console appears. You can now work in the **Computer Management** console like an administrator.

Figure 6-14 Accessing the Run as command

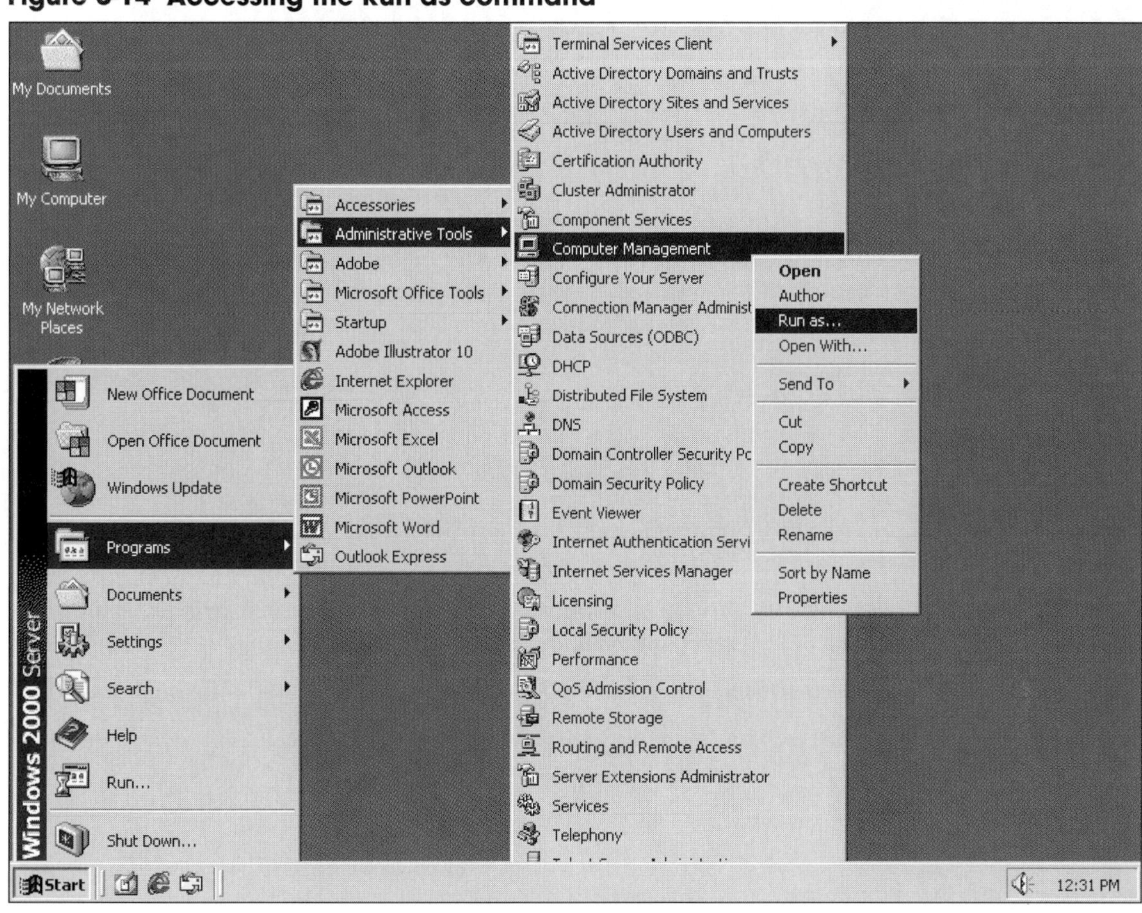

Figure 6-15 Running a program as another user

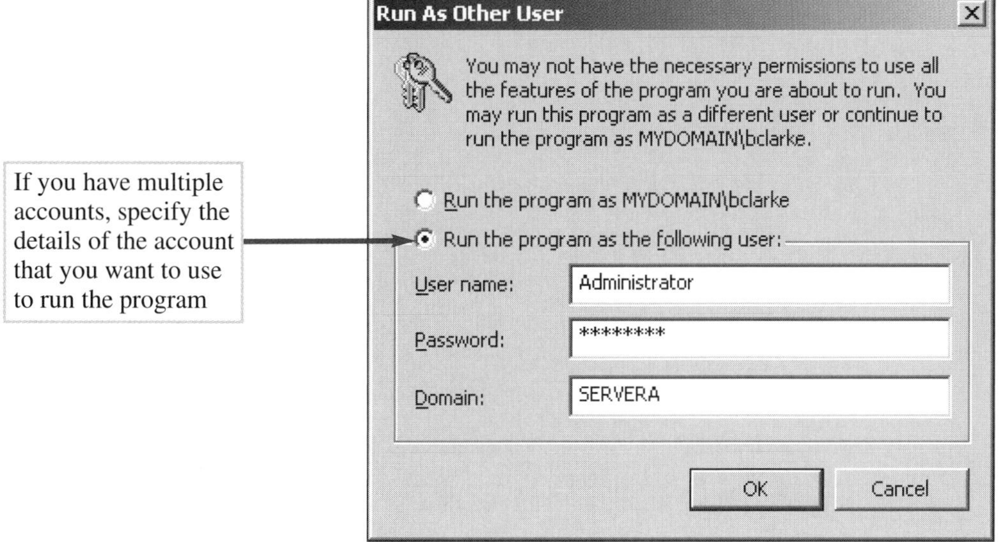

Exam 70-217

skill 8

Starting a Program Using the Run as Command *(cont'd)*

exam objective

Basic knowledge

more

You can access the **Run as** functionality from the command prompt, as well. To do this, you use the RUNAS command at the command prompt. The syntax for the RUNAS command is as follows: runas [/profile] [/env] [/netonly] /user:UserAccountName program

Where:

- /profile allows you to load the specified user's profile.
- /env specifies that the current environment be used instead of the user's environment.
- /netonly indicates that the user information specified is for remote access only.
- /user:UserAccountName specifies the name of the user account under which to run the program. The user account format should be user@domain or domain\user.
- program specifies the program or command to be executed.

For example, to start the **Computer Management** console using a domain administrator account called **mydomain\admin**, type (**Figure 6-16**):

runas /user:mydomain\admin "mmc %windir%\system32\compmgmt.msc"

Finally, the Run as command can also be invoked in a shortcut. Just go into Properties for the shortcut and check the "Run as different user" box.

Figure 6-16 Using Run as from the command prompt

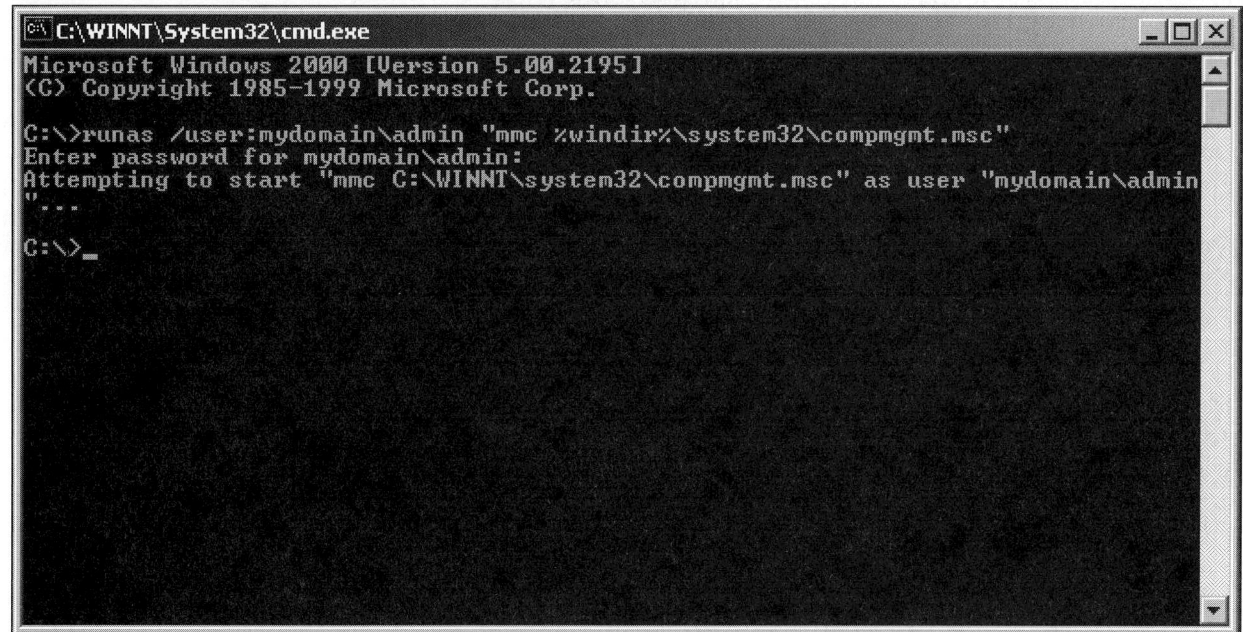

Summary

- A group is a collection of users, computers, contacts, and other groups in a forest. The two main functions of a group include managing administration and providing security to the resources of the network.
- While creating a group, you need to specify the type and scope of the group. Groups are of two types: distribution groups and security groups. Distribution groups are primarily used for e-mail. Security groups are used in Windows 2000 to assign permissions in order to gain access to the resources on a network.
- There are three types of group scopes: global, domain local, and universal. The global group scope is used to group users who share similar access profiles. The domain local group scope is used to assign permissions to resources. The universal group scope is used when several groups from several domains need the same access to several resources, also in several domains.
- Proper use of the Microsoft suggested group strategy will reduce administrative overhead as the company grows.
- You use the Active Directory Users and Computers console to create and manage groups. As part of managing groups, you can add members to the groups, add the group as a member of other groups, and specify the manager or contact for the group.
- When you create a group, each group is identified by a unique number called the SID. Windows 2000 Active Directory service uses the SID to identify a particular group and assign permissions to it.
- Changes in the requirements of an organization may call for the need to modify the properties of groups. For example, when a network is restructured, it may become necessary for the administrator to change the scope of the group, which might require changing a global or domain local group to a universal group. Similarly, with occasional changes in the role of a group, a group type may also need to be changed correspondingly. The type and scope of a group can be changed only when Windows 2000 Active Directory is operating in the native mode.
- A local group is used to access resources on a single server or a stand-alone computer. You can use the Computer Management console to create local groups.
- Windows 2000 Active Directory has three classes of default groups: predefined global, built-in domain local, and special identity groups.
- The Run as command allows you to access programs and other Windows 2000 administrative tools temporarily without logging off as the current user.

Key Terms

Built-in domain local groups
Built-in local groups
Distribution group
Domain local group scope
Global groups
Global group scope
Group
Local group
Mixed mode
Native mode
Nesting
Run as command
Security group
SID
Special identity groups
Universal group scope

Test Yourself

1. What are the properties of the two different group types? Choose all that apply.
   a. Security groups simplify administration by reducing administrative overhead related to applying permissions.
   b. Distribution groups are used solely for nonsecurity-related purposes.
   c. Distribution groups are used for security purposes.
   d. Distribution groups provide methods to group users who share similar network access requirements.
   e. Distribution groups facilitate coexistence of Windows NT and Windows 2000 domain controllers in the same domain.
2. Which of the following statements is true about group scopes in Active Directory?
   a. You can create domain local groups that can contain user accounts and global groups from any domain.
   b. You can convert global groups to domain local groups in native mode.
   c. You can assign global scope to groups to grant permissions only for the domain in which the global group exists.
   d. You can create domain local groups that can be members of universal, global, and domain local groups in any domain.

3. Universal groups can:
   a. Be members of domain local groups in the same domain only.
   b. Be created in any mode.
   c. Access only those resources that are in the same domain.
   d. Contain user accounts and global groups from any domain in the forest.
4. The Windows 2000 network of XYZ, Inc., has five domains. To increase security, you created a new account that you will use to administer the entire network. To which group would you add the account so that you can manage the entire network?
   a. Interactive
   b. Administrators
   c. Enterprise Admins
   d. Domain Admins
5. You are logged on to a Windows 2000 computer as a user with no administrative rights. You need to launch the Active Directory Sites and Services console to create a server object. How will you accomplish the task without logging out from your current user account and logging on again as an administrator?
   a. Create a remote session to a domain controller.
   b. Assign temporary administrative rights to access the Active Directory Sites and Services console.
   c. Use the Run as command to launch the Active Directory Sites and Services console.
   d. Use the DCPROMO command-line tool.
6. Which of following describes the recommended process for creating domain local groups and global groups?
   1. Assign users with common job responsibilities to global groups.
   2. Assign permissions and access rights to the domain local group.
   3. Identify the resources to which users need access and create a domain local group for these shared resources.
   4. Add global groups that need to access the resources to that domain local group.

   a. 2, 3, 1, 4
   b. 3, 4, 1, 2
   c. 1, 4, 2, 3
   d. 1, 3, 4, 2
7. You are the network consultant of GoodKnight Corp., which maintains seven domains spread across different branches. You need to create a group and add new users from two domains. Which tab would you use to add members to the group?
   a. Object tab
   b. Members tab
   c. Member Of tab
   d. Managed By tab
8. The Windows 2000 network of XYZ, Inc., has hired a new assistant in the network administration department. The assistant needs to create, manage, and delete user accounts on local computers. To which group should the user account be added so the new assistant can perform his role?
   a. Creator Owner
   b. Replicator
   c. Backup Operators
   d. Power Users
9. Which of the following statements is true about local groups in a mixed mode domain?
   a. Local groups cannot be members of any other group.
   b. Local groups can be created on any domain controller.
   c. The scope of a local group can be global or domain local.
   d. A local group and a domain local group are the same.

Projects: On Your Own

1. Create a group and add members to the group.
   a. Log on as a **Domain Administrator** on a domain controller.
   b. Open the **Active Directory Users and Computers** console.
   c. Access the **Users** container and display the **New Object-Group** dialog box.
   d. Name the group **Research**. Specify the group scope as **Global** and group type as **Security**.
   e. Create a domain user account for **ResearchStudent1**.
   f. Open the **Members** tab in the **Properties** dialog box of the **Research** group.
   g. Add the user **ResearchStudent1** to the **Research** group.
2. Change the scope and type of the Research group.
   a. Open the **Properties** dialog box of the Research group.
   b. Change the group scope to **Universal**.
   c. Change the group type to **Distribution**.
   d. Close the **Active Directory Users and Computers** console.
3. Create a local group and add members to the group.
   a. Log on as an **Administrator** on a member server.
   b. Open the **Computer Management** console.
   c. Create a local user account, **MarketingUser1**.
   d. Create a local user group **Marketing**.
   e. Add the user **MarketingUser1** to this group.
   f. Close the **Computer Management** console.

Problem Solving Scenarios

1. You are the Administrator of a Windows 2000 ADS-based network. Your network consists of three domains named Development, Admin, and Sales. Users in the Development domain need to access resources from the Admin and Sales domains for day-to-day activities. There are three user groups in the Development domain named GR1, GR2, and GR3. GR1 needs write access to the resources in the Admin domain and read access to the resources in the Sales domain. GR2 and GR3 need read access to the resources in the Admin domain and write access to the resources in the Sales domain.

   Prepare a PowerPoint presentation outlining how you will achieve this change.

2. You administer two Active Directory forests, which share a non-transitive two-way trust relationship. Due to recent modifications in user duties, you need to grant access to some users from three domains in forest2 for a resource located in the root domain in forest1 named Root.Forest.Msft.

   Prepare a PowerPoint presentation describing the most effective group management strategy to achieve this objective. Also specify the requirements for implementing this strategy.

LESSON

7 Performing Active Directory Administrative Tasks

As an administrator, you need to regularly monitor, maintain, and perform common administrative tasks to make sure Windows 2000 Active Directory works seamlessly. These tasks can range from locating Active Directory objects on the network to setting security permissions for objects. Additionally, you may need to ensure secure publication of network resources and provide easy access of information to users in need. You can accomplish these tasks by publishing objects in Active Directory using the Active Directory Users and Computers console. You can also publish network-enabled services information to help administrators locate and administer the services using the Active Directory Sites and Services console.

Another common task you may need to perform, due to structural or network changes in your organization, involves moving user or group objects within domains and between domains. Moving Active Directory objects between domains is significantly more complex and technical than moving them within a domain. Additionally, you might also need to move domain controllers between sites to create an efficient replication topology using the Active Directory Sites and Services console.

Finally, you can decentralize the network administration at various levels of your organization by distributing the administrative control of Active Directory objects and components among various users and administrators. The responsibility of carrying out specific tasks within the organizational units (OUs) or objects can be assigned to each administrator or user. You can use the Delegation of Control Wizard to delegate administrative tasks to designated users and groups. This will reduce the centralized administrative burden.

Goals

In this lesson, you will learn to perform various Active Directory administration tasks such as locating Active Directory objects, setting standard Active Directory permissions, and publishing Active Directory resources and network services. You will also learn to move Active Directory objects within the domain, between domains, and between sites, as well as delegate control of Active Directory objects to users and administrators. Finally, you will learn to troubleshoot Active Directory problems.

Lesson 7 Performing Active Directory Administrative Tasks

Skill	Exam 70-217 Objective
1. Searching for Active Directory Objects on a Network	Locate objects in Active Directory. Manage Active Directory objects.
2. Setting Standard Active Directory Object Permissions	Manage Active Directory objects. Control access to Active Directory objects.
3. Introducing Inheritance of Permissions	Control access to Active Directory objects.
4. Publishing Resources in Active Directory	Publish resources in Active Directory.
5. Publishing Network-enabled Services Using Active Directory	Publish resources in Active Directory.
6. Moving Active Directory Objects Within a Domain	Move Active Directory objects.
7. Moving Active Directory Objects Between Domains	Move Active Directory objects.
8. Moving a Domain Controller Between Sites	Move Active Directory objects.
9. Delegating Active Directory Permissions	Delegate administrative control of objects in Active Directory.
10. Troubleshooting Active Directory	Monitor, optimize, and troubleshoot Active Directory performance and replication.

Requirements

To complete the skills in this lesson, you will need administrative rights on three domain controllers. One computer should be the domain controller for the mydomain.com domain you created in Lesson 2 (Server01), and the other two should be domain controllers for the domain1.mydomain.com and domain2.mydomain.com domains. Create an Admin OU, Sales OU, and Human Resources OU, then create domain user accounts for users named Amanda Temple and Alfred Wilson in the Admin OU, Donna Smith in the Sales OU, and Jim Ford in the Human Resources OU on the mydomain.com server. Modify Jim Ford's account and enter "Human Resources" in his Department field. Finally, create two sites named Atlanta and NewYork.

skill 1 Searching for Active Directory Objects on a Network

exam objective

Locate objects in Active Directory. Manage Active Directory objects.

overview

Active Directory contains information on objects that are located on a network. Each Active Directory object has a unique set of attributes associated with it. For example, the attributes of a user account can include the user's address, telephone numbers, and organization details. **Table 7-1** describes some commonly used objects in Active Directory. In a network, which has a large number of Active Directory objects, it becomes difficult for an administrator to remember the exact locations of all the objects. The administrator then uses the help of the object attributes to locate the object.

To locate objects in Active Directory, you use the Find dialog box in the Active Directory Users and Computers console. The Find dialog box provides various options that you can use to search Active Directory objects. When you search Active Directory for an object, the Find dialog box helps generate a **Lightweight Directory Access Protocol (LDAP)** query. LDAP is the primary access protocol used to query and retrieve information about objects in Active Directory. The LDAP query searches the global catalog or the local domain (depending on the location listed in the "look in" box) for the specified object and returns the queried information. The Find dialog box thus helps administrators in locating objects from the entire forest.

While using the Find dialog box, you can specify a single attribute or multiple attributes to locate an object. You can even specify partial values for the objects you are trying to locate. For example, to locate a computer named BIGPC, you can just specify the first two letters of the computer name 'BI'. Note that computer names are not case sensitive.

It is important to note that you can locate objects using Active Directory only if:

- You have read permissions to the objects in question.
- Your computers have Windows 2000 Server, Windows NT with the Active Directory client, or Windows 95/98 with the Active Directory Client and Active Desktop enabled.

tip

Always supply an object's common attributes while creating the object. These common attributes help trace the object easily.

tip

Users should use the Search option in the Start menu, as users do not typically have access to Active Directory Users and Computers.

how to

Locate the user account of an employee named Jim Ford of the Human Resources department in the domain mydomain.com.

1. Log on to **Server01** as an **Administrator**.
2. Click **Start**, point to **Programs**, point to **Administrative Tools**, and then click the **Active Directory Users and Computers** command to open the **Active Directory Users and Computers** console **(Figure 7-1)**.
3. To initiate the search in the **Users** container of the **mydomain.com domain**, right-click the **Users** container, and then click the **Find** command. The **Find Users, Contacts, and Computers** dialog box appears.
4. By default, the **Find** list box contains the object types **Users**, **Contacts**, and **Groups**. The **In** list box contains the name of the domain or OU where the search will be carried out. To specify the attribute for searching the user object Jim Ford, type **Jim** in the **Name** text box (**Figure 7-2**).
5. Click the **Advanced** tab to filter the search by specifying the search conditions.
6. Click Field, point to **Users**, and then click the **Department** attribute.

tip

You can specify multiple conditions to search for an object by using the Add button.

Table 7-1 Commonly used objects in Active Directory

Objects	Description
User account	Represents a user who has the ability to log on to a Windows 2000 network.
Contact	Defines a person connected to the organization such as a service provider.
Group	Represents a grouping of user accounts or computers.
Computer	Stores details about the computers in the domain.
Printer	Stores information about the printer on a network.
Shared folder	Points to the computer and entry of the shared folder, rather than the folder itself. In other words, this searches for folders published to AD.
Organizational unit	Organizes other Active Directory objects for administrative purposes.

Figure 7-1 Various objects in Active Directory

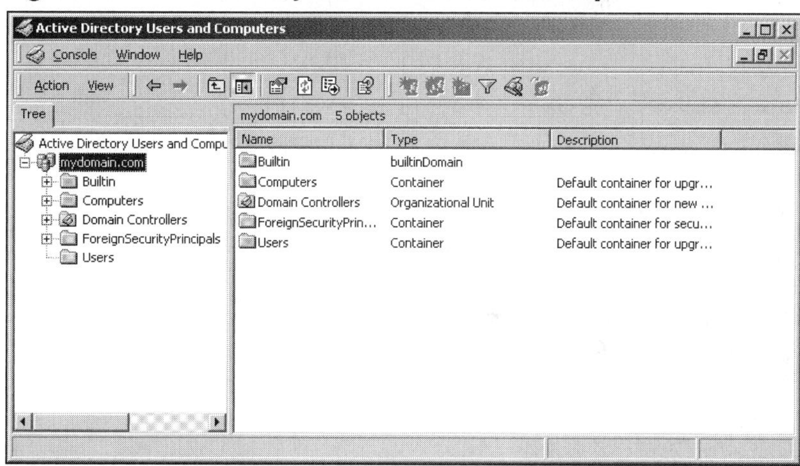

Figure 7-2 Specifying search attributes

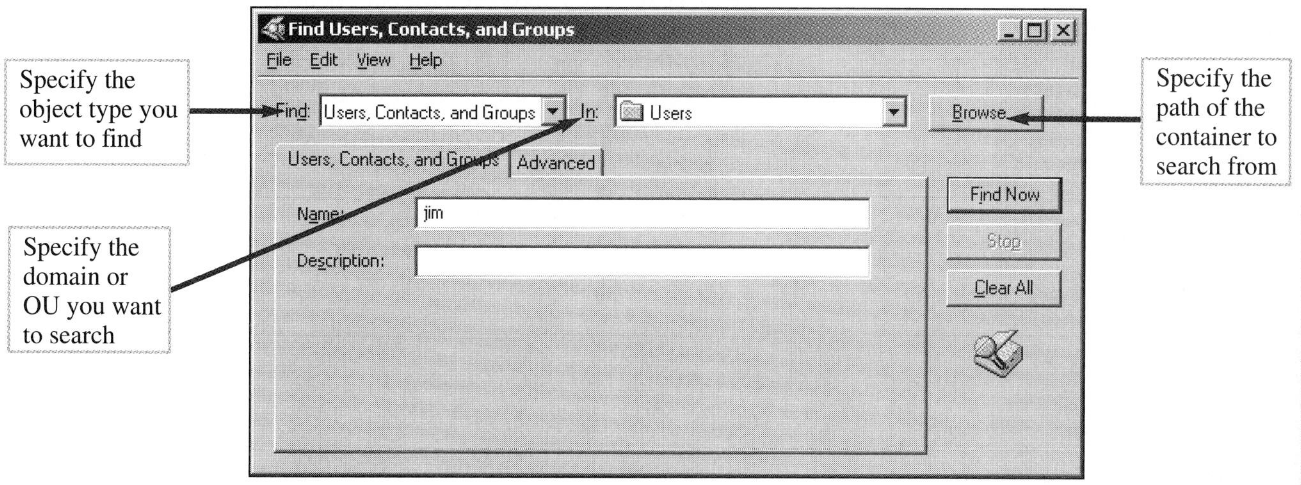

skill 1

Searching for Active Directory Objects on a Network *(cont'd)*

exam objective

Locate objects in Active Directory. Manage Active Directory objects.

how to

7. Accept the default setting of the **Starts with** operator in the **Condition** list box. Type **Human** in the **Value** text box to specify a value for the department attribute **(Figure 7-3)**.
8. Click [Add] to add the condition to the search criteria. The complete search criteria appears in the bottom panel.
9. Click [Find Now] to begin the search.
10. The search results display the user account for the employee named Jim Ford in the lower half of the **Find Users**, **Contacts**, **and Groups** dialog box **(Figure 7-4)**.
11. Click the **Close** button [X] to close the **Find Users**, **Contacts**, **and Groups** dialog box.

more

You can use the **Advanced** tab in the **Find** dialog box to make the search more specific. On this tab, you can search for an object based on multiple conditions. There are three search criteria you can specify:

- **Field:** You can specify the search field you are looking for based on the attribute of the object you are searching
- **Condition:** You can specify various conditions, such as **Starts with** and **Ends with**, to narrow the search.
- **Value:** Requires you to specify a value for the attribute.

tip

The attributes listed in the Field button change according to the object type.

Figure 7-3 Using the Advanced tab to search for an object based on a condition

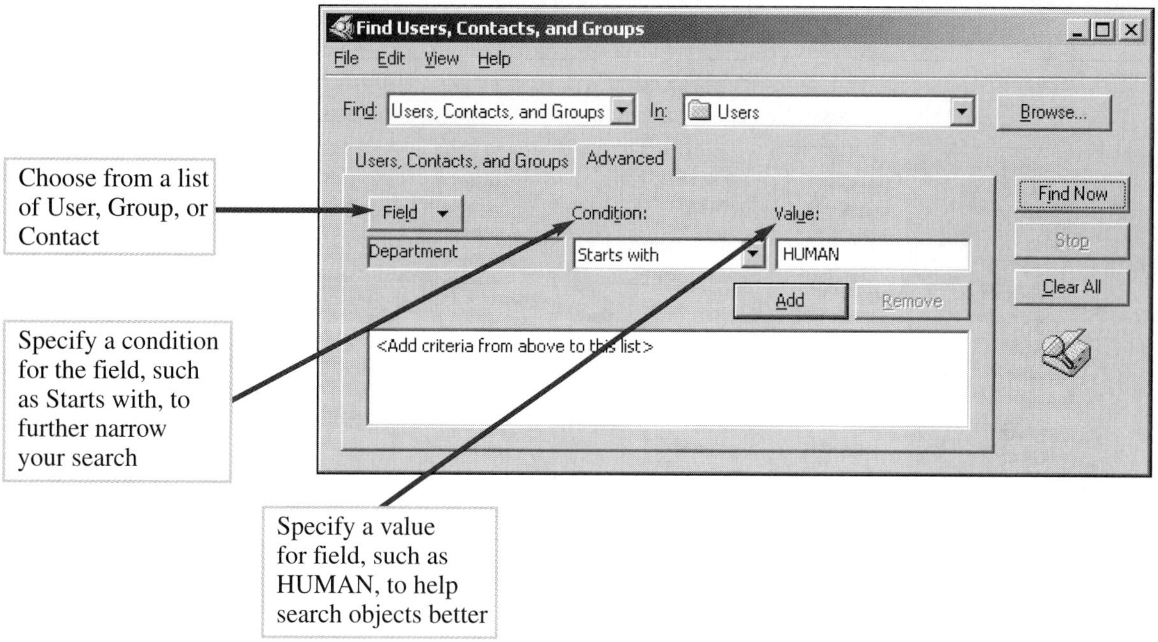

Find Users, Contacts, and Groups
File Edit View Help
Find: Users, Contacts, and Groups
In: Users
Browse...
Users, Contacts, and Groups
Advanced
Field
Condition:
Value:
Department
Starts with
HUMAN
Add
Remove
<Add criteria from above to this list>
Find Now
Stop
Clear All
Choose from a list of User, Group, or Contact
Specify a condition for the field, such as Starts with, to further narrow your search
Specify a value for field, such as HUMAN, to help search objects better

Figure 7-4 Filtering the search results

Find Users, Contacts, and Groups
File Edit View Help
Find: Users, Contacts, and Groups
In: Users
Browse...
Users, Contacts, and Groups
Advanced
Field
Condition:
Value:
Add
Remove
Department Starts with Human
Find Now
Stop
Clear All
Name
Type
Description
Jim Ford
User
Employee
1 item(s) found
Results appear in the bottom white panel

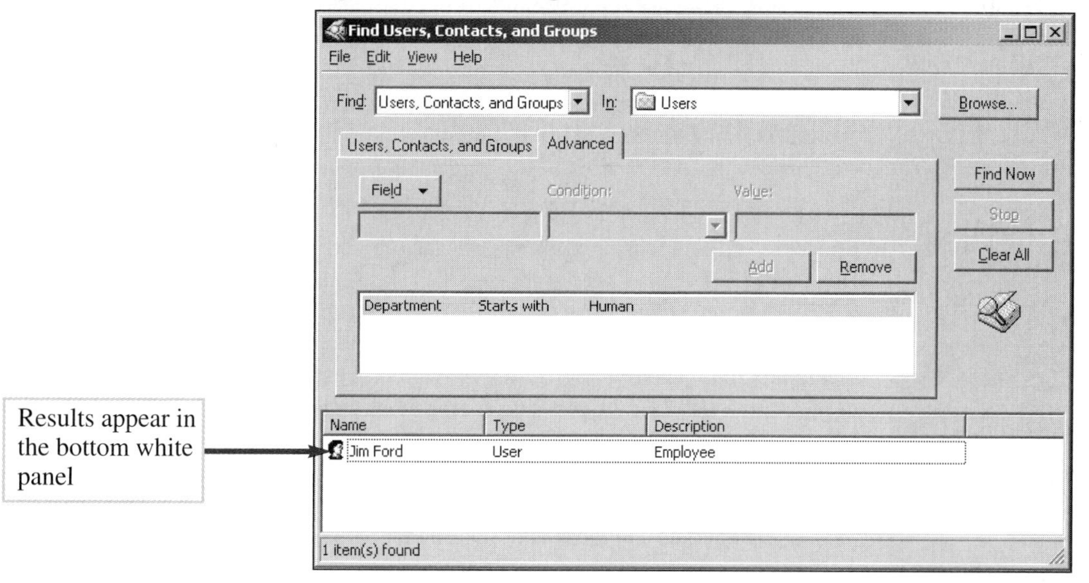

skill 2 Setting Standard Active Directory Object Permissions

exam objective

Manage Active Directory objects. Control access to Active Directory objects.

overview

Windows 2000 provides security access to Active Directory objects by using object permissions. Every Active Directory object has a **security descriptor** associated with it. This security descriptor controls access to objects by defining the permissions and the type of access allowed. As an administrator, you must assign permissions to an object so that users can access the object. The list of these user access permissions is stored in the **Discretionary Access Control List (DACL)** in Active Directory. Besides a list of all user accounts and groups that have access permissions to the Active Directory objects, the DACL also mentions the type of access granted. For every user who is assigned access to an object, the DACL for the object must contain an entry called an **access control entry (ACE)**. The user cannot gain access to the object if there is not an ACE for either the user, or groups the user is a member of, specified in the DACL.

caution

Always assign Full Control permission for objects to at least one user, such as the administrator. This will ensure that every object in Active Directory can be accessed by at least one user.

As part of managing Active Directory objects, you need to assign permissions to users and groups depending on the needs and policies of your organization. However, you need to be careful while assigning these permissions. Many users are members of multiple groups. Since a user's effective permissions are a combination of permissions for all groups, assigning different permissions to multiple groups can change the effective permissions of the user on objects. For example, assume that a user named Allan belongs to two groups. One group provides him with the Read permission for a folder, while the other provides him with the Write permission for the same folder. The effective permissions granted to him for the folder in this case would be both Read and Write. However, denied permissions take precedence over all other permissions you assign to users and groups. For example, if Allan, as part of one group, has been denied access permissions to the network printer, he will not be able to access the printer even if another group to which he belongs does have access.

tip

Note that the options in the Properties dialog box for each object type are different.

Active Directory provides two sets of permissions that you can either allow or deny to users and groups. These are standard and special permissions.

- **Standard permissions** include the most commonly assigned permissions such as Read and Write. **Table 7-2** describes the standard permissions. In reality, standard permissions are simply combinations of specific special permissions.
- **Special permissions** achieve a more specific level of control over objects than standard permissions do. For example, special permissions for the standard Read permission include Read Attributes and Read Extended Attributes.

You can assign security permissions for objects and their attributes using the **Active Directory Users and Computers** console. The **Security** tab of the **Properties** dialog box for an object in the **Active Directory Users and Computers** console provides options to assign security permissions to objects. You will be able to view the **Security** tab in the **Properties** dialog box only when you select the **Advanced Features** menu command in the **View** menu of the **Active Directory Users and Computers** console.

how to

Set standard permissions for the domain1.mydomain.com domain controller.

1. In the **Active Directory Users and Computers** console, click the **Domain Controllers** container in the left pane.
2. Click **View** on the menu bar and then click the **Advanced Features** command. A check mark appears next to the **Advanced Features** command **(Figure 7-5)**, indicating that you will now be able to view the **Security** tab in the **Properties** dialog box for the domain controller.

Table 7-2 Commonly used standard object permissions in Active Directory

Permissions	Description
Full Control	All permissions
Read	View objects, their attributes, object owner, and Active Directory permissions.
Write	Change the attributes of an object.
Create All Child Objects	Create all types of child objects in a parent object (such as an OU).
Delete All Child Objects	Delete all types of child objects from a parent object (such as an OU).

Figure 7-5 Setting the Advanced Features option

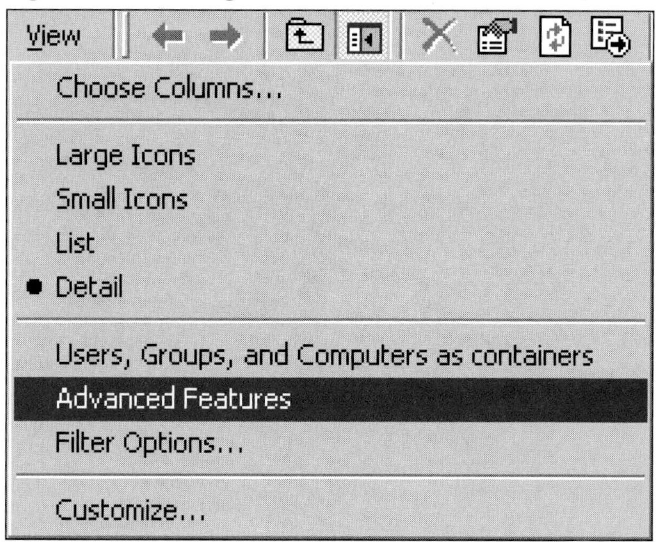

skill 2

Setting Standard Active Directory Object Permissions (cont'd)

exam objective

Manage Active Directory objects. Control access to Active Directory objects.

how to

3. Double-click **Domain Controllers** in the mydomain.com node to display the list of domain controllers in the Details pane **(Figure 7-6)**.
4. Right-click **ServerA** in the Details pane and then click the **Properties** command to open the **ServerA Properties** dialog box.
5. Click the **Security** tab and then click **Authenticated Users** in the **Name** list box.
6. Under the **Permissions** section, select the **Allow** check box for the **Change Password** permission **(Figure 7-7)**. This will allow authenticated users to change passwords on this domain controller.
7. Click [OK] to close the **Properties** dialog box.

more

In some cases, you might notice that the **Security** tab displays blank check boxes for all standard permissions assigned to an object. This implies that the object is granted special permissions. You can view these special permissions by using [Advanced...] in the **Security** tab of the **Properties** dialog box for the object. To see the details for an entry, select the entry by clicking it, and then click [View/Edit...]. In the **Permission Entry For** dialog box, use the **Object** tab to view special permissions assigned to the user or group.

Figure 7-6 Displaying the list of domain controllers

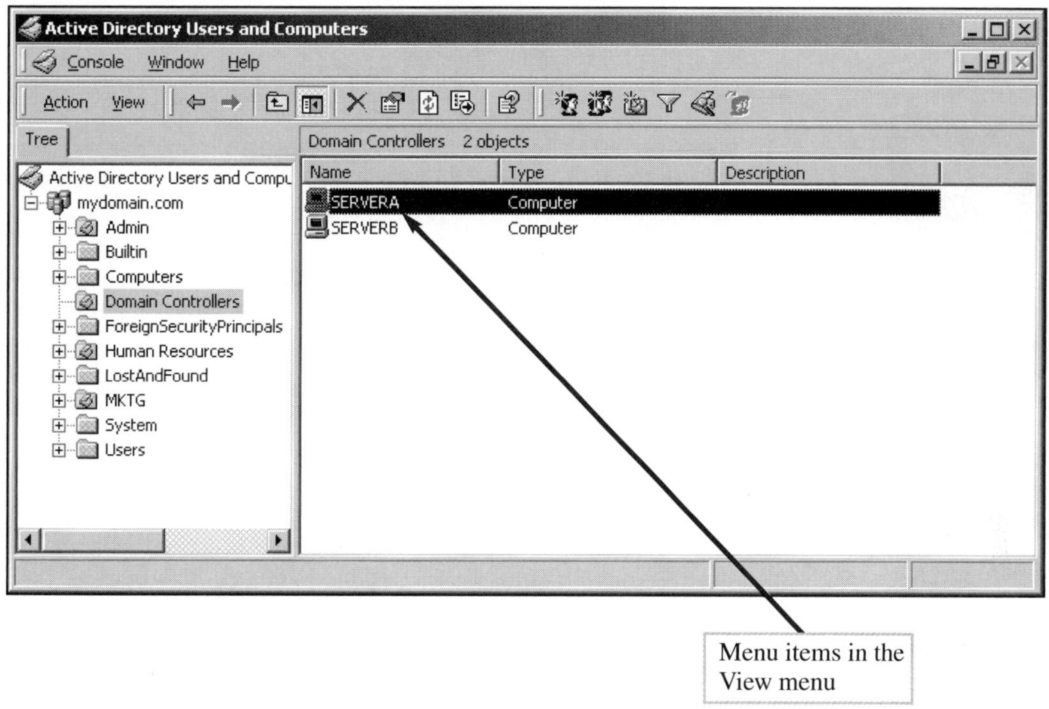

Figure 7-7 Setting permissions for a domain controller

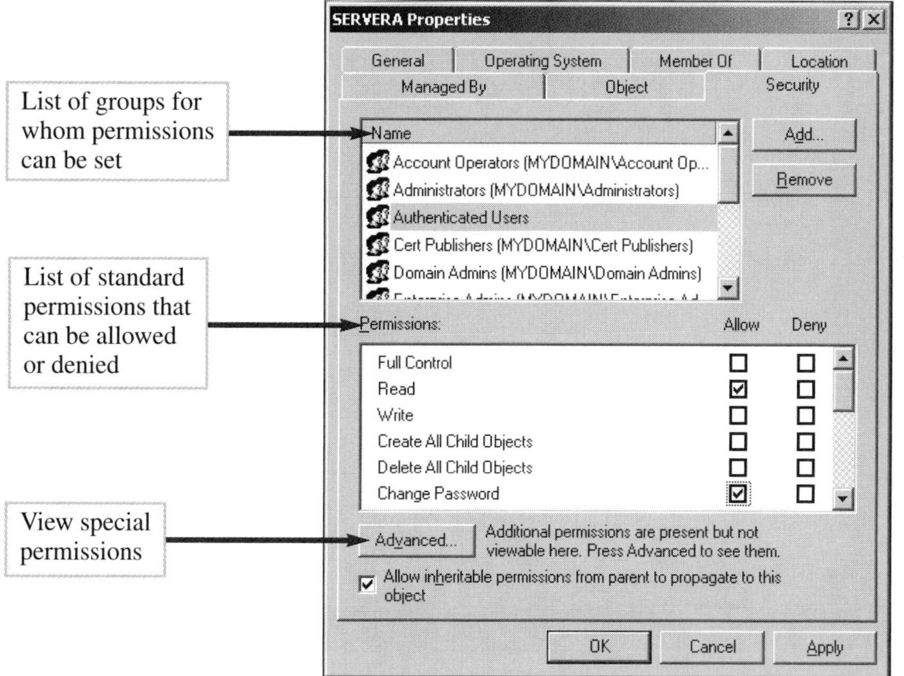

skill 3 Introducing Inheritance of Permissions

exam objective

Control access to Active Directory objects.

overview

Permission inheritance for Active Directory objects works the same way as that for files and folders. Inheritance simplifies the administration of objects. When you assign permissions to an object at the top of the hierarchy, all its child objects automatically inherit the permissions of the parent object. For example, you can group all network printers in an OU named Network Printers and assign the group of printer administrators Full Control over the Network Printers OU. This will enable the group of printer administrators to administer all printers in the OU.

Alternatively, you can choose to prevent an object from inheriting permissions from a parent object by clearing the Allow Inheritable Permissions from Parent to Propagate to this Object check box on the Security tab of the Properties dialog box of the object. For example, you may need to prevent inheritance of permissions at the domain or OU level. Although this option provides a finer degree of control over objects, the maintenance required increases the burden on the administrator so the option should be used cautiously. When you clear the Allow Inheritable Permissions from Parent to Propagate to this Object check box for a child object, a message box is displayed that provides you with two options **(Figure 7-8)**. The Copy button allows you to copy the permissions from the parent object. These permissions act as the base permissions for the child object. However, any permission you set for the parent object after removing inheritance will not apply to the child object. The Remove button removes all previously inherited permissions from the object. You can thus apply your set of permissions for the object based on your needs.

Once you remove inheritance, the object you removed the inheritance from becomes the root for inheritance for objects below it.

tip

You can easily identify inherited permissions in the Permissions section of the Security tab in the Properties dialog box by seeing which of the check boxes for an object are shaded.

Figure 7-8 Preventing inheritance of permissions

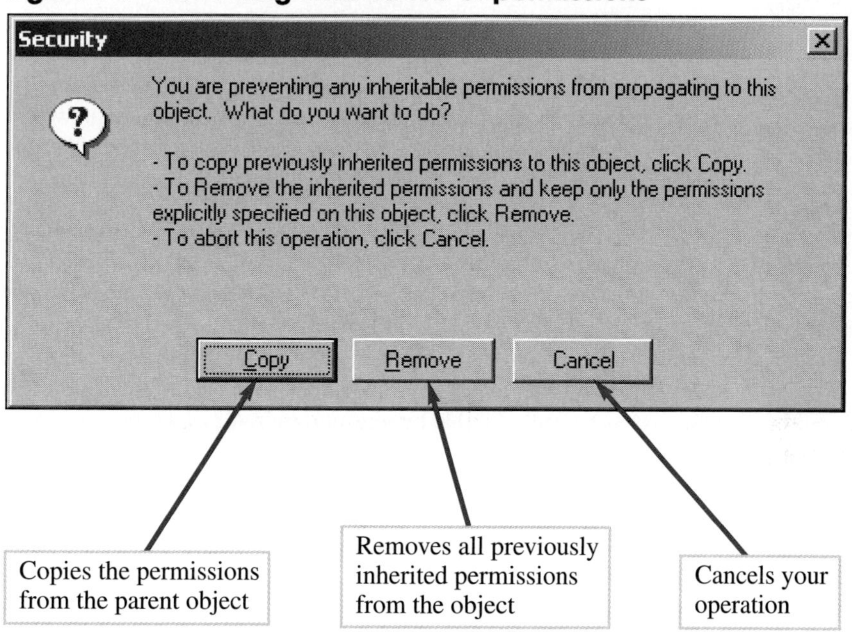
Security
You are preventing any inheritable permissions from propagating to this object. What do you want to do?
- To copy previously inherited permissions to this object, click Copy.
- To Remove the inherited permissions and keep only the permissions explicitly specified on this object, click Remove.
- To abort this operation, click Cancel.
Copy
Remove
Cancel
Copies the permissions from the parent object
Removes all previously inherited permissions from the object
Cancels your operation

skill 4

Publishing Resources in Active Directory

exam objective

Publish resources in Active Directory.

overview

Active Directory provides a centralized database for network resources, including printers and shared folders that have been published. This database can also be used as a single location where network users can find required information about network resources. Hence, you can use Active Directory to your benefit by adding your network resources to Active Directory. The process of adding resources to the directory is known as publishing. Publishing the network resources in Active Directory enables users to locate them easily, when required. It also helps provide selective and secure publication of network resources to users.

Besides allowing you to publish network resources and assign security attributes to objects in the directory, Active Directory also provides specific administrative controls for these directory objects so that you can assign users access to specific directory objects. The network resources that are published in Active Directory are called published resources. Some network resources, such as shared printers on Windows 2000 print servers, are published by default when they are created. Other resources, such as shared folders, need to be published manually. As a result of publishing resources in Active Directory, network users can locate the published resources quickly and easily.

You can publish network resources in Active Directory by using the Active Directory Users and Computers console.

how to

Publish a shared folder in Active Directory.

1. In the **Active Directory Users and Computers** console, right-click the **Users** container in the left pane, point to **New**, and then click the **Shared Folder** command to open the **New Object-Shared Folder** dialog box.
2. Type **C drive** in the **Name** text box.
3. In the **Network Path** text box, type the full path of the shared folder that you want to publish in Active Directory; for example, **\\server01\c$ (Figure 7-9)**.
4. Click OK to close the **New Object-Shared Folder** dialog box. The details pane of the **Active Directory Users and Computers** console displays the shared folder **General Stuff** in the **Users** container **(Figure 7-10)**.
5. Close the **Active Directory Users and Computers** console.

tip

Make sure that you follow the Universal Naming Convention (UNC) (\\server_name\share_name) while specifying the network path of the shared folder that you want to publish.

more

Only Windows 2000 network printers are published automatically in Active Directory. You need to manually publish information about printers running on non-Windows 2000 Server computers using the **Active Directory Users and Computers** console. To do this, right-click the container where you want to publish the printer, point to **New**, and then click the **Printer** command. In the **New Object-Printer** dialog box, specify the network path of the pre-Windows 2000 print share to publish the printer in Active Directory.

Figure 7-9 Publishing a shared folder

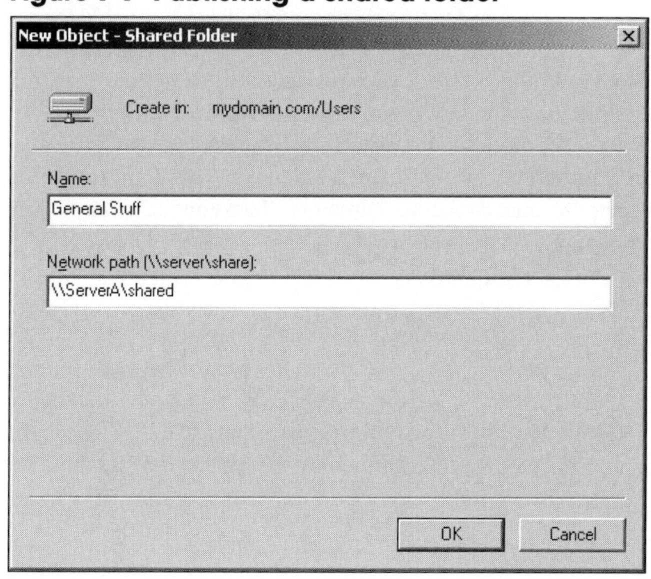

Figure 7-10 The published folder in the Users container

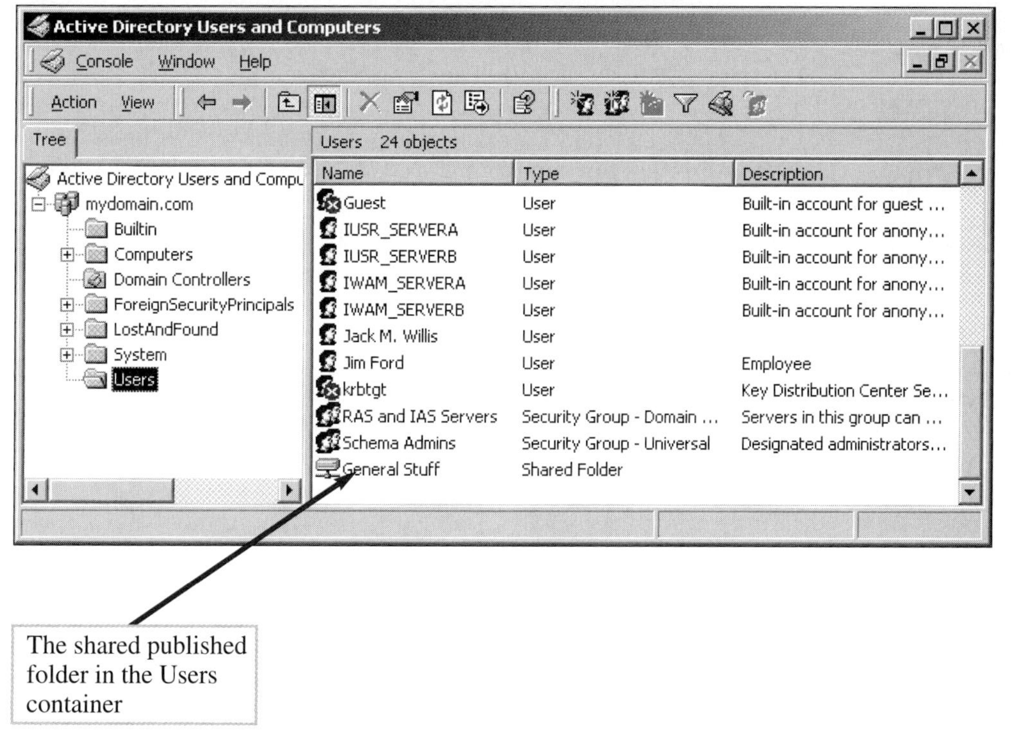

The shared published folder in the Users container

skill 5 Publishing Network-enabled Services Using Active Directory

exam objective

Publish resources in Active Directory.

overview

In older versions of Windows, managing network-enabled services was a tiresome task that had administrators regularly checking the status of services on the servers. However, with the arrival of Windows 2000, administration of these network services can be easily managed by publishing the network services information in Active Directory. By publishing service information, administrators can manage the service from a central location rather than from individual servers or computers. There are two types of service information that can be published in Active Directory. These include binding information and configuration information.

- **Binding information** can be published by using client desktops to connect to services following a service-centric model. The service-centric model uses a network service in contrast to the machine-centric model, which depends on specific computers to complete a task. Windows 2000 automatically establishes connections with services when bindings for these services are published.
- **Configuration information** can be published by distributing configuration information for a particular application to all the clients in a domain. The client applications can then access the configuration information as required.

Before publishing service information, you need to be aware of the characteristics of effective service information. **Table 7-3** describes these characteristics.

You need to use the Services container in the Active Directory Sites and Services console to publish and manage network services information. The Services container does not appear in the console by default. You need to select the Show Services command on the View menu to view it.

tip

Service publication is a relatively unused feature in most networks. While it may become popular in the future (as more applications integrate with AD), at present, you will only see it in isolated cases.

caution

Always remember that machine-centric services should not be published to Active Directory. These services are handled on a service-to-service basis.

how to

Publish a network service, namely, the WebServer certificate template in Active Directory, by setting its security permissions.

1. Click Start, point to **Programs**, point to **Administrative Tools**, and then click the **Active Directory Sites and Services** command to open the **Active Directory Sites and Services** console.
2. Click **View** on the menu bar, and then click the **Show Services Node** command. A check mark appears next to this command indicating that the left pane of the console now displays the **Services** container.
3. Click the **Services** container to view its contents in the details pane.
4. Double-click the **Public Key Services** container, and then the **Certificates Templates** container to view the templates available in the details pane.
5. Double-click the certificate template **WebServer** to open its **Properties** dialog box.
6. Click the **Security** tab to set security permissions.
7. Click **Enterprise Admins** in the **Name** section.
8. In the **Permissions** section, select the **Allow** check box for the **Read** permission (**Figure 7-11**). This will allow enterprise administrators to read the WebServer certificate.
9. Click OK to close the dialog box. The WebServer certificate has been published to the users of the Enterprise Admins group.
10. Close the **Active Directory Sites and Services** console.

tip

These changes apply to the certificate template within the current domain only.

Table 7-3 Characteristics of effective service information

Characteristics	Explanation
Service information should be stable	The information you publish in Active Directory is regularly replicated to every domain controller in Active Directory. Hence, frequent changes in service information will generate extra network traffic. This problem can easily outweigh the benefits caused by publishing the service, and require you to be careful to publish the information of services that are relatively stable.
Service information should have concise properties	It is easier to use service information that is relatively small and concise. Active Directory replicates service information based on a complete property and not on a portion of a property. For example, when you modify a word in the description field, the entire description field is replicated during replication, and not just the modified word.
Service information should be useful	Only publish services that are of widespread significance. In other words, the service information that is replicated should be of use to a large number of clients. The published information is replicated to every domain controller in the site. If the replicated information is of no relevant use to most clients, it causes unnecessary usage of network resources. Choosing information that is of use to a large number of clients ensures maximum benefit from the necessary network bandwidth and disk space.

Figure 7-11 Publishing a service certificate template

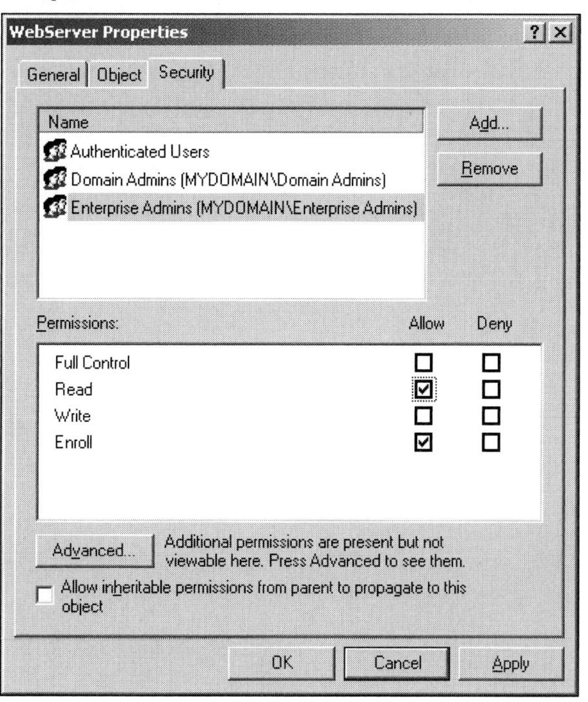

skill 6 Moving Active Directory Objects Within a Domain

exam objective

Move Active Directory objects.

overview

As an administrator, you may need to move objects in Active Directory from time to time. This could be due to a number of reasons such as employees moving from one department to another, or companies reorganizing their network and OU setup. Depending on the size and infrastructure of the organization, objects can be moved:

- Within a domain
- Between domains
- Between sites

We will study each of these in detail later in the lesson.

Moving Active Directory objects from one container to another within a domain is an easy procedure. To do this, you use the Active Directory Users and Computers console.

It is important to note the restrictions that apply to the movement of objects in Active Directory. After the object has moved to a new container, it ceases to retain the permissions of the old container and inherits the permissions of the new container. However, permissions assigned directly to the object remain with the object even after you move it to a new location. In short, the destination container permissions are inherited and original object permissions are retained.

tip

If required, you can select and move as many objects as you want in one single action.

how to

Move Active Directory objects, such as users, within a domain.

1. Click Start, point to **Programs**, point to **Administrative Tools**, and then click the **Active Directory Users and Computers** command to open the **Active Directory Users and Computers** console.
2. Click the Human Resources OU in the left pane to view the available users in the details pane.
3. Right-click the entry for **Jim Ford** in the details pane.
4. Click the **Move** command on the shortcut menu to open the **Move** dialog box.
5. To move the user object **Jim Ford** to the **MKTG** container, click **MKTG** in the **Container to move object to** section of the **Move** dialog box **(Figure 7-12)**.
6. Click OK to close the dialog box. **Figure 7-13** displays the new location of the user object.
7. Close the **Active Directory Users and Computers** console.

Figure 7-12 Selecting a new location

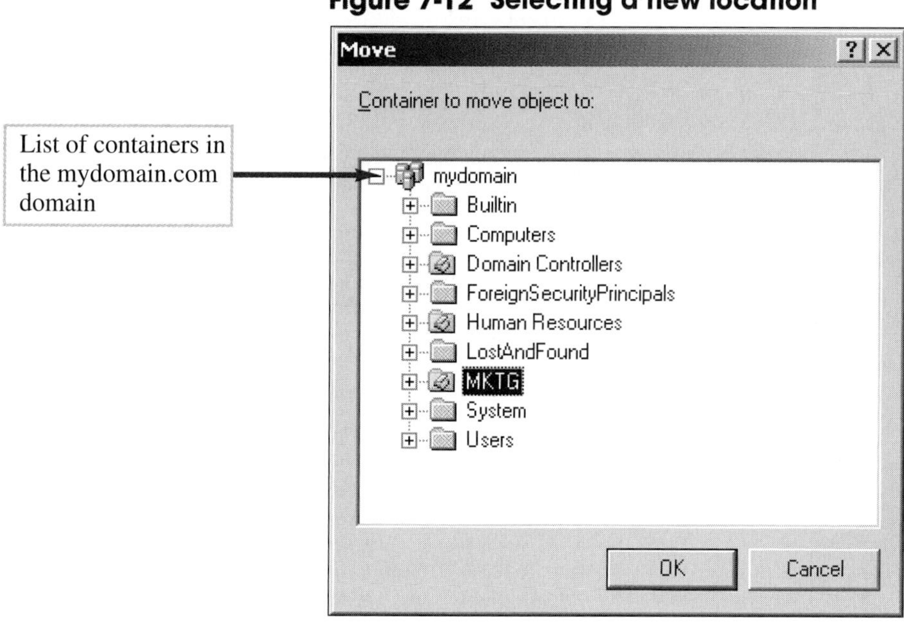

Figure 7-13 The new location of the user object

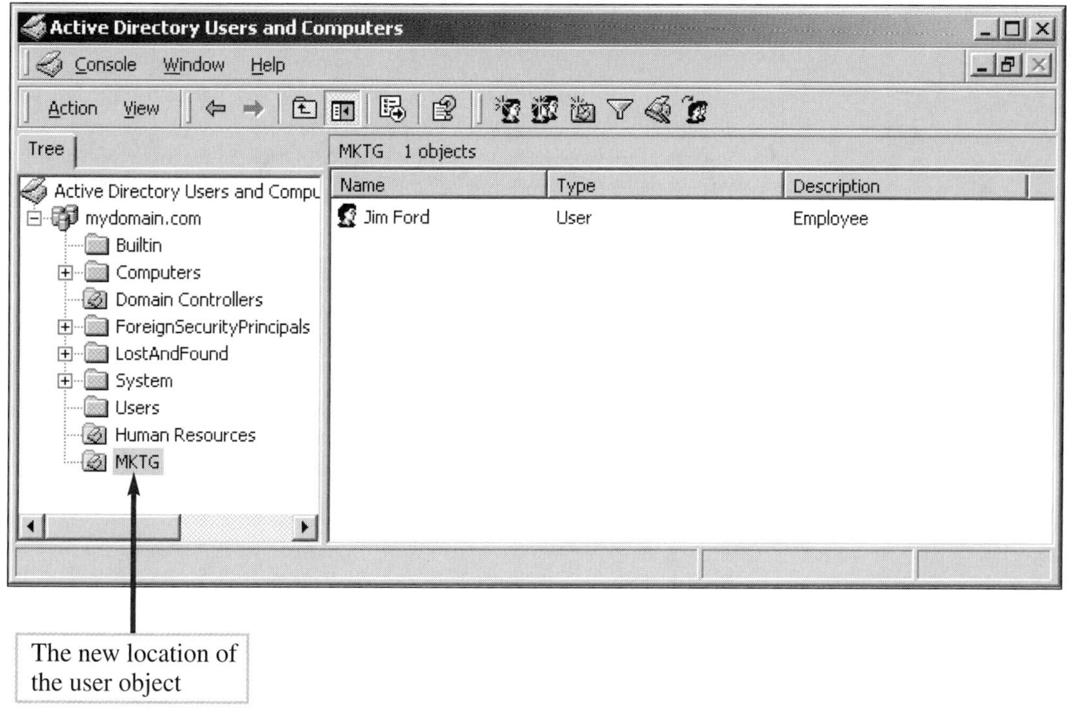

skill 7 Moving Active Directory Objects Between Domains

exam objective

Move Active Directory objects.

overview

caution

While MOVETREE is capable of moving computer objects between domains, the computer accounts are typically invalid after the move. The suggested tool for moving computer accounts is NETDOM.

caution

Because MOVETREE moves objects in closed sets, there is a good possibility that without proper planning, you may move significantly more between domains than you bargained for. In most cases, you should use a third party tool to move users between domains.

Moving Active Directory objects between domains is significantly more complex and technical than moving them within a domain. To move objects such as users, computers, and OUs across domains, you need to use the **MOVETREE** command-line utility. This utility is part of the support tools available in the \Support\Tools folder on the Windows 2000 Server CD-ROM. Note that in order to use MOVETREE, you need to install it, as it is not available by default.

Security objects in Active Directory have a unique security ID (SID) in the domain. However, when an object is moved between domains, the SID for that object becomes invalid and a new SID is created for the object in the new domain. The old SID information is stored in **SIDHistory**, a security field available in Windows 2000. The information in SIDHistory is used when users log on to a network. During logon, along with the new SIDs, the old SIDs in the SIDHistory field are also considered and added to the access token. This helps the users retain some of the old access permissions. [In contrast, the Globally Unique Identifier (GUID), which also represents a unique reference number for an object, remains unchanged and unaffected even after moving the object from one domain to another].

In order to move objects across domains, you need to run the MOVETREE utility from the command prompt. Alternatively, you can create a batch file and run the file from the **Start** menu. To view the complete syntax of the MOVETREE command, you can run it with the **/?** parameter. **Figure 7-14** displays the complete syntax of the MOVETREE command along with examples. You can run this command successfully only if you have permissions to move objects in both the source and destination domains. The MOVETREE utility can be used only when the destination domain is in native mode.

To use the MOVETREE utility effectively, you must understand the operations supported by this utility. Using the MOVETREE utility, you can move:

- Objects between domains in the same forest, even if the objects have child objects. The child objects move along with the parent objects.
- Global and local groups, as long as the groups contain no members, between domains.
- Universal groups across domains regardless of the presence of members.

One thing to keep in mind, however, is that MOVETREE always moves objects in what is known as closed sets. **Closed sets** include the object and all references to the object. For instance, moving a user will move all global groups the user is a member of. However, each of these groups will also have members, and because MOVETREE only works with closed sets, this means that it will also move all members of those groups. But again, those members may be members of other groups, so those groups would also be moved, and so on. For this reason, MOVETREE will not allow you to move users that are members of populated global groups.

There are several possible solutions for getting around the closed set issue involved with MOVETREE. In our scenario, we will take the simple route and remove all references to the object before moving it.

The MOVETREE utility also has some restrictions, which may cause the movement of Active Directory objects to fail.

The following objects cannot be moved using the MOVETREE utility:

- System objects such as those stored in the Configuration or Schema containers.
- Objects in special containers such as Built-in, LostAndFound, and System.
- Objects with names identical to those present in the destination domain.
- Attributes associated with the object such as user profiles, encrypted files, and users' personal data.

Figure 7-14 The complete syntax of the MOVETREE command

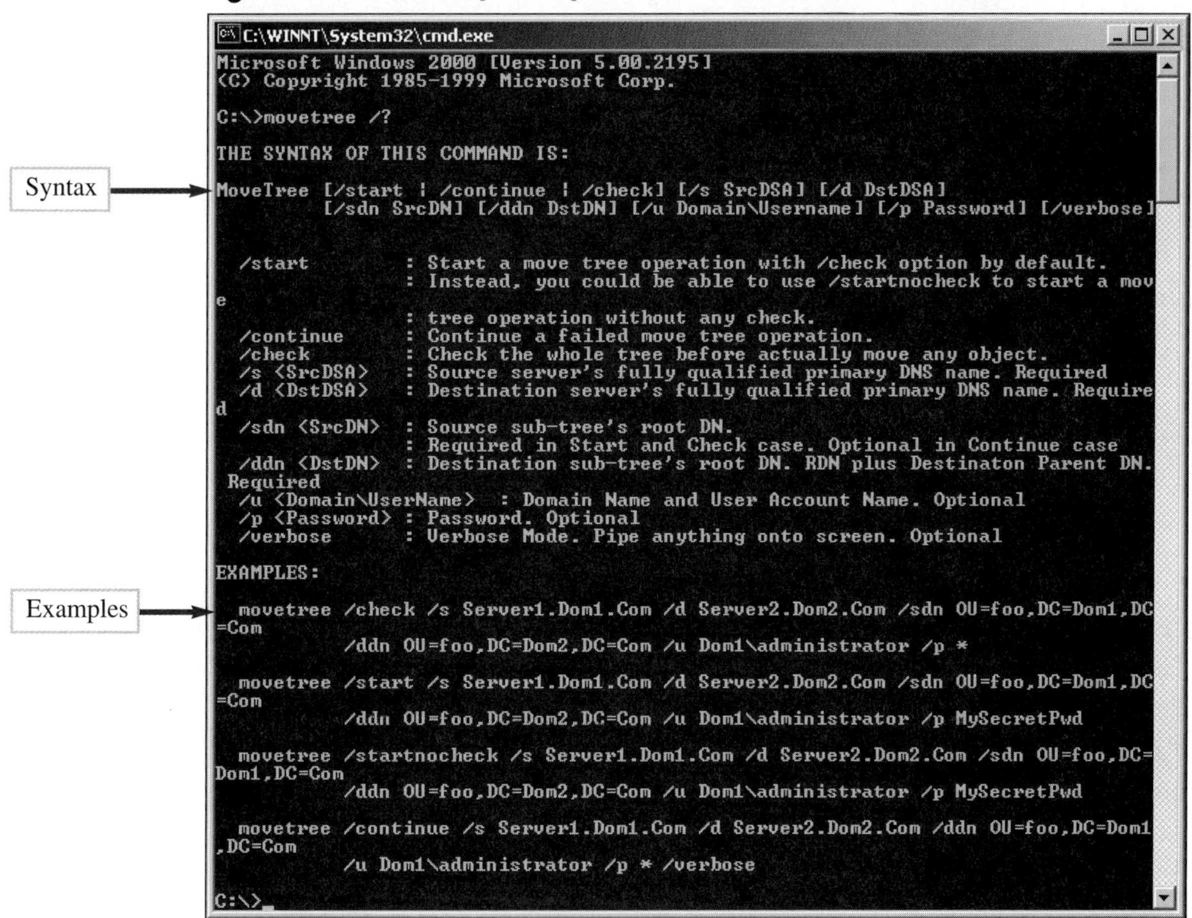

skill 7 Moving Active Directory Objects Between Domains (cont'd)

exam objective

Move Active Directory objects.

overview

- Domain controllers and other objects whose parents are domain controllers.

You should be familiar with some specific restrictions before moving users and groups between domains. These restrictions are described below.

- You cannot move users or groups if the length of their password is less than the minimum specified in the destination domain.
- In order to use MOVETREE, the destination domain *must* be in native mode.

Sometimes, objects fail to move from one domain to another during a MOVETREE operation. These objects are placed in a container in the **LostAndFound** container in the **Active Directory Users and Computers** console, in the source domain. As an Administrator, you need to monitor this container regularly and move any object in this container to its proper location.

If you are considering using MOVETREE in a production environment, you should examine the following reference and test your plan thoroughly, as MOVETREE is not very forgiving. You can find information on MOVETREE'S potential pitfalls here: http://www.microsoft.com/technet/treeview/default.asp?url=/technet/prodtechnol/windows2000serv/deploy/cookbook/cookchp3.asp.

how to

Move the user object Jim Ford into the Human Resources OU, then move MKTG OU you created in Lesson 2 to domain1.mydomain.com using the MOVETREE utility.

1. Click **Start**, point to **Programs**, point to **Administrative Tools**, and then click the **Active Directory Users and Computers** command to open the **Active Directory Users and Computers** console.
2. Click the **MKTG OU** in the left pane to view the available users in the details pane.
3. Right-click the entry for **Jim Ford** in the details pane.
4. Click the **Move** command on the shortcut menu to open the **Move** dialog box.
5. To move the user object **Jim Ford** to the **Human Resources** OU, click **Human Resources** in the **Container to move object to** section of the **Move** dialog box (**Figure 7-15**).
6. Click **OK** to close the dialog box. **Figure 7-16** displays the new location of the user object.
7. Close the **Active Directory Users and Computers** console.
8. Click **Start**, and then click the **Run** command to open the **Run** dialog box.
9. Type **cmd** in the **Open** text box, and click **OK**. This opens the command prompt.
10. At the command prompt, type movetree /start /s server01.mydomain.com /d server02.domain1.mydomain.com /sdn OU=MKTG, DC=mydomain, DC=com /ddn OU=MKTG, DC=domain1, DC=mydomain, DC=com /verbose and press **[Enter]**. Several pieces of information should flash across the screen, detailing each action MOVETREE makes. Finally, a message should appear saying that the command was executed successfully.
11. Close the Command Prompt window.

more

The MOVETREE command generates three log files that are stored in the folder where the command was run. The three files are described below.

- **MOVETREE.CHK** — Lists the errors encountered during the testing phase of the command. This file is created only when you use the /check option.
- **MOVETREE.ERR** — Lists the errors found during the running of this command.
- **MOVETREE.LOG** — Lists the statistics of the operation for future use in troubleshooting problems. These files are of great use to the administrator for troubleshooting purposes.

Figure 7-15 Selecting a new location for the user object

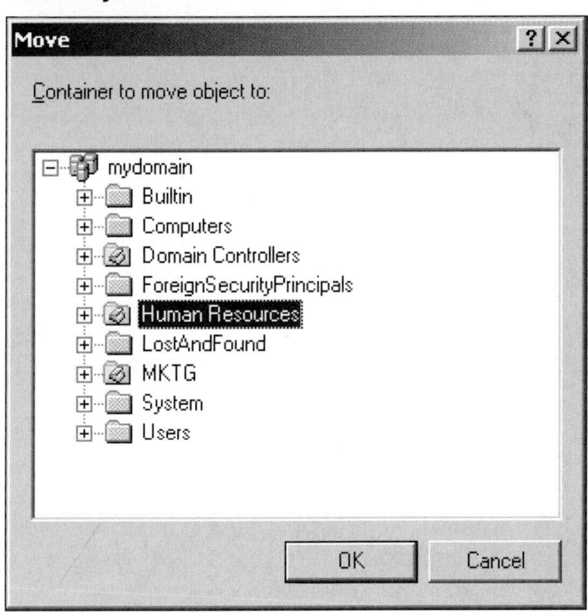

Figure 7-16 User object moved to new OU

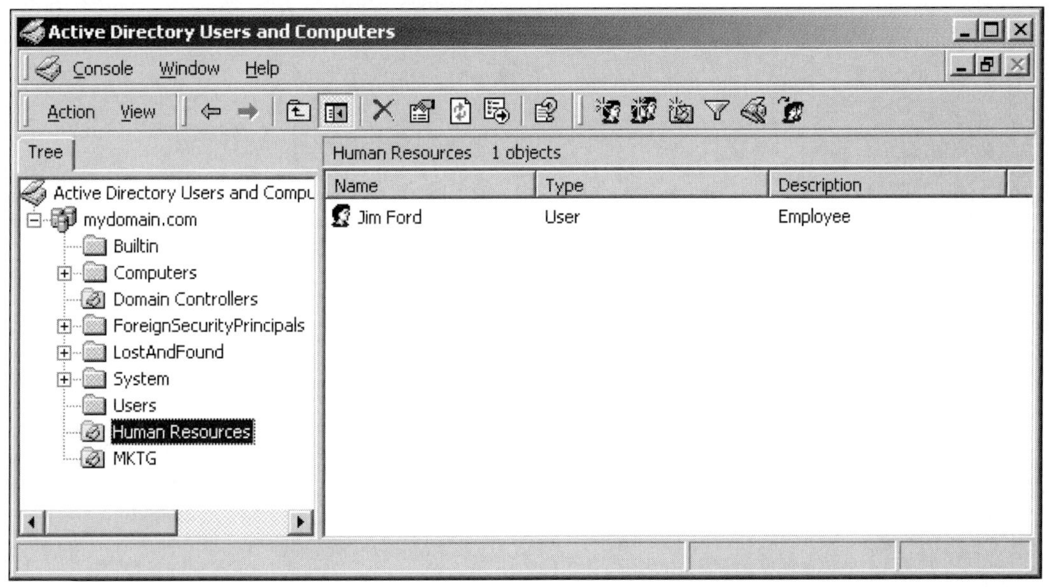

skill 8 Moving a Domain Controller Between Sites

exam objective

Move Active Directory objects.

overview

As an administrator, you need to control replication and monitor server performance to ensure that users are able to log on within a reasonable amount of time. In order to accomplish these tasks and create an efficient replication topology, you will need to move domain controllers between sites occasionally. Although the first domain controller is always created in the Default-First-Site-Name site, you can create subsequent domain controllers in any site and later move them to other sites based on the organizational network setup. To move domain controllers between sites, you need to use the Active Directory Sites and Services console.

how to

Move a domain controller between the sites named **NewYork and Atlanta**.

1. Click **Start**, point to **Programs**, point to **Administrative Tools**, and then click the **Active Directory Sites and Services** command to open the **Active Directory Sites and Services** console.
2. Click the **Servers** folder under the **Default-First-Site-Name** site in the **Active Directory Sites and Services** console.
3. In the details pane, right-click **ServerA**, and then click the **Move** command to open the **Move Server** dialog box.
4. To move the domain controller **ServerA** from the site **Default-First-Site-Name** to **Atlanta**, click **Atlanta** from the **Site name** list (**Figure 7-17**), and click **OK**.
5. Click **Atlanta** to expand the site **Atlanta** from the console tree. **Figure 7-18** displays the new location of the domain controller
6. Close the **Active Directory Sites and Services** console.

more

To move workstations and member servers between domains, you use a utility named **NETDOM**. This utility is also installed along with the MOVETREE utility as part of the support tools available on the Windows 2000 CD-ROM. The syntax of the NETDOM command is described in **Figure 7-19**.

tip

Domain controllers cannot be moved across domains. To move the system acting as the domain controller from one domain to another, first demote the domain controller to a member server, and then use the NETDOM utility to move it to the required domain.

Figure 7-17 Moving a domain controller across site

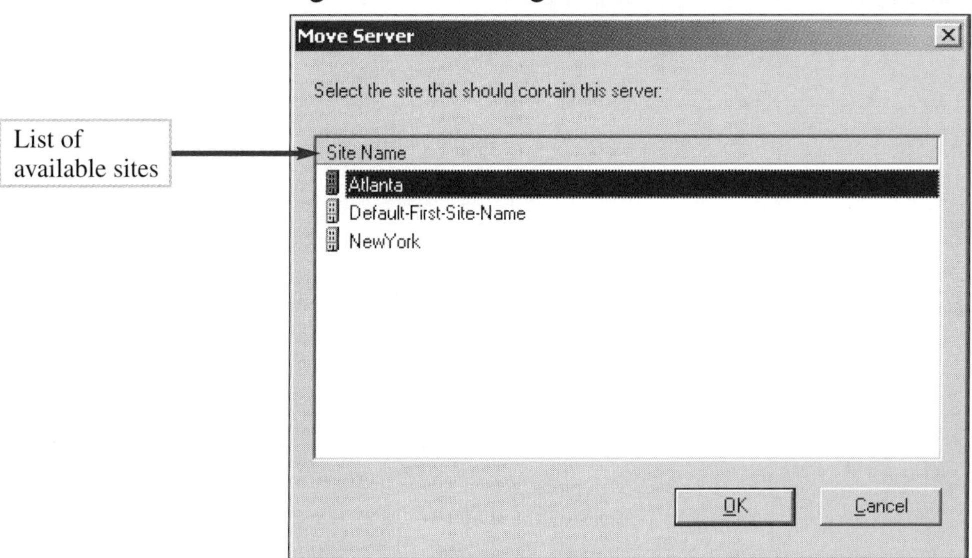

Figure 7-18 The new location of the domain controller

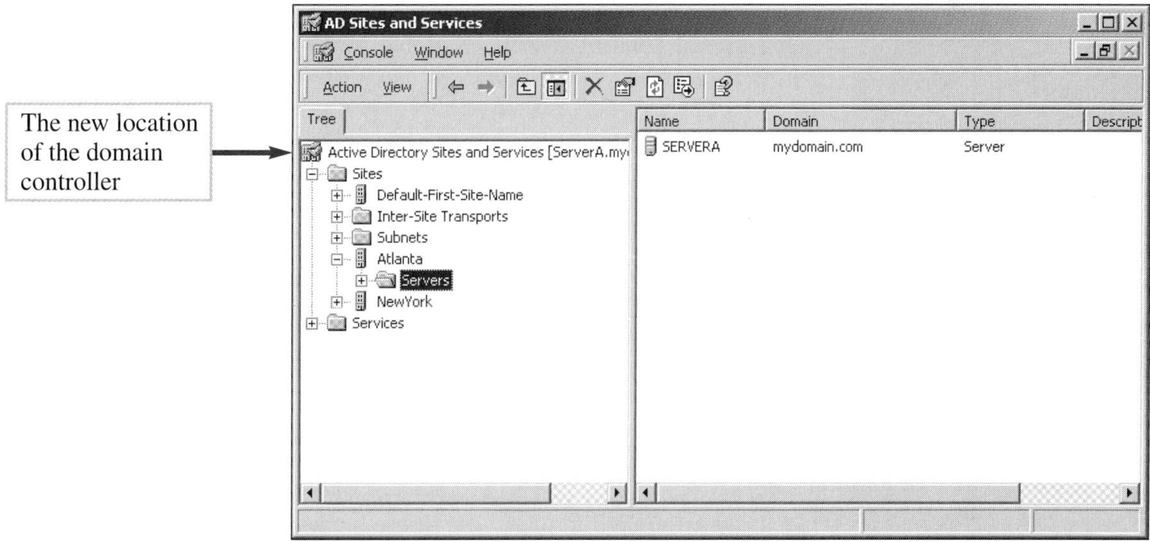

Figure 7-19 The complete syntax of the NETDOM command

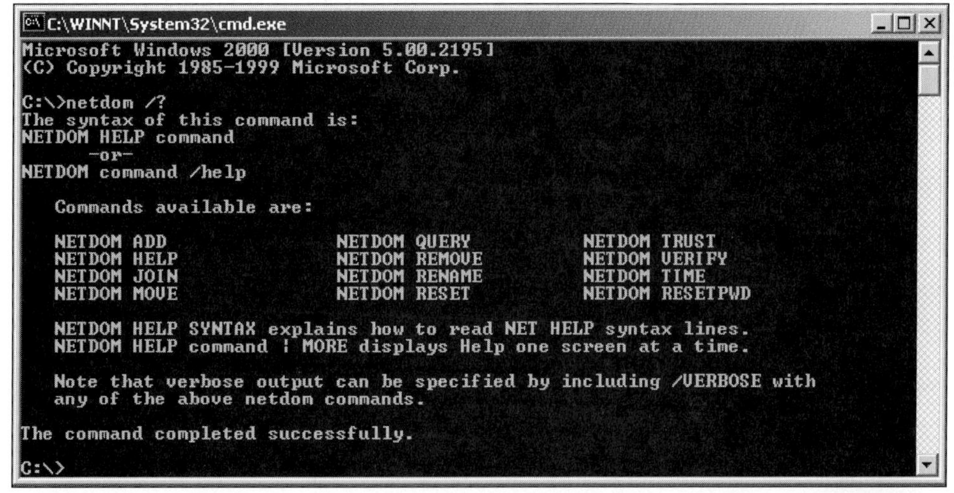

skill 9 Delegating Active Directory Permissions

exam objective

Delegate administrative control of objects in Active Directory.

overview

In large organizations, it becomes imperative for administrators to share administrative tasks, because it can be difficult for a single network administrator to handle all administrative functions. **Delegation of control** is the process of giving other users or administrators rights on Active Directory objects so that the load of administration tasks is distributed. One of the most significant benefits of implementing Active Directory is that the directory can be used to delegate administrative tasks. Delegation of control decentralizes the administration at various levels of the organization and helps reduce centralized administrative burden.

Delegation of control is available at all levels of the structure, meaning you can delegate the ability to modify all objects in the domain, all objects in an OU, or even delegate control over a single object. However, delegation at OU level is more common than delegation at object level, because it is easier to track permissions at the OU level than at the individual object level. Moreover, it is an extra burden for the administrator to manually track the delegations at the object level.

To assign permissions for delegation of control to OUs or containers, you can use the Delegation of Control Wizard, available in the Active Directory Users and Computers console.

tip

At its heart, delegating control is simply assigning permissions to one or more AD objects. Therefore, you can also simply set permissions on objects instead of using the wizard.

how to

Delegate Active Directory permissions and test the delegated permissions.

1. Click Start, point to **Programs**, point to **Administrative Tools**, and then click the **Active Directory Users and Computers** command to open the **Active Directory Users and Computers** console.
2. Right-click the **Admin** OU, and then click the **Delegate Control** command to initiate the Delegation of Control Wizard.
3. The **Welcome** screen of the Delegation of Control Wizard appears. Click Next > to continue to the **Users or Groups** screen.
4. Click Add... in the **Users or Groups** screen to open the **Select Users**, **Computers**, **or Groups** dialog box and select users for delegation.
5. Click **Amanda Temple** in the **Name** list box, and then click the Add button to select this user as the one who has been delegated the control of the **Admin** container (**Figure 7-20**).
6. Click OK to close the dialog box and return to the wizard.
7. The entry for Amanda Temple appears in the list of selected users and groups (**Figure 7-21**). Click Next > to move to the **Tasks to Delegate** screen and assign the delegated tasks.

Figure 7-20 Selecting the user for delegation

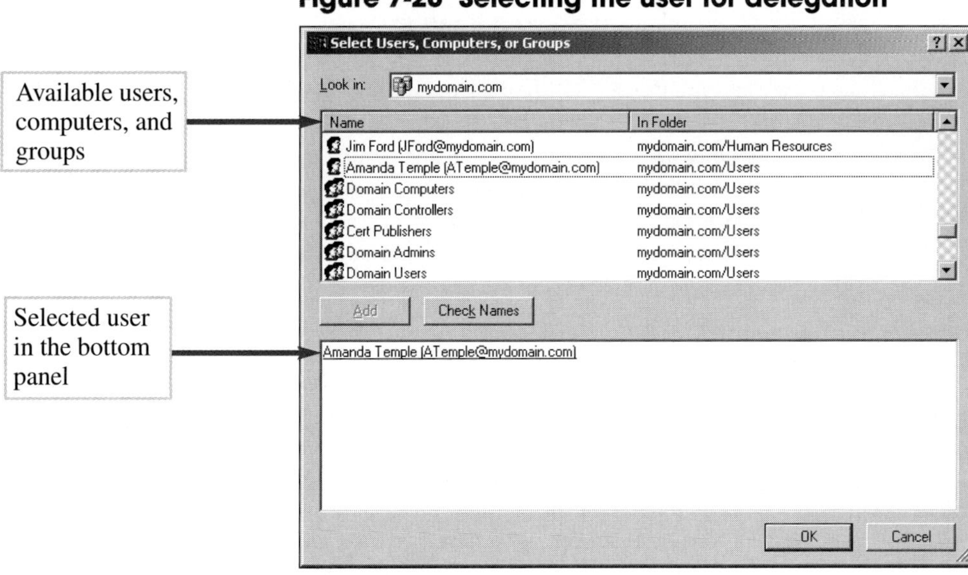

Figure 7-21 List of selected users and groups who will be assigned delegation of control

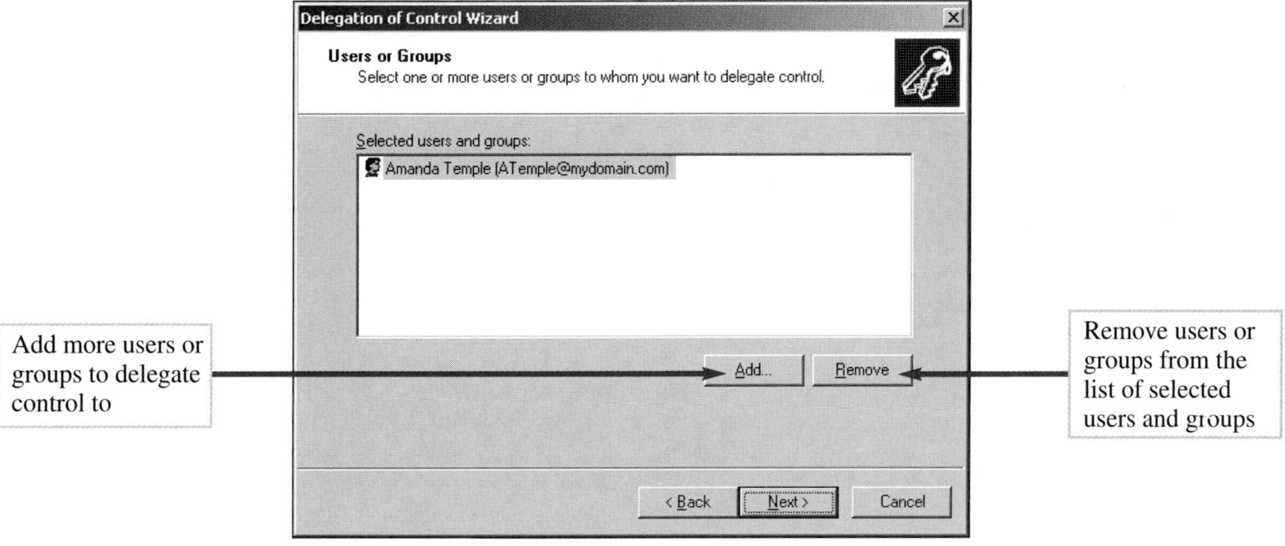

skill 9 Delegating Active Directory Permissions *(cont'd)*

exam objective

Delegate administrative control of objects in Active Directory.

how to

8. In the **Tasks to Delegate** screen, select the **Reset passwords on user accounts** check box under the **Delegate the following common tasks** section. Click Next > to move to the next screen of the wizard **(Figure 7-22)**.
9. The final screen of the Delegation of Control Wizard displays the summary of all the settings you have specified in the previous screens of the wizard **(Figure 7-23)**. Click Finish to close the wizard and complete the process of delegating control.
10. To test the delegated permissions, log off and then log on as Amanda Temple.
11. Open the **Active Directory Users and Computers** console and click the **Admin** OU.
12. Attempt to reset the password for a user in the Admin OU. Since you have been delegated the control of changing the passwords for all user accounts, you should be able to change the password successfully.

more

You can refer to the following guidelines for administering Active Directory.

- Understand the policies and the requirements of the organization before planning the delegation of control.
- Make sure that users who have been assigned the delegation of tasks are fully aware of Active Directory and its functions. If not, arrange training for them.
- Delegate control at the domain, site, or OU level, rather than on individual objects.
- Be very restrictive with using the Deny permission. See that you provide the correct permissions to users in order to enable them to perform their duties properly.
- Always document your Active Directory object control decisions. Documentation serves as a future reference for you and other administrators. Additionally, you can track the assignment of permissions in order to manage Active Directory objects better.

Figure 7-22 Selecting the tasks to be delegated

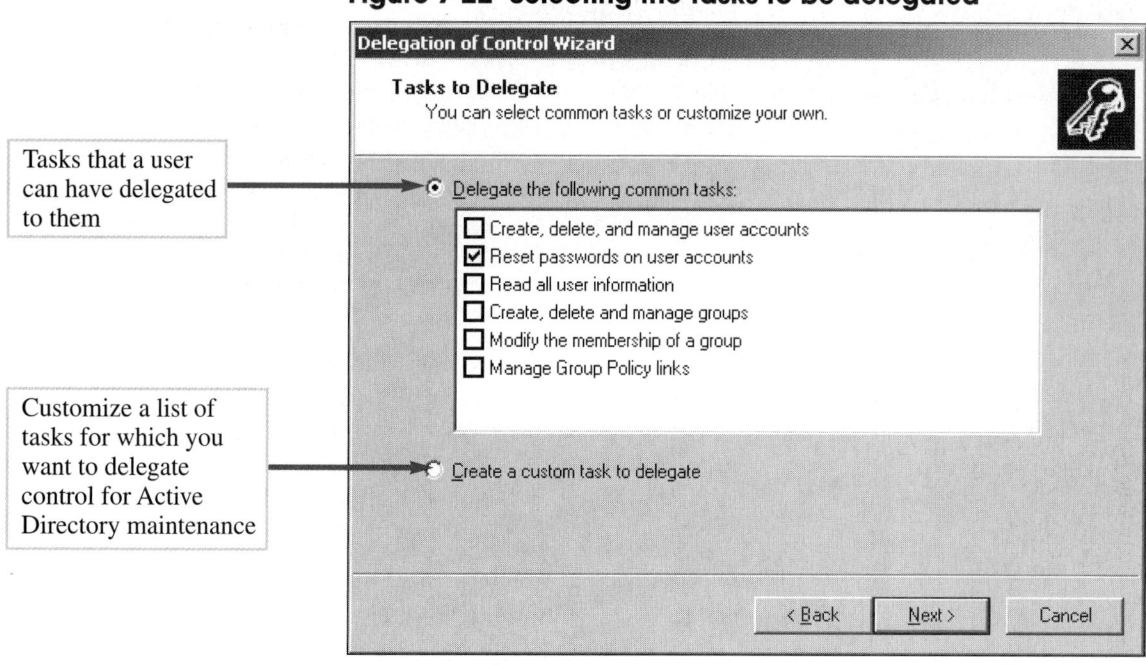

Figure 7-23 Summary screen of the Delegation of Control Wizard

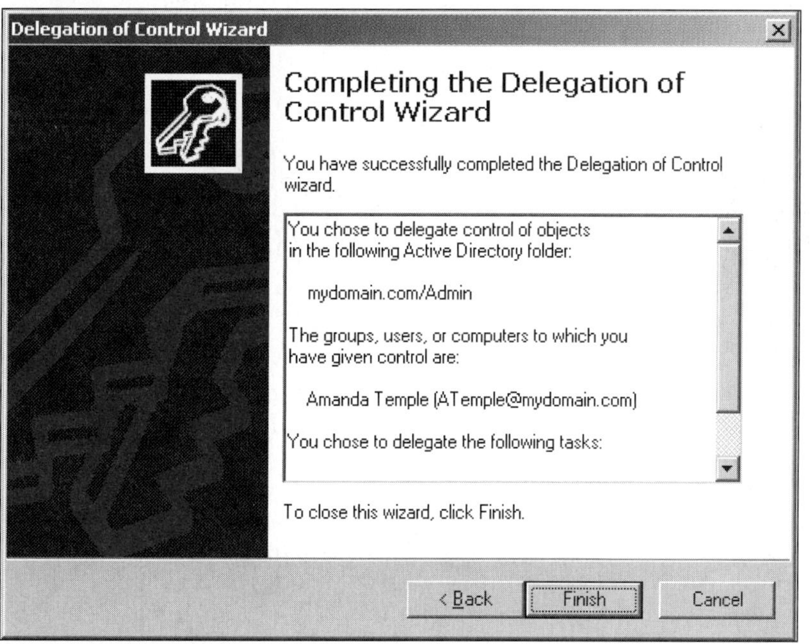

skill 10 Troubleshooting Active Directory

exam objective

Monitor, optimize, and troubleshoot Active Directory performance and replication.

overview

One of the most common jobs an administrator performs is managing Active Directory problems. Various useful tools are available in Windows 2000 with which you can analyze and troubleshoot problems in Active Directory. One such tool is the **Recovery Console**, a command-line feature that helps in resolving complex system problems when a full system boot is not available. The Recovery Console is not installed by default. To install it, you need to run the **winnt32/cmdcons** command, which is available in the **I386** folder of the Windows 2000 Server CD-ROM. Alternatively, you can launch the Recovery Console after starting the computer with the Windows 2000 Server CD-ROM (**Figure 7-24**). You can only access the Recovery Console by logging on to the computer using the Administrator account.

The Recovery Console performs a variety of tasks such as starting and stopping services, formatting drives, and copying files from the installation CD to the local hard disks.

Table 7-4 describes other Active Directory troubleshooting scenarios and their solutions.

Figure 7-24 The Recovery Console

```
Microsoft Windows 2000<TM> Recovery Console.

The Recovery Console provides system repair and recovery functionality.

Type EXIT to quit the Recovery Console and restart the computer.

M: C:\WINNT

Which Windows 2000 installation would you like to log onto
<To cancel, press ENTER>? 1
Type the Administrator password:
C:\WINNT>fix boot

The target partition is  C:.
Are you sure you want to write a new bootsector to the partition  C:  ?  y
The file system on the startup partition is NTFS.

FIXBOOT is writing a new boot sector.

The new bootsector was successfully written.

C:\WINNT>_
```

Table 7-4 Troubleshooting Active Directory problems

Problem	***Corrective action***
Down-level clients cannot log on in the absence of Active Directory client software	This problem occurs when the client's user account's password has expired and the PDC Emulator is unavailable. To temporarily resolve this problem, you can simply reset the user's password for them (but do not select the "user must change password" option).
An entire OU was deleted from Active Directory	Perform an authoritative restore of the deleted subtree to give the restored copy of the data the highest Update Sequence Number (USN).
Active Directory installed on the only domain controller of the network has become corrupt	Perform a non-authoritative restore.

Summary

- To locate objects in Active Directory, you use the Find dialog box in the Active Directory Users and Computers console. The Find dialog box provides various options that you can use to search the global catalog for the required object in Active Directory.
- Active Directory provides two sets of permissions that you can either allow or deny to users and groups. These are standard and special permissions.
- Standard permissions include the most commonly assigned permissions such as Read and Write. Special permissions achieve finer control over objects.
- Inheritance simplifies the administration of objects. You can assign permissions to an object at the top of the hierarchy, and all its child objects automatically inherit the permissions of the parent object. You can set the inheriting permissions of an object by selecting the Allow Inheritable Permissions from Parent to Propagate to the Object check box in the Security tab of the object's Properties dialog box.
- Active Directory allows you to publish network resources and assign security attributes to these resources. Some network resources such as shared printers are published by default when they are created. Other resources such as shared folders need to be published manually.
- Administration of the network can be easily managed by publishing network services information in Active Directory. The two types of service information that are published in Active Directory include binding information and configuration information.
- AD objects can be moved within the domain, between domains, and even between sites.
- To move objects such as users, groups, and OUs across domains, you use the MOVETREE command-line utility. You need to run the MOVETREE utility from the command prompt. You can also create a batch file and run the file from the **Start** menu.
- To move workstations and member servers between domains, you use a utility named NETDOM.
- Delegation of control is the process of giving other users or administrators rights on Active Directory objects so that the administration of the network is distributed.
- Various tools are available in Windows 2000 for you to use when you are analyzing and troubleshooting problems in Active Directory. One such tool is the Recovery Console. The Recovery Console is a command-line feature that helps in resolving complex system problems.

Key Terms

Lightweight Directory Access Protocol (LDAP)
Security descriptor
Access Control List (ACL)
Access control entry (ACE)
Standard permissions
Special permissions
Binding information
Configuration information
MOVETREE command-line utility
Security ID (SID)
SIDHistory
NETDOM utility
Delegation of control
Recovery Console

Test Yourself

1. Which of the following defines LDAP?

a. The entry in the Access Control List that specifies the type of access required for a user to gain access to a resource.
b. The database that stores information about each object in Active Directory.
c. The primary access protocol used to query and retrieve information about Active Directory objects.
d. The list of all user accounts and groups that have access permissions to Active Directory objects.

2. Which of the following best describes a security descriptor?

a. A security field available in Windows 2000 that stores the old SID information, including the security settings.
b. A list that controls access to objects by defining the permissions and the type of access allowed.
c. A unique reference number for an object that remains unchanged and unaffected even after moving the object from one domain to another.
d. An entry in the Access Control List that specifies the type of access required for a user to gain access to a resource.

3. You have created some objects in a new OU. You notice that some of the security permissions of the objects are shaded. This implies that:

a. These permissions are special.
b. These permissions cannot be modified.
c. These permissions are inherited.
d. These permissions are standard.

4. Greg is managing a printer that is attached to a Windows 2000 computer in the SYSTEMS department. He now needs to publish the printer in Active Directory. What does he need to do?
   a. Add the printer to Active Directory manually.
   b. Share the printer from the Windows 2000 computer.
   c. Share the printer from a Windows NT computer.
   d. Attach the printer to the Windows NT computer.
5. Which of the following do you need to publish manually in Active Directory?
   a. User accounts
   b. Network printers
   c. Group accounts
   d. Shared folders
6. Which of the following statements about publishing network services using Active Directory is false?
   a. Binding information can be published by using client desktops to connect to services following a machine-centric model.
   b. Configuration information can be published by distributing configuration information for a particular application to all clients in the domain.
   c. Only relatively stable services should be published.
   d. The published services should be of use to the maximum number of clients possible.
7. You need to move a user object from the Marketing OU to the Sales OU in the domain ABC.com. Which of the following should you use to move the object?
   a. MOVETREE utility
   b. NETDOM utility
   c. **Move Server** dialog box
   d. **Move** dialog box
8. Which of the following tasks can you perform using the MOVETREE utility?
   a. Move users, groups, and OUs across domains.
   b. Move users and their associated data.
   c. Move domain controllers across domains.
   d. Move domain controllers across sites.
9. You have moved an OU and its contents to a different domain. You find that although the OU has moved successfully, some of the objects of the previous domain are missing in the new domain. Where can you locate them?
   a. You cannot locate the missing objects because they were deleted.
   b. Missing objects are stored in the **LostAndFound** container in the source domain.
   c. Missing objects are stored in the **LostAndFound** container in the destination domain.
   d. Missing objects are renamed and are stored in the OU in the destination domain.
10. To move workstations and member servers between domains, you need to use the:
    a. **Move** command
    b. MOVETREE utility
    c. NETDOM utility
    d. Delegation of Control Wizard
11. Fred is managing an entire network of 300 users in his organization by himself. Employees in the Marketing team want permissions to handle their own user and group accounts. What should Fred do?
    a. Set permissions for each member of the Marketing team.
    b. Create a new site.
    c. Create a new domain.
    d. Delegate tasks using the Delegation of Control Wizard.
12. Greg is troubleshooting a boot problem with his server. Which of the following features can Greg use to resolve his problem?
    a. Recovery Console
    b. Active Directory Sites and Services console
    c. Active Directory Users and Computers console
    d. Computer Management console

Projects: On Your Own

1. Publish a shared folder named SHARE in Active Directory.
   a. Log on as **Administrator**.
   b. Open the **Active Directory Users and Computers** console.
   c. Create a shared folder named **SHARE** in the **Users** container using the network path **\\Server01\STANDARDS** where Server01 is the server name.
   d. Close the **Active Directory Users and Computers** console.
2. Move a user object TestStudent1 from one OU to another.
   a. Log on as **Administrator**.
   b. Open the **Active Directory Users and Computers** console.
   c. Create two OUs, **SALES** and **ADMIN**.
   d. Create a user account for **TestStudent1** in the **SALES** OU.
   e. Move the user **TestStudent1** from the **SALES** OU to the **ADMIN** OU.
   f. Close the **Active Directory Users and Computers** console.
3. Delegate the task of resetting passwords to the user TestStudent1.
   a. Log on as **Administrator**.
   b. Open the **Active Directory Users and Computers** console.
   c. Delegate the task of resetting passwords to the user **TestStudent1** using the Delegation of Control Wizard.
   d. Close the **Active Directory Users and Computers** console.

Problem Solving Scenarios

1. You administer a windows 2000 ADS-based network. There are three file servers on your network named FILESRV1, FILESRV2 and FILESRV3. All users use these file servers for storing and accessing all data on the network. Lately, there have been complaints about difficulty finding resources on the network. Users have pointed out that the share names of the folders frequently change, which creates significant inconvenience.

You now need to implement a better method of sharing resources. At the same time, the whole process has to be more secure. Write a memo outlining the steps you will take to achieve these goals.

2. You are the Administrator for your company's network. You are primarily responsible for managing Active Directory and all related administrative tasks. A junior employee, Anna, assists you, although she has no user rights suited for administrative duties. You need to assign Anna a specific level of access only to help you with the task of managing group memberships for 228 domain local and global groups in your domain. Outline the steps you need to take in order to change the level of access for Anna.

LESSON 8

Backing Up and Restoring Active Directory

Active Directory is the backbone of a Windows 2000-based network. It is a service that helps you in locating and accessing network objects. Active Directory uses files to provide these services. If these files get corrupted either due to hardware failures or due to virus attacks, users will not be able to use the services provided by Active Directory. In such cases, you may need to use the most recent backup of Active Directory to restore it.

Backup of the System State data includes Active Directory. This data is critical to the functioning of a domain controller. It is a good practice to back up Active Directory daily, even though this can be a monotonous task. To break the monotony of this task, you can use the Task Scheduler to schedule the backup operation to occur at specific intervals. This will make sure that you have the most recent System State data if Active Directory files get corrupted.

In case the Active Directory files are corrupted, you use the last backup of the System State data to restore them. The Windows 2000 operating system enables you to restore Active Directory files in two ways: nonauthoritative and authoritative. A nonauthoritative restore is a simple restoration of Active Directory. You use an authoritative restore when you need to overwrite a change that has taken place such as when you need to restore a deleted object.

Goals

In this lesson, you will learn to back up Active Directory and schedule the backup process. You will also learn to restore Active Directory both nonauthoritatively and authoritatively.

Lesson 8 Backing Up and Restoring Active Directory	
Skill	***Exam 70-217 Objective***
1. Using the Backup Wizard to Back Up Active Directory	Back up and restore Active Directory.
2. Scheduling Active Directory Backups	Back up and restore Active Directory.
3. Examining Different Ways to Restore the Active Directory Database	Back up and restore Active Directory.
4. Executing a Nonauthoritative Restore	Perform an authoritative and a nonauthoritative restore of Active Directory. Recover from a system failure.
5. Executing an Authoritative Restore	Perform an authoritative and a nonauthoritative restore of Active Directory.

Requirements

For this lesson, you need administrative rights on at least two Windows 2000 Server computers, one of which should be a domain controller for mydomain.com (ServerA). You will also need to create a shared folder, called ADBackup, on the other server (Server02). For this lesson, you need to map this shared folder as network drive F: on your mydomain.com domain controller. Create a user object, Doug, in the Users container of the mydomain.com domain.

skill 1 Using the Backup Wizard to Back Up Active Directory

exam objective

Back up and restore Active Directory.

overview

Active Directory is a transaction based database service that uses files, such as ntds.dit, and various log files in order to function. To prepare for a situation where these files get corrupted, you need to back up Active Directory using the Backup Wizard **(Figure 8-1)**. The Backup Wizard creates an archive with a '.bkf' extension, containing the files that have been selected for backup. To back up Active Directory, it is important to remember that you must be a member of the Backup Operators group or the Administrators group.

The Active Directory backup involves the Active Directory database file, ntds.dit, and the **shared system volume (SYSVOL)** folder. To back up Active Directory, you need to back up the **System State data** of a domain controller. In addition to the Active Directory database file and the SYSVOL folder, System State data has other components such as:

- **Registry**—This database stores the configuration of a computer such as user profiles and folder settings.
- **COM+ Class Registration database**—This database stores entries for dynamic link library (DLL) and executable (EXE) files on a computer.
- **System boot files**—These files are used to load and configure the Windows 2000 operating system.

Before you start the Active Directory backup operation, you should perform the following tasks:

- Choose the scope of backup based on your requirements. You can back up the entire contents of a computer, or select files or drives, network data, or System State data (which includes Active Directory).
- Choose the type of backup media you wish to use. You also need to decide whether you want to use a removable storage medium, such as a tape drive, or a file. If you choose a file as your storage medium, you can save the file on a floppy disk, a recordable CD-ROM, or a shared folder on the network.
- Decide the type of backup that is required. **Table 8-1** lists the types of backups and their descriptions. You can use this table to decide which type of backup suits your requirements.
- Notify users about the backup operation through e-mail or administrative messages.
- Make sure that the media device you have selected for storing the Active Directory backup is listed on the Hardware Compatibility List (HCL). Otherwise, you may not be able to store the backup on the media device. The HCL contains a list of devices tested by Windows Hardware Testing Labs and are supported by the Windows 2000 operating system. To check if a device is supported by the Windows 2000 operating system, you can view the 'hcl.txt' file in the Support folder of the Windows 2000 CD-ROM. Be aware that this file is not the most recent version, however. The most recent version of the HCL is always available on Microsoft's web site.
- Make sure that the backup media device is attached to the computer and the device is switched on.
- Make sure that the backup media is loaded in the media device. You can now start the Active Directory backup operation.

tip
A full backup of the computer also contains the System State data.

caution
The Backup Wizard allows you to back up the System State data of a local computer, but not of a remote computer.

tip
By default, the Backup Wizard uses the Normal type of backup to archive files.

Figure 8-1 Using the Backup Wizard

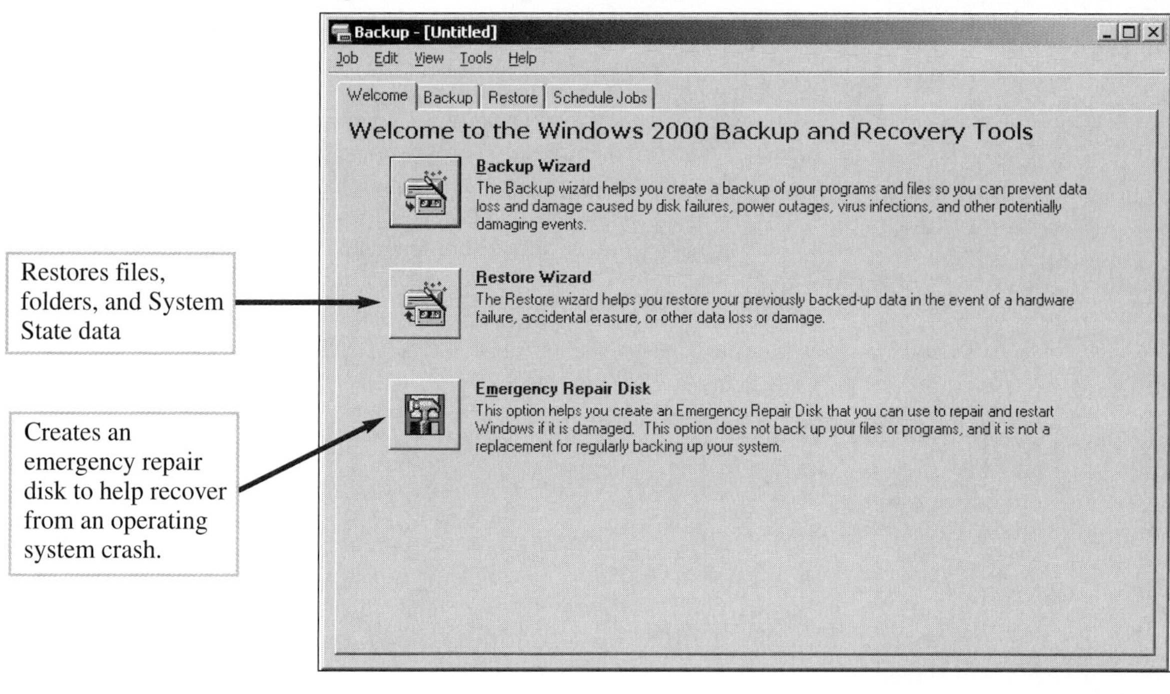

Table 8-1 Types of backup

Backup Type	Description
Normal	Archives all selected files, regardless of the state of the archive bit, and clears the archive bit for each file. An archive bit is a property of files and folders used by applications to track the backup status of files and folders. If the archive bit is set, the file has changed since the last backup. If the archive bit is cleared, the file has not changed, and will not be backed up by backup types that check the state of the archive bit.
Copy	Archives all selected files, regardless of the state of the archive bit, but does not clear the archive bit for each file.
Incremental	Archives the selected files. An incremental backup checks to see if the archive bit is set (meaning it will not backup files that are unchanged since the last backup), and clears the archive bit for each file.
Differential	Archives the selected files. A differential backup checks to see if the archive bit is set, but does not clear the archive bit for each file.
Daily	Archives the selected files that have changed on the day the back up is performed (regardless of the archive bit status), but does not clear the archive bit for each file.

skill 1

Using the Backup Wizard to Back Up Active Directory *(cont'd)*

exam objective

Back up and restore Active Directory.

how to

Perform a backup of Active Directory on ServerA and store the backup on a mapped, shared folder, ADBackup, on Server02.

1. Log on to ServerA as Administrator.
2. Click **Start**, point to **Programs**, point to **Accessories**, point to **System Tools**, and then click the **Backup** command. The **Backup – [Untitled]** window appears.
3. Click the **Backup Wizard** button to open the **Welcome to the Windows 2000 Backup and Recovery Tools** screen of the Backup Wizard.
4. Click **Next >** to open the **What to Back Up** screen **(Figure 8-2)**.
5. To back up Active Directory, select the **Only back up the System State data** option button, and then click **Next >** to open the **Where to Store the Backup** screen.
6. To specify the backup location, click **Browse...** to open the **Open** dialog box.
7. Click the **ADBackup on Server02 (F:)** option from the **Look in** list box, and then click **Open**. The **Where to Store the Backup** screen appears as shown in **Figure 8-3**. By default, the backup file will be saved as Backup.bkf in the specified location.
8. Click **Next >** to move to the **Completing the Backup Wizard** screen. This screen lists details such as the type of backup, the backup media, and the location of the backup.
9. Click **Finish** to start the backup process. This may take some time, as a typical System State backup for a simple domain typically takes around 200MB. A backup of a production DC typically takes *significantly* more.
10. Close the **Backup – [Untitled]** window. You have successfully backed up Active Directory on a mapped, shared folder, ADBackup.

tip

You can also run the Backup Wizard by running the **NTBACKUP** command from the command prompt.

caution

Make sure that the computer on which the shared folder exists is switched on.

more

The default settings of the **Backup Wizard** work well in most cases. However, you might want to specify additional advanced settings using the **Advanced...** button in the **Completing the Backup Wizard** screen of the Backup Wizard in order to:

- Specify a backup type other than the normal type.
- Verify data after the backup operation to ensure the success of the backup operation.
- Append the backup data to an existing archive or create a new archive.
- Specify a name and description to identify the backup operation.
- Schedule the backup process to occur at specified intervals.

tip

You should verify data after a backup operation to ensure the success of the operation.

Figure 8-2 Specifying the scope of backup

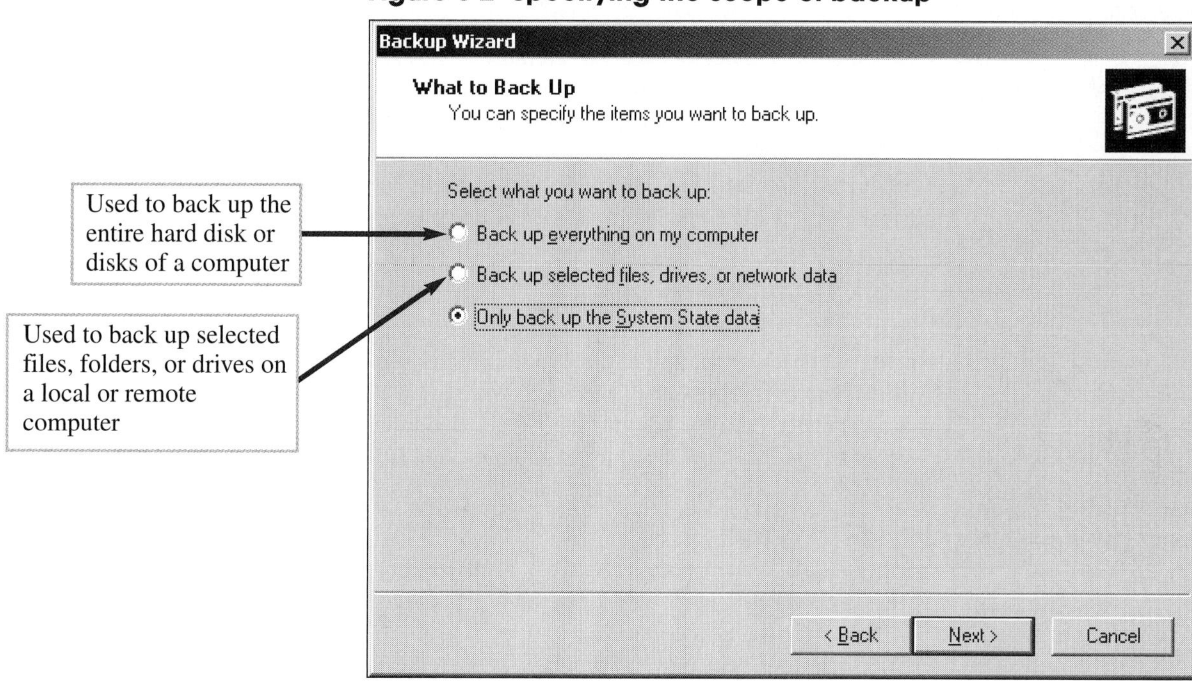

Figure 8-3 Specifying the backup location

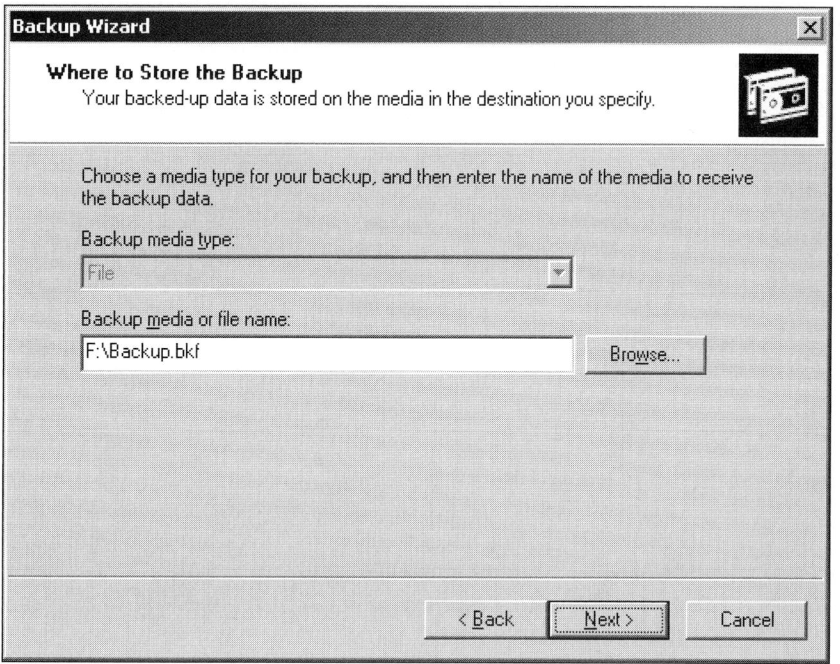

skill 2 Scheduling Active Directory Backups

exam objective

Back up and restore Active Directory.

overview

To be better prepared for recovering from a hardware failure or a virus attack, you should back up Active Directory daily, preferably after office hours. A typical scenario is to perform a normal backup (on Friday, for instance) followed by an incremental backup for each other day of the week. This method will ensure that the backup file occupies less disk space and that you have the most recent data in case of a hardware or software failure. However, most production networks have ample backup capacity to perform a full backup daily. A full daily backup makes life considerably easier when you need to restore.

Backing up servers, at times, can become a time-consuming and monotonous task. To avoid this cumbersome and repetitive task, you can program the backup operation to occur at specified intervals by using the **Task Scheduler** service of Windows 2000 Server. When you program a backup operation, the Task Scheduler service runs the Backup Wizard to carry out the backup operation at the scheduled date and time. This type of operation is also known as an unattended backup. You use the advanced options in the Completing the Backup Wizard screen of the Backup Wizard to schedule unattended Active Directory backups.

how to

Schedule unattended Active Directory backup to occur daily at 10:00 P.M. on ServerA.

1. Click Start, point to **Programs**, point to **Accessories**, point to **System Tools**, and then click the **Backup** command.
2. Click the **Backup Wizard** button to open the **Welcome to the Windows 2000 Backup and Recovery Tools** screen of the Backup Wizard.
3. Specify the scope of backup, the location to store the backup **(Figure 8-4)** and then move to the **Completing the Backup Wizard** screen by clicking Next > **(Figure 8-5)**.
4. Click Advanced... to specify additional backup options. The **Type of Backup** screen appears.
5. Accept the default settings and click Next > to open the **How to Back Up** screen.
6. Accept the default settings and click Next > to move to the **Media Options** screen.
7. Accept the default settings and click Next > to open the **Backup Label** screen.
8. Accept the default settings and click Next > to move to the **When to Back Up** screen.
9. Click the **Later** option button to schedule the backup operation. The **Set Account Information** dialog box appears. In this dialog box, you specify a valid password for the user who is a member of the **Administrators** group or the **Backup Operators** group.
10. Type the appropriate administrator password in the **Password** and **Confirm Password** text boxes, and then click OK **(Figure 8-6)**. The **When to Back Up** screen appears.
11. In the **Schedule entry** section, type **ServerASystemStateDataBackup** in the **Job name** text box, and then click Set Schedule... to open the **Schedule Job** dialog box. By default, the backup operation is scheduled to occur once at the current date and time.
12. To schedule the backup operation to occur daily at 10:00 P.M., click the **Daily** option in the **Schedule Task** list box, specify the start time in the **Start time** field as **10:00 PM (Figure 8-7)**, and then click OK to return to the **When to Back Up** screen. You can also schedule the backup operation to occur weekly, monthly, once, at system startup, at logon, or when the computer is idle.
13. In the **When to Back Up** screen, click Next > to move to the **Completing the Backup Wizard** screen.
14. Click Finish to close the Backup Wizard.
15. Close the **Backup – [Untitled]** window. You have scheduled the backup of Active Directory to occur daily at 10:00 P.M.

caution

Make sure that the Task Scheduler service is running before you schedule the Active Directory backup. You can check the status of this service using the Services command on the Administrative Tools menu.

Figure 8-4 Specifying a location in which to store the backup file

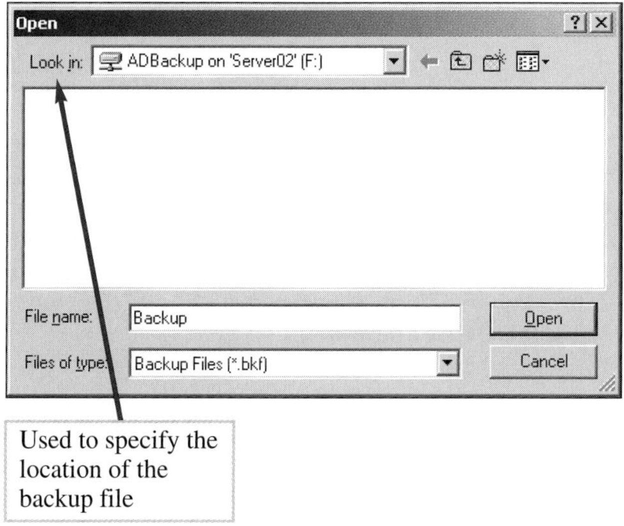

Figure 8-5 Completing the Backup Wizard screen

Figure 8-6 Specifying a password for the backup operation

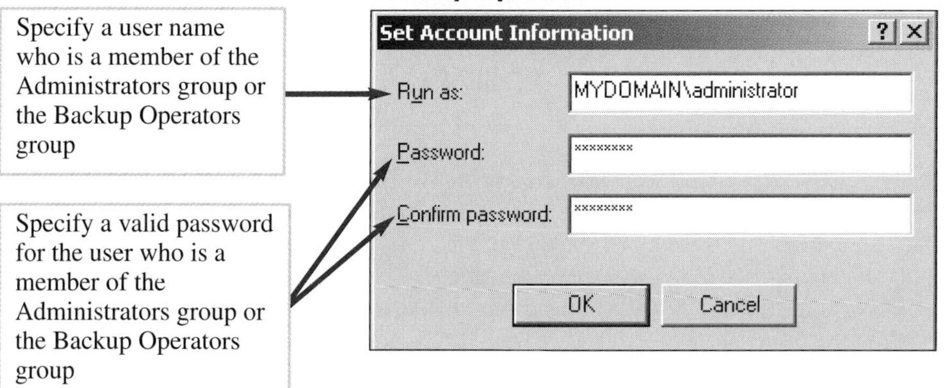

Figure 8-7 Scheduling a backup operation

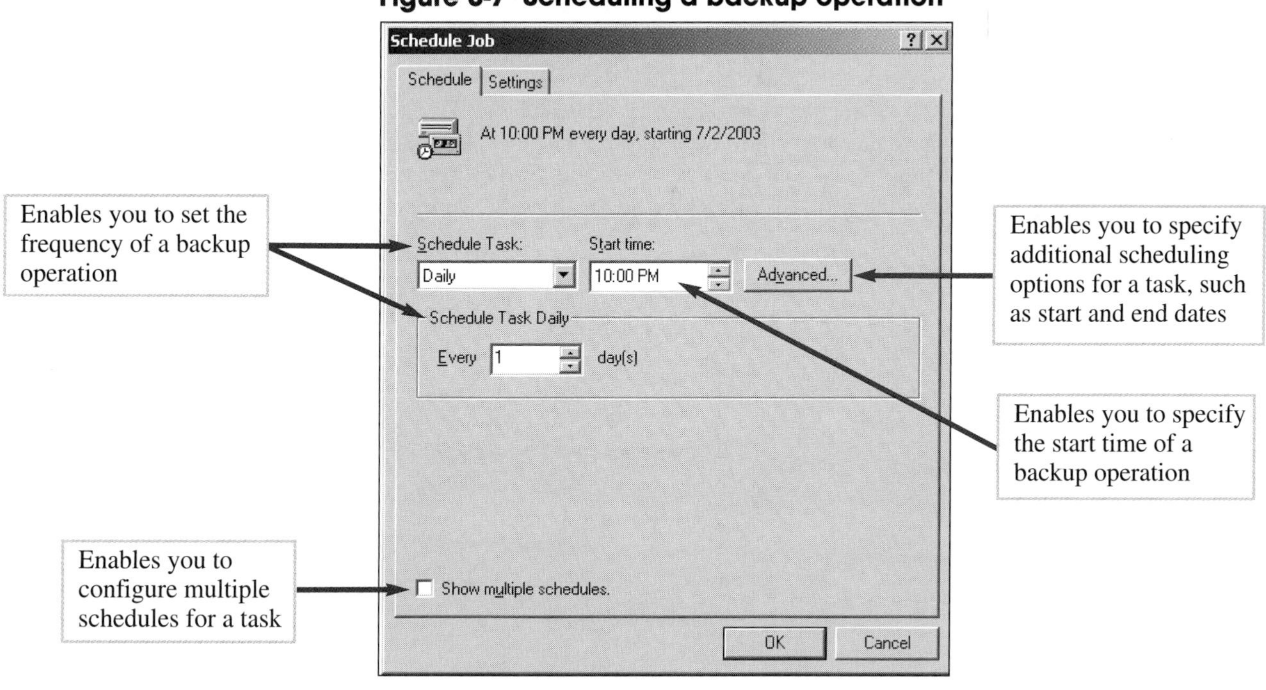

skill 3 Examining Different Ways to Restore the Active Directory Database

exam objective

Back up and restore Active Directory.

overview

Active Directory stores information about all the objects in a domain. If the files that make up Active Directory are corrupted due to a hardware or software failure, users and applications will not be able to access the objects. To overcome this problem, you may require a backup of the System State data to restore Active Directory. There are two methods of restoring Active Directory files: **nonauthoritative** and **authoritative (Table 8-2)**.

Nonauthoritative restore

The nonauthoritative restore method restores Active Directory on a domain controller to its last backup state. After Active Directory is restored on a domain controller, the replication process will update the database on the domain controller with the latest information about objects from other domain controllers in the domain.

Note that unless you only have one domain controller (a situation which should never happen in a production environment), or are at an isolated remote location, a nonauthoritative restore is not particularly useful. This is because, in order to perform a nonauthoritative restore on a server that has lost all data, you must first reinstall Windows 2000 and promote the server to a domain controller. As part of this process, the AD database is copied from the other servers onto your failed server, fully restoring AD. This makes a nonauthoritative restore redundant.

Authoritative restore

An authoritative restore is used to recover an Active Directory object that was accidentally deleted. During an authoritative restore, the **Update Sequence Number (USN)** of the deleted object is modified (increased by 100,000 for each day since the backup was performed) so that it is higher than the USNs of the existing objects. The Active Directory replication system uses USNs to track changes made to the database, like a version number (or serial number in DNS). When you create an object, Active Directory assigns a unique USN to the object. When you make changes to the object, Active Directory increments the object's USN by one. The copy of the object that has the highest USN is considered the latest and is replicated to other domain controllers.

more

Active Directory actually performs attribute level replication in most cases. This means that if you change a field in a user account, just the field is replicated and not the entire object. This feature means that, to allow for full replication functionality, AD actually assigns a USN to the database itself, each object in the database, and each attribute of each object.

Table 8-2 Methods of restoring Active Directory files

Method	Description
Nonauthoritative restore	◆ Restores Active Directory on a domain controller to its last backup state. ◆ Replication updates the database on the domain controller with the latest information from other domain controllers in the domain.
Authoritative restore	◆ Recovers an Active Directory object that was deleted. ◆ Modifies the Update Sequence Number (USN) of the object so that it is higher than the USNs of the existing objects. ◆ Replicates the copy of an object that has the highest USN to the other domain controllers.

skill 4 Executing a Nonauthoritative Restore

exam objective

Perform an authoritative and a nonauthoritative restore of Active Directory. Recover from a system failure.

overview

Nonauthoritative restore is a method to restore Active Directory in cases where no objects have been accidentally deleted and no other options are available. In a nonauthoritative restore, you use the backup of the System State data to restore Active Directory on a domain controller.

You use the Restore Wizard available in the Windows 2000 operating system to restore Active Directory. To begin, you need to start the computer in a special, safe mode called the **Directory Services Restore Mode**. This mode ensures that the domain controller remains offline while you restore the Active Directory database and the SYSVOL folder. In an offline mode, the Active Directory services on a domain controller are stopped to allow a successful restoration. After the completion of the Active Directory restoration process, the replication process updates the restored Active Directory database, with the help of other domain controllers.

caution

Just as you cannot back up the System State data on a remote computer, you cannot restore the System State data on it, either. You can restore System State data only on a local computer.

how to

Perform a nonauthoritative restore on the ServerA domain controller.

1. Start the computer.
2. On the **Starting Windows** screen, press the **F8** key to open the **Windows 2000 Advanced Options Menu** screen.
3. Select the **Directory Services Restore Mode (Windows 2000 domain controllers only)** option, and then press **[Enter]**. You choose this option to ensure that the directory service is not started on the domain controller. The startup procedure continues.
4. Log on as the local Administrator.
5. A **Desktop** message box informing you that Windows is running in safe mode appears. Click OK to close the message box. The desktop appears.
6. To start the Restore Wizard, click Start point to **Programs**, point to **Accessories**, point to **System Tools**, and then click the **Backup** command. The **Backup – [Untitled]** window appears.
7. Click the **Restore** button to initiate the **Restore Wizard**. The **Welcome to the Restore Wizard** screen appears.
8. Click Next > to open the **What to Restore** screen. The last entry in the left pane represents the most recent backup.
9. To restore Active Directory using the backup of the **System State data**, double-click the latest entry in the right pane. Two empty check boxes appear in both panes **(Figure 8-8)**. Notice that the shape of the mouse pointer changes to ✔ when you place it over the check boxes.
10. Select the **System State** check box in either of the panes to restore the System State data.
11. Click Next > to open the **Completing the Restore Wizard** screen.
12. Click Finish to start the restoration process. The **Enter Backup File Name** dialog box appears asking you to verify the source of the backup file **(Figure 8-9)**.
13. Accept the default settings and click OK to close the **Enter Backup File Name** dialog box. The **Restore Progress** window indicating the progress of the restoration process appears.
14. Click Close to close the **Restore Progress** window.
15. Close the **Backup – [Untitled]** window. Restart the computer in normal mode.

tip

To log on to the **Directory Services Restore Mode**, you should use the directory service restore mode administrator password that you specified during Active Directory installation. Do not specify the Active Directory password that you use to log on to a domain.

tip

By default, the Restore Wizard restores the System State data to its original location.

Figure 8-8 Restoring Active Directory

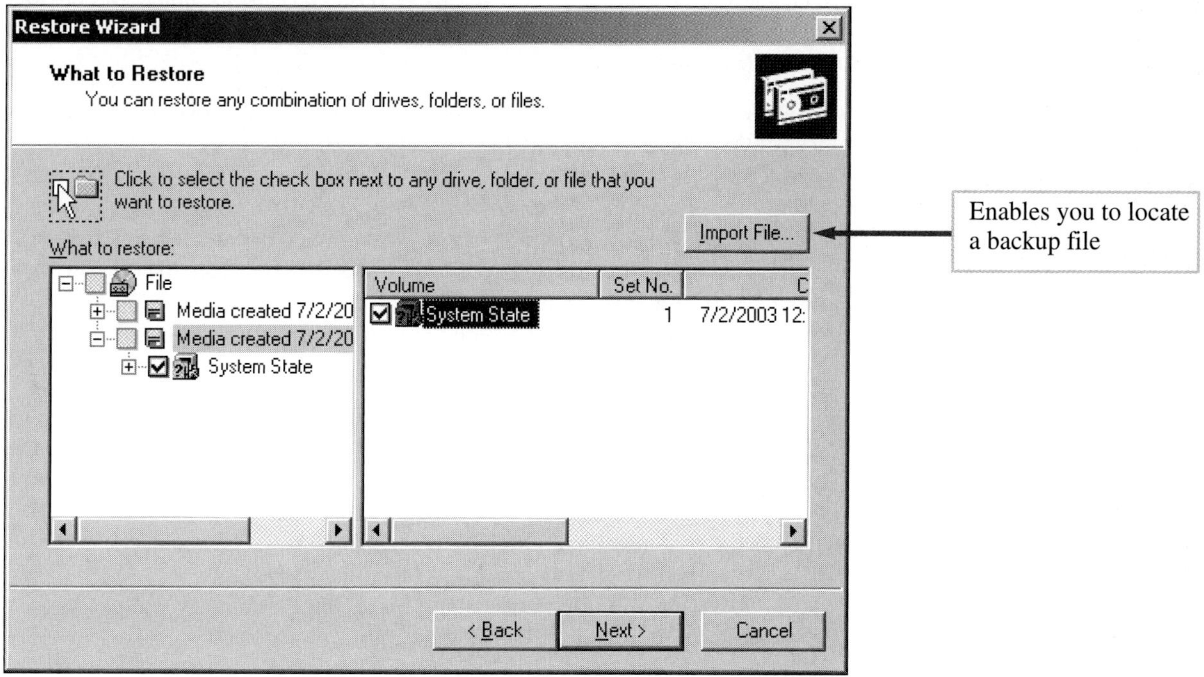

Figure 8-9 Confirming the location of the backup file

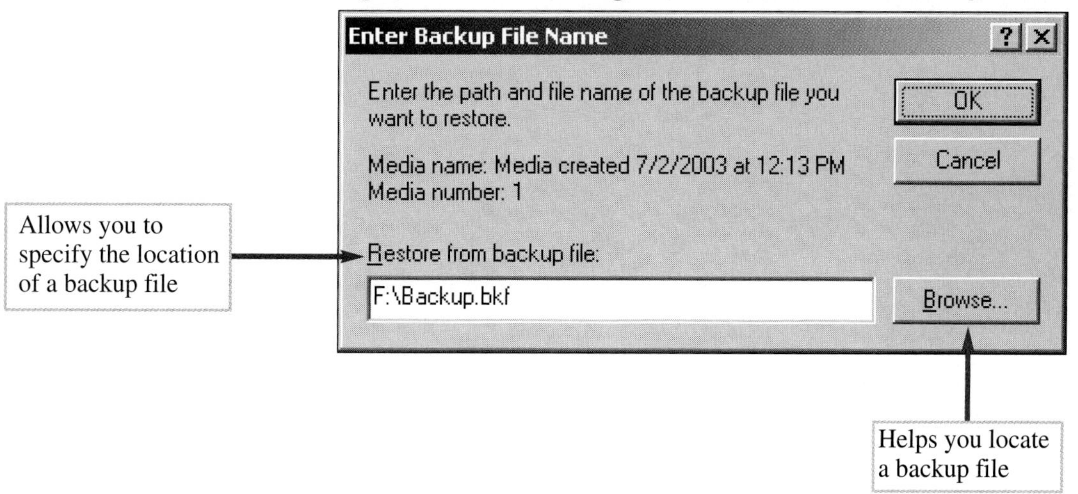

skill 5 Executing an Authoritative Restore

exam objective

Perform an authoritative and a nonauthoritative restore of Active Directory.

overview

You use an authoritative restore to recover selected Active Directory objects. For example, if you have erroneously deleted Active Directory objects, you use an authoritative restore to recover the deleted objects.

Before you perform an authoritative restore, you need to perform certain tasks. These preliminary tasks are as follows:

- Copying the Policies folder in the SYSVOL folder to an alternate location. **Figure 8-10** displays the location and contents of the Policies folder. You should copy the Policies folder from the alternate location back to its original location after you have performed an authoritative restore, and the SYSVOL share has been published. This is done to ensure that the proper elements are restored.
- Performing a standard (nonauthoritative) restore of the System State data. You can then use NTDSUTIL to perform an authoritative restore to recover the deleted object.

An authoritative restore involves running the **NTDSUTIL** command-line utility. This utility assigns the highest USN to the deleted object. To restore a deleted object, you need to specify the **distinguished name** of the object. A distinguished name uniquely identifies an object in a network. It includes the name of the domain that holds the object and the complete path to the object through the container hierarchy. The distinguished name of an object can consist of the common name (cn), the organizational unit (OU) name (ou), and the domain component name (dc). If you wanted to restore the full OU (and all objects in it), you would use the following DN: OU=Admin, DC=Mydomain, DC=com.

Similar to the nonauthoritative restore, an authoritative restore also requires a domain controller to be running in the **Directory Services Restore Mode**. After the restoration process is complete, the domain controller is brought online by starting the computer in the normal mode. In case the Active Directory database has changed on other domain controllers, the replication process will update the copy of the restored Active Directory database. The replication process will also distribute the information about the restored object to other domain controllers.

how to

On the ServerA domain controller, restore Active Directory authoritatively to recover the deleted user object, Doug, which existed in the Users container of the spearhead.com domain.

1. Perform a nonauthoritative restore and restart the computer in the **Directory Services Restore Mode**.
2. Log on as the Administrator using the Directory Services Restore Mode password.
3. Restore your System State backup using the NTBackup utility.
4. Click **Start**, point to **Programs**, point to **Accessories**, and then click the **Command Prompt** command to open the **Command Prompt** window. Alternatively, type **cmd** in the **Run** window.
5. Type **ntdsutil** at the command prompt, and then press **[ENTER]** to run the **NTDSUTIL** utility. The **ntdsutil** prompt appears.
6. Type **authoritative restore** at the **ntdsutil** prompt, and then press **[ENTER]**. The **authoritative restore** prompt appears.

caution

You should not restart after restoring the database until you run NTDSUTIL.

Figure 8-10 Copying the Policies folder to an alternate location

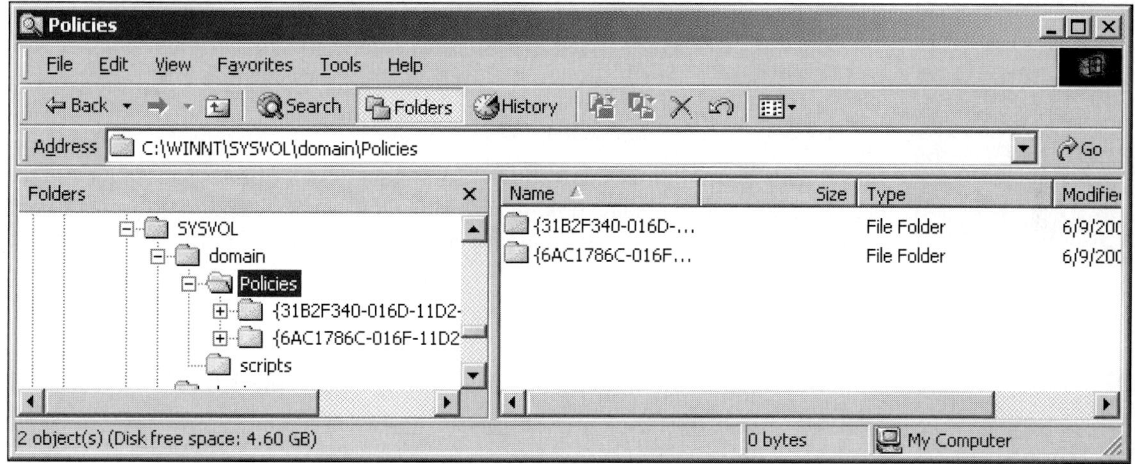

skill 5 Executing an Authoritative Restore

(cont'd)

exam objective

Perform an authoritative restore of Active Directory.

how to

7. To restore the deleted object, type **restore subtree cn=JWillis,cn=users,dc=mydomain,dc=com** at the authoritative restore prompt, and then press **[Enter]**. The **Authoritative Restore Confirmation Dialog** message box appears asking for your confirmation to continue with the restoration process **(Figure 8-11)**.
8. Click Yes to authoritatively restore the deleted object, Doug **(Figure 8-12)**.
9. Type **quit** at the authoritative restore prompt to return to the **ntdsutil** prompt.
10. Type **quit** at the **ntdsutil** prompt to return to the command prompt.
11. Type **exit** at the command prompt to close the command prompt window. You have authoritatively restored Active Directory to recover the deleted object, Doug.

more

Sometimes, you might accidentally delete a large number of objects. Manually recovering each object is a cumbersome task. In such situations, you can authoritatively restore the entire database. To do this, type the **restore database** command at the **authoritative restore** prompt.

However, be very careful not to perform an authoritative restore of the entire database on the servers holding the RID master or Schema master FSMO roles. The Schema cannot be authoritatively restored, and authoritatively restoring the RID master can lead to SID conflicts.

Figure 8-11 Confirming an authoritative restore

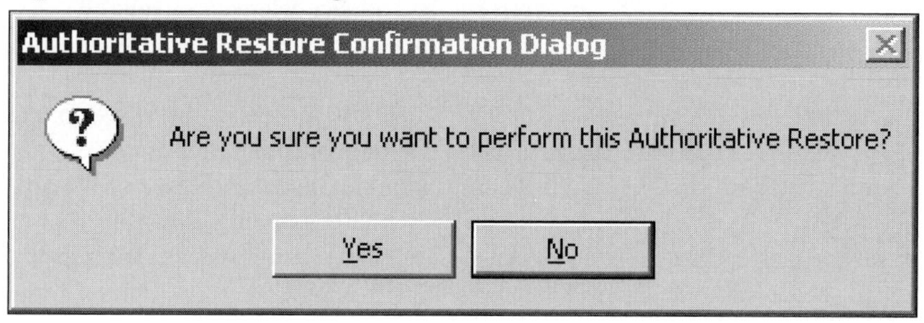

Figure 8-12 Using NTDSUTIL to recover a deleted object

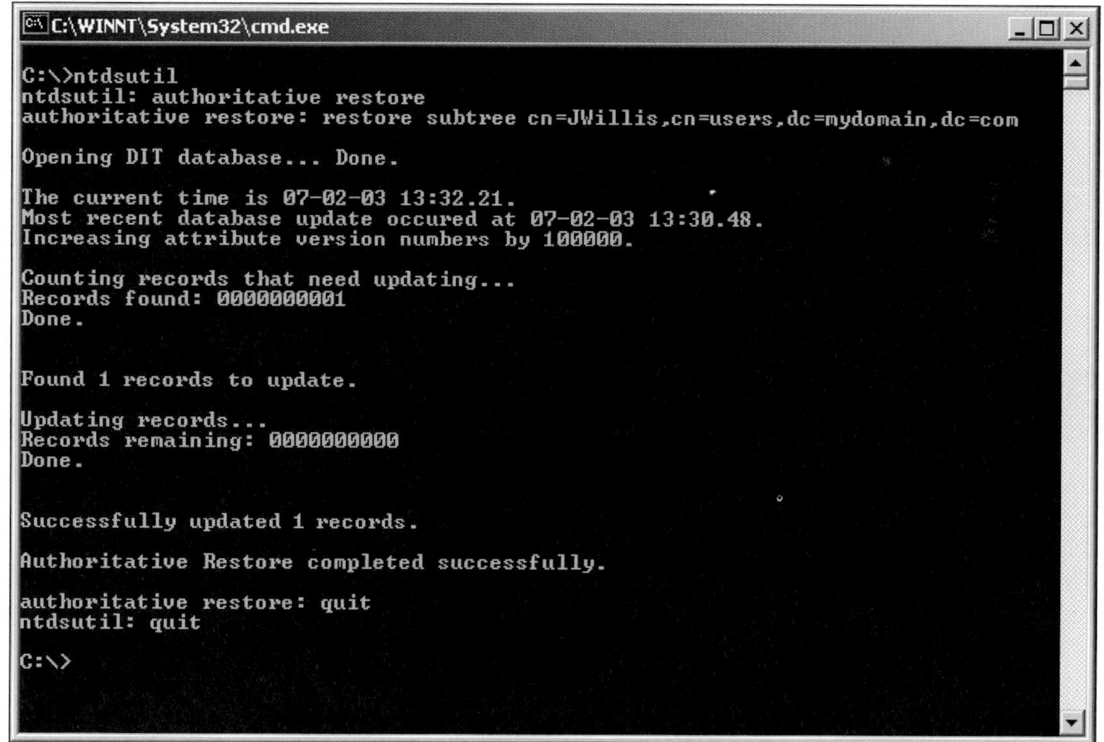

Summary

- The Backup Wizard is used to back up Active Directory. It creates an archive with a '.bkf' extension containing the files that have been selected for backup.
- You should be a member of the Backup Operators or the Administrators group in order to back up Active Directory.
- Back up of Active Directory involves backing up the System State data, which also includes the Active Directory database, the SYSVOL folder, the registry, the COM+ Class Registration database, and the system boot files.
- The Task Scheduler service is integrated with the Backup Wizard to enable you to schedule the backup operation to occur at a specified date and time.
- You can schedule Active Directory backup using the Advanced button available on the Completing the Backup Wizard screen of the Backup Wizard.
- A backup of the System State data is required to restore the Active Directory database.
- There are two methods of restoring the Active Directory database: nonauthoritative and authoritative.
- A nonauthoritative restore is the more frequently used method to restore Active Directory on a domain controller.
- An authoritative restore is used to recover any specific object deleted accidentally.
- During an authoritative restore, the update sequence number (USN) of the deleted object is modified so that it is higher than the USNs of the same object on other domain controllers.
- You use the Restore Wizard to restore the Active Directory database.
- To restore Active Directory, you need to start the computer in a special safe mode called the Directory Services Restore Mode.
- You use the NTDSUTIL utility to perform an authoritative restore.
- To recover a deleted object, you should perform a nonauthoritative restore before you run the NTDSUTIL utility.
- To restore a deleted object, you need to specify the distinguished name of the object.

Key Terms

Authoritative restore
COM+ Class Registration database
Directory Services Restore Mode
Distinguished name
Hardware Compatibility List (HCL)
Nonauthoritative restore
NTDSUTIL
Registry
Shared system volume (SYSVOL)
System boot files
System State data
Task Scheduler
Update Sequence Number (USN)

Test Yourself

1. The Backup Wizard allows you to: (Choose all that apply).
   a. Create an emergency repair disk.
   b. Archive Active Directory of a remote computer.
   c. Restore a deleted object authoritatively.
   d. Archive the entire content on a computer.

2. You are backing up Active Directory using the default settings. Which one of the following types will the Backup Wizard use to backup Active Directory?
   a. Incremental
   b. Daily
   c. Normal
   d. Differential

3. Which one of the following statements about nonauthoritative restore is correct?
   a. Modifies the USN of a deleted object.
   b. Restores Active Directory completely.
   c. Is followed by an authoritative restore.
   d. Helps recover a deleted object.

4. Which is the correct method to perform a nonauthoritative restore?
   a. Start the computer, run the Backup Wizard, specify the location to restore the Active Directory backup, and then restart the computer.
   b. Start the computer in the Directory Services Restore Mode, run the NTDSUTIL utility, and then restart the computer.
   c. Start the computer in the Directory Services Restore Mode, run the Restore Wizard, specify the location to restore the backup, and then restart the computer.

d. Start the computer, perform an authoritative restore, perform a nonauthoritative restore, and then restart the computer.

5. From an NTDSUTIL prompt, which one of the following commands would you use to recover a deleted object?
  a. Restore database
  b. Authoritative restore
  c. NTDSUTIL
  d. Restore subtree

6. You erroneously deleted the HR organizational unit (OU) belonging to the Admin OU in the domain spearhead.com. Which is the correct command to recover the HR OU?
  a. restore subtree ou=hr,ou=admin,dc=spearhead, dc=com
  b. restore subtree ou=admin,ou=hr,dc=spearhead, dc=com
  c. restore subtree dc=spearhead,dc=com,ou=admin, ou=hr
  d. restore subtree dc=com,dc=spearhead,ou=admin, ou=hr

Projects: On Your Own

1. Back up Active Directory.
  a. Start the Backup Wizard.
  b. Click the **Backup Wizard** button.
  c. Select the **Only back up the System State data** option.
  d. Specify the location to store the backup file.
  e. Click the **Finish** button to start the backup procedure.

2. Perform a nonauthoritative restore.
  a. Start the computer in the **Directory Services Restore Mode**.
  b. Log in as the Directory Service Restore Mode administrator.
  c. Start the **Backup Wizard**.
  d. Click the **Restore Wizard** button.
  e. Select the latest backup.
  f. Click the **Finish** button.
  g. Accept the default location of the backup file.

3. Perform an authoritative restore to recover a deleted object.
  a. Restart the computer in the **Directory Services Restore Mode**.
  b. Log in as the **Directory Services Restore Mode Administrator**.
  c. Perform a nonauthoritative restore.
  d. Run the **NTDSUTIL** utility from the command prompt.
  e. Specify the distinguished name of the deleted object to start the restoration process.

Problem Solving Scenarios

1. You administer your Windows 2000 domain. Your domain consists of three domain controllers. You have a backup policy, which backs up the system state on the domain controller once every day. Suddenly, you realize that one of your domain controllers has failed and the system can no longer boot up normally. You try starting your computer in safe mode and the system starts up. However, after restarting, the system fails again.

You need to get the domain controller up and running as soon as possible. Draft a memo listing the steps you need to follow to solve this problem.

2. You administer your company's ADS infrastructure. One day, you receive a call from a user who tells you that he has accidentally deleted a few AD objects. He asks you if you can recover the objects. You know that you have a recent backup of the system state that was completed that morning.

You need to complete the operation as fast as possible. List the steps required to complete the procedure.

LESSON

9 Implementing Group Policy in Windows 2000 Server

Managing the user environment is one of the most important tasks of an Active Directory administrator. In large organizations, an administrator may face problems in maintaining consistency in user and computer settings across the network, which can lead to cost and time overruns. Windows 2000 Server provides a feature called Group Policy to help administer large environments efficiently. Windows 2000 has provided about 450 Group Policy settings, which administrators can specify using one or more Group Policy Objects (GPOs). A GPO is an Active Directory object that represents a collection of Group Policy settings, which enable an administrator to control various aspects of a computing environment.

GPOs can be applied to various Active Directory containers such as sites, domains, and organizational units (OUs). Group Policy settings consist of Computer configuration settings and User configuration settings, which apply to computers at startup and shutdown, as well as users at logon and logoff, respectively. These settings are applied in a sequence with the Computer configuration settings taking precedence in case of a conflict. Similarly, the GPOs are also processed in the order local, sites, domains, and OUs (referred to as "LSDOU").

Before creating GPOs, it is very important to design and implement a Group Policy deployment. Creating multilevel OU structures with numerous GPOs can lead to a complex startup and logon structure that could adversely affect the performance of the logon process. The various types of Group Policy implementation strategies are based on factors such as location of GPOs, delegation of authority, and organization structure.

Finally, you can assign permissions to delegate the administrative control of individual GPOs, delegate the ability to apply GPOs (known as linking), and even delegate the ability to create new GPOs, dispersing the administrative burden associated with GPO administration.

Goals

In this lesson, you will be introduced to the concept of Group Policy, Group Policy Objects, and types of Group Policy settings. You will also learn about the role of a Group Policy at computer startup and user logon. Additionally, you will learn about the various implementation strategies for a Group Policy. Finally, you will create a GPO and delegate the administrative control for a GPO to a specific group of users.

Lesson 9 Implementing Group Policy in Windows 2000 Server

Skill	Exam 70-217 Objective
1. Introducing Group Policy	Basic knowledge
2. Introducing the Types of Group Policy Settings	Basic knowledge
3. Identifying the Role of a Group Policy at Startup and Logon	Basic knowledge
4. Planning a Group Policy Implementation	Basic knowledge
5. Creating a Group Policy Object	Implement and troubleshoot Group Policy. Create and modify a Group Policy Object (GPO). Manage network configuration by using Group Policy.
6. Assigning Control of a Group Policy Object to Administrators	Implement and troubleshoot Group Policy. Delegate administrative control of Group Policy.

Requirements

To complete this lesson, you will need administrative rights on a Windows 2000 Server domain controller that belongs to the mydomain.com domain (either ServerA or ServerB).

skill 1 Introducing Group Policy

exam objective

Basic knowledge

overview

An administrator of a Windows 2000 network needs to monitor user and computer settings regularly to make sure they conform to the corporate standards for different departments. **Group Policy** is the primary Active Directory feature that not only helps administrators specify the standard behavior of users' desktops, but also enforces those requirements. Using group policies, administrators need to define the settings for the work environment only once. These settings will always remain applicable regardless of the location of the user.

Group policies can be applied to various Active Directory containers, such as sites, domains, and organizational units (OUs), to implement rules at various levels of an organization. To do this, you need only to link the GPO to one of these containers.

Table 9-1 lists the main features of a Group Policy.

Group Policy is also referred to as a **Group Policy Object (GPO)** since Group Policy is an object of Active Directory. A GPO is a storehouse of a collection of Group Policy settings that enable an administrator to control various aspects of a computing environment.

A GPO is made up of two parts:

- **Group Policy Container (GPC):** A GPC is an Active Directory component and contains GPO attributes, extensions, and version information. Domain controllers in a network use this information to make sure they are using the most recent version of the GPO and to apply permissions to the GPO. For each GPO, there is a GPC container stored in the System\Policies folder in the **Active Directory Users and Computers console (Figure 9-1)**. Each GPC container contains the **Globally Unique Identifier (GUID)** of the GPO.
- **Group Policy Template (GPT):** A GPT is a collection of folders stored under %systemroot%\SYSVOL\sysvol\domainname\Policies on each Windows 2000 domain controller. For each GPO, a folder hierarchy composed of physical files and settings required by the GPO is created automatically. These files and settings include security settings, administrative templates, software installation information, scripts, and folder redirection settings. These settings are applied to the Windows 2000 clients on a network. Like the GPC container, the GPT folder is also named after the GUID of the created GPO.

Table 9-1 Important Features of Group Policy

Features of Group Policy	Explanation
Centralizes control	Group Policy centralizes control over computers and users within an organization.
Provides secure environment	Group Policy is written to a secure section of the registry. This prevents users from removing or modifying a policy through regedit32.exe or regedit.exe utilities.
Always contains the latest information	Group Policy is updated at specific intervals on each machine. This means that when you modify a Group Policy, it only takes a short period of time (90-120 minutes, by default) for your changes to take effect. For most settings in Group Policy, the user does not have to log off and log back on for the settings to take effect.
Ensures adherence to security requirements	Group Policy settings ensure that users adhere to all the security requirements, such as password length and duration.
Enhances administrative control	Group Policy is a tool that tremendously enhances administrative control. Numerous detailed settings can be applied throughout an organization by using Group Policy.
Reduces the total cost of ownership (TCO)	Group Policy helps in reducing the TCO of an organization by applying rules that automate administrative control. Furthermore, Group Policy helps prevent data and time loss due to inadvertent or intentional damage to the computing environment.

Figure 9-1 GPC containers in the Active Directory Users and Computers console

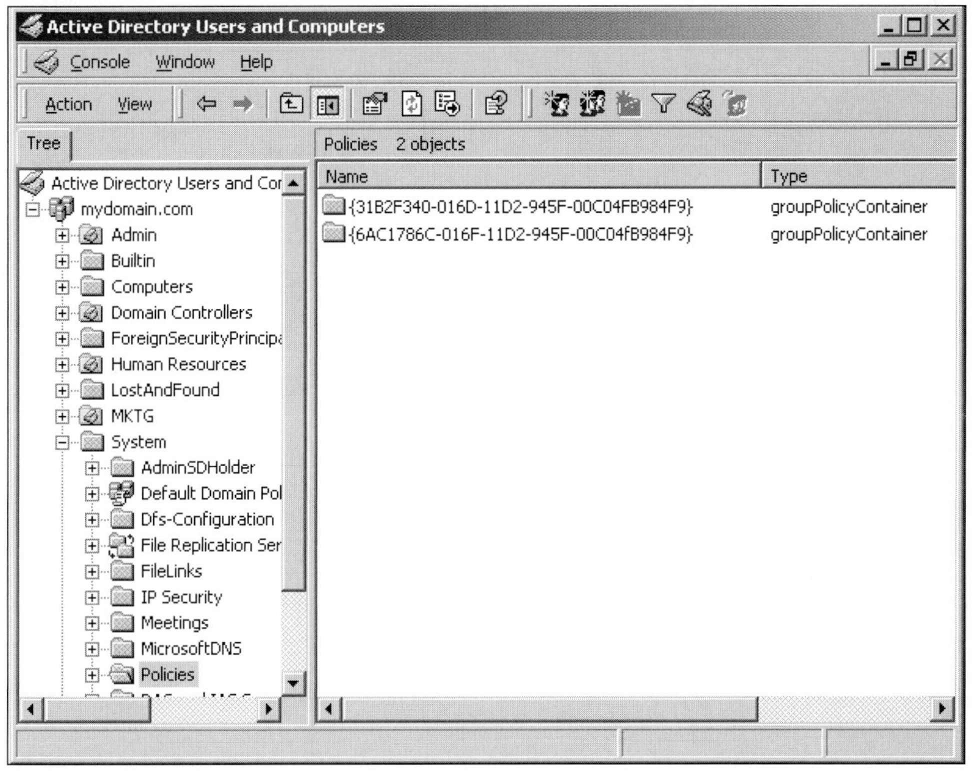

skill 1 Introducing Group Policy *(cont'd)*

exam objective

Basic knowledge

how to

Access the Group Policy snap-in for the local computer.

1. Log on to the ServerA or ServerB domain controller as an Administrator.
2. Click Start, and then click the **Run** command to open the **Run** dialog box.
3. Type **mmc** in the **Open** text box, and click OK to open the **MMC** console.
4. Click the **Add/Remove Snap-In** command from the **Console** menu to open the **Add/Remove Snap-In** dialog box.
5. Click Add... to open the Add Standalone Snap-In dialog box.
6. Click **Group Policy** in the **Available standalone snap-ins** list, and then click Add to open the **Select Group Policy Object** dialog box.
7. Accept the default entry **Local Computer** in the **Group Policy Object** text box.
8. Click Finish to close the **Select Group Policy Object** dialog box.
9. Click Close to close the **Add Standalone Snap-In** dialog box. The snap-in name, **Local Computer Policy**, appears in the **Add/Remove Snap-In** dialog box **(Figure 9-2)**.
10. Click OK to close the **Add/Remove Snap-In** dialog box. The Group Policy snap-in for the local computer is now available to you (**Figure 9-3**).
11. Close the MMC console window. Click Yes when prompted to save.

Figure 9-2 Adding the Group Policy snap-in to the console

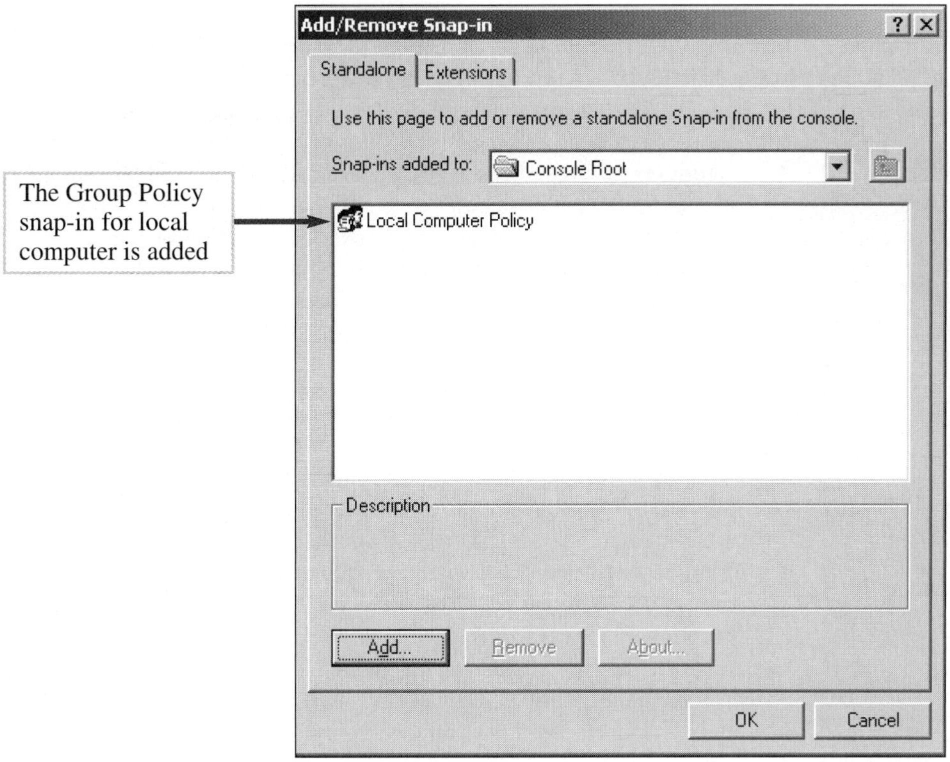

The Group Policy snap-in for local computer is added

Figure 9-3 Accessing the Group Policy snap-in

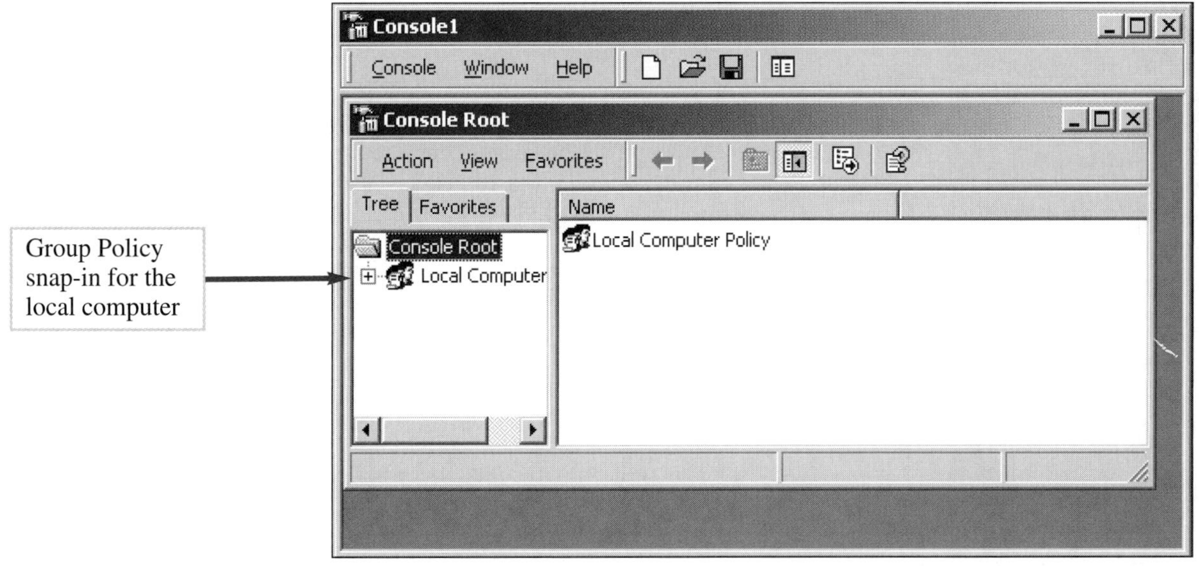

skill 2 Introducing the Types of Group Policy Settings

exam objective

Basic knowledge

overview

Group policies can be applied to both users and computers. To organize and manage the various Group Policy settings in each GPO efficiently, Windows 2000 provides two types of Group Policy settings in the Group Policy snap-in: Computer configuration settings and User configuration settings.

- **Computer configuration settings:** Computer configuration settings refer to the group policies for computers, irrespective of the users logging on to them. These settings apply to a computer during the initialization of the operating system.
- **User configuration settings:** User configuration settings refer to the group policies for users, irrespective of the computer the users log on to. These settings apply at the time of user logon.

Both Computer configuration settings and User configuration settings contain three containers, each of which includes several related policies. These containers are Software Settings, Windows Settings, and Administrative Templates **(Figure 9-4)**.

- **Software Settings:** This container contains the Software Installation extension. You can use the Software Installation extension to install software automatically from a central distribution point.
- **Windows Settings:** This container contains Scripts and Security Settings extensions. You can use the Scripts extension to specify startup/shutdown scripts for computers, and logon/logoff scripts for users in a network. The startup/shutdown scripts run when the computer starts up or shuts down, and the logon/logoff scripts run when a user logs on or off a computer. The Security Settings extension, on the other hand, is used by security administrators to configure the security aspects of the machine. This section also contains additional settings for Remote Installation Service (RIS) and Folder Redirection in the User Configuration container.
- **Administrative Templates:** This container contains all registry-based Group Policy settings, including settings for Windows Components, System, and Network. Other settings, such as Desktop and Control Panel, are available only in the User Configuration container.

more

The Group Policy snap-in is made up of many Microsoft Management Console (MMC) snap-in extensions. Although all the Group Policy setting folders are loaded by default when the Group Policy snap-in is started, you can create custom consoles for each of these Group Policy snap-in extensions. You need to use the Microsoft Management Console folder under the Administrative Templates container in the Group Policy snap-in in order to apply these policies.

caution

Some settings, such as Kerberos policies and the MMC folder, are not available in local policies.

Figure 9-4 Group Policy settings in the Group Policy snap-in

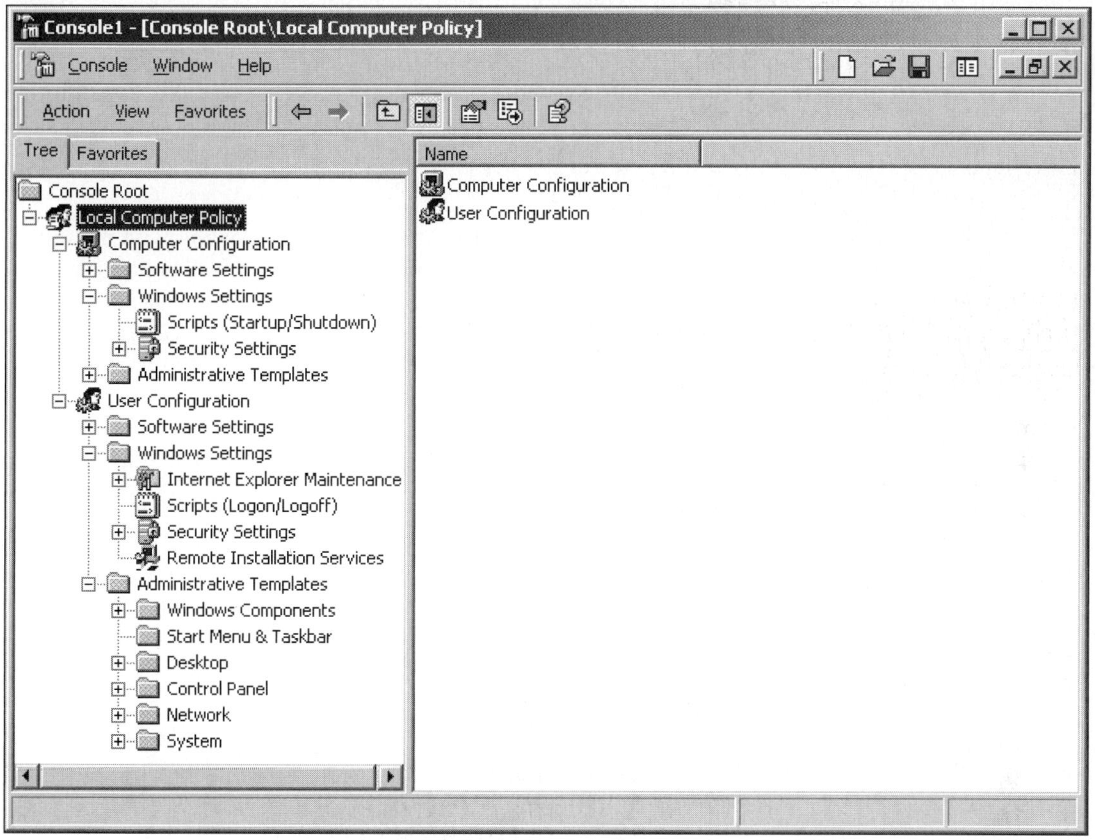

skill 3

Identifying the Role of a Group Policy at Startup and Logon

exam objective

Basic knowledge

overview

The role of a Group Policy begins when a computer starts up and a user logs on. During startup and logon, both the Computer Configuration and the User Configuration settings are applied in a specific sequence. In the event that computer settings and user settings conflict with each other, the computer settings take precedence. However, this is rare, as there are only a few settings that are exactly the same. Most settings in the Computers container have no peer in the Users container, and vice versa. **Figure 9-5** describes the complete process of the computer startup and user logon.

The processing sequence becomes very important when dealing with multiple policies. If there are no conflicts within the policies, then all settings from all policies apply. However, if a conflict occurs (such as one policy removing the start menu and another enabling the start menu), the policy to apply last wins. The sequence in which Group Policy settings are processed is as follows: local GPO, site GPOs, domain GPOs, and then OU GPOs. If more than one GPO is linked to a site, domain, or OU, the policies are processed in reverse order (bottom to top) for each individual container. This is done so that the "most important" policy, of all GPOs applied to a particular container, is displayed at the top of the list **(Figure 9-6)**.

There are certain exceptions to the order in which GPOs are processed:

- If a computer belongs to a workgroup, it only processes the local GPO.
- If the **No Override** option is set for a GPO, no configured policy setting in the GPO can be overridden. In case of multiple GPOs being set to No Override, the GPO that is the highest in the Active Directory hierarchy (the one that applies first) gets the highest priority. If there are multiple policies set to No Override in a single container, then the one at the bottom of the list (again, the one that is applied first) wins. While this initially sounds confusing, the easiest way to think of it is that the first GPO to say "you can't override my settings" wins.
- If the **Block Policy Inheritance** option is set for a domain or OU, the GPOs above that point in the structure do not affect users or computers in that structure; they are blocked. However, if there is a conflict between No Override and Block Inheritance, No Override always wins.
- If Loopback settings are applied to a GPO list, the default GPO processing order is not maintained. The Loopback setting modifies the default method by which the list of GPOs is prepared for the user and hence affects the default processing order of GPOs.

more

Like files and folders, group policies are also inherited from parent containers to child containers. In other words, a Group Policy assigned to a parent container applies to all sub-containers under the parent container. However, you can specifically set a separate Group Policy setting for a child container to override the settings that it inherits from its parent container. It is extremely important to realize, however, that just like OU structures, group policies do not flow between domains. A Group Policy applied to a parent domain will not apply to its child domain or domains. The only container that can apply group policies to multiple domains is the site container. A Group Policy applied to a site will affect all users and/or computers in the site, regardless of domain. For this reason, you must be an enterprise admin to apply a Group Policy to a site.

Figure 9-5 The sequence in which computer configuration and user configuration settings are applied

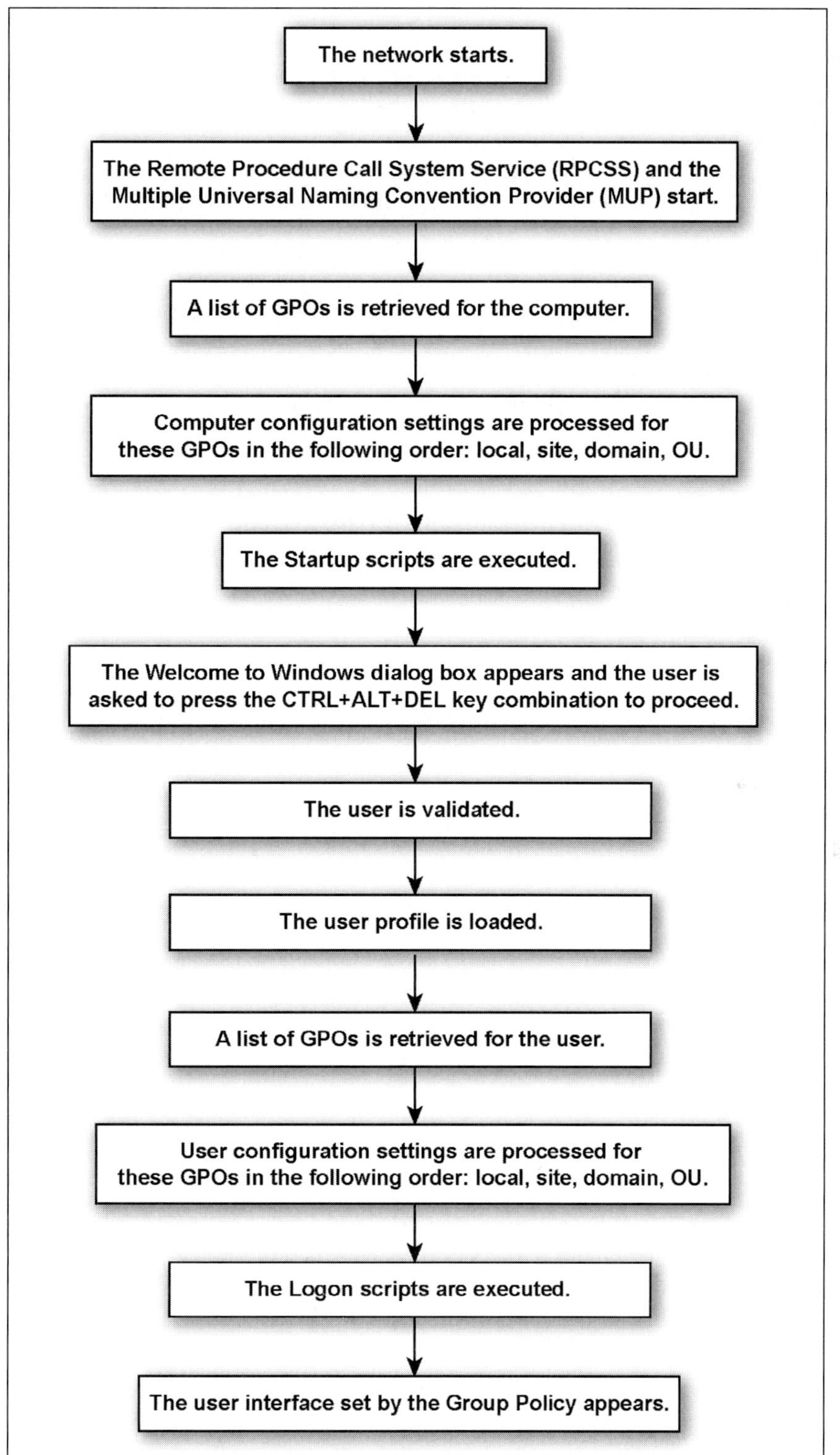

skill 4 Planning a Group Policy Implementation

exam objective

Basic knowledge

overview

It is very important to plan and design a Group Policy implementation carefully. Creating multilevel domain and OU structures, as well as numerous GPOs can lead to complex startup and logon structures, which could adversely affect the performance of your login speed. In order to manage group policies efficiently, you need to understand the three main design strategies of GPO setting types. **Table 9-2** lists and describes each strategy.

After deciding upon a Group Policy setting design for your organization, you need to consider the Group Policy implementation strategy. Various factors need to be considered before a strategy is chosen to implement Group Policy in an organization. These factors include:

- Location of GPOs
- Delegation of authority
- Organization structure

The major types of Group Policy implementation strategies based on each of these factors are described below.

Centralized vs. Decentralized GPO Design: This strategy is based on the centralized (monolithic) and decentralized (layered) location of GPOs. The **centralized GPO design approach** suggests that the organization network should be maintained by a small number of large GPOs. For example, if one GPO handles an entire domain, the logon process for this GPO would be faster, but it would be difficult to delegate this GPO because of its large number of settings.

The **decentralized GPO design approach** uses separate GPOs for specific policy settings. This is especially helpful in situations where you need to modify only one GPO for enforcing a change in one of the policy settings. This approach increases the number of GPOs, and hence lengthens the logon time. On the other hand, it simplifies administration due to its flexibility.

Functional Role or Team Design: The functional role strategy is based on the structure of the organization. The **functional role design approach** suggests that the functional roles of users be used in an organization to apply group policies. To do this, you first need to create an OU structure that corresponds to the actual team structure of your organization. Then, create a GPO for each OU, with each GPO customized to the OU's individual needs. This approach also minimizes the number of GPOs to be used because each GPO caters to the specific needs of a group.

Delegation with Central Control Design or Distributed Control Design: The central control design approach is based on delegating the administrative control of OUs to various administrators of an organization. The **central control design approach** suggests that you maintain a central control while delegating administration to various OU administrators. For example, you can create a GPO with specific desktop settings at the domain level. These settings would apply on all child containers, thus maintaining centralized control on the entire domain. Similarly, separate GPOs can be created for other policy settings, and delegated to different OU administrators.

Regardless of which approach (or combination) you choose, it is important to try and avoid using Block Inheritance as much as possible, as troubleshooting GPOs can be very difficult when these tools are used. Likewise, you should only use No Override and filtering (modifying permissions on a GPO so that only certain domain groups can apply the GPO) when explicitly required.

caution

Considering that on average client hardware, each GPO takes 5-30 seconds to process, logon delay considerations involved with GPO processing are not trivial concerns. With 20 or more GPOs applied, you could be adding 10+ minutes to each user's logon delay.

tip

A useful tool for troubleshooting group policies is gpresult.exe, contained in the Windows 2000 resource kit. With gpresult, you can see which policies are applying to a given user and in what order, which helps you determine where conflicts may be occurring.

Table 9-2 Design strategies of GPO setting types

GPO Setting	Description
Single Policy (Modular) Type	In this approach, one GPO represents only one type of Group Policy setting. For example, there will be one GPO for the software management settings, another for the security settings, and so on. You can assign the responsibility of such GPOs to specific users. This approach can be used in large organizations where administrative control is distributed among various individuals.
Multiple Policy (Consolidated) Type	In this approach, one GPO represents multiple types of Group Policy settings. For example, a single GPO can be used to store both software management and security settings. This approach can be used in small organizations where a single person administers multiple group policies.
Dedicated Policy Type	In this approach, separate GPOs represent the user configuration and the computer configuration group policies. This is an excellent way to control GPOs if your company has dedicated OU structures for users and computers. However, if you have both users and computers in the same OU, you are generally better off controlling both objects with a single policy.

skill 5 Creating a Group Policy Object

exam objective

Implement and troubleshoot Group Policy. Create and modify a Group Policy Object (GPO). Manage network configuration by using Group Policy.

overview

After you have identified the GPO implementation strategy for your organization, you need to create a GPO that best suits your requirements. When you install Active Directory on your network, two GPOs named Default Domain Policy (linked to the domain) and Default Domain Controller Policy (Linked to the Domain Controllers OU) are created automatically. You can use these policies to assign standard settings to the domain and the domain controllers in a domain, respectively. GPOs can be linked to sites, domains, and OUs. To link a GPO to a site, you need to use the Active Directory Sites and Services console. On the other hand, if you want to link GPOs to domains and OUs, you can use the Active Directory Users and Computers console.

how to

Create a GPO, mydomain object 1, for the mydomain.com domain.

1. Log on to the ServerA or ServerB domain controller as an Administrator.
2. Click **Start**, point to **Programs**, point to **Administrative Tools**, and then click the **Active Directory Users and Computers** command to open the **Active Directory Users and Computers** console.
3. Right-click **mydomain.com**, and then click the **Properties** command on the shortcut menu to open the **mydomain.com Properties** dialog box.
4. Click the **Group Policy** tab.
5. Click **New** to create a new GPO. A GPO link with the default name **New Group Policy Object** appears. Type the name **mydomain object 1** in place of this default name to specify the name for the new GPO. The new GPO is created (**Figure 9-6**).
6. Close the **mydomain.com Properties** dialog box.
7. Close the **Active Directory Users and Computers** console.

more

You can create a stand-alone GPO console for a GPO and access it directly from the **Administrative Tools** menu. To create a GPO console, open the **Add Standalone Snap-In** dialog box through the **MMC** console and select **Group Policy** from the list of available snap-ins. After adding the snap-in, click the **Browse** button in the **Select Group Policy Object** dialog box to open the **Browse For a Group Policy Object** dialog box, where you can specify the GPO for which you want to create a snap-in. The selected GPO name now appears in the **Group Policy Object** text box of the **Select Group Policy Object** dialog box (**Figure 9-7**). You can later save the GPO using the **Save** command on the **Console** menu to make it available on the **Administrative Tools** menu.

Figure 9-6 Creating a new GPO

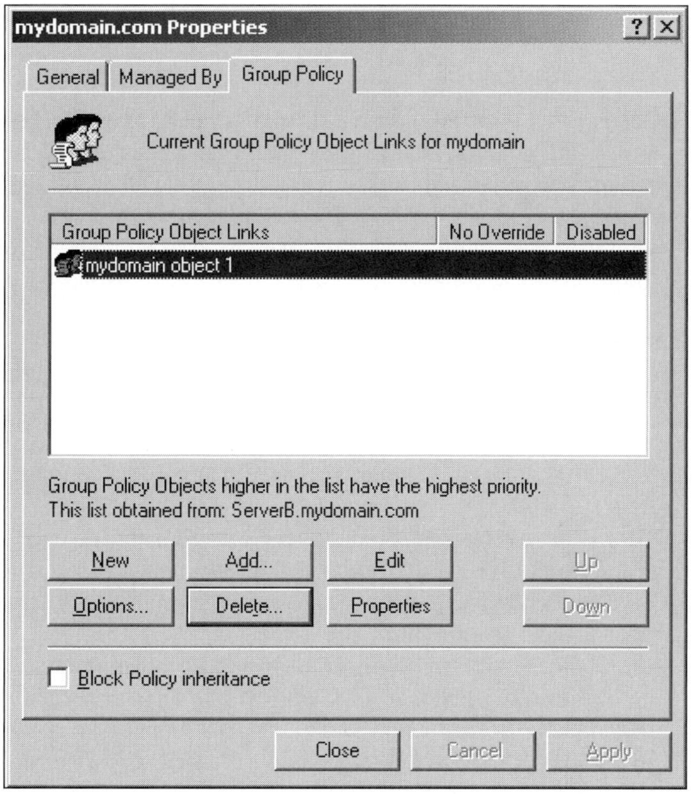

Figure 9-7 Creating a GPO console

skill 6

Assigning Control of a Group Policy Object to Administrators

exam objective

Implement and troubleshoot Group Policy. Delegate administrative control of Group Policy.

overview

Once a GPO is created, it usually becomes necessary to delegate the administrative control of the GPO to various administrators in the organization. This relieves the administrative burden that would fall on a single individual. You can assign permissions to delegate the administrative control of a GPO by using the Properties dialog box for the GPO. To provide administrative control of the GPO, you need to set both the Read and Write permissions to Allow.

tip

A user having only Read permissions cannot open the various extensions of the Group Policy snap-in.

how to

Delegate administrative control of the GPO **mydomain object 1** to the CREATOR OWNER group.

1. In the **Active Directory Users and Computers** console, right-click the domain **mydomain.com** and click the **Properties** command to open the **mydomain.com Properties** dialog box.
2. Click the **Group Policy** tab.
3. Click the GPO **mydomain object 1** in the **mydomain.com Properties** dialog box (**Figure 9-8**), and then click Properties to open the **Properties** dialog box for the GPO.
4. Click the **Security** tab.
5. Click **CREATOR OWNER** in the **Name** list to delegate administrative control to this group.
6. Now, set the Read and Write permissions to **Allow** (**Figure 9-9**). These permission settings will provide complete administrative control of the GPO to the CREATER OWNER group.
7. Click OK to save the settings and close the **Properties** dialog box for the GPO.
8. Close the **mydomain.com Properties** dialog box.
9. Close the **Active Directory Users and Computers** console.

Figure 9-8 Selecting the Group Policy object for which you want to assign control

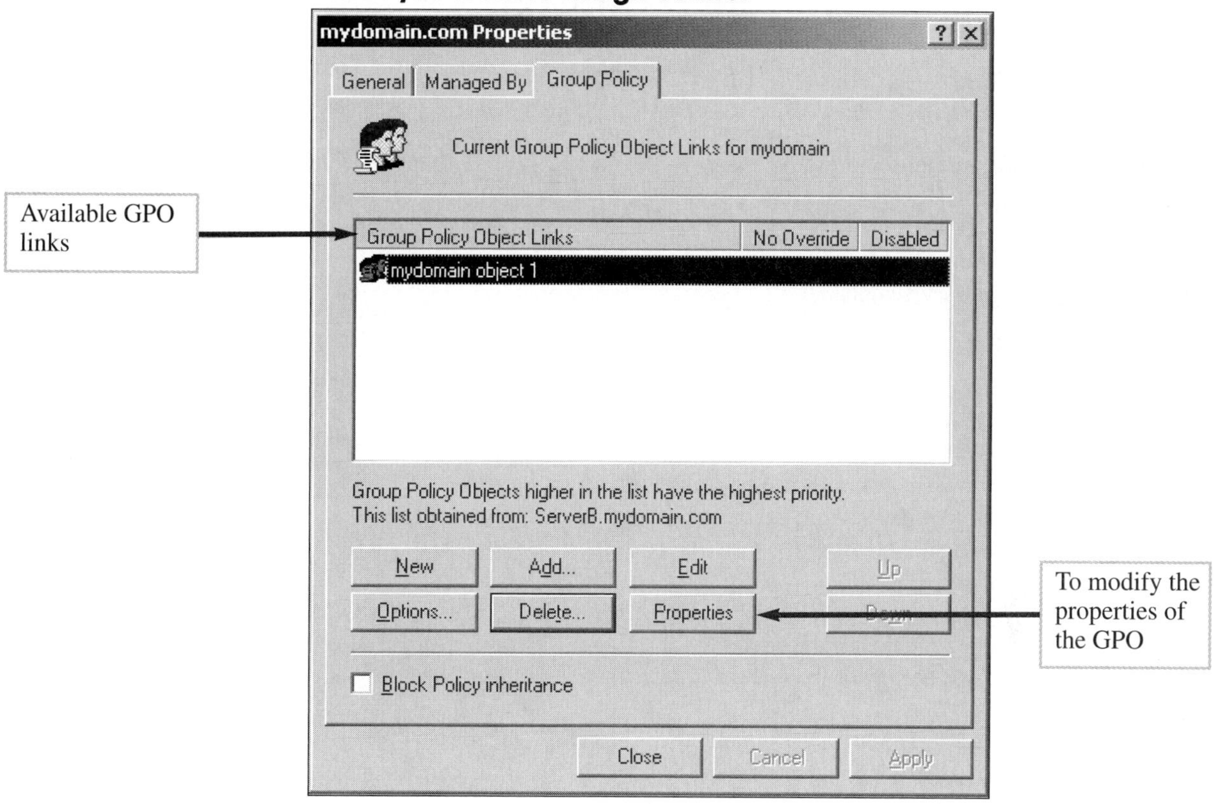

Figure 9-9 Setting permissions

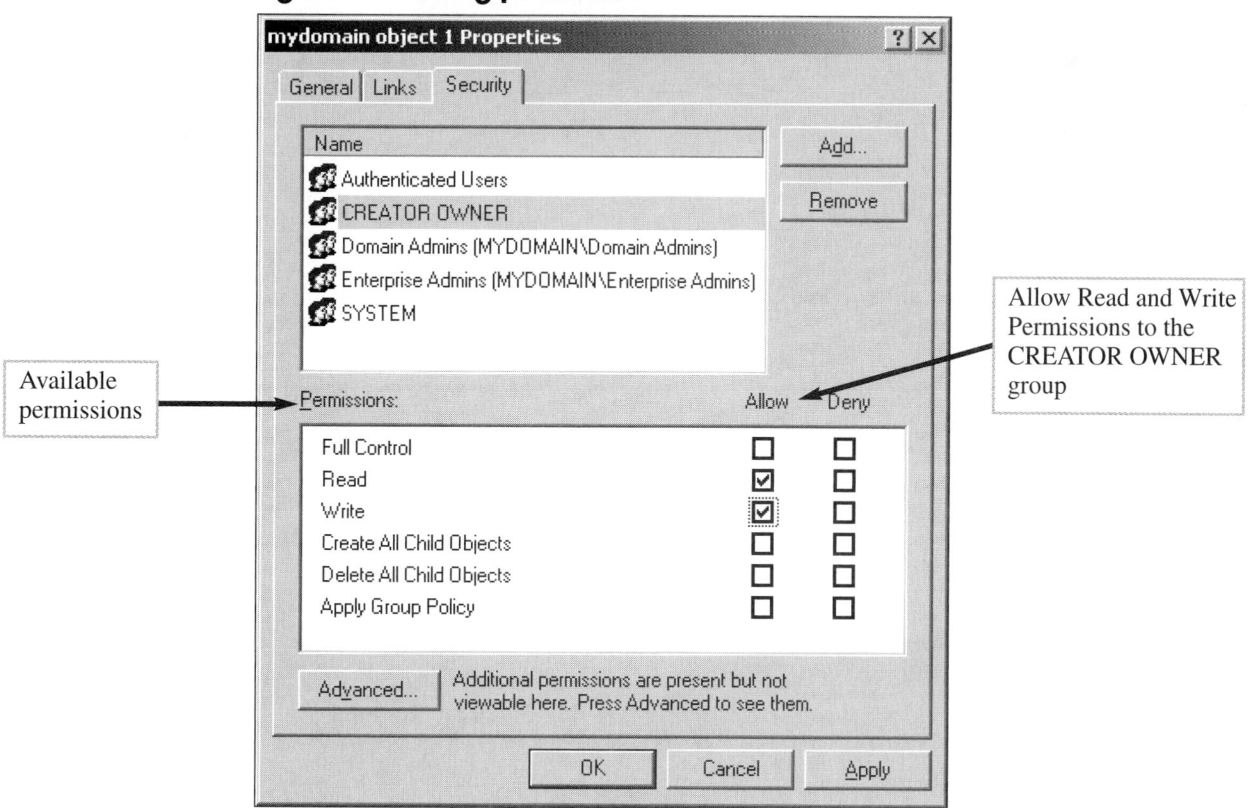

Summary

- Group Policy is the primary Active Directory feature that helps administrators decide and specify the behavior of users' desktops.
- A Group Policy Object (GPO) is a storehouse of the collection of Group Policy settings that enable an administrator to control various aspects of a computing environment.
- A GPO is made up of two parts: Group Policy Container (GPC) and Group Policy Template (GPT).
- A GPC is an Active Directory component and contains GPO attributes, extensions, and version information.
- A GPT is a collection of folders stored under %systemroot%\SYSVOL\sysvol\domainname\Policies on each Windows 2000 domain controller.
- Windows 2000 provides two types of Group Policy settings in the Group Policy snap-in: Computer configuration and User configuration.
- Computer configuration settings refer to the group policies for computers, irrespective of the users logging on to them. User configuration settings refer to the group policies for users, irrespective of the computer users log on to.
- The Computer configuration settings and the User configuration settings contain three containers: Software Settings, Windows Settings, and Administrative Templates, which include several related policies.
- The sequence in which Group Policy settings are processed is as follows: local GPO, site GPOs, domain GPOs, and OU GPOs (LSDOU).
- At startup and during logon, both the Computer Configuration and the User Configuration settings are applied in a specific sequence. In the event that computer and user settings conflict with each other, the computer settings take precedence.
- The major types of Group Policy implementation strategies based on each of these factors are listed below:
    - Centralized vs. Decentralized GPOs Design: Based on the centralized (monolithic) and decentralized (layered) location of GPOs.
    - Functional Role: Based on the structure of the organization.
    - Delegation with Central or Distributed Control Design: Based on delegating the administrative control of OUs to various administrators of an organization.
- To link a GPO to a site, you need to use the Active Directory Sites and Services console. On the other hand, if you want to link GPOs to domains and OUs, you need to use the Active Directory Users and Computers console.
- You can assign permissions to delegate the administrative control of a GPO by using the Properties dialog box for the GPO. To provide administrative control of the GPO, you need to set both the Read and Write permissions to Allow.

Key Terms

Group Policy
Group Policy Object (GPO)
Group Policy Container
Group Policy Template
Computer configuration settings
User configuration settings
Centralized GPO design approach
Decentralized GPO design approach
Functional role design approach
Team Design approach
Central control design approach
Distributed control design approach

Test Yourself

1. A Group Policy: (Choose all that apply.)
   a. Decentralizes control over computers, groups, and users in an organizational network.
   b. Enables users to remove and modify a policy using the regedit32.exe or regedit.exe utilities.
   c. Gets erased and rewritten with a policy change.
   d. Helps ensure that all security requirements, such as password length and duration, are being adhered to by the users.
   e. Is flexible in nature.

2. Group Policy Container (GPC): (Choose all that apply.)
   a. Is an Active Directory component.
   b. Contains GPO attributes, extensions, and version information.
   c. Is a collection of folders in the SYSVOL share on Windows 2000 domain controllers.
   d. Is identified by the Globally Unique Identifier (GUID) of the GPO.
   e. Includes physical files and settings required by the GPO and gets created every time a GPO is created.

3. Which of the following correctly represents the default processing order of a GPO?
   a. Site GPO, domain GPO, OU GPO, local GPO
   b. Domain GPO, site GPO, OU GPO, local GPO
   c. Local Policy, site GPO, domain GPO, OU GPO
   d. Local Policy, domain GPO, site GPO, OU GPO

4. Which of the following items can be set using the Administrative Templates container in the Group Policy snap-in? (Choose all that apply.)
   a. Network
   b. Printers
   c. Software Installation
   d. Desktop
   e. Scripts
   f. Security Settings

5. Which one of the following GPO setting designs should be used in large organizations where policy administration is duly delegated among different individuals?
   a. Single policy type
   b. Multiple policy type
   c. Dedicated policy type

6. You, as a member of the Marketing group, have been assigned only Read permissions for a GPO in the organization. With these permissions, you can use the Group Policy snap-in to access its extensions, although you cannot modify its settings.
   a. True
   b. False

Projects: On Your Own

1. Create a GPO named Marketing for the mydomain.com domain.
   a. Access the **Active Directory Users and Computers** console.
   b. Access the **mydomain.com Properties** dialog box.
   c. Create a GPO named Marketing.
   d. Close the **Active Directory Users and Computers** console.
2. Add the **Group Policy** snap-in for the **Marketing GPO** to the **Administrative Tools** menu.
   a. Open the **Microsoft Management Console**.
   b. Add the Group Policy snap-in.
   c. Link the Marketing GPO to the Group Policy snap-in.
   d. Save the console settings to make the snap-in available in the **Administrative Tools** menu.
   e. Close the Microsoft Management Console.
3. Delegate the administrative control of the Marketing GPO to a user named **Greg Hunter**.
   a. Open the **Active Directory Users and Computers** console.
   b. Add a user object named Greg Hunter.
   c. Open the **Properties** dialog box for the **Marketing** GPO.
   d. Set the **Read** and **Write** permissions to **Allow**.
   e. Close the **Active Directory Users and Computers** console.

Problem Solving Scenarios

1. You are administering your Windows 2000 network. Currently you are using Local Security Policies to secure individual desktops. Recently, the company has added another 75 systems to the network due to which you have suggested the implementation of Group Policies for easier management and multi-level administration. Your boss is a bit reluctant about implementing Group Policies, since he is used to working on Windows NT 4.0.

Write a memo explaining the features and advantages of using Group Policies over conventional Local Security Policies.

2. You are the Assistant Administrator for your company's Windows 2000-based ADS network. Currently, you have two domains operating in native mode: mydomain.com and business.mydomain.com. The business.mydomain-.com domain has two top-level OUs: Marketing and Sales. Each of these top-level OUs contain two child OUs: Project and Product. The various policies that apply to the domains and OUs in your company are:

- mydomain.com: Domain Policy
- business.mydomain.com: Business Policy
- Marketing: Marketing Policy
- Sales: Sales Policy
- Project: Project Business Policy
- Product: Product Business Policy

Your network administrator would like to know what policies would apply for a user in the Project OU.

Prepare a memo listing the correct order in which the policies will apply and describe the reasons behind the same. Also explain the exceptions that can be brought in using the No Override option and the Block Policy Inheritance option, and by applying Loopback settings to a GPO list.

LESSON

10 Specifying Group Policy Settings

In order to enable you to manage the desktop settings of various users in the network, and make sure that the availability of desktop items for a user remains intact once set, Windows 2000 provides a feature called Group Policies. These policies enable the Administrators to manage desktop configurations for a group of users and computers. You set properties for a Group Policy, which are then checked by the operating system at the time of startup and logon. The operating system then applies these policies to the Windows 2000 computers in order to maintain consistency in the desktop configuration.

The Group Policy properties are stored in Group Policy Objects (GPOs). GPOs are further associated with sites, domains, or organizational units. GPOs are processed in a particular order beginning with local policies, then site policies, then domain policies, and finally, OU policies (LSDOU). If multiple GPOs are applied to a given container, then the GPOs are processed in reverse of the order that they are listed in the container. When GPOs conflict, the last policy to apply wins, unless No Override, Block Inheritance, or filtering are used to modify the application of a particular policy or policies.

You can apply a single GPO to more than one container by creating the required links to the additional containers. You might need to do so in order to apply the same settings contained in a GPO to more than one container. There is no limit the number of links a container or a GPO can have.

You might encounter situations where a GPO is not serving any purpose at a certain time. In such a situation, you need to remove either the link to the GPO or the GPO itself. To decide whether to remove the GPO link or the GPO, you should remember that removing a GPO link only removes the GPO link, whereas deleting a GPO removes the GPO from Active Directory, deleting it permanently.

Goals

In this lesson, you will learn various ways of administering Group Policies. You will learn to specify GPO properties, alter the order of GPOs, filter the scope of a GPO, link and unlink GPOs, and delete a GPO.

Lesson 10 Specifying Group Policy Settings	
Skill	***Exam 70-217 Objective***
1. Setting Group Policy Object Properties	Create and modify a Group Policy Object (GPO). Configure Group Policy options.
2. Modifying the Order of Group Policy Objects	Modify Group Policy prioritization.
3. Filtering the Scope of a Group Policy Object	Filter Group Policy settings by using security groups.
4. Linking Group Policy Objects	Link to an existing GPO.
5. Delinking and Deleting Group Policy Objects	Create and modify a Group Policy Object (GPO).

Requirements

To complete this lesson, you will need administrative rights on Server B, the Windows 2000 Server domain controller for mydomain.com. Additionally, you need to have an OU named Domain Controllers, which should contain four GPOs named Customized group policy 1, Customized group policy 2, Customized group policy 3, and Customized group policy 4. Finally, you will need to create a GPO named object 1 and link it to mydomain.com (the entire domain).

skill 1

Setting Group Policy Object Properties

exam objective

Create and modify a Group Policy Object (GPO). Configure Group Policy options.

overview

The desktop environment for a user defines the availability and appearance of the desktop items. **Group Policies** define a user's desktop environment by managing its various components. Using the Group Policy settings, you can alter the User Configuration and Computer Configuration settings, which affect the administration of users, as well as the computers, respectively. The Group Policy settings are stored in the **Group Policy Objects (GPOs)**, which are the most basic units of Group Policies. The GPOs further apply the stored settings on the Active Directory objects contained in sites, domains, or organizational units (OUs). For example, imagine a situation where you are administering a group of computers using one OU named Team1. You want to prevent the members of the team who belong to the OU Team1 from being able to set screen saver passwords on their systems. To do this, you can create a policy named 'Password protect the screen saver' on a GPO of the Team1 OU.

You can customize a GPO using the Group Policy snap-in for that GPO by locating the GPO in a container, selecting it, and clicking edit.

caution

Do not confuse policies with profiles. There is a small amount of overlap between the two, but they serve very different purposes. Policies are used to restrict, allow, or modify functionality of certain components of the operating system, while profiles are used to store a user's preferences.

how to

Set Group Policy properties for the **object 1** GPO created for the **mydomain.com** container.

1. Log on to the domain controller as an Administrator.
2. Click **Start**, point to **Programs**, point to **Administrative Tools**, and then click the **Active Directory Users and Computers** command to open the **Active Directory Users and Computers** console.
3. Right-click the **mydomain.com** container, and then click the **Properties** command on the shortcut menu to open the **mydomain.com Properties** dialog box.
4. Click the **Group Policy** tab.
5. Click the GPO **object 1**, and then click **Edit...** to open the **Group Policy** snap-in.
6. In the console tree of the **Group Policy** snap-in, double-click the **User Configuration** node to view the **Administrative Templates** folder.
7. Double-click the **Administrative Templates** folder to view the **Control Panel** folder.
8. Expand the **Control Panel** folder by double-clicking it. This displays the **Add/Remove Programs** folder.
9. Click the **Add/Remove Programs** folder to view the list of group policies in the details pane.
10. Right-click the **Hide Add New Programs page** policy, and then click the **Properties** command to open the **Hide Add New Programs page Properties** dialog box.
11. Click the **Enabled** option button to enable this policy as shown in **Figure 10-1**. Then click **OK** to close the **Hide Add New Programs page Properties** dialog box for the policy.
12. The setting for this policy changes to **Enabled (Figure 10-2)**. This removes the **Add New Program** icon from the **Add/Remove Programs** window. After rebooting, you can open the **Add/Remove Programs** window from the Control Panel to verify that the **Add New Programs** icon is no longer visible in this window.
13. Click **X** to close the **Group Policy** snap-in.
14. Click **OK** to close the **Properties** dialog box.
15. Click **X** to close the **Active Directory Users and Computers** console.

tip

There might be some nodes for which the policy settings are not configured. Since the policies in Windows 2000 are checked and applied from beginning to end at the time of startup and logon, you can disable unused portions of group policy to speed up the logon process.

Figure 10-1 Setting Group Policy Object Properties

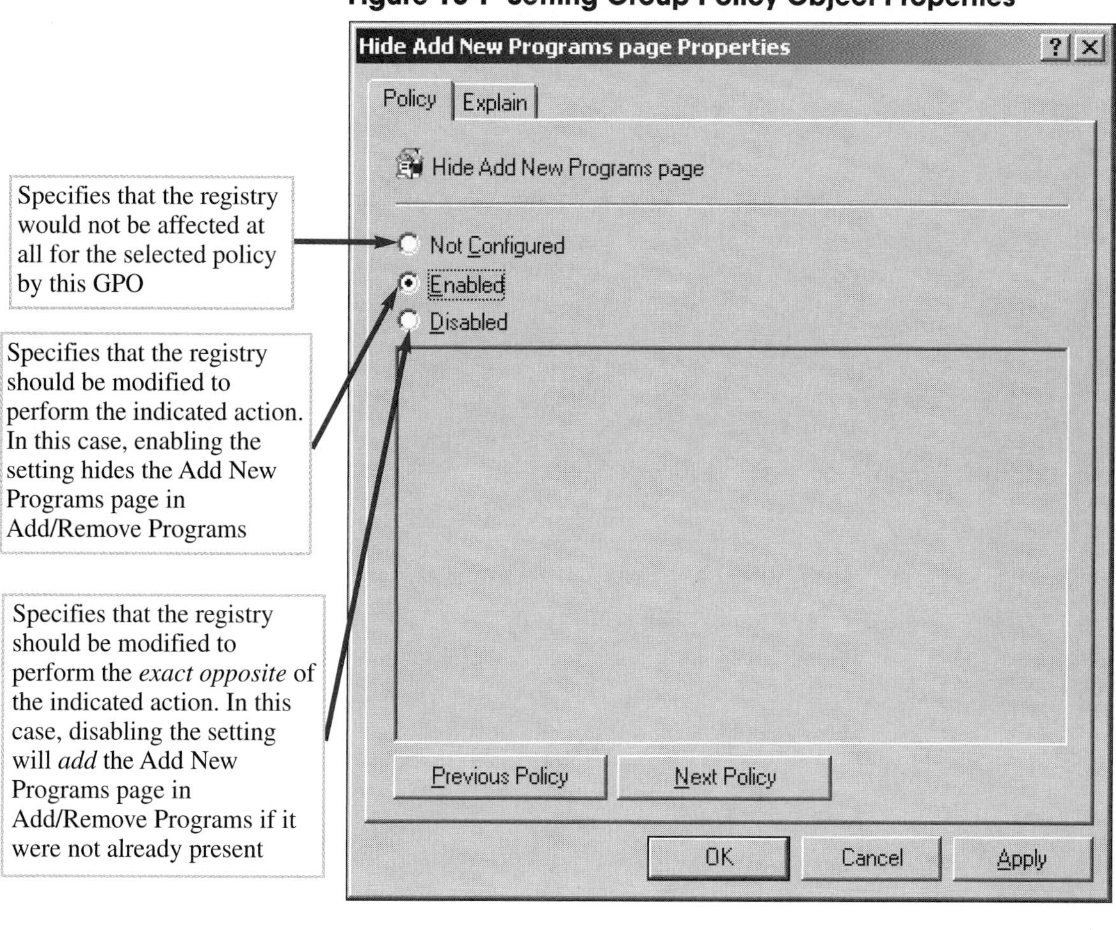

Figure 10-2 Setting changed to Enabled

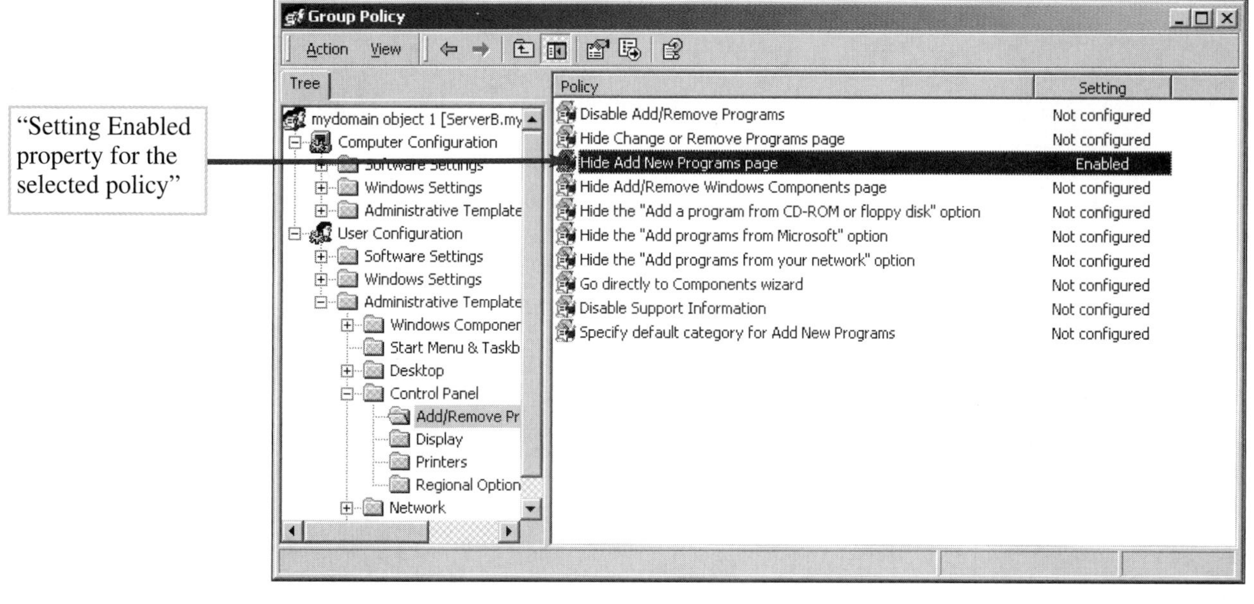

skill 2 Modifying the Order of Group Policy Objects

exam objective

Modify Group Policy prioritization.

overview

The order in which the Group Policy settings actually apply to a user or computer depends on the order of prioritization of GPOs, i.e., the order in which they are placed in the GPO list. GPOs, by default, are processed (mostly) in accordance with the Active Directory hierarchy, that is, the local policy is applied, then the site, then the domain, and finally, OU policies are applied (LSDOU). However, the policies at each level (except local) can be given preference by using No Override. Additionally, you can block the application of all policies applied at higher levels for a specific container by using block inheritance. Finally, you can specify that a particular GPO only applies to one or more specific group of users within a container by using filtering (modifying the "apply group policy" permission on the GPO).

To change the order of prioritization of GPOs for a domain or an OU, you need to use the Active Directory Users and Computers console. If you need to modify the order of GPOs for a site, you use the Active Directory Sites and Services console. Local policies have no prioritization options, as they are always overwritten when a conflict occurs.

how to

Change the order of GPOs for the **Domain Controllers** container.

1. Click Start, point to **Programs**, point to **Administrative Tools**, and then click the **Active Directory Users and Computers** command to open the **Active Directory Users and Computers** console.
2. In the console tree, right-click the **Domain Controllers** container, and then click the **Properties** command to open the **Domain Controllers Properties** dialog box.
3. Click the **Group Policy** tab. In the **Group Policy Object Links** list, select the GPO **Customized Policy 2**, and click Up to bring the selected GPO to the top **(Figure 10-3)**.
4. Click OK to apply the changed order and close the **Domain Controllers Properties** dialog box.
5. Close the **Active Directory Users and Computers** console.

tip

In Windows 2000 Server, GPOs are processed from the bottom of the list to the top of the list. The GPO listed at the top of the list is actually applied last, making it the "most important" policy.

Figure 10-3 Changing the order of GPOs

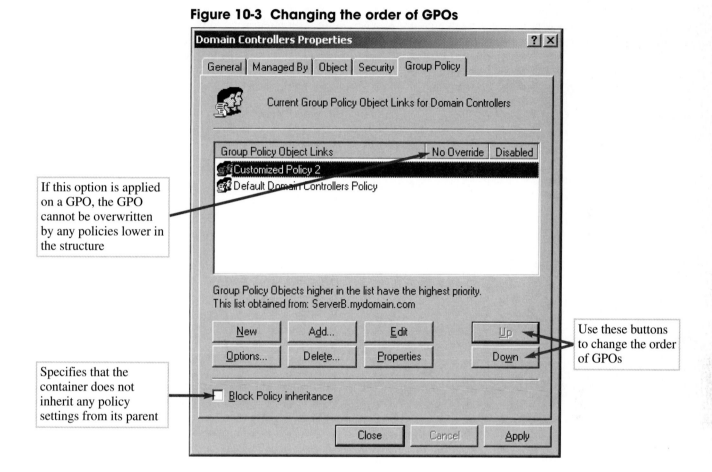

If this option is applied on a GPO, the GPO cannot be overwritten by any policies lower in the structure

Use these buttons to change the order of GPOs

Specifies that the container does not inherit any policy settings from its parent

skill 3

Filtering the Scope of a Group Policy Object

exam objective

Filter Group Policy settings by using security groups.

overview

There may be a situation in which you have to apply a certain GPO to specific users or computers in a group. In other words, you might need to restrain the scope of a GPO by applying permissions to specific users and/or computers, just like you would apply permissions to access a share, for instance. This is called filtering the GPO scope. To filter the scope of a GPO, you use the **Windows 2000 security groups**. These groups enable you to specify exactly which groups are to be affected by a particular GPO. The Security page on the Properties dialog box of a GPO enables you to specify different permissions for different security groups on a network. As a Windows 2000 administrator, you need to assign the Read and Apply Group Policy permissions for a particular GPO to users and computers on which the Group Policy needs to be applied (by default, the Authenticated Users group has both of these permissions for all GPOs). However, you can specify that a policy should not apply to a specific group by setting its Apply Group Policy permission to Deny. Similarly, if you only want a single group of users to apply the GPO (instead of all users in the structure), you can remove the Authenticated Users group's Apply Group Policy permission and add an entry to allow the Apply Group Policy permission for your special group.

When filtering, only two of a GPO's permissions are applicable: Read and Apply Group Policy. **Table 10-1** describes various situations, as well as the required permissions for filtering the scope of an applicable GPO.

how to

Set the scope of a GPO to exempt the members of the **CREATOR OWNER** group from the GPO.

1. In the **Active Directory Users and Computers** console, right-click the **Domain Controllers** container to access the **Domain Controllers Properties** dialog box.
2. Click the **GPO Customized Policy 1** in the **Domain Controllers Properties** dialog box, and then click Edit... to open the **Group Policy** snap-in for this GPO.
3. Right-click the root node of the console, **Customized Policy 1 [ServerB.mydomain.com] Policy**, and then click the **Properties** command to open the **Customized Policy 1 Properties** dialog box.
4. Click the **Security** tab, and then click the **CREATOR OWNER** security group through which this GPO is to be filtered.
5. Now, set the **Apply Group Policy (AGP)** permissions to **Deny (Figure 10-4)**. Such permission settings will make sure that the members of the group **CREATOR OWNER** are exempted from the impact of the GPO **Customized Policy 1**.
6. Click OK to save the settings.
7. Close the **Group Policy** snap-in.
8. Close the **Domain Controllers Properties** dialog box.
9. Close the **Active Directory Users and Computers** console.

Table 10-1 Filtering the Scope of a Group Policy Object

Cases	Permissions
When the members of the selected security group should have the GPO applied to them	**Authenticated Users Group** Apply Group Policy: Blank (Not allowed) Read: Allowed **Your selected group** Apply Group Policy: Allowed Read: Allowed
When the members of the selected security group are to be exempted from the GPO	**Authenticated Users Group** Apply Group Policy: Allowed Read: Allowed **Your selected group** Apply Group Policy: Denied Read: Allowed

Figure 10-4 Setting permissions for the security groups

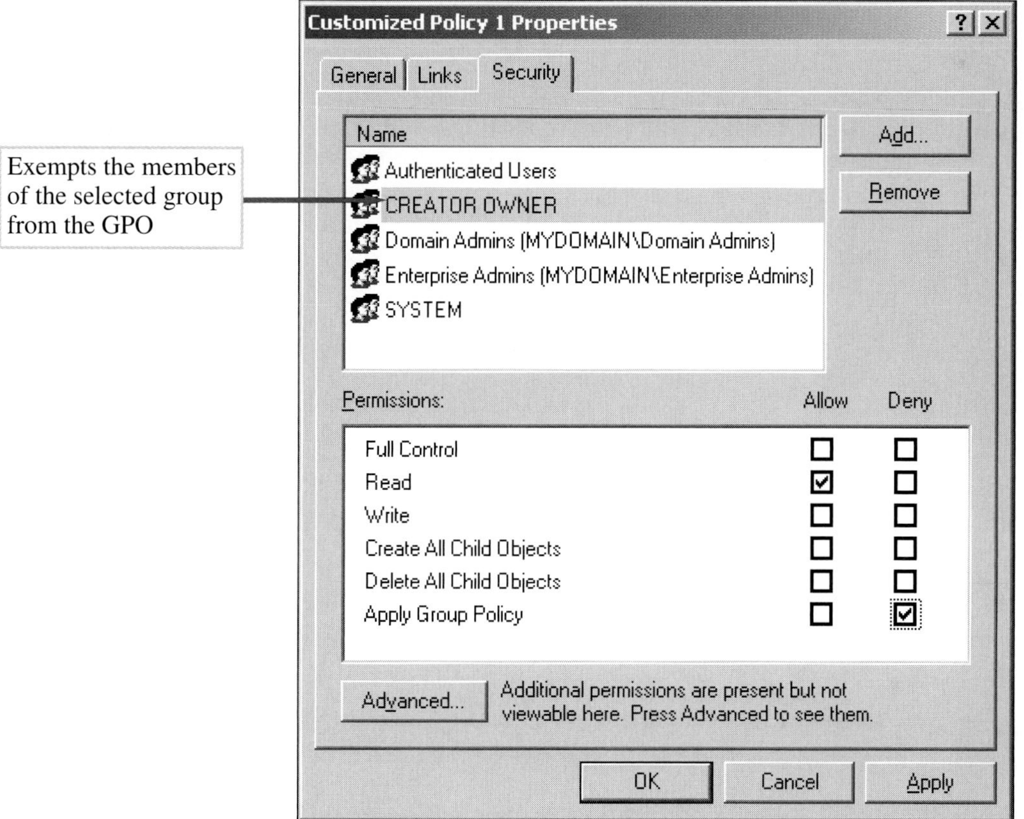

skill 4 Linking Group Policy Objects

exam objective

Link to an existing GPO.

overview

Before you set the scope of a GPO for the targeted users and computers, you should apply the GPO to a site, a domain, or an OU by linking it to that particular Active Directory object. A GPO, by default, is linked to the container in which it is created. However, you might want to link GPOs to additional sites, domains, or OUs in order to increase the scope of the GPO. For instance, you might have created a GPO to affect one team in an organization by implementing the GPO on a container. If you want another team in the organization to have the same effect, you can apply the same GPO to the container associated with the users of the second team. To do this, you need to link the GPO to the second container object associated with the second team.

To link a GPO to an additional container, you use the Group Policy tab in the Properties dialog box for that container.

how to

Link the **Customized Policy 3 GPO** created for the **Domain Controllers** container to the container **mydomain.com**.

1. In the **Active Directory Users and Computers** console, right-click the container **mydomain.com** to access the **mydomain.com Properties** dialog box.
2. Click the **Group Policy** tab in the **mydomain.com Properties** dialog box (**Figure 10-5**). It already contains a **GPO** named **object 1**.
3. Now, click [Add...] to open the **Add a Group Policy Object Link** dialog box. This dialog box enables you to link this container to the GPO Customized Policy 3, created for the **Domain Controllers** container.
4. Click the **All** tab to view a list of all the GPOs stored in this domain.
5. Click the **Customized Policy 3** GPO (**Figure 10-6**), click [OK] to link this GPO to the **mydomain.com** container, and then close the **Add a Group Policy Object Link** dialog box.
6. The GPO Customized Policy 3 is linked to the container **mydomain.com** and appears in the **Group Policy Object Links** list in the **mydomain.com Properties** dialog box.
7. Close the **Properties** dialog box by clicking [OK].
8. Close the **Active Directory Users and Computers** console.

Figure 10-5 Adding a GPO to an additional container

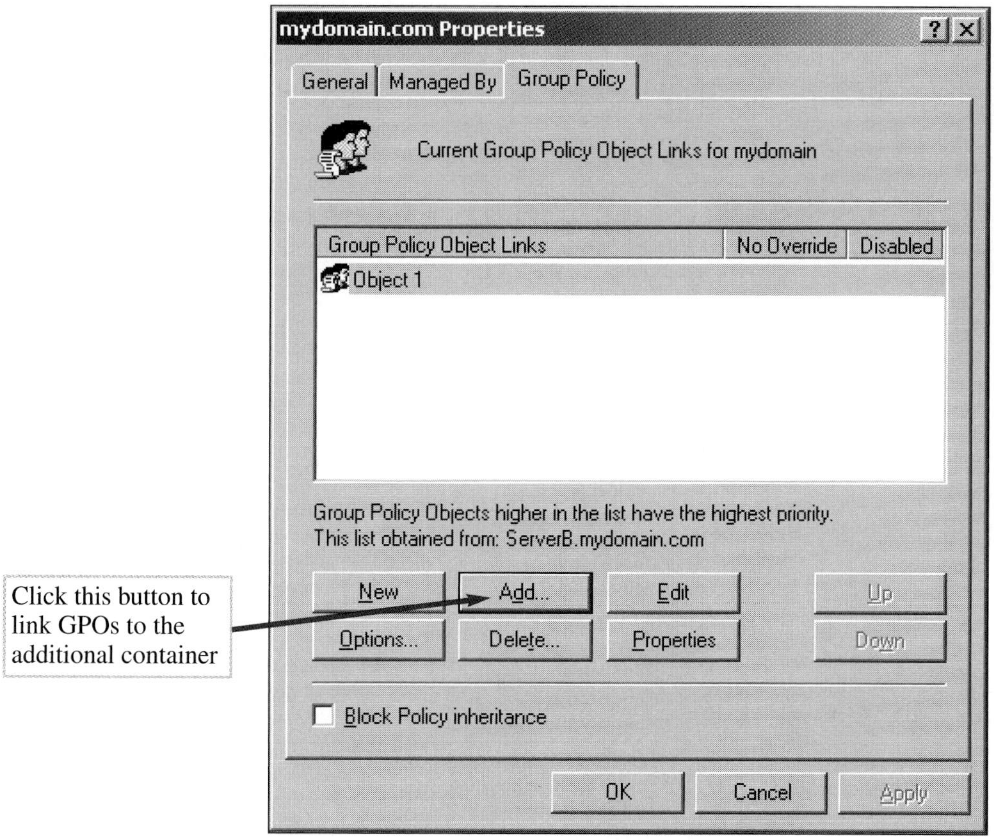

mydomain.com Properties
General | Managed By | Group Policy
Current Group Policy Object Links for mydomain

Group Policy Object Links	No Override	Disabled
Object 1		

Group Policy Objects higher in the list have the highest priority.
This list obtained from: ServerB.mydomain.com

New | Add... | Edit | Up
Options... | Delete... | Properties | Down

Block Policy inheritance

OK | Cancel | Apply

Click this button to link GPOs to the additional container

Figure 10-6 Selecting the desired GPO

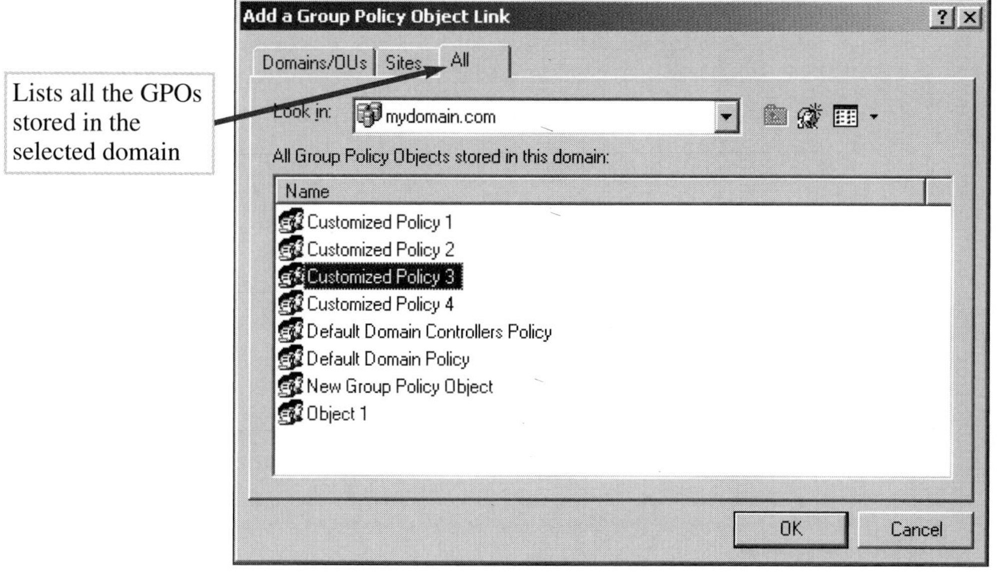

skill 5 Delinking and Deleting Group Policy Objects

exam objective

Create and modify a Group Policy Object (GPO).

overview

In certain situations, you might need to link a GPO to additional containers for a certain period of time. There can also be situations where certain policies no longer apply to a GPO. In these situations, you may want to remove the GPO link from that object, or even delete the GPO. It is important to remember that if there is more than one GPO link associated with the object, then you should not delete the GPO. Instead, you should only remove the GPO link to that object. However, if the GPO is associated with a single object, you could delete the GPO itself.

caution

It is generally recommended that you do not delete the GPO unless you are absolutely sure that it will never be needed again.

how to

Remove the GPO link **Customized Policy 3** from the **mydomain.com** container.

1. In the **Active Directory Users and Computers** console, right-click the container **mydomain.com** to access the **mydomain.com Properties** dialog box.
2. Click the **Group Policy** tab, click the GPO **Customized Policy 3** in the **Group Policy Object Links** list (**Figure 10-7**), and then click [Delete...] to remove the selected GPO link.
3. In the **Delete** dialog box, click the **Remove the link from the list** option button (**Figure 10-8**), and then click [OK] to apply the selection and close the **Delete** dialog box. The GPO is now unlinked, but still exists in Active Directory.
4. Click **Close** to close the **mydomain.com Properties** dialog box.
5. Close the **Active Directory Users and Computers** console.

more

Deleting a GPO removes it from **Active Directory** permanently. The sites, domains, or OUs that were earlier linked to the GPO are no longer controlled by the GPO. To delete a GPO permanently, access the **Group Policy** tab in the **Properties** dialog box for the container from which the GPO needs to be deleted. Select the desired GPO and click **Delete** to open the Delete dialog box. Click **Remove the link** and delete the **Group Policy Object permanently** option, and then click **OK** to delete the selected GPO from **Active Directory** permanently.

Figure 10-7 Delinking or deleting a GPO

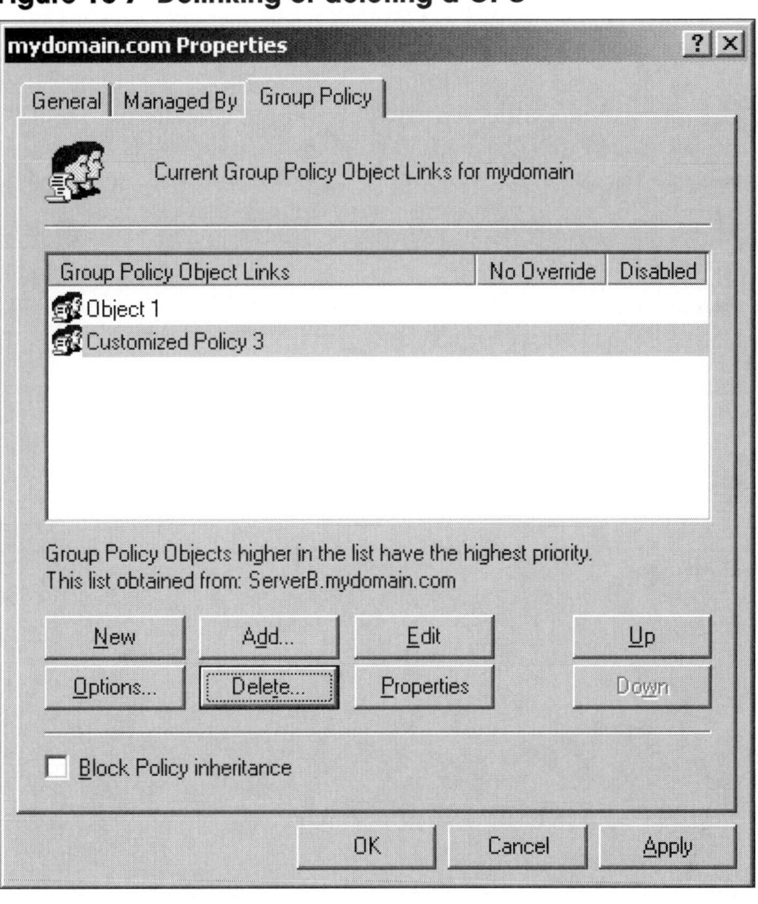

Figure 10-8 Removing a Group Policy Object link

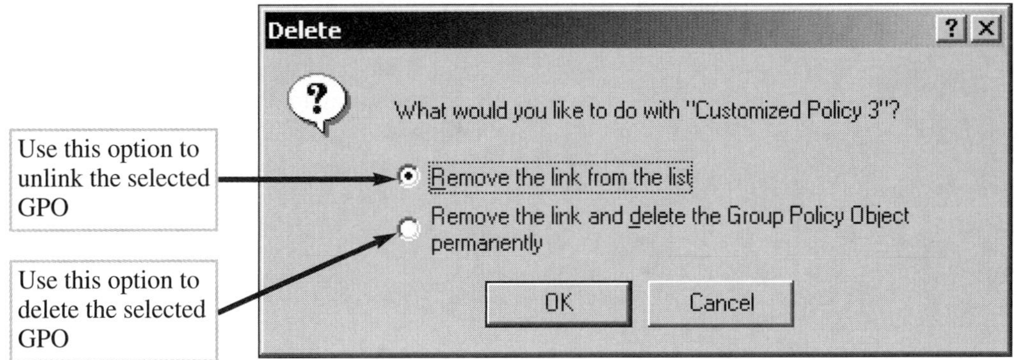

Summary

- The Group Policy Objects (GPOs) store all the Group Policy settings that you set for administering users or computers. You can set Group Policy properties for customizing the GPO as per your requirements.
- GPOs are processed mostly in accordance with the Active Directory hierarchy. Local policies are applied first, then site, then domain, and finally, OU (LSDOU).
- Windows 2000 security groups enable you to specify exactly which groups are to be affected by a particular GPO. You use the Security tab on the Properties page of the GPO for this purpose.
- Filtering is the act of selectively modifying the Apply Group Policy permission on a GPO to reduce the scope of the GPO.
- You use the Group Policy tab on for the respective site, domain, or OU Properties page for linking a GPO to additional sites, domains, or OUs.
- You can unlink the GPO from the specified site, domain, or OU by removing the concerned GPO link using the Properties dialog box for that particular object.
- Removing a GPO link disassociates the GPO from its OU, and does not remove the GPO from Active Directory. However, deleting a GPO removes it from the Active Directory.

Key Terms

Group Policies

Group Policy Objects (GPOs)

Windows 2000 security groups

Test Yourself

1. Which of the following options in a Group Policy Properties dialog box indicates that the Group Policy Object will not affect the registry for that policy?

a. Enabled
b. Not Configured
c. Disabled

2. The ________ stores all the Group Policy settings that you specify for administering users or computers.

a. Windows 2000 security groups
b. Computer Configuration node
c. Group Policy Object
d. Group Policy snap-in

3. Which is the correct order for GPO processing?

a. Site, OU, domain
b. OU, domain, site
c. Domain, site, OU
d. Site, domain, OU

4. Which of the following statements about GPOs are correct? (Choose all that apply)

a. When you create a new GPO, it is linked to the container and domain controllers.
b. Group Policy Objects, by default, are processed mostly in accordance with the Active Directory hierarchy.
c. The order in which the Group Policy settings apply to a user or a computer depends on the container for which the GPO was created.
d. The Windows 2000 security groups enable you to specify exactly which groups are to be affected by a particular Group Policy Object.
e. A GPO is deleted from the Active Directory when unlinked.

5. Joe, the network administrator of XYZ Consultants Pvt. Ltd., is required to assign different levels of access to different computer groups on the network. He has created different GPOs with different policies for the various working groups of the company. He is instructed to keep the group named MANAGERS exempted from the GPO access level 1. For this group, he should set the GPO permissions as:

a. Apply Group Policy to Allow.
b. Apply Group Policy to Deny.
c. Apply Group Policy to neither Allow nor Deny.

6. You can specify that a policy should not apply to a specific group by setting:

a. AGP to Deny.
b. Read to neither Allow nor Deny.
c. Read to Deny.
d. AGP to neither Allow nor Deny.

Projects: On Your Own

1. Set permissions for the GPO **object 1** in the **mydomain.com** domain such that the membership in the **Authenticated Users** group is irrelevant to whether the GPO should be applied.

a. Access the **mydomain.com Properties** dialog box.

b. Open the **Group Policy** snap-in for the GPO **object 1**.

c. Open the **Security** tab of the **object 1 Properties** dialog box.

d. Click the **Authenticated Users** security group and set both AGP and READ permissions to neither **Allow** nor **Deny**.

2. Delete the GPO **Customized Domain Policy 1** from the container **Domain Controllers**.

a. Access the **Group Policy** tab in the **Domain Controllers Properties** dialog box.

b. Select the GPO **Customized Domain Policy 1** and open the **Delete** dialog box.

c. Remove the GPO link and delete the GPO permanently.

Problem Solving Scenarios

1. You administer your company's Windows 2000 ADS-based network. You are required to create a policy that will prevent users from adding and removing programs on their computers. The need for the policy arose recently, following a number of system crashes due to incorrect configuration changes. The Administrators group and the Group Leaders domain local group should not be subject to this policy setting. At the same time, only the Administrators Group should be able to make changes to the policy.

Draft a document with the guidelines for setting up this new policy. Give reasons for the choice of procedures and the exact steps to be followed.

2. Your Windows 2000-based network consists of a Marketing and a Sales container. The Marketing Policy, created primarily to affect the marketing team in your organization, has been implemented on the Marketing container. The same policy has been linked to the Sales container to affect the Sales team as well. However, with the changes in your organizational policies, the Marketing Policy is no longer applicable to the Sales team. You now want to remove the GPO link from the Sales object.

Prepare a memo listing the steps you will take to remove the policy linkage, while ensuring that the Marketing container polices are not affected.

LESSON

11 Using Group Policy to Manage Software

In all previous versions of Windows, the process of deploying software was a tedious job for an administrator. This process has also affected organizations tremendously in terms of productivity and cost-effectiveness. However, using the Group Policy feature of Windows 2000, the entire process of software deployment is automated and can be performed remotely from an administrator's workstation. Group Policy combined with Windows 2000 Active Directory enables an administrator to manage software by formulating and implementing a Group Policy-based plan, involving the phases of preparation, installation, management, and removal of software from a central location.

Deployment of software begins with setting up a software distribution point, which acts as the central location for applications that need to be installed. Next, you set software installation defaults to maintain consistency in all applications. Finally, you deploy applications using group policy. Windows 2000 uses two important features of the IntelliMirror technology to allow automated deployment of software. These features include the Software Installation extension of the Group Policy snap-in and the Windows Installer service.

Applications deployed using Group Policy can be customized by specifying various properties and modification files. You can also set properties to install, upgrade, and uninstall applications at the time of deployment itself. Additionally, you can use Group Policy to implement Folder Redirection, a feature used to store the contents of special folders such as My Documents at alternate locations on the network, especially when the special folders become overloaded.

Group Policy also includes event logging for troubleshooting software deployment. All events related to software deployment are logged in the Event Viewer. This information can help you diagnose problems with your policies.

Goals

In this lesson, you will learn to use Group Policy to deploy, configure, and manage applications on Windows 2000 machines. This lesson also introduces you to the software installation tools. Finally, you will learn to implement folder redirection settings, as well as troubleshoot Group Policy-related issues.

Lesson 11 Using Group Policy to Manage Software

Skill	Exam 70-217 Objective
1. Introducing the Software Installation Tools	Basic knowledge
2. Setting Up a Software Distribution Point	Manage and troubleshoot user environments by using Group Policy. Install, configure, manage, and troubleshoot software by using Group Policy.
3. Setting Up Software Installation Defaults	Manage and troubleshoot user environments by using Group Policy. Install, configure, manage, and troubleshoot software by using Group Policy.
4. Deploying Software Applications	Manage and troubleshoot user environments by using Group Policy. Install, configure, manage, and troubleshoot software by using Group Policy.
5. Using Modifications to Customize Software Applications	Manage and troubleshoot user environments by using Group Policy. Install, configure, manage, and troubleshoot software by using Group Policy.
6. Setting Automatic Installation Options and Application Categories	Manage and troubleshoot user environments by using Group Policy. Install, configure, manage, and troubleshoot software by using Group Policy.
7. Setting Installation Properties of Software Applications	Manage and troubleshoot user environments by using Group Policy. Install, configure, manage, and troubleshoot software by using Group Policy.
8. Upgrading Software Applications	Install, configure, manage, and troubleshoot software by using Group Policy.
9. Uninstalling Software Applications	Install, configure, manage, and troubleshoot software by using Group Policy.
10. Using Group Policy to Manage Folder Redirection	Basic knowledge
11. Troubleshooting Group Policy-Related Problems	Implement and troubleshoot Group Policy.

Requirements

To complete the skills in this lesson, you will need to have administrative rights on a domain controller in the mydomain.com domain (either ServerA or ServerB). In addition, you require the installation files for MS Office 2000.

skill 1 Introducing the Software Installation Tools

exam objective

Basic knowledge

overview

A Group Policy allows you to deploy software applications remotely to users and computers in a site, domain, or an organizational unit (OU). It also allows you to manage software applications that you have installed using group policy. The Group Policy snap-in of Windows 2000 provides the **Software Installation extension**, a built-in feature that you can use for installing and maintaining software.

The Software Installation extension is used to set up a Group Policy-based software management system that enables the administrator to manage various features such as installation of software, upgrades, patches, and software removals. This is done using the Group Policy snap-in (**Figure 11-1**).

The Software Installation extension of the Group Policy snap-in uses Windows Installer, a Windows 2000 component that defines and manages a standard format for setup and installation of applications, as well as tracking components such as registry entries and shortcuts. Windows Installer is made up of three main components as described in **Table 11-1**. In addition, Windows Installer consists of Windows Installer package files that contain instructions on the installation and removal of an application.

Windows Installer can be used for **software diagnostics** (information about the software that helps in troubleshooting), auto-repair, complete uninstallation of software, and multiple operating system platform capability. For example, if Windows Installer detects that a program file for the application is missing, it immediately uses the auto-repair function to reinstall the damaged or missing file, thereby fixing the application automatically.

You can use Windows Installer to install software applications with various file types. **Table 11-2** describes these file types in detail.

tip

IntelliMirror is a Windows 2000 native set of features that uses Active Directory, Group Policy, and Windows Installer technologies for desktop change and configuration management technology, including software installation and maintenance.

Figure 11-1 Software Installation extension of the Group Policy snap-in

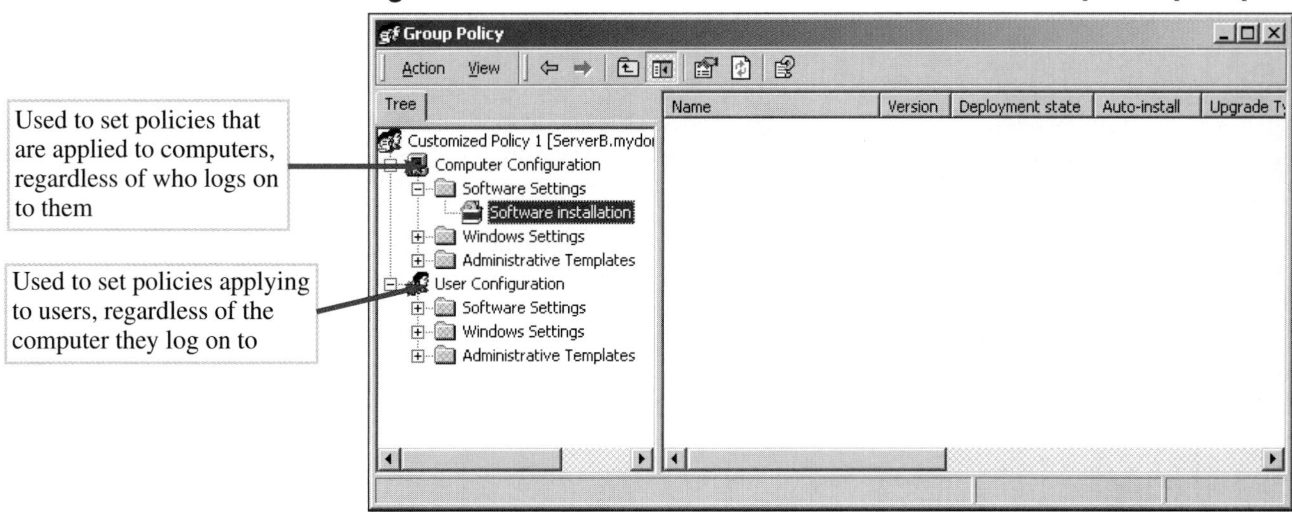

Table 11-1 Components of Windows Installer

Part	Function
Application Programming Interface (API)	An interface provided by the application to interact with Windows Installer for the purpose of modifying and customizing settings for the software.
Operating system service	Installs, modifies, and removes the software using the information in the Windows Installer package.
Windows Installer package	Consists of a database containing information used to install the application.

Table 11-2 File types used by the Software Installation extension

Types of programs	File type	Description
Native Windows Installer package	(.msi)	Files developed as a part of the application.
Repackaged applications	(.msi)	Files that allow you to repackage applications that do not have a native Windows Installer package.
Existing setup program	(.zap)	A file that installs an application using its original SETUP.exe file.
Transform files (modifications)	(.mst)	Files used to modify an application, perhaps to add additional functionality such as a statistics component for a spreadsheet application.
Patch files	(.msp)	Files that are used for bug fixes and service packs.

skill 1 Introducing the Software Installation Tools (cont'd)

exam objective

Basic knowledge

overview

Another tool used by users to manage the installation of software on their machines is the Add/Remove Programs item in the Control Panel. When a user double-clicks the Add/Remove Programs icon in the Control Panel window, the Add/Remove Programs window (**Figure 11-2**) appears along with the list of available software. This list is based on your group membership and the Group Policy created for you. Once you select the software you want to install, Windows Installer proceeds to install the application if it is not already installed.

how to

Administrators can use various methods to deploy software applications with the help of Group Policy snap-in. These methods include:

- Assigning applications to users.
- Assigning applications to computers.
- Publishing applications to users.

After an application is assigned to a user, notification of the application appears in the **Start** menu the next time the user logs on to a computer, regardless of the physical computer he or she actually uses. The application icon is also available for the user on the computer desktop. This is known as **advertising** the application. The user can then install the application either by using the **Start** menu or by double-clicking the application icon on the desktop. Additionally, the user can install the application by document invocation. Document invocation is the automatic installation of an application when a user double-clicks a file with an extension associated with the application.

tip

No notifications regarding the application are displayed to the user when an application is published. Additionally, the desktop shortcuts, Start menu, and the local registry are not affected.

After an application is assigned to a computer, the installation is automatically carried out at the next computer boot. This application will then be available to all users who use the machine, making assigning an application to a computer particularly useful for dedicated workstations.

Assigning an application also adds one particular benefit that is extremely useful: assigned applications are resilient. This means if files that the application requires are removed, the application will automatically reinstall itself.

Publishing an application, on the other hand, doesn't provide resiliency or advertisement. After an application is published to a user, the application's name, file associations, and notification settings are stored in Active Directory. A user can only install the application by document invocation or by using the Add/Remove Programs utility in the Control Panel. While these points may all seem to be disadvantages of publishing, these same points bring about publishing's major advantage: publishing helps keep users from inadvertently installing the application, which has considerable ramifications when disk space and licensing costs are considered. **Table 11-3** describes the various methods of deployment of applications and their installation and removal considerations. The software deployment phase consists of analysis, planning, and implementation phases.

Figure 11-2 Add/Remove Programs Window

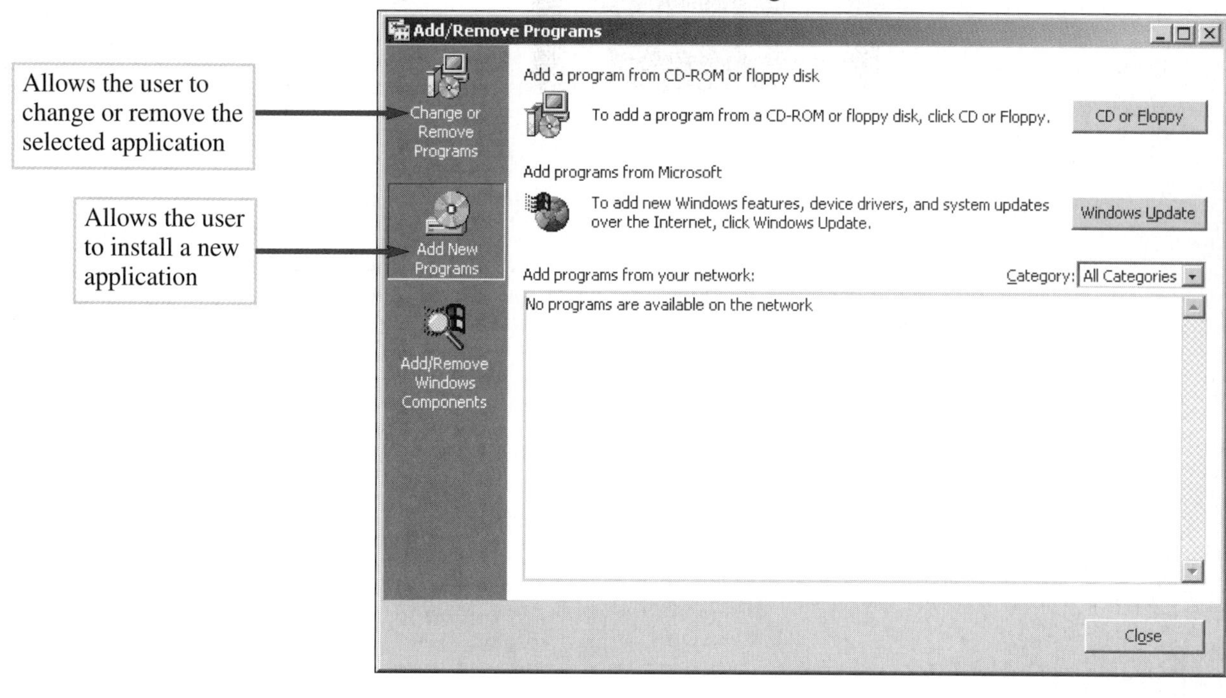

Table 11-3 Methods of deployment of software applications

Deployment methods	Installed from	Uninstalled from
Applications assigned to users	Start menu	Add/Remove Programs item in the Control Panel
	Application icon on the desktop	
	Document invocation	
Applications assigned to computers	Automatically installed when computer restarts	Cannot be uninstalled by the user
Applications published to users	Add/Remove Programs item in the Control Panel	Add/Remove Programs item in the Control Panel
	Document invocation	

skill 2 Setting Up a Software Distribution Point

exam objective

Manage and troubleshoot user environments by using Group Policy. Install, configure, manage, and troubleshoot software by using Group Policy.

overview

Once you are familiar with the tools available for installing and maintaining software, you need to formulate a Group Policy-based software installation plan for the software installation process. This plan should be based on the requirements and available resources of your organization. **Figure 11-3** describes a sample process used for preparing for a software installation.

The next step after preparing a plan for software installation is setting up a **Software Distribution Point (SDP)**. An SDP is a shared folder on the network from which users can get the software that they need. The process of setting up an SDP is described in **Figure 11-4**. In Windows 2000, only the administrators should have Full Control permissions to the SDP folder. Users of the SDP folder are assigned only Read and Execute permissions. Some software applications support special commands to facilitate the creation of an SDP. For example, running the command SETUP /A during the setup of Microsoft Office 2000 allows you to specify the software license key just once for all users. This makes the process of installation more efficient, if most users in an organization use a core set of applications.

more

A few strategies that you can use to implement a software installation are listed below:

- Create OUs to allocate particular applications to target groups depending on the organization's needs.
- Deploy the software at the site level. Using this method, you can deploy a single Group Policy Object (GPO) to provide users in each location, regardless of domain, with access to the most commonly used applications rather than creating the object in multiple OUs and multiple domains. In addition, deploying at the site level significantly reduces the headache associated with ensuring that software is not installed over slow WAN links.
- Create a single GPO rather than multiple GPOs to manage multiple applications. A single GPO deploying multiple applications processes faster than multiple GPOs each deploying a single application. Hence, the logon process in the former case is faster than the process in the latter.

Figure 11-3 Plan for preparing software installation

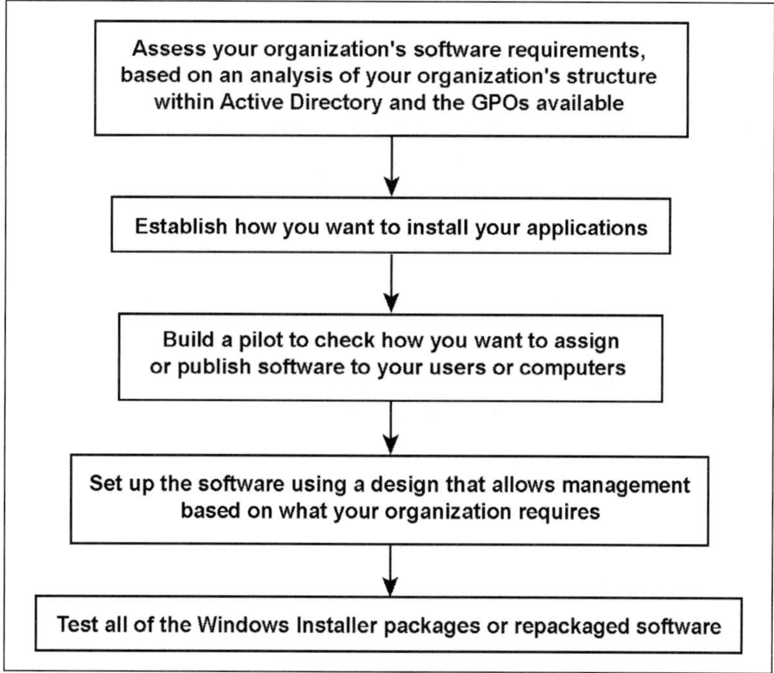

Figure 11-4 The process of setting up an SDP

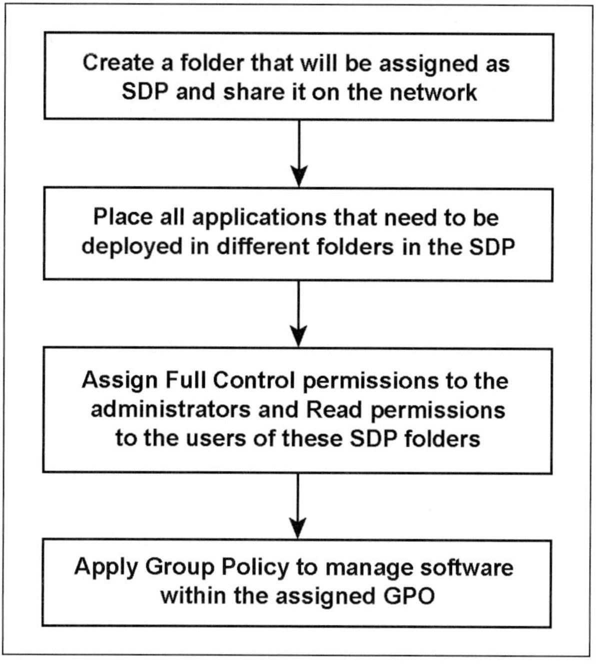

skill 3 Setting Up Software Installation Defaults

exam objective

Manage and troubleshoot user environments by using Group Policy. Install, configure, manage, and troubleshoot software by using Group Policy.

overview

Once you have set up SDPs and placed applications in them, you can define the default settings for all installed applications. These settings help in the management and uninstallation of applications. Specifying default settings includes setting up SDPs, placing the applications in these SDPs, and specifying initial deployment settings. These settings can be specified by accessing the Software Settings node in the Group Policy snap-in.

how to

Set up a Software Distribution Point and specify Software Installation defaults.

1. Log on to the domain controller as an Administrator.
2. To create a default SDP to which you can copy the Installer (.msi) files of the applications, create a folder named **Installs** on the **C:\ drive** of the computer.
3. Enable sharing of the **Installs** folder. Assign **Full Control** permissions to the administrators and **Read** permissions only to the users of the folder.
4. Insert MS Office 2000 disk 1 into your CD-ROM drive. Cancel the Autorun process.
5. Click Start, Run, and type "D:\ setup.exe /a data1.msi", where "D:" is the drive letter associated with your CD-ROM.
6. Enter your CD Key and organization name, click Next >>, accept the license agreement and click Next >> again (**Figure 11-5**).
7. Type **C:\installs** when prompted for the installation location (**Figure 11-6**).
8. Click Install Now to install the software. Complete any additional Install Wizard steps if prompted.
9. When the installation is complete, click Start, point to **Programs**, point to **Administrative Tools**, and then click **Active Directory Users and Computers**.
10. Right-click on **mydomain.com** and choose **Properties**.
11. Click on the **group policy** tab, click on **Default Domain Policy**, and click **edit**.
12. Double-click **Computer Configuration** under **Default Domain Policy** to view its contents.
13. Double-click the **Software Settings** container to view the **Software Installation** node.
14. Right-click **Software Installation**, and then click the **Properties** command to open the **Software installation Properties** dialog box.
15. Type **\\ServerA\Installs** in the **Default package location** text box to specify the location of the default SDP.
16. Accept the default option **Display the Deploy Software dialog box** in the **New Packages** section. Setting this option will display the **Deploy Software** dialog box as soon as an application is added as a package to the GPO.
17. Accept the default option **Basic** in the **Installation User Interface Options** section. The **Basic** option does not display any alerts and messages during the installation. It provides only a basic display of the installation progress.
18. Select the **Uninstall the applications when they fall out of the scope of management** check box to automatically remove the application when the GPO is no longer applicable to the users or computers (**Figure 11-7**).
19. Click the **Categories** tab, and add a new category labeled **Office**.
20. Click OK to apply the settings and close the **Software installation Properties** dialog box.
21. Close the Group Policy snap-in. You have now specified the software installation defaults to be applied for all applications deployed in the GPO.

tip

Since the installation is for computers, the **Publish** option will be disabled, given that software cannot be published to computers.

Figure 11-5 Accepting the license agreement

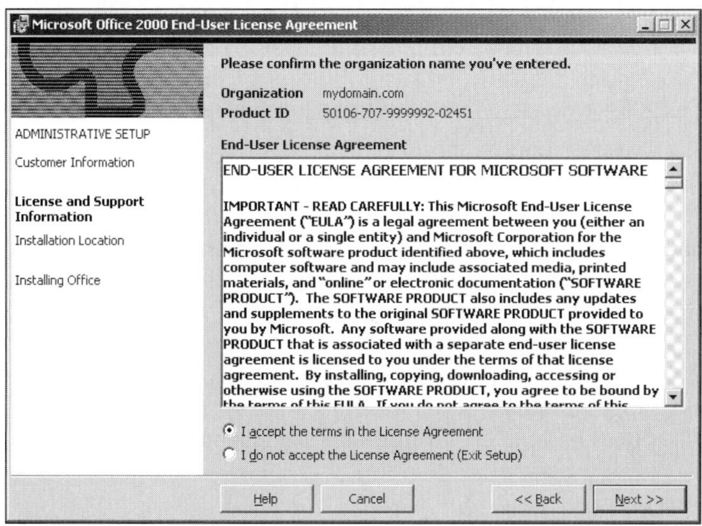

Figure 11-6 Specifying the installation location

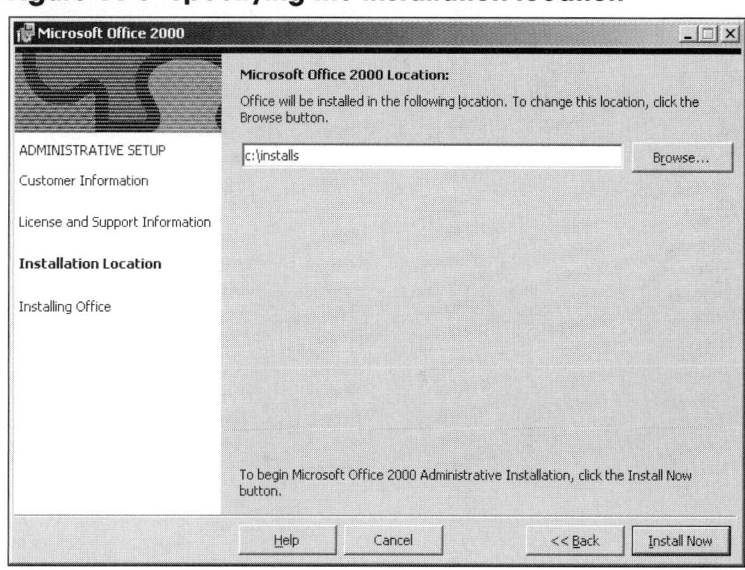

Figure 11-7 Specifying Software Installation defaults

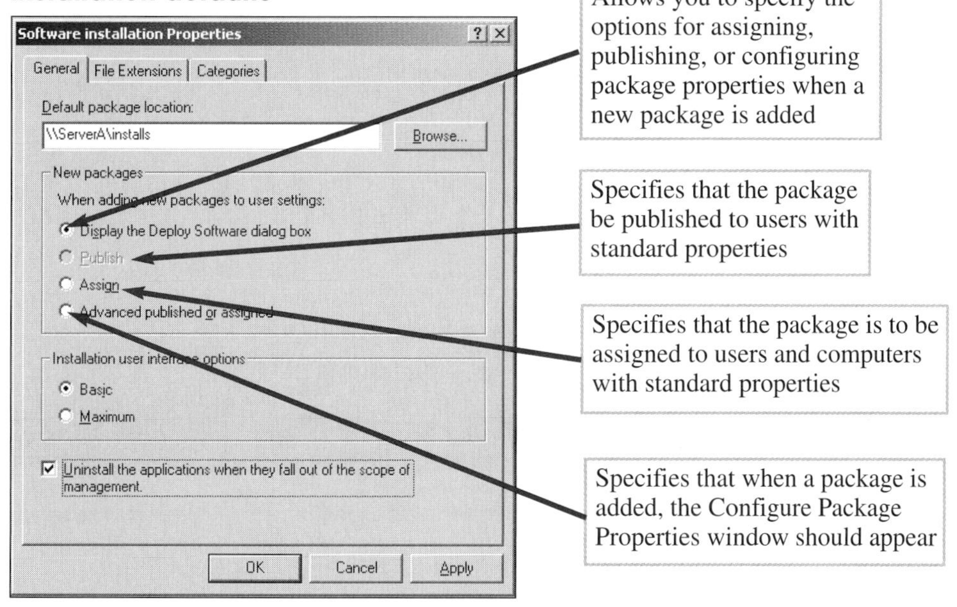

skill 4 Deploying Software Applications

exam objective

Manage and troubleshoot user environments by using Group Policy. Install, configure, manage, and troubleshoot software by using Group Policy.

overview

Once you have set up default installation settings for managing applications in a Group Policy Object (GPO), you can start deploying applications to users and computers by either assigning or publishing the applications. You can use different combinations of these deployment methods based on the needs of your organization. For example, you can assign an application to users when you want all users to install an application on their machines. Alternatively, you can publish applications when you want to leave it to the users to decide if they need the application. In both cases, the GPO manages the application.

how to

Assign the application named MS Office 2000 to users.

1. Log on to the domain controller as an Administrator.
2. Click **Start**, point to **Programs**, point to **Administrative Tools**, and then click **Active Directory Users and Computers**.
3. Right-click on **mydomain.com** and choose **Properties**.
4. Click on the **group policy** tab, click on **Default Domain Policy**, and click **edit**. The **Group Policy** console appears.
5. In **User Configuration**, click **Software Settings** to view the **Software Installation** node.
6. Right-click **Software Installation**, click **New**, and then click the **Package** command to open the **Open** dialog box.
7. Type **\\ServerA\Installs** in the **Look in** list box to specify the SDP location, if it does not appear there already.
8. To assign an application, in this case the MS Office 2000 application, to users, click **Data1** from the list of available .msi files **(Figure 11-8)**.
9. Then, click **Open** to open the **Deploy Software** dialog box.
10. Click the **Assigned** option button to assign the application to users **(Figure 11-9)**.
11. Click **OK** to close the **Deploy Software** dialog box.
12. Close the Group Policy snap-in. You have now assigned MS Office to the users of the GPO.

tip

If you do not have a copy of MS Office (any version) available, you can substitute the adminpak.msi file from your Windows 2000 Server CD. Adminpak.msi installs the administrative tools.

Figure 11-8 Selecting a file for deployment from the SDP

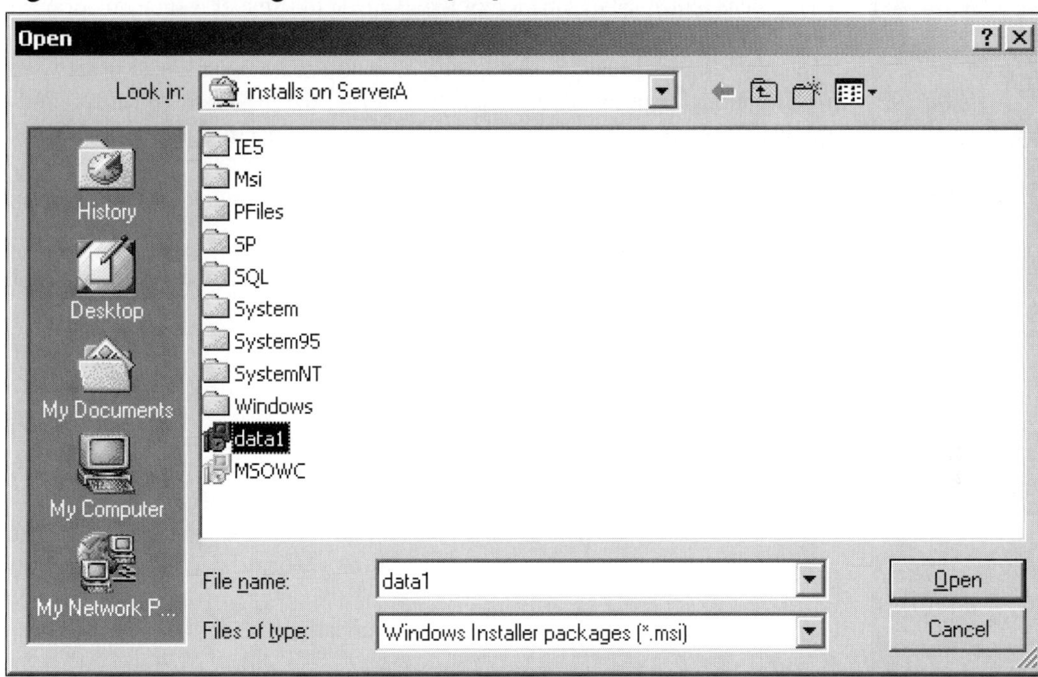

Figure 11-9 Deploying an application

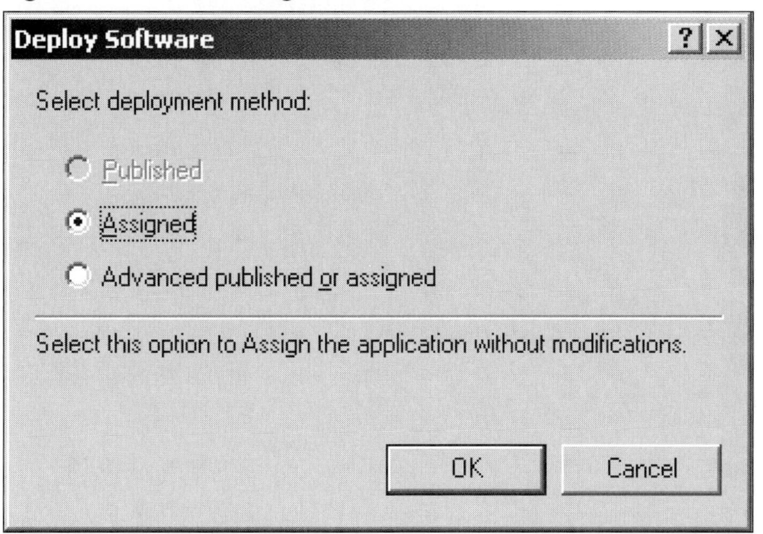

skill 5 Using Modifications to Customize Software Applications

exam objective

Manage and troubleshoot user environments by using Group Policy. Install, configure, manage, and troubleshoot software by using Group Policy.

overview

You can customize the installation of a package at the time of assignment or publication using modifications. **Modifications** are .mst files that allow you to customize the installation of Windows Installer packages at the time of deployment. Modifications also enable a user to install optional features of an application during the installation process. For example, the graphics tool Adobe Photoshop allows the user to install optional features such as extra palettes and fonts. You can add the required .mst file in the Group Policy, which installs these features. Since modification files help you transform the original package, these files are also known as transform files.

To apply modifications, you need to use the Modifications tab in the Properties dialog box for an application (**Figure 11-10**).

caution

Once a software package has been installed, it cannot be modified using an .mst file. In this case, you would need to uninstall the application using group policy and then reinstall it with the required .mst files.

more

If the application has already been deployed, you can specify modifications by editing the properties of the GPO that is deploying the application. To do this, you need to open the GPO software installation snap-in, and right-click the application listed in the details pane of the Software Installation node. Click the Properties command on the shortcut menu to open the Properties dialog box, and then click the Modifications tab to add modifications.

tip

To apply a modification to an existing application in an organization, you must redeploy the package after the modifications have been applied.

Figure 11-10 Applying modifications to an application

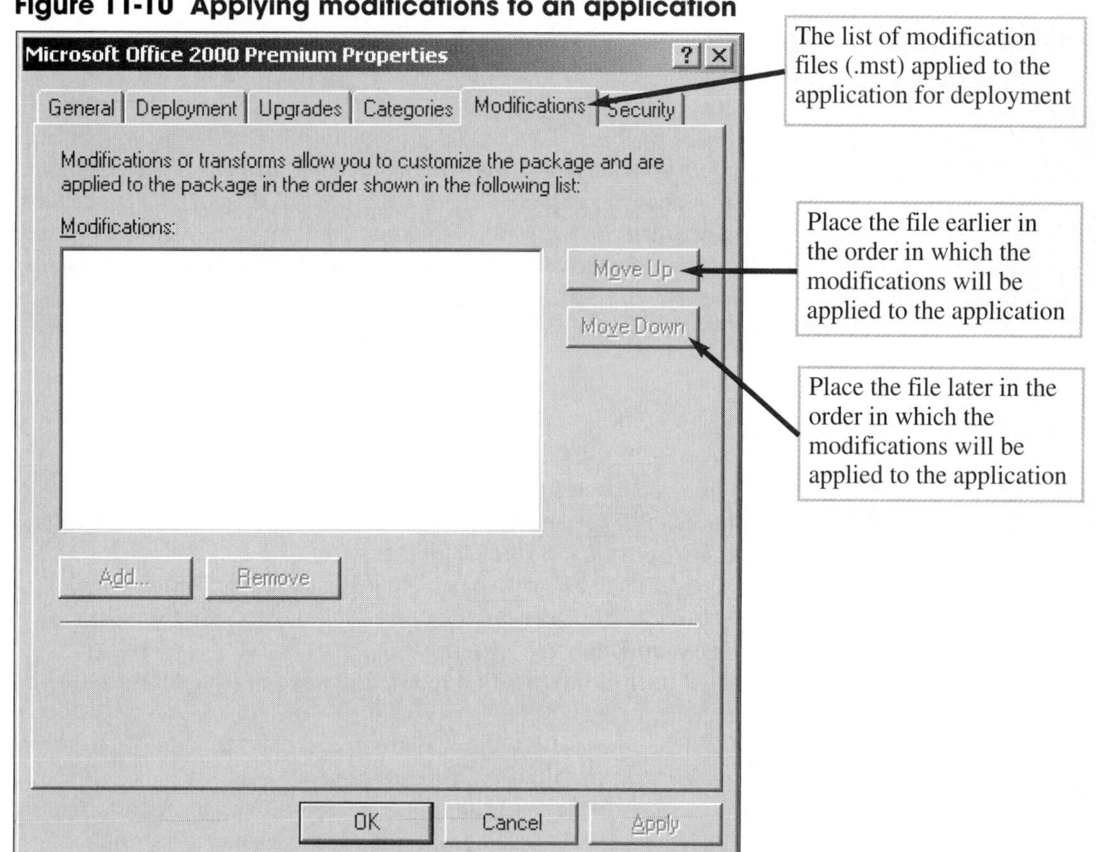
Microsoft Office 2000 Premium Properties
General
Deployment
Upgrades
Categories
Modifications
Security
Modifications or transforms allow you to customize the package and are applied to the package in the order shown in the following list:
Modifications:
Move Up
Move Down
Add...
Remove
OK
Cancel
Apply
The list of modification files (.mst) applied to the application for deployment
Place the file earlier in the order in which the modifications will be applied to the application
Place the file later in the order in which the modifications will be applied to the application

Exam 70-217

skill 6 Setting Automatic Installation Options and Application Categories

exam objective

Manage and troubleshoot user environments by using Group Policy. Install, configure, manage, and troubleshoot software by using Group Policy.

overview

It is very common for users to install applications using document invocation. However, many times you will find that a single file extension is often associated with multiple applications. For example, a .doc file can be opened using Microsoft Word, WordPad, or even Microsoft Internet Explorer. This causes a problem for users using document invocation to install a particular application. To solve this problem, you can set automatic installation options that define application precedence for the file extensions. The application at the top of the list becomes the default application associated with a particular file extension. If the top-most application is part of a GPO that is not applied to the user or computer, the next application listed is examined, and so on, until a match is found. This ensures smooth functioning of a document invocation installation of the required application.

how to

Set automatic installation options.

1. Log on to the domain controller as an Administrator.
2. Click [Start], point to **Programs**, point to **Administrative Tools**, and then click **Active Directory Users and Computers**.
3. Right-click on **mydomain.com** and choose **Properties**.
4. Click on the **group policy** tab, click on **Default Domain Policy**, and click **edit**. The **Group Policy** console appears.
5. In **User Configuration**, click **Software Settings** to view the **Software Installation** node.
6. Right-click **Software Installation**, and then click the **Properties** command to open the **Software installation Properties** dialog box.
7. Click the **File Extensions** tab of the **Software installation Properties** dialog box **(Figure 11-11)**, and then click the file extension **.doc** from the **Select file extension** list. The applications that are associated with the file extension will be listed in the **Application precedence** pane.
8. Click the application **Microsoft Office 2000**, and then click the Up button [Up] to move the selected application to the top of the list. Now, **Microsoft Office 2000** will be installed if the user opens a .doc file after the application is deployed to the user.
9. Click [OK] to apply the settings and close the **Software installation Properties** dialog box.
10. Click [X] to close the Group Policy snap-in. You have now set Microsoft Office 2000 to be installed automatically using document invocation by a .doc file.

more

By default, Windows 2000 displays all applications in one list in the Add/Remove Programs item in the Control Panel. This can lead to confusion. To overcome this confusion, you can organize the various assigned and published applications into application categories. Application categories enable users to install software in a more systematic and logical manner. A single application can appear in more than one category and needs to be defined only once for the entire domain. You can create application categories using the Categories tab of the Software installation Properties dialog box **(Figure 11-12)**.

Figure 11-11 Specifying file precedence using the File Extensions tab

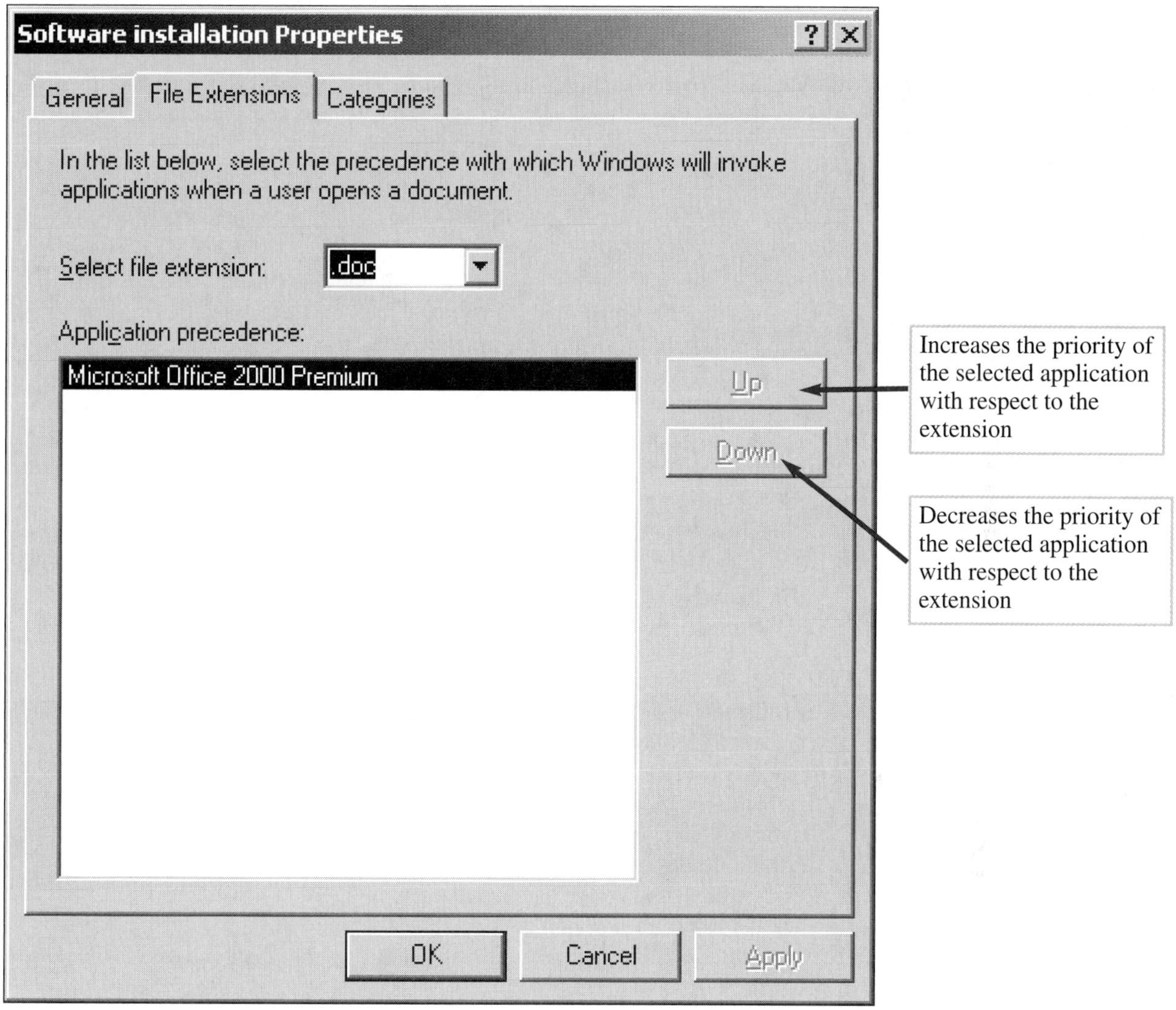

Software installation Properties

General | File Extensions | Categories

In the list below, select the precedence with which Windows will invoke applications when a user opens a document.

Select file extension: .doc

Application precedence:

Microsoft Office 2000 Premium

Up

Down

OK | Cancel | Apply

Increases the priority of the selected application with respect to the extension

Decreases the priority of the selected application with respect to the extension

Figure 11-12 Creating an application category

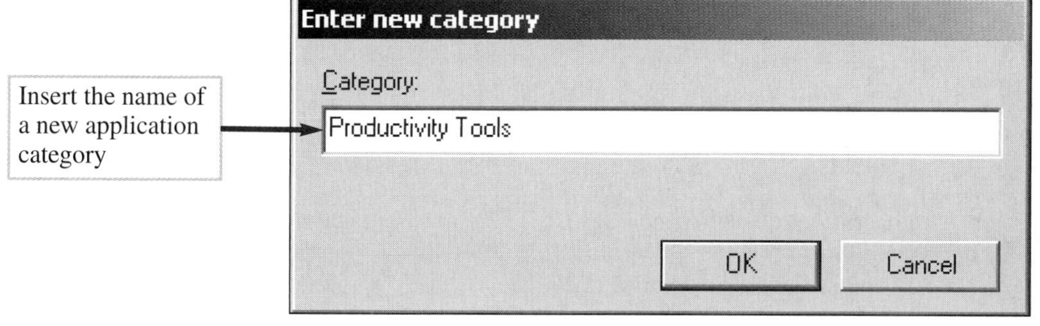

skill 7 Setting Installation Properties of Software Applications

exam objective

Manage and troubleshoot user environments by using Group Policy. Install, configure, manage, and troubleshoot software by using Group Policy

overview

After you have deployed an application, you can configure and fine-tune its installation properties depending on organizational requirements. You can also add the application to an application category if needed in order to reduce confusion.

You use the Software installation Properties dialog box in the Group Policy snap-in to set installation properties of software applications. Setting software application properties involves the following tasks:

- Editing installation defaults — Using the Deployment tab.
- Specifying application properties — Using the Categories tab.
- Setting permissions for software installation — Using the Security tab.

how to

Modify installation options, such as Deployment settings, specify application categories, and set permissions, for software installation of the MS Office application.

1. Log on to the domain controller as an Administrator.
2. Click Start, point to **Programs**, point to **Administrative Tools**, and then click **Active Directory Users and Computers**.
3. Right-click on **mydomain.com** and choose **Properties**.
4. Click on the **group policy** tab, click on **Default Domain Policy**, and click **edit**.
5. In **User Configuration**, click the **Software Settings** container to view the **Software Installation** node. Double-click the **Software Installation** node to view the list of applications deployed.
6. To modify the installation options for the MS Office application, right-click **MS Office** in the details pane, and then click the **Properties** command to open the **MS Office Properties** dialog box.
7. Click the **Deployment** tab.
8. Click the **Assigned** option button in the **Deployment type** section.
9. Click the **Maximum** option button in the **Installation user interface options** to view all installation screens and messages during the installation of the application (**Figure 11-13**).
10. Click the **Categories** tab of the **MS Office Properties** dialog box to assign application categories to the application.
11. Click **Office** on the **Available categories** list, and then click Select > to add the application MS Office to the **Selected categories** list, as shown in **Figure 11-14**.
12. Click the **Security** tab to set software installation permissions.
13. Click **Administrators** from the **Name** list box and select the **Allow** check box for Full Control permission, thus giving administrators full control to manage the deployment of the application.
14. Click **Authenticated Users** from the **Name** list and select the **Allow** check box for Read and Execute permissions since the users of the GPO only need read and execute level access.
15. Click OK to apply the settings and close the **MS Office** dialog box. The properties of the application MS Office are now set, and the application is ready to be deployed.
16. Click X to close the Group Policy snap-in.

Figure 11-13 Modifying installation options for an application

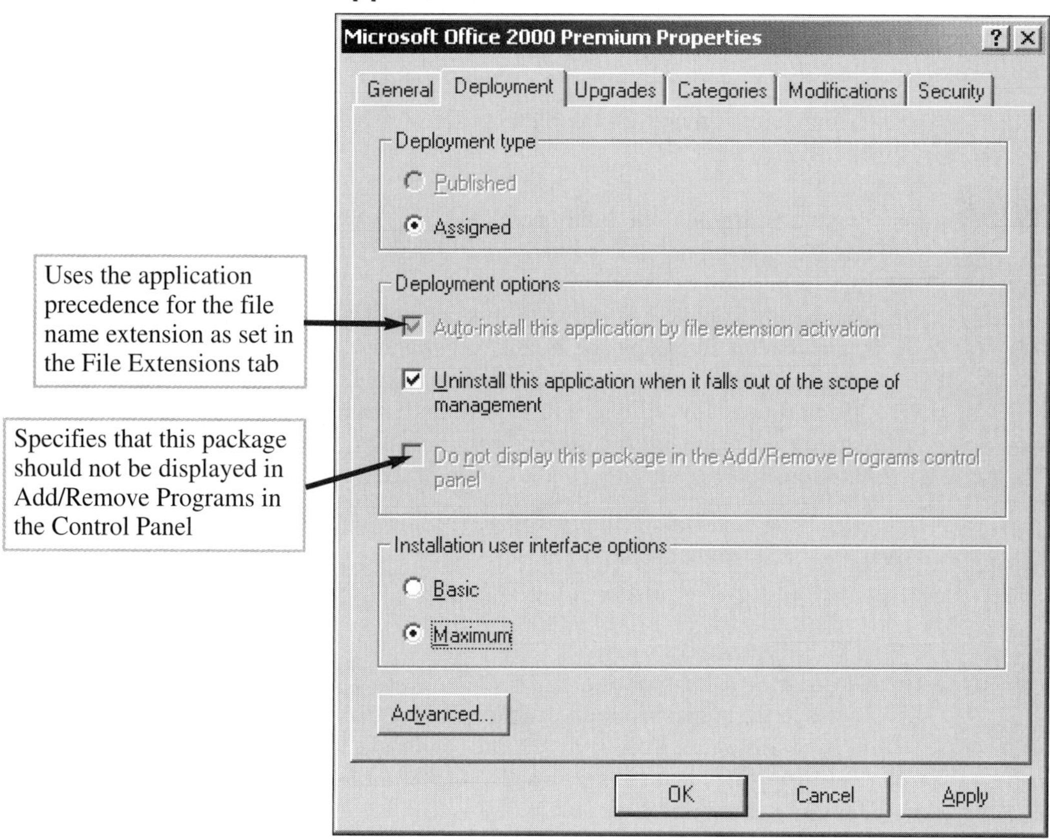

Figure 11-14 Specifying the category for an application

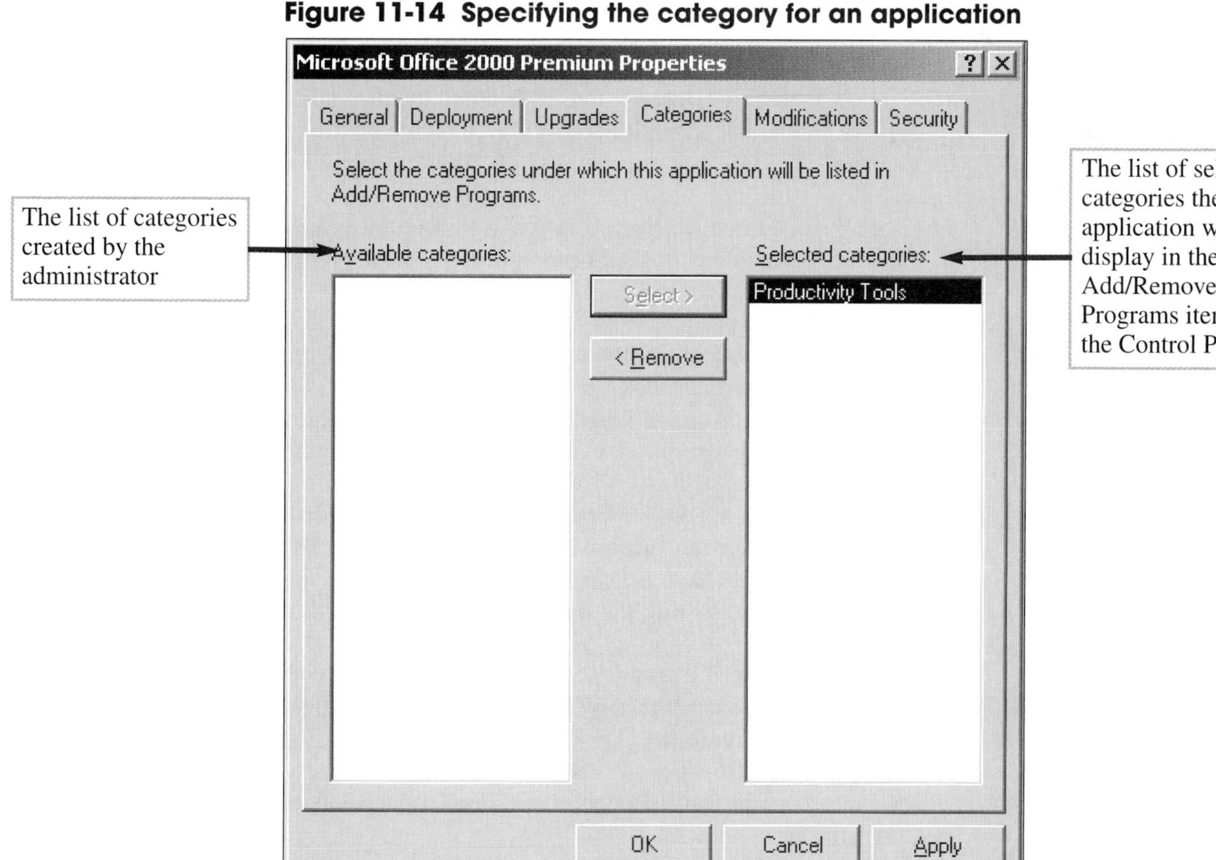

skill 8 Upgrading Software Applications

exam objective

Install, configure, manage, and troubleshoot software by using Group Policy.

overview

Installing software is a one-time operation, but software will also need to be upgraded regularly. Thus, upgrades are an integral part of every software application. Administrators can typically perform two kinds of upgrades:

- **Mandatory upgrade:** Used when it is compulsory to install the latest versions of the application on all computers. In this type, the new version of the software is automatically installed the next time a user invokes the application.
- **Optional upgrade:** Provides flexibility to the user by allowing the user to install the upgrade when he or she requires it. The user can install the upgrade from the Add/Remove Programs item in the Control Panel.

Both Mandatory and Optional upgrades are specified on the Upgrades tab of the Application Properties dialog box in the GPO.

tip

To install Windows 2000 Professional over a network, you first connect to a distribution server and then run the Setup program.

overview

Upgrade the MS Office application.

1. Log on to the domain controller as an Administrator.
2. In C:\Installs, make a copy of **data1.msi** and name it **data2.msi**.
3. Click Start, point to **Programs**, point to **Administrative Tools**, and then click **Active Directory Users and Computers**.
4. Right-click on **mydomain.com** and choose **Properties**.
5. Click on the **group policy** tab, click on **Default Domain Policy**, and click **edit**. The **Group Policy** console appears.
6. In **User Configuration**, click the **Software Settings** container to view the **Software Installation** node.
7. Right-click **Software Installation**, click **New**, and then click the **Package** command to open the **Open** dialog box. If necessary, type **\\ServerA\Installs** in the **Look in** list box.
8. To upgrade the MS Office application, click the file **data2.msi** from the list of available .msi files.
9. Click Open to select the file and open the **Deploy Software** dialog box.
10. Click the **Advanced published or assigned** option button to open the **Properties** dialog box for the application.
11. Click the **Upgrades** tab.
12. Click Add... to add the package to which this upgrade will be applicable. The **Add upgrade package** dialog box opens.
13. Accept the default option **Current Group Policy Object (GPO)** in the **Choose a package from** section since the package to which the upgrade is to be applied exists in the same GPO.
14. Click the package **MS Office** from the **Package to upgrade** list.
15. Click the **Package can upgrade over the existing package** option button since the upgrade is a service pack and can be installed over the existing package **(Figure 11-15)**.
16. Click OK to close the **Add upgrade package** dialog box and return to the **Upgrades** tab.
17. Select the **Required upgrade for existing packages** check box to make the upgrade mandatory for the users **(Figure 11-16)**. Not selecting this check box will make this upgrade optional for users.
18. Click OK to close the **Properties** dialog box. You have now set up the service pack upgrade to be applied to the existing application McAfee VirusScan.
19. Close all open windows.

Figure 11-15 Specifying the package to upgrade

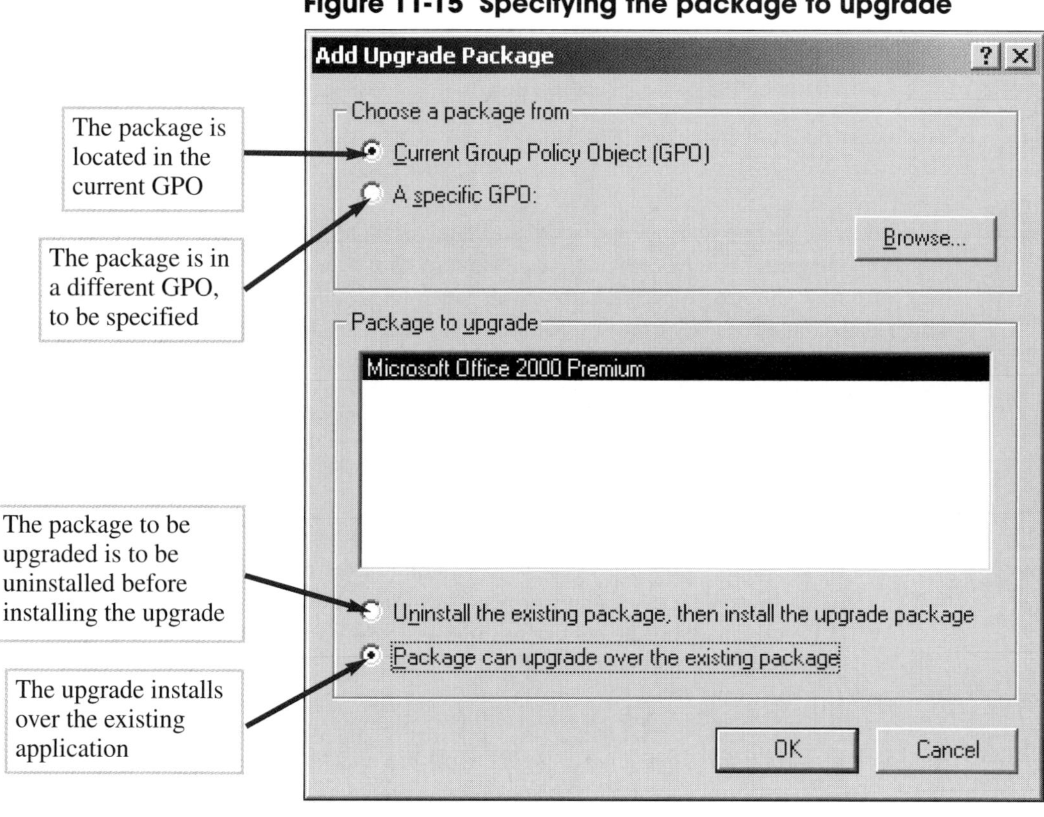

Figure 11-16 Specifying the upgrade options in the Upgrades tab

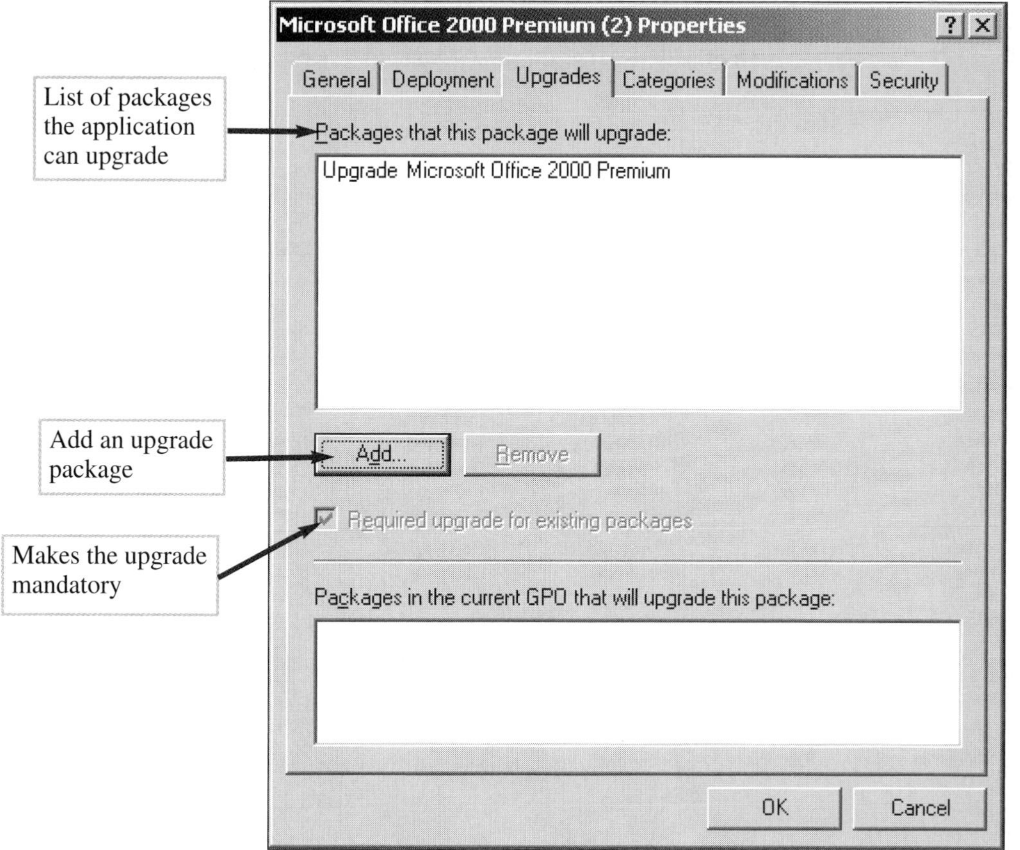

skill 9 Uninstalling Software Applications

exam objective

Install, configure, manage, and troubleshoot software by using Group Policy.

overview

It is as easy to remove software using Group Policy in Windows 2000 as it is to install. In this industry, software becomes redundant or outdated very quickly. Additionally, users may resign from or shift departments, leaving the software installed on their computers behind, which leads to unnecessary usage of valuable disk space. As an administrator, you can handle this problem effectively by specifying removal settings for applications during deployment.

As an administrator, you may uninstall software using two modes:

- **Mandatory removal** — The application is uninstalled automatically from the computer the next time a user logs on or the computer restarts. This is also known as forced removal.
- **Optional removal** — The existing application is left as is on users' machines, but no users are allowed to perform any new installation of the application. Additionally, users will not be allowed to install the software from the Add/Remove Programs item in the Control Panel. Finally, if the application was assigned, it is no longer resilient.

how to

Uninstall the MS Office application using the Optional removal mode.

1. Log on to the domain controller as an Administrator.
2. Click **Start**, point to **Programs**, point to **Administrative Tools**, and then click **Active Directory Users and Computers**.
3. Right-click on **mydomain.com** and choose **Properties.**
4. Click on the **group policy** tab, click on **Default Domain Policy**, and click **edit**.
5. In **User Configuration**, click the **Software Settings** container to view the **Software Installation** node.
6. Double-click **Software Installation** to view the list of deployed applications in the details pane.
7. Right-click **MS Office**, point to **All tasks**, and click **Remove** to open the **Remove Software** dialog box, as shown in **Figure 11-17**.
8. Click the option labeled **Allow users to continue to use the software**, **but prevent new installations**, as shown in **Figure 11-18**.
9. Click **OK** to close the **Remove Software** dialog box.
10. Close the Group Policy snap-in. You have now uninstalled the MS Office application using the Optional removal mode.

more

The two modes of application removal function only with applications installed by Group Policy deployment.

Figure 11-17 Removing a deployed application

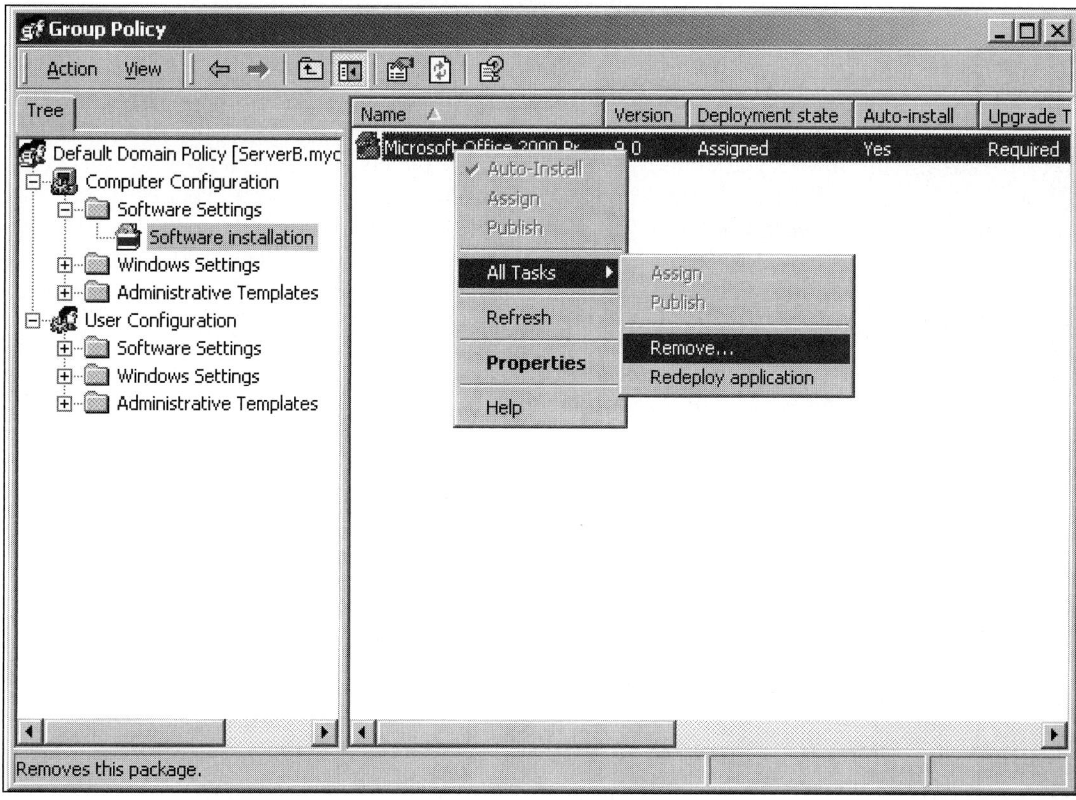

Figure 11-18 Selecting a removal method

skill 10 Using Group Policy to Manage Folder Redirection

exam objective

Basic knowledge

overview

Group Policy can also be used to help resolve the most common problem with roaming user profiles: network bandwidth waste. A new feature in group policy, called **Folder Redirection**, allows you to take the most common folders and redirect them to a network server. This means that, instead of downloading the full folder at logon, your users are instead browsing the remote folder, just as if they were browsing a network share. When a user opens an item in a redirected folder, the individual item is downloaded. This functionality saves considerable network bandwidth and can considerably reduce the logon time for users with large profiles.

You can redirect folders over a network using the **Folder Redirection** extension located in the Windows Settings folder. This folder resides in the **User Configuration** node in the Group Policy snap-in, as shown in **Figure 11-19**.

The Folder Redirection feature proves especially beneficial to users. Some of these benefits are listed below.

- The users' documents, being on the network, are always available as long as the user is connected to the network, regardless of the computer the user logs on to.
- Systems that need to be reconfigured at the system level or require reinstallation of the operating system can redirect their data safely to a location different than the local computer's hard disk.
- Using roaming user profiles makes the process of logging on and off quicker compared to other operating systems, as roaming user profiles must download the entire folder structure at logon.
- Backing up data on a shared network server can be scheduled as a routine system administrative task. The Folder Redirection feature is safer and less user-dependent than manually backing up data, as it does not involve any user action.

how to

Redirect the My Documents folder to a location for the user account for Jack M. Willis that you created in Lesson 5, according to security group membership. You will require a shared folder on ServerA named 'share'.

1. Log on to the domain controller as an Administrator.
2. Click Start, point to **Programs, point to Administrative Tools**, and then click **Active Directory Users and Computers**.
3. Right-click on **mydomain.com** and choose **Properties**.
4. Click on the **group policy** tab, click on **Default Domain Policy**, and click **edit**.
5. In **User Configuration**, click the **Windows Settings** folder, and then click the **Folder Redirection** folder to view its contents.
6. In the details pane, right-click the **My Documents** folder, and then click the **Properties** command to open the **Properties** dialog box for the My Documents folder.
7. Click the **Advanced - Specify locations for various user groups** option from the **Settings** list box. This will allow you to specify different locations for redirection over the network for different user groups.
8. Click Add... to open the **Specify Group and Location** dialog box.
9. Click Browse... in the **Security Group Membership** section to open the **Select Group** dialog box.
10. Click **Users**, and then click OK to specify the user group for folder redirection.
11. Type **\\ServerA\Share\%username%** to specify the location of the redirection folder on the network, where **ServerA** is the name of the server, **Share** is the name of the shared folder, and **%username%** is the user who will own the redirected folder.

tip

Always enter a full UNC (Universal Naming Convention) path using the format \\Server\share\%username%. as the redirection folder location. Specify the user name variable only if you want to give each user in the group his or her own subfolder.

Figure 11-19 Special folders available for redirection

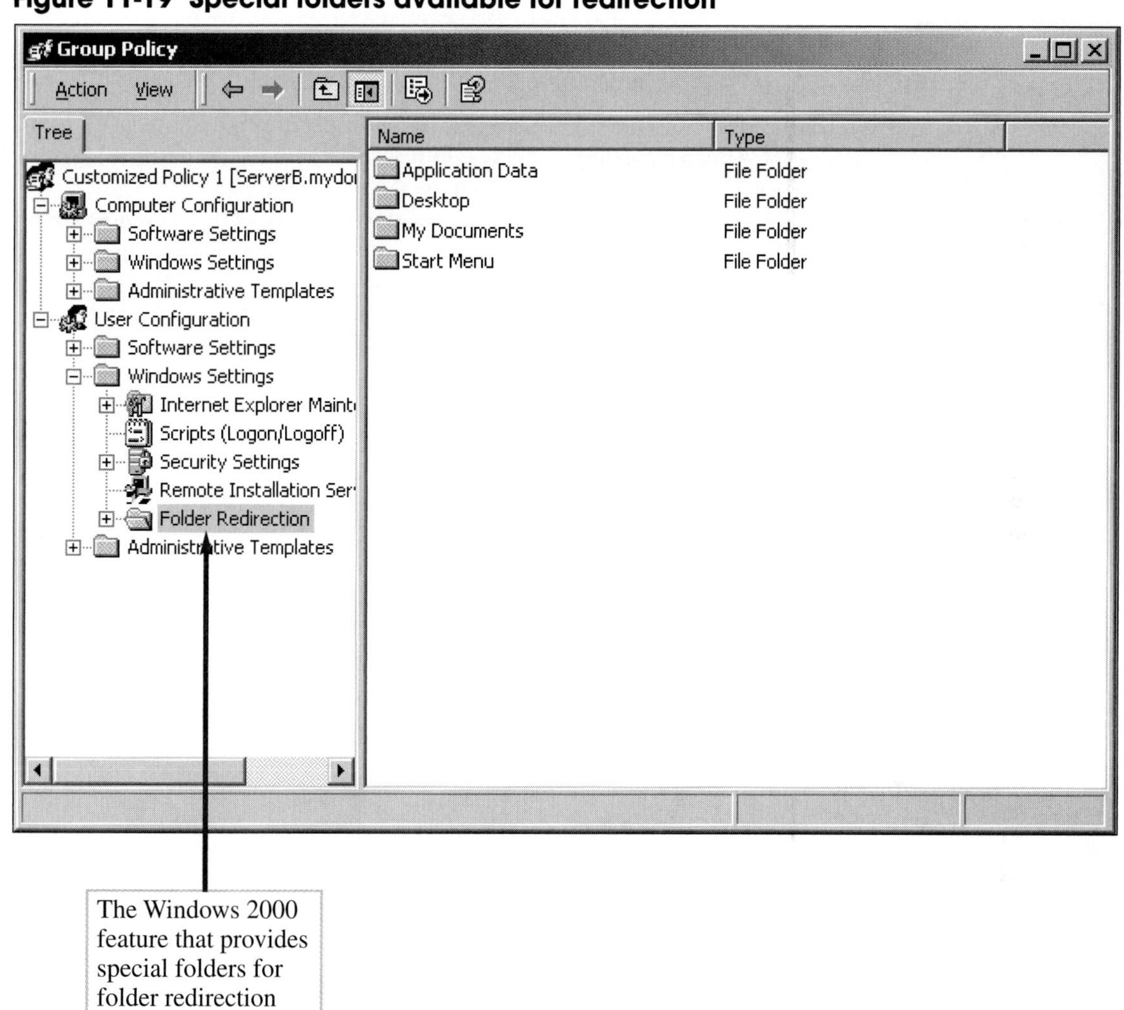

The Windows 2000 feature that provides special folders for folder redirection

skill 10 Using Group Policy to Manage Folder Redirection *(cont'd)*

exam objective

Basic knowledge

how to

12. Click OK to close the **Specify Group and Location** dialog box and return to the **Properties** dialog box **(Figure 11-20)**.
13. Click the **Settings** tab to specify the redirection settings for the My Documents folder.
14. Accept the default setting of the **Grant user exclusive rights to the folder** check box to make the folder accessible exclusively to the user of the folder.
15. Accept the default setting of the **Move the contents of My Documents to the new location** check box to move the files from the My Documents folder to the specified network location.
16. In the **Policy Removal** section, click the option labeled **Redirect the folder back to the local userprofile location when policy is removed** in order to allow the folder contents to be moved back to the original location after the removal of the policy **(Figure 11-21)**.
17. Click OK to close the **Properties** dialog box.
18. Close the Group Policy snap-in. You have now redirected the special folder My Documents for Jack M. Willis to a location on the network.

Figure 11-20 Folder redirection settings

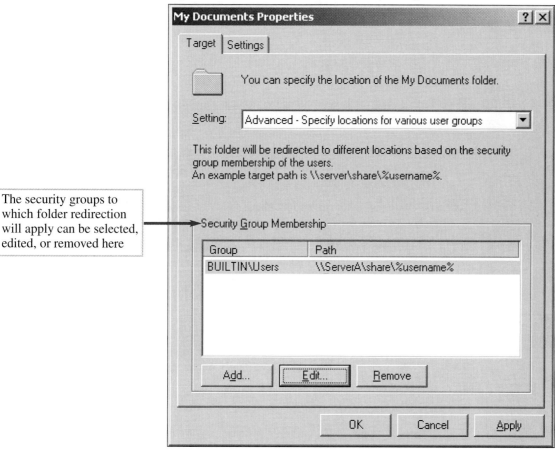

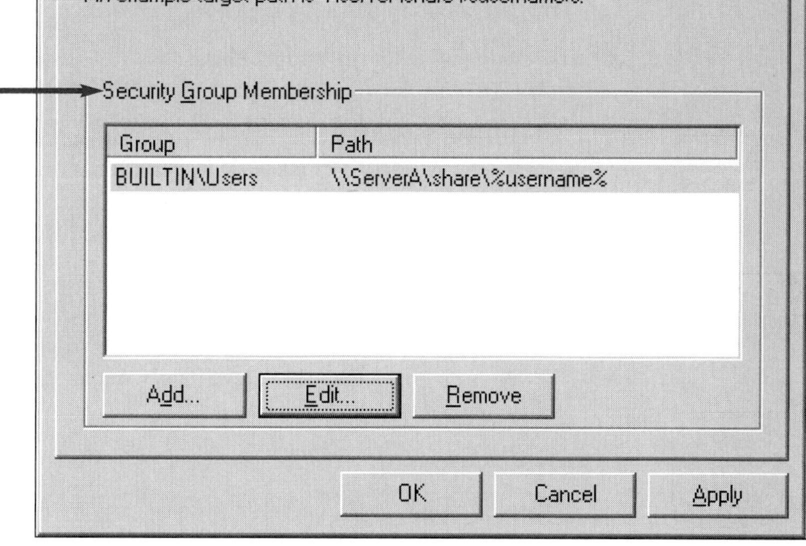

The security groups to which folder redirection will apply can be selected, edited, or removed here

Figure 11-21 Folder redirection properties

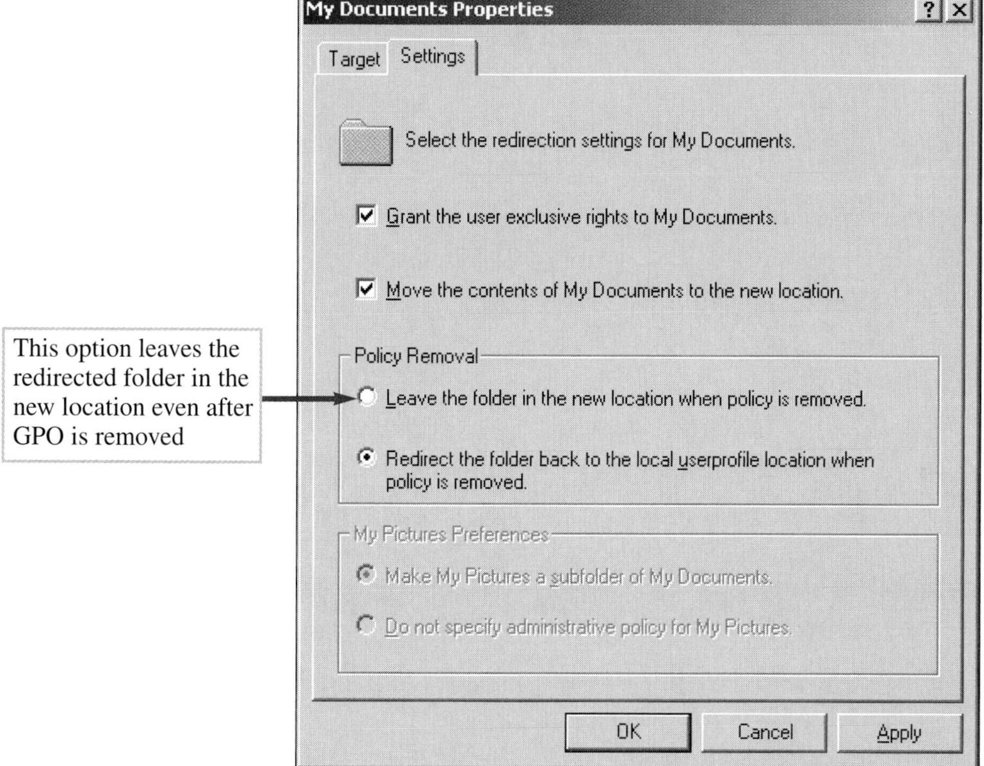

skill 11 Troubleshooting Group Policy-Related Problems

exam objective

Implement and troubleshoot Group Policy.

overview

Group Policy has greatly simplified the process of software deployment, maintenance, and removal. However, there might be times when errors occur in spite of these processes being in place in Group Policy. As an administrator, you can troubleshoot these problems and get the system back in place. Some problems associated with the deployment, maintenance, and removal of software are linked to Group Policy issues. **Table 11-4** describes a few common Group Policy-related problems, their causes, and their solutions.

tip

Group Policy does not provide complete logging of the installation. If you need this feature, you are advised to examine Systems Management Server for software installation.

Another common issue that one might encounter while using the Software Installation feature of Windows 2000 involves improper packaging. This could result in packages not installing properly, or installing and then causing a GPF when it runs.

Finally, improper settings in the software installation extension can cause several varied problems. Luckily, these are, typically, easily solved. Some of the issues involving the Software Installation extension are described in **Table 11-5**.

You can further troubleshoot package installation errors using the Application Log in the Event Viewer. Event Viewer logs all events related to package installation and contains event logs that you can use to begin your troubleshooting. You can view these events by opening Event Viewer from the **Administrative Tools** menu, or by typing **EVENTVWR** at the command prompt.

Table 11-4 Problems related to Group Policy settings

Problems	Causes	Possible solutions
1. Group Policy does not affect users and computers in a site, domain, or OU.	Group Policy settings are blocked.	Make sure that the policy is not blocked.
	The No Override option is applied applied to a GPO, which prevents the Group Policy from being applied.	Make sure the No Override option for the policy is not set.
	Appropriate permissions are not set for the users or computers.	Verify that the user or computer is part of at least one group for which the Apply Group Policy (AGP) and Read permissions are set to Allow. Also ensure that they are not members of any groups that deny those same permissions.
2. Users are not able to open a GPO.	User has not been assigned the right permissions.	Make sure that the user has been assigned both Read and Write permissions for the GPO.
3. Group Policy is not being applied to the users and computers of a particular Active Directory container.	You are not able to link GPOs to Active Directory containers other than sites, domains, and OUs.	Link the GPO to a parent OU of the Active Directory container. In accordance with the law of inheritance, parent settings will be applied to the Active Directory containers, as well.
4. The local computer policy settings are not being applied.	All non-local GPOs can overwrite local policies (LSDOU).	Make sure there are no contradictory settings between the local and the non-local GPOs.

Table 11-5 Problems related to Software Installation

Problems	Causes	Possible solutions
1. Package does not install.	Permission problems.	Make sure that the user has Read and AGP permissions for the GPO, as well as Read permission for the SDP and the application.
2. Document Invocation does not function.	The administrator did not set auto-install while specifying deployment settings.	Make sure that the Auto-Install option is enabled in the Deployment tab of the application's Properties dialog box during deployment.
3. Published applications do not appear in the Add/Remove Programs item in the Control Panel.	Group Policy is not applied properly. The "Do not list in Add/Remove programs" check box has been set on the application.	Make sure the right permissions have been assigned. Clear the check box.
4. The application has been removed. However, the application shortcut still appears on the user's desktop.	The shortcuts may be user-created; therefore, Windows Installer has no knowledge of them.	The shortcuts must be removed manually.

Summary

- Group Policy can be used to manage software deployment and maintenance within an organization in an effective and systematic manner.
- Windows 2000 contains the following built-in tools for installing and maintaining software:
  - Software Installation extension of Group Policy snap-in
  - Windows Installer
  - Add/Remove Programs in the Control Panel
- Methods used for the deployment of software applications include assigning the applications to users, assigning the applications to computers, and publishing the applications to users.
- After preparing a plan for software installation, you need to set up a Software Distribution Point (SDP). An SDP is a network location from which users can get the software that they need.
- You can define default settings for all installed applications to help in the management of applications. Specifying default settings includes placing the applications in these SDPs and specifying initial deployment settings.
- You can customize the installation of a package at the time of assignment or publication using modifications. Modifications are .mst files that allow you to customize the installation of Windows Installer packages at the time of deployment.
- As an administrator, you can relieve yourself of administrative burden by defining application precedence for file extensions, as well as organizing the various assigned and published applications into application categories.
- You can fine-tune software installation properties depending on organizational requirements by using the Software installation Properties dialog box in the Group Policy snap-in.
- The two kinds of upgrades an administrator can perform include mandatory and optional upgrades.
- The two kinds of removals of an application include mandatory and optional removals. These two modes of application removal can function only with applications installed by Group Policy deployment.
- Group Policy can be used to organize files in folders with the help of Folder Redirection, a feature provided by Windows 2000. Folder Redirection lets users redirect special folders to alternate locations on the network, especially in cases when these folders become overloaded and difficult to manage.
- Most of the problems associated with the deployment of software are linked to Group Policy issues and packaging problems.
- All events related to package installation are logged in Event Viewer. The information in Event Viewer can help you diagnose problems in Group Policy.

Key Terms

Windows Installer
Software Installation extension
Modifications
Mandatory upgrade
Optional upgrade
Mandatory removal
Optional removal
Folder Redirection
Software diagnostics
IntelliMirror
Software Distribution Point (SDP)

Test Yourself

1. Which of the following are Software Installation and Maintenance tools? (Choose all that apply.)
   a. Software Installation extension
   b. Containers
   c. Microsoft Management Console (MMC)
   d. Windows Installer
   e. Add/Remove Programs in the Control Panel

2. Which of the following processes occurs when an application is published to a user?
   a. The application is installed on the computer the next time the user logs on.
   b. A notification is displayed to the user the next time the user logs on and the application is installed on document invocation.
   c. The application is installed on document invocation or using the Add/Remove Programs item in the Control Panel.
   d. The application displays a notification and is automatically installed the next time the computer is started.

3. Which of the following security group attributes should be set when an application is copied to a Software Distribution Point (SDP)? (Choose all that apply.)

a. The users are assigned Read and Write permissions for the SDP.
b. The administrators are assigned Read and Write permissions for the SDP.
c. The users are assigned only Read and Execute permissions for the SDP.
d. Everyone is assigned Read and Write permissions for the SDP.
e. Everyone is assigned Read permissions for the SDP.

4. Which of the following option buttons on the General tab of the Software installation Properties dialog box would you choose to enable the user to configure package properties at the time of deployment?
a. Publish
b. Assign
c. Advanced published or assigned
d. Enable

5. You want to deploy a mandatory application on all users of a domain using the Software Installation feature of Windows 2000. You have created a Windows Installer package for the application and are ready to configure automatic deployment options for the application. How should you deploy the application so users need not install the application manually?
a. Assign the application to users.
b. Publish the application to users.
c. Assign the application to computers.
d. Publish the application to computers.

6. You want to deploy Microsoft Office 2000 to Windows 2000 Professional clients using the Software Installation feature and Group Policy Objects. You also need to apply modifications to the application so that unwanted features are removed and other features are customized as per organizational requirements. Which file type should you use to modify the Office 2000 Windows Installer package?
a. .mst files
b. .msp files
c. .zap files
d. .msi files

7. You are the network administrator of RainDrop Consultants. You need to deploy an application that currently has multiple file associations. How will you specify default file associations for this application?
a. By creating an application category and adding the application under that category.
b. By selecting the application with the highest precedence on the File Extensions tab of the Software Properties dialog box with respect to the file extension.
c. By pressing the [Shift] key and right-clicking a file with the extension, and then selecting the Open With command.
d. By selecting the Auto-install option.

8. A new version of a software package used in your firm has been released. You need to install the package using Group Policy after removing the existing version of the software. Which is the right method to achieve this?
a. Upgrade the existing package.
b. Add a modification to the package while deploying the application.
c. Select the Auto-install this application by file extension activation check box in the Deployment tab of the Software Properties dialog box.

9. You need to publish an application to the users of the Graphics department. The application is an Image Viewer utility. You open the Application Properties dialog box, add the Graphics category in the Categories tab, and then open the Security tab. What do you need to do on this tab in order to publish the application?
a. Select the Allow inheritable permissions from parent to propagate to this object check box.
b. Add the security group of the graphics department and allow Read permissions to the group, then remove the authenticated users group from the security list.
c. Add the security group Everyone and allow Read permissions to the group and deploy the application.
d. Add the security group Administrators and allow Full Control to the group.

10. You publish a package to upgrade an application in the organization. However, the old application does not appear in the Upgrade tab list. Which of the following could be a cause for this error?
a. The .msi files cannot upgrade 16-bit applications.
b. The application was not deployed using Group Policies.
c. You cannot publish an upgrade.
d. The application might have been deployed using a .zap extension.

11. You modify a Group Policy to remove an application that had been installed using Group Policy. However, users continue to use the application. Which of the following could be possible causes for this?
a. The users did not uninstall the application after the Group Policy was applied.
b. The users reinstalled the application from an SDP.
c. There was a conflict between the removal Group Policy and another existing Group Policy.
d. The option to remove the package immediately was not selected.

12. You want to improve the accessibility of documents for users who log in from multiple locations in the organization, as well as minimize the possibility of loss of data. Using Group Policy, choose the folders you can redirect to network server locations. (Choose all that apply.)
a. Application Data
b. My Documents
c. Control Panel
d. Start Menu
e. My Network Places
f. Desktop

13. The directors of the organization Happylife Insurance want their document folders in the network to be accessed solely by them. As an administrator, how can you ensure this?
   a. Select the Grant the user exclusive rights to My Documents option in the Settings tab of the My Documents Properties dialog box.
   b. Create a new security group and specify a target location for the new group.
   c. Use share permissions to only allow internal employees access to the share.
   d. Hide the folders.

Projects: On Your Own

1. Set up an **SDP** named **SHARE** and set software installation defaults for an application to be installed on the computers of the users of the **GPO ABC**. Finally, deploy the application to the user.
   a. Log on as an **Administrator** on the domain controller that contains the GPO ABC.
   b. Create a folder **SHARE** in the primary drive of the server and enable sharing of the folder with **Read** permissions to the users security group and **Full Control** permissions to the group of administrators. Copy the installation file of the application to the folder.
   c. Open the **Group Policy** snap-in.
   d. Set the software installation defaults using the **Software installation Properties** dialog box to assign the application.
   e. Deploy the application to the users of the GPO.
   f. Close the **Group Policy** snap-in.

2. Create an application category named **Utilities** and add the application above to the category. Also, specify the default installation option for the application such that the application installs itself when any file with the file extension .apx is opened.
   a. Log on as an **Administrator** on the domain controller that contains the GPO ABC.
   b. Open the **Group Policy** snap-in.
   c. Create an application category named **Utilities**.
   d. Specify the application under the **Utilities** category.
   e. Assign the topmost priority to the application for the file extension **.apx**.
   f. Close the **Group Policy** snap-in.

3. A new version of the application has been released. Remove the application immediately to allow for a fresh installation.
   a. Log on as an **Administrator** on the domain controller that contains the GPO ABC.
   b. Open the **Group Policy** snap-in.
   c. Open the **Remove software** dialog box and specify the software to be removed from users and computers immediately.
   d. Close the **Group Policy** snap-in.

Problem Solving Scenarios

1. You administer your company's network. All users on the network require the Microsoft Project 2000 application, which is vital to their work. Recently your company has recruited a lot of new staff, and you are required to set up the workstations to be used by these new employees.

You need to work out an efficient method for installing the required application on all the workstations to be used. All of the new employees will belong to an OU named Trainees in the domain Vertex.co.in. Additionally, the new employees are neither experienced with using Windows 2000 nor with installing applications on Windows. You are planning to use group policy objects to install the required application.

Draft a plan of action explaining how the group policy needs to be configured for installing the required application.

2. You administer your company's Windows 2000 ADS-based network. Your network consists of two domains named DOMAINA and DOMAINB. DOMAINA is mostly administered since all development team members belong to this domain. DOMAINA is further categorized into four OU's for better resources management. The Managers OU and the Group Leads OU usually have some members shifting amongst each other's OU.

The members of the Managers OU need to use Microsoft Office 2000 Professional for their work, whereas the members of the Group Leads OU need to use Microsoft Visual Studio. NET. You need to work out an efficient plan that automates the installation process for the users in the Managers OU, since those users are not very comfortable with application installation procedures. On the other hand, members of the Group Leads OU must be able to install the application only if required. Also, if any members of one OU are shifted to another OU, the related applications must automatically be uninstalled.

Prepare a PowerPoint presentation explaining your plan of action to achieve the necessary organization.

LESSON

12 Performing Security Configuration for Active Directory

The systems and personnel data in an organization should function at optimal levels in a secure environment in order to achieve maximum productivity. One of your duties as an administrator may be to maintain a secure and efficient network. You need to ensure that the network in your organization is secure enough to prevent unauthorized users from accessing resources. You must also provide easy access to the network and resources for authorized users.

Windows 2000 Server provides you with tools that enable you to monitor and manage the security of a network. The Windows 2000 Auditing tool allows you to monitor user activities such as access to resources on the network, as well as events such as a system startup and policy changes.

You can also configure Windows 2000 to log information about directory and file access attempts and server events. For example, you can record security events such as valid and invalid logon attempts, as well as events that are related to resource use such as creating, opening, or deleting files on the server. These events are logged in the Windows Security log and can be analyzed later.

One tool you can use to help secure resources in a Windows 2000 network is Group Policy. Windows 2000 Server provides the Security Templates tool and the Security Configuration and Analysis tool that are used to set up and manage security templates, which affect the security portions of Group Policy. These security templates can then be applied to multiple computers on a network by importing the settings into a group policy and linking it.

The Security Configuration and Analysis tool allows you to apply the restrictions defined in a security template to a system. However, its best feature is that it allows you to analyze the existing security setup of a system and to compare these settings with security templates. This comparative analysis will assist you in determining the optimal security settings for a specific system. Based on these settings, you can then configure an optimal security template for your needs.

Goals

In this lesson, you will learn about the security settings in Windows 2000 Server. You will learn to set up an audit policy for computers, such as a domain controller and a stand-alone server, and to audit access to resources on your network. You will also learn to use the Security Templates tool and the Security Configuration and Analysis tool to set up and manage network security.

Lesson 12 Performing Security Configuration for Active Directory

Skill	Exam 70-217 Objective
1. Introducing Security Configuration	Apply security policies by using Group Policy.
2. Introducing the Windows 2000 Auditing Tool	Basic knowledge
3. Setting Up an Audit Policy for a Domain Controller	Implement an audit policy.
4. Setting Up an Audit Policy for a Stand-Alone Server or Computer	Implement an audit policy.
5. Creating an Audit Policy for Files and Folders	Implement an audit policy.
6. Auditing User Access to Active Directory Objects	Implement an audit policy.
7. Using Security Logs to Handle Events	Monitor and analyze security events.
8. Assigning User Rights to Users and Groups	Apply security policies by using Group Policy.
9. Implementing Security Templates	Create, analyze, and modify security configurations by using the Security Configuration and Analysis snap-in and the Security Templates snap-in.
10. Using the Security Configuration and Analysis Console	Create, analyze, and modify security configurations by using the Security Configuration and Analysis snap-in and the Security Templates snap-in.
11. Configuring Security by Using the Security Configuration and Analysis Console	Create, analyze, and modify security configurations by using the Security Configuration and Analysis snap-in and the Security Templates snap-in.
12. Troubleshooting Security Configuration Issues	Monitor and analyze security events.

Requirements

To complete the skills in this lesson, you need administrative rights on the ServerA domain controller for the mydomain.com domain. You also need a stand-alone server named Server3. In addition, you will need a shared printer on ServerA.

skill 1

Introducing Security Configuration

exam objective

Apply security policies by using Group Policy.

overview

You need to protect your network both from unauthorized users within your organization and from external threats. Windows 2000 Server enables you to set up a number of security policies to enhance the security of both individual systems and the entire network. The process of setting up a security policy for an individual system or network is called **security configuration**. Security configuration allows you to set up security policies (account and local), access control policies (services, registry, and files), event logs settings, group membership settings (restricted groups), Public Key policies, and Internet Protocol (IP) security policies.

When determining the security policy for computers in an enterprise, you need to consider the organizational and functional characteristics of the network. These characteristics include the physical distribution of the network, the business models the organization uses, the network load due to inter-computer dataflow and access, and the overall computer usage.

tip

Group Policy-based security is predominantly done in the Computer Configuration node of the Group Policy Object (GPO).

Windows 2000 Server provides you with several different tools that can be used to configure the security policy in a computer, or across computers in a site, domain, or Organizational Unit (OU). You can use the Group Policy snap-in as a tool to apply security settings centrally for the computers in a domain using Group Policy Objects based on the security level of the computers. To apply security policy, you can use the Security Settings extension of the Group Policy snap-in. (**Figure 12-1**). In configuring the security settings of a GPO, you should be aware of the available security areas

- **Account Policies:** The account policy area includes the attributes for the Password Policy (Figure 12-2), Account Lockout Policy, and Kerberos Policy (refer to **Table 12-1** for the usage of the policies). These policies are particular in that they can only be set for the entire domain. If you modify these settings in a GPO and apply them to an OU, they will not take effect on domain accounts.
- **Local Policies:** These policies are local to a computer and are used to define security settings on the computer. The local policies are Audit policy, User rights assignment, and Security options (Refer to **Table 12-1** for the usage of the policies).
- **Event Log:** Security-related events, such as audit policy events, are stored in the security event log of the Event Viewer console. You can specify security log settings such as the maximum size of the event log file, logging options, and event log access rights.
- **Restricted Groups:** Restricted Groups are a new feature of Windows 2000 that allow you to place some additional control over the membership of key groups. When you define a group as a restricted group, you set the membership for the group and configure which groups the restricted group is a member of. From then on, after applying the policy, if someone modifies the membership of that group, the next time Group Policy applies the membership is reverted back to whatever you have set in the group policy.

Figure 12-1 Security extension of the Group Policy snap-in

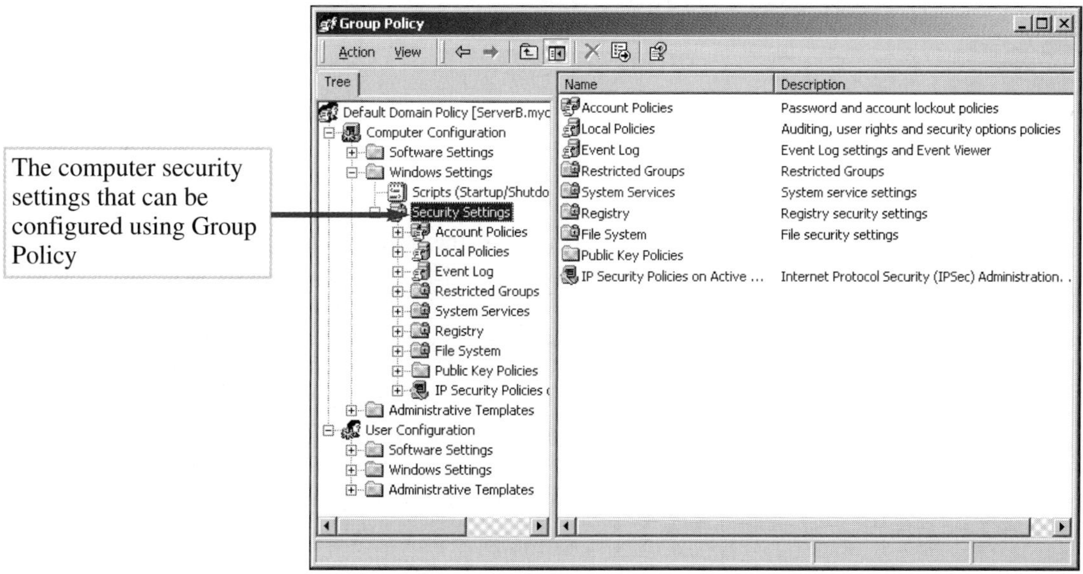

Figure 12-2 Password Policy settings

Table 12-1 Account and Local Security Policies

Policy	***Function***
Password Policy	Sets account password-related settings such as password lifetimes and password usage enforcement.
Account Lockout Policy	Sets account lockout duration as well as threshold and reset values.
Kerberos Policy	Kerberos authenticates the identity of a user, and issues tickets that are used in the user authorization process in Active Directory. Ticket lifetimes and other Kerberos settings can be configured in this section.
Audit policy	Establishes which security events are to be audited.
User rights assignment	Determines what rights user accounts have on the computer; for instance, "act as part of the operating system", "log on locally", "log on as a service", and so on.
Security options	Allows or disallows specific computer security settings such as logon display messages and CD-ROM access.

skill 1

Introducing Security Configuration (cont'd)

exam objective

Basic knowledge

overview

- **System Services:** You can configure the startup settings for services such as the Windows Installer service on a computer. The three settings are Automatic, Manual, and Disabled (**Figure 12-3**). You can also specify which security group or user can modify a service's properties, including the ability to start, stop or pause a service.
- **Registry:** The registry security settings allow you to specify who can read, modify, and add new keys to the registry.
- **File System:** You can set access permissions for the folders and files of the computer (**Figure 12-4**). Note that these settings only apply to machines with NTFS drives.
- **Public Key Policies:** These policies are used to set up public key encryption settings on a computer. Public key policy enables the computer to add encrypted data recovery agents, and to set automatic certificate request settings, trusted root certification authorities, and enterprise trust settings. Public key policy is the only security setting available in user configuration.
- **IP Security Policies:** These policies are used to configure IP security for TCP/IP-based communication between Windows 2000 servers, clients, and domain controllers.

Figure 12-3 System Services security settings

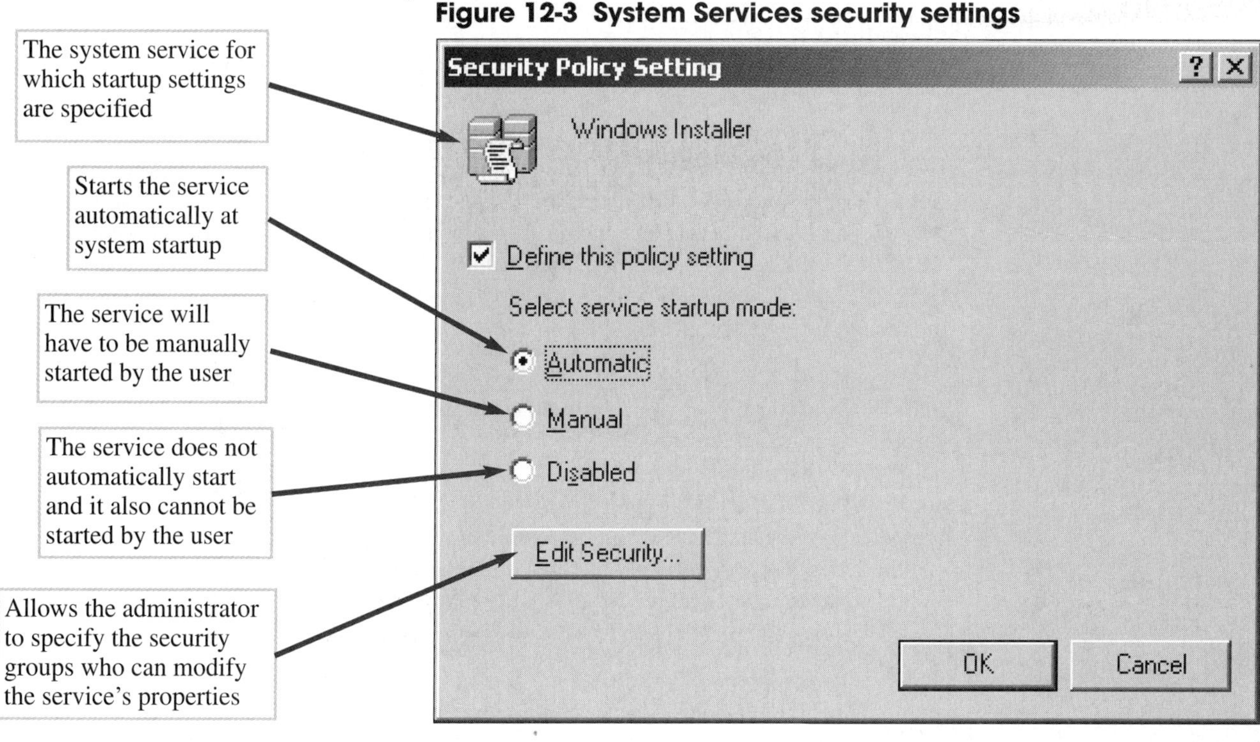
The system service for which startup settings are specified
Starts the service automatically at system startup
The service will have to be manually started by the user
The service does not automatically start and it also cannot be started by the user
Allows the administrator to specify the security groups who can modify the service's properties
Security Policy Setting
Windows Installer
Define this policy setting
Select service startup mode:
Automatic
Manual
Disabled
Edit Security...
OK
Cancel

Figure 12-4 Files and Folders permissions settings

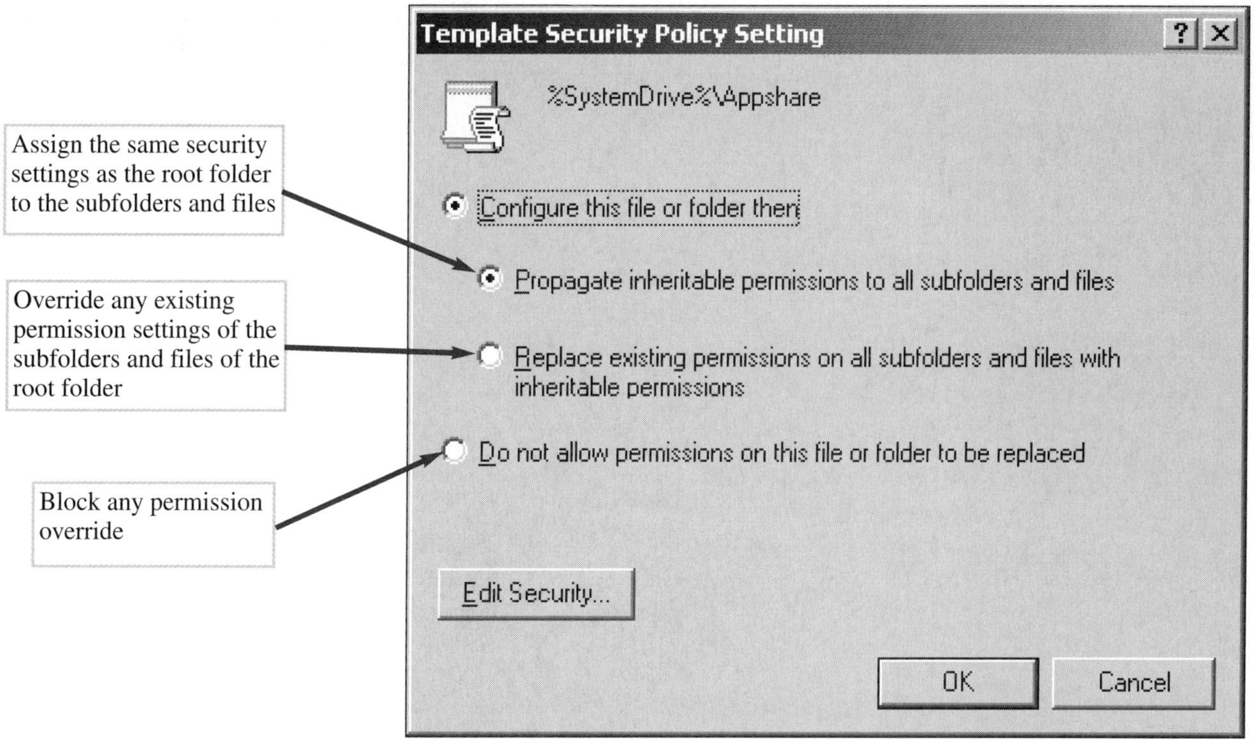

Assign the same security settings as the root folder to the subfolders and files

Override any existing permission settings of the subfolders and files of the root folder

Block any permission override

Template Security Policy Setting

%SystemDrive%\Appshare

Configure this file or folder then:

Propagate inheritable permissions to all subfolders and files

Replace existing permissions on all subfolders and files with inheritable permissions

Do not allow permissions on this file or folder to be replaced

Edit Security...

OK

Cancel

skill 2 Introducing the Windows 2000 Auditing Tool

exam objective

Basic knowledge

overview

In addition to setting up security policies in an enterprise, you need to monitor security-related events on the network. Security events include system events, account creation, network logon attempts, object access attempts, and policy changes. You can monitor these security events by using the Windows 2000 **Auditing** tool to set **audit policy** for the computers in the network. Audit policy defines which user activities and system events to monitor on a computer.

Setting audit policies helps you log intrusions into a network by unauthorized users. In some cases, these logs can help you determine when someone is trying to gain unauthorized access before they actually do, allowing you to take preventive action. In other cases, logging may help you define which resources should have additional protection against attacks. After an attack is detected, auditing analysis can help you determine the extent to which network resources have been affected. You can correlate information, such as the method of the attack and the security policy currently in effect on the network, to identify which security measures should be taken in order to reduce risk in the future.

While planning an audit policy for your organization, you need to consider the security level of the systems. **Table 12-2** discusses the general guidelines to be followed, while planning an audit policy and the scope of each of these guidelines.

Audit results are stored as log entries in the security log of Event Viewer (**Figure 12-5**). The entries consist of details of activities performed such as account logon attempts and file access attempts by users. Details about the user who performed the activity, the time of activity, and the result of the activity, either successful, failed, or both, are stored in the entries. The security log audit results allow you to identify existing security problems in the overall network, as well as on individual computers.

Table 12-2 Guidelines for an Audit Policy Plan

Scope
This allows you to maintain a balance between auditing requirements and system resources, since auditing is a process that uses a lot of resources.
Successful events show the users who accessed and used a resource successfully. Failed events alert you to potential security intrusions because they show failed attempts by a user, which could mean an unauthorized attempt by that user. Monitoring both events allows you to track all access attempts to the object.
Monitoring the trends can help you project future system requirements.
Auditing allows you to analyze system usage over a period of time, and take preventive or corrective measures against future security problems.
Typically, you will want to audit only high-risk services, as auditing uses disk space, and sorting through the logs takes considerable administrative resources.
Auditing allows you to keep a track of all administrative changes in a domain such as new policies and permission changes.

Figure 12-5 Storing the audit results

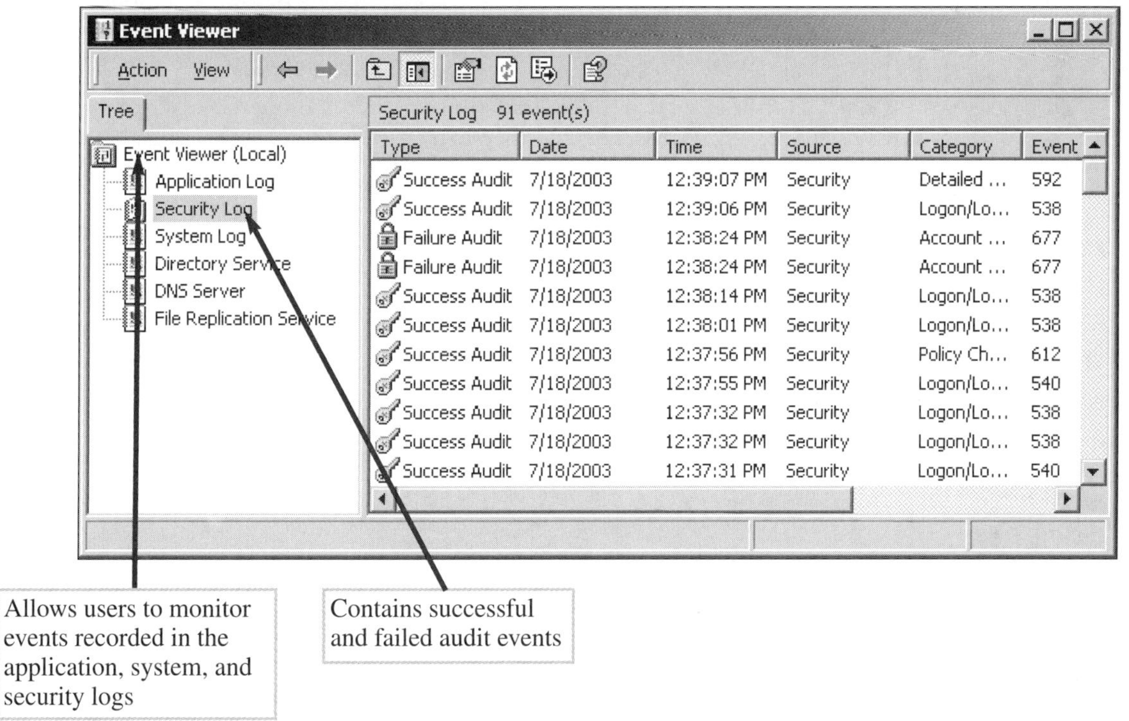

skill 3

Setting up an Audit Policy for a Domain Controller

exam objective

Implement an audit policy.

overview

Events, such as user logons, need to be monitored in order to track unauthorized users who attempt to access the domain through a domain controller. A domain controller is used to validate user logons and store user accounts and network details. You can set an audit policy to monitor such events on the domain controller.

Windows 2000 Server enables you to set up an audit policy for a domain controller using Group Policy. To enable audit policies for domain controllers, you will typically link the GPO to the default Domain Controllers OU.

Setting up auditing is a two-step process. Before setting an audit policy, you need to ensure that you have the Manage Auditing And Security Log right for the system. Then, you should modify the audit policy to track particular events, listed in **Table 12-3** by selecting to audit successful events, failed events, or both. Next, you need to go into the specific resource you wish to audit, such as files on the drive, and enable auditing by selecting what type of event you would like to track, and the user group or groups you would like to track that event for. For instance, you might wish to track file deletions, but not read events, and only track those events performed by the Administrators group. A good practice is to be as selective as possible in your auditing, as each audited event adds clutter to the logs and requires time to sort through and examine.

tip

The Manage Auditing and Security log is a default right for the Administrators user group.

how to

Set up an Audit Policy for a domain controller.

1. Log on to the mydomain.com domain from ServerA as an Administrator.
2. Click **Start**, point to **Programs**, point to **Administrative Tools**, and then click the **Active Directory Users and Computers** command.
3. Right-click the **Domain Controllers** container in the **Console** tree, and then click the **Properties** command to open the **Domain Controllers Properties** dialog box.
4. Click the **Group Policy** tab, and then click **New** to create a new Group Policy object. A new listing named **New Group Policy Object** appears in the **Group Policy Object Links** window (**Figure 12-6**).
5. Type **DCSecGPO** as the new name of the GPO and press **[Enter]** to accept the change.
6. Click “Options” and then click the “No Override” check box.
7. Select **DCSecGPO**, and then click **Edit...** to open the **Group Policy** snap-in.
8. Click the **Computer Configuration** node, double-click the **Windows Settings** node under **Computer Configuration**, and then double-click the **Security Settings** node.

Table 12-3 Windows 2000 Audit Events and Their Parameters

Event	Monitoring parameters	Example
Account logon	Logon validation requests from users and computers to the domain controller.	A user attempts to log on to a computer and specifies a domain-level account.
Account management	User or group accounts in the domain created, modified, removed, or disabled. Account password creation, deletion, and modification are also managed.	The administrator creates a new user account for a domain.
Directory service access	User access to specific Active Directory objects. To enable this policy you must select individual AD objects to audit.	A user accesses the properties of a user object.
Logon	User logon/logoff attempts to a local computer using the local accounts database.	A user logs on to a computer by selecting the "this computer" option in the domain drop-down box, and any time a user logs on locally to a Domain Controller.
Object access	User access attempts to files and folders on an NTFS drive or a printer. The policy is applied on an individual object basis.	A user prints a document on a network printer.
Policy change	User security option changes, user rights changes, and audit policies changes.	A user modifies a machine's auditing settings.
Privilege use	Usage of privileges and user rights by a member of the domain.	A user changes the system date of a computer.
Process tracking	Application program execution details.	A programmer tracks the execution of an application during testing of the application.
System events	System events such as startup or shutdown, and events that affect Windows security or the security log.	The security log is cleared.

Figure 12-6 Creating a GPO for a domain controller

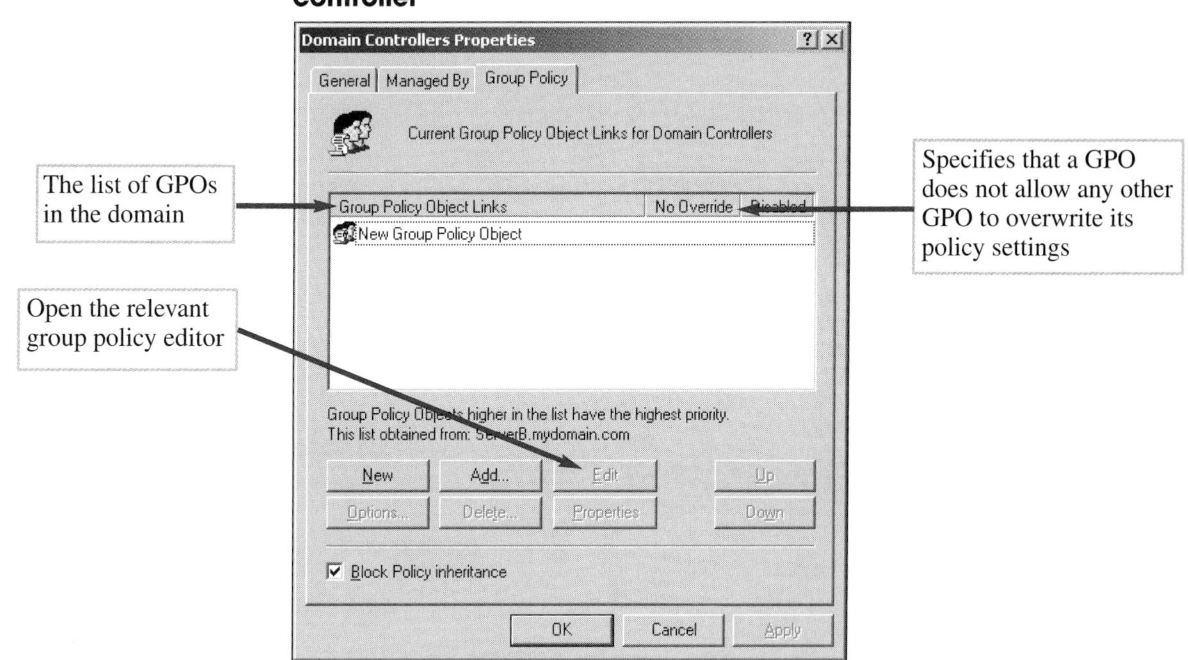

Exam 70-217

skill 3 Setting up an Audit Policy for a Domain Controller (cont'd)

exam objective

Implement an audit policy.

how to

9. Double-click the **Local Policies** node, and then click the **Audit Policy** node to list the audit policy settings in the details pane as shown in **Figure 12-7**.
10. Right-click the **Audit account logon events** policy in the details pane and click the **Security** command to open the **Security Policy Setting** dialog box. This setting will track logon attempts made by users to a domain.
11. Select the **Define these policy settings** check box to activate this audit policy setting.
12. Under **Audit these attempts**, select both the **Success** and **Failure** check boxes to enable auditing of both successful and failed logon attempts, as shown in **Figure 12-8**.
13. Click OK to add the settings to the audit policy.
14. Click the **Close** button ☒ to close the **Group Policy** snap-in.
15. Click Close to close the **Domain Controllers Properties** dialog box.
16. Close the **Group Policy** console.
17. Close the **Active Directory Users and Computers** console. You have created a GPO and set up an audit policy for a domain controller to audit logon attempts.

more

An audit policy takes effect once it is applied to the computer. By default, an audit policy is applied to computers in a domain every 90-120 minutes, and to domain controllers every five minutes. This is because the default group policy refresh interval for computers is 90 minutes with a 30 minute randomized offset, and the interval for domain controllers is a flat five minutes. If the audit policy needs to be applied immediately, you either can restart the computer or run the secedit command at the command prompt with the /refreshpolicy machine_policy or /refreshpolicy user_policy flags (**Figure 12-9**).

You can perform auditing on member servers and workstations remotely by configuring a GPO to apply to those machines, and linking it to an appropriate container in AD such as an OU created for the server computer accounts. Using OU's, you can selectively apply audit policies to affect only those machines that contain sensitive information.

caution

Once domain-level policy settings are defined and propagated, they override any conflicting local policy settings.

Figure 12-7 List of audit policy settings

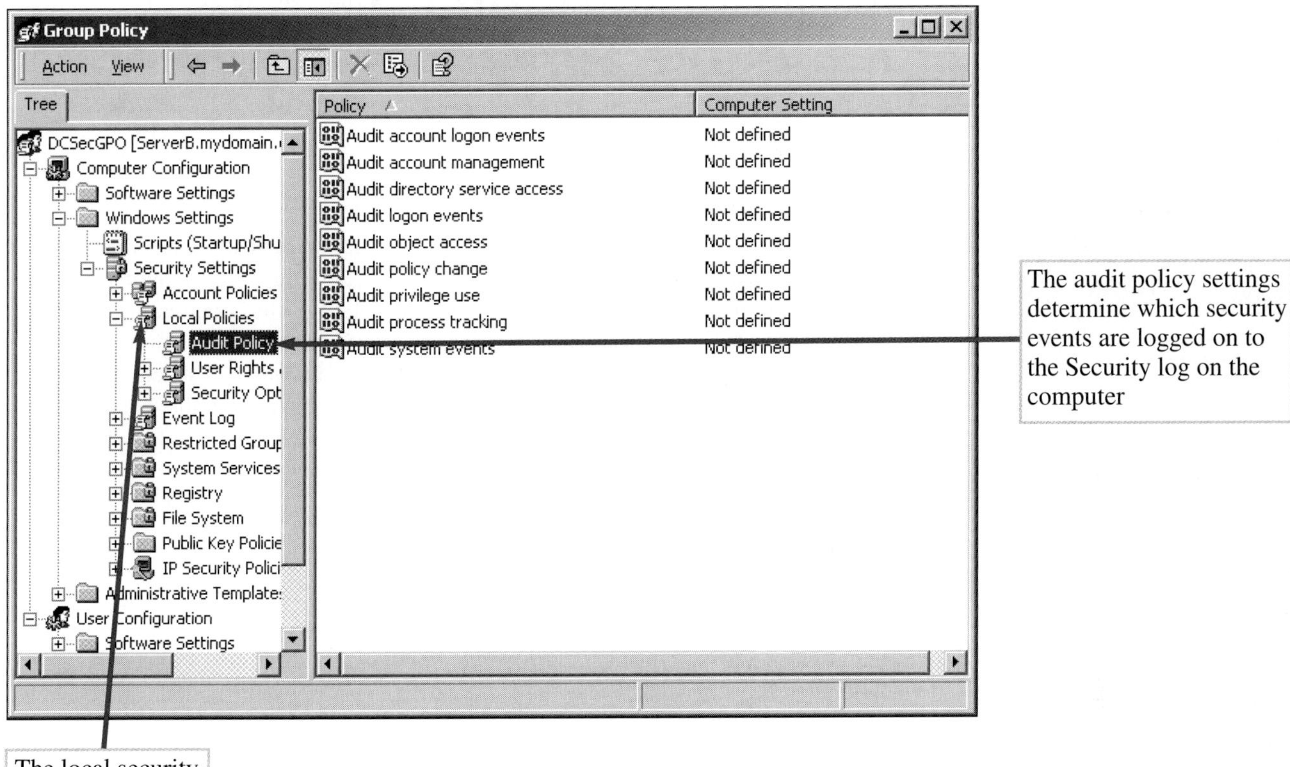

Figure 12-8 Enabling auditing of logon attempts

Figure 12-9 Immediate policy propagation

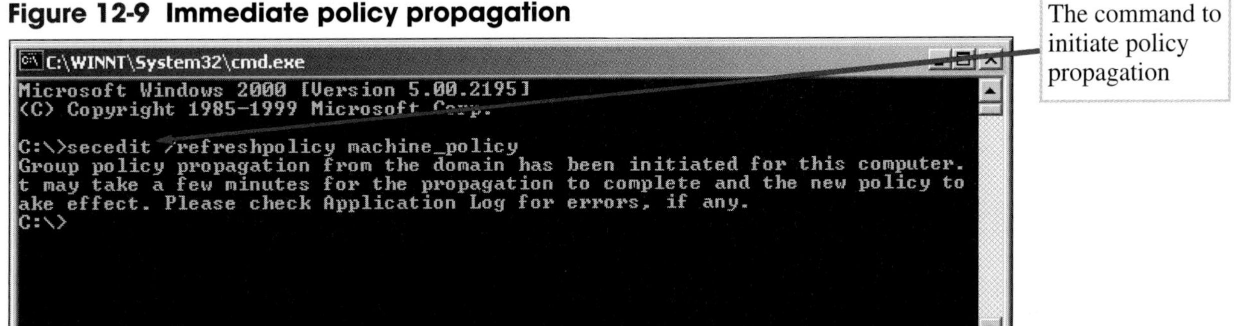

skill 4 Setting up an Audit Policy for a Stand-Alone Server or Computer

exam objective

Implement an audit policy.

overview

Stand-alone servers and computers running Windows 2000 Professional are not part of a domain. Therefore, you cannot use a domain controller-based audit policy to audit events and activities on these computers. You should still set audit policy for the stand-alone computers to monitor network access attempts and local security events, because stand-alone computers and the network computers will still be able to access each other. You can set auditing for the stand-alone computers using a local audit policy that is applicable only to that computer.

how to

Set up an audit policy for a stand-alone server.

1. Log on to the server [Server1] as an Administrator.
2. Click Start, point to **Programs**, point to **Administrative Tools**, and then click the **Local Security Policy** command to open the **Local Security Settings** console.
3. In the **Local Security Settings** console tree, double-click the **Local Policies** node, and then double-click the **Audit Policy** node to view the security settings that can be audited **(Figure 12-10)**.
4. In the details pane, double-click the **Audit logon events** setting to open the **Local Security Policy Setting** dialog box.
5. Select both the **Success** and **Failure** check boxes as shown in **Figure 12-11**. This setting will enable auditing of successful and failed logon attempts by users on the computer.
6. Click OK to apply the setting.
7. Click the Close button X to close the **Local Security Settings** console.
8. Click Start, and then click the **Run** command to open the **Run** dialog box.
9. Type the **"secedit /refreshpolicy machine_policy"** command in the **Open** text box to refresh the policy settings. The audit policy settings are immediately applied to the stand-alone server for auditing logon attempts.
10. Close the command prompt when finished.

Figure 12-10 Security settings in the Local Security Settings console

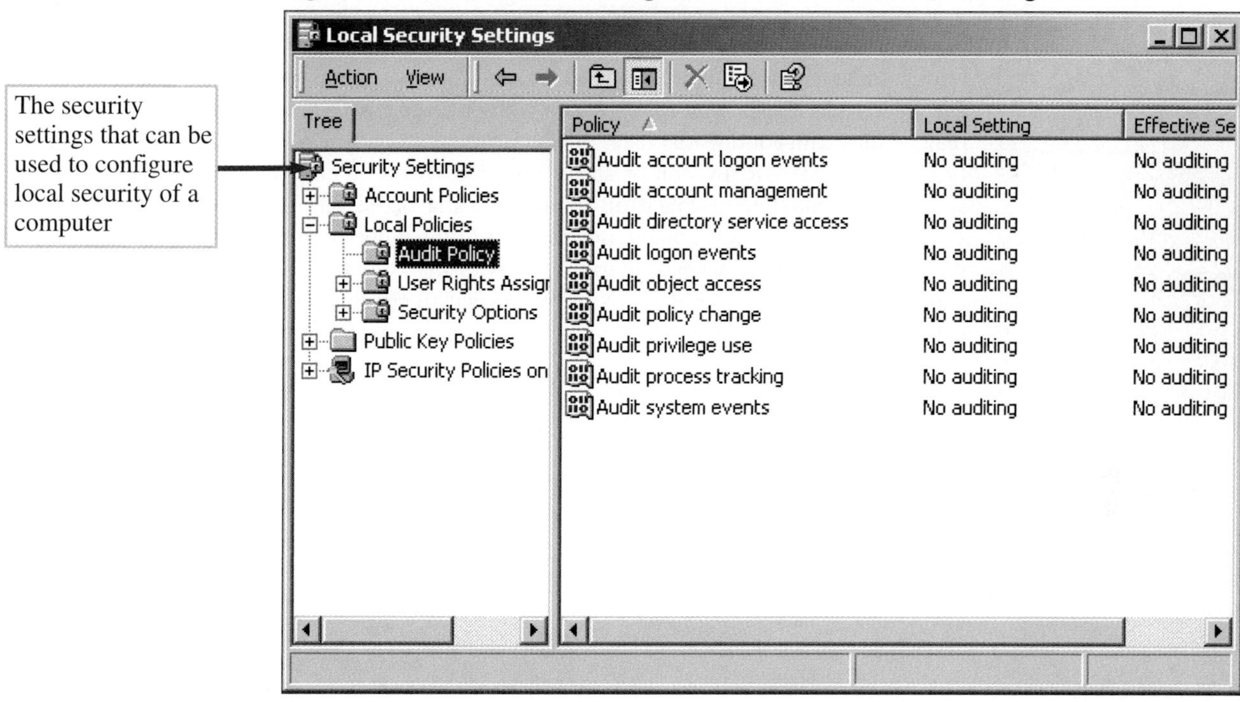

Figure 12-11 Enabling auditing of logon attempts

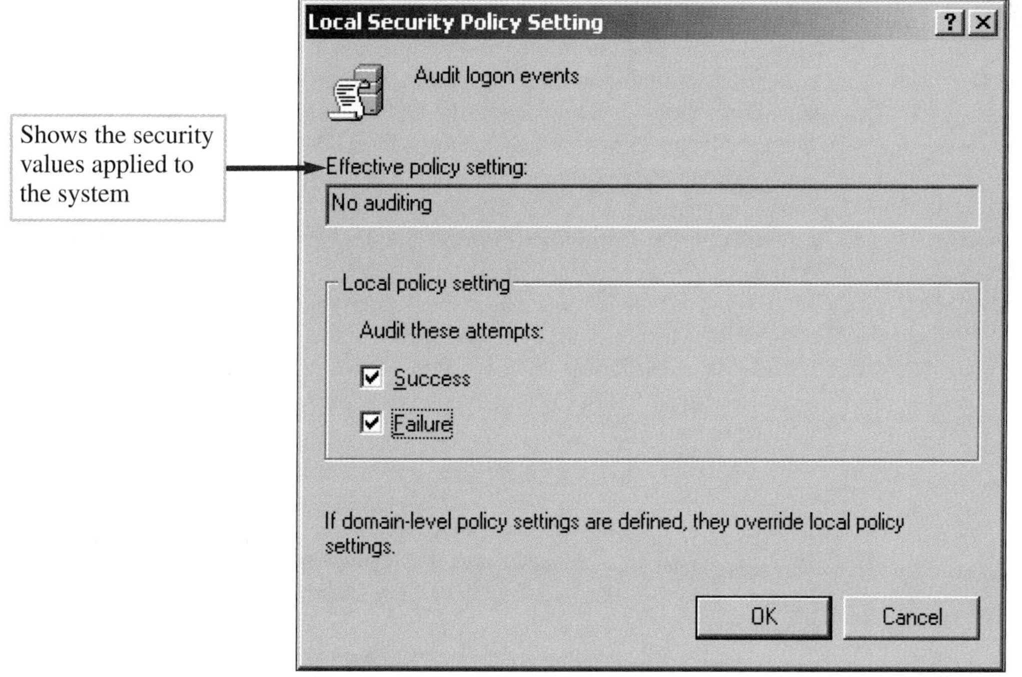

skill 5 Creating an Audit Policy for Files and Folders

exam objective

Implement an audit policy.

overview

Files and folders form an integral part of all operations you perform using your computer. Files contain the data you need to work on, and folders contain files arranged logically. Files and folders also enable you to share data with other users in an organization. However, there may be files with confidential data, to which you will not want all employees to have access. For example, the HR division of an organization will have employee information files that should not be made accessible to all employees in the organization. Therefore, the folders that store these files should be made inaccessible to unauthorized users. For example, our HR folder should only be accessible to members of the Human Resources group. Creating an audit policy for files and folders is an effective way to maintain the confidentiality of sensitive data.

Windows 2000 Server enables you to apply security permissions to files and folders so that you can assign or deny permissions to users who attempt to access them. To audit files and folders, you first need to enable the Audit Object Access event category in the security policy of the computer or GPO **(Figure 12-12)**. You then set audit policies for these files and folders to ensure that access is only obtained by authorized users.

The security events that you can monitor for files and folders include permission settings for folder access, directory traversal, folder creation, folder deletion, file deletion, and read attributes.

caution

You can set audit policies on NTFS but not on FAT files, because a FAT file system does not include permissions assignment capabilities.

how to

Create an audit policy for a folder.

1. Log on to the mydomain.com domain from ServerA as an Administrator.
2. Click **Start**, point to **Programs**, point to **Administrative Tools**, and then click the **Active Directory Users and Computers** command to open the **Active Directory Users and Computers** console.
3. Right-click the **Domain Controllers** container in the console tree and then click the **Properties** command to open the **Domain Controllers Properties** dialog box. This dialog box will allow you to access the GPOs linked to the Domain Controllers OU.
4. Click the **Group Policy** tab, click the **DCSecGPO** GPO link in the list, and then click **Edit...** to open the Group Policy snap-in console. You can edit the GPO settings using the snap-in console.
5. In the **Computer Configuration** node of the Group Policy snap-in, double-click the **Windows Settings** node, and then double-click the **Security Settings** node.
6. Click the **Local Policies** node under the **Security Settings** node, and then click the **Audit Policy** node to list the audit policy settings in the details pane.
7. Right-click the **Audit object access** setting in the details pane, and then click **Security** to open the **Security Policy Setting** dialog box. This setting will enable auditing of files and folders **(Figure 12-13)**.
8. Select the **Define these policy settings** check box to activate the audit policy setting.
9. In the **Audit these attempts** section, select both the **Success** and **Failure** check boxes to enable auditing of both successful and failed object access attempts.
10. Click **OK** to add the settings to the audit policy. This audit setting will activate object access auditing, which is necessary before setting audit policies for files and folders.
11. Right-click the **File System** node of the Security Settings container, and then click the **Add File** command to open the **Add a file or folder to this template** dialog box.

Figure 12-12 Enabling the Audit Object Access event

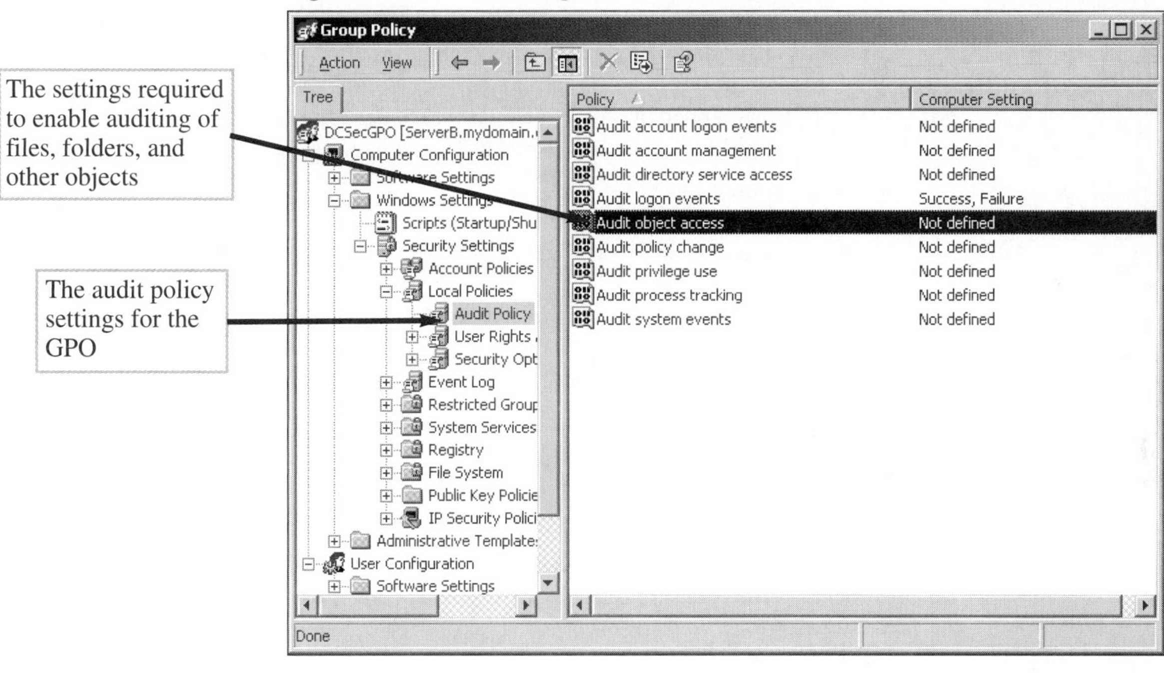

Figure 12-13 Enabling access attempts for files and folders

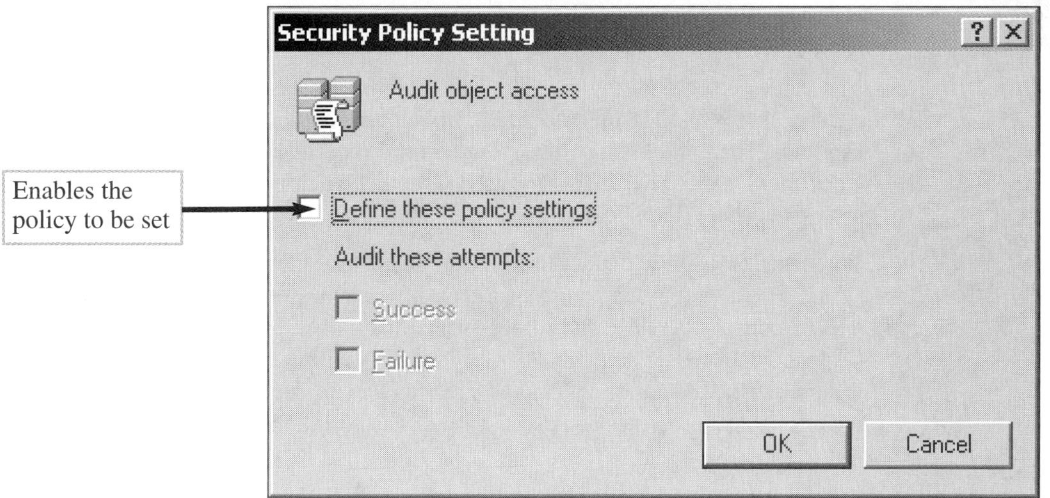

skill 5

Creating an Audit Policy for Files and Folders *(cont'd)*

exam objective

Implement an audit policy.

how to

12. Type **C:\WINNT** in the text box, and then click [OK]. The **Database Security for %SystemRoot%** dialog box opens. This dialog box allows you to modify the properties of the folder.
13. Click [Advanced...] to open the **Access Control Settings for %SystemRoot%** dialog box.
14. Click the **Auditing** tab. Click [Add...] to add security groups that auditing will be enabled for on this object.
15. In the **Select User**, **Computer**, **or Group** dialog box, click the **Backup Operators** security group listing, and then click [OK] to add the **Backup Operators** security group to the Auditing Entries list.
16. In the **Access** pane of the **Auditing Entry for WINNT** dialog box, select both the **Successful** and **Failed** check boxes for the **Create folders/Append Data**, **Delete Subfolders and Files**, and **Change Permissions** access settings, as shown in **Figure 12-14**. This will monitor both the successful and failed states of the audit.
17. Click [OK] to close the **Auditing Entry** dialog box, click [OK] to close the **Access Control Settings** dialog box **(Figure 12-15)**, and then click [OK] to close the **Database Security** dialog box.
18. The **Template Security Policy Setting** dialog box opens, enabling you to set the policy inheritance permissions for the folder. Accept the default settings and click [OK] to save these settings.
19. Click [X] to close the GPO. You have activated Object Access Auditing and set up an audit policy for the WINNT folder.
20. Close the Domain Controllers Properties window and the Active Directory Users and Computers console.

more

You can also set Auditing for files and folders by using Windows Explorer. For example, right-click the WINNT folder on the C drive of the computer in the Folders pane of Windows Explorer. Then, click Properties to open the Properties dialog box for the WINNT folder. Click the Security tab, click Advanced, and then click the Auditing tab to specify the audit settings for the WINNT folder.

Whenever an audit event set to monitor files and folders is triggered by user activity or a system event, a detailed record of the audit event is stored in the security log in the Event Viewer console. The file and folder events that can be audited in a computer are displayed **(Figure 12-14)**. User activities that can trigger auditing include events such as unauthorized folder access, viewing of documents, creating new folders and files within a folder, changing of file or folder attributes and permissions, and file and folder deletions.

Figure 12-14 Setting Audit Object Access security policy

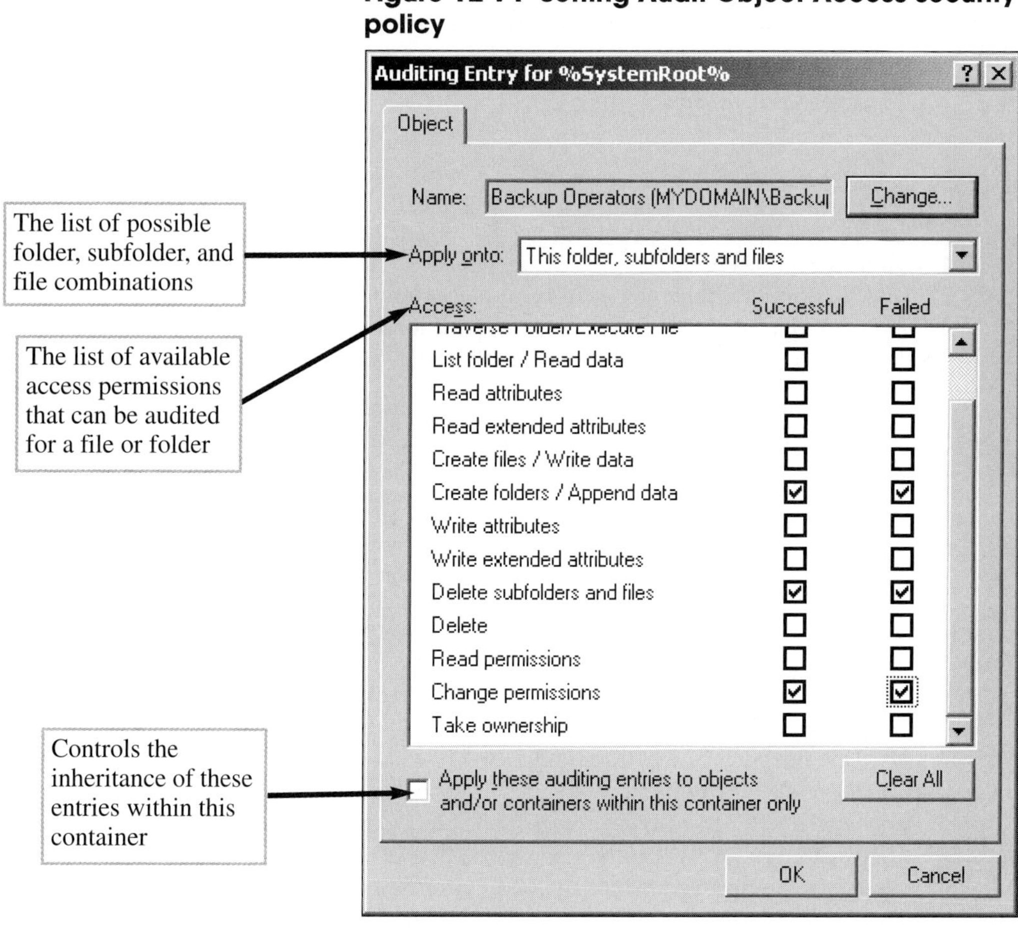

Figure 12-15 Setting up auditing for groups

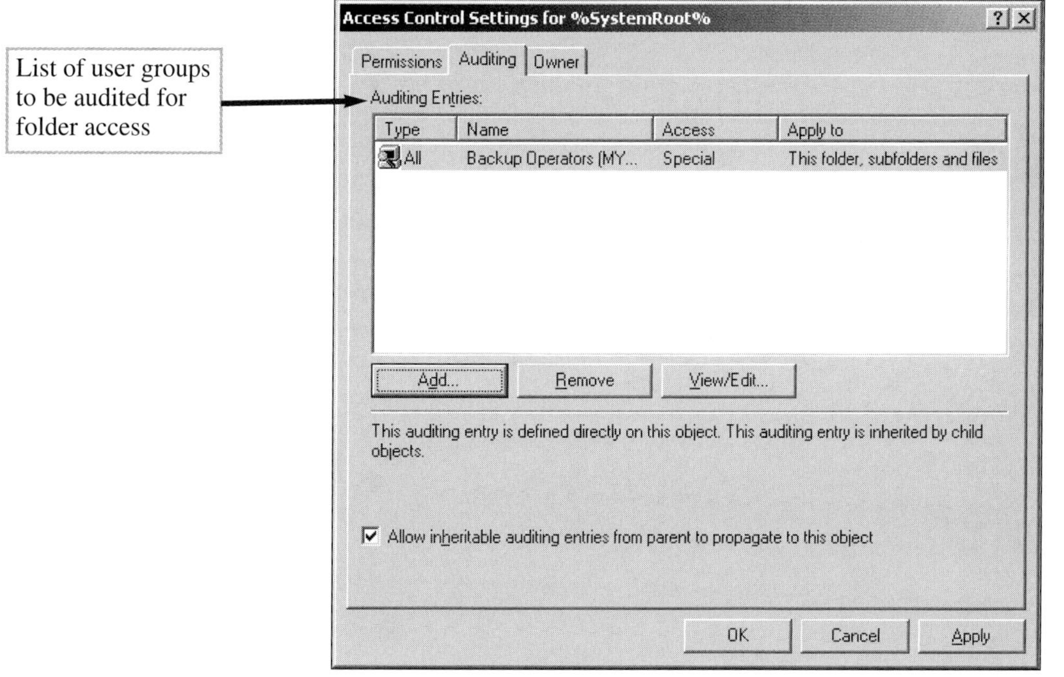

skill 6 Auditing User Access to Active Directory Objects

exam objective

Implement an audit policy.

overview

Active Directory objects, such as users, computers, OUs, groups, and published printers, are the essential building blocks of a Windows 2000 network. You can set audit policies for Active Directory objects to monitor the Windows 2000 network. An audit policy set for an Active Directory object is inherited by its child object through **Policy Inheritance** by default. Since certain Active Directory objects are of a critical nature, you need to specify audit policy for the Active Directory object based explicitly on the functionality of the object.

Consider an example in which you need to audit a specialized printer such as a high-end color laser printer. You would want to audit failed print jobs, successful and failed permission changes, successful delete permissions, and other such critical printer events in order to ensure security of the printer and to optimize its usage. You can use the results of the printer audit policy to analyze printer access attempts and prevent unauthorized access to printers.

how to

Set up auditing for user access on a printer.

1. Log on to the mydomain.com domain on ServerA as an Administrator.
2. Click Start, point to **Programs**, point to **Administrative Tools**, and click on **Active Directory Users and Computers**.
3. Right click **mydomain.com** at the very top and click **Find**.
4. Use the **Objects of type** drop down box to choose **Printers** and then click Find Now.
5. Right-click on **NWPrinter** and choose **Properties**.
6. Click the **Security** tab of the **NWPrinter Properties** dialog box to view the list of permitted security groups who can access the active directory object associated with this published printer and their associated permissions.
7. Click Advanced... to open the **Access Control Settings for NWPrinter** dialog box.
8. Click the **Auditing** tab (**Figure 12-16**), and then click Add... to add a group to be audited.
9. In the **Select User**, **Computer**, **or Group** dialog box, click the **Domain Users** security group, and then click OK to monitor access to the printer by users of the domain.
10. In the **Access** pane of the **Auditing Entry for NWPrinter** dialog box, select both the **Successful** and **Failed** check boxes for the **Print** access setting (**Figure 12-17**). This will monitor both the successful and failed states of the event.
11. Click OK to close the **Auditing Entry for NWPrinter** dialog box.
12. Click OK to close the **Access Control Settings for NWPrinter** dialog box.
13. Click OK to close the **NWPrinter Properties** dialog box. You now have set up an audit policy for an Active Directory printer on the network.
14. Close the Active Directory Users and Computers window.

caution

You may receive a Security message box if you have not configured auditing for directory service access on your domain.

Figure 12-16 Add a group to be audited

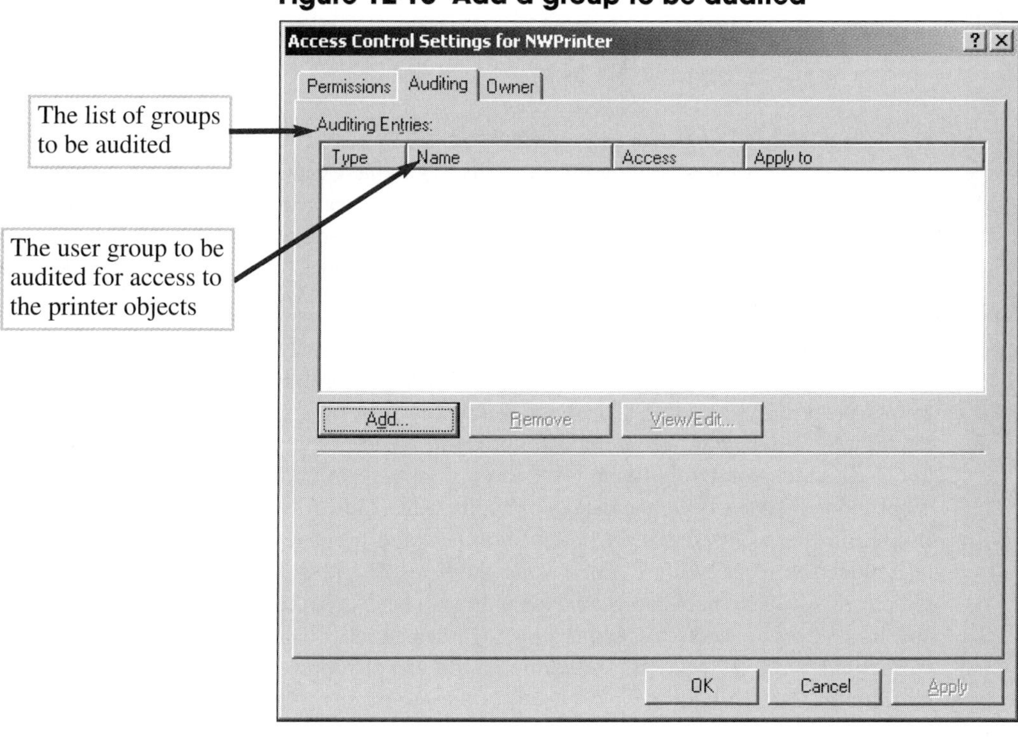

Figure 12-17 Select the events to be audited

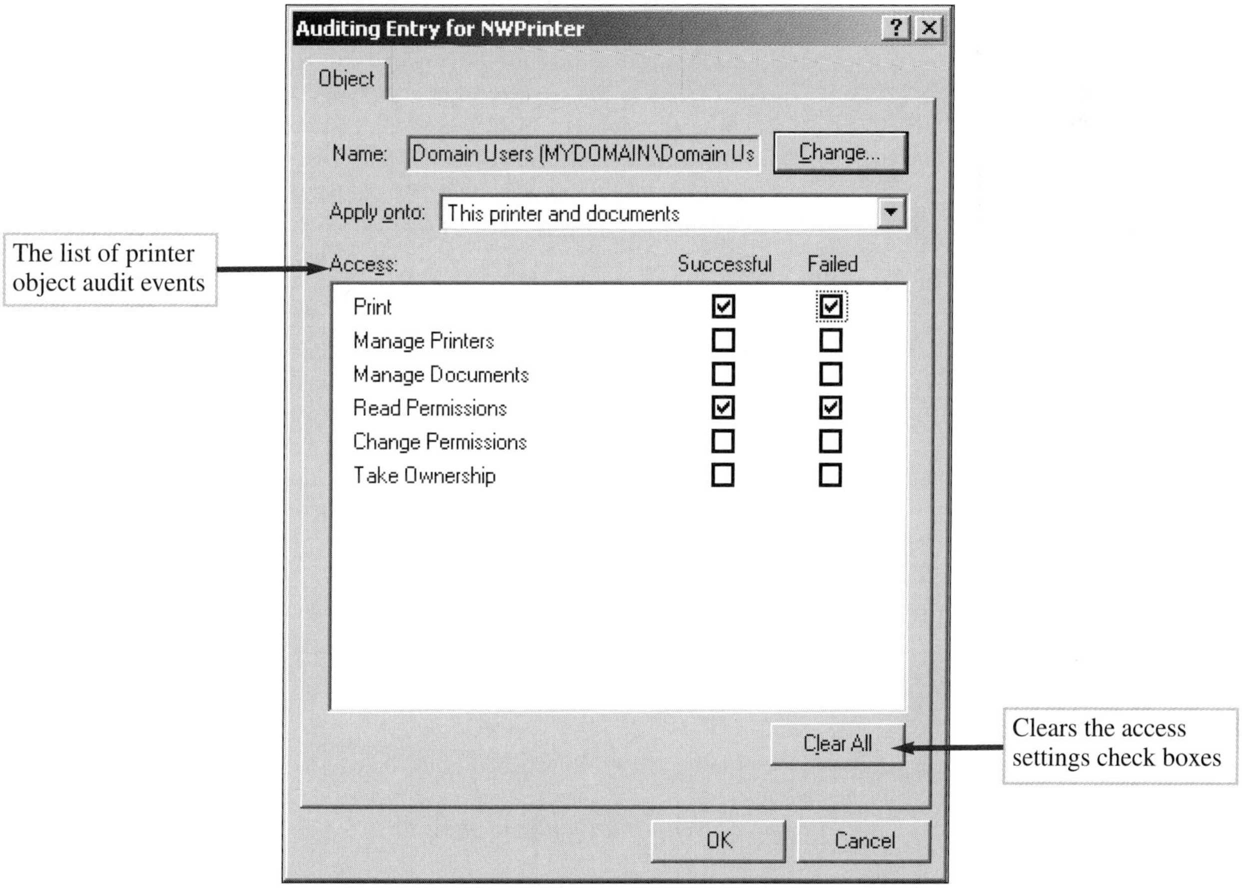

Auditing Entry for NWPrinter

Object

Name: Domain Users (MYDOMAIN\Domain Us Change...

Apply onto: This printer and documents

Access: Successful Failed

Access	Successful	Failed
Print	☑	☑
Manage Printers	☐	☐
Manage Documents	☐	☐
Read Permissions	☑	☑
Change Permissions	☐	☐
Take Ownership	☐	☐

Clear All

OK Cancel

The list of printer object audit events

Clears the access settings check boxes

skill 7

Using Security Logs to Handle Events

exam objective

Monitor and analyze security events.

overview

Windows 2000 provides you with the security log in the Event Viewer, which enables you to store the details of audit event results of a computer as log entries. Each log entry is a summary of an audit with information about the type of audit event (successful or failed), the date and time of the event, the user, and the computer **(Figure 12-18)**. You can view the details of an event in the Event Properties window. Note that auditing must be enabled in Group Policy.

The Security log is a 512 kilobyte (KB) file by default with a capacity to store up to three events per kilobyte. If this size is too small for your needs, you can increase it up to a maximum of 4GB.You need administrator rights to access the security log. As soon as you apply an audit policy to a computer and configure specific objects or events to audit, the security log begins storing the details of audit events. However, the storage of these details is limited to the events the audit policy monitors and the size of the security log. You can customize the security log by increasing the log size and the log event overwrite settings, which allow you to enable or disable log entries to be overwritten by new events. You can also specify that the connection speed is slow to indicate that you are accessing a security log file stored on a network location. Furthermore, you can also prevent the log file from filling up and failing to store later events by setting the log events to be overwritten after a certain amount of time or after the log fills to capacity. You can make these setting changes in the Security Log Properties dialog box.

If you clear the log manually or the events are overwritten, the events are erased permanently from the log. In order to maintain a track of audit events, you need to archive the security log from time to time.

You can locate specific events in the security log by using the Find tool **(Figure 12-19)**. You can also view specific events in the security log by applying the Filter tool from the Event Viewer console. The filtered results are displayed as log entries; all other entries are hidden. You can return later to the original list from the Filter tool window, if required. Both the Find and Filter tools allow you to specify options, such as event type, event source, event category, event ID, user, and the computer on which the event occurred, to locate an event.

tip

In high-security computers, such as servers, you can enable the security policy option to shut down the computer when the security log is full. This is done to prevent someone from filling the log with insignificant events (such as repeated attempts to log on as guest), and then accessing resources unaudited.

how to

Locate, filter, configure, and archive events in a log using the Event Viewer console.

1. Log on to the mydomain.com domain from ServerA as an Administrator.
2. Click Start, point to **Programs**, point to **Administrative Tools**, and then click the **Event Viewer** command to open the **Event Viewer** console.
3. Click **Security Log** in the **Console** tree to view the security log events in the details pane.
4. Double-click the first log entry to open the **Event Properties** window. Here, you can view the details of the first audit event entry.
5. Click OK to close the **Event Properties** window.
6. Open the **View** menu and click the **Find** command to open the **Find in local Security Log** dialog box.
7. Click **Security** in the **Event source** list box and **Object Access** in the **Category** list box. The **Security event source** and **Object access category** options will be the basis for the Find operation.
8. Click Find Next to view the results one after the other. The results will be highlighted in the details pane.
9. Click Close to close the **Find in local security log** dialog box.

Figure 12-18 Summary of an audit of events in the Security log

Event Viewer

Action View

Tree: Event Viewer (Local) — Application Log, Security Log, System Log, Directory Service, DNS Server, File Replication S

Security Log 325 event(s)

Type	Date	Time	Source	Category	Event	User
Failure Audit	7/18/2003	12:38:24 PM	Secu...	Account Log...	677	SYSTEM
Failure Audit	7/18/2003	12:38:24 PM	Secu...	Account Log...	677	SYSTEM
Success Audit	7/18/2003	1:39:07 PM	Secu...	Policy Change	612	SYSTEM
Success Audit	7/18/2003	1:39:06 PM	Secu...	Directory Se...	565	SYSTEM
Success Audit	7/18/2003	1:39:06 PM	Secu...	Directory Se...	565	SYSTEM
Success Audit	7/18/2003	1:37:43 PM	Secu...	Policy Change	612	SYSTEM
Success Audit	7/18/2003	1:37:38 PM	Secu...	Privilege Use	576	SYSTEM
Success Audit	7/18/2003	1:37:38 PM	Secu...	Privilege Use	576	SYSTEM
Success Audit	7/18/2003	1:37:38 PM	Secu...	Privilege Use	576	SYSTEM
Success Audit	7/18/2003	1:37:38 PM	Secu...	Privilege Use	576	SYSTEM
Success Audit	7/18/2003	1:32:35 PM	Secu...	Policy Change	612	SYSTEM

List of summaries of all audit entries in the security log

Logs the unsuccessful attempt to perform an activity

Figure 12-19 Using the Find tool to view a specific event

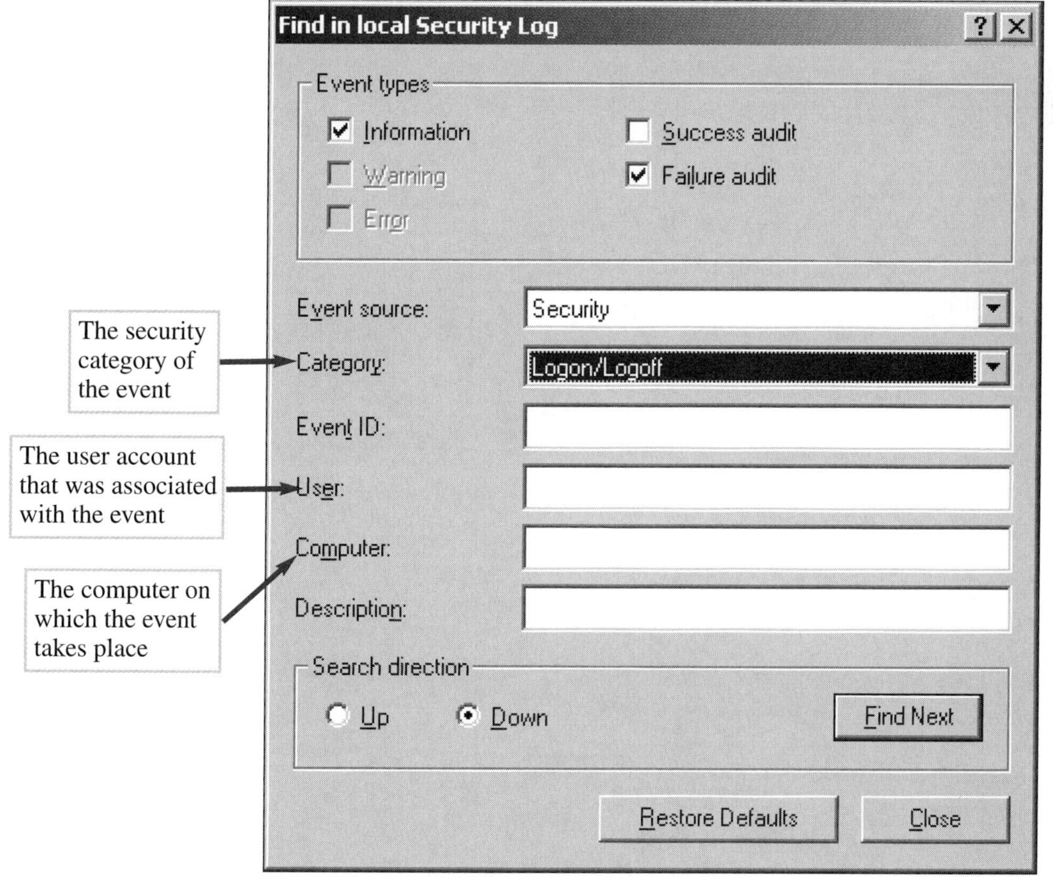

skill 7 Using Security Logs to Handle Events (cont'd)

exam objective

Monitor and analyze security events.

how to

10. Click **Filter** on the **View** menu to open the **Security Log Properties** dialog box. This dialog box will allow you to specify settings for the Filter operation.
11. Click the **Filter** tab, and then click the **Security Account Manager** option in the **Event source** list box to select it.
12. Type **CIPHER** in the **Computer** text box to filter only the events generated by the CIPHER computer.
13. Click the **Events On** option in the **From** drop-down list, and then click a week-old date in the date section **(Figure 12-20)**. These options will be the basis for the Filter operation.
14. Click [Apply]. The existing log entries will be cleared and the results of the Filter operation will be displayed in the details pane.
15. Click [OK] to close the **Security Log Properties** dialog box. Thus, you have used the Filter tool to view selected events.
16. Click **All Records** on the **View** menu of the **Event Viewer** to list all of the event log entries in the details pane once again.
17. Right-click the **Security Log** node in the **Console** tree, and then click the **Properties** command to open the **Security Log Properties** dialog box.
18. Type **1024** in the **Maximum log size** text box to increase the capacity of the security log **(Figure 12-21)**.
19. Click [OK] to save the new configuration of the security log settings.
20. Right-click the **Security Log** node in the **Console** tree, and then click the **Save Log File As** command to create a record of all the security log entries to date.
21. In the **Save Security Log As** dialog box that opens, type **ServerA-SecLog-date**, and click [Save] to save the security archive file as an .evt file. This is the default event log file extension. This allows you to archive the security event log **(Figure 12-22)**.
22. Click [X] to close the **Event Viewer** console. You now have located security log entries, applied filters to view selected entries, configured the security log settings, and archived the log entries using the Event Viewer.

Figure 12-20 Setting the parameters to view filtered events

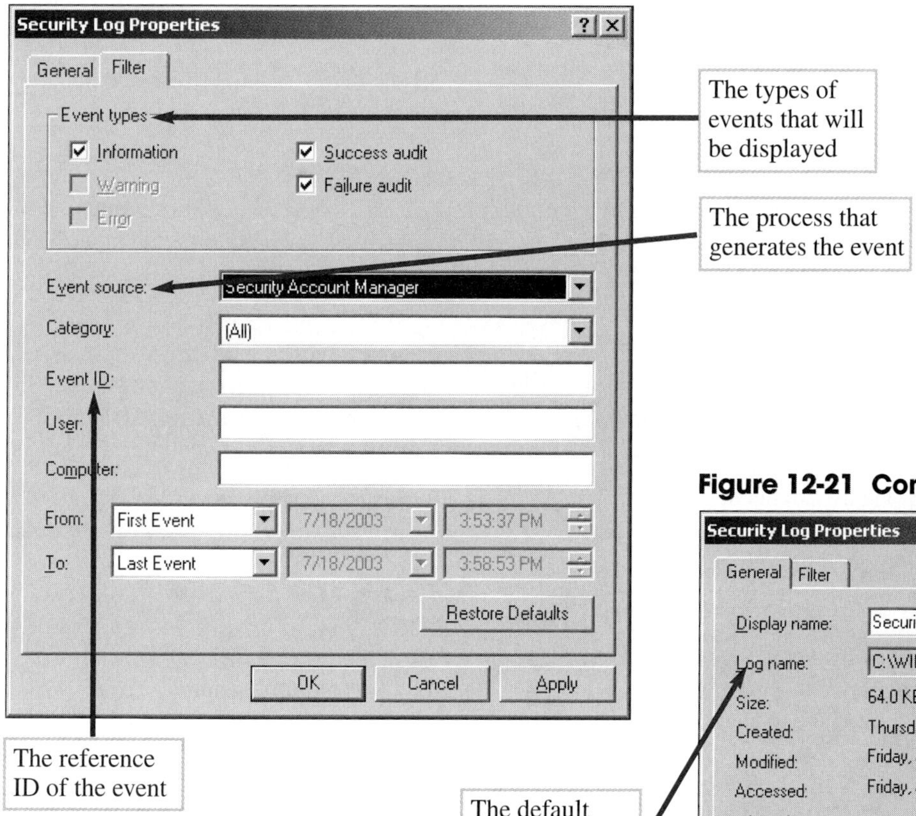

Security Log Properties

General | Filter

Event types: Information, Warning, Error, Success audit, Failure audit

Event source: Security Account Manager

Category: (All)

Event ID:

User:

Computer:

From: First Event 7/18/2003 3:53:37 PM

To: Last Event 7/18/2003 3:58:53 PM

Restore Defaults

OK Cancel Apply

The types of events that will be displayed

The process that generates the event

The reference ID of the event

Figure 12-21 Configuring Security log settings

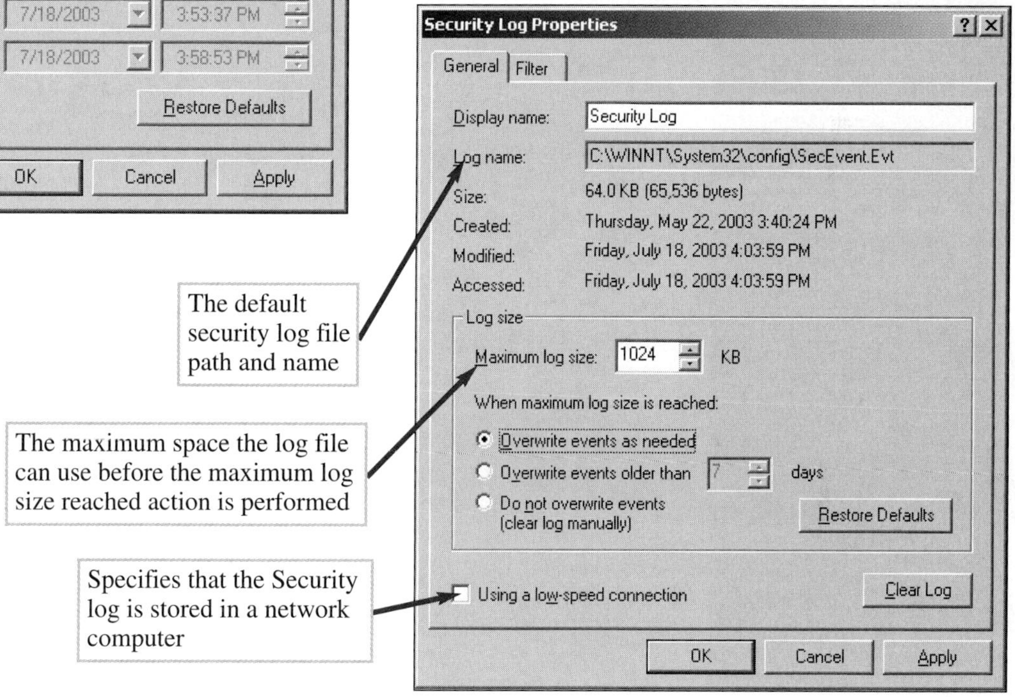

Security Log Properties

General | Filter

Display name: Security Log

Log name: C:\WINNT\System32\config\SecEvent.Evt

Size: 64.0 KB (65,536 bytes)

Created: Thursday, May 22, 2003 3:40:24 PM

Modified: Friday, July 18, 2003 4:03:59 PM

Accessed: Friday, July 18, 2003 4:03:59 PM

Log size

Maximum log size: 1024 KB

When maximum log size is reached:

Overwrite events as needed

Overwrite events older than 7 days

Do not overwrite events (clear log manually)

Restore Defaults

Using a low-speed connection

Clear Log

OK Cancel Apply

The default security log file path and name

The maximum space the log file can use before the maximum log size reached action is performed

Specifies that the Security log is stored in a network computer

Figure 12-22 Archiving the security event log

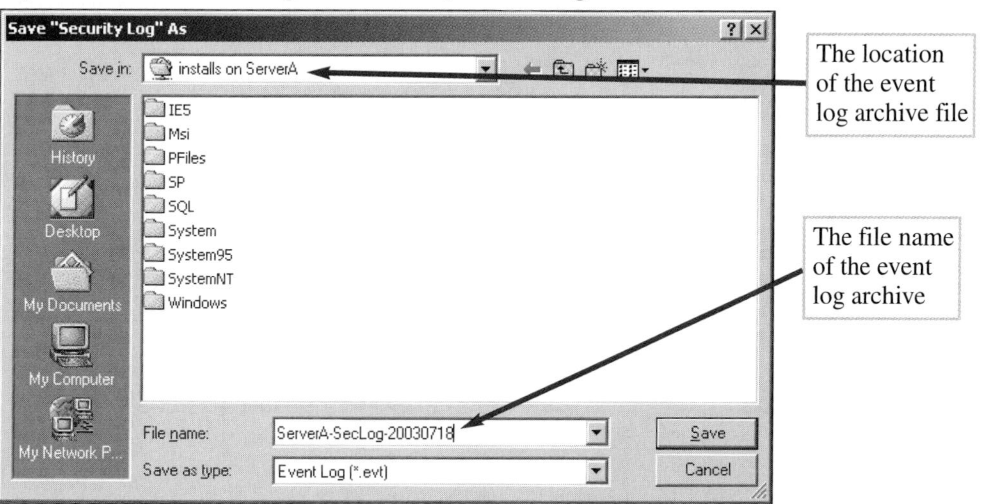

skill 8 Assigning User Rights to Users and Groups

exam objective

Apply security policies by using Group Policy.

overview

User rights are very different from, but often confused with, permissions. Permissions, as we have already seen, allow a user access to certain resources. **User rights**, on the other hand, allow the user to perform certain restricted actions such as shutting down the system, or logging on locally.

The User Rights Assignment local policy allows an administrator to grant users rights. These rights should be assigned to user groups rather than to individual users in order to make administration easier. Once a user group is assigned these user rights, a user can be added to that user group in order to grant the user the same user rights. A user can be a part of multiple user groups.

Assigning user rights in this fashion helps you to allocate particular users to carry out specific functions. This increases the security of the system, because only specific users are authorized to carry out specific functions.

how to

tip
In a production network, you typically do not want to give the everyone group rights on your domain controller.

Assign a user right to the Everyone user group.

1. Log on to the mydomain.com domain from ServerA as an Administrator.
2. Click Start, point to **Programs**, point to **Administrative Tools**, and then click the **Active Directory Users and Computers** command to open the **Active Directory Users and Computers** console.
3. Right-click the **Domain Controllers** container in the console tree, and then click the **Properties** command to open the **Domain Controllers Properties** dialog box.
4. Click the **DCSecGPO** GPO in the **Group Policy Object links** list, and then click Edit... to open the Group Policy snap-in.
5. In the **Computer Configuration** node of the Group Policy snap-in, double-click the **Windows Settings** node, and then double-click the **Security Settings** node.
6. Click the **Local Policies** node, and then click the **User Rights Assignment** node to list the user rights settings in the details pane **(Figure 12-23)**.
7. Right-click the **Access this computer from the network** user right in the details pane to allow other users to remotely access this computer over the network. Click **Security** to open the **Security Policy Setting** dialog box.
8. Select the **Define these policy settings** check box to activate the policy setting.
9. Click Add... to open the **Add user or group** dialog box.
10. Click Browse... to open the **Select Users or Groups** dialog box.
11. Click the **Everyone** user group, and click Add... to add the user group Everyone. This will allow the members of the Everyone user group to access this computer over the network **(Figure 12-24)**.
12. Click Close to close the **Select Users or Groups** dialog box.
13. Click OK to close the **Add user or group** dialog box, and then click Close to close the **Security Policy Setting** dialog box.
14. Click X to close the Group Policy snap-in.
15. Click OK to close the **ServerA Properties** window.
16. Click X to close the **Active Directory Users and Computers** console. You have set user rights to audit user access to a computer over the network.

more

The user account **LocalSystem** is a special account created by Windows 2000 to access the operating system processes as a service. It is, therefore, associated with all the application and system procedures, and is automatically assigned most logon rights and privileges.

Figure 12-23 User rights assignment options

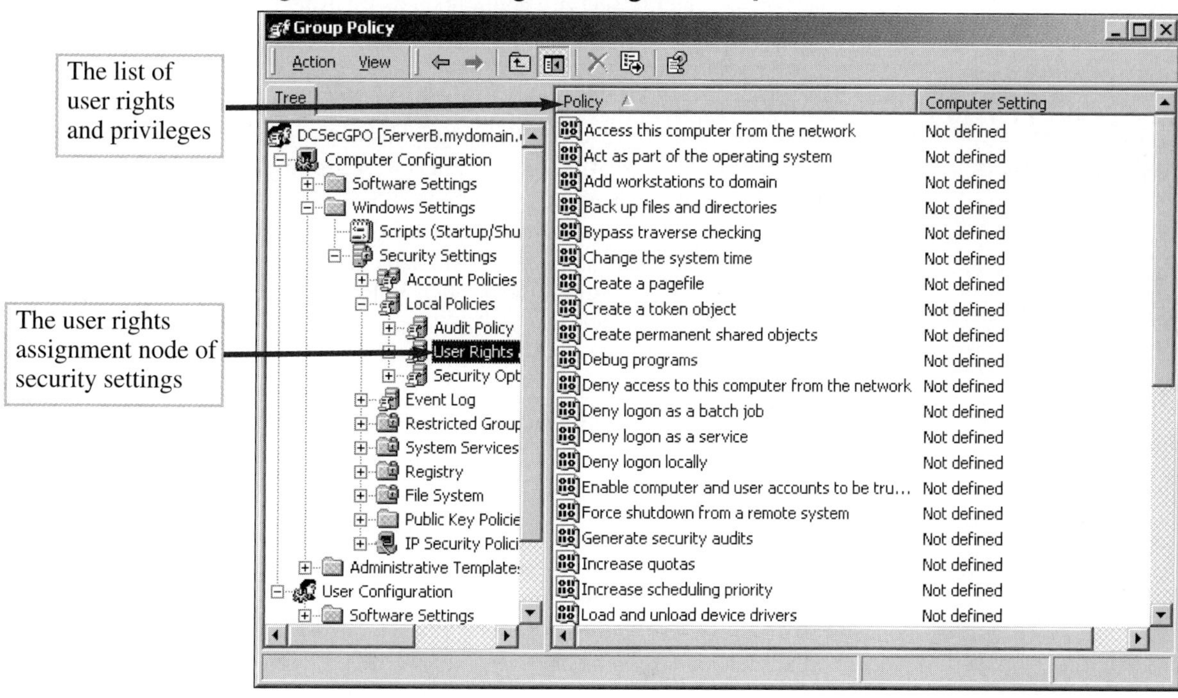

Figure 12-24 Security policy setting to grant the network access to the computer privilege to the Everyone user group

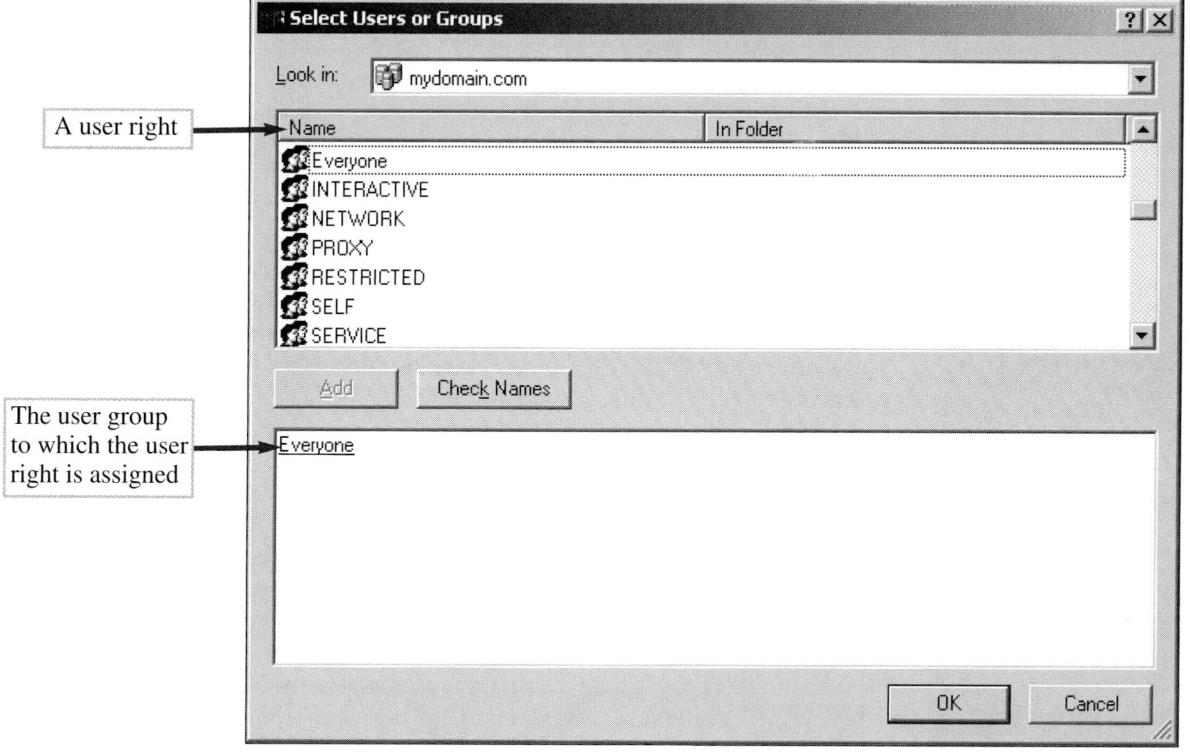

skill 9 Implementing Security Templates

exam objective

Create, analyze, and modify security configurations by using the Security Configuration and Analysis snap-in and the Security Templates snap-in.

overview

Different types of computers should typically have different security configuration settings. For example, security configuration settings for a domain controller should typically be more restrictive than the settings of a workstation. For a group of similar computers such as workstations, you can create a group of common security settings. Such settings are stored as security templates in a text-based file with a .inf file extension. A **security template** is a group of security settings that can be used to implement security in Windows 2000 computers. You can import these templates into GPOs, and apply the set of common security settings to other computers with similar functionality. This enables uniformity of security across multiple computers, and makes security administration easier and quicker. You can also use security templates to configure the security of a stand-alone computer using a local policy. In addition, you can save the initial security settings of a computer in a security template. If the security settings are changed in the future, and if there is a need to revert to the original security settings of the computer, the security template can be used to restore the settings.

Windows 2000 Server provides several predefined security templates that can be used to apply security configuration settings to different computers. These templates are designed and configured based on the general security policies for computers performing specific roles such as domain controllers, servers, and workstations. You can modify these templates according to your specific organizational requirements. These templates are located in the %systemroot%\security\templates folder (**Figure 12-25**). The predefined security templates that Windows 2000 provides allows for four standard security levels: Basic, Compatible, Secure, and Highly Secure. In addition, other security templates are provided to enhance the security of specific components.

Once you determine the level of security required for a computer, you can specify security policy for the computer using a security template. For example, a highly secure template for a computer, such as a domain controller, will specify the high levels of security for Windows 2000-only networks. However, a computer with this template applied will not be able to communicate with non-Windows 2000 computers, so care must be taken before implementing this policy. Implementing security templates consists of the following five main parts:

1. **Accessing the Security Templates console:** You can access the Security Templates console in an existing console by adding the Security Templates snap-in to it. You can also create a new Microsoft Management Console (MMC), and then add the Security Templates snap-in to it.
2. **Customizing a predefined security template:** You can edit a predefined security template **(Figure 12-26)** and save the modified template as a new template. This allows you to fine-tune certain security settings based on the requirements of the computer. Either of these templates can be applied to the computer at any given time.
3. **Defining a new security template:** You can define security settings in a new customized security template according to the specific security requirements of your organization. For example, computers such as e-mail servers may require additional security against Denial of Service attacks. The predefined security templates do not meet the security requirement of such a computer. You can create a new security template exclusively for that computer.
4. **Importing a security template to a GPO:** To apply the same security settings for multiple objects using a GPO, you can import an appropriate security template into the GPO. For example, the predefined security template domain controller security can be imported into a GPO to apply the security settings across the domain. This makes security administration easier.
5. **Exporting security settings to a security template:** The initial security configuration of a computer can be exported to a security template. Similarly, the effective security settings (the security settings currently applied on the computer) of the computer can be exported to a security template. In case the initial security settings need to be applied to the computer, the initial security template can be used to restore the settings.

Figure 12-25 Predefined Windows 2000 security templates

Console1 - [Console Root\Security Templates\C:\WINNT\Security\Templates]

List of predefined and new security templates

Name	Description
basicdc	Default Security Settings. Requires environment va...
basicsv	Default Security Settings. User Rights\Restricted G...
basicwk	Default Security Settings. User Rights\Restricted G...
compatws	Assumes clean-install NTFS file\reg acls. Relaxes A...
DC security	Default security settings updated for domain contr...
hisecdc	Assumes clean-install NTFS file\reg ACLs. Includes ...
hisecws	Increases SecureWS Settings. Restricts Power Us...
notssid	Removes the Terminal Server User SID from Windo...
ocfiless	Optional Component File Security. Many of the files...
ocfilesw	Optional Component File Security. Many of the files...
securedc	Assumes clean-install NTFS file\reg ACLs. Secures r...
securews	Assumes clean-install NTFS file\reg ACLs. Secures r...
setup security	Default security settings updated for domain contr...

Brief explanation of the functionality of the template

Figure 12-26 Editing a predefined Windows 2000 security template

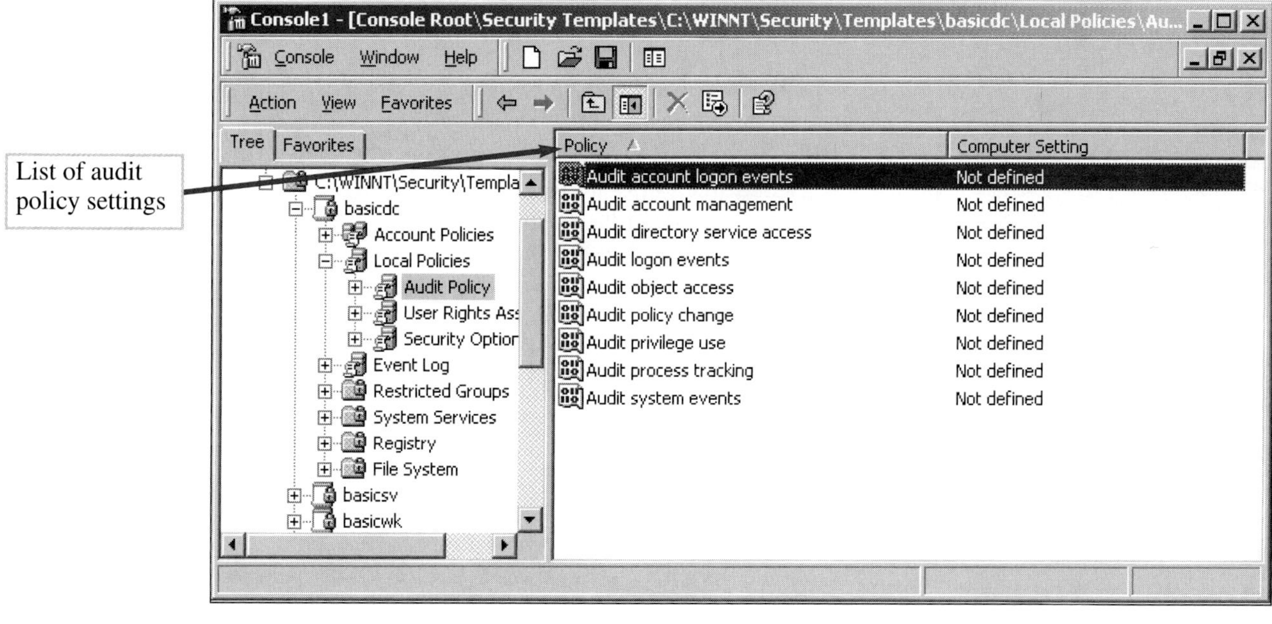

skill 9

Implementing Security Templates (cont'd)

exam objective

Create, analyze, and modify security configurations by using the Security Configuration and Analysis snap-in and the Security Templates snap-in.

how to

Create a new security template.

1. Log on to the mydomain.com domain on ServerA as an Administrator.
2. Click Start, and then click the **Run** command to open the **Run** dialog box.
3. Type **mmc** in the **Open** text box, and then click OK to open a new console.
4. Click the **Add/Remove Snap-in** command on the **Console** menu to open the **Add/Remove Snap-in** dialog box.
5. Click Add... to open the **Add Standalone Snap-in** dialog box.
6. Click the **Security Templates** snap-in from the list of available snap-ins, and then click Add... to add Security Templates to the list of **Console Root** snap-ins.
7. Click Close to close the **Add Standalone Snap-in** dialog box.
8. Click OK to close the **Add/Remove Snap-in** dialog box. The Security Templates snap-in will be listed under the console root of the MMC console.
9. Double-click the **Security Templates** node to view the path of the default security templates and the list of predefined security templates available in Windows 2000 Server.
10. Right-click the **template path** node, and then click the **New Template** command to open the **%systemroot%\Security\Templates** dialog box.
11. Type **trialsecdc** in the **Template name** text box and **security template trial** in the **Description** text box **(Figure 12-27)**
12. Click OK to add the new template to the existing list of templates.
13. In the **Console** tree, double-click the **trialsecdc** security template to view the security policies.
14. Double-click the **Account Policy** node, and then double-click the **Password Policy** node to view the password policy settings.
15. Double-click the **Minimum password length** setting to open the **Template Security Policy Setting** dialog box. Select the **Define this policy setting in the template** check box to activate the policy.
16. Type **6** in the **Password must be at least** text box, and click OK to update the minimum password length setting.
17. Click X to close the security template. The **Save Security Template** dialog box opens.
18. Click Yes to save the new security template.
19. Type **trialsecdcpol** in the **File name** text box to specify the name for the file.
20. Click Save to save the console.

more

Once you define or modify the security settings of a computer, you can export them to a security template as a .inf file. You can use such templates to restore the security settings on the computer later, and to apply the settings on a different computer or a set of computers that have the same security requirement. You can export security settings to a security template using the **Local Security Policy** administrative tool. The **Local Policy** (the security settings of the local computer) and the **Effective Policy** can be exported using the **Export Policy** command from the **Security Settings** node **(Figure 12-28)**. Similarly, a security template **(Figure 12-29)** can be imported into a GPO using the **Import Policy** command to apply the security template settings to the GPO.

Figure 12-27 Creating a new security template

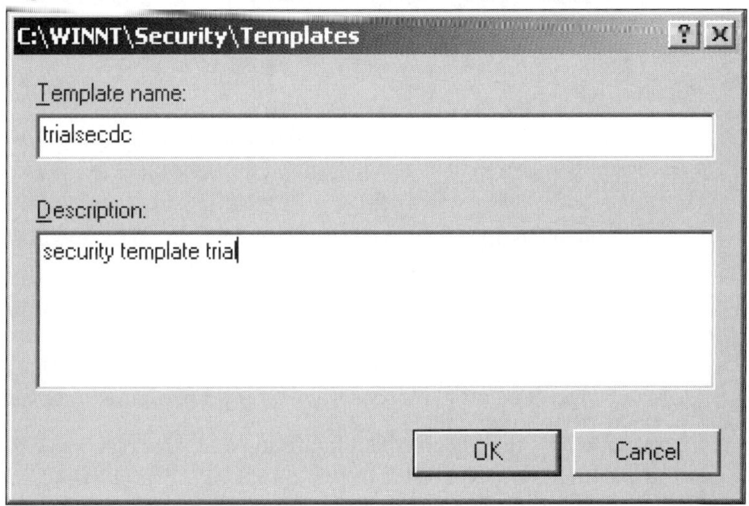

Figure 12-28 Exporting policy settings to a template

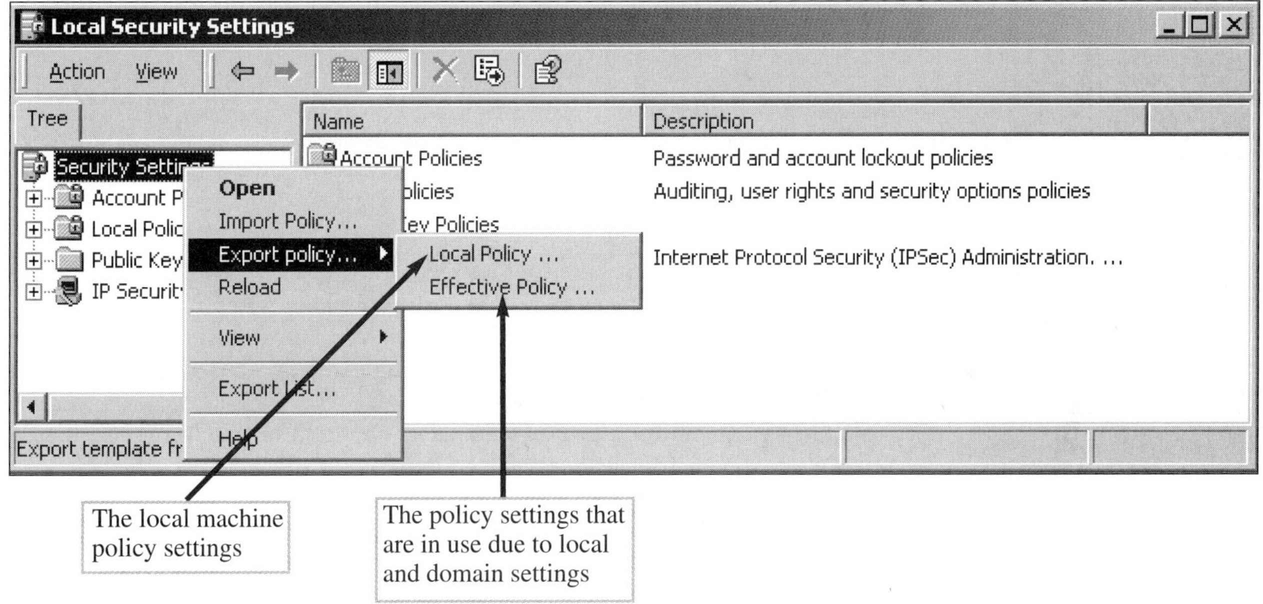

Figure 12-29 Importing a security template into a GPO

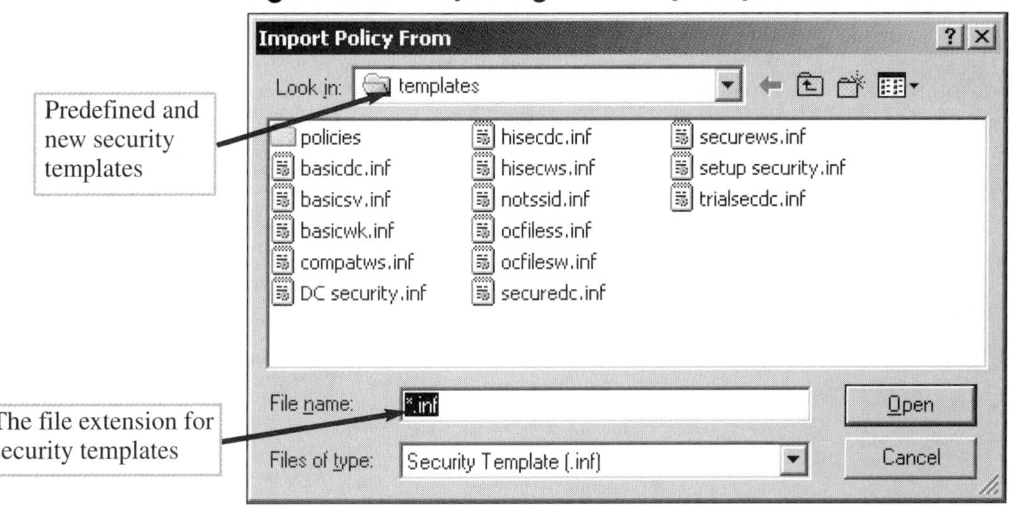

skill 10 Using the Security Configuration and Analysis Console

exam objective

Create, analyze, and modify security configurations by using the Security Configuration and Analysis snap-in and the Security Templates snap-in.

overview

In addition to Group Policy and Security Templates, Windows 2000 provides another tool, the **Security Configuration and Analysis** snap-in **(Figure 12-30)**, to configure the local security settings on a computer. The Security Configuration and Analysis snap-in uses databases to import a security template and compare the template to the currently configured computer settings. This functionality allows for a kind of "what-if" scenario, where you can see what exact changes are going to occur if you apply a particular template.

You can access the Security Configuration and Analysis console through an MMC console. You can create a new MMC console or use an existing MMC console. You can then open a security database in the Security Configuration and Analysis console, and import security templates into the database. Using the database template, you run the Security Configuration and Analysis tool to carry out analysis of the computer security settings. Thus, you can verify the consistency in the effective security settings with the actual security requirements of the computer using the Security Configuration and Analysis console.

The consistent and inconsistent settings are marked in the Security Configuration and Analysis console by a green check mark icon and a red x icon, respectively. You can then use the analysis results to update the inconsistent security settings of the computer.

how to

Set a working database in the Security Configuration and Analysis console, analyze the security settings of the computer, and view the analysis results.

1. Log on to the mydomain.com domain from ServerA as an Administrator.
2. Click **Start**, point to **Programs**, point to **Administrative Tools**, and then click the **TrialSecDCPol** command to open the console.
3. Click the **Add/Remove Snap-in** command on the **Console** menu to open the **Add/Remove Snap-in** dialog box.
4. Click **Add...** to open the **Add Standalone Snap-in** dialog box.
5. To add the **Security Configuration and Analysis** snap-in, click the **Security Configuration and Analysis** option from the list of available snap-ins, and then click **Add**.
6. Click **Close** to close the **Add Standalone Snap-in** dialog box.
7. Click **OK** to close the **Add/Remove Snap-in** dialog box. The **Security Configuration and Analysis** snap-in is listed under the **Console** root of **TrialSecDCPol**.
8. Click **Save** on the **Console** menu to save the console.
9. Right-click the **Security Configuration and Analysis** node, and then click the **Open database** command to view the **Open database** dialog box.
10. Type **ServerASecDb** in the **File name** text box, and click **Open**. The **Import template** dialog box opens.
11. Click the **DC security.inf** file, and then click **Open** to load the security template into the database. The database is now functional as the security database. This set of security settings will function as a benchmark during analysis.
12. Right-click the **Security Configuration and Analysis** node **(Figure 12-31)**, and then click the **Import Template** command to open the **Import Template** dialog box.

Figure 12-30 Security Configuration and Analysis snap-in

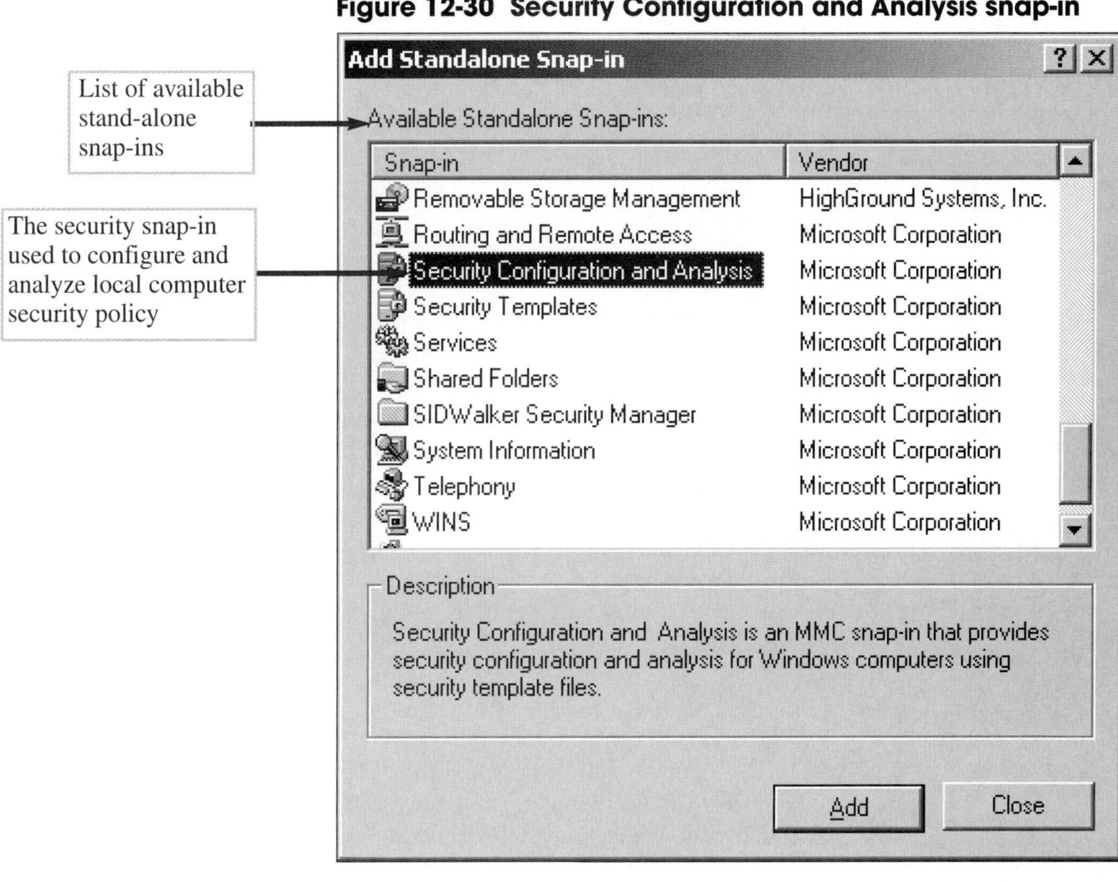

Figure 12-31 Security Configuration and Analysis console menu commands

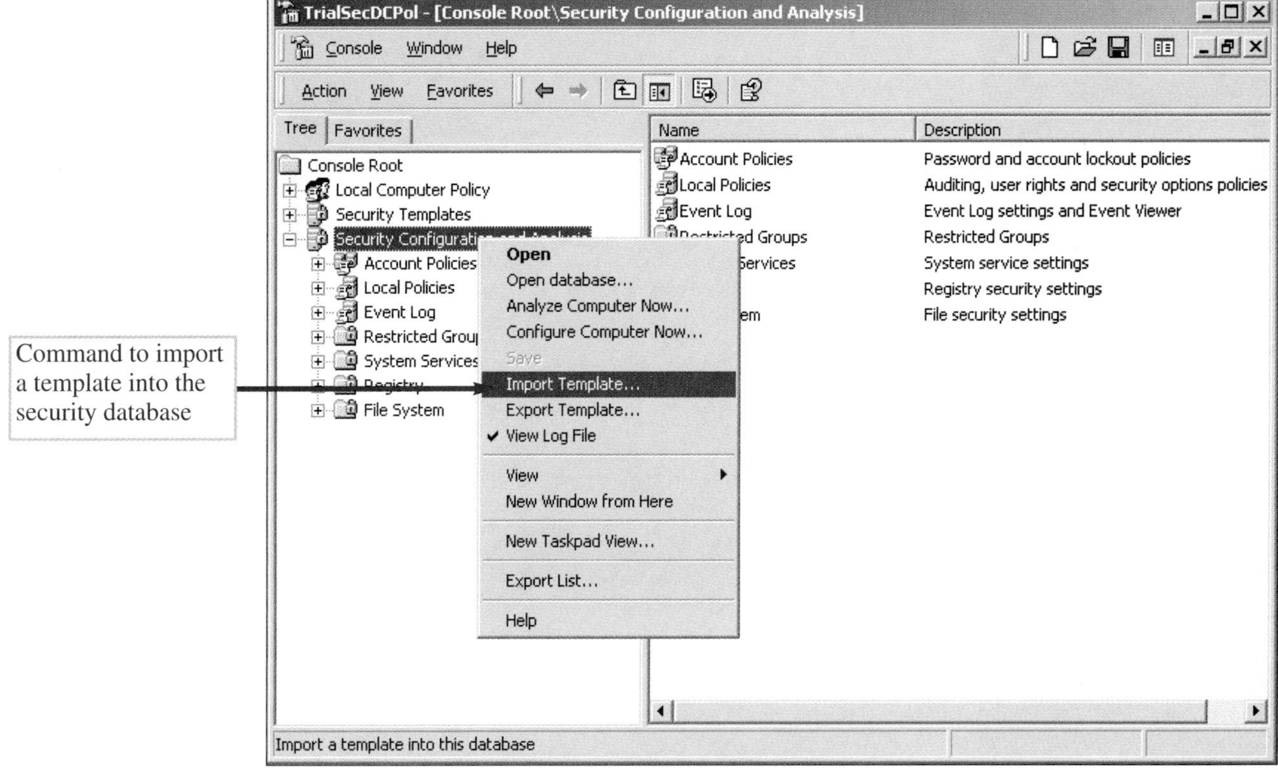

skill 10 Using the Security Configuration and Analysis Console *(cont'd)*

exam objective

Create, analyze, and modify security configurations by using the Security Configuration and Analysis snap-in and the Security Templates snap-in.

how to

13. Click the **trialsecdc.inf** file, and then click Open to add the template.
14. Right-click the **Security Configuration and Analysis** node, and then click the **Analyze Computer Now** command to begin the security analysis of the computer. The **Perform Analysis** dialog box opens.
15. Accept the default path specified in the **Error log file path** text box, and click OK.
16. The **Analyzing System Security** window displays the analysis progress of the different security events **(Figure 12-32)**.
17. Double-click the **Security Configuration and Analysis** node, double-click the **Account Policies** node, and then double-click the **Password Policy** node to view the results of the analysis for the password policy settings. The computer settings that show a difference are displayed with a red x mark **(Figure 12-33)**.
18. Click X to close the console, and then click Yes to save the console. You now have accessed the Security Configuration and Analysis console, analyzed the security settings of the computer against the benchmark security template, and viewed the analysis results.

more

Multiple security templates can be imported into a security database to be compiled as a composite template. The last template imported has the highest priority when it comes to inconsistent settings among the imported templates. You can also set the existing database to be cleared while importing a new template by selecting the Clear This Database Before Importing check box in the Import Template dialog box.

Figure 12-32 Analyzing System Security window

List of audit categories being analyzed

Analyzing System Security	
Analyzing:	
✔ User Rights Assignment	Active Directory Objects
✔ Restricted Groups	System Services
➡ Registry	Security Policy
File System	

Figure 12-33 System security analysis results

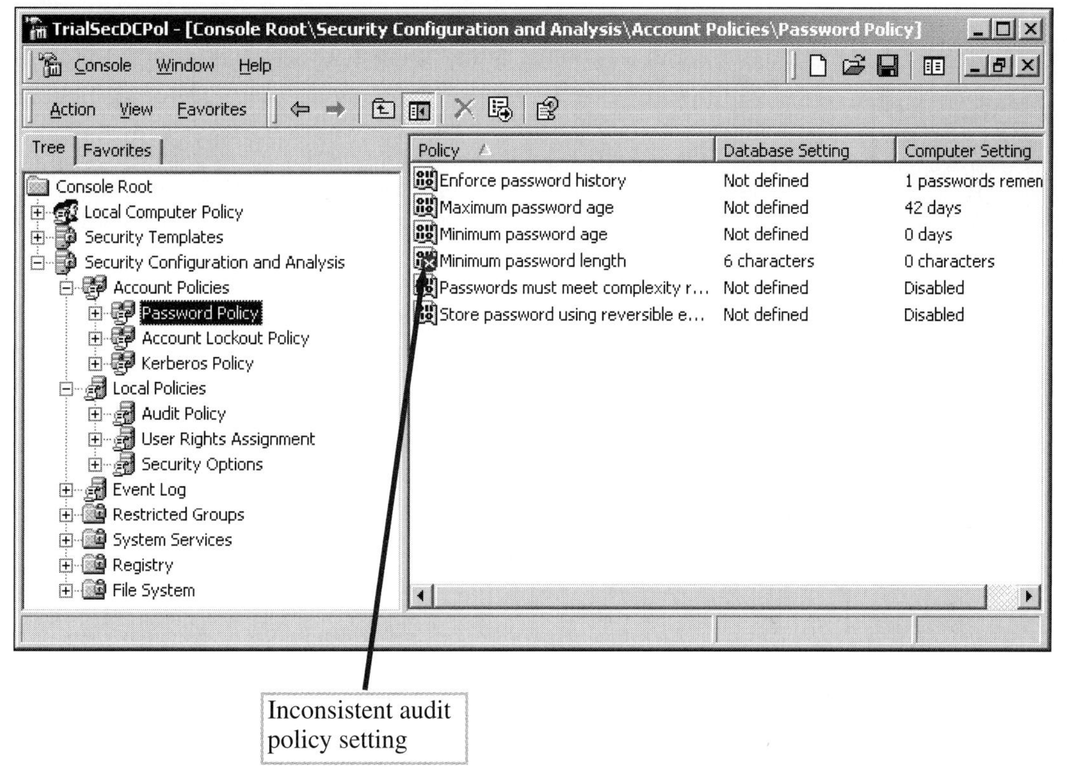

skill 11 Configuring Security by Using the Security Configuration and Analysis Console

exam objective

Create, analyze, and modify security configurations by using the Security Configuration and Analysis snap-in and the Security Templates snap-in.

overview

You can use the Security Configuration and Analysis console to analyze the security settings of a computer. After you analyze the security of your computer, you can configure the computer security settings using the Security Configuration and Analysis console. You need to do this to optimize the security of the computer by removing or updating any inconsistencies displayed by the analysis results. You can also enhance the security of your computer by changing the values of the security settings. Additionally, if you think another template meets the security needs of the computer, you can import more templates (either predefined or customized) into the database in order to make a composite database security template.

This database security template can be used to apply the updated security settings to a computer. Once the configuration is done, the effective settings of the computer become the same as the database security settings. The security of the computer is now updated using the Security Configuration and Analysis tool. The Security Configuration and Analysis tool is primarily used to configure the security of individual computers.

tip

After configuring the security settings of the computer, you can use the Analysis tool to verify that the newly applied security settings of the computer are consistent with the settings in the database template.

how to

Configure and edit the system security and view the results.

1. Log on to the mydomain.com domain from ServerA as an Administrator.
2. Click **Start**, point to **Programs**, point to **Administrative Tools**, and then click the **TrialSecDCPol console** to open it.
3. In the **Console** root, right-click the **Security Configuration and Analysis** node, and then click the **Configure Computer Now** command to run the configuration tool. The **Configure System** dialog box opens with the default log file path.
4. Accept the default log file path setting, and click OK **(Figure 12-34)**. The security configuration log file can be accessed from this location later.
5. The **Configuring Computer Security** window opens, showing the progress of the computer configuration process in the different security areas **(Figure 12-35)**.
6. On completion of the configuration process, right-click the **Security Configuration and Analysis** node, and then click the **Analyze Computer Now** option. This will run the computer security analysis tool, enabling you to view the updated security settings made in the system.
7. In the **Security Configuration and Analysis** node, double-click the **Account Policies** node, and then double-click the **Password Policy** node to view the results of the analysis for the password policy settings.
8. Double-click the **Minimum password age** setting to open the **Analyzed Security Policy Setting** dialog box.
9. Select the **Define this policy in the database** check box to allow editing of the policy setting, and then type **1** in the **Password can be changed after** text box **(Figure 12-36)**. This will allow the password to be changed only one day since the last password change once the policy has been applied to the computer.

tip

You can also right-click the Security Configuration and Analysis node, and click the View Log File command to display the configuration results in the details pane.

Figure 12-34 Default configuration log file path

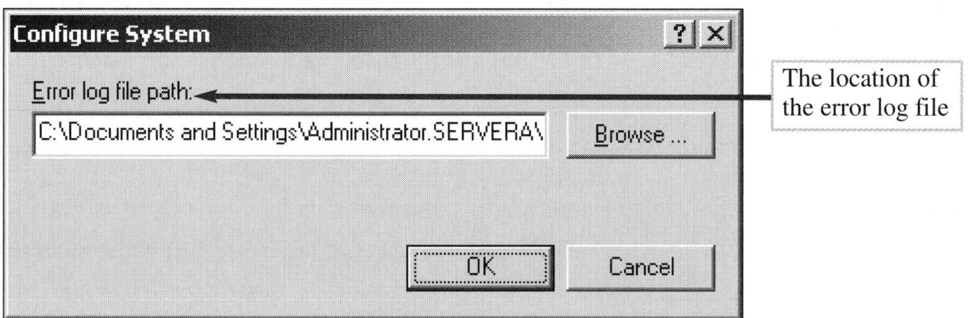

Figure 12-35 Configuring Computer Security

The list of security categories being configured

Configuring Computer Security

Configuring:

User Rights Assignment

Active Directory Objects

Restricted Groups

System Services

Registry

Security Policy

File System

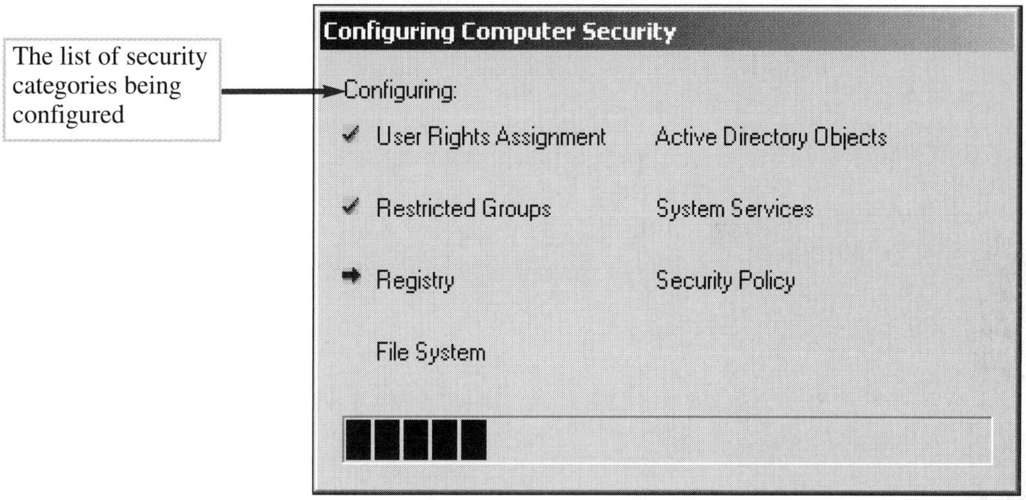

Figure 12-36 Editing a configuration setting

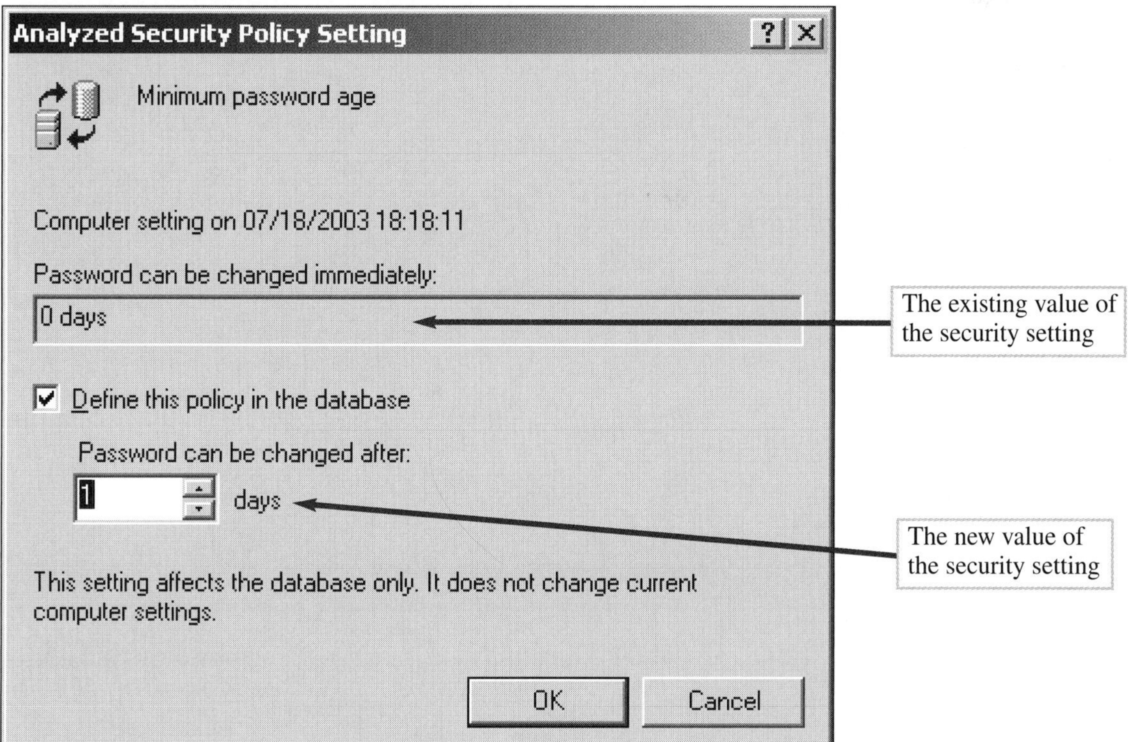

skill 11

Configuring Security by Using the Security Configuration and Analysis Console (cont'd)

exam objective

Create, analyze, and modify security configurations by using the Security Configuration and Analysis snap-in and the Security Templates snap-in.

how to

10. Click OK to apply the setting and close the **Analyzed Security Policy Setting** dialog box.
11. A **Suggested Value Changes** message box appears, suggesting that the maximum password age be set to 30 days **(Figure 12-37)**. Click **OK**.
12. Double-click the **Enforce password history** setting to open the **Analyzed Security Policy Setting** dialog box.
13. Clear the **Define this policy in the database** check box to disable the current setting of password history.
14. Click OK to close the **Analyzed Security Policy Setting** dialog box and to apply the new setting.
15. Click the **Enforce password history** setting to view the details of the setting update in the details pane **(Figure 12-38)**.
16. Click X to close the console. You will be prompted to save the console. Click Yes to save it. You have configured the system, edited the security settings, and viewed the configuration results using the Security Configuration and Analysis console.

caution

In order to modify account policies and have them actually take effect, you must import these settings into a GPO and link that GPO to the domain. Account policies are domain-wide changes that can only be applied at the domain level.

more

Once you define and configure the optimal security settings for one computer, you can implement the same settings for another computer on the network. You can export the security database configuration to a new template file using the Security Configuration and Analysis console Export Template command. This template can be applied to other individual computers. You can also import the template into a GPO to be applied to all the computers targeted by the GPO.

Figure 12-37 The Suggested Value Changes message box

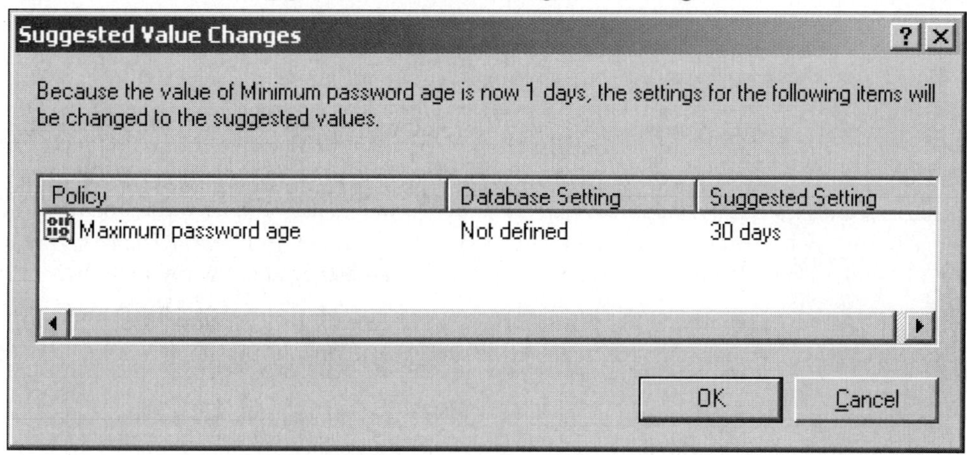

Figure 12-38 The edited security setting

TrialSecDCPol - [Console Root\Security Configuration and Analysis\Account Policies\Password Policy]

Console Window Help

Action View Favorites

Tree | Favorites

- Console Root
  - Local Computer Policy
  - Security Templates
  - Security Configuration and Analysis
    - Account Policies
      - Password Policy
      - Account Lockout Policy
      - Kerberos Policy
    - Local Policies
    - Event Log
    - Restricted Groups
    - System Services
    - Registry
    - File System

Policy	Database Setting	Computer Setting
Enforce password history	Not defined	1 passwords remen
Maximum password age	30 days	42 days
Minimum password age	1 days	0 days
Minimum password length	6 characters	6 characters
Passwords must meet complexity r...	Not defined	Disabled
Store password using reversible e...	Not defined	Disabled

Done

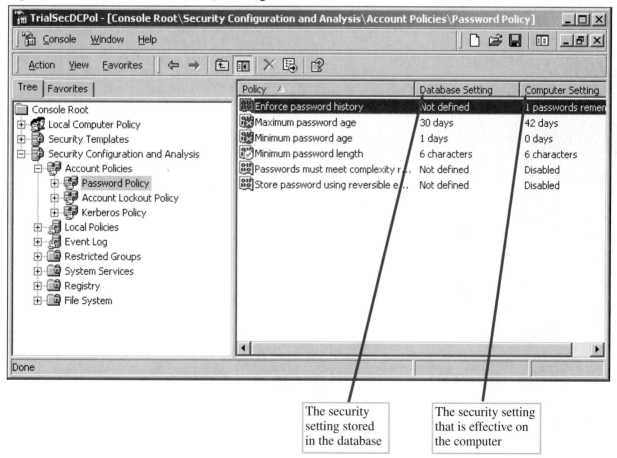

The security setting stored in the database

The security setting that is effective on the computer

skill 12 Troubleshooting Security Configuration Issues

exam objective Monitor and analyze security events.

overview

Group Policy, Security Templates, and the Security Configuration and Analysis tool enable you to define, implement, and monitor the configuration of security settings of computers easily and effectively. However, while managing a network, you may encounter a number of problems related to security configuration. You need to analyze these problems and find effective solutions to keep network efficiency and security at its peak at all times.

Following certain practices while configuring security for a network and its individual computers will improve the success rate of your configuration. You should take a close look at your security requirements before implementing a security policy. Most networks do not require ultra-high levels of security, but all networks require some level of security. Remember that all security settings end up costing, typically by reducing efficiency and increasing administrative effort. However, unauthorized access will also have repercussions, so you need to walk a fine line between overdoing the security settings and reducing administrative effort.

You should configure auditing for the computers based on the security level of that computer. This will assist you in ensuring that the security policies of the computers are effective at all times. You need to identify the existing and potential problems from the audit results and update the appropriate security settings. Additionally, periodic monitoring of the Event Viewer security log is necessary to ensure that the system has not been affected and to spot network usage, as well as security patterns that may cause problems in the future. The audit event details provide in-depth information on the security audit events **(Figure 12-39)**.

Some of the errors that may arise while configuring security, the causes of these errors, and their solutions, are described in **Table 12-4**.

Figure 12-39 Security audit event details

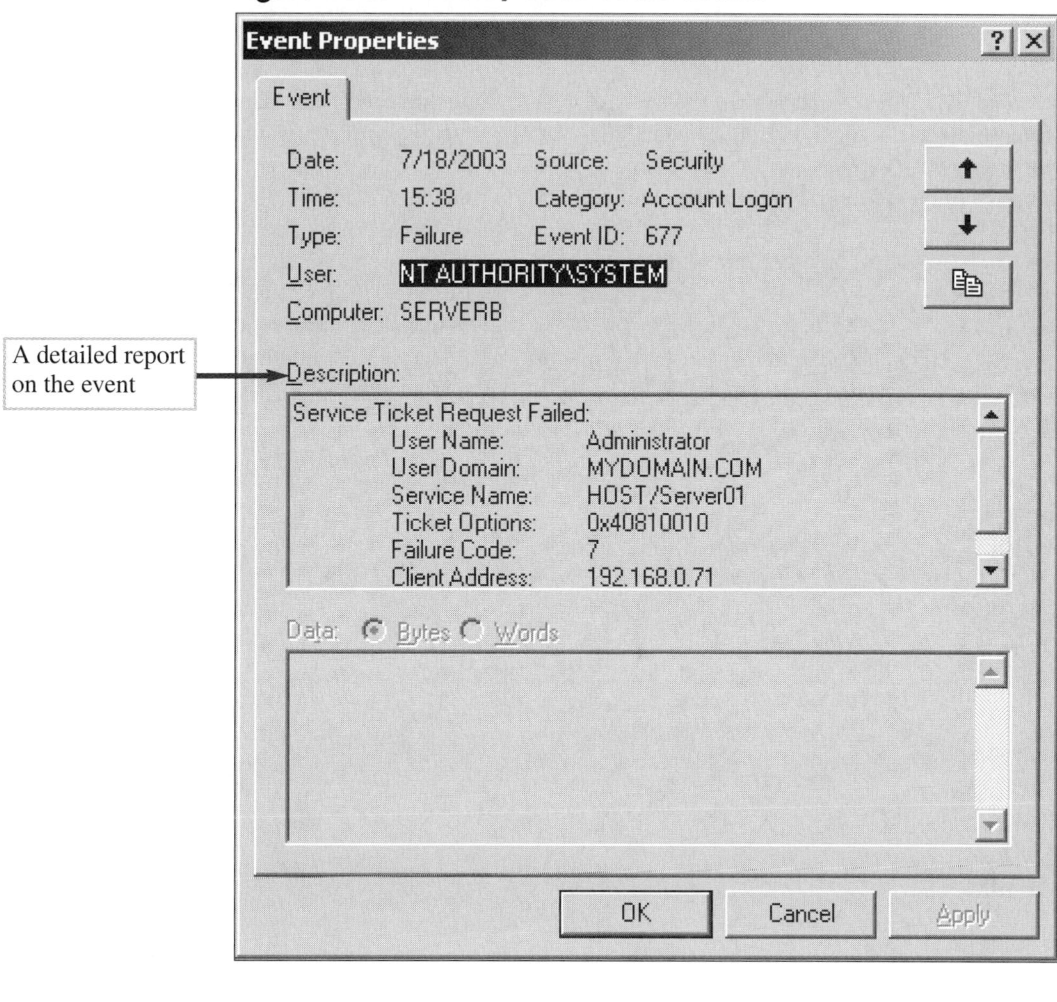

Table 12-4 Errors Encountered While Configuring Security

Error	Cause	Solution
Security settings are not applied	Policy has not been propagated.	Manually apply the policy using the secedit command. Also check for GPO conflicts to ensure a lower level policy is not overwriting your new policy.
Certain local security settings are not applied	The policy of the setting is being overridden by a lower level policy.	Verify the policy conflict, and then modify your policies as necessary.
Windows 2000 Group Policies will not apply to legacy operating systems (such as NT 4.0)	Active Directory handles group policies much differently than Windows NT 4.0 handles system policies.	You must continue to use system policies for legacy operating systems.
Error message: Object access failure	The user or computer does not have the required privileges to access the object.	Configure the object security settings to provide the user or computer access to the object.

Summary

- Windows 2000 provides tools, such as Group Policy, Security Templates, and Security Configuration and Analysis, to configure and manage system security.
- Windows 2000 Auditing allows you to monitor user activities and system events across the network.
- Several types of audit policies can be applied to a system, such as account policies, local policies, event log policies, system service policies, public key policies, restricted groups policies, file system policies, and IP security policies.
- Group Policy can be used to implement an audit policy for domain controllers.
- Domain-wide security is set up in a two-step process: first, creating a new GPO, and then editing the GPO to configure the security settings for the computers.
- Audit policy for stand-alone computers is done locally.
- Audit policies for file access can be set only for NTFS drives.
- The Event Viewer is used to view the security log for security audit event details.
- Policy can be propagated manually to the computers using the secedit command.
- Security Templates can be used to define the security settings of the computer.
- Windows 2000 provides predefined security templates for different types of computers.
- Security templates can be edited and the new settings can be exported to a new template, which can be imported into other computers.
- The Security Configuration and Analysis console can be used to analyze, configure, and view the security settings for individual computers.

Key Terms

Auditing
Security Configuration and Analysis console
Security configuration
Policy inheritance
Privileges
Logon right
Security template
Security log
Audit policy
Local security policy
Nonlocal GPO

Test Yourself

1. Your organization has decided to implement security on the Windows 2000 computers in the network. Which of the following tools provided by Windows 2000 Server would you use to configure security for these computers? (Choose all that apply)
   a. Kerberos security policy
   b. Security Templates
   c. Microsoft Management Console
   d. Security Configuration and Analysis snap-in
   e. Security log of Event Viewer

2. How will you set account policies for a domain spread across three locations in the domain?
   a. Create an account policy for all three locations.
   b. Create an account policy for each user group in each location.
   c. Apply the policy to the domain.
   d. Apply a local policy for each location.

3. Which security group will you audit to ensure that all possible intruders are monitored by a particular security policy?
   a. The Domain Users group
   b. The Users group
   c. The Administrator group
   d. The Everyone security group

4. You have set audit policies for a computer. Which command will you run to manually propagate security policy for the computer?
   a. secedit /refreshpolicy machine_policy
   b. secedit /refreshpolicy user_policy
   c. secedit /validate securedc.inf
   d. secedit /configure securedc.inf

5. Which of the following consoles do you use to configure the audit settings for a stand-alone server?
a. Active Directory Users and Computers
b. Active Directory Domains and Trusts
c. Domain Controller Security Policy
d. Local Security Policy

6. You have certain important files on a computer. How will you enable monitoring of which user reads these files?
a. Set the Audit privilege policy.
b. Set the Audit object access policy.
c. Set the Audit logon events policy.
d. Set the Audit system events policy.

7. Which of the following file systems support Auditing?
a. A FAT-16 file system
b. A FAT-32 file system
c. An NTFS file system
d. A Distributed file system

8. You need to review the security audit events that have occurred over the last month. Which of the following Event Viewer options would you use to display only the event entries in the security log over the last month?
a. Use the Find option.
b. Use the Newest first option.
c. Use the Filter option.
d. Use the New log view option.

9. Which of the following is the best method for maintaining the security log without increasing the file size?
a. Archive the security log events weekly, and then clear the log.
b. Select the Overwrite events option.
c. Set the value of the Overwrite events older than x days option to 7.
d. Click the Restore defaults button to clear the log file.

10. You want to grant special rights to a certain set of users that will allow them to view security audits on any of the computers in the domain. Which of the following is the best method to do this?
a. Assign the Manage security audits user right to the users individually.
b. Create a user group containing these users and assign the manage security audits user right to the user group.
c. Create an OU containing these users and apply a security policy on the OU allowing the users to manage security audits.
d. Add these users to the Administrator group to allow them to manage security audits on the computers.

11. You have edited certain security settings in a predefined security template based on the security requirement of a computer. You have to propagate the security template policies on all computers in the domain. Which of the following do you need to do for the policies to take effect?
a. Apply the settings and restart the computer.
b. Run the secedit command.
c. Apply the template to an active GPO at the domain level.
d. Select the Define this policy setting option in the template.

12. In a Security Configuration and Analysis snap-in, what happens to a security template file after it is imported into a database, edited, and saved?
a. The security template file is deleted from the computer.
b. The security template file is overwritten.
c. The security template file is unchanged.
d. The security template file is moved to a different location.

13. You need to perform system security analysis of a computer to verify the correct application of the security settings. The results are displayed in the details pane of the Security Configuration and Analysis snap-in. Some of the policy settings are marked with a red x icon. What does it indicate?
a. The setting was not included in the template, and therefore, not analyzed.
b. The setting was not configured for the computer.
c. The setting is the same as the setting in the database.
d. The setting is less secure than the setting in the database.

14. Which of the following does the Security Configuration and Analysis tool use to analyze and configure the security of a computer?
a. Active Directory
b. Log files
c. Policy propagation
d. Computer-specific database

15. You need to apply security settings on a computer using the Security Configuration and Analysis tool. Which of the following commands will you use?
a. The Analyze Computer Now command
b. The View Log File command
c. The Configure Computer Now command
d. The Export Template command

16. You have configured the local security policy of a computer. Which of the following solutions will you implement when the local security policy fails to apply on the computer?
a. Log off, and then log on again.
b. Manually apply policy propagation using the secedit command.
c. Check the DNS settings of the computer.
d. Analyze the computer security settings.

Projects: On Your Own

1. Set an audit policy for a local computer to monitor failed access attempts to the Documents and Settings folder.
   a. Log on to the computer as an Administrator.
   b. Open the **Local Security Settings** console.
   c. Set the **Audit object access** policy for files and folders.
   d. Close the Local Security Settings console.
   e. Open the **Windows Explorer** window to access the Documents and Settings folder.
   f. Set the Documents and Settings folder to be audited for access by the Everyone user group.
   g. Close the **Windows Explorer** window.
2. Create a new security template to be applied to a GPO, SecPol. The template should have the minimum password length set to 10.
   a. Log on to the **domain controller** as an Administrator.
   b. Open the **Group Policy Object SecPol** snap-in.
   c. Add the stand-alone **Security Templates** snap-in to the GPO.
   d. Update the **Set minimum password length** policy setting to 10.
   e. Save the new template as **newsectmpl**.
   f. Close the Group Policy snap-in.
3. Analyze the computer security settings with the predefined security template basicsv.inf.
   a. Log on to the computer as an Administrator.
   b. Open a new **MMC** console.
   c. Add the stand-alone **Security Configuration and Analysis** snap-in.
   d. Open a new database and import the basicsv.inf template into it.
   e. Run the **Analyze Computer Now** command.
   f. View the analysis results in the details pane.
   g. Save the MMC console and close it.

Problem Solving Scenarios

1. You administer your company's Windows 2000 network. Recently there have been reports of unauthorized logon attempts after normal office working hours. To tackle this problem, you want to implement a security policy to track logon events. This policy must be applicable to all domains and OU's within your network's site. Also, as a specific security requirement, you would like to track the usage for a shared folder named SALES_DATA.

Write a memo explaining how you will implement security policies for achieving these goals.

2. You administer your Windows 2000 ADS network. Recently, some members of the development team pointed out that they do not have the rights to shut down or restart their computers, which is sometimes required for software testing purpose. In addition, these users do not have enough privileges to change the system time.

You need to solve the problem as soon as possible. Your network is divided into two sites. You administer the first site named CORP_SITE1, which consists of four domains; the users needing assistance are members of the CORP_SITE1_DEV domain. There exists a group policy at the domain level, which is used for setting password restrictions.

Explain the steps you will follow to solve the development team members' problem.

LESSON

13 Monitoring Active Directory Performance

In order to ensure high availability and adequate response times, you need to ensure that your domain controllers, and the network infrastructure that supports them, are operating at peak performance. A large increase in traffic over WAN links, for instance, can cause serious problems with AD replication. However, if you are consistently monitoring the network's performance, you can find and resolve problems like this before they become critical.

To monitor Active Directory performance, the Microsoft Windows 2000 operating system provides you with a number of tools such as the Performance console and the Event Viewer console. The Performance console consists of two snap-ins: the System Monitor snap-in and the Performance Logs and Alerts snap-in. The System Monitor snap-in helps you view performance data with the help of graphs and reports. The Performance Logs and Alerts snap-in enables you to record performance data into logs and configure alerts when specific events occur. You can use the information obtained from these snap-ins to pinpoint bottlenecks and use this information to reconfigure your infrastructure for optimal performance. You can also use the information to diagnose and troubleshoot problems relating to Active Directory. In addition, you can use various support tools, such as LDP and REPLMON, for monitoring and troubleshooting Active Directory.

Goals

In this lesson, you will be introduced to various Active Directory performance-monitoring and support tools. You will learn to monitor Active Directory performance counters and create performance logs and alerts. In addition, you will learn to control access to network resources.

Lesson 13 Monitoring Active Directory Performance

Skill	*Exam 70-217 Objective*
1. Introducing Active Directory Performance-Monitoring Tools	Basic knowledge
2. Monitoring Active Directory Performance Counters	Monitor, optimize, and troubleshoot Active Directory performance and replication.
3. Creating Performance Logs and Alerts	Monitor, optimize, and troubleshoot Active Directory performance and replication.
4. Identifying the Active Directory Support Tools	Basic knowledge

Requirements

For this lesson, you need administrative rights on two Windows 2000 domain controllers in the mydomain.com domain, named ServerA and ServerB, with Active Directory and support tools installed on them. ServerA should have two shared folders called Backup and Public.

skill 1 Introducing Active Directory Performance-Monitoring Tools

exam objective

Basic knowledge

overview

For the smooth functioning of any Windows 2000-based network, you need to monitor the performance of Active Directory. By periodically monitoring Active Directory performance, you can anticipate problems that you might encounter and take preventive measures. To monitor Active Directory, you can use various tools provided by the Windows 2000 operating system. You can use these tools to:

- **Collect baseline data**. Baseline data is the load placed on your resources over time, which is averaged to show you what is considered 'normal' for your particular environment. A baseline gives you something to compare future performance data against to determine if performance is improving or deteriorating **(Figure 13-1)**. Baseline data should typically be recorded over, at least, one week of time, and should only include activity during working hours. For instance, if your company's normal working hours are from 8AM to 5PM, Monday through Friday, then those are the periods in which you should establish your baseline.
- **Troubleshoot problems**. You can use the information obtained from the tools to diagnose and solve performance bottlenecks and problems.
- **Understand the effects of Active Directory performance on the hardware resources of a computer**. If you observe that the resources are not performing efficiently, you should consider upgrading the hardware.

The two most widely used tools for monitoring Active Directory performance are as follows:

Performance console

This console enables you to collect and monitor information about system resources. You can use performance monitor to view performance statistics on both local and remote machines. Be advised, however, that viewing performance data does impact the machine slightly, as it adds an additional load. In addition, when viewing remote machines, network traffic will increase due to the additional demands caused by transferring this performance information.

caution

In order to monitor the performance of Active Directory on a remote computer, make sure you have appropriate permissions on it.

The **Performance** console consists of two snap-ins: the **System Monitor** snap-in and the **Performance Logs and Alerts** snap-in. You use the System Monitor snap-in to view previously collected and real-time performance data in the form of a graph, histogram, or report. You use the Performance Logs and Alerts snap-in to store performance data in log files and to create alerts. You use the System Monitor snap-in in conjunction with the Performance Logs and Alerts snap-in to analyze and optimize Active Directory performance. To do so, you need two data samples. You can obtain one sample using the Performance Logs and Alerts snap-in to act as a baseline. The other sample can be collected during working hours using the System Monitor. You should calculate baseline as the average of Active Directory performance statistics collected over a period of time. The baseline data represents the typical level of performance. You can then compare the baseline data with the sample. Any deviation of the sample from the baseline data should be analyzed to determine the cause, even if it appears that the deviation is an improvement. For instance, you may notice that network traffic in your sample is markedly reduced from the baseline. While this may appear to be a positive change, it could in fact be an indicator that a network service is not working properly. If you analyze your traffic in more detail at this point, you may find that AD has not been replicating changes properly, which is a significant problem.

Figure 13-1 Comparing the current data with the baseline data

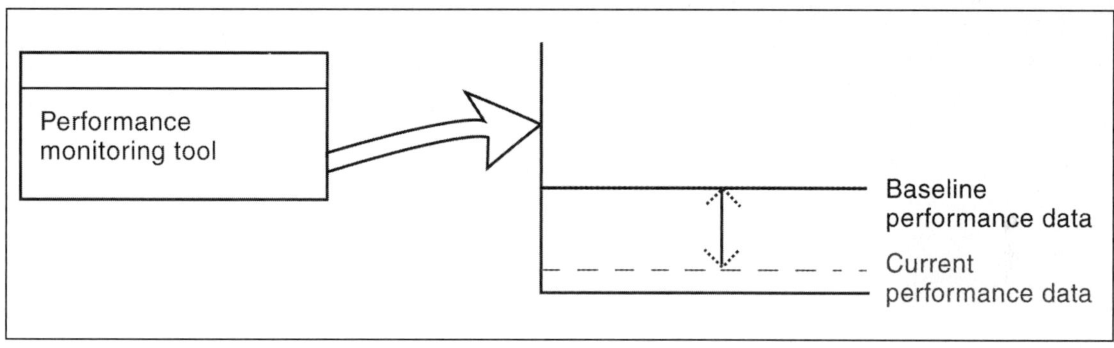

skill 1

Introducing Active Directory Performance-Monitoring Tools (cont'd)

exam objective

Basic knowledge

overview

Event Viewer

The **Event Viewer** console contains messages generated by applications and the operating system in different **event logs**. By studying the sequence of events in the logs available in the Event Viewer console, you can understand and solve problems relating to applications, services, and operating system. The different types of event logs are as follows:

- **Application log:** Stores information, errors, or warnings generated by applications present on a computer.
- **Security log:** Stores auditing entries. You can use this log to track users who are trying to access objects for which they do not have permissions.
- **System log:** Stores information, errors, or warnings generated by the Windows 2000 operating system. If you are facing difficulties in starting a service, such as Task Scheduler, you should study this log to identify the cause of the problem.
- **Directory Service log:** Stores information, errors, or warnings generated by Active Directory **(Figure 13-2)**. The Directory Service log is available only on domain controllers.
- **DNS log:** Stores information, errors, or warnings generated by the Domain Name Service (DNS) server.
- **File Replication Service log:** Stores information, errors, or warnings generated by the File Replication Service, which is the service used to replicate the shared system volume (Sysvol folder).

Each event log records five types of messages. **Table 13-1** lists the types of messages and their descriptions.

Figure 13-2 Using the Event Viewer to track events

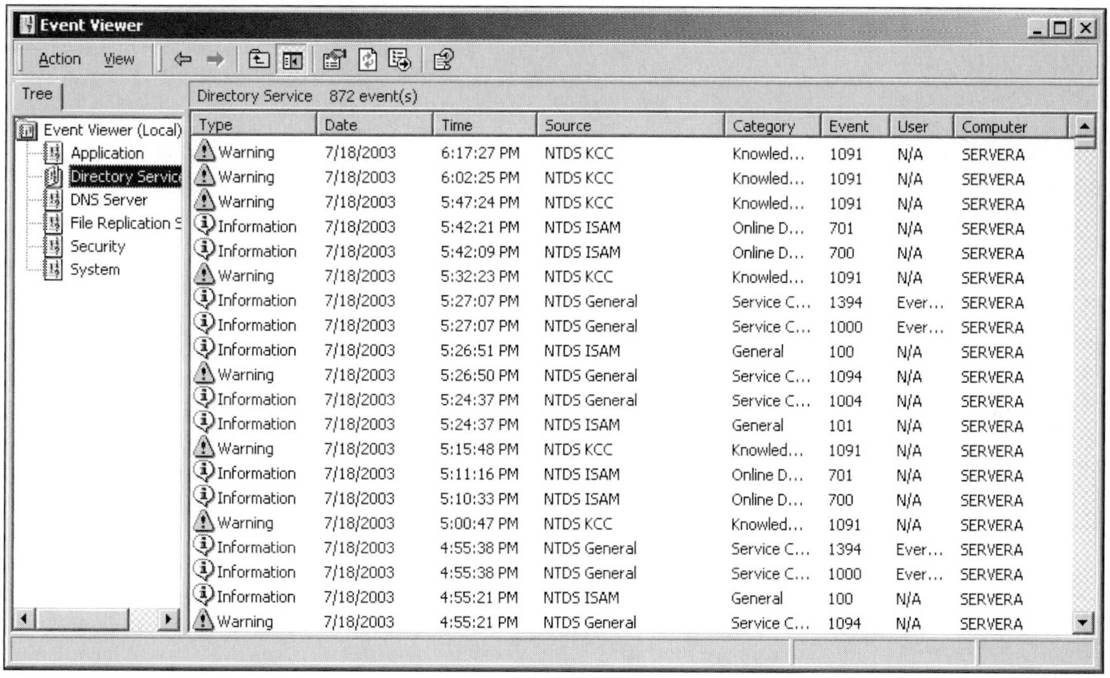

Event Viewer

Action View

Tree

Event Viewer (Local)
Application
Directory Servic
DNS Server
File Replication S
Security
System

Directory Service 872 event(s)

Type	Date	Time	Source	Category	Event	User	Computer
Warning	7/18/2003	6:17:27 PM	NTDS KCC	Knowled...	1091	N/A	SERVERA
Warning	7/18/2003	6:02:25 PM	NTDS KCC	Knowled...	1091	N/A	SERVERA
Warning	7/18/2003	5:47:24 PM	NTDS KCC	Knowled...	1091	N/A	SERVERA
Information	7/18/2003	5:42:21 PM	NTDS ISAM	Online D...	701	N/A	SERVERA
Information	7/18/2003	5:42:09 PM	NTDS ISAM	Online D...	700	N/A	SERVERA
Warning	7/18/2003	5:32:23 PM	NTDS KCC	Knowled...	1091	N/A	SERVERA
Information	7/18/2003	5:27:07 PM	NTDS General	Service C...	1394	Ever...	SERVERA
Information	7/18/2003	5:27:07 PM	NTDS General	Service C...	1000	Ever...	SERVERA
Information	7/18/2003	5:26:51 PM	NTDS ISAM	General	100	N/A	SERVERA
Warning	7/18/2003	5:26:50 PM	NTDS General	Service C...	1094	N/A	SERVERA
Information	7/18/2003	5:24:37 PM	NTDS General	Service C...	1004	N/A	SERVERA
Information	7/18/2003	5:24:37 PM	NTDS ISAM	General	101	N/A	SERVERA
Warning	7/18/2003	5:15:48 PM	NTDS KCC	Knowled...	1091	N/A	SERVERA
Information	7/18/2003	5:11:16 PM	NTDS ISAM	Online D...	701	N/A	SERVERA
Information	7/18/2003	5:10:33 PM	NTDS ISAM	Online D...	700	N/A	SERVERA
Warning	7/18/2003	5:00:47 PM	NTDS KCC	Knowled...	1091	N/A	SERVERA
Information	7/18/2003	4:55:38 PM	NTDS General	Service C...	1394	Ever...	SERVERA
Information	7/18/2003	4:55:38 PM	NTDS General	Service C...	1000	Ever...	SERVERA
Information	7/18/2003	4:55:21 PM	NTDS ISAM	General	100	N/A	SERVERA
Warning	7/18/2003	4:55:21 PM	NTDS General	Service C...	1094	N/A	SERVERA

Table 13-1 Types of event log messages

Message Type	Description
Information (icon)	Represents an occurrence of an event.
Warning (icon)	Reports an event completed with problems. This type of message indicates low-severity events. You must check events of this type while troubleshooting problems relating to applications, services, and the operating system.
Error (icon)	Reports an event stopped due to critical problems such as failure of the replication process. This type of message indicates high-severity events.
Failure (icon)	Reports failure audits. This type of message occurs only in the Security log.
Success (icon)	Reports success audits. This type of message only occurs in the Security log.

skill 2 Monitoring Active Directory Performance Counters

exam objective

Monitor, optimize, and troubleshoot Active Directory performance and replication.

overview

The Performance console is perhaps the most useful tool at your disposal for tracking the performance of a machine. When tracking the performance of AD using this tool, there are a large number of specific metrics you can monitor. Before you decide which are most useful for tracking your environment, you need to understand how the Performance console organizes all of the different metrics that it can track.

The Performance console arranges the various data sources it can monitor into objects, and then arranges all of the individual types of data it can monitor from that source into counters. For instance, the NTDS (NT Directory Services) object contains all data related to Directory Services. However, there are lots of different types of data you could analyze regarding directory services. Each of these is organized into counters within the NTDS object. For instance, if you wanted to track inbound replication traffic sent to your bridgehead server from other sites, you would use the "Directory Replication Agent (DRA)—Inbound Bytes Compressed (Between Sites, Before Compression)/sec" counter of the NTDS object.

Table 13-2 lists the most widely used performance counters of the **NTDS** performance object and their descriptions.

how to

Monitor the DRA Inbound Bytes Total/sec counter on the **ServerA** domain controller. The DRA Inbound Bytes Total/sec counter tells us how many bytes per second are being used for inbound replication traffic of all types.

1. Log on to **ServerA** as an Administrator.
2. Click **Start**, point to **Programs**, point to **Administrative Tools**, and then click the **Performance** command to open the **Performance** console. By default, the **System Monitor** node is selected and a blank chart is displayed.
3. To add performance objects and counters, click the **Add** button + on the **System Monitor** toolbar. The **Add Counters** dialog box appears. By default, the name of the local computer and the **Processor** performance object appear in the **Add Counters** dialog box.
4. Click the arrow for the **Performance object** list box ▾, scroll up the list, and then click the **NTDS** option to monitor the performance of Active Directory. By default, the DRA Inbound Properties Total/sec counter appears in the **Select counters from list** list box.
5. Scroll up the **Select counters from list** list box and click the **DRA Inbound Bytes Total/sec** counter to observe the total number of bytes received in a second by **ServerA** through the replication process. **(Figure 13-3)**.

tip

You can also open the Performance console by running the perfmon command from the Run dialog box.

caution

Using performance counters does add some load to the server, so be judicious in their use.

Table 13-2 Performance counters

Performance counter	Description
Directory Replication Agent (DRA) Inbound Bytes Total/sec	Performance counters beginning with DRA provide statistics on the replication process. The DRA Inbound Bytes Total/sec counter indicates the total number of bytes received in a second through the replication process.
DRA Inbound Full Sync Objects Remaining	This counter indicates the number of objects that still need to be replicated before the database is fully synchronized.
DRA Inbound Objects Applied/sec	This counter indicates the rate at which replication updates are received from other domain controllers and incorporated on a domain controller. You use this counter to measure the amount of replication activity occurring on a domain controller due to changes made on other domain controllers.
DRA Inbound Object Updates Remaining in Packet	This counter indicates the number of objects that have not been updated on a domain controller. A higher value of this performance counter than the baseline implies that the server is experiencing poor performance.
DRA Pending Replication Synchronizations	This counter records the number of replication requests that have not been processed by a domain controller. A higher value of this performance counter than the baseline denotes a replication backlog.
Lightweight Directory Access Protocol (LDAP) Client Sessions	Performance counter names beginning with LDAP provide statistics on events involving LDAP, which is an access protocol used to locate and access objects in an AD. The LDAP Client Sessions counter indicates the number of existing clients that are connected to a domain controller using LDAP.
LDAP Bind Time	This counter indicates the time taken by a domain controller, in milliseconds, to connect to another domain controller.

Figure 13-3 Specifying performance objects and counters

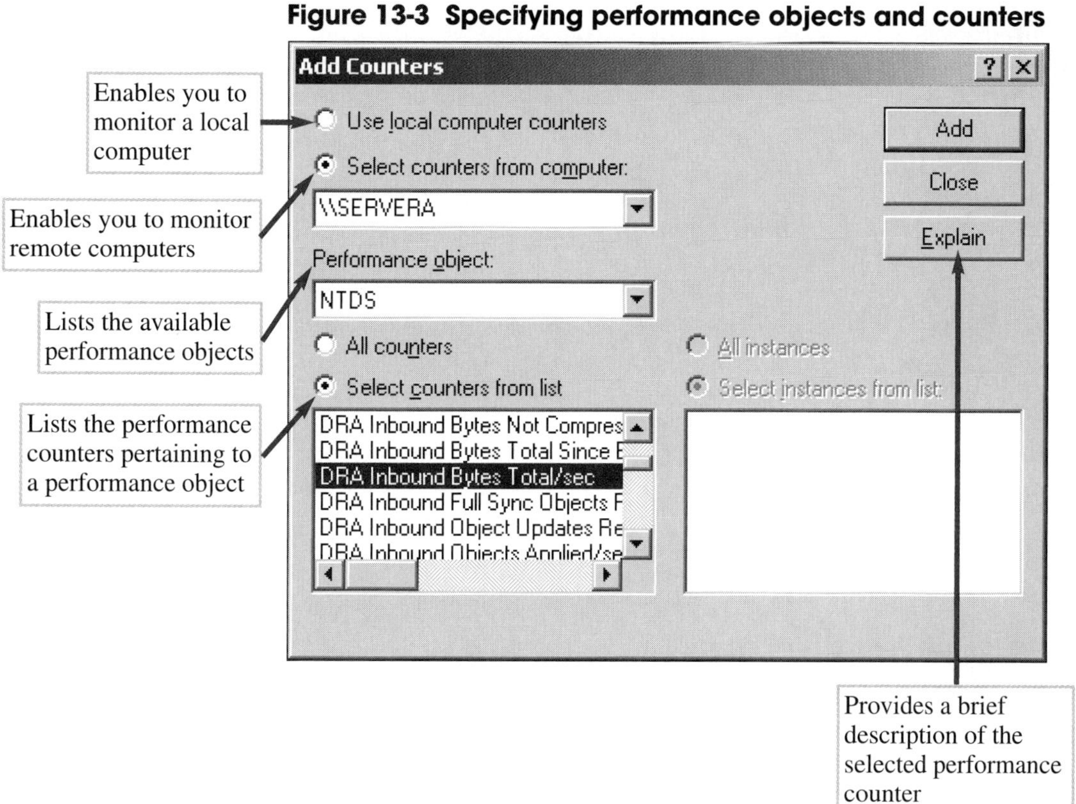

Exam 70-217

skill 2 Monitoring Active Directory Performance Counters *(cont'd)*

exam objective

Monitor, optimize, and troubleshoot Active Directory performance and replication.

how to

6. Click [Add] to add the selected performance counter.
7. Click [Close] to close the **Add Counter** dialog box. The **System Monitor** node displays a chart that graphically represents the statistics of the DRA Inbound Bytes Total/sec performance counter (**Figure 13-4**).
8. Click the **Close** button [X] to close the **Performance** console.

more

The hardware configuration of a domain controller can also affect the performance of Active Directory. To track such hardware bottlenecks, the System Monitor provides you with a number of performance objects and performance counters. **Table 13-3** lists the recommended performance objects and counters for monitoring hardware resources.

Figure 13-4 Monitoring the performance of Active Directory

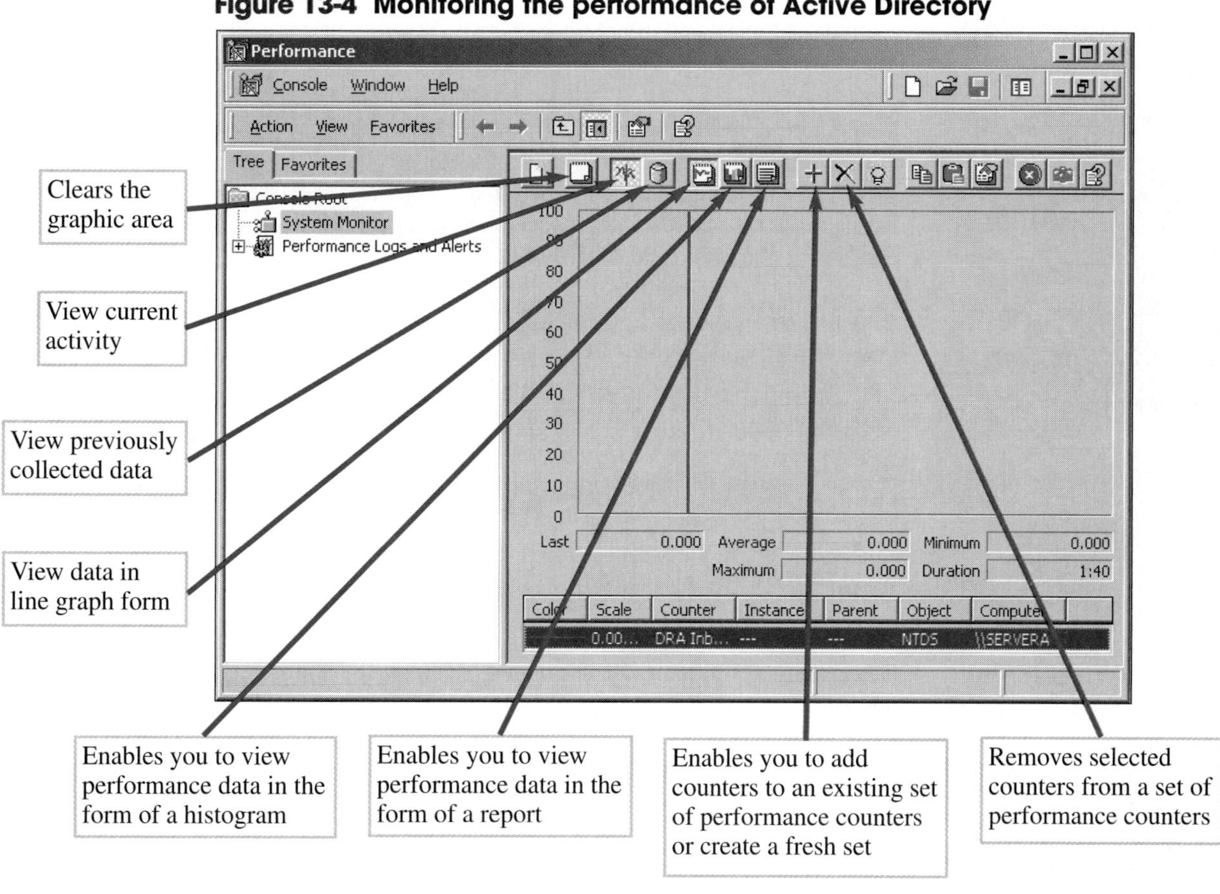
Performance
Console Window Help
Action View Favorites
Tree Favorites
Console Root
System Monitor
Performance Logs and Alerts
Last 0.000 Average 0.000 Minimum 0.000
Maximum 0.000 Duration 1:40
Color Scale Counter Instance Parent Object Computer
0.00... DRA Inb... --- --- NTDS \\SERVERA
Clears the graphic area
View current activity
View previously collected data
View data in line graph form
Enables you to view performance data in the form of a histogram
Enables you to view performance data in the form of a report
Enables you to add counters to an existing set of performance counters or create a fresh set
Removes selected counters from a set of performance counters

Table 13-3 Recommended performance objects and counters for hardware resources

Resource	Performance object	Performance counters
Memory	Memory	Pages/sec, Committed Bytes, Pool Nonpaged Bytes, Pool Nonpaged Allocs, Available Bytes
	Paging File	% Usage
	PhysicalDisk	Avg. Disk Queue Length
	Server	Pool Paged Bytes, Pool Nonpaged Bytes
Processor	Processor	Interrupts/sec, % Processor Time
	System	Processor Queue Length
Hard Disk	PhysicalDisk	Current Disk Queue Length, % Disk Time, Avg. Disk Bytes/Transfer, Disk Reads/sec, Disk Writes/sec
Network	Network Interface	Bytes Received/sec, Bytes Sent/sec, Packets Outbound Errors
	Server	Bytes Total/sec, Work Item Shortages

skill 3 Creating Performance Logs and Alerts

exam objective

Monitor, optimize, and troubleshoot Active Directory performance and replication.

overview

In addition to viewing active performance data of hardware resources and services, you can use the Performance console to collect and record data specific to hardware resources and services. You can achieve this using the Performance Logs and Alerts snap-in of the **Performance** console. The Performance Logs and Alerts snap-in enables you to create counter logs, trace logs, and alerts.

Counter logs

Counter logs are logs that use performance objects and performance counters to record hardware resource- and Active Directory-specific performance data. Counter logs store performance data in log files, which you can import to spreadsheet or database programs for reporting purposes. You can configure a counter log to record statistics of a performance counter at a specified interval for a specified period to collect Active Directory performance data to act as baseline data. This baseline data can be compared with randomly collected performance data while analyzing Active Directory performance.

Trace logs

Trace logs record data only when an event supported by an operating system or an application occurs. For example, you can create a trace log to collect and record data when a read operation is performed on a hard disk. You can use the information stored in trace logs to study the effects of hardware resources on the performance of Active Directory. If you notice that a hardware resource is hampering Active Directory performance, you should consider upgrading the hardware.

Alerts

Alerts are messages that trigger when a resource- or service-related performance counter exceeds or falls below a specified threshold value. The threshold value should be based on the baseline value. Any deviations from the baseline value imply problems relating to the performance of Active Directory and various resources. For example, you may want to set an alert on the Memory, Available Bytes counter. In case a threshold value is breached, you can configure an alert to log an entry in the **application log**, send a message to a computer, start an existing performance log, or run a specified program.

how to

Create a counter log, called **AD**, to collect statistics of the DRA Inbound Objects Applied/sec counter on **ServerA**.

1. Open the **Performance** console.
2. Double-click the **Performance Logs and Alerts** node to expand it, and then click the **Counter Logs** node.
3. Click the **New Log Settings** command on the **Action** menu to open the **New Log Settings** dialog box.
4. Type the counter log file name, **AD**, in the **Name** text box and click OK to open the **AD** dialog box. By default, the log file will be saved as a binary file with a '.blg' extension in a folder named C:\Perflogs (**Figure 13-5**).
5. Click Add... to choose the **NTDS** performance object. The **Select Counters** dialog box appears.
6. Click the arrow for the **Performance object** list box, scroll up the list, and then click the **NTDS** option.

tip

You should have administrative permissions for the HKEY_LOCAL_MACHINE\SYSTEM\CurrentControlSet\Services\SysmonLog\Log Queries registry key to create or modify counter and trace logs.

Figure 13-5 Adding performance counters

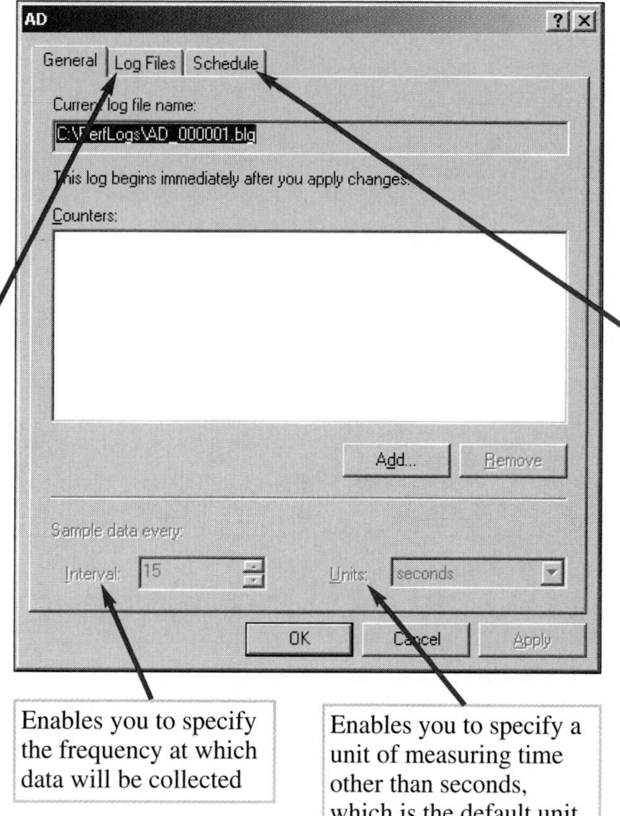

Enables you to specify a different location, file name, file naming convention, type, and size

Enables you to specify the starting and stopping time and date, logging period, and the action to be taken when a log file closes

Enables you to specify the frequency at which data will be collected

Enables you to specify a unit of measuring time other than seconds, which is the default unit

skill 3

Creating Performance Logs and Alerts *(cont'd)*

exam objective

Monitor, optimize, and troubleshoot Active Directory performance and replication.

how to

7. Scroll up the **Select counters from list** list box and click the **DRA Inbound Objects Applied/sec** counter to select it. You use this counter to monitor the rate at which replication updates are received from other domain controllers and incorporated on a domain controller.
8. Click Add to add the selected performance counter, and then click Close to close the **Select Counters** dialog box.
9. Click Apply to save the settings. If this is the first time that a log file is being saved, a message box appears asking you if you want to create the C:\PerfLogs folder now **(Figure 13-6)**. Click **Yes**.
10. Click OK to close the **AD** dialog box. The counter log, called **AD**, appears in the **Performance** console **(Figure 13-7)**.
11. Click the **Close** button ☒ to close the **Performance** console.

more

You can also use the Performance Logs and Alerts snap-in of the Performance console to diagnose and troubleshoot problems relating to Active Directory. The steps for creating trace logs and alerts are similar to the steps for creating counter logs. To create a trace log, click the Trace Logs node in the Performance console, and then click the New Log Settings command on the Action menu. To configure a trace log, you can then specify events you want to track, and change the default log file and the scheduling settings in the respective log file dialog box. To create alerts, click the Alerts node in the Performance console, and then click the New Alert Settings command on the Action menu. To configure an alert, you can then specify counters, alert triggering actions, and scheduling options in the respective dialog boxes.

Figure 13-6 AD Message box

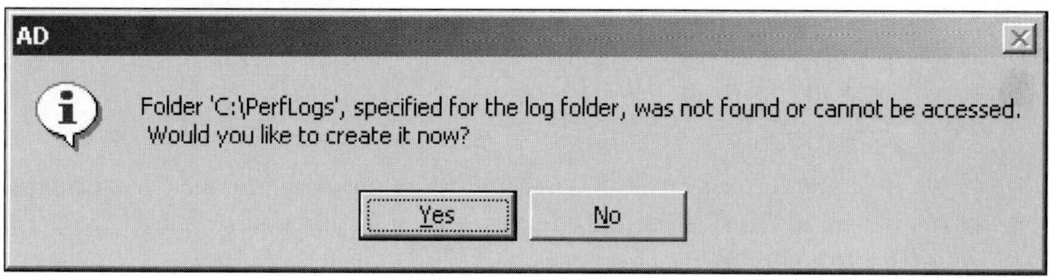

Figure 13-7 Creating a counter log

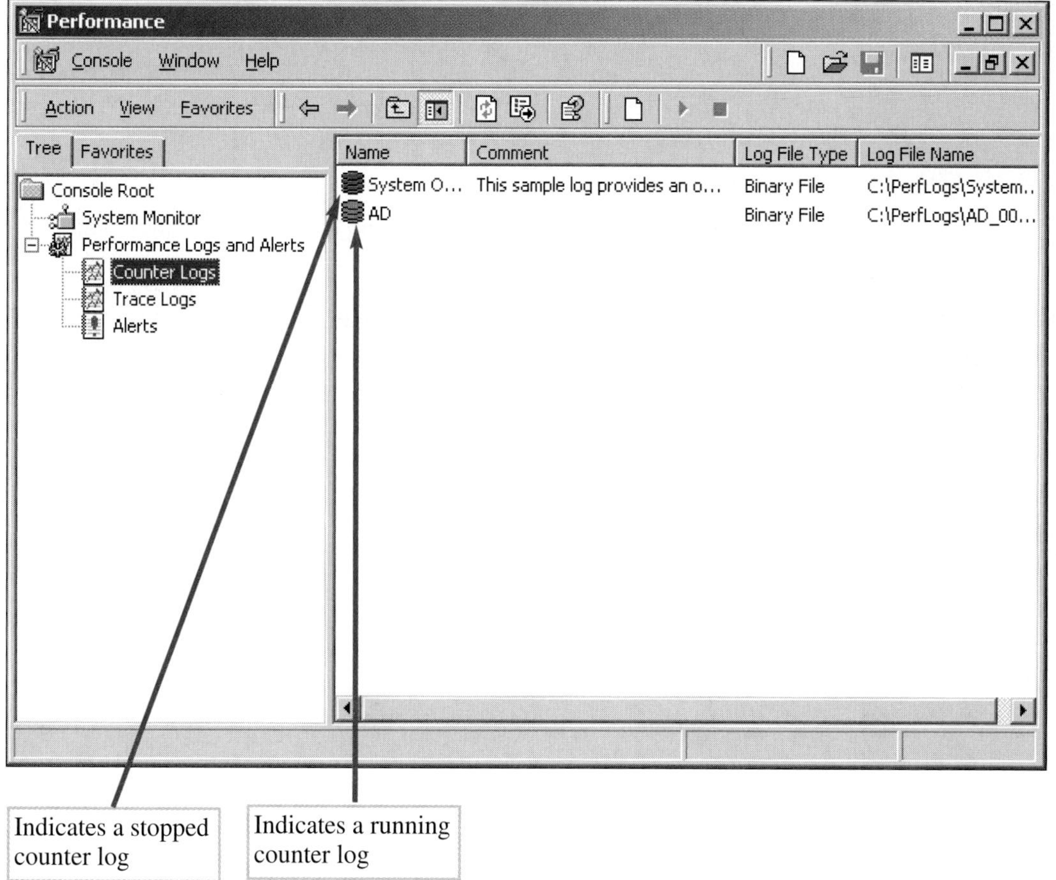

skill 4 Identifying the Active Directory Support Tools

exam objective

Basic knowledge

overview

Besides the performance-monitoring tools, there are various other advanced support tools available for you to monitor the performance of Active Directory, and troubleshoot problems relating to it. The support tools are **LDP.EXE**, **REPLMON.EXE**, **REPADMIN.EXE**, **DSASTAT.EXE**, **SDCHECK.EXE**, **NLTEST.EXE**, **ACLDIAG.EXE**, and **DSACLS.EXE**.

LDP.EXE

LDP.EXE is a graphical tool that provides you with information about objects. This tool also enables you to connect to domains, search, modify, add, delete, and bind to LDAP-compatible directories. Active Directory uses LDAP to locate and access objects in a network. If you are experiencing a problem with Active Directory, you can use this tool to troubleshoot the problem.

tip

The support tools are not installed during Active Directory installation. You need to manually install the support tools on a computer using the Windows 2000 CD-ROM.

REPLMON.EXE

REPLMON is another tool that can graphically represent the replication status, replication topology, and performance of domain controllers. REPLMON can also report on changes that have not replicated from a specified domain controller. Using this tool, you can troubleshoot replication-related problems, and force synchronization between domain controllers. The synchronization process maintains the consistency of Active Directory information by ensuring that the domain controllers participating in the replication process receive Active Directory updates.

REPADMIN.EXE

REPADMIN **(Figure 13-8)** is a command-line tool used to diagnose replication problems. You use this tool to modify and view your replication topologies, view replication information, and force replication between domain controllers. You will need to force replication if you want to propagate important Active Directory updates to other domain controllers immediately.

caution

In normal circumstances, you should not use the REPADMIN tool to change the existing replication topology because it may hamper the replication process.

DSASTAT.EXE

DSASTAT is also a command-line tool used to diagnose replication problems. This tool compares Active Directory replicas on various domain controllers, as well as global catalog servers in a forest. Discrepancies in Active Directory replicas may imply replication-related problems.

SDCHECK.EXE

SDCHECK is a command-line tool that lists the **security descriptors** for Active Directory objects. Security descriptors store discretionary access control lists (DACLs). You can use this tool to verify successful propagation of changes made to the DACLs of objects.

NLTEST.EXE

NLTEST is a command-line tool used to perform network administrative tasks. You can use this tool to check the status of trust relationships between domains and the connectivity and flow of traffic between domain controllers and computers in a network.

ACLDIAG.EXE

ACLDIAG is a command-line tool that you can use to diagnose and troubleshoot problems related to permissions set on AD objects.

DSACLS.EXE

DSACLS is a command-line tool used to manage ACLs. Using this tool, you can query and modify security attributes of Active Directory objects to troubleshoot problems relating to permissions.

Figure 13-8 REPADMIN.EXE

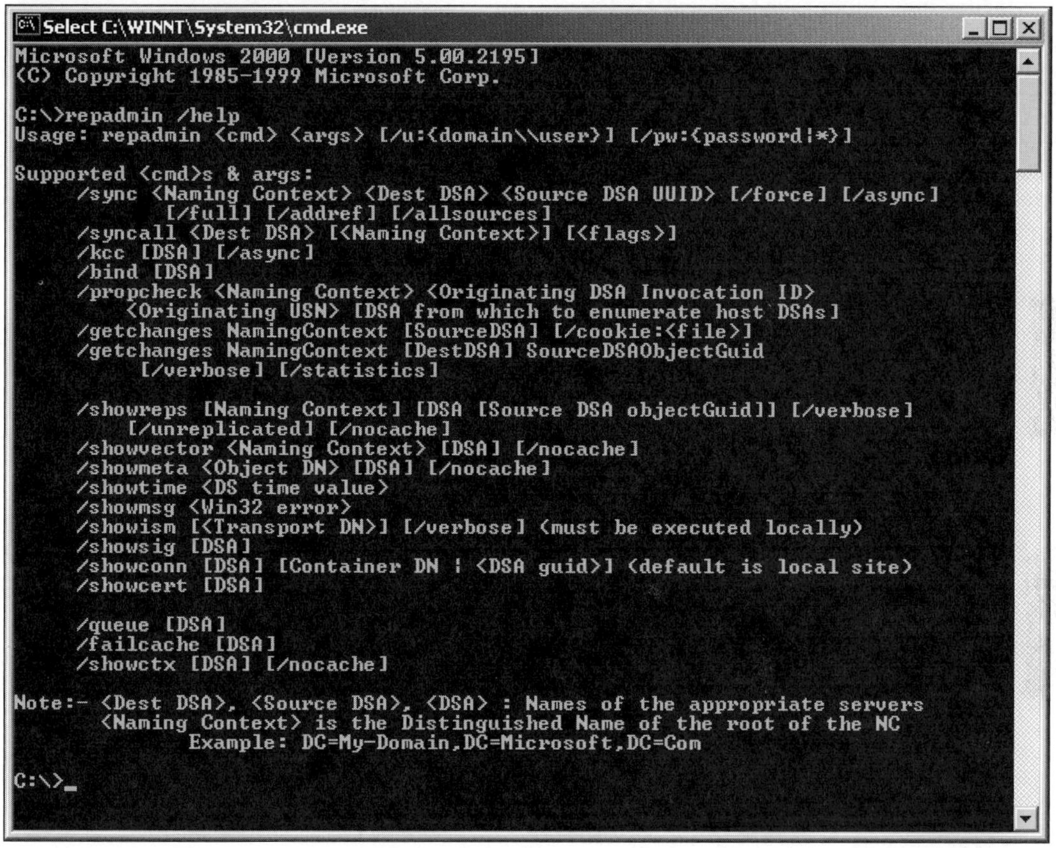

```
Select C:\WINNT\System32\cmd.exe
Microsoft Windows 2000 [Version 5.00.2195]
(C) Copyright 1985-1999 Microsoft Corp.

C:\>repadmin /help
Usage: repadmin <cmd> <args> [/u:<domain\\user>] [/pw:<password|*>]

Supported <cmd>s & args:
     /sync <Naming Context> <Dest DSA> <Source DSA UUID> [/force] [/async]
          [/full] [/addref] [/allsources]
     /syncall <Dest DSA> [<Naming Context>] [<flags>]
     /kcc [DSA] [/async]
     /bind [DSA]
     /propcheck <Naming Context> <Originating DSA Invocation ID>
         <Originating USN> [DSA from which to enumerate host DSAs]
     /getchanges NamingContext [SourceDSA] [/cookie:<file>]
     /getchanges NamingContext [DestDSA] SourceDSAObjectGuid
          [/verbose] [/statistics]

     /showreps [Naming Context] [DSA [Source DSA objectGuid]] [/verbose]
         [/unreplicated] [/nocache]
     /showvector <Naming Context> [DSA] [/nocache]
     /showmeta <Object DN> [DSA] [/nocache]
     /showtime <DS time value>
     /showmsg <Win32 error>
     /showism [<Transport DN>] [/verbose] (must be executed locally)
     /showsig [DSA]
     /showconn [DSA] [Container DN | <DSA guid>] (default is local site)
     /showcert [DSA]

     /queue [DSA]
     /failcache [DSA]
     /showctx [DSA] [/nocache]

Note:- <Dest DSA>, <Source DSA>, <DSA> : Names of the appropriate servers
       <Naming Context> is the Distinguished Name of the root of the NC
              Example: DC=My-Domain,DC=Microsoft,DC=Com

C:\>_
```

Exam 70-217

Summary

- Monitoring the performance of Active Directory is crucial for the smooth functioning of any Windows 2000-based network.
- The two most widely used tools for monitoring Active Directory performance are the Performance console and the Event Viewer console.
- You use the performance-monitoring tools to collect baseline data and troubleshoot problems.
- The Performance console consists of two snap-ins: System Monitor and Performance Logs and Alerts.
- The System Monitor graphically represents the current or previously recorded performance data relating to Active Directory and hardware resources.
- Performance counters provide statistics on the performance of a resource or a service.
- Performance counters are logically grouped together to form performance objects, which represent the resources and services on a computer.
- To monitor the performance of Active Directory, you primarily use the NTDS performance object.
- The Performance Logs and Alerts snap-in enables you to create counter logs, trace logs, and alerts.
- Counter logs store performance data in log files, which you can import to spreadsheet or database programs.
- Trace logs record data only when an event supported by an operating system, or an application, occurs.
- Alerts are messages that trigger when a resource- or service-related performance counter exceeds or falls below a specified threshold value.
- The Event Viewer console enables you to track various events.
- The support tools that enable you to monitor the performance of Active Directory, and troubleshoot any problems relating to it are LDP.EXE, REPLMON.EXE, REPADMIN.EXE, DSASTAT.EXE, SDCHECK.EXE, NLTEST.EXE, ACLDIAG.EXE, and DSACLS.EXE.

Key Terms

ACLDIAG.EXE
Alert
Application log
Console message
Counter log
Directory Service log
DSACLS.EXE
DSASTAT.EXE
Event log
Event Viewer
LDP.EXE
NLTEST.EXE
Performance console
Performance counter
Performance Logs and Alerts
Performance object
REPADMIN.EXE
REPLMON.EXE
SDCHECK.EXE
Security descriptor
System Monitor
Trace log

Test Yourself

1. Which of the following statements about the Event Viewer is correct?
   a. Enables you to create logs and alerts.
   b. Logs alerts and messages generated by applications and services.
   c. Enables you to collect and view real-time performance data.
   d. Represents the replication status and topology.

2. You will check the Directory Service log when:
   a. A user is unable to access an object.
   b. Replication between domain controllers is not occurring.
   c. A user query on an object has failed.
   d. The Task Scheduler service is not responding.

3. Which of the following tools is used to monitor Active Directory performance data in real-time mode?
   a. Event Viewer
   b. Performance Logs and Alerts
   c. REPLMON
   d. System Monitor

4. Performance objects:
   a. Represent the resources and services on a computer.
   b. Provide statistics on the performance of a resource.
   c. Verify successful propagation of changes made to the ACLs of objects.
   d. Study the effects of hardware resources on Active Directory performance.

5. You use the DRA Inbound Objects Applied/sec performance counter if you want to:
   a. Ascertain the total number of bytes received in a second through the replication process.
   b. Measure the amount of replication activity due to updates occurring on a domain controller.
   c. Ascertain the number of objects that have not been updated on a domain controller.
   d. Estimate the number of replication requests that are not processed by a domain controller.

6. Which of the following combinations will enable you to collect and compare baseline and randomly collected Active Directory performance data?
   a. Trace log and alert
   b. Directory Service log and REPLMON
   c. LDP and REPADMIN
   d. Counter log and System Monitor

7. Which of the following is the correct sequence of steps to create a counter log?
   a. Open the System Monitor snap-in, select the performance object and the performance counter, and then save the settings.
   b. Open the Event Viewer console, select the performance counter and the performance object, and then save the settings.
   c. Open the Performance Logs and Alerts snap-in, select the performance object and the performance counter, and then save the settings.
   d. Open the Computer Management console, select the performance object and the performance counter, and then save the setting.

8. You use the DSASTAT tool to:
   a. Compare Active Directory replicas on domain controllers.
   b. Verify successful propagation of changes made to ACLs.
   c. Check the status of trust relationships between domains.
   d. Diagnose and troubleshoot permission-related problems.

9. You use the Computer Management console to:
   a. Query and manipulate security attributes of objects.
   b. Check the status of replication between domains.
   c. Change the access permissions on a shared folder.
   d. Bind to LDAP-compatible directories.

Projects: On Your Own

1. Monitor the Active Directory performance counter named **LDAP Bind Time** on a domain controller.
   a. Log on to the domain controller as an Administrator.
   b. Open the **Performance** console.
   c. Select the **NTDS** performance object.
   d. Select the **LDAP Bind Time** performance counter.
   e. Close the **Performance** console.
2. Create a counter log named **LOGS** to record the statistics provided by the **LDAP Client Sessions** performance counter on a domain controller.
   a. Open the **Performance** console.
   b. Select the **Counter Log** node.
   c. Specify a name for the log file.
   d. Add the **NTDS** performance object and LDAP Client Sessions performance counter.
   e. Accept the default interval settings.
   f. Save the settings.

Problem Solving Scenarios

1. You administer your company's domain controller array located at the company's headquarters. The network is divided across two sites, which jointly service six domains. You have implemented a custom-made Replication Topology for complete pass-through access and authentication, and to reduce replication traffic.

Recently, you have received complaints from users on the other site that ADS data for a couple of domains is not being fully replicated. Changes made to the database two days ago are being reflected now, whereas changes made today are nowhere to be seen.

You are required to analyze the cause of the problem. Draft a document explaining the steps you need to take to correctly analyze the directory database replication process.

2. You administer your company's network. Lately, you have been receiving several complaints regarding incorrect/incomplete directory replication requests from the users. You have been analyzing the network for about a week now and have also implemented a solution for the problem. However, you now want to implement a mechanism that is capable of generating alerts in case a similar problem crops up in the future.

Write a memo describing your proposed plan for the implementation of the alert mechanism.

LESSON

14 Implementing Remote Installation Services (RIS) in Windows 2000

While setting up or expanding the network of an organization, you may need to install an operating system on multiple machines. If this process were automated, it would save time for system administrators, and allow them to perform other activities such as troubleshooting network problems and performing server maintenance. Windows 2000 Server provides the Remote Installation Services (RIS) feature, which automates the installation process to a great extent. RIS enables you to install the Windows 2000 Professional operating system on multiple computers without any user intervention, beyond logging in and selecting an image. In addition to the operating system, RIS enables you to install applications and customize desktop settings on several client computers simultaneously using the RIPrep imaging option. This saves the time and effort of installing the operating system and required software individually on each computer. RIS functions in combination with Active Directory, Dynamic Host Configuration Protocol (DHCP), and Domain Name System (DNS) to provide remote installation of an operating system, as well as applications on new computers without operating systems. Overall, RIS reduces the effort required for operating system installation.

To use RIS, you first need to add the RIS component to the computer that you want to set up as a RIS server. You then need to authorize the RIS server that you set up before it can service RIS clients. Since RIS supports various installation options, you also need to configure RIS so that the required installation and image options are available to users. You can control the installation options available to users by modifying the settings applied to Group Policy Objects (GPOs).

Additionally, it is important to understand the hardware and software requirements for computers to function as RIS servers and RIS clients. Depending on the hardware of the client machines, you might have to create a RIS boot disk before performing a RIS-based installation. Once you have installed and configured RIS, you might also need to check the integrity of the configurations that you have set. To verify RIS configuration, Windows 2000 Server provides the Check Server Wizard, which detects and corrects errors in the configuration.

Goals

In this lesson, you will learn the advantages of RIS, the hardware and software requirements of RIS servers and clients, as well as the steps involved in RIS installation. In addition, this lesson teaches you how to create a RIPrep image and a RIS boot disk. You will also learn how to modify the properties of RIS servers and verify RIS configuration.

Lesson 14 Implementing Remote Installation Services (RIS) in Windows 2000

Skill	Exam 70-217 Objective
1. Introducing Remote Installation Services	Basic knowledge
2. Understanding the Remote Operating System Installation Process	Basic knowledge
3. Setting Up RIS On Windows 2000 Server	Configure Active Directory to support Remote Installation Services (RIS).
4. Authorizing a RIS Server	Configure Active Directory to support Remote Installation Services (RIS).
5. Customizing Properties for a RIS Server	Configure RIS options to support remote installations.
6. Customizing Options for RIS Client Installation	Configure RIS options to support remote installations.
7. Creating a RIPrep Image	Basic knowledge
8. Creating a RIS Boot Disk	Basic knowledge
9. Verifying RIS Configuration	Basic knowledge

Requirements

To complete this lesson, you need administrative rights on ServerA, the domain controller of the mydomain.com domain. ServerA should be running the DHCP and DNS services with Active Directory. It should also have a second NTFS partition or volume with at least 2 GB of space configured. Active Directory should contain an empty Group Policy named Users applied to the domain, and another empty GPO named Advanced Users applied to the Domain Controllers OU. You will also need administrative rights on a Windows 2000 Professional computer that is a client in the domain.

skill 1 Introducing Remote Installation Services

exam objective

Basic knowledge

overview

Remote Installation Services (RIS) enables you to automate the installation of the Windows 2000 Professional operating system. This is particularly useful in cases where you need to install the operating system on multiple machines simultaneously, especially in large organizations. In addition to reducing the time required for installation, this service enables you to perform the installation without physically going to each machine. To perform an installation using RIS, you need a DHCP server, a Windows 2000-compliant DNS server, and an Active Directory service. The DHCP server provides the Internet Protocol (IP) address to the client computer. DNS is needed to allow the RIS server to find and use Active Directory. Active Directory enables the RIS server to determine user rights and permissions.

RIS has two major components: RIS servers and RIS clients. The information required for the installation, such as computer names, time zone settings, and network settings, is specified on RIS servers. RIS clients are the machines on which Windows 2000 Professional is to be installed. The following services are added when RIS is installed on a server (**Figure 14-1**):

- **Boot Information Negotiation Layer (BINL)**. The BINL service manages the working of RIS. It controls the response to network service requests from RIS clients. On receiving these requests, BINL ensures that the correct files and configuration and policy settings are sent to the client.
- **Trivial File Transfer Protocol (TFTP)**. The TFTP service manages the file transfer requests from RIS clients during a remote installation. This service is used to download initial files such as the bootstrap files required for installation to start. TFTP is also used for downloading the Client Installation Wizard (CIW). This wizard prompts RIS clients to provide information that is required during operating system installation such as user name, password, and domain name.
- **Single Instance Store (SIS)**. The SIS service minimizes the disk space required for storing RIS installation images on the RIS server. SIS searches for duplicate files in the RIS volume, which is the location on the RIS server where RIS has been installed. SIS tries to identify all files related to the installation and links them together. It removes redundant copies, thereby saving space on the server. The file links contain information such as the name and the location of the original file in the SIS store, its size, and its attributes.

The above three services are installed on the RIS server when you install RIS. These services then work in combination with one another to enable remote installation of Windows 2000 Professional on computers.

Figure 14-1 Components of RIS

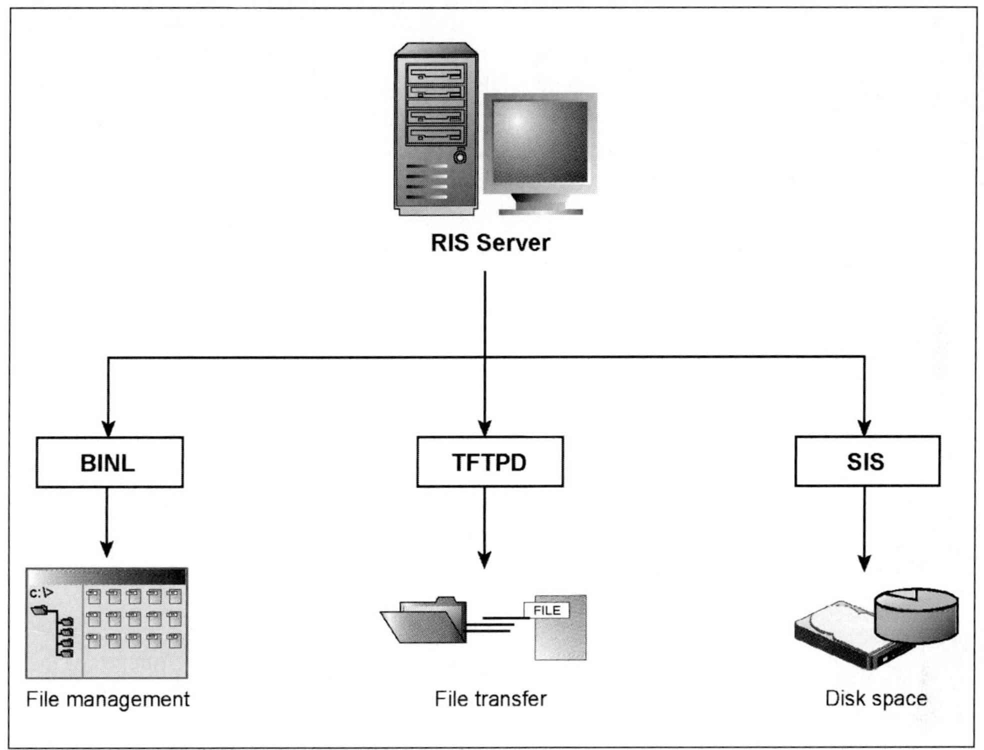

skill 1 Introducing Remote Installation Services *(cont'd)*

exam objective

Basic knowledge

overview

RIS clients can be of the following two types (**Figure 14-2**):

- **Computers that support Preboot Execution Environment (PXE) DHCP-based remote boot ROMS**. The PXE DHCP-based remote boot technology enables computers to start operating system installation from a remote source. This remote source is a RIS server in the case of RIS. It enables computers to connect to the network and execute programs by booting directly from a network image. Computers using the PXE technology send a DHCP discovery packet as a network broadcast. On receiving a response from a DHCP server, the client computer sends a request for an IP address for itself, as well as the IP address of a RIS server. On receiving this information, the computer sends a network service request to the RIS server, which sends the location and filename of the bootstrap files to the computer. PXE support is typically provided by a boot ROM on the NIC. This PXE boot ROM must be version .99c or higher to support RIS.
- **Computers with network cards that the RIS boot disk supports**. If a computer does not support the PXE DHCP-based remote boot technology, then you can use RIS with the help of the RIS boot disk. This disk can be created using a tool provided by Windows 2000 Server known as RBFG.EXE (**Figure 14-3**). It emulates the PXE remote boot technology and enables computers to boot directly from the network image. The boot disk includes drivers that are compatible with around 30 different models of network cards, all defined by their chipset. Since most network cards use similar chipsets, even if your card isn't listed, it may still be compatible.

more

In addition to the basic operating system, you can also create images of the operating system that include the application and desktop settings required by users. You can then use this image for remote installation of the required operating system, applications, and desktop settings on several computers simultaneously.

Figure 14-2 RIS clients

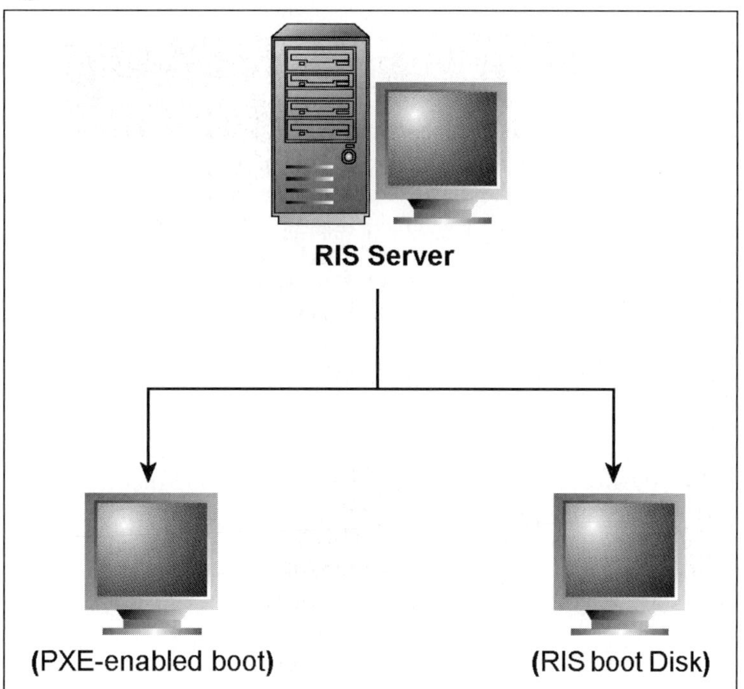

Figure 14-3 Creating an RIS boot disk

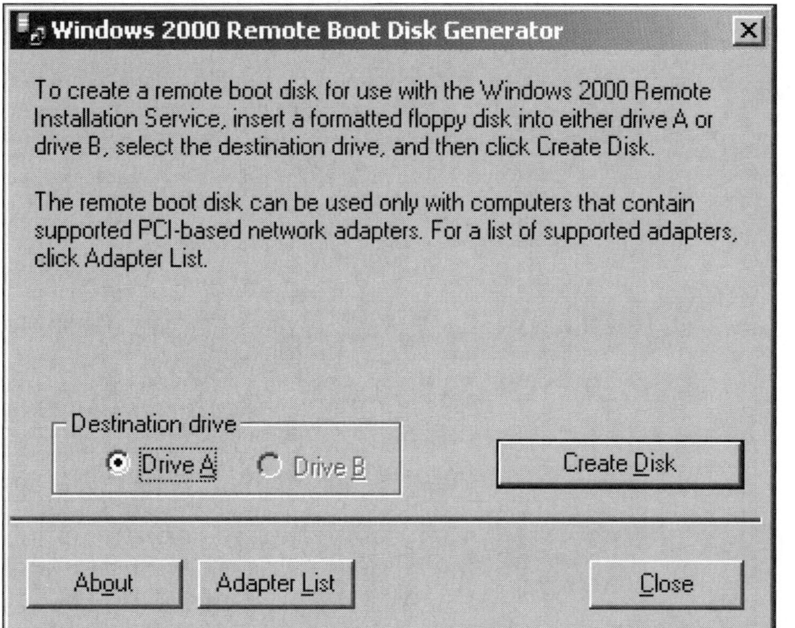

skill 2 Understanding the Remote Operating System Installation Process

exam objective

Basic knowledge

overview

tip

If multiple servers exist on the network, any RIS server can send its IP address to the computer. Typically, the first RIS server to respond is used in this case.

During a RIS-based remote installation of Windows 2000 Professional RIS, the following steps are performed:

1. When a computer connected to the network is switched on, and the computer does not have an operating system, the computer will typically display a message indicating that you need to press a key to boot from the network. Once this is done, the machine sends a DHCP discover packet that requests an IP address. This packet also includes a request for the IP address of any RIS server present on the network, and contains the Globally Unique Identifier (GUID) or Universally Unique ID (UUID) of the computer without the operating system. The DHCP server allocates an IP address to the computer and sends it in response to the packet. The RIS server on the network sends its IP address to the computer along with the name of the boot file. The system then prompts the user to press the F12 key to start the installation.
2. The selected RIS server then checks the pre-staged computer accounts in Active Directory for an account with a GUID that matches that of the computer without an operating system. Then, the Client Installation Wizard (CIW) is downloaded to the computer. From there, the CIW prompts the user to log on to the network.
3. When the user logs on, the RIS server checks the account information. The RIS server determines the installation options, as well as the operating system images to be presented to the user based on the Group Policy settings related to RIS. If the machine is pre-staged, the GUID/UUID of the computer account is also checked at this time.
4. The user is then prompted to select the required operating system image based on a brief description that is associated with each image. Next, the CIW displays a warning that the hard disk will be reformatted, and previous data will be lost. After this, the user can start the remote installation of the operating system.
5. The CIW displays a summary of the specified installation settings. Once the user confirms these settings, the installation starts. If, at this stage, the computer has not been pre-staged and its account is not created in Active Directory, the BINL service creates the computer account. The operating system will now be fully installed and can be configured to be performed without any further user intervention.

more

To use RIS, you need to fulfill certain hardware and software requirements for computers to function as RIS servers and RIS clients. These requirements are listed in **Table 14-1**.

Table 14-1 Hardware and software requirements for using RIS

	RIS Server	RIS Client
Hardware Requirements	• Pentium or Pentium II 166 MHz (200 MHz or faster processor recommended) • 64 MB RAM (128 MB if Active Directory, DHCP, and DNS are to be installed) • 2 GB hard disk or partition dedicated to the RIS directory tree • 10 or 100 mbps network card	• Pentium 166 MHz • 32 MB RAM (64MB recommended) • 800 MB hard disk • Supported PCI Plug and Play network adapter card • Optional: PXE-based remote boot ROM version .99c or later
Software Requirements	The following services should be running on individual servers or the same server: • DNS • DHCP • Active Directory	

skill 3

Setting Up RIS on Windows 2000 Server

exam objective

Configure Active Directory to support Remote Installation Services (RIS).

overview

Before you can use RIS, you need to set it up. Setting up RIS on a server involves adding the RIS component to the server and installing RIS. During the installation of RIS, the system performs various tasks **(Figure 14-4)**.

tip

It is important to note that RIS installation is performed on a Windows 2000 Server computer in order to create a RIS server. This installation is different from the RIS-based installation, which is used for installing Windows 2000 Professional on RIS clients.

how to

Set up RIS.

1. Log on to ServerA as an Administrator.
2. Click Start, point to **Settings**, and then click the **Control Panel** command. This displays the **Control Panel** window.
3. Double-click the **Add/Remove Programs** icon to display the **Add/Remove Programs** window. Click the **Add/Remove Windows Components** icon to initiate the Windows Components Wizard.
4. Select the **Remote Installation Services** check box in the **Components** section, and click Next > to start copying the installation files.
5. The **Files Needed** dialog box opens to prompt you for the location of the installation files. Type **E:\i386** (you are going to need your Windows 2000 CD-ROM, and E:\ is the address of your CD-ROM drive) in the **Copy files from** text box, and click OK.
6. When the installation files have been copied, click Finish on the last screen of the Windows Component Wizard. This adds the RIS component **(Figure 14-5)**. You can now close the **Add/Remove Programs** window and the **Control Panel** window.
7. Click **Yes** to restart your system.
8. After adding the RIS component, you need to configure RIS. Close the Control Panel window, and then click Start, point to **Programs**, point to **Administrative Tools**, and then click the **Configure Your Server** command. This displays the **Windows 2000 Configure Your Server** dialog box.
9. Click the **Finish setup** hyperlink to display the **Add/Remove Programs** window.
10. To start the Remote Installation Services Setup Wizard, click Configure in the **Configure Remote Installation Services** section.

Figure 14-4 Installing RIS

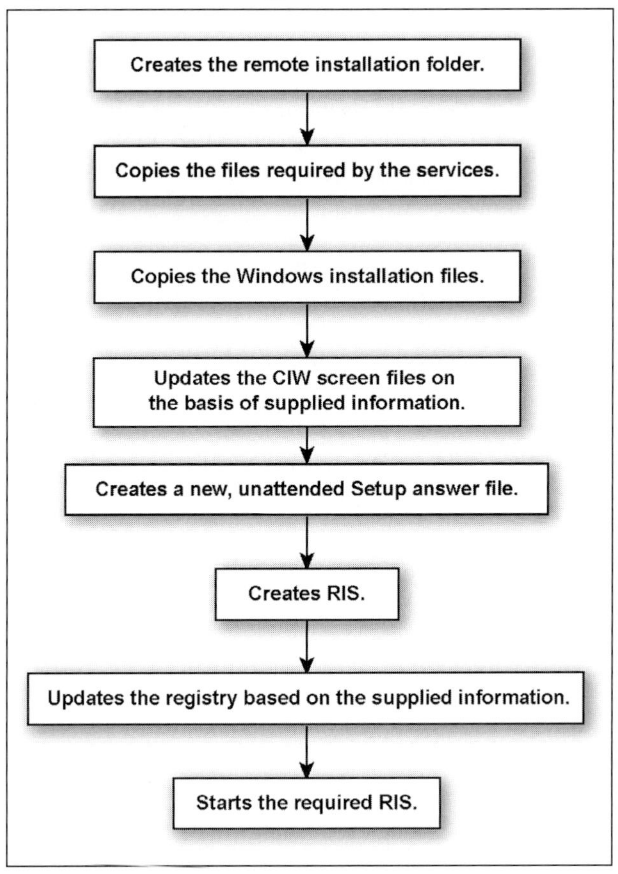

Figure 14-5 RIS component added

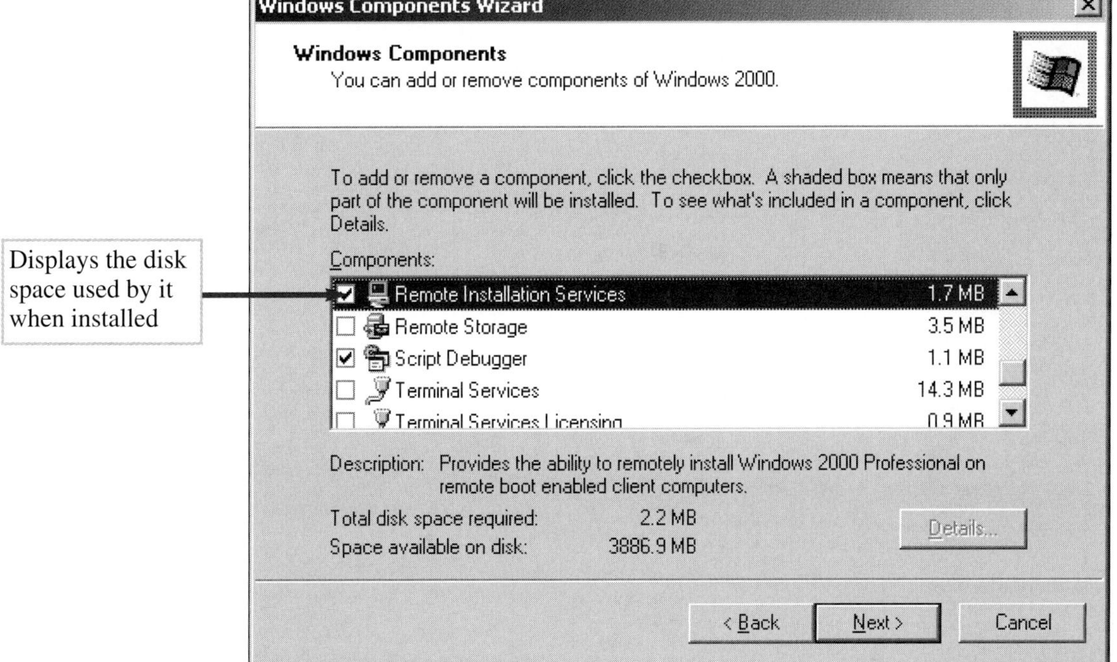

skill 3

Setting Up RIS on Windows 2000 Server (cont'd)

exam objective

Configure Active Directory to support Remote Installation Services (RIS).

how to

11. The first screen of this wizard lists the requirements for using RIS (**Figure 14-6**). Click [Next >] to move to the **Remote Installation Folder Location** screen of the wizard.
12. Type **D:\RemoteInstall** in the **Path** text box to specify the location to which the RIS files should be copied. Then, click [Next >] to display the **Initial Settings** screen of the wizard.
13. Select the **Respond to client computers requesting service** check box in order to configure the RIS server to start servicing client requests immediately. Click [Next >] to specify the location of source files.
14. Type **E:\i386** in the **Path** text box to specify the location of the source files, and click [Next >] to move to the **Windows Installation Image Folder Name** screen of the wizard.
15. Accept the default name **win2000.pro** in the **Folder name** text box, and click [Next >]. The **Friendly Description And Help Text** screen of the wizard appears.
16. Accept the default description and help text, and click [Next >]. This displays the **Review Settings** screen, which shows a summary of the RIS settings you have specified. Click [Finish] to finish the configuration process. Once the configuration is complete, click [Done] to exit the Remote Installation Services Setup Wizard (**Figure 14-7**).
17. Close the **Add/Remove Programs** window and the **Windows 2000 Configure Your Server** dialog box.

more

To specify the location of the installation files in the **File Needed** dialog box while adding the RIS component, you can also click [Browse...] to browse and select the location of the installation files.

Figure 14-6 Remote Installation Services Setup Wizard

Figure 14-7 Please Wait screen of Remote Installation Services Wizard

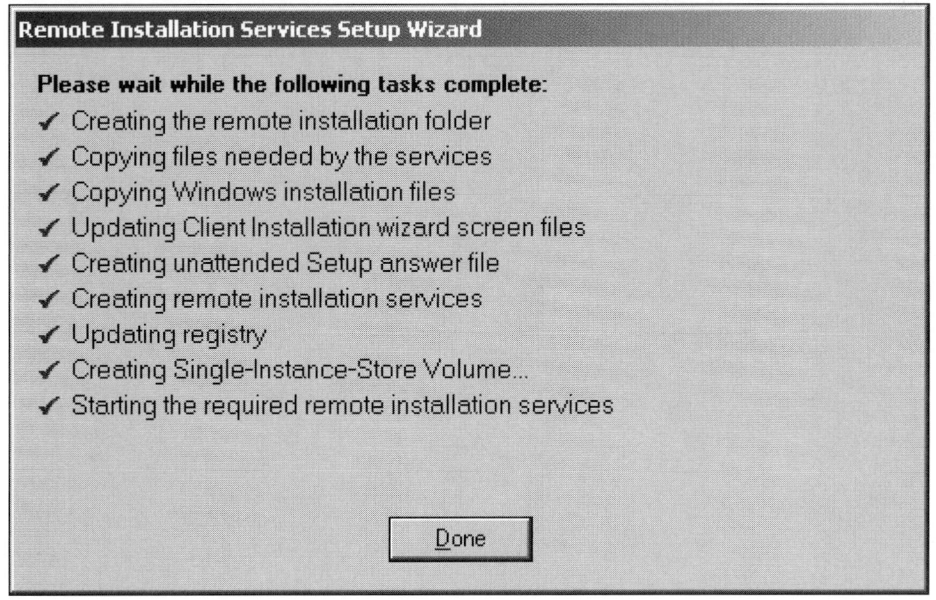

Exam 70-217

skill 4 Authorizing a RIS Server

exam objective

Configure Active Directory to support Remote Installation Services (RIS).

overview

After setting up RIS on a server, you need to authorize the RIS server. Authorizing a RIS server enables it to service RIS client requests. Also, authorizing RIS servers helps prevent unauthorized servers on the network from acting as RIS servers. If unauthorized RIS servers were started on the network, it would automatically be shut down. You authorize RIS servers in the same way that you authorize A DHCP server: in the DHCP server console.

how to

Authorize an RIS server on a DHCP server.

1. Log on to ServerA as an Administrator.
2. Click Start, point to **Programs**, point to **Administrative Tools**, and then click the **DHCP** command. This displays the **DHCP** console.
3. Right-click the **DHCP** node in the left pane, and then click the **Manage authorized servers…** command to display the **Manage Authorized Servers** dialog box. This dialog box lists the names and IP addresses of the authorized servers, if any.
4. Click Authorize... to open the **Authorize DHCP Server** dialog box **(Figure 14-8)**. Type **ServerA** in the **Name or IP address** text box and click OK to view a message displaying the name and IP address of the specified server **(Figure 14-9)**.
5. Click Yes to authorize the server. The **ServerA** server is added to the list of authorized servers (**Figure 14-10**). Select the server in the list, and click OK to add the RIS server to the **DHCP** node.
6. Close the **DHCP** console.

more

Only a user with Enterprise Administrator privileges can authorize a DHCP or RIS server. This is because these services can potentially impact multiple domains.

Figure 14-8 Specifying the name of the server to authorize

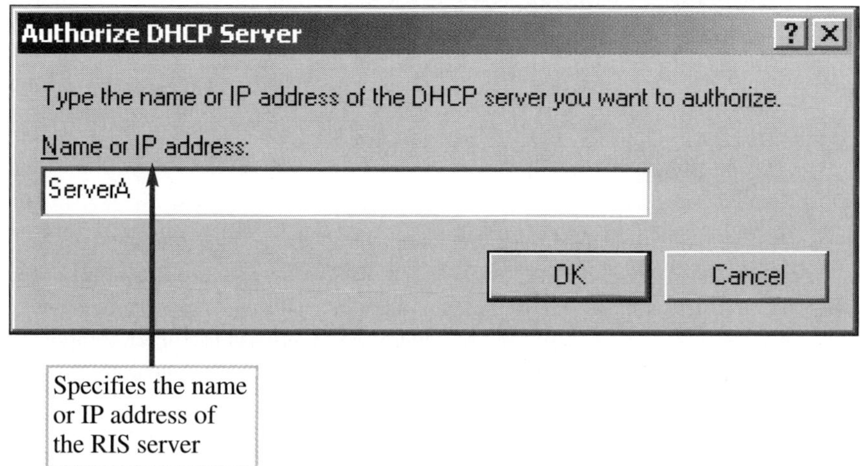

Figure 14-9 Confirming the name and IP address of the server to authorize

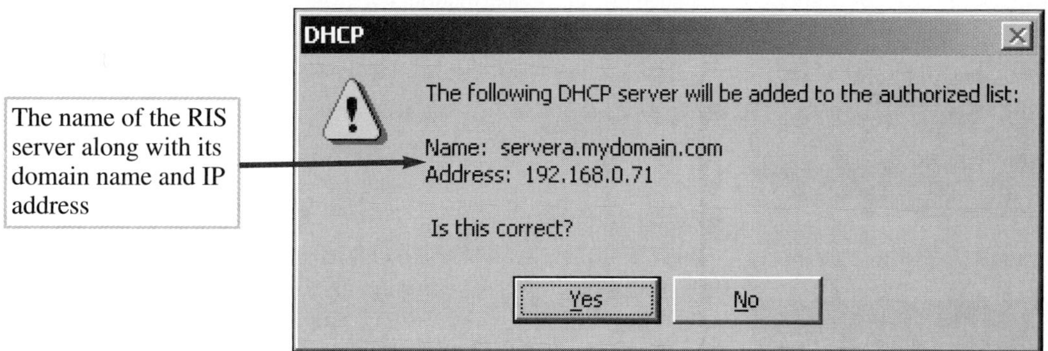

Figure 14-10 Viewing authorized servers

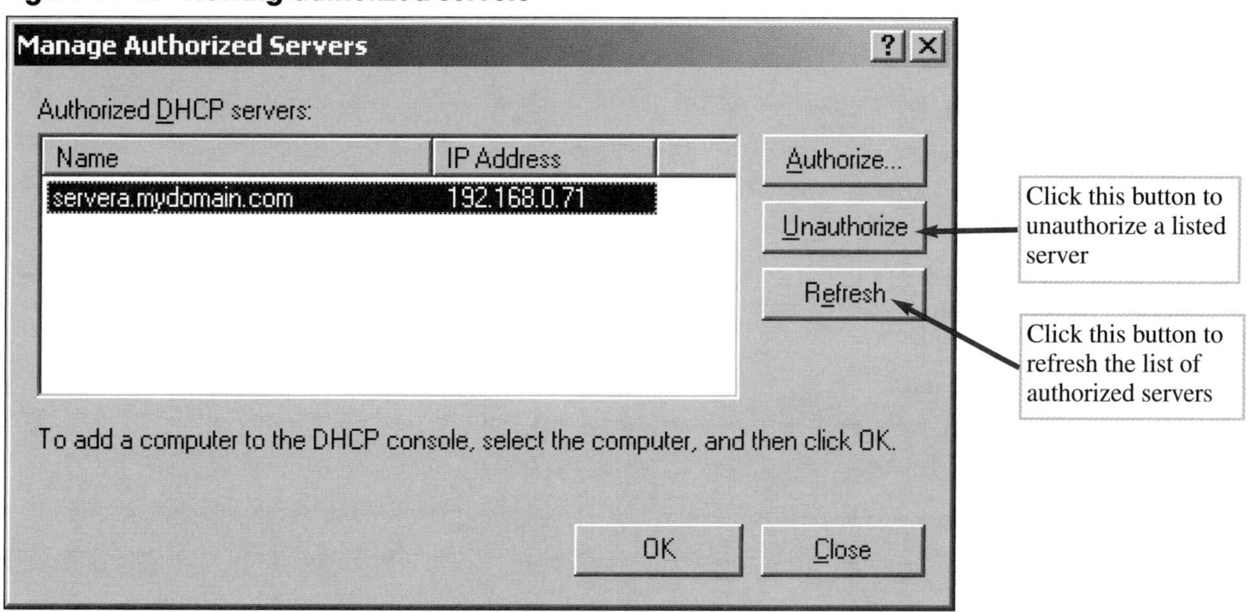

skill 5 Customizing Properties for a RIS Server

exam objective

Configure RIS options to support remote installations.

overview

After installing RIS, you can customize the way in which a RIS server handles client requests. Suppose you have to install Windows 2000 Professional on 50 computers for developers and 10 computers for managers. You might want to perform the installation on the managers' computers manually and use RIS for installing the operating system on the other computers. To accomplish this, create computer accounts for the developers' computers and configure the server to service requests only of computers whose accounts have been created in Active Directory. In such a situation, you can modify the RIS server settings using the Active Directory Users and Computers console. In this console, you can locate the RIS server and modify its properties, as required. Besides specifying selected clients to be serviced, you can modify the RIS properties to a RIS in order to determine which RIS server will service the pre-staged clients. This might be required in certain situations such as if you wish to load balance the image distribution across several RIS servers. In the case where there is a problem with a particular RIS server, you may stop the RIS server service. To stop the RIS server from servicing RIS clients at all, clear the Respond to client computers requesting service check box on the Remote Install tab of the Properties dialog box.

how to

Modify the properties of an RIS server so that it responds only to known computers, and generates computer names using the first initial and last name of users.

1. Log on to ServerA as an Administrator.
2. Click Start, point to **Programs**, point to **Administrative Tools**, and then click the **Active Directory Users and Computers** command to open the **Active Directory Users and Computers** console.
3. Select the **Domain Controllers** container in the left pane to view its contents in the details pane.
4. Right-click the **ServerA** server in the details pane, and then click the **Properties** command. This displays the **Properties** dialog box for the selected server **(Figure 14-11)**.
5. Click the **Remote Install** tab to view and modify RIS settings **(Figure 14-12)**.
6. Select the **Do not respond to unknown client computers** check box in order to configure the RIS server to respond only to known clients.

Figure 14-11 Selecting the RIS server in the Active Directory Users and Computers console

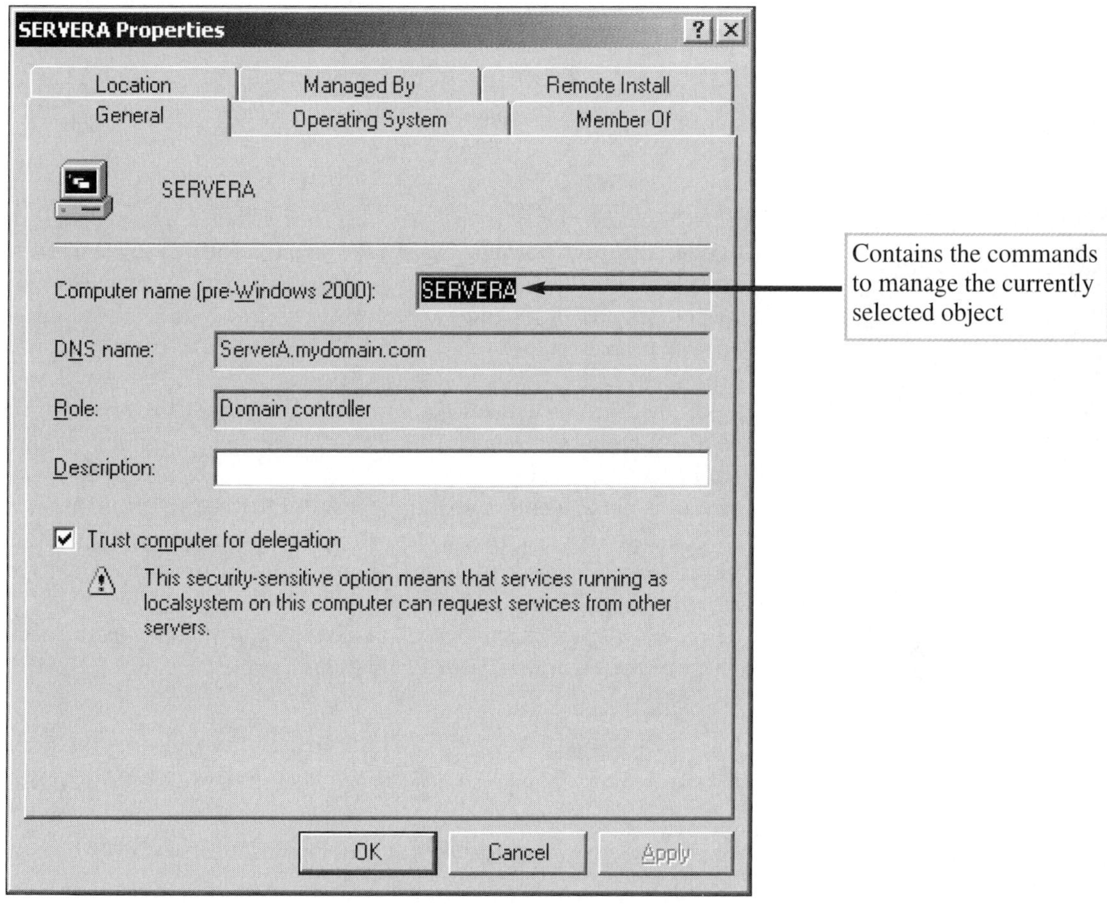

Figure 14-12 Viewing the properties of a RIS server

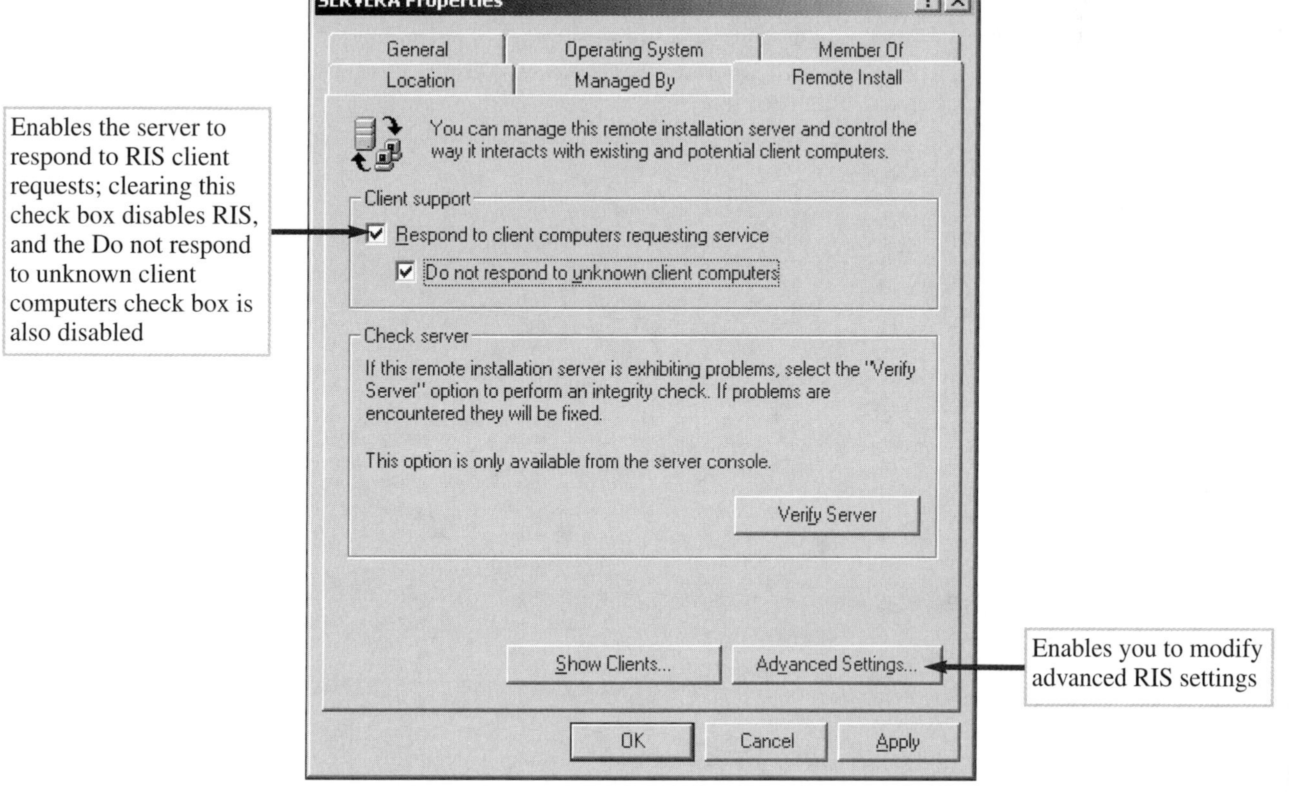

skill 5 Customizing Properties for a RIS Server *(cont'd)*

exam objective

Configure RIS options to support remote installations.

how to

7. Click Advanced Settings... to display the **New Clients** tab of the **Remote Installation Services Properties** dialog box for the selected server. You can use the **New Clients** tab to specify how the names for the new clients should be generated. Computer names are generated by the RIS server and used during RIS-based installations. The **New Clients** tab also enables you to specify the location where the client account should be created **(Figure 14-13)**.
8. Select the **First initial**, **Last name** option from the **Generate client computer names using** list box. An example of this type of naming convention is displayed below the list box.
9. Select the **Same location as that of the user setting up the client computer** option.
10. Click the **Images** tab. This tab lists the various operating system images available on the server. Besides a description of each image, the platform and language of each image is also displayed **(Figure 14-14)**.
11. Select the **win2000pro** image, and click Properties to display the details of the selected image. Type **Windows 2000 Professional** in the **Friendly Description** text box, and click OK.
12. Click OK to close the **Remote Installation Services Properties** dialog box for the selected server and click OK again to close the **Properties** dialog box for the selected server.
13. Close the **Active Directory Users and Computers** console.

more

You can customize the values that the RIS server uses to generate computer names. To create a customized naming scheme, select Custom from the Generate client computer names using list box, or click Customize in the Remote Installation Services Properties dialog box. Clicking this button displays the Computer Account Generation dialog box, where you can specify a customized format for the generation of computer names. This dialog box also lists descriptions of the different variables that can be used for defining the format.

Figure 14-13 Specifying how the RIS server should create client computer accounts

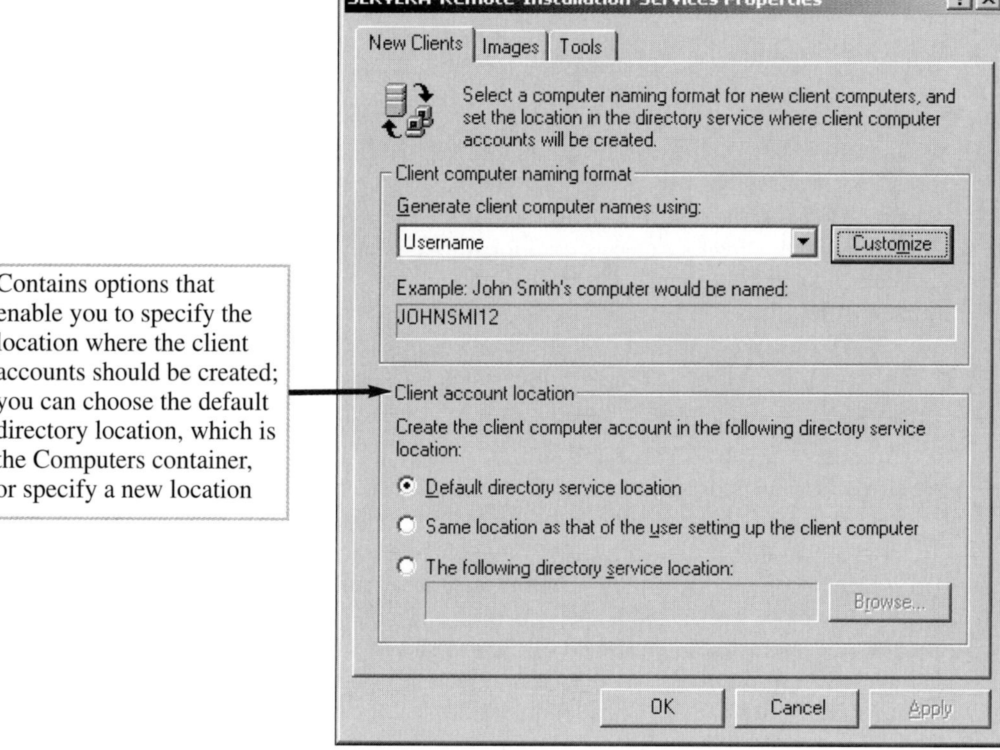

Figure 14-14 Viewing the list of images stored on the RIS server

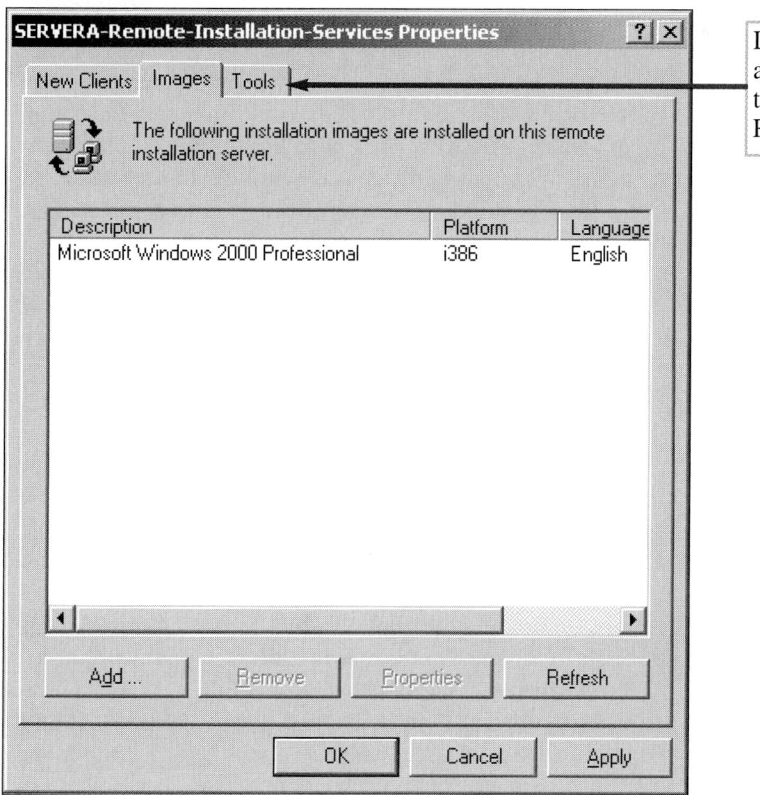

skill 6 Customizing Options for RIS Client Installation

exam objective

Configure RIS options to support remote installations.

overview

While configuring a RIS server, you can also customize the client installation options that should be available to users. Suppose you have a Group Policy Object (GPO) named Advanced Users applied to an OU, and another GPO named Novices applied to the domain. GPOs are Active Directory objects used for storing policy settings. Since the Novices GPO applies to all users, you might not want an installation option that requires user input to be available to Novices. However, if you want all the installation options to be available to the Advanced Users GPO, you can modify the RIS settings accordingly. To view and modify the installation option settings for a GPO, use the Choice Options Properties dialog box.

There are four installation options that you can make available to users:

- **Automatic Setup** — This is the default installation option. The installation starts as soon as the user logs on. This option prevents users from being prompted for the various settings, such as computer names, network settings, and time zone settings, that are normally available during the installation of an operating system. However, you can still present the user with various operating system images from which to choose. Therefore, the user can select the set of applications that should be installed on his computer. When the user selects the automatic setup, the RIS server generates the machine name, and the client account is created in the location specified in the RIS server settings.
- **Custom Setup** — This installation option enables the user to override the computer names generated by the RIS server. For instance, if you want the operating system to be installed on a manager's computer automatically but you also want him to be able to specify a computer name of his choice, you can make this option available to him. Additionally, the user can specify a location other than the one specified in the RIS server settings for the client account.
- **Restart Setup** — This installation option helps users if there is an incomplete setup attempt. If a user cancelled a previous setup event after specifying a few options, or if the setup fails, the user can select this option to restart the setup. When this option is selected, the complete installation begins again. However, the option does not prompt the user for any values that have already been specified such as network settings and time zone settings. Therefore, this option saves the time required for specifying the same values again. Availability of this installation option can be set using the options in the Restart Setup section of the Choice Options Properties dialog box.
- **Tools:** This option enables users to use troubleshooting tools before the operating system has been installed. These tools could include system BIOS flash updates and memory virus scanners. Availability of this installation option can be set using the options in the Tools section of the Choice Options Properties dialog box.

how to

Modify the client installation options for a GPO.

1. Log on to ServerA as an Administrator.
2. Click Start, point to **Programs**, point to **Administrative Tools**, and then click the **Active Directory Users and Computers** command to open the **Active Directory Users and Computers** console.
3. Right-click the **Domain Controllers** organizational unit (OU), and then click the **Properties** command to view the properties of the domain controllers.
4. Click the **Group Policy** tab to view the list of GPOs (**Figure 14-15**).
5. Click **Advanced Users**, and then click Edit... to edit the **Advanced Users** GPO. This displays the **Group Policy** console.

Figure 14-15 Editing GPO properties

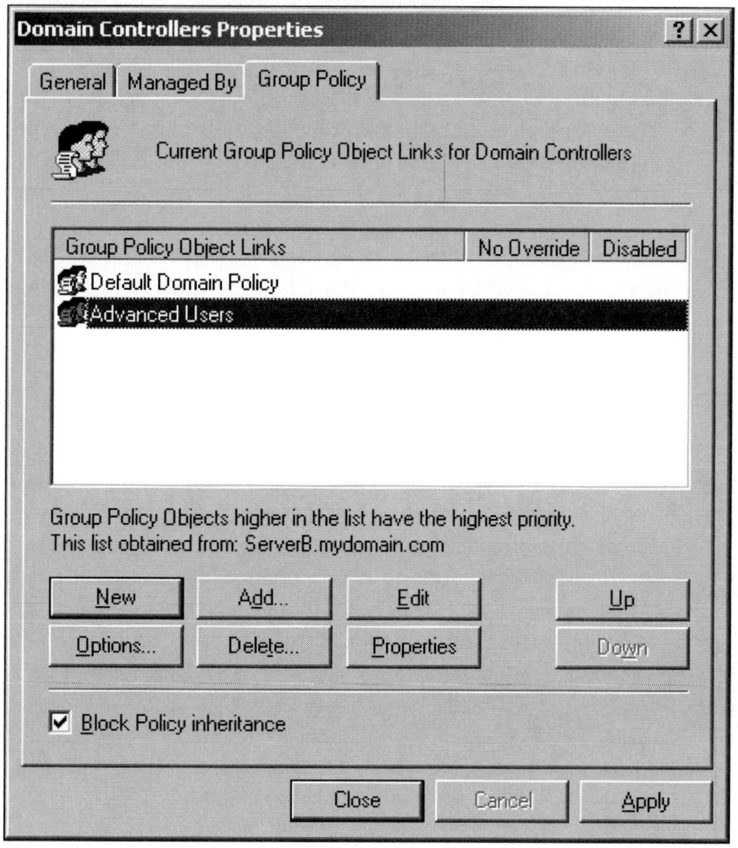

skill 6

Customizing Options for RIS Client Installation (cont'd)

exam objective

Configure RIS options to support remote installations.

how to

6. In the **Group Policy** console, double-click the **User Configuration** node to expand it, and then click the **Window Settings** node to expand it, as well.
7. In the **Windows Settings** node, double-click the **Remote Installation Services** node to view the **Choice Options** object in the details pane of the **Group Policy** console **(Figure 14-16)**.
8. Double-click the **Choice Options** object to display the **Choice Option Properties** dialog box. This dialog box displays the policy settings for each of the four installation options **(Figure 14-17)**.
9. Select the **Allow** option in the **Custom Setup** section to make the **Custom Setup** installation option available to all users associated with the **Advanced Users** GPO. This setting overrides the setting applied to the parent GPO.
10. Click OK to close the **Choice Option Properties** dialog box. Then, close the **Group Policy** console and the **Active Directory Users and Computers** console.

more

When you modify an installation option setting for a GPO, the change takes effect only after the automatic policy propagation. Automatic policy propagation applies changes made to user policies. It occurs at default intervals of 90-120 minutes. However, if you want to apply the changes immediately, you can either log off and log back on, or you can execute the secedit/refreshpolicy user_policy command at the command prompt. You would typically perform this action after a modification to group policies, however, certain policy settings (such as RIS, application installation, and logon scripts) will only take effect during the next startup or logon.

Figure 14-16 Selecting RIS settings in the Group Policy console

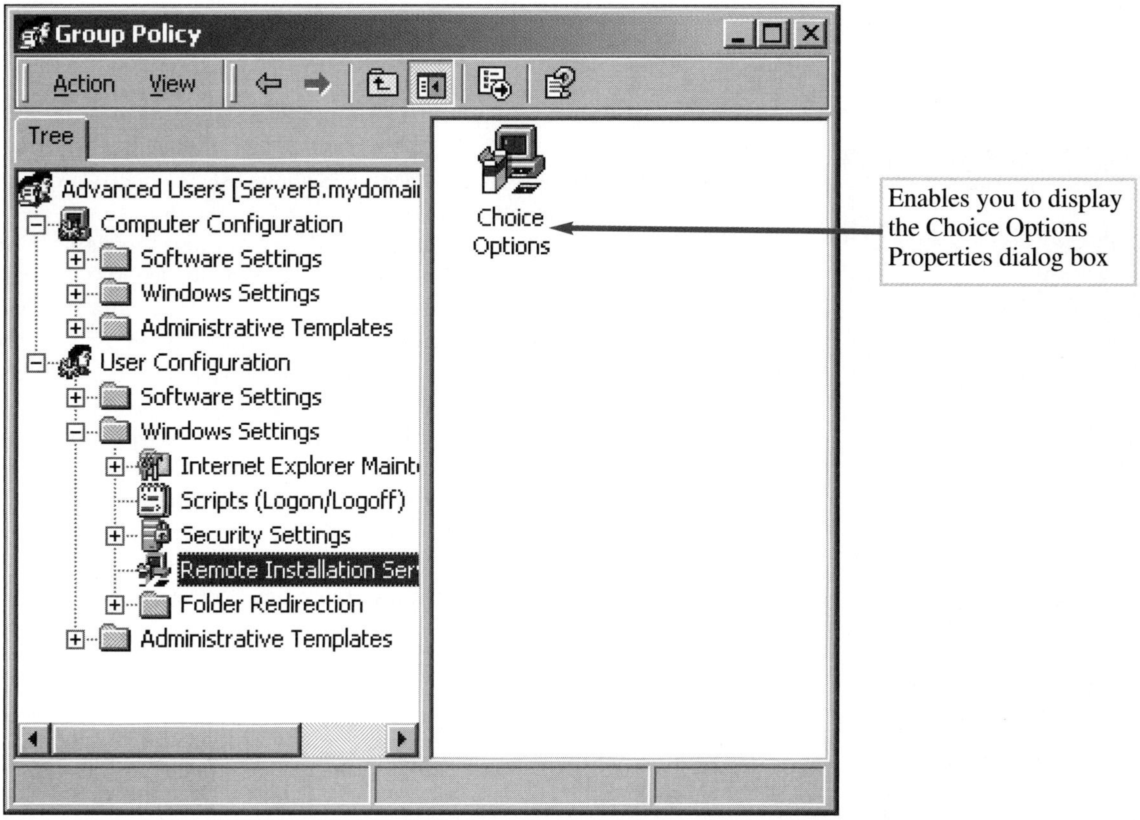

Group Policy

Action View

Tree

Advanced Users [ServerB.mydomai

Computer Configuration

Software Settings

Windows Settings

Administrative Templates

User Configuration

Software Settings

Windows Settings

Internet Explorer Maint

Scripts (Logon/Logoff)

Security Settings

Remote Installation Ser

Folder Redirection

Administrative Templates

Choice Options

Enables you to display the Choice Options Properties dialog box

Figure 14-17 Modifying installation choice options

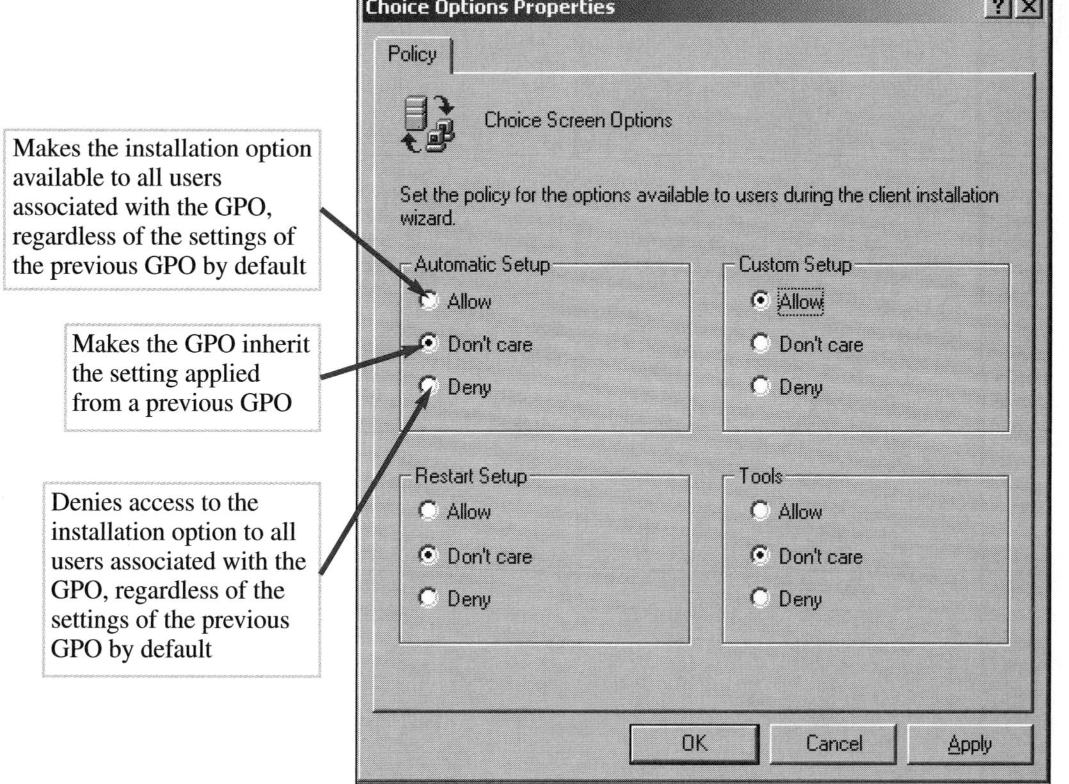
Choice Options Properties
Policy
Choice Screen Options
Set the policy for the options available to users during the client installation wizard.
Automatic Setup
Allow
Don't care
Deny
Custom Setup
Allow
Don't care
Deny
Restart Setup
Allow
Don't care
Deny
Tools
Allow
Don't care
Deny
OK
Cancel
Apply
Makes the installation option available to all users associated with the GPO, regardless of the settings of the previous GPO by default
Makes the GPO inherit the setting applied from a previous GPO
Denies access to the installation option to all users associated with the GPO, regardless of the settings of the previous GPO by default

skill 7 Creating a RIPrep Image

exam objective

Basic knowledge

overview

tip

A default CD-based image is created and stored on the RIS server automatically when you install RIS. While you cannot include application installation with a CD-based image, you can use Group Policy to push out applications as required after the installation.

caution

You need to close all programs and stop all services while creating a RIPrep image.

caution

RIPrep images cannot be stored on the boot or system partition of a machine. These images consist of Windows 2000 Professional source files, as well as RIS-related files, and require 2 GB of hard disk space. Also, these need to be stored on an NTFS partition.

In addition to the various installation types, RIS allows you to create various operating system images, called **RIPrep images**, along with the default CD-based image. CD-based images enable you to install only the basic Windows 2000 Professional operating system without any applications, and with settings defined by a standard unattended answer file. RIPrep images enable you to include various applications and desktop settings in a RIS-based installation. This is particularly useful in situations where multiple users require a definite set of applications, and the set varies based on their roles. For instance, managers might require software such as Microsoft Project, while developers might require Microsoft Word. In such cases, you can create a RIPrep image for each type of system. RIPrep images can include all the applications and desktop settings commonly required by users. Since these RIPrep images are a compressed form of the operating system and applications, and since the files associated with each image are never duplicated, they decrease the server disk space required for image storage, as opposed to other imaging techniques such as Ghost. On the other hand, a RIS install is a full install, meaning it can take more time to install on each client than a Ghost image.

To create a RIPrep image, you use the RIPrep tool. While creating a RIPrep image, you install the operating system along with the required applications, and configure the required desktop settings on a computer. Then, you copy the Administrator profile to the default user profile and allow all users to use it. Next, you test the image. Finally, you create a RIPrep image of this computer and store the image on a RIS server. Once you have created a RIPrep image, it can be reused multiple times. When the operating system is installed using RIS, the required applications and configured settings are installed with it.

The RIPrep tool creates an image of the operating system and applications installed on the computer. Note, however, that the RIPrep tool creates an image of only the drive on which the operating system files are located. Therefore, all required applications should be installed on the same drive. The tasks performed by the system during image creation are shown in **Table 14-2**.

RIPrep images use the default CD-based image already present on the RIS server by applying the differences in the RIPrep image on top of the default image. This functionality conserves significant disk space on the RIS servers.

Both CD-based images and RIPrep images contain associated answer files. These answer files are .SIF files and contain the answers to the various prompts that a user receives during a normal installation of the operating system such as network settings and time zone settings. You can control access to images by setting permissions on the associated .SIF files. Therefore, you can limit the images that are available to a user during a RIS installation so that the user does not select an incorrect image during installation.

how to

Create a RIPrep image.

1. Log on a computer running Windows 2000 Professional as an Administrator.
2. Click **Start**, and then click **Run** to display the **Run** dialog box.
3. To access the RIPrep tool stored in the shared folder containing the RIS files on the RIS server, type **\\ServerA\REMINST\Admin\I386\RIPREP.EXE** in the **Open** text box, and click **OK**. This displays the first screen of the **Remote Installation Preparation Wizard**.
4. The first screen of this wizard provides an introduction to the wizard **(Figure 14-18)**. Click **Next >** to display the second screen of the wizard. Type **ServerA** in the **Server name** text box to specify the name of the RIS server on which you want the images to be stored, and then click **Next >**.

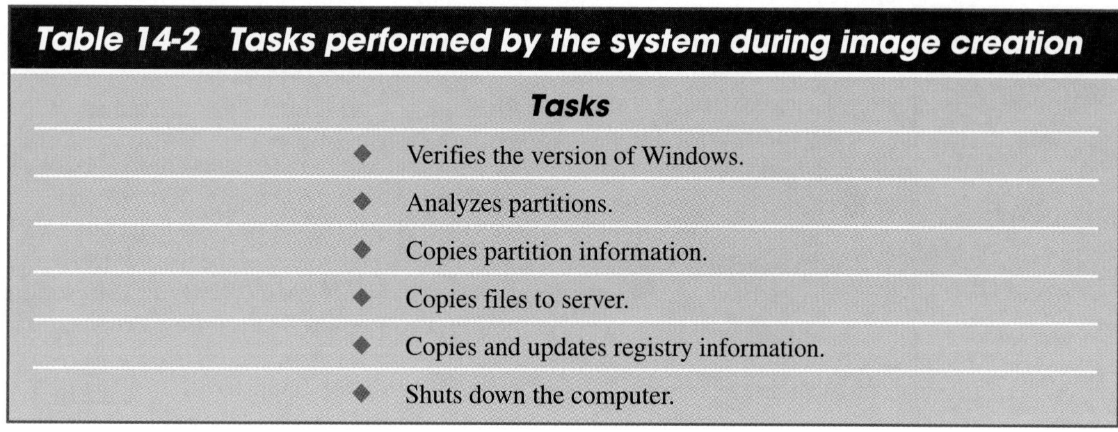

Table 14-2 Tasks performed by the system during image creation

Tasks
◆ Verifies the version of Windows.
◆ Analyzes partitions.
◆ Copies partition information.
◆ Copies files to server.
◆ Copies and updates registry information.
◆ Shuts down the computer.

Figure 14-18 Starting the Remote Installation Preparation Wizard

The first screen of the Remote Installation Preparation Wizard lists some important points related to RIPrep images

skill 7

Creating a RIPrep Image (cont'd)

exam objective

Basic knowledge

how to

5. Type **RIPrepImages** in the **Folder name** text box to specify the folder on the RIS server to which the images should be copied **(Figure 14-19)**. This folder is created in the **RemoteInstall\Setup\English\Images** folder. Then, click Next > to display the **Friendly Description and Help Text** screen of the wizard. This screen enables you to specify a brief description and help text to identify the image **(Figure 14-20)**.
6. To specify a description, type **For Developers** in the **Friendly description** text box. Type **Contains applications required by developers** in the **Help text** text box.
7. Click Next > to display the **Review Settings** screen of the wizard, which summarizes the settings specified by you **(Figure 14-21)**. After verifying the settings, click Next > to view the **Completing The Remote Installation Preparation Wizard** screen.
8. To start the creation of the RIPrep image on the computer, click Next >. After the image has been created, it is copied to the RIS server, and is available to RIS clients for installation. Click Done to close the wizard.

tip

If you receive a "Programs or Services are Running" message before the review screen, ensure that all applications are closed before continuing.

more

While creating a RIPrep image, you can also specify the product ID for the operating system. This prevents the installation program from prompting the user for the product ID when the operating system is being installed. You need to specify the product ID as: **ProductID = "<product_ID>"** in the **[UserData]** section of the .SIF file. Note that there may be licensing restrictions on this practice, and you should ensure that you are legally capable of entering the product ID in this manner.

Figure 14-19 Specifying a folder for storing the RIPrep image

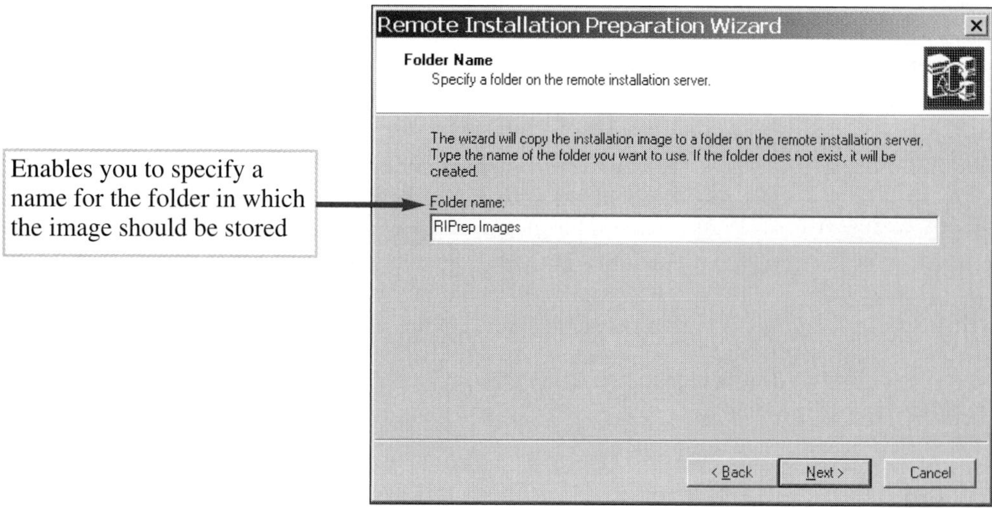

Figure 14-20 Specifying a description and help text for the image

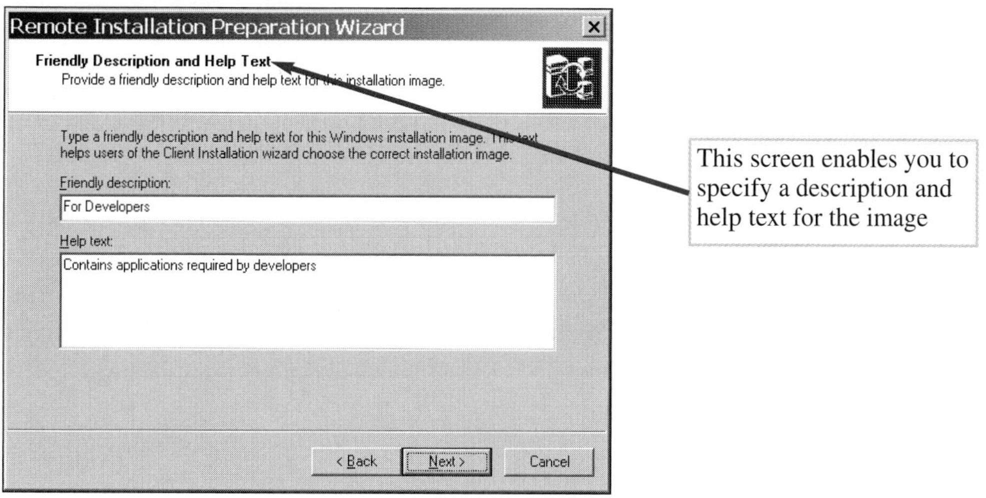

Figure 14-21 Viewing a summary of the RIPrep settings

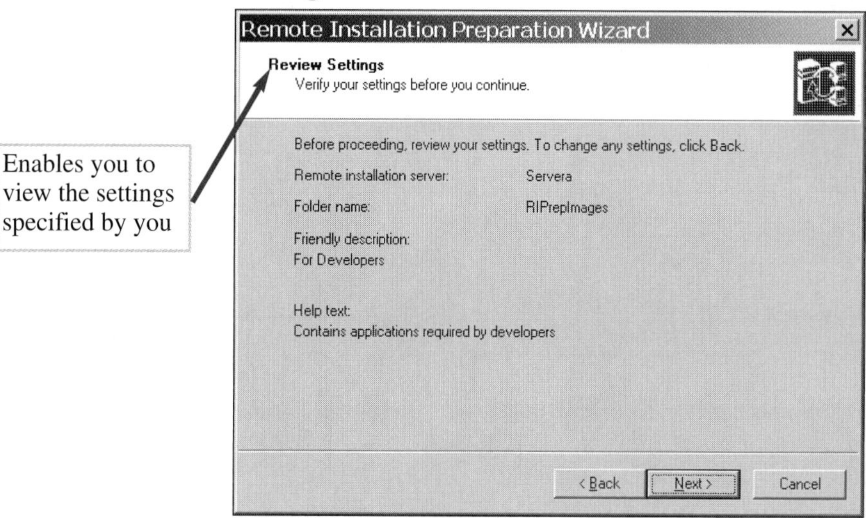

skill 8 Creating a RIS Boot Disk

exam objective

Basic knowledge

overview

If your computer does not have a PXE DHCP-based boot ROM, you need to create a RIS boot disk before you can use RIS. The RIS boot disk supports certain network cards, which can be viewed by clicking Adapter List in the Windows 2000 Remote Boot Disk Generator dialog box (**Figure 14-22**). If the network cards or the chipsets of the RIS clients are supported by the RIS boot disk, then a RIS-based installation can be performed on the RIS clients. Windows 2000 Server provides the Remote Boot File Generator (RBFG) utility for creating the RIS boot disk.

caution

The RIS boot disk works only with selected plug and play PCI network interface cards. Therefore, before using the RIS boot disk for RIS, you need to verify whether your network interface card is supported by the RIS boot disk.

how to

Create a RIS boot disk on the RIS server.

1. Click Start, and then click **Run** to display the **Run** dialog box.
2. Type **D:\RemoteInstall\Admin\I386\RBFG.EXE** in the **Open** text box, and click OK to display the **Windows 2000 Remote Boot Disk Generator** dialog box (**Figure 14-23**).
3. Insert a floppy disk in the A: drive.
4. Click Create Disk to start the creation of the RIS boot disk. Once the disk is created, a message box appears asking you if you want to create another disk. Click No to return to the **Windows 2000 Remote Boot Disk Generator** dialog box, and then click Close to close the **Windows 2000 Remote Boot Disk Generator** dialog box.

more

The RIS boot disk works only with plug and play PCI network cards. Therefore, in the case of laptop computers, the disk works only if the laptop is docked to a station that has a supported PCI network card.

Figure 14-22 Viewing the list of supported network interface cards

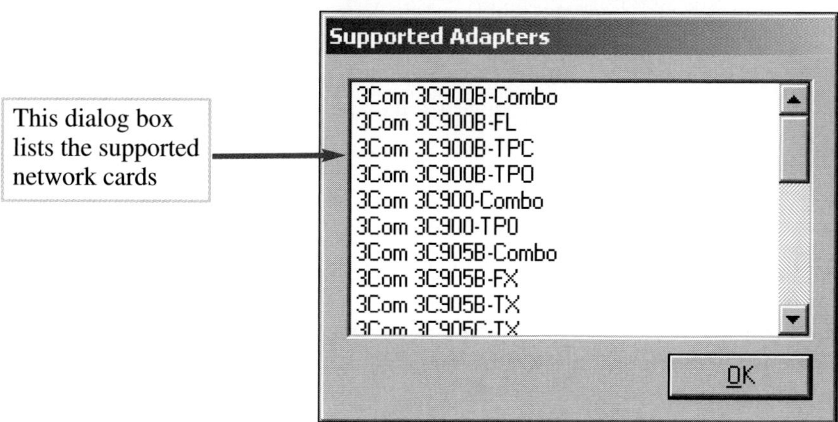

Figure 14-23 Creating the RIS boot disk

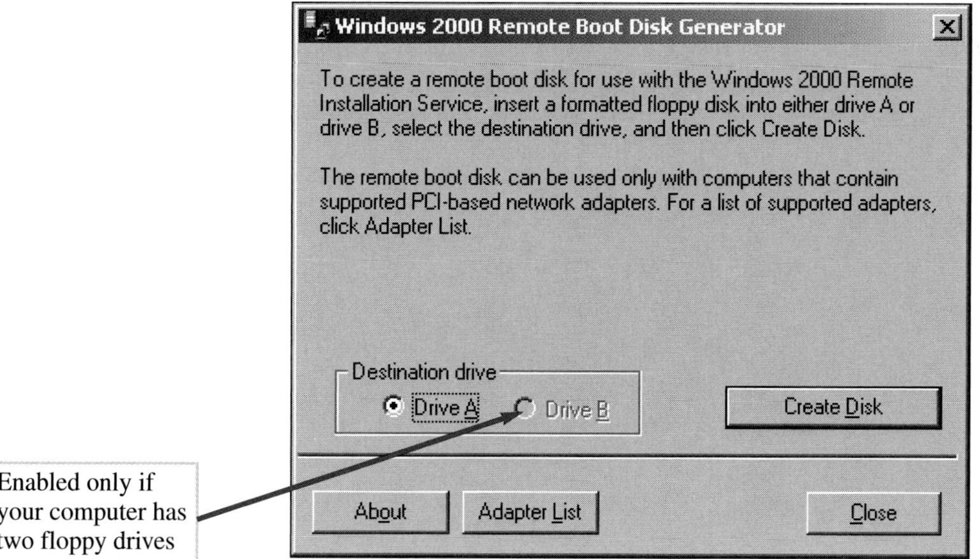

skill 9 Verifying RIS Configuration

exam objective

Basic knowledge

overview

At times, after setting up your RIS server, you may notice that the server is not servicing RIS client requests properly. For example, you might notice that the RIS server is not responding to the network service requests of RIS clients. In such situations, you might want to verify the configuration of RIS. To check the settings of the RIS server, Windows 2000 Server provides the **Check Server Wizard**. This wizard tests the settings of the RIS server, noting problems with the BINL, SIS, or TFTP service. The wizard then fixes the problems, if any, and displays a summary of the RIS configuration. However, the Check Server Wizard does not validate the RIPrep images stored on the server.

tip

If the wizard is not able to fix the problems that it detects, then it logs the errors in the server's event log.

how to

Verify the RIS configuration of a domain controller.

1. Log on to ServerA as an Administrator.
2. Click **Start**, point to **Programs**, point to **Administrative Tools**, and then click the **Active Directory Users and Computers** command to open the **Active Directory Users and Computers** console.
3. Right-click the server named **ServerA** in the **Domain Controllers** node in the left pane, and then click the **Properties** command to open the **Properties** dialog box for the selected server.
4. Click the **Remote Install** tab, and click **Verify Server** to initiate the Remote Installation Services Setup Wizard. The **Welcome to the Check Server Wizard** screen of the wizard contains information about the functionality of the wizard **(Figure 14-24)**.
5. Click **Next >** to start the verification process. After the verification is complete, the **Remote Installation Services Verification Complete** screen is displayed **(Figure 14-25)**.
6. After viewing the information about the RIS configuration, click **Finish** to exit the wizard.
7. Close the **Active Directory Users and Computers** console.

Figure 14-24 Welcome to the Check Server Wizard

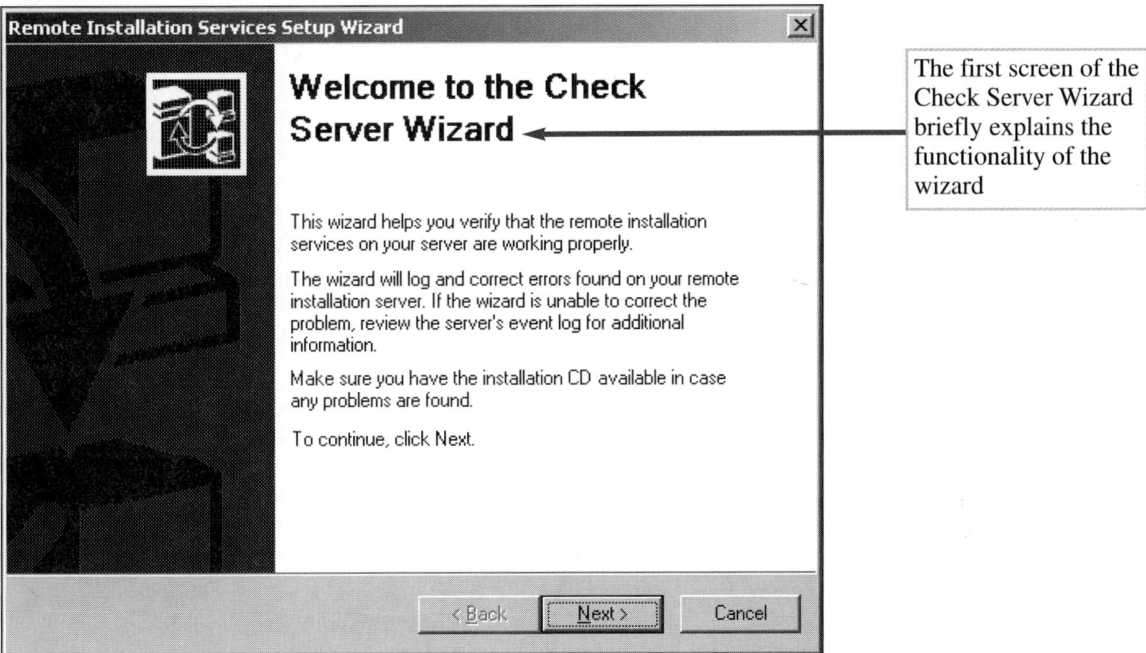

The first screen of the Check Server Wizard briefly explains the functionality of the wizard

Figure 14-25 Remote Installation Services Verification Complete screen

The final screen of the Wizard displays a summary of the verification of the RIS settings

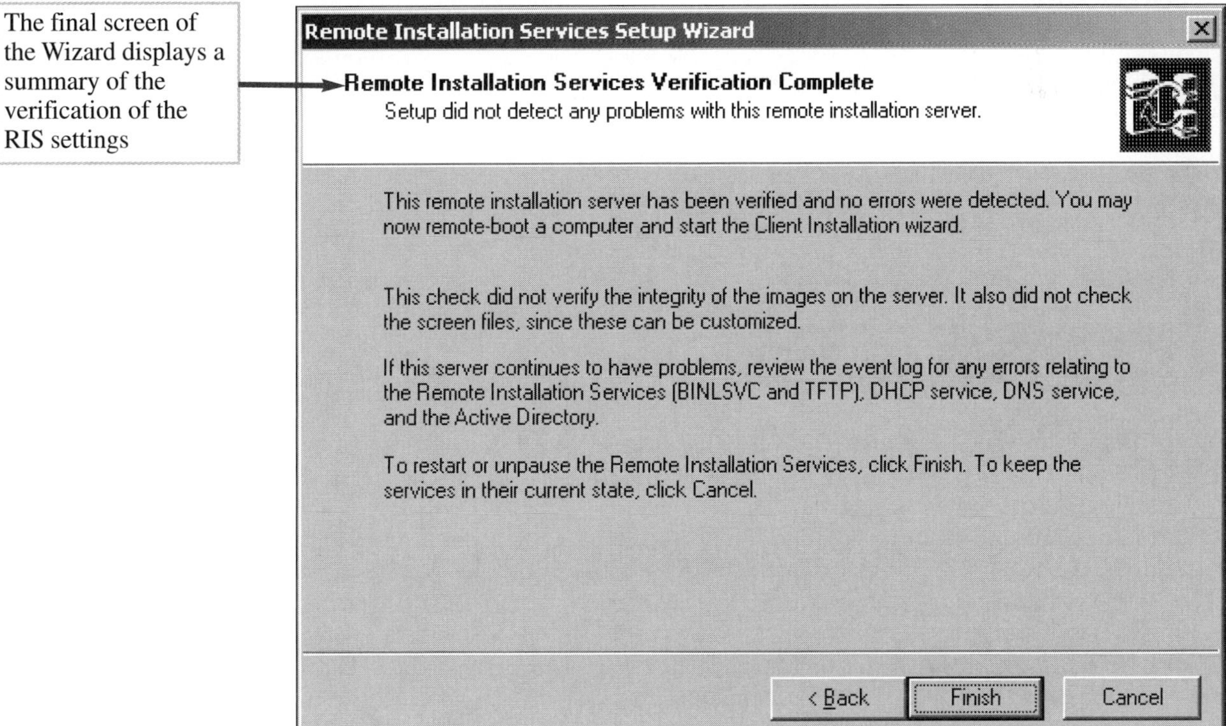

Summary

- Remote Installation Service (RIS) enables you to automate the installation of an operating system, and install the operating system on multiple computers simultaneously.
- A RIS-based installation involves a RIS server running Windows 2000 Server, as well as RIS clients on which the operating system is to be installed.
- To use RIS, Active Directory, DNS, and DHCP should be installed on the RIS server or another server.
- RIS clients should either support Preboot Execution Environment (PXE) DHCP-based remote boot ROMS or contain network cards supported by the RIS boot disk.
- RIS consists of three component services: Boot Information Negotiation Layer (BINL), Trivial File Transfer Protocol Daemon (TFTP), and Single Instance Store (SIS).
- BINL manages the overall working of RIS, TFTP manages file transfer requests during a remote installation, and SIS minimizes the disk space required for storing RIS installation images.
- In a RIS-based installation, a RIS client, when switched on, sends out a network service request in response to which it receives an IP address and the IP address of a RIS server. It can then connect to the RIS server for the installation of the operating system.
- While setting up a RIS server, you first need to add the RIS component, and then install RIS.
- After setting up a RIS server, you need to authorize it to prevent other servers from acting as RIS servers.
- You can modify the default RIS settings to customize the way in which computer names are generated and client requests are serviced.
- There are four installation options available in a RIS-based installation: automatic setup, custom setup, restarting a previous setup, and maintenance and troubleshooting. You can use Group Policy Objects to control the installation options that are available to a user during a remote installation.
- RIS also enables you to create images of workstations after the operating system and required applications have been installed on them. These images are called RIPrep images and can be used for installing the operating system, as well as the entire set of applications on a RIS client.
- Windows 2000 Server includes the Check Server Wizard, which enables you to verify RIS configuration settings.

Key Terms

Remote Installation Service (RIS)
Boot Information Negotiation Layer (BINL)
Trivial File Transfer Protocol Daemon (TFTPD)
Single Instance Store (SIS)
Automatic Setup
Custom Setup
Restart Setup
Maintenance and Troubleshooting
RIPrep (Remote Installation Preparation) image
RIS boot disk
Check Server Wizard

Projects: On Your Own

1. The Boot Information Negotiation Layer (BINL) service:

a. Manages the overall functioning of RIS.
b. Manages file transfers that occur during a RIS-based installation.
c. Reduces the disk space required for storing multiple operating system images.
d. Enables RIS-based installation on computers that do not support the PXE DHCP-based remote boot technology.

2. Which one of the following is the correct sequence of steps that occurs during a remote installation of Windows 2000 Professional using RIS?

1. Client Installation Wizard (CIW) is downloaded to the RIS client.
2. The RIS server checks the user information and presents the installation options accordingly.
3. The user logs on to the network.
4. The RIS client sends a network service request that includes its Globally Unique Identifier (GUID) and a Dynamic Host Configuration Protocol (DHCP) discover packet.

a. 1, 2, 4, 3
b. 4, 3, 1, 2
c. 4, 3, 2, 1
d. 4, 1, 3, 2

3. You have configured RIS for performing remote installation of Windows 2000 Professional. However, when Alice logs on to her machine, she is not prompted to select the operating system image. Which of the following could be the possible reasons for this? (Choose all that apply.)
   a. The Group Policy settings for Alice's user account do not allow her to select the operating system image to be installed.
   b. The TFTP service is not running properly and CIW has not been downloaded.
   c. You have not created any operating system images, and only the default image is available.
   d. Alice's computer has not been able to contact the RIS server.

4. You are using RIS to install Windows 2000 Professional on multiple client machines. Mary, James, and Timothy are required to run a memory virus scanner on their machines before the operating system is installed. These three user accounts are placed in an OU Experts, which has a group policy applied, also named Experts. The domain also has a group policy named AllUsers, which applies to all user accounts. Which of the following steps will you perform to enable these three users and restrict all other users from running the memory virus scanner before installing the operating system? (Choose all that apply.)
   a. Edit the choice options for the AllUsers GPO, and select the Allow option in the Tools section of the Choice Options Properties dialog box.
   b. Edit the choice options for the Experts GPO, and select the Allow option in thc Tools section of the Choice Options Properties dialog box.
   c. Edit the choice options for the AllUsers GPO, and select the Deny option in the Custom Setup section of the Choice Options Properties dialog box.
   d. Edit the choice options for the Experts GPO, and select the Don't care option in the Tools section of the Choice Options Properties dialog box.

5. Your organization is in the expansion phase. It has just recruited 100 developers. You need to set up machines for them. All these developers require Windows 2000 Professional and a definite set of applications installed on their machines.

   Primary goal: To install the operating system without visiting each client computer.
   Secondary goal: To install all the applications without visiting each client computer.
   Proposed solution: Set up a RIS server and use the CD-based image for installation of the software.

   What does the proposed solution achieve?

   a. The proposed solution achieves both the primary and secondary goals.
   b. The proposed solution achieves only the secondary goal.
   c. The proposed solution achieves only the primary goal.
   d. The proposed solution achieves neither the primary goal nor the secondary goal.

6. The RIS files are stored in the D drive of your server. To create a RIS boot disk, which one of the following commands will you execute?
   a. secedit /refreshpolicy user_policy
   b. D:\RemoteInstall\Admin\I386\RIPREP.EXE
   c. D:\RemoteInstall\Admin\I386\RBFG.EXE
   d. dcpromo

7. Which of the following steps does the system perform during the installation of RIS? (Choose all that apply.)
   a. Updates the CIW screens.
   b. Creates a new setup answer file.
   c. Creates a new RIPrep image.
   d. Applies the Group Policy settings.
   e. Creates a RIS boot disk.

8. Which one of the following is used for authorizing a RIS server?
   a. DHCP console
   b. Active Directory Users and Computers console
   c. Remote Installation Services Setup Wizard
   d. Client Installation Wizard

9. You plan to use RIS to install Windows 2000 on 100 computers. 20 computers need to be installed with the default CD-based image, while the others need to be installed with a RIPrep image that you have created. To prevent the users on the 20 computers from accessing the RIPrep image that you have created, you will:
   a. Use the Remote Installation Services Properties dialog box.
   b. Use the Choice Options Properties dialog box.
   c. Set appropriate permissions on the .SIF file.
   d. Set appropriate permissions using Group Policy Objects.

10. The Remote Installation Services Properties dialog box enables you to: (Choose all that apply.)
   a. Specify the format that the RIS server should use for generating client computer names.
   b. Add maintenance and troubleshooting tools on the RIS server.
   c. Specify which installation options should be available to users.
   d. Specify the location where client computer accounts should be created.
   e. Authorize a RIS server.

11. You had set up a RIS server a few days back and have been using it for remote installations. However, you observe that the server is functioning inconsistently lately. To detect and correct the problem, you will use the:
   a. Remote Installation Services Setup Wizard.
   b. Client Installation Wizard.
   c. Remote Installation Preparation Wizard.
   d. Check Server Wizard.

12. Jim is using RIS for performing remote installation on multiple client machines. He observes that multiple users are trying to supply identical computer names. Jim decides to restrict the users from specifying computer names. To do so, he needs to:
    a. Disable the Custom Setup installation option.
    b. Use only the default CD-based image.
    c. Stop the RIS server from servicing unknown clients.
    d. Disable the Tools option.
13. If the computers on which you want to perform a RIS-based installation do not support the PXE DHCP-based remote boot technology, you need to: (Choose all that apply.)
    a. Create a RIS boot disk.
    b. Install the operating system manually on each client computer.
    c. Check whether the RIS boot disk supports the network cards installed on the computers.
    d. Create a RIPrep image.
    e. Authorize the RIS server.
14. For storage, RIPrep images require:
    a. A FAT partition.
    b. The boot partition.
    c. At least 2 GB disk space.
    d. The system partition.

Projects: On Your Own

1. Set up RIS.
    a. Log on as an **Administrator**.
    b. Start the **Windows Components Wizard**.
    c. Add the **Remote Installation Services** component using the source files present in **E:\i386**, where E: is your CD-ROM drive.
    d. Initiate the **Remote Installation Services Setup Wizard**.
    e. Install RIS in the D drive and accept the default description, help text, and name for the image.
2. Authorize a RIS server.
    a. Log on as an **Administrator**.
    b. Open the **DHCP** console.
    c. Authorize the computer as a RIS server.
3. Set the properties of a RIS server such that it generates client computer names using the first names and last initials of users. Then, verify the RIS configuration.
    a. Log on as an **Administrator**.
    b. Open the **Active Directory Users and Computers** console.
    c. Configure the server to generate client computer names using the first names and last initials of users.
    d. Verify the RIS configuration of the server.

Problem Solving Scenarios

1. You administer the company network. Recently your company purchased 150 new computers for a fresh batch of employees expected to join within the next three days. You are required to install Windows 2000 Professional on all these computers as soon as possible. You suggest to your Senior Network Administrator that you should implement RIS for the task, but he does not really seem convinced.

Draft a complete plan of action outlining how RIS can help automate the installation process. Explain the steps required for installing and activating RIS on your network. Also, specify the hardware requirements for the RIS clients to be.

2. You administer the company's network. Your company is setting up a new branch office. You are required to install the operating systems and all related applications on the new computers. To make things easier for you, your Senior Network Administrator has told you the requirements beforehand: Computers in the management department must be running the Windows 2000 Professional operating system with Microsoft Project 2000 and Microsoft Office 2000 Professional installed. Computers in the CSB department must be running the Windows 2000 Server operating system with Microsoft Visual Studio 6.0 and Microsoft SQL Server 2000.

You need to work out an efficient plan for installing the required software quickly with minimal administration and user intervention. Write a memo outlining your plan of action.

LESSON

15 Managing a Remote Installation Services (RIS) Implementation

Remote Installation Services (RIS) is used to perform remote installations on a Windows 2000 network. To make sure that remote installations are performed correctly, you need to manage the use of RIS. RIS management involves working with three components: the client installation images, the RIS clients, and the user permissions and rights.

- **Client installation images:** CD-Based Images are the default image type, and the files involved with CD-based images are typically installed when RIS is installed. Answer files enable you to specify values for various settings such as network settings, time zone settings, and display settings. These values are used by the system when an unattended installation is performed. Therefore, you need separate answer files if you want to specify different settings, such as time zone settings or display settings, for different images. Each answer file uses the same CD-based image. You may also have RIPrep images, which also used the CD-based image as a base image, and have their own answer files.
- **RIS clients:** RIS clients can be pre-staged, which allows you to specify various settings for each specific machine. In addition, you can allow any machine to connect and get an image.
- **User permissions:** You need to manage user permissions to enable users to manage their computers. Also, if you do not pre-stage RIS clients, users installing the RIS clients need to be granted the right to join the RIS clients to the domain.While managing RIS, if you incorrectly modify RIS configuration, it might cause RIS-based installations to fail. In addition to incorrect configuration, RIS-based installations can fail if RIS client requirements are not met. In order to manage RIS, it is important to understand the common problems you might face.

Goals

In this lesson, you will learn how to manage RIS installation images, RIS clients, and security permissions related to RIS. You will also learn how to search for RIS clients being serviced by a particular RIS server. Finally, you will learn about the common problems that occur in RIS-based installations, along with their causes and solutions to these problems.

Lesson 15 Managing a Remote Installation Service (RIS) Implementation

Skills	*Exam 70-217 Objective*
1. Managing CD-based Images	Basic knowledge
2. Pre-staging a RIS Client	Basic knowledge
3. Searching for a RIS Client	Basic knowledge
4. Setting Permissions for Managing Pre-staged Computer Accounts	Configure RIS security.
5. Setting Permissions for Joining Computer Accounts in an OU to a Domain	Basic knowledge
6. Troubleshooting RIS Problems	Basic knowledge

Requirements

To complete this lesson, you need administrative rights on ServerA, the Windows 2000 Server computer that is the domain controller for the mydomain.com domain. For this lesson, ServerA should be an authorized RIS server. A user group named RIS Admin, a Group Policy Object (GPO) named RIS Policies, and an organizational unit (OU) named RIS Clients should be present in the domain. The RIS server should have a RIS client named ClientA. You also need the Windows 2000 Professional CD.

skill 1

Managing CD-based Images

exam objective

Basic knowledge

overview

CD-based images enable you to install the basic Windows 2000 Professional operating system on RIS clients using the RIS feature of Windows 2000. To make sure that RIS functions properly, you may need to manage these images. Managing CD-based images includes performing tasks such as adding CD-based images and associating answer files with CD-based images. It might be necessary to add a new image if the default image gets corrupted.

While adding a new CD-based image, you need the Windows 2000 Professional source files. The system copies the installation files, creates a standard unattended setup answer file, and starts the required remote access services. To add CD-based images and associate answer files, you use the **Add Wizard (Figure 15-1)**.

tip

To create an unattended answer file, use the Setup Manager tool.

how to

Add a new CD-based image and store it in a folder named **Win2KPro**. Include the description **For computers in the Mydomain domain** for the image.

1. Click Start, point to **Programs**, point to **Administrative Tools**, and then click the **Active Directory Users and Computers** command to open the **Active Directory Users and Computers** console.
2. Select the **Domain Controllers** container in the left pane to view its contents in the details pane.
3. Right-click the **ServerA** server in the details pane, and then click the **Properties** command to open the **Properties** dialog box for the **ServerA** server **(Figure 15-2)**.
4. Click the **Remote Install** tab to view and modify RIS settings.
5. On this tab, click Advanced Settings... . The **Remote Installation Services Properties** dialog box appears with the **New Clients** tab selected by default.
6. Click the **Images** tab, and then click Add... to initiate the Add Wizard.
7. Select the **Add a new installation image** option, and click Next > to initiate the Add Installation Image Wizard.
8. The first screen of the Add Installation Image Wizard lists a brief introduction to the wizard. Click Next > .
9. The **Installation Source Files Location** screen appears and prompts you for the location of the Windows 2000 Professional source files.
10. Type **E:\I386** in the **Path** text box to specify the location of the source files. Then, click Next > to open the **Windows Installation Image Folder Name** screen.

Figure 15-1 Adding images and associating answer files

Enables you to add CD-based images and to associate unattended setup answer files with existing images

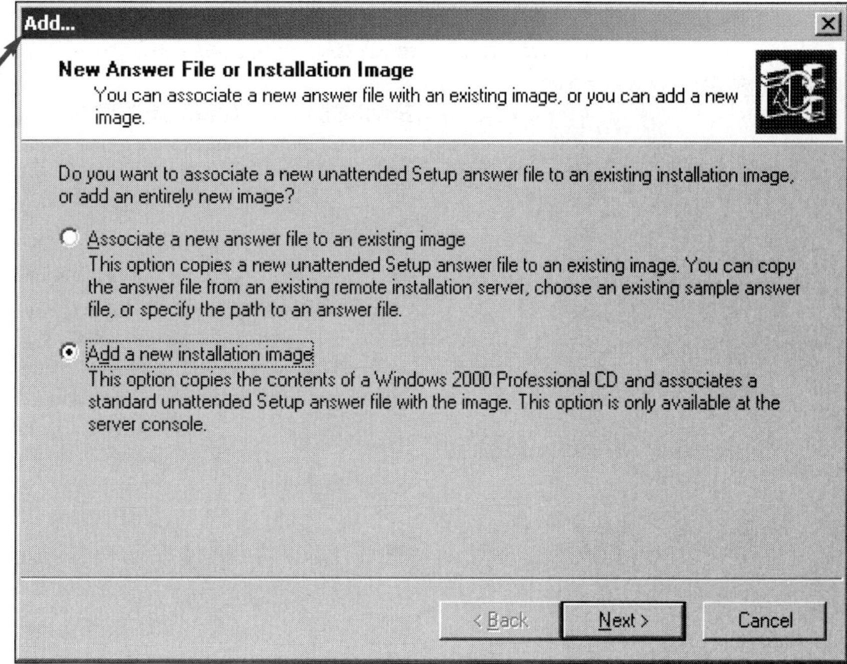

Figure 15-2 Adding a new CD-based image

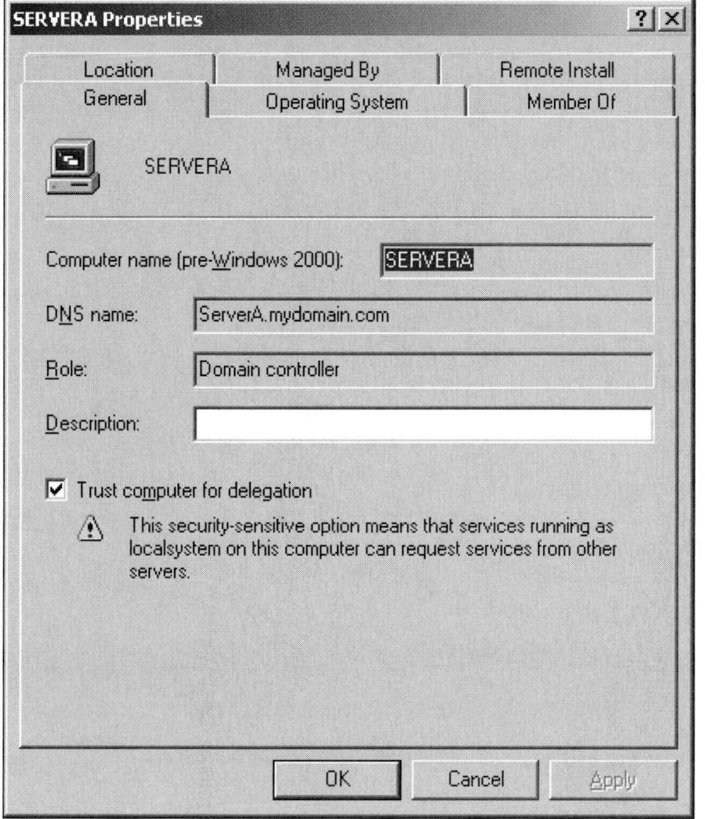

skill 1 Managing CD-based Images (cont'd)

exam objective

Basic knowledge

how to

11. Type **Win2KPro** in the **Folder name** text box. This folder will be created in the RemoteInstall\Setup\English\Images folder.
12. Click Next > to open the **Friendly Description and Help Text** screen.
13. Type **For computers in the Mydomain domain** in the **Friendly description** field.
14. Click Next > to open the **Previous Client Installation Screens Found** screen. This screen enables you to specify whether the new client installation screens should be created in addition to old client installation screens, if the old client installation screens should be overwritten, or if the old client installation screens should be used as is. **(Figure 15-3)**.
15. Select the **Use the old client installation screens** option button.
16. Click Next > to open the **Review Settings** screen, which lists a summary of the settings you specified **(Figure 15-4)**.
17. Click Finish to start the creation of the installation image using the displayed settings.
18. Once the image is created, a list of tasks performed by the system appears with check marks. Click Done to close the wizard.
19. Click OK to close the **Remote Installation Services Properties** dialog box.
20. Click OK to close the **Properties** dialog box for the ServerA server.
21. Close the **Active Directory Users and Computers** console.

tip

The Previous Client Installation Screens Found screen appears only if Client Installation Wizard (CIW) screens of an image exist on the RIS server.

more

Managing CD-based images also involves associating unattended setup answer files with existing images. You can use the Add Wizard to associate setup answer files with existing images. In the wizard, click the Associate a new answer file to an existing image option button on the New Answer File or Installation Image screen. The subsequent screens enable you to specify the source that contains the required answer file and the image with which you want to associate the answer file. Then, you need to select a sample answer file and specify a description, as well as a help text, for the image. Finally, after reviewing the settings, you can finish the process of associating the answer file with the image.

Figure 15-3 Specifying the client installation screens to be used

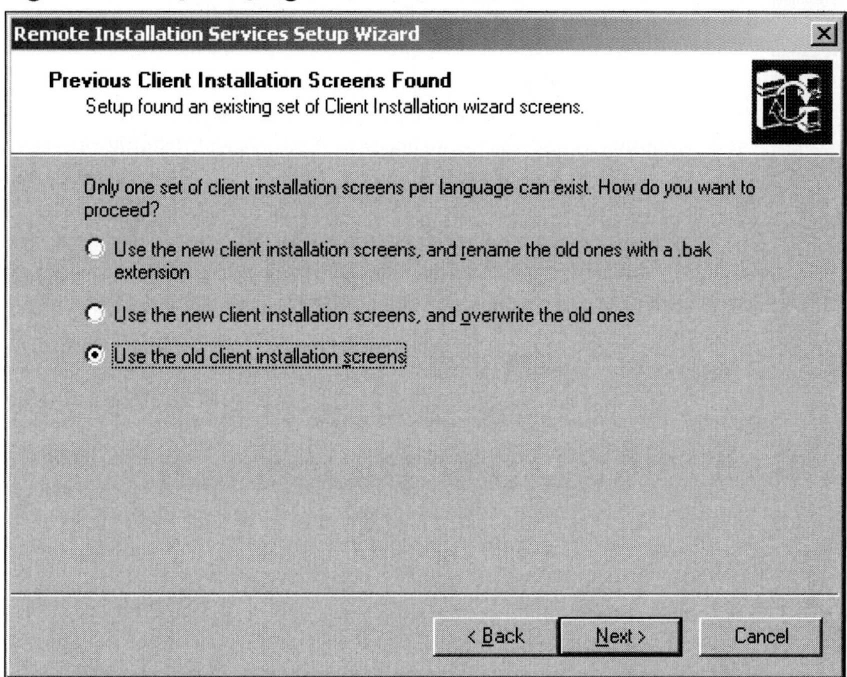

Figure 15-4 Viewing a summary of the CD-based image settings

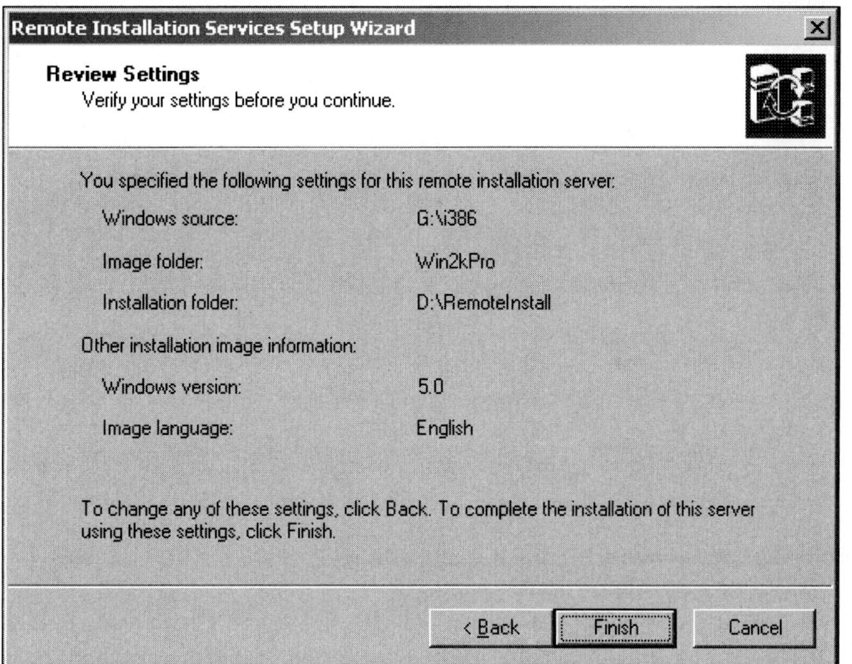

skill 2 Pre-staging a RIS Client

exam objective

Basic knowledge

overview

In a RIS environment, you need to delegate permissions to users of RIS clients for joining computers to the domain. By enabling users to join the RIS clients to the domain, you allow them to access network resources after performing a RIS-based installation. However, this delegation of permissions to the user presents a security hazard, because users can connect any computer to the network, perform a RIS-based installation, join a domain, and access network resources. To prevent this, you can **pre-stage** the computers on which you want a RIS-based installation to be performed, and configure the RIS server to respond only to these computers. Pre-staging involves identifying RIS clients using their globally unique identifiers (GUIDs) or Universally Unique IDs (UUIDs) and creating computer accounts for them. Since the computer accounts are created in the domain during pre-staging, you do not need to delegate permissions to users for joining computers to the domain. This also enables you to designate the computers that the RIS server should service.

tip

Not all machines have a GUID/UUID. In this case, you may also use the MAC address of the machine's NIC.

When you pre-stage a RIS client, you can also specify the RIS server that should be used for servicing requests from the client. Therefore, pre-staging is also useful in situations where multiple RIS servers exist on a network **(Figure 15-5)**, and you want to make sure that only a specific RIS server services the requests of a RIS client. Then, pre-stage the managers' and developers' computers and specify the appropriate RIS servers to service their requests. This will ensure that managers and developers access the appropriate RIS server for their images.

how to

Pre-stage a RIS client having the GUID 921BF974-ED42-11DE-BACD-00AA0057A223. Name the RIS client **RobertS**. Make sure that the ServerA RIS server services the requests of this RIS client.

1. Click **Start**, point to **Programs**, point to **Administrative Tools**, and then click the **Active Directory Users and Computers** command to open the **Active Directory Users and Computers** console.
2. Right-click the **Computers** container in the left pane, click **New**, and then click the **Computer** command to open the **New Object—Computer** dialog box.
3. Type **RobertS** in the **Computer name** text box to specify a name for the RIS client **(Figure 15-6)**.
4. Click **Next >** to open the **Managed** dialog box in order to specify the GUID of the client to which you want to assign the computer name **(Figure 15-7)**. The names of users or groups that should be able to join the computer to a domain are displayed in the **User or group** text box. If you do not select the **This is a managed computer** check box, the computer name is assigned to any RIS client randomly.
5. To specify the GUID, select the **This is a managed computer** check box and type **{921BF974-ED42-11DE-BACD-00AA0057A223}** in the **Computer's unique ID (GUID/UUID)** text box. If you specify a GUID that is associated with an existing computer account, an error message appears when you click **Next >** in the **Managed** dialog box.

tip

To open the New Object-Computer dialog box, you can also click Action on the menu bar, point to New, and then select the Computer command.

Figure 15-5 Using Pre-staging in a multiple RIS server environment

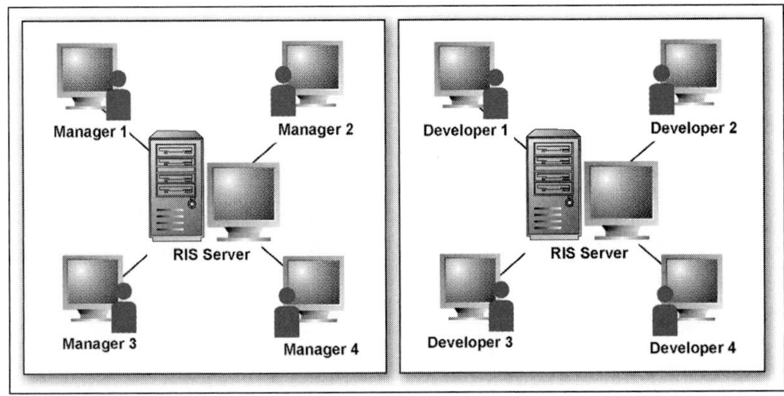

Figure 15-6 Specifying the computer name to be assigned to the RIS client

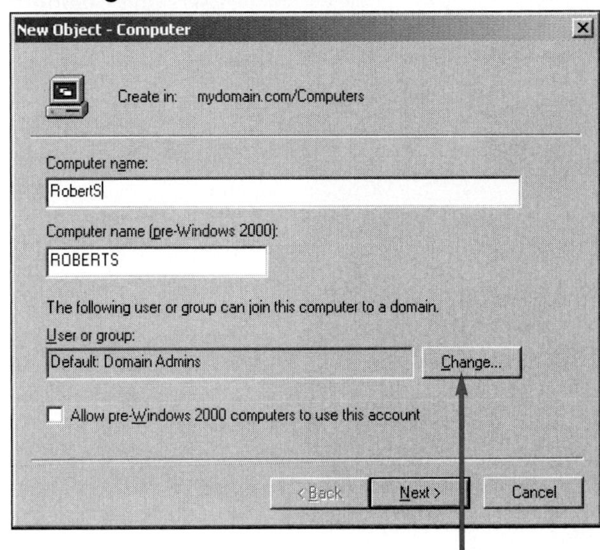

Figure 15-7 Specifying the GUID of a RIS client

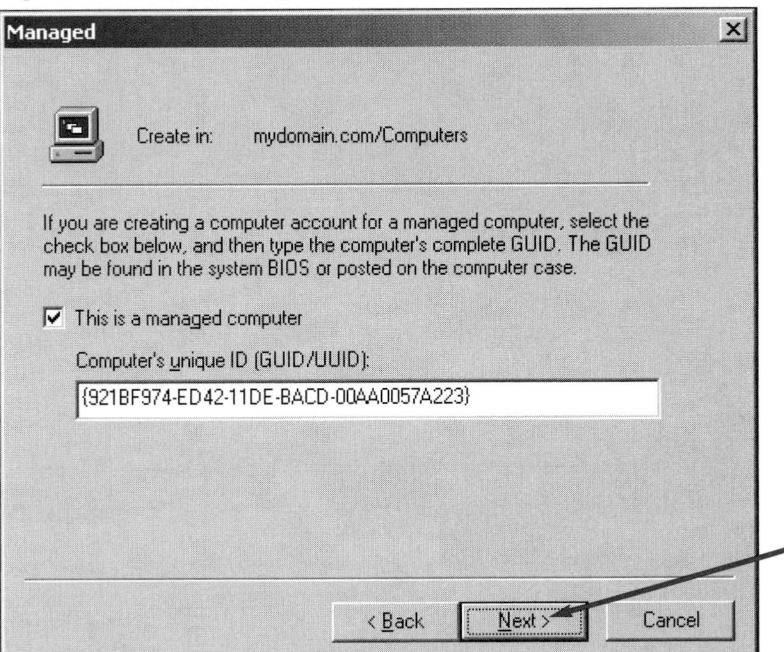

skill 2 Pre-staging a RIS Client (cont'd)

exam objective

Basic knowledge

how to

6. Click Next > to open the **Host server** dialog box, which is for specifying the name of the RIS server that should service the RIS client. If you do not want a specific RIS server to service the request of the RIS client, leave the **Any available remote installation server** check box selected.
7. To specify the name of the RIS server that should service the requests of the RIS client, type **SERVERA** in the **The following remote installation server** text box.
8. Click Next > to open the **New Object — Computer** screen, which shows a summary of the settings you specified **(Figure 15-8)**.
9. Click Finish to create the computer account, and then close the **Active Directory Users and Computers** console.

more

The GUID of a computer is generally written on a label on the side of the computer or inside the computer case. If the GUID is not written on one of these labels, you can view the Basic Input Output System (BIOS) settings to see the GUID of a computer. You can also find out the GUIDs of computers by using the Network Monitor tool to view the Dynamic Host Configuration Protocol (DHCP) request packets sent by the computers. These packets request an IP address from the DHCP server and contain the GUID of the host computer.

Figure 15-8 Reviewing pre-stage settings

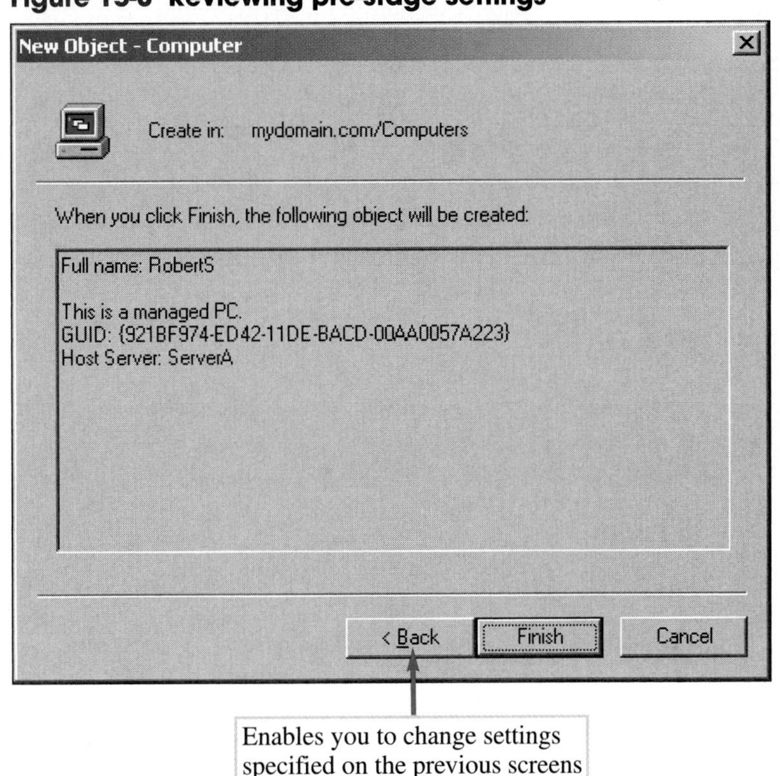

Enables you to change settings specified on the previous screens

skill 3 Searching for a RIS Client

exam objective

Basic knowledge

overview

If you work in a large organization that uses multiple RIS servers, it might be difficult to remember which RIS server services which RIS client. Under such circumstances, you can use the RIS client search feature. Search results include the names of RIS clients and their GUIDs. The GUIDs are displayed in wire format. This format stores GUIDs by reordering the first 16 characters of the GUID. Windows converts the GUIDs into this format because it is optimal for sending data over the network.

how to

Search for all RIS clients serviced by the ServerA RIS server.

1. Click Start, point to **Programs**, point to **Administrative Tools**, and then click the **Active Directory Users and Computers** command to open the **Active Directory Users and Computers** console.
2. Select the **Domain Controllers** container in the left pane to view its contents in the details pane.
3. Right-click the **ServerA** server in the details pane, and then click the **Properties** command to open the **Properties** dialog box for the **ServerA** server.
4. Click the **Remote Install** tab, and then click Show Clients... **(Figure 15-9)**. The **Find Remote Installation Clients** dialog box opens and automatically searches for RIS clients serviced by the selected RIS server. The search results appear in the list box at the bottom of the dialog box **(Figure 15-10)**.
5. Close the **Find Remote Installation Clients** dialog box.
6. Close the **Properties** dialog box for the **ServerA** server.
7. Close the **Active Directory Users and Computers** console.

Figure 15-9 Searching for RIS clients serviced by the selected RIS server

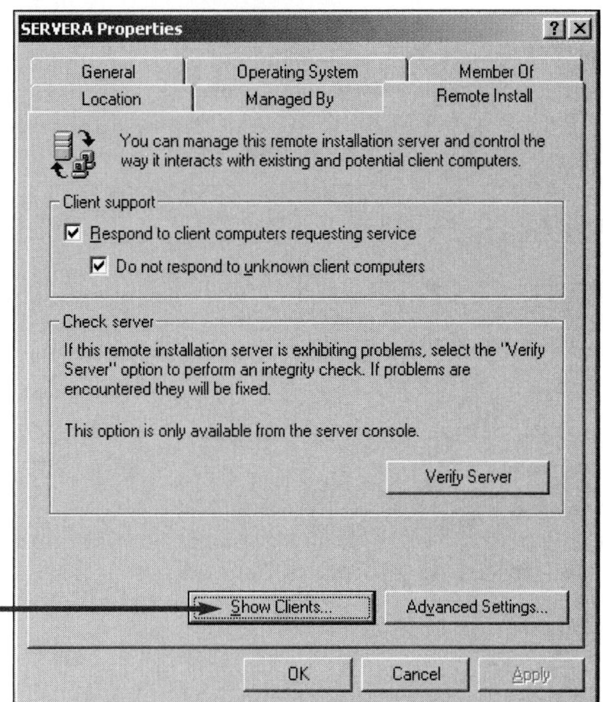

Enables you to view the names, as well as GUIDs of RIS clients serviced by this RIS server

Figure 15-10 Viewing the names and GUIDs of RIS clients

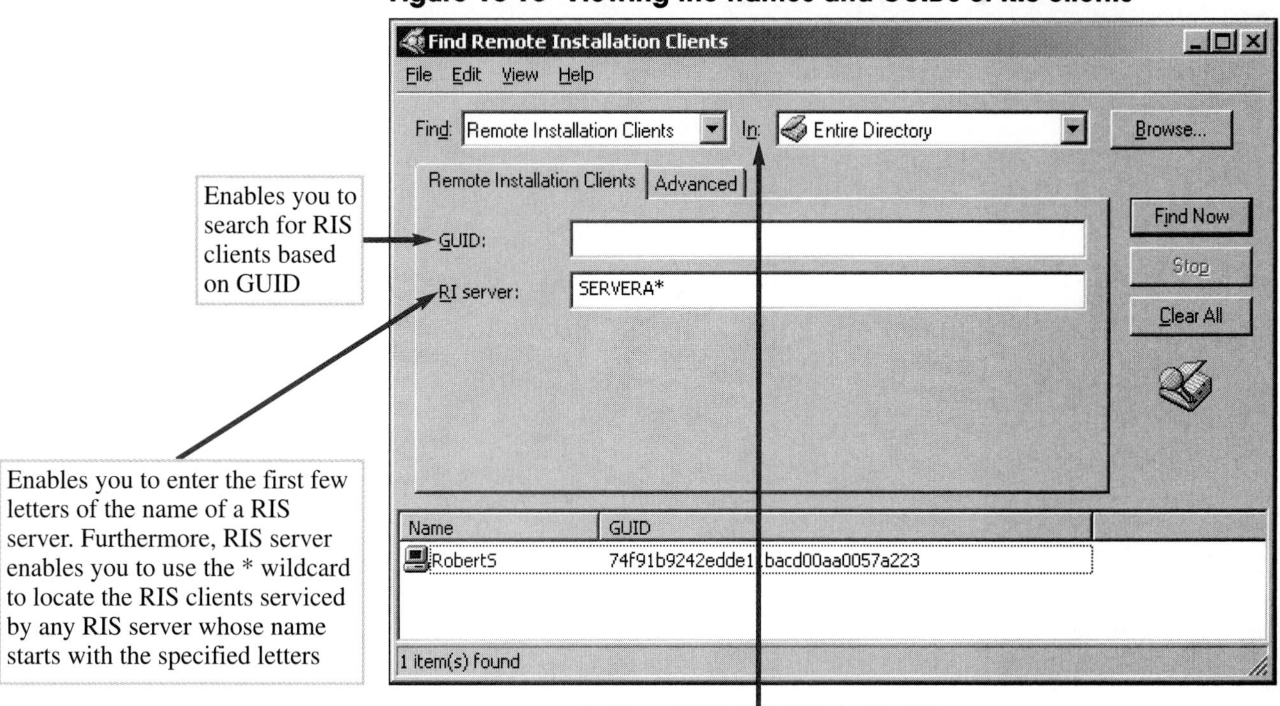

Enables you to search for RIS clients based on GUID

Enables you to enter the first few letters of the name of a RIS server. Furthermore, RIS server enables you to use the * wildcard to locate the RIS clients serviced by any RIS server whose name starts with the specified letters

Enables you to specify whether you want to search for RIS clients on the entire Active Directory or just on the domain

skill 4 Setting Permissions for Managing Pre-staged Computer Accounts

exam objective

Configure RIS security.

overview

An important aspect of managing RIS is overseeing its security. Managing RIS security involves granting appropriate permissions to users and groups. For instance, you need to grant permissions to specific users or groups responsible for managing pre-staged RIS clients. To set permissions for managing pre-staged RIS clients, it is advisable to create a group of users who need to be granted permissions. Once you create a group of users that require the same permissions, you can grant this group the required permissions using the **Active Directory Users and Computers** console. For granting management permissions of a pre-staged client, you need to assign Read and Write and Reset Password permissions for the client to the group. These permissions enable users to modify the properties of the RIS clients once the RIS clients have been set up.

how to

Assign permissions to the group named **RIS Admin** for managing the pre-staged RIS client named **RobertS**.

1. Click Start, point to **Programs**, point to **Administrative Tools**, and then click the **Active Directory Users and Computers** command to open the **Active Directory Users and Computers** console.
2. Select the **Advanced Features** command on the **View** menu. This lists the users, groups, and computers in Active Directory as containers, and enables you to view and modify advanced features such as permissions.
3. Click the **Computers** container to view its contents. In the details pane, right-click the computer named **RobertS**, and then click the **Properties** command to open the **Properties** dialog box for the computer named **RobertS**.
4. Click the **Security** tab.
5. Click Add... to open the **Select Users, Computers, or Groups** dialog box. This dialog box enables you to add groups to which you want to assign permissions.
6. Click the **RIS Admin** group in the **Name** list, and then click Add **(Figure 15-11)**. The group is added to the list box.
7. Click OK to close the **Select Users, Computers, or Groups** dialog box. The **RIS Admin** group is added to the list of groups associated with the **RobertS** computer.
8. To assign permissions for managing the pre-staged computer, select the **Read**, **Write**, and **Reset Password** check boxes in the **Allow** column of the **Permissions** list box **(Figure 15-12)**.
9. Click OK to apply the changes and close the **Properties** dialog box.
10. Close the **Active Directory Users and Computers** console.

Figure 15-11 Selecting the group to be assigned permissions

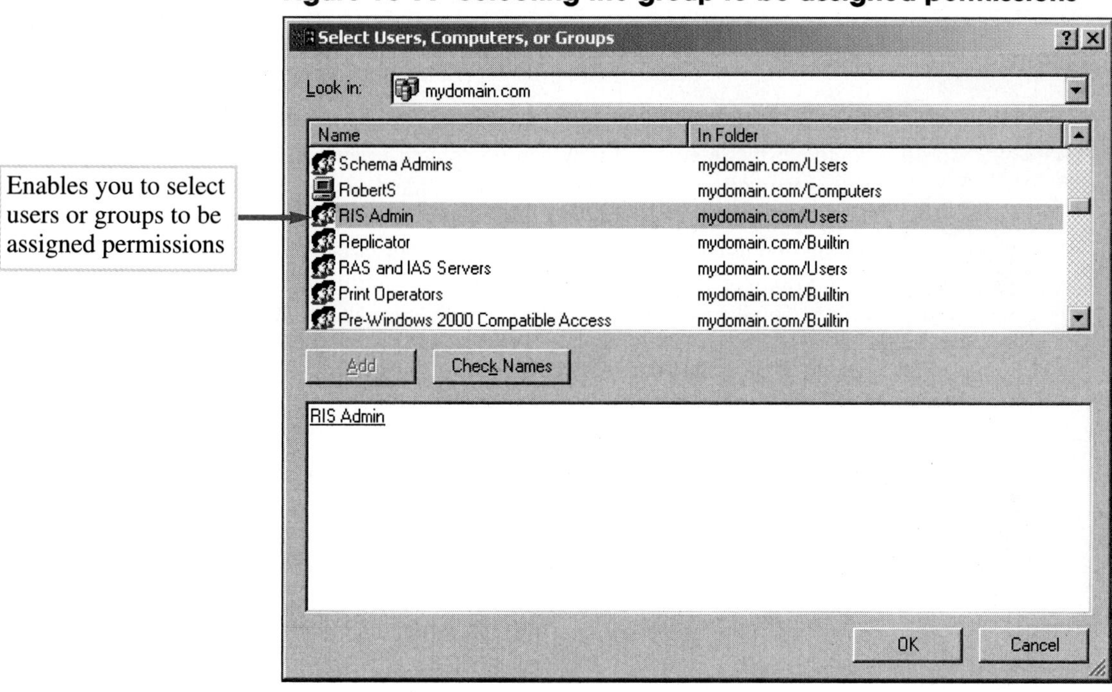

Figure 15-12 Assigning rights to users for managing pre-staged computers

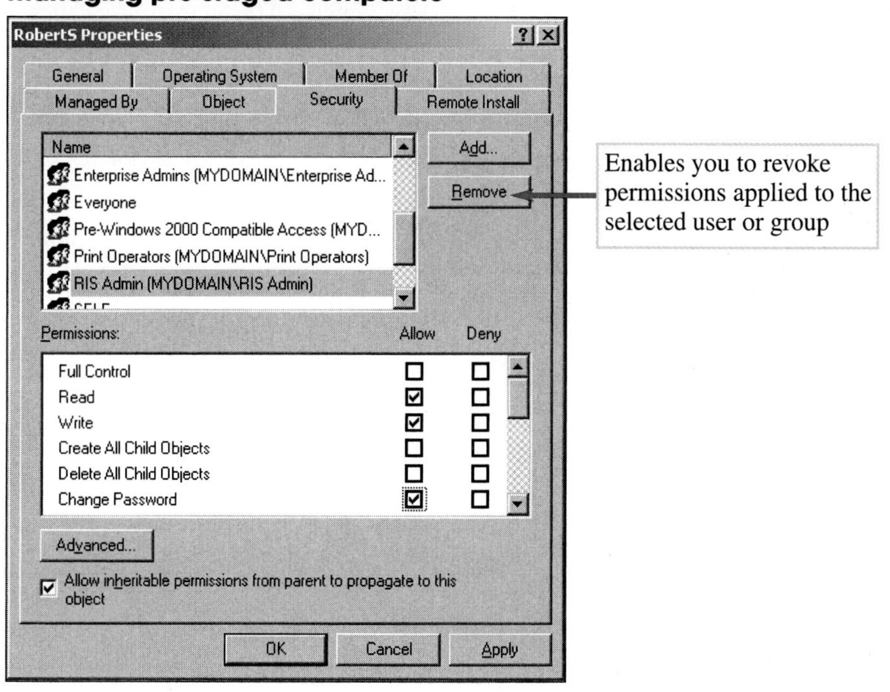

skill 5

Setting Permissions for Joining Computer Accounts in an OU to a Domain

exam objective

Basic knowledge

overview

If you do not pre-stage RIS clients, then all RIS computer accounts are created in the same container during the RIS-based installation. Computer accounts are created in the Computers container by default, but they can be created in any organizational unit (OU). However, to access network resources, these computers must be joined to the domain. Therefore, you need to grant users the right to join these computers to the domain, as well as give them the permission to add computer objects to the appropriate OU. Giving users the "Add computers to the domain" right, you typically need to modify the user rights assignment in a group policy. To give users the permission to add computer objects to the OU, you need to modify the properties of the OU within which the computer accounts should be created.

how to

Assign rights to the **RIS Admin** group to add the computers in the **RIS Clients** OU to the domain.

1. Click Start, point to **Programs**, point to **Administrative Tools**, and then click the **Active Directory Users and Computers** command to open the **Active Directory Users and Computers** console.
2. Right-click the **Domain Controllers** OU, and then click the **Properties** command to open the **Properties** dialog box for the OU named **Domain Controllers**. Click the **Group Policy** tab to view the list of GPOs linked to the OU.
3. Select the **Default Domain Controllers** GPO, and click Edit... to open the **Group Policy** console.
4. Double-click **Computer Configuration** in the details pane of the console. Then, double-click **Windows Settings** in the details pane.
5. Double-click the **Security Settings** option in the details pane of the console. Next, double-click the **Local Policies** option.
6. Double-click the **User Rights Assignment** option to list the rights that can be assigned to users in the details pane of the console.
7. Double-click the **Add workstations to domain** permission in the details pane of the console to open the **Security Policy Setting** dialog box.
8. Select the **Define these policy settings** check box to enable Add... and Remove.
9. Click Add... to open the **Add user or group** dialog box.
10. Type **MYDOMAIN\RIS Admin** in the **User and group names** text box, and click OK **(Figure 15-13)**.
11. Click OK to close the **Security Policy Setting** dialog box. The name of the group appears in the **Group Policy** console **(Figure 15-14)**.
12. Close the **Group Policy** console and the **Active Directory Users and Computers** console.

more

When you modify the permissions of a user or group by using Group Policy Objects (GPOs) that contain security policies, the changes take effect only after the automatic policy propagation. Automatic policy propagation applies the policies at default intervals of 90-120 minutes for clients and 5 minutes for domain controllers. However, if you want to apply the changes immediately, you can either restart your computer or execute the secedit/ refreshpolicy machine_policy command at the command prompt.

Figure 15-13 Assigning the permission to add workstations to the domain

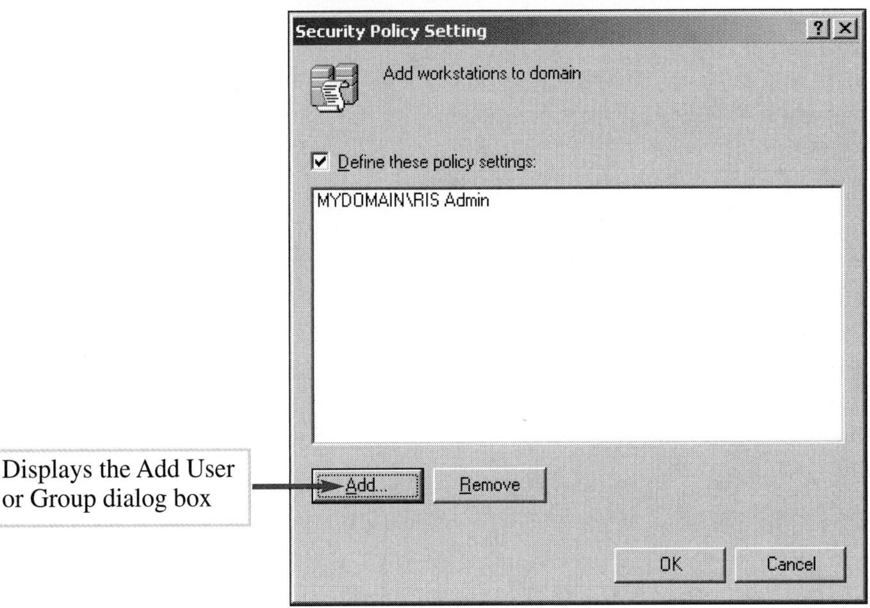

Figure 15-14 Group Policy console

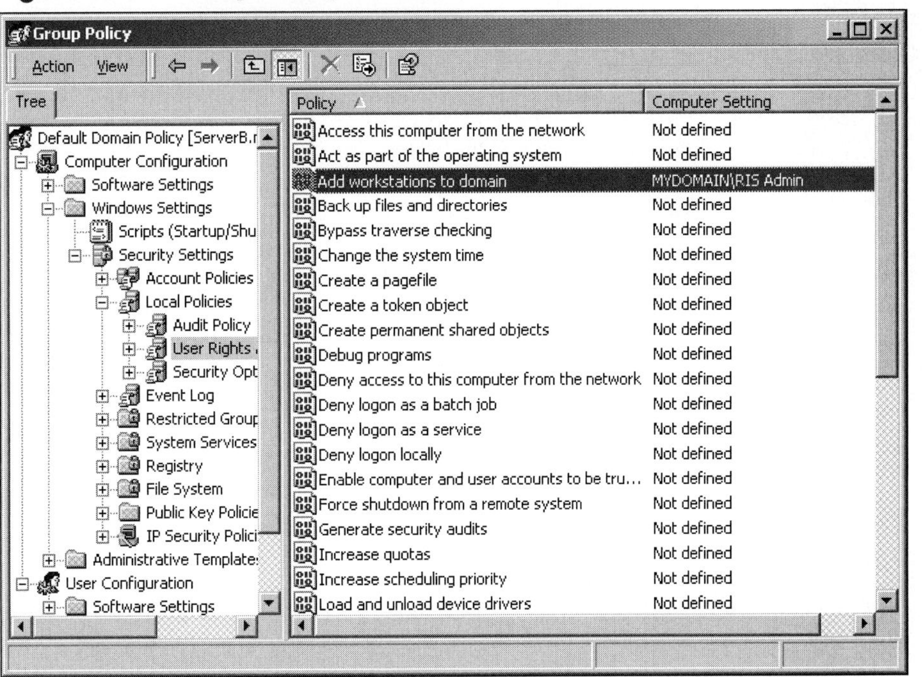

skill 6 Troubleshooting RIS Problems

exam objective

Basic knowledge

overview

RIS is an advanced service of Windows 2000 Server that enables you to perform remote installations easily. However, like any other service, it might not work smoothly all the time. For example, if the hardware requirements of RIS clients are not met fully, RIS-based installations cannot start. **Table 15-1** lists some problems related to client requirements and describes their causes, as well as their solutions.

RIS functions in combination with other services such as Dynamic Host Configuration Protocol (DHCP), Active Directory, and Domain Name System (DNS). Therefore, an incorrect setting related to any of these services can also cause a RIS-based installation to fail. Some problems related to RIS and associated services are discussed in **Table 15-2**.

Sometimes, the appropriate RIS-based installation and image options might not be available to users if the GPO permissions or image permissions have been assigned incorrectly. These problems are generally related to security settings. **Table 15-3** describes some common problems of this kind.

Table 15-1 Problems related to RIS client requirements

Problem	Cause	Solution
Installation fails on clients using RIS boot disks	The network cards of the clients are not supported by the RIS boot disk	Use the Remote Boot Disk Generator dialog box to check whether the RIS boot disk supports the network cards. If the cards are not supported, then replace them with cards that are supported by the RIS boot disk.
The remote boot sequence starts, but the RIS client cannot connect to the RIS server	The PXE-based network card has a boot ROM earlier than version .99c	Change the network card to one with a later version of boot ROM.

Table 15-2 Problems related to RIS and associated services

Problem	Cause	Solution
The DHCP message is not displayed during the boot process	DHCP server not available	Check whether the DHCP service is running. Verify that the DHCP server is a Windows 2000 DHCP server. If the DHCP server and the RIS client are on different subnets, ensure that a DHCP relay agent is present, or that Boot P forwarding is enabled and available for the client's subnet. Check that the DHCP server is authorized. Verify that a DHCP scope is activated and has available addresses.
The Boot Information Negotiation Layer (BINL) message is not displayed after the RIS client has obtained an IP address	RIS server is offline RIS server has not been authorized	Bring the RIS server online and authorize it in Active Directory
The BINL message is displayed, but the CIW is not being downloaded	The NetPC Boot Service Manager (BINLSVC) is not functioning properly	Stop and restart the NetPC Boot Service Manager service by executing the following commands: Net Stop BINLSVC and Net Start BINLSVC.

Table 15-3 Problems related to security settings

Problem	Cause	Solution
The expected installation options are not available to users	The OU GPO has the Don't care permission applied to it, and an upper level GPO has the Deny permission applied to it	To override the permissions of the previous GPO, you need to select the Allow option for the OU GPO
The required images are not available to users	Permissions have not been set correctly for the .SIF files associated with the images	Verify and correct the permissions for the .SIF file
Installation fails on clients that have not been pre-staged	The RIS server is configured to respond to known computers only	Clear the Do not respond to unknown client computers check box in the Properties dialog box of the RIS server

Summary

- While using RIS, you need to manage CD-based images, RIS clients, and user permissions.
- A CD-based image enables you to install the basic Windows 2000 Professional operating system.
- While adding a new CD-based image, you require the Windows 2000 Professional source files.
- To add CD-based images and associate answer files, you use the Add Wizard.
- To prevent users from being able to connect any RIS client to the network and access resources, you can pre-stage RIS clients.
- Pre-staging involves identifying RIS clients using their globally unique identifier (GUID) and creating computer accounts for them.
- Pre-staging ensures that RIS servers service only specific RIS clients.
- In a multiple RIS server environment, you can also specify the RIS server to be used for servicing a pre-staged RIS client.
- You can search for all the clients serviced by a RIS server.
- You can also search for RIS clients based on GUIDs.
- After pre-staging RIS clients, you need to assign permissions to users for managing RIS clients.
- If you do not pre-stage RIS clients, you need to grant permissions to users for joining the RIS clients to the domain.
- You can grant permissions using the Active Directory Users and Computers console.
- RIS-based installations can fail due to problems related to client requirements, component services, and user permissions.

Key Terms

Pre-staging

Add Wizard

Test Yourself

1. The Add Wizard in the Remote Installation Services Properties dialog box enables you to:
   a. Add new CD-based images.
   b. Add new RIPrep images.
   c. Create new unattended setup answer files.
   d. Add remote installation options.

2. Jim is pre-staging a RIS client. When he specifies the GUID of the RIS client in the Manage dialog box to identify the RIS client, the Next button remains disabled. Which one of the following could be the reason for this?
   a. Jim needs to specify the IP address of the RIS client.
   b. Jim needs to clear the This is a managed computer check box.
   c. The GUID is associated with an existing computer account.
   d. The GUID needs to be enclosed within brackets.

3. Pre-staging a RIS client:
   a. Requires the GUID of the RIS client.
   b. Enables users to perform RIS-based installations on unknown computers.
   c. Decreases security.
   d. Requires you to select a specific RIS server for servicing requests.

4. You have assigned permissions to Jim in order to enable him to add computers in an OU to a domain. You want these permissions to take effect immediately. Which one of the following actions will you perform?
   a. Execute the command secedit/refreshpolicy user_policy.
   b. Execute the command secedit/refreshpolicy machine_policy.
   c. Use automatic policy propagation.
   d. Log off and log on again.

5. Jim is searching for all the RIS clients being serviced by a RIS server. He can search for these RIS clients:
   a. In the RIS server's domain only.
   b. Based on GUIDs.
   c. Based on IP addresses.
   d. Only by specifying the full name of the RIS server.

6. Which one of the following is used for identifying RIS clients while pre-staging them?
   a. Computer name
   b. IP address
   c. GUID

7. Timothy needs to grant user rights to Jim in order to manage a pre-staged RIS client. Which of the following sets of permissions should Timothy assign to Jim?

a. Full Control
b. Read, Write, and Reset Password
c. Read
d. Change Password and Reset Password

8. Mary is the systems administrator of a large organization. She wants to view the GUIDs of the RIS clients serviced by a RIS server. Which of the following would enable her to do so? (Choose all that apply.)
a. Search for RIS clients serviced by the RIS server.
b. View the BIOS setting of each RIS client.
c. View the GUID on the label inside the cover of each RIS client computer.
d. View the details of RIS clients in the right pane of the Active Directory Users and Computers console. View the Properties dialog box of the RIS server servicing the RIS clients.

9. CD-based images:
a. Need not be associated with an answer file.
b. Can be created using Windows 2000 Server source files.
c. Need to be created manually after RIS has been installed.
d. Use answer files for specifying network settings and time zone settings.

10. James is performing a RIS-based installation on a RIS client. After the Boot Information Negotiation Layer (BINL) message is displayed, nothing happens, and the CIW is not downloaded.What could be the possible reason for this?
a. The RIS server is offline.
b. The DHCP server is not available.
c. The NetPC Boot Service Manager is not functioning properly.
d. The RIS server has not been authorized.

11. While performing a RIS-based installation, you observe that the BINL message is not being displayed on any RIS client. Which one of the following commands should you execute on the RIS server to correct this problem?
a. Net Stop BINLSVC
b. secedit /refreshpolicy machine_policy
c. secedit /refreshpolicy user_policy
d. Net Stop BINLSVC and Net Start BINLSVC

Projects: On Your Own

1. Add a CD-based image in a folder named New Image.
a. Log on as an administrator.
b. Open the **Active Directory Users and Computers** console.
c. Initiate the **Add Wizard**.
d. Add the CD-based image in a folder named **New Image**.
e. Accept the default description and help text for the image.
f. Select the option to use the old client installation screens—refer to this option by proper name.
g. Close the **Active Directory Users and Computers** console.

2. Pre-stage the RIS client named **ClientA** that has the GUID **954BF985-EF42-11DE-BACD-00AA0075A227**.
a. Log on as an **Administrator**.
b. Open the **Active Directory Users and Computers** console.
c. Add a new computer object.
d. Specify the name and GUID of the computer as mentioned above.
e. Select the option to enable any available RIS server to service the request of the computer—refer to this option by proper name.
f. Close the **Active Directory Users and Computers** console.

3. Assign permissions to the group named **RIS Installers** for managing the pre-staged computer account named **ClientA**.
a. Log on as an **Administrator**.
b. Open the **Active Directory Users and Computers** console.
c. Open the **Properties** dialog box for the computer named **ClientA**.
d. Add the **RIS Installers** group to the list of users and groups that have permissions on **ClientA**.
e. Assign permissions to the group **RIS Installers**.
f. Close the **Active Directory Users and Computers** console.

Problem Solving Scenarios

1. You are planning a mass installation of Windows 2000 Professional for your company's new branch in the city. You are thinking of implementing RIS for the mass installation process. The users in the development department are quite technology savvy and therefore sometimes create a nuisance when it comes to installing applications. You do not want to grant these users the permissions for adding new computers to the domain, nor do you want to be physically present all the time when the new network is put in place. At the same time, you want to increase the speed of the installation process, as the number of computers is high. Draft a plan of action outlining the solution to the above problems and the steps involved in configuring solution.

2. You are administering a RIS-based installation setup of Windows 2000 Professional. You realize that the installation is failing on some computers. You inspect the situation and realize that the installation is successful only on computers that have been pre-staged. Additionally, you are also facing a problem on another RIS server, which is simply not starting the install process on any of its clients whether pre-staged or not. Draft a memo discussing the cause of the problems and the solutions you can provide.

Glossary

ACE See Access Control Entry.

Access Control Entry (ACE) A specific permission setting defining a single permission applied to a single SID.

Access Control List (ACL) Allows you to restrict access to specific zones or resource records in the zone.

ACLDIAG.EXE Tool used to diagnose and troubleshoot permission-related problems.

AD See Active Directory.

ADSI See Active Directory Services Interfaces.

Active Directory (AD) The directory service of Windows 2000 Server.

Active Directory Domains and Trusts console Helps in managing the trust relationships between two or more domains in the same forest or different forests. This is also where you add alternative UPN suffixes.

Active Directory Schema snap-in Helps in viewing and modifying Active Directory schema.

Active Directory Services Interfaces (ADSI) Used to create scripts that interact with AD.

Active Directory Sites and Services console This is where you create sites, subnets, site links, connection objects, and add or remove global catalog servers.

Active Directory Users and Computers console Helps in creating and deleting most objects, modifying their properties, and setting their permissions.

Active Directory zone replication This technique is only used for ADI zones. With ADI zones, each domain controller may act as a primary DNS server, and replication between these servers is automatically performed by Active Directory.

Active Directory-integrated zone When the zone data is stored and replicated as a part of the Active Directory database, the zone type is Active Directory integrated.

Add Wizard Enables you to add CD-based images and associate unattended setup answer files with existing images.

Advertising Displaying the start menu shortcut and/or desktop icons for the application making it appear as if it is already installed. When an application is advertised, however, it is not installed until the first time the user attempts to run it.

Alert Message that triggers when a resource or service-related performance counter exceeds or falls below a specified threshold value.

All Users folder Used to add settings to all profiles used on this specific machine.

Application log An event log in the Event Viewer console that stores messages generated by applications.

Attributes Distinct characteristics that represent an object.

Audit policy A policy that defines which user activities and system events to monitor.

Auditing A Windows 2000 tool to monitor user activities and system events.

Authoritative restore Process that allows you to recover deleted objects.

Automatic Setup Allows the operating system to be installed without user intervention.

Binding information Can be published by using client desktops to connect to services following a service-centric model.

BINL See Boot Information Negotiation Layer.

Boot Information Negotiation Layer (BINL) Controls the responses sent to RIS clients.

Bridgehead server The primary server for inter-site replication. Acts as the contact point for sending and receiving replication information between sites.

Built-in user accounts Created automatically during installation of Windows 2000 Server. Examples of such accounts are Administrator and Guest. Built-in accounts cannot be deleted, but they can be disabled and renamed. Renaming the Administrator account is a common security practice.

Caching-only name servers DNS servers that do not have their own local zone database file.

Central control design approach Suggests that you maintain a central control while delegating administration to various OU administrators.

Centralized GPO design approach Suggests that the organization network should be maintained by a small number of large GPOs.

Check Server Wizard Enables you to verify the configuration of a RIS server.

Child domain (subdomain) A domain created under a parent domain.

Closed Set The object, and all references to the object.

COM+ Class Registration database Database stores entries for dynamic link library (DLL) and executable (EXE) files on a computer.

Computer configuration settings These settings refer to the group policies for the computers, irrespective of the users logging on to them.

Computer objects Store information about computers that are members of a domain.

Configuration information Can be published by distributing configuration information for a particular application to all clients in the domain.

Connection objects One-way, individual communications channels that the KCC typically creates between individual servers for replication.

Connections Use physical network connections to replicate directory information.

Contacts Used to store information about any person or organization that has business relations with your organization.

Contiguous naming scheme A naming scheme where every child domain in a tree derives its name from the parent domain.

Counter log Stores performance data relating to hardware resources and Active Directory in log files.

Custom Setup Allows users to specify computer names of their choice.

DACL See Discretionary Access Control List.

Data Store (NTDS.DIT file) Files that hold the records that make up the Active Directory database.

Database Layer Acts as an abstraction layer between the applications that make the access calls and the database.

DC See Domain controller.

DDNS See Dynamic Domain Name System.

Decentralized GPO design approach Uses separate GPOs for specific policy settings.

Default User profile The profile that all profiles are copied from the first time you log on. The default user profile is stored under documents and settings like all other profiles, but the folder it is contained in is marked as a hidden folder by default. You must change your display settings in order to view the folder.

Delegation of control The process of giving other users or administrators rights on Active Directory objects so that the administration of the network is distributed.

DHCP Server Server that runs the DHCP service. This service automatically provides clients with IP addresses, subnet masks, and can provide additional IP configuration (such as DNS server addresses), thus saving the administrator from manually configuring static IP addresses for each machine.

Direct replication partner A domain controller for which the originating domain controller has a connection object.

Directory database Repository of information about network objects.

Directory service A database that stores information about users and resources in a network and provides ways to access and distribute that information.

Directory Service log Stores alerts and messages relating to Active Directory.

Directory Services Restore Mode Special mode that allows you to restore the System State data on a domain controller.

Directory System Agent (DSA) Provides the interface for the application calls that are made to the directory. Also supports the following protocols that enable clients to gain access to the Active Directory LDAP/ADSI, MAPI, SAM, and REPL.

Discretionary Access Control List (DACL) A list of ACEs defining various levels of access to Active Directory objects. Essentially, a list of permissions.

Disjointed naming scheme A naming scheme where the names of domain trees are not related.

Distinguished name (DN) Includes the name of the domain that holds the object and the complete path to the object through the container hierarchy.

Distribution groups Used for nonsecurity-related purposes such as sending e-mail messages to a group of users.

DN See Distinguished name.

DNS name server A server that runs the DNS server service and is used to resolve host names to IP addresses or vice versa.

DNS namespace A contiguous collection of domains.

DNS notification A feature of the DNS service that uses a push mechanism for notifying a selected set of secondary servers for a zone whenever the zone is updated.

DNS server log Contains basic events logged by the DNS server service, including the status on the starting and stopping of the DNS server.

DNS zone An area of authority over a namespace or collection of contiguous namespaces.

Domain A collection of network resources grouped together under a single domain name and security boundary.

Domain controller (DC) Windows 2000 server that stores a writable copy of the domain database, and authenticates user logon.

Domain local group scope Used to grant access rights to network resources such as printers and shared folders. This scope of group may include members from any domain, but it is only visible in its own domain.

Domain namespace Naming scheme used by DNS to organize domains in a hierarchical structure.

Domain Naming Master role The domain controller holding the domain naming master role can add or remove domains in a forest. Only one domain naming master role can exist in the entire forest at once.

Domain user accounts Allow users to log on to and gain access to resources anywhere on the network.

Domain-wide operations master roles Tasks that are controlled by a single server for each domain.

DSA See Directory System Agent.

DSACLS.EXE Tool used to query and manipulate security attributes of objects.

DSASTAT.EXE Tool used to compare Active Directory replicas on domain controllers and global catalog servers in a forest.

Dynamic Domain Name System (DDNS) The capability to dynamically create and modify records in a DNS zone. This feature is included in Windows 2000 and BIND (8.1.1 or higher) DNS servers.

Environment subsystem Allows operating system to run applications not otherwise compatible with the operating system.

ESE See Extensible Storage Engine.

Event log Stores alerts and messages specific to a service, an application, or an operating system.

Event Viewer Used to view the information contained in event logs.

Executive Performs I/O functions, object management, and security functions.

Extensible Storage Engine (ESE) Has a direct contact with the records in the directory data.

Firewall A combination of hardware and software security systems that secures a network from unauthorized access from outside the network, usually using stateful packet filtering techniques.

Floating/Flexible Single Master of Operations (FSMO) A server which performs one of the specific AD roles which require single-master replication.

FSMO See Floating/Flexible Single Master of Operations.

Folder Redirection A Group Policy extension that allows you to redirect the Windows 2000 special folders to network locations.

Forest Collection of domains that share a common schema, global catalog, and configuration.

Forest-wide operations master roles Tasks that are controlled by a single server for the entire Forest.

Forward lookup zones These help to resolve host names to IP addresses using forward lookup queries.

Forwarders Servers that your DNS server should query to resolve addresses that are not locally resolvable. Forwarders are used in situations where root hints are unusable or deemed inefficient for resolving other domains.

FQDN See Fully Qualified Domain Name.

Fully Qualified Domain Name (FQDN) The full DNS path name, containing all domains and subdomains along the path to the host. For example, www.sales.corp.com. is an example of a FQDN. www is the hostname (the name of the computer), sales is a subdomain, corp is the second level domain, com is the top level domain, and the "." at the end signifies the root of DNS.

Functional role design approach Suggests that the functional roles of users be used in an organization to apply group policies.

Global catalog Database that stores a full replica of the directory data for its own domain and a partial replica for every other domain in the forest.

Global catalog server Domain Controller that stores a full copy of its own domain database, and a partial copy of all other domain databases in the forest. The partial databases include all objects, but do not include all attributes of each object. Global catalog servers are required in Active Directory to facilitate enterprise searching, User Principal Name (UPN) lookups, and Universal group storage.

Global group scope Used to group users of a specified domain who share a similar access profile based on their role in the organization. Global groups may only contain members from their own domain, but are visible in all domains.

Globally unique identifier (GUID) A unique 128-bit number assigned to an object at the time of its creation.

GPO See Group Policy Object.

Group Objects used to apply permissions across large numbers of users, computers, and even other groups.

Group Policy An Active Directory feature that helps administrators specify the behavior of users' desktops. A group policy is essentially a set of rules that apply to a part of the directory structure, such as an OU, Domain, or Site.

Group Policy Container An Active Directory component that contains GPO attributes, extensions, and version information.

Group Policy Object Stores the collection of Group Policy settings that enable an administrator to control various aspects of the computing environment. Consists of a Group Policy Container (GPC) and a Group Policy Template (GPT).

Group Policy Template A collection of folders stored under %systemroot%\SYSVOL\sysvol\domainname\Policies on each Windows 2000 domain controller. The GPT contains all of the registry entries and associated files and folders required to implement the various GPO functions.

GUID See Globally unique identifier.

HAL See Hardware Abstraction Layer.

Hardware Abstraction Layer (HAL) Provides the interface between the other software layers and the core hardware, allowing the Windows 2000 operating system to run on multiple hardware platforms.

Home folder Alternate default location for storage.

in-addr.arpa Special domain created for DNS to ease the problem of resolving IP addresses to names.

Infrastructure master role The domain controller holding this role is responsible for updating all cross-domain object references (such as a group from Domain A being added as a member of another group in Domain B).

Integral subsystems Perform important operating system functions such as security and session management.

IntelliMirror A set of powerful features native to Microsoft Windows 2000 for desktop change and configuration management.

Interrupt Request for attention from the processor coming from hardware devices.

Inter-site replication Active Directory replication that occurs between sites.

Inverse query Client sends request to name server to resolve an IP address to a name. Also known as a reverse lookup query.

IP replication Replication using the Remote Procedure Call protocol. Also known as RPC over IP.

Iterative query A query allowing the receiver to give a reference to where to find the requested record instead of simply looking up the record.

KCC See Knowledge Consistency Checker.

Kernel mode Has direct access to system data and hardware.

Kernel mode drivers Take requests from applications and translate them into hardware functions.

Knowledge Consistency Checker (KCC) Active Directory process responsible for creating connection objects.

LDAP See Lightweight Direct Access Protocol.

Lightweight Direct Access Protocol (LDAP) The primary access protocol used to query and retrieve information about objects in Active Directory.

LDP.EXE Enables you to connect to domains, bind to, search, modify, add, and delete LDAP-compatible directories.

Local group Used to manage local user accounts on a single server or a stand-alone computer.

Local policy The security settings of the local computer.

Local user accounts Allow users to log on only to the computer where the local user account was created.

Local user profile Created the first time you log on to a computer and stored on a system's local hard disk.

Logical structure Reflects the logical setup of an organization and is made up of domains, OUs, trees, and forests.

Mandatory removal The application is uninstalled automatically from the computer the next time the user logs on or the computer restarts.

Mandatory upgrade Used when the latest versions of the application compulsorily need to be installed on the computers.

Mandatory user profile A roaming profile that can be used to specify particular settings for individuals or an entire group of users.

Master name server The DNS server from which the secondary name server gets the copy of the zone database.

Microkernel Manages the computer's processors.

Mixed mode Allows coexistence of Windows NT and Windows 2000 domain controllers in the same domain. You can switch from mixed mode to native mode, but this process is irreversible.

Modifications .mst files that allow you to customize the installation of Windows Installer packages at the time of deployment.

MOVETREE Utility to move objects such as users, computers, and OUs across domains.

Multimaster replication Arrangement in which there are no master domain controllers. All the domain controllers in a domain act as peers while replicating directory information.

Multiple domain model A type of domain model in which the network objects are placed in more than one domain.

Name resolution Process of mapping a name to an IP address.

Name server Contains address information about network hosts.

Native mode Supports only Windows 2000 domain controllers. You cannot switch from native mode to mixed mode.

Nesting The process of adding a group to other groups or consolidating the groups within a network.

NETDOM utility Used to move workstations and member servers between domains.

NLTEST.EXE Tool used to test and check the status of trust relationships and replication between domains.

Nonauthoritative restore Process that allows you to recover Active Directory, while keeping any changes that have occurred since the last backup.

No-Refresh Interval The period of time during which a record may be updated, but not refreshed. By default, this is seven days.

NSLookup A command-line utility that can be used to test the DNS domain namespace.

NTDS.DIT file See Data Store.

NTDSUTIL Active Directory support tool that manages the directory database files. It also lists sites, domains, and server information, manages operations masters, performs authoritative restore, and creates domains. The primary uses of NTDSUTIL are as follows authoritative restorations, database copying, database moving, offline defragmentations, and metadata cleanups.

Object Domain resource defined by a named set of attributes.

Operations masters Servers that control single-master functionality in Active Directory.

Optional removal The existing application is left as it is, but no new users can install the software.

Optional upgrade Provides flexibility to the user by allowing the user to install the upgrade when he or she needs it.

Organizational unit (OU) Container objects that can store groups, users, computers, and other OUs.

OU See Organizational unit.

Performance console Enables you to collect and monitor information about system resources.

Performance counter Provides statistics on the performance of a resource or a service.

Performance Logs and Alerts Enable you to store performance data in log files and to create alerts.

Performance object Logical collection of performance counters.

Physical structure Reflects the physical locations of components in an organization and is made up of sites and domain controllers.

Policy Inheritance Allows policy settings to pass down from parent objects to child objects.

Pre-staging Involves identifying RIS clients using their globally unique identifier (GUID) and creating computer accounts for them.

Primary DNS server Another name for a Primary name server.

Primary domain controller (PDC) emulator role The domain controller holding this role acts as a Windows NT primary domain controller to any Windows NT 4.0 backup domain controllers, processes password change requests from Windows NT clients, and replicates updates to the Windows NT backup domain controllers. In native mode, it receives preferential replication of security. The PDC emulator is responsible for clock synchronization between domain controllers in a domain, which is an extremely important function in an AD, as the primary method AD uses to resolve conflicts is to accept the last modification.

Primary name server The name server with the primary copy of the zone. Modifications are made on this server, and the changes are forwarded to secondary name servers. Also called a Primary DNS server.

Published folders Shared folders that have been listed in Active Directory.

RDN See Relative distinguished name.

Recovery Console A command-line feature that helps in resolving complex system problems when a full system boot is not available.

Recursive query A query requesting the receiver, not the sender, to perform recursion as necessary to retrieve the requested record.

Refresh A refresh of the timestamp on a DNS record. Used solely to keep the record from being scavenged due to a lack of updates.

Refresh Interval (SOA Properties) How often a secondary server will query a primary server for changes to the zone, and refresh or update a record. This process is accomplished by a transfer and comparison of the serial number field in the SOA record. By default, this is seven days.

Registry Database that stores the configuration of a computer.

Relative distinguished name (RDN) Derived from the distinguished name of an object. It is an attribute of the object itself.

Relative identifier (RID) master role The domain controller responsible for this role issues unique blocks of RIDs to each domain controller in the domain. RIDs are a part of each object's SID (Security ID), and are required to ensure domain-wide uniqueness of SIDs.

Remote Installation Service (RIS) Allows automatic installation of the Windows 2000 operating system.

REPADMIN.EXE Tool used to modify and view replication topologies, force replication between domain controllers, and view replication information.

Replication Process of exchanging directory information between the domain controllers of a domain.

Replication topology Defines the path for replication of Active Directory from one domain controller to another until all the domain controllers have the same directory information. The total topology is built from individual connection objects.

REPLMON.EXE Tool that can graphically represent the replication status, replication topology, and performance of domain controllers.

Requests for Comments (RFCs) A regularly growing series of technical reports, proposals for protocols, and protocol standards used by the Internet community.

Resolver The service responsible for formulating the initial DNS query.

Resource record Entries in a DNS database that contain information about the resources in a DNS domain.

Restart Setup Allows users to continue a previous setup attempt.

Reverse lookup zones These help to resolve IP addresses to host names using reverse lookup queries.

RFCs See Requests for Comments.

RIPrep (Remote Installation Preparation) image A copy of the basic Windows 2000 CD-based image along with applications and desktop settings. Once this image has been created, it can be used for installing the operating system, applications, and desktop settings simultaneously on multiple clients using RIS.

RIS See Remote Installation Service.

RIS boot disk Simulates the PXE remote boot ROMs and enables computers without these ROMs to use RIS for remote installation.

Roaming user profile Used where users need to work on multiple computers.

Root domain The first domain in a structure. The Forest Root is the first domain created in the forest. The Tree Root is the first domain created in a given tree, from which all other domains in the tree will derive their names.

Run as command Allows you to run particular programs under a different user account.

Schema Definition of object classes and attributes allowed, as well as the rules regarding the relationships between them.

Schema master role The domain controller performing this role controls all updates and modifications to the schema.

SDCHECK.EXE Tool used to display security descriptors for Active Directory objects.

Secondary DNS server Another name for a secondary name server.

Secondary name server The name server that maintains a copy of the zone database file from the primary DNS server of the zone. Also called a Secondary DNS server.

Security configuration The process of setting up security levels for a system.

Security Configuration and Analysis snap-in A Windows 2000 auditing tool used to analyze and configure local machine security policy.

Security descriptor Store discretionary access control lists (DACLs) that control user access on objects.

Security groups Used to assign permissions to access or share the resources on a network.

Security ID (SID) A unique number (usually 80 bits in size) used by Active Directory to represent the identity of a user account or group.

Security template A group of security configuration settings that can be used to implement security in Windows 2000 computers.

Shared system volume (SYSVOL) Folder that stores a copy of public files of domains such as scripts and group policy objects.

SID See Security ID.

SIDHistory A security field available in Windows 2000 that stores the old SID.

Single domain model A type of domain model in which only one domain stores the network objects.

Single Instance Store (SIS) Minimizes the disk space required for storing RIS installation images.

SIS See Single Instance Store.

Site license server In Windows 2000 Server, the License Logging service in a site replicates the licensing information to a centralized database on a server called the site license server for the site.

Site link attributes Include the site link cost, replication frequency, and replication schedule.

Site link bridges A means of linking two or more sites' links to allow replication when a direct site link does not exist between two sites.

Site links Logical representations of your physical connections between locations (sites).

Site A logical representation of a physical location within Active Directory.

SMTP replication Uses e-mail messages to transmit replication data. SMTP can only be used for replicating between domain controllers of different domains that are located in different sites.

Software diagnostics Provides information about software that helps in troubleshooting it.

Software Distribution Point The network location from which users can get the software that they need.

Software Installation extension The administrator's main tool for managing software throughout its life cycle within the organization.

Special permissions Used to achieve finer control over object security.

Standard permissions Made up of the most commonly assigned permissions, such as Read and Write.

Standard primary zone When a DNS server is the primary server for a zone, the zone type is configured as standard primary. All updates are made on the primary zone.

Standard secondary zone When a DNS server is the secondary server for a zone, the zone type is standard secondary. The changes in standard primary zone are replicated through a one-way zone transfer on the secondary zone.

Standard zone replication The act of copying the text-based database using a process known as zone transfers. It is used by standard primary and standard secondary zones.

Subnet A collection of host computers on a TCP/IP network that are not separated by routers. Also known as a segment.

System boot files Files that are used to load and configure the Windows 2000 operating system.

System Monitor Enables you to collect and view real-time or previously collected performance data.

System state data Information that is critical to the functioning of a domain controller.

SYSVOL See Shared system volume.

Task Scheduler Service that allows you to program tasks to run at a specified date and time.

Tools Allows users to use maintenance and troubleshooting tools before the operating system has been installed.

Trace log Records an event supported by the default system providers or the nonsystem providers.

Transitive site links Site links that are combined to create a site link bridge.

Tree A collection of domains that have a contiguous namespace.

Trivial File Transfer Protocol (TFTP) Manages the file transfer requests of RIS clients during a remote installation.

Trust relationship A logical relationship between domains to facilitate exchange of authentication information.

TFTP See Trivial File Transfer Protocol.

Unicode characters A standard for encoding text that is compatible with multiple character sets, unlike ASCII, which is only useful for Latin-based character sets (most notably, American English).

Universal group Contains global groups, other universal groups, and user accounts from any domain in a domain tree or forest.

Universal group scope Used under very specific cases. Universal groups are stored on global catalog servers, and are only available in native mode. Universal groups can contain members from any domain and are visible in all domains.

Update Sequence Number (USN) Unique number assigned by Active Directory to a new or modified object and its attributes.

Update An update of both record data and the timestamp. Used when the data associated with the record (such as the IP address for a host record) needs to be updated to reflect changes.

UPN See User principal name.

User account Contains information about a user such as user logon name, first name, last name, and password.

User configuration settings These settings refer to the group policies for the users, irrespective of the computer they log on to.

User mode Interface between the application and the kernel mode.

User principal name (UPN) An easy-to-remember name of a user account composed of first name and last name attributes of a user and the UPN suffix, which is usually DNS name of the domain where the user is situated.

User profile A collection of folders that stores a user's customized desktop environment.

User rights Allow a user to perform a specific restricted action.

USN See Update Sequence Number.

Windows 2000 security groups Enable you to specify exactly which groups are to be affected by a particular GPO, by assigning permissions for those groups.

Windows Installer A Windows 2000 component that defines and manages a standard format for application setup and installation, as well as tracks components such as registry entries and shortcuts.

Zone An area of authority consisting of one or more contiguous domains.

Zone database file Contains all of the DNS records associated with a given zone.

Zone delegation The process of assigning responsibility of a section of the DNS namespace to a separate zone.

Zone file The file on the DNS server that contains information about a zone.

Zone replication The process of replicating zone data to all secondary zones at each server.

Zone transfer Process of synchronization of standard secondary zones with primary zone.

Index

B

C

D

E

F

G

H

I

J-K-L

M

N

O

S

T

U-V

W-Z

Test with Pearson VUE and Save Over 50%!

Get Certified Through the Microsoft Authorized Academic Testing Center (AATC) Program:

You invested in your future with the purchase of this textbook from Prentice Hall. Now, take the opportunity to get the recognition your skills deserve. Certification increases your credibility in the marketplace and is tangible evidence that you have what it takes to provide top-notch support to your employer.

Save more than 50%!

Take advantage of this money-saving offer now. The cost of taking the exam is $60.00 with this offer.

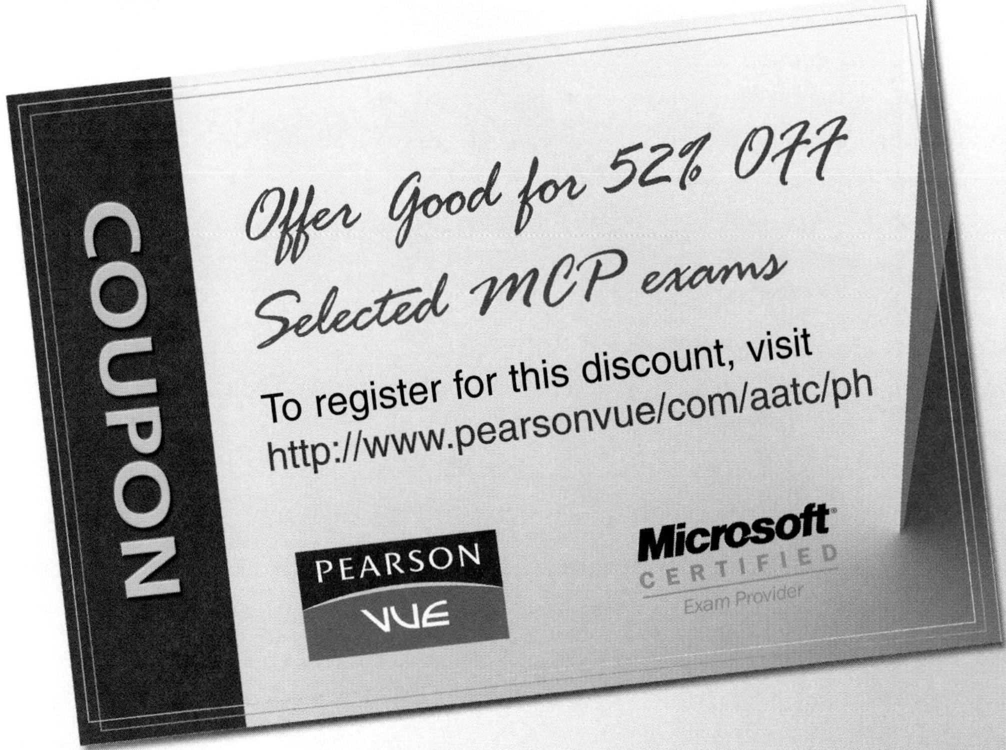

AATC discounted exams are offered only to students and instructors that currently attend, or are employed by, a high school or accredited post-secondary school. Students can take advantage of the offer regardless of whether or not their school is an AATC. The only requirement is that you are a full-time student.

MCSA	
72-210	Installing, Configuring, and Administering Microsoft Windows 2000 Professional
72-270	Installing, Configuring, and Administering Microsoft Windows XP Professional
72-215	Installing, Configuring, and Administering Microsoft Windows 2000 Server
72-218	Managing a Microsoft Windows 2000 Network Environment
72-216	Implementing and Administering a Microsoft Windows 2000 Network Environment
72-224	Installing, Configuring, and Administering Microsoft Exchange Server 2000
72-227	Installing, Configuring, and Administering Microsoft Internet Security and Acceleration (ISA) Server 2000
72-228	Installing, Configuring, and Administering Microsoft SQL Server 2000 Enterprise Edition
72-086	Implementing and Supporting Microsoft Systems Management Server 2.0
72-244	Supporting and Maintaining a Microsoft Windows NT Server 4.0 Network
MCAD	
72-305	Developing and Implementing Web Applications with Microsoft Visual Basic .NET and Microsoft Visual Studio .NET
72-315	Developing and Implementing Web Applications with Microsoft Visual C# .NET and Microsoft Visual Studio .NET
72-306	Developing and Implementing Windows-based Applications with Microsoft Visual Basic .NET and Microsoft Visual Studio .NET
72-316	Developing and Implementing Windows-based Applications with Microsoft Visual C# .NET and Microsoft Visual Studio .NET
72-310	Developing XML Web Services and Server Components with Microsoft Visual Basic .NET and the Microsoft .NET Framework
72-320	Developing XML Web Services and Server Components with Microsoft Visual C# .NET and the Microsoft .NET Framework
72-229	Designing and Implementing Databases with Microsoft SQL Server 2000, Enterprise Edition
72-230	Designing and Implementing Solutions with Microsoft BizTalk Server 2000, Enterprise Edition
72-234	Designing and Implementing Solutions with Microsoft Commerce Server 2000

***For more information on Prentice Hall textbooks for MCSA and MCAD, visit* www.prenhall.com.**

Take advantage of this great offer! Go to www.pearsonvue.com/aatc/ph for complete details and to schedule a discounted exam at an AATC near you!